Learn to Read
in Japanese

A Japanese Reader

including

a Catalogue of 608 Target Kanji,

an Index to 1,300 Kanji Pronunciations,

and 4,200 Practice Sentences

by
Roger Lake and Noriko Ura

Learn to Read in Japanese

A Japanese Reader

Contents

Introduction

For those of us who grew up speaking and reading Western languages, the task of learning to read in Japanese can seem overwhelming. We are accustomed to using relatively few characters (26, in English) to express our thoughts. In contrast, the Japanese people use three different alphabets in everyday writing: hiragana (46 characters), katakana (46 characters) and kanji (more than 2,000 characters).

Fortunately for Western students of Japanese, there is also romaji. Romaji can be defined as the use of Western characters to write phonetic equivalents of Japanese words and sentences.

Japanese people often use romaji to input Japanese words into electronic devices when writing emails and so forth, but they are not very fond of it. Foreign students of Japanese are generally encouraged to abandon romaji early in their studies and to rely solely on Japanese text as they progress. If romaji equivalents and English translations are provided in intermediate-level Japanese reading textbooks, they are usually hidden, requiring a student to turn pages in order to verify that he or she is reading the Japanese text correctly.

The purpose of this *Japanese Reader* is to make it relatively easy for Western students to start reading in Japanese, and to that end it uses romaji freely. In addition, it employs a few practical innovations.

In the first place, this book doesn't hide romaji text and English translations on distant pages. Instead it places all such Western text in a separate column on each page and prints it in a much smaller font, compared to the Japanese text. When students want to challenge themselves by reading in Japanese without assistance, they find it easy to ignore this small romanized text. On the other hand, when they need help with the Japanese text, they have ready access to romaji equivalents and translations.

In the second place, the only kanji that this book asks students to read are 608 carefully selected "target" kanji, and it makes a serious effort to teach these kanji via an informative Kanji Catalogue. Admittedly, 608 kanji are quite a few, but this is only about a third of the kanji that Japanese high school graduates are expected to know, and we think that students will find this number manageable.

The Kanji Catalogue divides its 608 target kanji into groups of characters sharing characteristics in common, so that similar kanji may be compared side by side. It provides memorable descriptions of the kanji as images, focusing on their "radicals," or subcomponents. In addition, it provides homophones, which are English (or sometimes Japanese or, rarely, Spanish) words that are pronounced in the same way that the kanji are pronounced. Students who pay close attention to these three kinds of memory aides (kanji groups, descriptions and homophones) should find it relatively easy to remember the kanji.

Finally, this book provides a Kanji Pronunciation Index, listing 1380 pronunciations that are associated with the 608 kanji in the Catalogue. When a student encounters an unfamiliar kanji in this book, he or she can determine its pronunciation by referring to its romaji pronunciation in the adjacent column. Then the student can look up this pronunciation in the Index and identify the kanji's reference number, which can be used in turn to locate the kanji in the Catalogue.

We sincerely hope that this book will help Western students to master the basics of reading in Japanese.

Preface

In 1981, I attended my first Japanese language course, which was taught at San Jose City College by a very good teacher, Professor Kimie Mushiaki. I still treasure her textbook, *A Linguistic Approach to Conversational Japanese*, which employs a format that is similar to the one used in this book, with a column of Japanese text on the left side of each page and a column of romaji on the right side. Since that time I have acquired more than 50 additional Japanese textbooks and have found valuable information in all of them.

In my efforts to learn the Japanese language, I have relied on my wife, Noriko Ura, as a teacher and friend. She is a native of Japan who now teaches shodo (Japanese calligraphy) in San Jose.

One of my Japanese study practices has been to write down interesting Japanese sentences borrowed from a number of sources, including the textbooks mentioned above and Japanese-language TV programs and movies. My routine has been to write these sentences in romaji, and Noriko has kindly corrected them and converted them back to proper Japanese text.

In the fall of 2015, after we had collected more than 7,500 authentic Japanese sentences in this way, it occurred to us that we might be able to use some of them to create this Japanese reading textbook. Our objectives were 1) to provide readers with a large selection of Japanese text, consisting of hiragana, katakana and 608 essential kanji printed in a large legible font; 2) to give them ready access to romaji equivalents and English translations, making it easy for them to correct reading errors as they read; 3) to help them learn the "target" kanji used in the book by providing a Kanji Catalogue, with memorable kanji descriptions and with homophones for each kanji's different pronunciations; and 4) to help them quickly locate information about each kanji by including a comprehensive Pronunciation Index linked to reference numbers in the Catalogue.

After selecting the target kanji that we wanted to teach, as described below, we sifted through our sentences using computer software and eliminated those that could not be spelled with the kanji that we had selected. We changed many names in the material, to provide students with more exposure to target kanji when reading Japanese names and more exposure to katakana when reading foreign names, and we also added a number of additional sentences, to ensure that each of our target kanji would be well represented.

The 4,200 Japanese sentences and phrases that we have selected for this book are spelled using only hiragana, katakana and the target kanji, except for a few words for which we provide furigana – see the discussion of furigana on the next page. These sentences and phrases illustrate many subtle features of Japanese grammar, and they contain thousands of useful Japanese words.

Readers may be interested to know that, in addition to this book, we have a web site, japaneseaudiolessons.com, where we provide more than 26 hours of free Japanese audio lessons, based on the learning method known as flashcards, or "active recall." This method employs "questions" consisting of sentences or phrases that students are asked to translate. In the audio lessons, each question is spoken in English. After hearing a question, students pause playback and try to translate the question into Japanese. They then resume playback and hear the correct answer. Active recall has been shown to be more effective for building strong memories, compared to "passive" learning methods like reading textbooks or merely listening to spoken Japanese.

In this book, we use the same learning method, active recall, but the language order is reversed. "Questions" are written on the left side of each page, but this time they appear in Japanese. Students do their best to translate them into English, and the correct answers are shown in a small font on the right side of each page.

To put it another way, our audio lessons are designed to help people learn to *speak* Japanese by giving them opportunities to translate from spoken English to spoken Japanese, and they also teach a considerable amount of Japanese grammar and vocabulary. In contrast, this book is designed to help people learn to *read* Japanese by giving them opportunities to translate from Japanese text to English, and it assumes that students already know some Japanese vocabulary and the basics of Japanese grammar.

Since this Japanese Reader is partly based on the same collection of sentences that was used to create the audio lessons, students who have studied the lessons will find a great deal of familiar material as they read. Hearing, speaking and reading the same material will create a synergistic learning experience, enhancing these students' confidence and morale.

Whether students choose to use our audio lessons or not, we suggest that those who need assistance with the grammar in this book refer to the transcript of the audio lessons and to the other explanatory literature that is available online. Please note that the transcript and other online materials are searchable, making it possible for motivated students to find answers to questions about grammar that may arise as they read these pages.

Readers will notice that many of the English translations provided in the following pages are quite literal. For example, consider the sentence: "Shorui wa hikidashi ni haitte imasu yo." I have translated this as: "As for the document, it is being entered in the drawer, for sure." Although this sentence simply means that the document is *in* the drawer, I think that a literal translation is preferable for someone who is trying to understand what the Japanese text means, word for word. In cases where there may be confusion as to what a sentence actually means in English, I have tried to provide more comprehensible translations in parentheses.

In compiling the list of kanji used in this book, we initially decided to include all of the 518 kanji that are taught by Koishi Nishiguchi in *Minna no Nihongo*, Volumes 1 & 2, two books that I had found to be very helpful in my own studies. We then added 90 more kanji characters – some because they are used as radicals, or components, in other kanji and others because they occurred frequently in our Japanese sentences. While preparing this book, I often consulted another textbook, *The Key to Kanji,* by Noriko Kurosawa Williams, and gained many valuable insights from it.

Students will see a few kanji in the Japanese text of this book that are *not* taught in the Kanji Catalogue, but these kanji always appear with furigana, tiny hiragana characters that tell a reader how to pronounce the kanji. In this book, kanji with furigana are primarily used to spell the names of important geographical locations in Japan. When students see furigana above a word, these should serve to alert them to the fact that at least one of the kanji in the word is not included in the Catalogue, and therefore they are not expected to read it unassisted.

If you are not yet completely comfortable reading in hiragana and katakana, you are not alone. Please use the Hiragana Review on page 509 and the Katakana Review on page 512 whenever you want to brush up on those skills.

If you are serious about learning to read in Japanese, please do not look at the romaji and the English translations that appear in the right column of each page of the Japanese Reader in this book until it is necessary for you to do so. Use a piece of paper, or at least your thumb, to cover this information while you first try to read the Japanese text in the left column.

If you look at the romaji and the translations *before* you try to read the Japanese text, you will allow your brain to take a vacation from the hard work that is required to learn to read in Japanese. Although this book may seem long, it actually contains a limited number of opportunities for you to read the kanji without assistance, and I hope that you will take advantage of each one.

Roger Lake
San Jose, California
December 28, 2016

Acknowledgments

We will always be grateful to Mihoko Hayashi, Nowa Mori, and Yu Mori, three wonderful Japanese friends who spent many hours reviewing the text of this book and who provided hundreds of thoughtful suggestions for correcting and improving it. Their kindness, energy and enthusiasm for the project were amazing, and we benefited enormously from their expertise.

We also want to acknowledge our immense debt to the authors of the many textbooks, dictionaries and reference books that we have used in preparing this book. In particular, we want to thank Professor Susumu Nagara and his nine colleagues, the authors of the excellent textbook *Japanese for Everyone*, where we found a treasure trove of authentic and instructive Japanese sentences, together with many clear explanations of Japanese grammar.

How to Use this Book

If you want to learn to read fluently in Japanese, you will need to spend quite a lot of time in reading practice. In this Japanese Reader, we have assembled 4,200 authentic Japanese sentences and phrases with the goal of helping you to derive the maximum benefit from the time that you spend in such practice. In order to facilitate prompt access to feedback while you are reading, tiny romaji equivalents and translations are printed in a separate column on each page of the Reader, readily available when you need them but easy to ignore when you don't.

If you follow our suggestion and hide the romaji text while you are reading the Japanese text, you will often discover Japanese characters that you are unable to read well, and you will probably want to look up those characters in the back of this book. To look up hiragana characters, please see page 509. For katakana characters, see page 512.

In order to look up *kanji* characters, you will first need to determine their reference numbers. These numbers can often be found in the list of new kanji that appears at the beginning of each of the first 61 chapters. If a particular kanji that you want to look up doesn't appear in the list of new kanji at the beginning of a chapter, you can determine the kanji's pronunciation by referring to its romaji equivalent in the column on the right side of the page and then look up this pronunciation in the Kanji Pronunciation Index, starting on page 516. The Pronunciation Index will provide you with a reference number, and this will allow you to find the Catalogue entry that describes that kanji.

Since each kanji character can be associated with more than one pronunciation, reading kanji is much more challenging than reading hiragana and katakana. In this book, we list 1380 pronunciations that are associated with the 608 kanji in our Kanji Catalogue.

A person's short-term memories last for no more than twenty to thirty seconds. To transfer your short-term memory of a kanji's image and its pronunciation into long-term memory, you should pay close attention to the image and to the particular pronunciation that you are trying to learn. It's helpful to repeat the word that contains the pronunciation several times, so that your brain will begin to associate the kanji with that pronunciation.

Another way to increase the chances that your short-term memory of a kanji's image and its pronunciations will become established in long-term memory is to use retrieval cues, which can be either visual or verbal. Visual cues include memorable descriptions of the kanji as images. Verbal cues include homophones, which are words that are pronounced in the same way that the kanji are pronounced. When you associate such cues with your memories of a kanji's image and its pronunciations, you make those memories more "chunky" and "sticky" and allow your brain to cross-reference them in more than one way.

As mentioned in the Introduction, the Kanji Catalogue in this book contains three kinds of mnemonics: 1) kanji groupings, by which similar kanji are grouped together in the Catalogue; 2) kanji descriptions; and 3) homophones. For the sake of simplicity, in the Kanji Catalogue we refer to homophones simply as "cues" (an abbreviation of "verbal retrieval cues").

Kanji descriptions are provided in the **DESCRIPTION** sections of the kanji listings in the Catalogue. Cues are provided in the **CUES** sections, in bold capitalized text. In addition, the **CUES** sections include some kanji pronunciations, written in a combination of bold text and underlining. A complete list of kanji pronunciations can be found in the **EXAMPLES** sections of the listings.

The most efficient way to create and reinforce associations between sounds (pronunciations) and kanji images in your memory is simply to read, pausing briefly to look things up when necessary. As you read this book, you will have ready access to feedback on your reading accuracy and to information that will help you to remember each character. As a result, the characters in this book and their pronunciations will gradually find a home in your long-term memory. By simply reading, you will learn to read fluently without having to spend a lot of time on tedious activities like kanji flashcard drills.

Suppose that you encounter a kanji that you don't know very well, such as 見, which is found in the first sentence on page 1-2 of the Reader. By referring to the romaji text on the right side of that page, you can

xvi

quickly discover that the pronunciation of 見 in this sentence is "mi." To determine 見's reference number, you can locate it in the list of new kanji at the beginning of Chapter 1 or, alternatively, you can look up "mi" in the Pronunciation Index, where you will find "Mi*ru 見 – 53."

Once you have determined that the reference number for 見 is 53, you can look it up in the Kanji Catalogue starting on page 401, where you will be able to compare it with other similar kanji. You will find its pronunciations, its meanings, and examples of words that include it. In the DESCRIPTION section, you will see: "目 me (eye, # 51) on sturdy legs." In the CUES section, you will see: "this 目 (eye) on sturdy legs 見る miru (looks) in a **Mi**rror and 見る **mi**ru (sees) **Ken** and Barbie."

After you have spent a few moments fixing this information in your memory, please go back to the Reader and keep reading. The next time that you see 見, your brain may think of "**Mi**rror," the cue for this pronunciation, but this connection will probably not become well-established in your memory until you have practiced reading this kanji several times. Don't worry. You will have other opportunities to reinforce this connection as you read.

Understandably, you may feel that you don't need to bother with our suggested retrieval cues, especially for kanji that you feel you already know. However, it's likely that you are able to read such kanji more easily in the context of familiar sentences in this book, and if you encounter them in other contexts, you may have trouble remembering them and their pronunciations. To increase the chances that you will remember the kanji in other situations, please consider linking all of them in your memory to the cues that we provide, in order to make your long-term memories of them more "chunky" and "sticky."

For example, the word 日本 nihon (Japan) is a combination of simple kanji, and you will probably recognize it easily after seeing it a few times in this book. If you look up 日 ni (reference # 32) in the Kanji Catalogue, you will see a description of the kanji, and you will also find a sentence under CUES that reads, in part, "日光 **ni**kkou (sunshine) brings **Hea**t to...**Ne**anderthals..." If you also look up 本 hon (reference # 123), you will find a description of it as an image, and you will see a sentence that reads, in part, "the 本 **hon** (book) near the bottom of this tree in **Hon**duras..." Please take a moment to remember the two retrieval cues **Ne**anderthals and **Hon**duras whenever you encounter the word 日本 in this book.

With respect to the two kanji in 日本 nihon (Japan), you will discover that there are 11 possible pronunciations of 日 listed in the Kanji Catalogue, and 4 possible pronunciations of 本. Although we provide retrieval cues for all of these pronunciations, we suggest that you focus on just one at a time. In other words, when you look up a pronunciation for a kanji that you encounter as you read, please pay attention primarily to the kanji's description and then to the pronunciation cue for the word that you are reading. You will almost certainly encounter other pronunciations for the kanji as you continue reading, and you can give your attention to the cues for those pronunciations as you need them.

Another important technique that many people use to strengthen their memories of Japanese characters is to practice writing them in accordance with their prescribed stroke orders. By becoming familiar with the order in which Japanese characters are written, you will improve your chances of recognizing them when they are written in non-standard fashion, as they often are in Japan. For example, on the next page, Noriko illustrates the gyosho style, a common writing style that may be difficult to read without a knowledge of stroke orders.

You can access the stroke orders for hiragana, katakana and our 608 target kanji at japaneseaudiolessons.com, on the page titled "Learn to Read in Japanese." In addition, stroke orders can be found in Japanese dictionary apps that are widely available for electronic devices.

When you are able to read the characters in this book, you will almost certainly want to learn additional kanji. As you do so, we encourage you to invent your own memory aides, in the form of kanji descriptions, homophones and so forth.

We hope that you enjoy deciphering the mysteries of written Japanese, and we wish you tremendous success with your Japanese studies!

One Master, Two Styles

To get an idea of the importance of stroke orders when reading Japanese characters, consider the word shujin (master), written below in the standard print font that we are using for all of the Japanese characters in this book. We have added numbers to show the stroke orders for these two kanji.

Now consider the same word, shujin (master), which Noriko has written below in gyosho (semi-cursive) style. Note that the second stroke in 人 always passes from left to right, but it can originate at any point along the course of the first stroke. The reason that we are showing you both of these styles is to make the point that, if you didn't know the correct kanji stroke orders, it might be difficult for you to realize that both of these words use the same kanji and have the same meaning.

Please take a moment to download the stroke orders for the target characters in this book and save them for future reference. They are available on our website, japaneseaudiolessons.com, on the page titled "Learn to Read in Japanese." If you practice writing Japanese characters in accordance with their prescribed stroke orders, you will find it easier to read the Japanese language as it is commonly written in Japan.

Part One: Introducing the Kanji

New kanji characters are introduced in each of the first 61 chapters of this Reader, and these new kanji are listed at the beginning of each chapter, in the order in which they first appear. Using the reference numbers provided, you can find information about each kanji character in the Kanji Catalogue, starting on page 401. This information includes kanji pronunciations, meanings, descriptions, homophones, examples and comparisons to other similar kanji.

If you need information about a particular kanji and cannot locate it in the list of new kanji at the beginning of the chapter you are reading (suggesting that it was introduced in a previous chapter), you may determine the kanji's pronunciation by referring to its romaji equivalent in the right column and use the Kanji Pronunciation Index starting on page 516 to determine the reference number that is associated with that kanji. You can then use this reference number to look up the kanji's information in the Kanji Catalogue.

Please be careful to keep the romaji text in the right column covered with a piece of paper, or at least with your thumb, until *after* you have done your best to read the Japanese text in the left column. If you are reading an even-numbered page (2, 4, 6, etc.), another way to conceal the text in the right column is to fold the page over gently as you read.

Chapter 1

New Kanji in this Chapter

# 53 見	# 23 手	# 221 紙	# 415 書	# 338 何
# 123 本	# 105 分	# 172 下	# 162 名	# 157 前

1. パスポートを見せてください。

Pasupooto wo misete kudasai.
Please show the passport.

2. はい、どうぞ。

Hai, douzo.
Yes, go ahead.

3. 手紙をすぐ書きます。

Tegami wo sugu kakimasu.
I will write the letter soon.

4. これは何ですか。

Kore wa nan desu ka.
As for this, what is it?

5. ハチミツです。

Hachimitsu desu.
It's honey.

6. 本を見せてください。

Hon wo misete kudasai.
Show me the book please.

7. あれは何ですか。

Are wa, nan desu ka.
As for that over there, what is it?

8. 分かりません。

Wakarimasen.
I don't know/understand.

9. 手を下げてください。

Te wo sagete kudasai.
Please put the hand (i.e., your hand) down.

10. 紙に名前を書きます。

Kami ni namae wo kakimasu.
I will write the name (i.e., my name) to the paper (i.e., on the paper).

11. 本を見せて下さいませんか。

Hon wo misete kudasaimasen ka.
Won't you show the book and give?

12. はい、分かりました。

Hai. Wakarimashita.
Yes, I understood. (this also = "I understand," in the exclamatory tense)

13. いいえ、だめです。

Iie, dame desu.
No, it's bad.

14. ちょっと見せて。

Chotto misete.
Show me for a second.

15. 手紙を書いてください。

Tegami wo kaite kudasai.
Please write the letter.

16. サマンサさんのそばに何が
ありますか。

Samansa-san no soba ni, nani ga arimasu ka.
At Samantha's proximity, what exists?

17. 名前が書けます。

Namae ga kakemasu.
It's possible to write the name.

18. 10分もかかりません。

Juppun mo kakarimasen.
It doesn't even take 10 minutes.

19. 本の下に手紙があります
よ。

Hon no shita ni tegami ga arimasu yo.
Under the book there is a letter, for sure.

20. あなたの名前は何ですか。

Anata no namae wa nan desu ka.
As for your name, what is it?

Chapter 2

New Kanji in this Chapter

#399 飲	#239 好	#292 今	#398 食	#493 店
#253 小	#416 事	#291 朝	#188 大	#510 私

1. ジュースを飲みたいです。

   Juusu wo nomitai desu.
   I want to drink juice.

2. 前はあまり好きじゃありませんでしたが、今は何でも食べます。

   Mae wa amari suki ja arimasen deshita ga, ima wa nandemo tabemasu.
   As for before, she didn't like it very much, but as for now, she eats anything.

3. あの店は小さいです。

   Ano mise wa chiisai desu.
   That store over there is small.

4. ここで食事をしましょう。

   Koko de shokuji wo shimashou.
   Let's do a meal here.

5. ニューヨークは今、朝ですね。

   Nyuuyooku wa ima, asa desu ne.
   As for New York, now, it's morning huh.

6. その店は大きいですか。

   Sono mise wa ookii desu ka.
   As for that store, is it big?

7. いいえ、大きくありませんが、すぐ分かりますよ。

   Iie, ookiku arimasen ga, sugu wakarimasu yo.
   No, it isn't big, but you will soon know/understand it, for sure.

8. 私はビールが好きでよく飲みます。

   Watashi wa biiru ga suki de yoku nomimasu.
   As for me, since I like beer, I drink it often.

9. 今朝、私はレストランで食事をしました。

   Kesa, watashi wa resutoran de shokuji wo shimashita.
   This morning, I did a meal at a restaurant.

10. タイラーさん、テニスが好きなんですね。

    Tairaa-san, tenisu ga suki nan desu ne.
    Tyler, you like tennis huh.

11. 私は小さいのでいいから、あなたが大きいのを食べてください。

Watashi wa chiisai no de ii kara, anata ga ookii no wo tabete kudasai.
As for me, because I'm OK with the small one, you please eat the big one.

12. 私はビールは飲みたくありません。

Watashi wa biiru wa nomitaku arimasen.
As for me, as for beer, I don't want to drink it.

13. もっと大きいのはありませんか。

Motto ookii no wa arimasen ka.
As for a larger one, doesn't it exist?

14. 私はどれも好きです。

Watashi wa dore mo suki desu.
As for me, I like all of them.

15. 小さな店でビールを飲みました。

Chiisana mise de biiru wo nomimashita.
I drank beer at a small store (i.e., restaurant).

16. あそこの小さい店ですか。

Asoko no chiisai mise desu ka.
Is it that over there place's small store?

17. いいえ、あの小さい店じゃありません。

Iie, ano chiisai mise ja arimasen.
No, it's not that small store over there.

18. その前のきれいな店です。

Sono mae no kirei na mise desu.
It's the that front's pretty store. (i.e., the pretty store in front of that)

19. 大事なことは何でしょうか。

Daiji na koto wa nan deshou ka.
As for the important thing, what is it probably?

20. フランスのを飲みます。

Furansu no wo nomimasu.
I'll drink the French one.

21. 私は今朝、パンを食べました。

Watashi wa kesa, pan wo tabemashita.
As for me, this morning, I ate bread.

22. 前は大きかったですが、今は大きくありません。

Mae wa ookikatta desu ga, ima wa ookiku arimasen.
Before it was big, but now it isn't big.

Chapter 3

New Kanji in this Chapter

#32 日	#189 天	#321 気	#109 男	#13 人
#51 目	#194 狭	#161 多	#334 行	#460 有

1. 今日は天気がいいです。
Kyou wa tenki ga ii desu.
As for today, the weather is good.

2. あの男の人は目が見えません。
Ano otoko no hito wa me ga miemasen.
As for that man over there, the eyes can't see. (i.e., he's blind)

3. ちょっと狭いですね。
Chotto semai desu ne.
It's a little tight, or narrow.

4. ずいぶん人が多いですね。
Zuibun hito ga ooi desu ne.
Extremely, people are numerous, huh.

5. あの人は目が大きいです。
Ano hito wa me ga ookii desu.
As for that person over there, the eyes are big.

6. ここは狭くありませんよ。
Koko wa semaku arimasen yo.
Here isn't tight or narrow, for sure.

7. 今日はタクシーで行きましょう。
Kyou wa takushii de ikimashou.
As for today, let's go by taxi.

8. 日本では有名ですが、アメリカでは有名じゃありません。
Nihon de wa yuumei desu ga, amerika de wa yuumei ja arimasen.
In Japan he's famous, but in the U.S. he isn't famous.

9. バレーボールをする人はテニスをする人ほど多くありません。
Bareebooru wo suru hito wa tenisu wo suru hito hodo ooku arimasen.
As for people who do volleyball, compared to people who do tennis, they are not numerous.

10. あの男の人はレストランで食事をするつもりです。
Ano otoko no hito wa resutoran de shokuji wo surutsumori desu.
Those men over there plan to do a meal at a restaurant.

11. 10ページの5行目を見なさ
い。

Juppeeji no go gyou me wo minasai.
Look at page 10's fifth line.

12. いい天気ですね。テニスでも
しませんか。

Ii tenki desu ne. Tenisu demo shimasen
ka.
It's nice weather, huh. Won't we play
tennis or something?

13. その人は男じゃなかった。

Sono hito wa otoko ja nakatta.
That person was not a male.

14. 静岡(しずおか)はミカンで有名ですね。

Shizuoka wa mikan de yuumei desu ne.
Shizuoka is famous for mandarin
oranges, huh.

15. すばらしい天気ですね。

Subarashii tenki desu ne.
It's wonderful weather, huh.

16. あの狭い店に多くの男の人が
行きました。

Ano semai mise ni ooku no otoko no hito
ga ikimashita.
A lot of men went to that narrow store
over there.

17. この店は有名ですね。

Kono mise wa yuumei desu ne.
This restaurant is famous, huh.

Chapter 4

New Kanji in this Chapter

#215 時	#293 会	#41 昨	#125 林	#271 社
#127 森	#88 員	#566 帰	#8 中	#411 間

1. ３時にアレクサスさんと会います。

Sanji ni, arekusasu-san to aimasu.
At 3:00, I will meet with Alexis.

2. 昨日ビールを何本飲みましたか。

Kinou biiru wo nanbon nomimashita ka.
Yesterday, beer, how many bottles did you drink?

3. 小林さんのうちから会社までどのくらいかかりますか。

Kobayashi-san no uchi kara kaisha made, dono kurai kakarimasu ka.
From Kobayashi's home until the company, about how long does it take?

4. 森さんがあなたに会いたがっていますよ。

Mori-san ga anata ni aitagatte imasu yo.
Apparently, Mori wants to meet you, for sure.

5. ライアンさんはアメリカ人で会社員です。

Raian-san wa amerika jin de kaishain desu.
Ryan is an American and a company employee. (de = both "desu" and "and" in this sentence)

6. 今、３時ですね。

Ima, sanji desu ne.
Now, it's 3:00, huh.

7. じゃ、行きましょう。

Ja, ikimashou.
Well, let's go.

8. 何時にうちに帰りますか。

Nanji ni uchi ni kaerimasu ka.
At what time will you return to the home (i.e., your home)?

9. 店の中に森さんがいます。

Mise no naka ni, mori-san ga imasu.
Inside the store, Mori exists.

10. あの会社員は何時間テレビを見ましたか。

Ano kaishain wa nanjikan terebi wo mimashita ka.
As for that company worker over there, how many hours did she watch TV?

11. 林さんは本を書いています。

Hayashi-san wa hon wo kaite imasu.
As for Hayashi, she is writing a book.

12. 森の中でおしっこしている男の人を見ました。

Mori no naka de oshikko shite iru otoko no hito wo mimashita.
Inside the woods, I saw a urinating man.

13. 昨日はいい天気でしたか。

Kinou wa, ii tenki deshita ka.
As for yesterday, was it good weather?

14. 店員：いらっしゃいませ。

Tenin: Irasshaimase.
Clerk: Welcome.

15. 5時です。うちへ帰りましょうか。

Goji desu. Uchi e kaerimashou ka.
It's 5:00. Shall we return to the home?

16. ジョシュアさんはコーヒーを飲んで帰ることにした。

Joshua-san wa koohii wo nonde kaeru koto ni shita.
Joshua decided to drink coffee and return.

17. バスでも行けますが時間がかかります。

Basu demo ikemasu ga, jikan ga kakarimasu.
One can go by bus also, but it takes time.

18. 時間がありましたら、このレポートを見ていただきたいんですが。

Jikan ga arimashitara, kono repooto wo mite itadakitain desu ga...
If there is time, I would like you to look at this report and I to humbly receive, but...

19. 森さんと林さん、昨日会社にいませんでした。

Mori-san to hayashi-san, kinou kaisha ni imasen deshita.
Mori and Hayashi, were not at the company yesterday.

20. うちの中にエリザベスさんがいます

Uchi no naka ni erizabesu san ga imasu.
Elizabeth is inside the home (i.e., her home).

21. 1時。2時。3時。

Ichiji. Niji. Sanji.
1:00. 2:00. 3:00.

22. 4時。

Yoji.
4:00. (yonji, *not* OK)

23. 5時。6時。8時。

Goji. Rokuji. Hachiji.
5:00. 6:00. 8:00.

24. 7時。

Shichiji, or Nanaji.
7:00. (two different ways to say 7:00)

25. 9 時。

Kuji.
9:00. (kyuuji, *not* OK)

26. 10 時。11 時。12 時。

Juuji. Juuichiji. Juuniji.
10:00. 11:00. 12:00.

27. 1 分。2 分。3 分。4 分。

Ippun. Nifun. Sanpun.
Yonfun, or yonpun.
One minute. Two minutes.
Three minutes. Four minutes.

28. 5 分。6 分。7 分。

Gofun. Roppun. Nanafun.
Five minutes. Six minutes. Seven
minutes. (shichifun, *not* OK)

29. 8 分。9 分。10 分。30 分。

Happun. Kyuufun. Jippun, or juppun.
Sanjippun, or sanjuppun.
Eight minutes. Nine minutes.
Ten minutes. Thirty minutes.

30. 1 時間。2 時間。3 時間。
4 時間。

Ichijikan. Nijikan. Sanjikan. Yojikan.
One hour. Two hours. Three hours.
Four hours. (yonjikan, *not* OK)

31. 5 時間。6 時間。7 時間。
8 時間。

Gojikan. Rokujikan. Shichijikan, or
nanajikan. Hachijikan.
Five hours. Six hours.
Seven hours. Eight hours.

32. 9 時間。

Kujikan.
Nine hours. (kyuujikan, *not* OK)

33. 10 時間。30 時間。

Juujikan. Sanjuujikan.
Ten hours. Thirty hours.

34. 今、何時ですか。

Ima, nanji desu ka.
Now, what time is it?

35. 10 時 42 分です。

Juuji yonjuu nifun desu.
It's 10:42.

Chapter 5

New Kanji in this Chapter

# 301 金	# 147 出	# 34 早	# 114 方	# 190 犬
# 327 来	# 184 学	# 208 生	# 200 曜	# 142 箱

1. お金を出さない。

   Okane wo dasanai.
   I won't take the money out.

2. 早くうちへ帰った方がいいで
   すよ。

   Hayaku uchi e kaetta hou ga ii desu yo.
   It would be better to return home early.

3. 犬が出た。

   Inu ga deta.
   The dog exited.

4. 昨日はどうして来なかったん
   ですか。

   Kinou wa doushite konakattan desu ka.
   As for yesterday, why didn't you come?

5. その学生の名前は林さんで
   す。

   Sono gakusei no namae wa hayashi-san
   desu.
   As for that student's name, it's Hayashi.

6. ソフィア、早く来て。

   Sofia, hayaku kite.
   Sophia, come quickly.

7. 金曜日に林さんがうちに来ま
   した。

   Kinyoubi ni hayashi-san ga uchi ni
   kimashita.
   On Friday, Hayashi came to the home
   (i.e., my home).

8. 昨日会社に来ませんでした
   ね。なぜですか。

   Kinou kaisha ni kimasen deshita ne.
   Naze desu ka.
   Yesterday you didn't come to the
   company, huh. Why is it?

9. この箱の方があの箱より大き
   くありませんか。

   Kono hako no hou ga ano hako yori
   ookiku arimasen ka.
   As for this box, compared to that box
   over there, isn't it bigger?

10. きれいな方ですね。

    Kirei na kata desu ne.
    She's a pretty person, huh.

11. お金を下ろしに行きます。

Okane wo oroshi ni ikimasu.
He will go for the purpose of withdrawing money.

12. 昨日は何曜日でしたか。

Kinou wa nanyoubi deshita ka.
As for yesterday, what day of the week was it?

13. ああ、すみません。今、小さいお金がないんですよ。

Aa, sumimasen. Ima chiisai okane ga nain desu yo.
Ah, excuse me. Now there is no small money, for sure.

14. 早くうちを出た方がいいですよ。

Hayaku uchi wo deta hou ga ii desu yo.
It would be better to leave home early.

15. その学生は大きな箱から犬を出しました。

Sono gakusei wa ookina hako kara inu wo dashimashita.
As for that student, she took the dog out from the large box.

16. 金曜日は朝6時に出かけましょうか。

Kinyoubi wa asa rokuji ni dekakemashou ka.
As for Friday, shall we depart at 6:00 in the morning?

17. それじゃ、早すぎますよ。7時にしませんか。

Sore ja, hayasugimasu yo. Shichiji ni shimasen ka.
In that case, it's too early, for sure. Won't you choose 7:00?

18. 私は学生なのであまりお金がありません。

Watashi wa gakusei na node amari okane ga arimasen.
As for me, because I'm a student, there isn't much money.

19. 犬は箱の中にいます。

Inu wa hako no naka ni imasu.
As for the dog, it exists at the box's inside.

20. スポーツはたくさんした方がいいです。

Supootsu wa takusan shita hou ga ii desu.
As for sports, it's better to play a lot.

21. 昨日は日曜日でした。

Kinou wa nichiyoubi deshita.
As for yesterday, it was Sunday.

22. 森さんは学生に本をあげました。

Mori-san wa gakusei ni hon wo agemashita.
As for Mori, to the student, he gave a book.

23. その社員は朝早く会社に行きました。

Sono shain wa asa hayaku kaisha ni ikimashita.
As for that employee, early in the morning, he went to the company.

Chapter 6

New Kanji in this Chapter

#263 電	#433 話	#63 屋	#432 読	#435 語	#283 車
#211 花	#481 便	#564 利	#176 不	#1 一	

1. 電話はタバコ屋の前にありま
す。

Denwa wa tabakoya no mae ni arimasu.
As for the telephone, it exists in front of
the tobacco shop.

2. いつも本を読みます。

Itsumo hon wo yomimasu.
I always read books.

3. エマさんは日本語を話すこと
ができます。

Ema-san wa nihongo wo hanasu koto ga
dekimasu.
Emma can speak Japanese.

4. ここからホテルまでどのくら
いかかりますか。

Koko kara hoteru made dono kurai
kakarimasu ka.
From here, until the hotel, about how
long will it take?

5. 2時間ぐらいかかります。

Nijikan gurai kakarimasu.
It will take about two hours.

6. 私はいつも電車の中で本を読
みます。

Watashi wa itsumo densha no naka de
hon wo yomimasu.
As for me, always, inside the train, I read
a book.

7. 花屋はそこにもあそこにもあ
ります。

Hanaya wa soko ni mo asoko ni mo
arimasu.
As for flower shops, also at there, also at
over there they exist.

8. このパソコンはとても便利で
す。

Kono pasokon wa totemo benri desu.
This personal computer is very
convenient.

9. この本を読んでください。

Kono hon wo yonde kudasai.
Please read this book.

10. 電車はちょっと不便です。

Densha wa chotto fuben desu.
The train is a little inconvenient.

11. 今日は車がずいぶん多いです
ね。

Kyou wa kuruma ga zuibun ooi desu ne.
As for today, cars are very numerous, huh.

12. 電話が一つだけだから不便で
すね。

Denwa ga hitotsu dake dakara fuben desu ne.
Because it's only one phone, it's inconvenient, huh.

13. 日本語ができる。

Nihongo ga dekiru.
I can do Japanese. (i.e., I can understand it or speak it)

14. 一人だけ来ました。

Hitori dake kimashita.
Only one person came.

15. どんな本が読みたいですか。

Donna hon ga yomitai desu ka.
What kinds of books would you like to read?

16. 日本語の手紙はまだ書いたこ
とがありません。

Nihongo no tegami wa mada kaita koto ga arimasen.
As for a Japanese language letter, I still have never written one.

17. 本屋はどこですか。

Honya wa doko desu ka.
As for the bookstore, where is it?

18. きれいでとても便利です。

Kirei de totemo benri desu.
It's clean and very convenient.

19. 来るかもしれません。

Kuru kamoshiremasen.
He might come.

20. 花屋さんで森さんと話をしま
した。

Hanayasan de mori-san to hanashi wo shimashita.
At the Mr. Flowershop (i.e., at the flower shop), I did talking with Mori (i.e., I talked to him).

21. もし電話がなければ不便だろ
うね。

Moshi denwa ga nakereba fuben darou ne.
If the phone doesn't exist, it will be inconvenient, probably, huh. (i.e., if we didn't have phones, it would probably be inconvenient)

22. 花についての本を読みました
か。

Hana ni tsuite no hon wo yomimashita ka.
Did you read a book about flowers?

23. 一時ですね。

Ichiji desu ne.
It's 1:00, huh.

24. 電車はとても便利です。

Densha wa totemo benri desu.
The train is very convenient.

Chapter 7

New Kanji in this Chapter

#67 仕	#233 終	#217 待	#96 頃	#59 土
#68 田	#430 言	#498 度	#459 友	#347 達

1. 仕事が終わらなかったんです。
Shigoto ga owaranakattan desu.
Work didn't finish.

2. ところで、今何時ですか。
Tokoro de, ima nanji desu ka.
By the way, now, what time is it?

3. えーと、あー、10時10分ですよ。
Eeto, aa, juuji jippun desu yo.
Er... Ah, it's 10:10, for sure.

4. ちょっと待ってください。
Chotto matte kudasai.
Please wait for a moment.

5. ニューヨークは今、朝の8時頃ですね。
Nyuuyooku wa ima, asa no hachiji goro desu ne.
As for New York, now, it's morning's about 8:00, huh.

6. 何時まで会社にいますか。
Nanji made kaisha ni imasu ka.
Until what time will you be at the company?

7. この仕事が終わるまでいます。
Kono shigoto ga owaru made imasu.
I'll be there until this work will finish.

8. 土田さんはどこにいますか。
Tsuchida-san wa, doko ni imasu ka.
As for Tsuchida, where does he exist?

9. 3時に来ると言っていたからもうすぐ来るはずです。
Sanji ni kuru to itte ita kara mou sugu kuru hazu desu.
Since he was saying that he would come at 3:00, he ought to come pretty soon.

10. お仕事はこの頃どうですか。
Oshigoto wa konogoro dou desu ka.
As for the honorable work, these days, how is it?

11. もう一度言います。

Mou ichido iimasu.
I'll say once again.

12. 今度の日曜日に何をします
か。

Kondo no nichiyoubi ni nani wo shimasu ka.
What will you do on next Sunday?

13. 今度の土曜日ですか。

Kondo no doyoubi desu ka.
Is it this Saturday?

14. ベンチで友達と話している人
は花田さんです。

Benchi de tomodachi to hanashite iru hito wa hanada-san desu.
On the bench, the person talking to a friend is Hanada.

15. その仕事は4時までに終わり
ますか。

Sono shigoto wa yoji made ni owarimasu ka.
As for that work, will it finish by 4:00?

16. 終わるかどうか分からない
けれどやってみます。

Owaru ka douka wakaranai keredo yatte mimasu.
Whether it will finish I don't know, but I will do and see.

17. 私はここで待っています。

Watashi wa koko de matte imasu.
As for me, I'll be waiting here.

18. 友達がたくさんいました。

Tomodachi ga takusan imashita.
Friends, a lot, existed.

19. すみませんが、もう一度名前
を書いて下さいませんか。

Sumimasen ga, mou ichido namae wo kaite kudasaimasenka.
Excuse me, but one more time, won't you write the name and give?

20. 土田さんとジョセフさんはど
こでアリッサさんを待ってい
ますか。

Tsuchida-san to josefu-san wa doko de arissa-san wo matte imasu ka.
As for Tsuchida and Joseph, at where are they waiting for Alyssa?

21. バーで待っています。

Baa de matte imasu.
They are waiting at a bar.

22. 土田さんはハンバーガーが好
きじゃないかもしれません。

Tsuchida-san wa hanbaagaa ga suki ja nai kamoshiremasen.
Tsuchida might not like hamburgers.

23. いつまで待ちますか。

Itsu made machimasu ka.
Until when will you wait?

24. 友達が来るまで待ちます。

Tomodachi ga kuru made machimasu.
I'll wait until the friend comes.

25. 昨日友達が私に会いに来ました。

Kinou tomodachi ga watashi ni ai ni kimashita.
Yesterday a friend came to meet me.

26. 10時頃だった。

Juuji goro datta.
It was about 10:00.

27. この仕事は今日までに終わるでしょう。

Kono shigoto wa kyou made ni owaru deshou.
This work will finish by today, probably.

28. 友達が「早く来る」と言いました。

Tomodachi ga "hayaku kuru" to iimashita.
The friend said, "I will come early."

29. すみません。この仕事、今日中にはできないんですが。

Sumimasen. Kono shigoto, kyoujuuni wa, dekinain desu ga...
Excuse me. This work, as for by the end of today, cannot be accomplished, but...

30. じゃ、今日中でなくてもいいです。

Ja, kyoujuu de nakute mo ii desu.
Well, of by the end of today, it isn't necessary.

31. 昨日私は友達に会ってきました。

Kinou watashi wa tomodachi ni atte kimashita.
Yesterday, as for me, I met the friend and came.

Chapter 8

New Kanji in this Chapter

#140 机	#171 上	#422 先	#198 難	#514 京
#277 都	#294 合	#154 明	#494 広	#336 毎

1. 日本語の本はどこにあります か。

Nihongo no hon wa doko ni arimasu ka.
As for the Japanese language book, where does it exist?

2. そこの机の上にあります。

Soko no tsukue no ue ni arimasu.
It exists on that place's desk's top. (i.e., on top of that desk)

3. 先に会社に帰ったらどうです か。

Saki ni kaisha ni kaettara dou desu ka.
How is it if you return to the company ahead of me?

4. ペンはどこにありますか。

Pen wa doko ni arimasu ka.
As for the pen, where does it exist?

5. あそこの机の中にあります。

Asoko no tsukue no naka ni arimasu.
It exists in that place over there's desk's inside.

6. テストは難しいですか。

Tesuto wa muzukashii desu ka.
As for the test, is it difficult?

7. いいえ、難しくありません。

Iie, muzukashiku arimasen.
No, it isn't difficult.

8. 机の上にアビゲイルさんのペ ンがあります。

Tsukue no ue ni abigeiru-san no pen ga arimasu.
At the desk's top (i.e., on top of the desk), Abigail's pen exists.

9. 先に会社に帰った方がいいで すよ。

Saki ni kaisha ni kaetta hou ga ii desu yo.
It would be better for you to return to the company ahead of me, for sure.

10. 日本語があまり上手じゃない 人が京都に来ました。

Nihongo ga amari jouzu ja nai hito ga kyouto ni kimashita.
A person whose Japanese is not very good came to Kyoto.

11. どうも有難う。

Doumo arigatou.
Thanks a lot.

12. 今日は都合がいいですが、明日はだめです。

Kyou wa tsugou ga ii desu ga, ashita wa dame desu.
Today the circumstances are good, but tomorrow they're bad.

13. 私は明日テニスをします。

Watashi wa ashita tenisu wo shimasu.
As for me, tomorrow, I will do tennis.

14. 広くて明るいです。

Hirokute akarui desu.
It's spacious and well-lighted.

15. もう一ついかがですか。

Mou hitotsu ikaga desu ka.
Another piece, how is it? (i.e., please have another one)

16. 有難うございます。いただきます。

Arigatou gozaimasu. Itadakimasu.
Thank you a lot. I will humbly receive (i.e., I'll have some).

17. イザベラさんのバッグはどこにありますか。

Izabera-san no baggu wa doko ni arimasu ka.
As for Isabella's bag, where does it exist?

18. 今日は都合がいいですか。

Kyou wa tsugou ga ii desu ka.
As for today, are the circumstances good? (i.e., is it convenient for you?)

19. 毎日、何時間仕事をしますか。

Mainichi, nanjikan shigoto wo shimasu ka.
Every day, how many hours work do you do?

20. 8時間仕事をします。

Hachijikan shigoto wo shimasu.
I do eight hours work.

21. 広田さんは毎日、何時間仕事をしますか。

Hirota-san wa mainichi, nanjikan shigoto wo shimasu ka.
As for Hirota, every day, how many hours does she do work?

22. 10時間仕事をします。

Juujikan shigoto wo shimasu.
She does ten hours work.

23. ブリアンナさんは新幹線に間に合いましたか。

Burianna-san wa shinkansen ni maniaimashita ka.
As for Brianna, was she on time for the bullet train?

24. 私は京都へ行きます。

Watashi wa, kyouto e ikimasu.
As for me, I will go to Kyoto.

25. 大阪へも行きます。

Oosaka e mo ikimasu.
I will go to Osaka also.

26. 私は先生から本をいただきました。

Watashi wa sensei kara hon wo itadakimashita.
I received a book from the teacher.

27. 先生は広田さんに本を下さいました。

Sensei wa hirota-san ni hon wo kudasaimashita.
As for the teacher, she gave Hirota a book. (Hirota is in the speaker's in-group)

28. 毎朝ジョギングをしていますか。

Maiasa jogingu wo shite imasu ka.
Every morning are you jogging?

29. いいえ、したりしなかったりです。

Iie. Shitari shinakattari desu.
No. Sometimes I do, sometimes I don't do.

30. 私の会社は京都にあります。

Watashi no kaisha wa kyouto ni arimasu.
As for my company, it exists in Kyoto.

Chapter 9

New Kanji in this Chapter

#130 校	#365 通	#405 家	#396 内	#302 銀
#340 向	#369 病	#424 院	#329 隣	#437 訳

1. ジョシュアさんは今どこにいますか。

Joshua-san wa ima doko ni imasu ka.
As for Joshua, now, where does he exist?

2. 学校にいますか。

Gakkou ni imasu ka.
Does he exist at school?

3. 日本人に日本語で話してみたら通じました。

Nihonjin ni nihongo de hanashite mitara tsuujimashita.
To a Japanese person, when I spoke in Japanese to see, I communicated.

4. 家のそばです。

Ie no soba desu.
It's close to the house.

5. 家内のハナです。

Kanai no hana desu. (i.e., it's my wife Hannah)
It's the wife's Hannah.

6. 土田さん、銀行はどこにありますか。

Tsuchida san, ginkou wa doko ni arimasu ka.
Tsuchida, as for a bank, at where does it exist?

7. えーと、この通りの向こうに病院があります。

Eeto, kono toori no mukou ni byouin ga arimasu.
Uh, at this road's far end, there's a hospital. (i.e., there's a hospital down the road)

8. 銀行はその病院の隣です。

Ginkou wa sono byouin no tonari desu.
As for the bank, it's that hospital's neighbor.

9. そうですか。どうも有難う。

Sou desu ka. Doumo arigatou.
Is that so? Thanks a lot.

10. お待たせしました。あれ！家内がいませんね。どこに行ったのでしょう？

Omatase shimashita. Are! Kanai ga imasen ne. Doko ni itta no deshou?
I humbly made you wait. Hey, the wife doesn't exist, huh. Where did she go, probably?

11. オリビアさんはあそこの本屋にいますよ。

Oribia-san wa asoko no honya ni imasu yo.
Olivia exists in that place over there's bookstore, for sure.

12. 学校の向こうに病院があります。

Gakkou no mukou ni byouin ga arimasu.
On the far side of the school, a hospital exists.

13. 前に何か仕事をしたことがありますか。

Mae ni, nanika shigoto wo shita koto ga arimasu ka.
At before, something work has she done?

14. アルバイトで通訳をしたことがあります。

Arubaito de tsuuyaku wo shita koto ga arimasu.
For part-time work, she has done interpretation.

15. 訳がわかんないね。

Wake ga wakannai ne.
Reason I don't understand, huh. (i.e., it doesn't make sense; wakannai is a contracted form of wakaranai)

16. 銀行の隣はレストランじゃありません。

Ginkou no tonari wa resutoran ja arimasen.
The bank's neighbor is not a restaurant.

17. 家内が病気です。

Kanai ga byouki desu.
The wife is sick.

18. 病院に行った方がいいですよ。

Byouin ni itta hou ga ii desu yo.
You'd better go to the hospital.

19. 学校の隣の銀行にアンソニーさんがいます。

Gakkou no tonari no ginkou ni Ansonii-san ga imasu.
At the school's neighbor's bank (i.e., at the bank next to the school) Anthony exists.

20. 銀行の向こうに大きな本屋があります。

Ginkou no mukou ni ookina honya ga arimasu.
At the far side of the bank, a large bookstore exists.

21. そういう訳で私の友達は来ません。

Sou iu wake de watashi no tomodachi wa kimasen.
From that to-say reason (i.e., for that reason), my friend won't come.

Chapter 10

New Kanji in this Chapter

#267 部	#538 台	#216 持	#236 安	#418 静
#19 高	#391 所	#440 誰	#512 料	#78 理

1. あなたの部屋は広いですか。

Anata no heya wa hiroi desu ka.
Is your room spacious?

2. いいえ、広くありません。

Iie, hiroku arimasen.
No, it isn't spacious.

3. 車を3台持っています。

Kuruma wo san dai motte imasu.
I have three cars. (dai = counter for cars
& other manufactured items)

4. そのレストランは安くておいしかったです。

Sono resutoran wa yasukute oishikatta desu.
That restaurant was cheap and delicious.

5. あの店は静かですか。

Ano mise wa shizuka desu ka.
Is that store over there quiet?

6. はい、静かです。

Hai, shizuka desu.
Yes, it's quiet.

7. タクシーは便利ですが高いです。

Takushii wa benri desu ga takai desu.
Taxis are convenient, but they are
expensive.

8. この花は安かったんですよ。

Kono hana wa yasukattan desu yo.
These flowers were inexpensive, for sure.

9. もっと静かな所へ行きましょう。

Motto shizuka na tokoro e ikimashou.
Let's go to a quieter place.

10. あなたの台所はとてもきれいですね。

Anata no daidokoro wa totemo kirei desu ne.
Your kitchen is very clean, huh.

11. 誰に会いたいですか。

Dare ni aitai desu ka.
Whom would you like to meet?

12. 日本料理はみんな好きです。

Nihon ryouri wa minna suki desu.
As for Japanese cooking, I like it all.

13. あのレストランは高いです
が、このレストランは安いで
す。

Ano resutoran wa takai desu ga, kono
resutoran wa yasui desu.
That restaurant over there is expensive,
but this restaurant is cheap.

14. この店は静かじゃありませ
ん。

Kono mise wa shizuka ja arimasen.
This store is not quiet.

15. 部屋が広くて気持ちがいいで
すね。

Heya ga hirokute kimochi ga ii desu ne.
Since the room is big, the feeling is good,
huh.

16. 静かだからいい所ですよ。

Shizuka dakara ii tokoro desu yo.
Since it's quiet, it's a good place, for sure.

17. 台所で料理をしているのは誰
ですか。

Daidokoro de ryouri wo shite iru no wa
dare desu ka.
As for the one who is doing cooking in
the kitchen, who is it?

18. イタリアから来た料理人で
す。

Itaria kara kita ryourinin desu.
It's a came-from-Italy cook.

19. それは誰のスーツケースです
か。

Sore wa dare no suutsukeesu desu ka.
As for that, whose suitcase is it?

20. 私のスーツケースです。

Watashi no suutsukeesu desu.
It's my suitcase.

21. フォークとナイフを持ってき
てください。

Fooku to naifu wo motte kite kudasai.
Please bring a fork and a knife.

22. ここは静かですが、あそこは
うるさいです。

Koko wa shizuka desu ga, asoko wa
urusai desu.
Here is quiet, but over there is noisy.

23. この部屋はどうですか。

Kono heya wa, dou desu ka.
As for this room, how is it?

24. そうですね。広いですがちょ
っと高いですよ。

Sou desu ne. Hiroi desu ga chotto takai
desu yo.
That's so huh. (i.e., let me see) It's
spacious but it's a little expensive, for
sure.

Chapter 11

New Kanji in this Chapter

# 401 物	# 484 価	# 16 公	# 279 園	# 101 真	# 335 後
# 118 木	# 363 建	# 508 東	# 351 遠	# 308 思	

1. 日本の物価は安いですか。

Nihon no bukka wa yasui desu ka
Are Japanese prices cheap?

2. いいえ、安くありません。

Iie, yasuku arimasen.
No, they aren't cheap.

3. これから出かけるところなんです。

Kore kara dekakeru tokoro nan desu.
From now, I'm on the verge of leaving.

4. ここは公園です。

Koko wa kouen desu.
As for here, it's a park.

5. 公園の真ん中にベンチがあります。

Kouen no mannaka ni benchi ga arimasu.
In the middle of the park, benches exist.

6. ベンチの後ろに大きい木があります。

Benchi no ushiro ni ookii ki ga arimasu.
At the benches' rear, big trees exist.

7. 大きい木の下のベンチにエリザベスさんがいます。

Ookii ki no shita no benchi ni erizabesu-san ga imasu.
On the big tree's underneath bench, Elizabeth exists.

8. あっ、あれが見えますか。

A! Are ga miemasu ka.
Ah! Is that over there visible ?

9. あの大きい建物ですか。

Ano ookii tatemono desu ka.
Is it that big building over there?

10. いいえ、あの建物じゃありません。

Iie, ano tatemono ja arimasen.
No, it isn't that building over there.

11. その隣です。

Sono tonari desu.
It's that neighbor. (i.e., it's next to that)

12. 何ですか。

Nan desu ka.
What is it?

13. ディズニーランドですよ。

Dizuniirando desu yo.
It's Disneyland, for sure.

14. ああ、あれが東京ディズニーランドですか。

Aa, are ga toukyou dizuniirando desu ka.
Ah, is *that* over there Tokyo Disneyland?

15. 大きいですね。

Ookii desu ne.
It's big, huh.

16. 東京の物価が高いのでびっくりしました。

Toukyou no bukka ga takai node bikkuri shimashita.
Since Tokyo prices are high, I got surprised.

17. 公園は家から遠いです。

Kouen wa ie kara tooi desu.
The park is far from the house.

18. 静かですがちょっと不便です。

Shizuka desu ga chotto fuben desu.
It's quiet, but it's a little inconvenient.

19. 大きい箱の真ん中に小さい箱があります。

Ookii hako no mannaka ni chiisai hako ga arimasu.
At the big box's middle, a small box exists.

20. 公園の中は静かですね。

Kouen no naka wa shizuka desu ne.
As for the park's inside, it's quiet, huh.

21. 病院は学校の後ろにありますよ。

Byouin wa, gakkou no ushiro ni arimasu yo.
As for the hospital, it exists at the school's rear, for sure.

22. すみません。後で来てください。

Sumimasen. Ato de kite kudasai.
Excuse me. Of later, please come.

23. 日本の物価は高いと思いますか。

Nihon no bukka wa takai to omoimasu ka.
Do you think Japanese prices are high?

24. 公園のまわりに大きな建物がたくさんあります。

Kouen no mawari ni ookina tatemono ga takusan arimasu.
Around the park, big buildings, a lot, exist.

25. 箱の中に犬がいますよ。

Hako no naka ni inu ga imasu yo.
At the box's inside, a dog exists, for sure.

26. 真さんはいいと思っていま
す。

Makoto-san wa ii to omotte imasu.
Makoto thinks that it's good.

27. 毎日、東京に行きます。

Mainichi, toukyou ni ikimasu.
Every day, I go to Tokyo.

28. 明日は東京に行きません。

Ashita wa toukyou ni ikimasen.
As for tomorrow, I will not go to Tokyo.

29. この本をどう思いますか。

Kono hon wo dou omoimasu ka.
How do you think of this book?

30. いいと思います。

Ii to omoimasu.
I think it's good.

31. ニコラスさんは明日行くと言
っていました。

Nikorasu-san wa ashita iku to itte
iimashita.
As for Nicholas, he was saying that he
will go tomorrow.

32. ずいぶん遠いですね。

Zuibun tooi desu ne.
To a great degree, it's far, huh.

33. 電車もありますがあまり便利
じゃありません。

Densha mo arimasu ga, amari benri ja
arimasen.
A train also exists, but it isn't very
convenient.

34. 物価は高いとは思いません。

Bukka wa takai to wa omoimasen.
As for prices, I don't think they're high.
(use wa after to in negative sentences)

35. 私の家から学校まであまり遠
くありません。

Watashi no ie kara gakkou made amari
tooku arimasen.
From my house, until the school, it isn't
very far. (i.e., the school isn't very far
from the house)

36. 車の後ろです。

Kuruma no ushiro desu.
It's behind the car.

37. 公園にきれいな木がたくさん
ある。

Kouen ni kirei na ki ga takusan aru.
In the park, pretty trees, a lot, exist.

Chapter 12

New Kanji in this Chapter

#49 昼	#122 休	#52 着	#370 疲	#254 少
#400 飯	#372 寝	#248 空	#549 港	#390 近

1. 昼休みは何時から何時までですか。

Hiruyasumi wa nanji kara nanji made desu ka.
As for the lunch rest (i.e., lunch break) from what time until what time is it?

2. さあ、着きました。

Saa, tsukimashita.
Well, we arrived.

3. ここは東京インターナショナルホテルです。

Koko wa toukyou intaanashonaru hoteru desu.
As for here, it's Tokyo International Hotel.

4. 土田さん、私はちょっと疲れました。

Tsuchida san, watashi wa chotto tsukaremashita.
Tsuchida, as for me, I got a little tired.

5. 少し休んだ方がいいですね。

Sukoshi yasunda hou ga ii desu ne.
It would be better to rest a bit, huh.

6. お昼ご飯はもう食べた？

Ohirugohan wa mou tabeta?
As for honorable lunch, did you already eat it?

7. ううん、まだ食べてない。

Uun, mada tabetenai.
No, I still am not eating. (i.e., I haven't eaten; shortened for speech)

8. 電車が着きましたよ。

Densha ga tsukimashita yo.
The train arrived, for sure.

9. 昼休みは何時間ですか。

Hiruyasumi wa nanjikan desu ka.
As for the lunch break, how many hours is it?

10. 疲れたので少し寝たいです。

Tsukareta node sukoshi netai desu.
Since I got tired, I would like to sleep a little.

11. 明日学校へ行く？

Ashita gakkou e iku?
Will you go to school tomorrow?

12. 毎日公園へ行きますが、今日は行けませんでした。

Mainichi kouen e ikimasu ga, kyou wa ikemasen deshita.
Every day, I go to the park, but, as for today, I could not go.

13. 誰が疲れましたか。

Dare ga tsukaremashita ka.
Who got tired?

14. 12時です。お昼ご飯を食べましょうか。

Juuniji desu. Ohirugohan wo tabemashou ka.
It's 12:00. Shall we eat honorable lunch?

15. 小田さんは毎日何時に寝ますか。

Oda-san wa mainichi nanji ni nemasu ka.
As for Oda, every day, at what time does he sleep? (i.e., go to bed)

16. 成田空港から東京までは近いですか。
<small>なりた</small>

Narita kuukou kara toukyou made wa chikai desu ka.
From Narita airport, as for until Tokyo, is it close?

17. アンソニーさんはよく寝ますが、タクシーの中では寝ません。

Ansonii-san wa yoku nemasu ga, takushii no naka de wa nemasen.
As for Anthony, he sleeps often, but as for in the taxi's inside, he doesn't sleep.

18. とても大きい空港ですが、少し遠いです。

Totemo ookii kuukou desu ga, sukoshi tooi desu.
It's a very big airport, but it's a little far.

19. ソフィアさんは疲れました。

Sofia-san wa tsukaremashita.
As for Sophia, she got tired.

20. ご飯を食べる。

Gohan wo taberu.
I will eat rice.

21. 林さんは、空港にいます。

Hayashi-san wa, kuukou ni imasu.
Hayashi exists at the airport.

22. 病院の近くに何がありますか。

Byouin no chikaku ni nani ga arimasu ka.
At the hospital's closely, what exists?

23. どうも有難うございました。

Doumo arigatou gozaimashita.
Thank you very much for what you did.

24. 銀行はあそこにあります。

Ginkou wa asoko ni arimasu.
As for the bank, it exists at over there.

25. 木のまわりにベンチがあります。

Ki no mawari ni benchi ga arimasu.
The benches are around the tree.

26. メガネはテレビの上にあります。

Megane wa terebi no ue ni arimasu.
As for the eye glasses, they exist on the TV's top.

27. 病院は学校の後ろにあります。

Byouin wa gakkou no ushiro ni arimasu.
As for the hospital, it exists at the school's rear.

28. 成田空港は東京の近くにありません。

Narita kuukou wa Toukyou no chikaku ni arimasen.
As for Narita airport, it doesn't exist at Tokyo's closely. (i.e., it isn't close to Tokyo)

29. パソコンは便利ですか。

Pasokon wa benri desu ka.
Is a personal computer convenient?

30. ええ、便利ですが難しいですね。

Ee, benri desu ga muzukashii desu ne.
Yeah, it's convenient, but it's difficult, huh.

31. 疲れたからもう寝ます。

Tsukareta kara mou nemasu.
Because I got tired, already I'm going to bed.

32. 日本の着物を着たことがありますか。

Nihon no kimono wo kita koto ga arimasu ka.
Have you ever worn a Japanese kimono?

33. きれいですよ。一度着てみてください。

Kirei desu yo. Ichido kite mite kudasai.
It's pretty, for sure. Please try wearing one once and see.

Chapter 13

New Kanji in this Chapter

# 261 雨	# 178 降	# 76 黒	# 339 同	# 434 計
# 58 取	# 173 止	# 603 靴	# 89 買	# 5 品

1. 雨はいつまで降りますか。

Ame wa itsu made furimasu ka.
As for the rain, until when will it precipitate?

2. 花田さんと黒田さんは同じバッグを持っています。

Hanada-san to Kuroda-san wa onaji baggu wo motte imasu.
As for Hanada and Kuroda, they have the same bags.

3. 時計を取ります。

Tokei wo torimasu.
I will take off the watch.

4. もしも雨が降ったらお花見は止めます。

Moshimo ame ga futtara ohanami wa yamemasu.
If it rains, as for the honorable flower viewing, it will be stopped by someone.

5. 黒い車が 3 時から止まっています。

Kuroi kuruma ga san ji kara tomatte imasu.
The black car is being parked since 3:00.

6. 先生と学生は時計と靴とハンドバッグが同じです。

Sensei to gakusei wa tokei to kutsu to handobaggu ga onaji desu.
As for teacher and student, watch and shoes and handbag are the same.

7. 昨日は雨でしたか。

Kinou wa, ame deshita ka.
As for yesterday, was it rain?

8. どうぞ好きなのを取ってください。

Douzo suki na no wo totte kudasai.
Please go ahead and take the ones you like.

9. どうして買わなかったんですか。

Doushite kawanakkatan desu ka
Why didn't you buy it?

10. 高かったんです。

Takakattan desu.
Because it was expensive.

11. その品物は安くても買わない
方がいいですよ。

Sono shinamono wa yasukutemo kawanai hou ga ii desu yo.
As for that merchandise, even though inexpensive, it would be better not to buy, for sure.

12. その靴は高いですか。

Sono kutsu wa takai desu ka.
Are those shoes expensive?

13. いいえ、高くない。

Iie, takakunai.
No, they aren't expensive.

14. 雨が降ります。

Ame ga furimasu.
It will rain.

15. テレビを買いたいので秋葉原
へ行きます。

Terebi wo kaitai node akihabara e ikimasu.
Because I want to buy a TV, I'm going to Akihabara.

16. この靴は私には小さいようで
す。

Kono kutsu wa watashi ni wa chiisai you desu.
As for these shoes, as for to me, they appear to be small.

17. 黒田さんはその店で時計を買
いました。

Kuroda-san wa sono mise de tokei wo kaimashita.
Kuroda bought a watch in that store.

18. 雨は明日の朝まで降ります。

Ame wa ashita no asa made furimasu.
As for the rain, it will precipitate until tomorrow morning.

19. ハチミツを取ってください。

Hachimitsu wo totte kudasai.
Please pick up the honey. (or, please pass the honey)

20. 同じ品物をたくさん買って安
くなった。

Onaji shinamono wo takusan katte yasuku natta.
Identical merchandise a lot I buy, and cheaply it became.

21. 雨が止むまで待ちましょう。

Ame ga yamu made machimashou.
Let's wait until the rain stops.

22. ちょっとそこの本を取ってく
れ。

Chotto soko no hon wo totte kure.
For a second, pass that place's book and give. (kure is the imperative form of kureru)

23. この店にはたくさんの品物が
あります。

Kono mise ni wa takusan no shinamono ga arimasu.
As for in this store, a lot of merchandise exists.

Chapter 14

New Kanji in this Chapter

#413 開	#521 薬	#195 実	#503 地	#281 図
#355 違	#77 画	#348 送	#349 道	#36 映

1. スーツケースを開けてくださ
   い。

Suutsukeesu wo akete kudasai.
Please open the suitcase.

2. 薬ですか。

Kusuri desu ka.
Is it medicine?

3. いいえ、薬じゃありません。

Iie, kusuri ja arimasen.
No, it isn't medicine.

4. 何ですか。開けてください。

Nan desu ka. Akete kudasai.
What is it? Please open it.

5. これは... あの、実はハムで
   す。

Kore wa... Ano, jitsu wa hamu desu.
As for this... Say, as for the truth, it's
ham.

6. ハムですか。ハムは、だめで
   すよ。

Hamu desu ka. Hamu wa dame desu yo.
Is it ham? As for ham, it's bad, for sure.

7. ドアを開けてください。

Doa wo akete kudasai.
Please open the door.

8. 薬を飲んでください。

Kusuri wo nonde kudasai.
Please drink the medicine.

9. この木の実は食べれますか。

Kono kinomi wa taberemasu ka.
As for this nut, is it edible?

10. これは地図です。

Kore wa chizu desu.
As for this, it's a map.

11. いいえ、違います。

Iie, chigaimasu.
No, it's different. (i.e., the other person's
suggestion is incorrect)

12. 計画の実行を見送ることにし
    た。

Keikaku no jikkou wo miokuru koto ni
shita.
We decided to postpone the plan's
implementation.

13. あれ、道を間違えたのかな。

Are, michi wo machigaeta no kana.
Hey, I wonder if I mistook the street?
(michi = "way" in this sentence)

14. ちょっと地図を見てみます。

Chotto chizu wo mite mimasu.
I'll look at a map for a second and see.

15. 今日は何をしましょうか。

Kyou wa nani wo shimashou ka.
As for today, what shall we do?

16. テニスをしましょうか。

Tenisu wo shimashou ka.
Shall we do tennis?

17. 昨日しましたよ。

Kinou shimashita yo.
Yesterday we did it, for sure.

18. 今日は映画に行きましょう。

Kyou wa eiga ni ikimashou.
As for today, let's go for the purpose of a movie.

19. 私はちょっと疲れました。

Watashi wa, chotto tsukaremashita.
As for me, I got a little tired.

20. 友達が車で送ってくれました。

Tomodachi ga kuruma de okutte kuremashita.
A friend by car dropped me off and gave.

21. このレポートは間違いだらけだ。

Kono repooto wa machigai darake da.
As for this report, it's full of mistakes.

22. 道が分かりません。

Michi ga wakarimasen.
I don't understand the street. (i.e., I don't know the way)

23. 地図を見た方がいいですよ。

Chizu wo mita hou ga ii desu yo.
You'd better look at a map.

24. 私は昨日映画を見ました。

Watashi wa, kinou, eiga wo mimashita.
As for me, yesterday, I saw a movie.

25. この店は開いています。

Kono mise wa aite imasu.
This store is open.

26. 東京の道はあまりきれいじゃありません。

Toukyou no michi wa amari kirei ja arimasen.
Tokyo's streets are not very clean. (or, not very pretty)

27. 薬を飲みます。

Kusuri wo nomimasu.
I take medicine, or I will take medicine.

28. 成田空港は東京の東にあります。

Narita kuukou wa toukyou no higashi ni arimasu.
Narita Airport exists east of Tokyo.

29. 地図を見ておきます。

Chizu wo mite okimasu.
I will look at a map in advance.

30. 東京から成田まで、車で2時間ぐらいかかります。

Toukyou kara narita made, kuruma de nijikan gurai kakarimasu.
From Tokyo, until Narita, by car, it takes about two hours.

31. 電車もありますが、少し不便です。

Densha mo arimasu ga, sukoshi fuben desu.
There is also a train, but it's a little inconvenient.

32. 友達に薬を送ってもらいました。

Tomodachi ni kusuri wo okutte moraimashita.
By the friend, she sent medicine, and I received.

33. この店は小さくありません。

Kono mise wa chiisaku arimasen.
This store is not small.

34. この映画を見たことがある。

Kono eiga wo mita koto ga aru.
I've seen this movie.

Chapter 15

New Kanji in this Chapter

#90 貸	#313 悪	#31 当	#10 申	#426 口
#304 鉄	#357 込	#18 十	#39 円	#169 玉

1. お金を貸してください。

Okane wo kashite kudasai.
Please lend me some money.

2. 悪いけど。

Warui kedo...
Bad, but... (i.e., I really can't, said in response to a request)

3. 本当に申し訳ありません。

Hontou ni moushiwake arimasen.
Truly, there's no excuse. (i.e., I'm sorry)

4. 林さんに会ったことある？

Hayashi-san ni atta koto aru?
Have you ever met Hayashi? (colloquial speech)

5. ちょっと口を開けてください。

Chotto kuchi wo akete kudasai.
A little, open the mouth please.

6. 東京の地下鉄は不便ですか。

Toukyou no chikatetsu wa fuben desu ka.
As for the Tokyo subway, is it inconvenient?

7. いいえ、不便じゃありません。便利ですよ。

Iie, fuben ja arimasen. Benri desu yo.
No, it isn't inconvenient. It's convenient, for sure.

8. 人の悪口は言ってもらいたくないですね。

Hito no warukuchi wa itte moraitakunai desu ne.
As for a person's slander, I don't want you to say and I receive it, huh.

9. 道がすいていますね。

Michi ga suite imasu ne.
The streets are being uncrowded, huh.

10. ええ、あまり込んでいませんね。

Ee, amari konde imasen ne.
Yeah, they aren't being very crowded, huh.

11. ビールは十分あります。

Biiru wa juubun arimasu.
As for beer, there's enough.

12. ここは狭いです。

Koko wa semai desu.
As for here, it's tight or narrow.

13. 申し訳ないんですが。

Moushiwake nain desu ga...
There's no excuse, but... (i.e., I'm sorry)

14. 黒田さんのけがはどうですか。

Kuroda-san no kega wa dou desu ka?
As for Kuroda's injury, how is it?

15. 今、あっちで手当てをしています。

Ima, atchi de teate wo shite imasu.
Now, at over that way, they are doing medical treatment.

16. 花田さん、100円玉を貸してくれませんか。

Hanada-san, hyaku en dama wo kashite kuremasen ka.
Hanada, won't you lend and give me a 100-yen coin?

17. 地下鉄は込んでいるけれど、便利です。

Chikatetsu wa konde iru keredo, benri desu.
The subways are crowded, but they are convenient.

18. その店は本当に安いんですか。

Sono mise wa hontou ni yasuin desu ka.
As for that store, is it truly cheap?

19. ここで十分待ちましょう。

Koko de juppun machimashou.
Let's wait here for 10 minutes.

20. ペンを貸してください。

Pen wo kashite kudasai.
Please lend me the pen.

21. ここは狭くないです。

Koko wa semaku nai desu.
As for here, it isn't tight or narrow.

22. 日曜日は家内とデパートへ買い物に行くことになっているので都合が悪いんですが…

Nichiyoubi wa kanai to depaato e kaimono ni iku koto ni natte iru node tsugou ga waruin desu ga...
As for Sunday, since I'm scheduled to go to a department store for shopping with my wife, the circumstances are bad, but...

23. あれは地下鉄です。

Are wa chikatetsu desu.
As for that over there, it's the subway.

24. ここは静かです。

Koko wa shizuka desu.
As for here, it's quiet.

25. ジョンソンさんにテレフォンカードを貸してあげました。

Jonson-san ni terefon kaado wo kashite agemashita.
I lent and gave a telephone card to Johnson.

26. キャベツとレタスと玉ねぎ
   を買いにスーパーに行く。

Kyabetsu to retasu to tamanegi wo kai ni suupaa ni iku.
For the purpose of to buy cabbage, lettuce and onions, I will go to the supermarket.

27. ごめんね。100円玉がなかっ
   たから電話ができなかった
   よ。

Gomen ne. Hyaku en dama ga nakatta kara denwa ga dekinakatta yo.
Forgive huh. Since there wasn't a 100-yen coin, I couldn't do the phone, for sure.

28. ここは静かじゃありません。

Koko wa shizuka ja arimasen.
As for here, it isn't quiet.

29. コピーは十時までにできる？

Kopii wa juuji made ni dekiru?
As for the copying, will it be ready by 10:00?

30. 花田さんにテレフォンカード
   を貸してもらいました。

Hanada-san ni terefon kaado wo kashite moraimashita.
By Hanada, she lent a telephone card, and I received.

31. 今日は道が込んでいますか。

Kyou wa michi ga konde imasu ka.
As for today, are the streets being crowded?

32. 今日のレートは1ドル110円
   です。

Kyou no reeto wa ichidoru hyaku juu en desu.
As for today's rate, it's one dollar 110 yen (i.e., 110 yen to the dollar).

Chapter 16

New Kanji in this Chapter

# 607 寿	# 608 司	# 197 漢	# 183 字	# 596 掛
# 243 帽	# 182 子	# 377 祭	# 280 困	# 104 初

1. アンドリューさんはお寿司が好きですか。

Andoryuu-san wa osushi ga suki desu ka.
As for Andrew, is honorable sushi liked?
(i.e., do you like it?)

2. 漢字は難しいですか。

Kanji wa muzukashii desu ka.
Are kanji difficult?

3. いいえ、難しくありません。

Iie, muzukashiku arimasen.
No, they aren't difficult.

4. 小さい字はめがねを掛けて見ます。

Chiisai ji wa megane wo kakete mimasu.
As for the small characters, I'll look at them wearing glasses.

5. あそこに帽子が掛かっています。

Asoko ni boushi ga kakatte imasu.
The hat is hanging over there.

6. 寿司はおいしいですが高いです。

Sushi wa oishii desu ga, takai desu.
Sushi is delicious, but it's expensive.

7. ひな祭りは何曜日でしたか。

Hinamatsuri wa nan youbi deshita ka.
What day of the week was the Doll's (i.e., Girl's) Festival?

8. 明日会社を休みたいんですが。

Ashita kaisha wo yasumitain desu ga...
Tomorrow, I'd like to rest the company, but... (i.e., I'd like to be off)

9. いや、休んじゃ困りますよ。

Iya, yasun ja komarimasu yo.
Nah, taking time off would inconvenience, for sure. (yasunja = yasunde wa)

10. お寿司が好きです。

Osushi ga suki desu.
Honorable sushi is liked. (i.e., I like it)

11. 道子さんはそう言わなかった。

Michiko-san wa sou iwanakatta.
Michiko didn't say so.

12. え！ 銀行は３時までですか。困ったなぁ。

E! Ginkou wa sanji made desu ka. Komatta naa.
Eh! As for the bank, it's until 3:00? I got inconvenienced.

13. お金を下ろしたいのに。

Okane wo oroshitai noni.
In spite of the fact that I want to withdraw money.

14. これはあなたの帽子じゃないんですか。

Kore wa anata no boushi ja nain desu ka.
Isn't this your hat?

15. 土田さんは誰に電話を掛けましたか。

Tsuchida-san wa dare ni denwa wo kakemashita ka.
As for Tsuchida, to whom did he call on the phone?

16. 日本に来るのは初めてです。

Nihon ni kuru no wa hajimete desu.
As for to come to Japan, it's the first time.

17. 帽子を取る。

Boushi wo toru.
I will take off the hat. (or, I will take the hat)

18. 漢字が分からなくて困っています。

Kanji ga wakaranakute komatte imasu.
Since I don't understand kanji, I am getting inconvenienced.

19. 寿司を食べてください。

Sushi wo tabete kudasai.
Please eat the sushi.

20. 日本のお祭りを見たことがありますか。

Nihon no omatsuri wo mita koto ga arimasu ka.
Have you ever seen an honorable Japanese festival?

21. いいえ、ありません。初めてです。

Iie, arimasen. Hajimete desu.
No, I haven't. It's the first time.

22. お祭りで多くの人を見ました。

Omatsuri de ooku no hito wo mimashita.
At the honorable festival, I saw a lot of people.

23. 帽子を取られた。

Boushi wo torareta.
The hat was taken on him.

24. 家内もお寿司が好きです。

Kanai mo osushi ga suki desu.
The wife also likes honorable sushi.

25. 黒田さんはパーティーの前にアビゲイルさんに会ったことがある。

Kuroda-san wa paatii no mae ni abigeiru-san ni atta koto ga aru.
As for Kuroda, she has met Abigail at before the party.

26. 雨でお祭りが中止になりました。

Ame de omatsuri ga chuushi ni narimashita.
Due to rain, the honorable festival to cancellation became. (i.e., it was cancelled)

27. あなたはどこから来ましたか。

Anata wa doko kara kimashita ka.
As for you, where did you come from? (i.e., where do you come from?)

28. 私は東京です。

Watashi wa toukyou desu.
As for me, it's Tokyo. (i.e., I came from Tokyo)

29. 寿司は何を食べたいですか。

Sushi wa nani wo tabetai desu ka.
As for sushi, what would you like to eat?

30. 私はトロ。

Watashi wa toro.
As for me, fatty tuna.

31. じゃあ、私はエビがいいわ。

Jaa, watashi wa ebi ga ii wa.
Well, as for me, shrimp is good.

32. どうですか。東京の寿司は。

Dou desu ka. Toukyou no sushi wa.
How is it, as for Tokyo sushi?

33. 今日初めて漢字を書いてみました。

Kyou hajimete kanji wo kaite mimashita.
Today, for the first time, I wrote kanji and saw. (i.e., I tried writing kanji)

Chapter 17

New Kanji in this Chapter

#380 駅	#474 勉	#478 強	#148 月	#448 光
#389 新	#282 面	#44 白	#177 年	#232 緒

1. 駅の近くです。

Eki no chikaku desu.
It's near the station.

2. 私は毎日勉強します。

Watashi wa mainichi benkyou shimasu.
As for me, every day, I study.

3. 道は月曜日より日曜日の方がもっと込んでいます。

Michi wa getsuyoubi yori nichiyoubi no hou ga motto konde imasu.
As for the roads, compared to Monday, they are more crowded on Sundays.

4. どれがジェイコブさんの靴ですか。

Dore ga jeikobu-san no kutsu desu ka.
Which are Jacob's shoes?

5. 東京駅から日光まで電車で2時間ぐらいかかります。

Toukyou eki kara nikkou made densha de nijikan gurai kakarimasu.
From Tokyo station, until Nikkou, by train, it takes about 2 hours.

6. あなたの日本語の本は新しいですか。

Anata no nihongo no hon wa atarashii desu ka.
Is your Japanese language book new?

7. ええ、新しいです。

Ee, atarashii desu.
Yeah, it's new.

8. 日本語は難しいですが面白いです。

Nihongo wa muzukashii desu ga, omoshiroi desu.
The Japanese language is difficult, but it's interesting.

9. ブラウンさんは鎌倉へも日光へも行きました。

Buraun-san wa kamakura e mo nikkou e mo ikimashita.
As for Brown, he went to Kamakura also, to Nikkou also.

10. ろうそくの光はきれいだ。

Rousoku no hikari wa kirei da.
As for the candle's light, it's pretty.

11. 十月中にアメリカに行くことになりました。

Juugatsu chuu ni amerika ni iku koto ni narimashita.
Sometime in October, I was scheduled to go to America.

12. この家はいつ頃できたんですか。

Kono ie wa itsu goro dekitan desu ka.
As for this house, about when was it accomplished?

13. もう十年になりますね。

Mou juu nen ni narimasu ne.
It will already become 10 years, huh.

14. この新しい靴はジェイコブさんの靴です。

Kono atarashii kutsu wa jeikobu-san no kutsu desu.
These new shoes are Jacob's shoes.

15. 来月駅の前に大きいスーパーができるんですよ。

Raigetsu eki no mae ni ookii suupaa ga dekirun desu yo.
Next month, in front of the station, a large supermarket will accomplish, for sure.

16. アッシュリーさん、いつか一緒に行きましょう。

Asshurii-san, itsuka issho ni ikimashou.
Ashley, sometime together let's go.

17. 面白いですよ。

Omoshiroi desu yo.
It's interesting, for sure.

18. 来年からフランス語を勉強することになりました。

Rainen kara furansugo wo benkyou suru koto ni narimashita.
It was scheduled that I'll study French starting next year.

19. 今年のクリスマスは何曜日ですか。

Kotoshi no kurisumasu wa nan youbi desu ka.
As for this year's Christmas, what day of the week is it?

20. 明日はテストがあります。

Ashita wa tesuto ga arimasu.
As for tomorrow, a test exists.

21. 一緒に勉強しましょうか。

Issho ni benkyou shimashou ka.
Shall we study together?

22. ちょっとビールを飲んで帰りませんか。

Chotto biiru wo nonde kaerimasen ka.
Won't you drink beer for a short time and return?

23. 今日はうちに早く帰ることにしています。

Kyou wa uchi ni hayaku kaeru koto ni shite imasu.
As for today, I am decided to return home early.

24. そうですか。あなたに話して
おきたいことがあったんです
けど。

Sou desu ka. Anata ni hanashite okitai
koto ga attan desu kedo...
Is that so? To you, wanting to talk in
advance thing existed, but...

25. じゃ、一緒に行くことにしま
しょう。

Ja, issho ni iku koto ni shimashou.
Well, let's decide to go together.

26. ちょっとうちに電話をして来
ますから...

Chotto uchi ni denwa wo shite kimasu
kara...
Because I will do a phone call to home
for a short time and come.

27. 東京は面白いですが物価が高
いです。

Toukyou wa omoshiroi desu ga bukka ga
takai desu.
As for Tokyo, it's interesting, but the
prices are high.

Chapter 18

New Kanji in this Chapter

# 502 長	# 324 短	# 412 聞	# 588 課	# 346 週
# 300 全	# 501 髪	# 103 切	# 361 過	# 129 枚

1. 少しスカートが長いですね。

Sukoshi sukaato ga nagai desu ne.
A little, the skirt is long, huh.

2. そうですね。少し短くしましょうか。

Sou desu ne. Sukoshi mijikaku shimashou ka.
That's so, huh. Shall we shorten it a little?

3. スミスさん、この間のレポートはどうなりましたか。

Sumisu-san, kono aida no repooto wa dou narimashita ka.
Smith, as for this recent report, how did it develop?

4. ええ、部長に見ていただきました。

Ee, buchou ni mite itadakimashita.
Yeah, by the division manager he looked at it, and I received.

5. 先生に聞きましょうか。

Sensei ni kikimashou ka.
Shall we ask the teacher?

6. 新聞を読む人です。

Shinbun wo yomu hito desu.
It's a person who reads a newspaper.

7. 課長さんは困っています。

Kachou-san wa komatte imasu.
As for Mr. Section Manager, he is being inconvenienced.

8. 来週の日曜日にはどんなことをしたいですか。

Raishuu no nichiyoubi ni wa donna koto wo shitai desu ka.
As for on next week's Sunday, what kinds of things would you like to do?

9. 一つ50円ですから全部で250円になります。

Hitotsu gojuuen desu kara zenbu de nihyaku gojuen ni narimasu.
Since it's 50 yen apiece, altogether it amounts to 250 yen.

10. 髪を短く切ってください。

Kami wo mijikaku kitte kudasai.
Please cut the hair short.

11. 社員：課長の話をもうお聞きになりましたでしょうか。

Shain: Kachou no hanashi wo mou okiki ni narimashita deshou ka.
Company employee: Did you already probably honorably hear the section manager's speech? (speaking to the president)

12. 社長：いや、まだ何も聞いていないよ。

Shachou: Iya, mada nanimo kiite inai yo.
President: Naa, I still am not hearing nothing, for sure.

13. ビールを飲み過ぎて少し気分が悪い。

Biiru wo nomi sugite sukoshi kibun ga warui.
Since I drank too much beer, a little, the health-related feeling is bad.

14. 髪が長かった人を見ました。

Kami ga nagakatta hito wo mimashita,
I saw a person who had long hair.

15. 私の小学校の校長先生は、白髪の品のいい方だった。

Watashi no shougakkou no kouchou sensei wa hakuhatsu no hin no ii kata datta.
As for my primary school's principal teacher, it was a grey hair's refinement-is-good person. (i.e., the principal was a grey-haired, highly refined person)

16. 課長、来週のパーティーにいらっしゃいますか。

Kachou, raishuu no paatii ni irasshaimasu ka.
Section Manager, to next week's party, will you honorably come?

17. 62円の切手と200円の切手を5枚ずつください。

Roku juu ni en no kitte to nihyaku en no kitte wo gomai zutsu kudasai.
62-yen stamps and 200-yen stamps, five of each please.

18. 全部で1310円になります。

Zenbu de sen sanbyaku juu en ni narimasu.
Altogether, it comes to 1310 yen.

19. このセーターは私には大き過ぎます。

Kono seetaa wa watashi ni wa, ooki sugimasu.
As for this sweater, as for to me, it's too big.

20. はさみなしで紙を切れません。

Hasami nashi de kami wo kiremasen.
Without scissors, I cannot cut the paper.

21. 来週の土曜日は何日ですか。

Raishuu no doyoubi wa nan nichi desu ka.
What day (of the month) is Saturday of next week?

22. 全部、私のペンです。

Zenbu, watashi no pen desu.
All are my pens.

23. 切手をもらったんですか。

Kitte wo morattan desu ka.
Did you get stamps?

24. ええ、62円のと41円のを5枚ずつもらったんです。

Ee, rokujuu ni en no to yonjuu ichi en no wo gomai zutsu morattan desu.
Yeah, I got 5 each of the 62-yen and 41-yen ones.

25. 日本の新聞を読んでいるんですか。

Nihon no shinbun wo yonde irun desu ka.
Are you reading a Japanese newspaper?

26. ええ、でも漢字が難し過ぎて分からないんですよ。

Ee, demo kanji ga muzukashisugite wakaranain desu yo.
Yeah, but because the kanji are too difficult, I don't understand it, for sure.

27. 課長はパーティにいらっしゃるかしら。

Kachou wa paatii ni irassharu kashira.
As for the section manager, to the party, he will honorably come, I wonder.

28. 短い時間で本を読み終わった。

Mijikai jikan de hon wo yomiowatta.
In a short time, I finished reading the book.

29. 白い紙を一枚買いました。

Shiroi kami wo ichimai kaimashita.
I bought one sheet of white paper.

Chapter 19

New Kanji in this Chapter

#303 良	#480 使	#524 客	#583 無	#350 遅
#166 主	#35 晩	#532 奥	#535 欲	#385 幸

1. 天気はあまり良くありまん。
Tenki wa amari yoku arimasen.
As for the weather, it isn't very good.

2. 食べるとき、はしを使う。
Taberu toki hashi wo tsukau.
When one eats, one uses chopsticks.

3. クリストファーさんはどこでも良く寝ます。
Kurisutofaa-san wa dokodemo yoku nemasu.
Christopher sleeps well anywhere.

4. この間はお客さんの前で寝ていましたよ。
Kono aida wa okyaku-san no mae de nete imashita yo.
As for the other day he was sleeping in front of honorable guests, for sure.

5. お金を無くしました。
Okane wo nakushimashita.
I lost money.

6. 道が込んでいたので遅れました。
Michi ga konde ita node okuremashita.
Because the streets were crowded, I was delayed.

7. 主人は今晩、遅いと言ってましたから、どうぞごゆっくり。
Shujin wa konban osoi to ittemashita kara, douzo goyukkuri.
Since my husband was saying tonight late (i.e., he said he would be late), go ahead, take your honorable time.

8. お金が無くなっています。
Okane ga nakunatte imasu.
The money is missing.

9. そんなにたくさんのお金を何に使うんだろう。
Sonna ni takusan no okane wo nani ni tsukaun darou.
So much a lot of money, to what will he use it probably?

10. 奥さんが前から欲しがってい
たダイヤのネックレスをプレ
ゼントするそうです。

Okusan ga mae kara hoshigatte ita daiya no nekkuresu wo purezento suru sou desu.
The wife-since-before-appeared-to-be-wanting diamond necklace he will do a present reportedly.

11. まぁ、いいご主人を持って奥
さん、幸せですねぇ。

Maa, ii goshujin wo motte okusan, shiawase desu nee.
My, since have a good husband, wife, it's happiness, huh.

12. このフォークはきれいです
か。

Kono fooku wa kirei desu ka.
Is this fork clean?

13. まだ誰も使っていないから、
きれいなはずです。

Mada daremo tsukatte inai kara, kirei na hazu desu.
Since no one still isn't using it, it ought to be clean.

14. お客さんが来るまでには終わ
るでしょう。

Okyaku-san ga kuru made ni wa owaru deshou.
As for by the time the honorable guest comes, it will probably finish (referring to the cleaning of a room).

15. 本を無くした。

Hon wo nakushita.
I lost a book.

16. 奥さんからのプレゼントは
白いエプロンでした。

Okusan kara no purezento wa shiroi epuron deshita.
The from-the-honorable-wife's present was a white apron.

17. 紙を大切にして欲しい。

Kami wo taisetsu ni shite hoshii.
I desire that you make paper precious. (i.e., don't waste it)

18. とても幸せです。

Totemo shiawase desu.
It's very much happiness. (i.e., I'm very happy)

19. ホテルで良く寝ました。

Hoteru de yoku nemashita.
I slept well in the hotel.

20. アッシュリーさんは仕事が終
わったら、ホテルに電話して
欲しいといった。

Asshurii-san wa shigoto ga owattara, hoteru ni denwa shite hoshii to itta.
As for Ashley, when the work finishes, she said that she desires me to do a phone call to the hotel.

21. お客さんはなぜ帰ると言いま
したか

Okyakusan wa naze kaeru to iimashita ka.
As for the honorable customer, why did he say he will return?

22. もう遅くなりましたから。

Mou osoku narimashita kara.
Because it already became late.

23. バスが無くなりましたから。

Basu ga nakunarimashita kara.
Because there wasn't a bus. (it disappeared)

24. 今晩何をするつもりですか

Konban nani wo surutsumori desu ka.
What are you planning to do tonight?

25. 私の主人はとても幸せです。

Watashi no shujin wa totemo shiawase desu.
As for my husband, it's very much happiness (i.e., he's very happy).

26. 今晩一緒に食事をしましょ
う。

Konban issho ni shokuji wo shimashou.
Tonight, together, let's do a meal.

Chapter 20

New Kanji in this Chapter

#93 頭	#153 胃	#368 痛	#262 雪	#146 山
#100 具	#452 起	#438 議	#330 洋	#513 和

1. 頭の上です。
Atama no ue desu.
It's above the head.

2. ちょっと胃が痛い。
Chotto i ga itai.
A little, the stomach hurts.

3. じゃ、病院に行った方がいいですよ。
Ja, byouin ni itta hou ga ii desu yo
Well, you'd better go to the hospital.

4. 1時間ぐらい待った方がいいんじゃありませんか。
Ichijikan gurai matta hou ga iin ja arimasen ka.
Wouldn't it be better if you waited about an hour?

5. ええ、でも今、行きます。
Ee, demo ima ikimasu.
Yeah, but I'll go now.

6. まだ痛いですか。
Mada itai desu ka.
Does it still hurt?

7. 雪子さん、山に行きたいですか。
Yukiko-san, yama ni ikitai desu ka.
Yukiko, do you want to go to the mountains?

8. いいえ、行きたくありません。
Iie, ikitaku arimasen.
No, I don't want to go.

9. 雪子さん、山に行きませんか。
Yukiko-san, yama ni ikimasen ka.
Yukiko, won't you go to the mountains?

10. ええ、でもちょっと都合が悪いんです。
Ee, demo chotto tsugou ga waruin desu.
Yeah, but a little bit, the circumstances are bad.

11. 気分はどうですか。
Kibun wa dou desu ka.
As for health-related feeling, how is it?

12. ええ、胃の具合が悪いんです。

Ee, i no guai ga waruin desu.
Yeah, the stomach's condition is bad.

13. 朝起きたら雪が降っていました。

Asa okitara yuki ga futte imashita.
Morning, when I got up, it was snowing.

14. 私は明日会議に出ることになっています。

Watashi wa asu kaigi ni deru koto ni natte imasu.
As for me, I am scheduled to attend a meeting tomorrow.

15. 胃がシクシクする。

I ga shikushiku suru.
The stomach does upset.

16. 洋子さんの手は雪みたいに白い。

Youko-san no te wa yuki mitai ni shiroi.
Youko's hands are, like snow, white.

17. 明日は早く起きます。

Ashita wa hayaku okimasu.
As for tomorrow, I will get up early.

18. 具合が悪いんでしょう？

Guai ga waruin deshou?
The condition is bad probably?

19. 明日は休んだらどうですか。

Asu wa yasundara dou desu ka.
As for tomorrow, if you rest, how is it?

20. 明日は大切な会議があるから、どんなに具合が悪くても休めないんです。

Asu wa taisetsu na kaigi ga aru kara, donna ni guai ga warukutemo yasumenain desu.
As for tomorrow, since an important meeting exists, whatever kind of condition bad even though, I am not able to rest.

21. もう痛くありません。

Mou itaku arimasen.
It doesn't hurt any more.

22. 和食が好きな人と洋食が好きな人とどちらが多いですか。

Washoku ga suki na hito to youshoku ga suki na hito to dochira ga ooi desu ka.
People who like Japanese food vs. people who like Western food, which are more numerous?

23. 山下さんはハンサムだし頭もいいし、とても人気があります。

Yamashita-san wa hansamu da shi atama mo ii shi, totemo ninki ga arimasu.
As for Yamashita, he is handsome, and his head is also good (i.e., intelligent), and a lot of popularity exists.

24. 洋子さんは飲まない。

Youko-san wa nomanai.
As for Youko, she won't drink.

25. 日曜日は昼ご飯ができるまで寝ているんですよ。

Nichiyoubi wa hirugohan ga dekiru made nete irun desu yo.
As for Sundays, until lunch is ready, I'm sleeping, for sure.

26. 10時頃までには起きた方がいいですよ。

Juuji goro made ni wa okita hou ga ii desu yo.
As for by about 10:00, it would be better to get up, for sure.

27. 私は明日会議に出るつもりです。

Watashi wa asu kaigi ni derutsumori desu.
As for me, tomorrow, I plan to attend the meeting.

28. 頭が痛いんです。

Atama ga itain desu.
The head hurts.

29. 和光へはどう行ったらいいでしょうか。

Wakou e wa dou ittara ii deshou ka.
As for to Wakou, how when you go is probably good? (asking for directions to Wakou, a luxury department store in Ginza)

30. 成田（なりた）は新しい空港ですが少し不便です。

Narita wa atarashii kuukou desu ga sukoshi fuben desu.
As for Narita, it's a new airport, but it's a bit inconvenient.

31. 和食が好きですか、それとも洋食が好きですか。

Washoku ga suki desu ka, soretomo youshoku ga suki desu ka.
Do you like Japanese food, or do you like Western food?

Chapter 21

New Kanji in this Chapter

#206 失	#275 礼	#94 願	#14 入	#133 符
#593 拝	#592 押	#29 点	#414 閉	#38 暖

1. あのう、失礼ですがスミスさんですか。

Anou, shitsurei desu ga sumisu-san desu ka.
Say, It's a discourtesy, but is it Smith? (i.e., are you Smith?)

2. はい、そうです。どなたですか。

Hai, sou desu. Donata desu ka.
Yes, it's so. Who is it?

3. 初めまして。どうぞよろしく。

Hajimemashite. Douzo yoroshiku.
How do you do? Go ahead be good to me.

4. こちらこそ。どうぞよろしく。こちらは、奥さんですか。

Kochira koso. Douzo yoroshiku. Kochira wa, okusan desu ka.
The pleasure's all mine. Please be good to me. As for this way, is it the honorable wife?

5. はい、家内のオリビアです。

Hai. Kanai no oribia desu.
Yes, it's the wife's Olivia. (i.e., my wife Olivia)

6. 初めまして、オリビアです。どうぞよろしくお願いします。

Hajimemashite, oribia desu. Douzo yoroshiku onegai shimasu.
How do you do? I'm Olivia. Please be good to me.

7. 箱に入れない。

Hako ni irenai.
I won't put it in a box.

8. 切符を拝見いたします。

Kippu wo haiken itashimasu.
I will humbly look at your ticket.

9. お待ちしていました。

Omachi shite imashita.
We were humbly waiting. (i.e., we've been expecting you)

10. どうぞお入りください。

Douzo ohairi kudasai.
Go ahead, please come in.

11. では失礼します。

Dewa shitsurei shimasu.
Well, I will commit a discourtesy. (i.e., I'll inconvenience you)

12. あっ、シーツがまだ出ていませんね。

A, shiitsu ga mada dete imasen ne.
Ah, the sheets aren't gone out yet, huh.
Meaning, they aren't out yet.

13. すみませんが押入れから出してください。

Sumimasen ga oshiire kara dashite kudasai.
Excuse me, but please take them out of the bedding closet.

14. 電気が点きました。

Denki ga tsukimashita.
The light came on.

15. ドアが閉まる。

Doa ga shimaru.
The door will close.

16. 部屋は暖かそうです。

Heya wa atataka sou desu.
As for the room, it appears to be warm.

17. パスポートを拝見してもよろしいですか。

Pasupooto wo haiken shite mo yoroshii desu ka.
Is it all right if I look at your passport?

18. あのう、すみません。切符を買いたいんですけど。

Anou. Sumimasen. Kippu wo kaitain desu kedo...
Say. Excuse me. I'd like to buy a ticket, but...

19. そろそろ失礼します。

Sorosoro shitsurei shimasu.
Gradually, I'll commit a discourtesy. (i.e., I'll be going)

20. 今日はどうも有難うございました。

Kyou wa doumo arigatou gozaimashita.
As for today, thank you very much for what you did.

21. 失礼します。さようなら。おやすみなさい。

Shitsurei shimasu. Sayounara. Oyasuminasai.
I will commit a discourtesy. Good-bye. Good night.

22. 飲み物は何にしますか。

Nomimono wa nani ni shimasu ka.
As for drinks, what will you choose?

23. ビールとジュースを4本ずつお願いします。

Biiru to juusu wo yonhon zutsu onegai shimasu.
Beer and juice four bottles each, I beg.

24. 全部で8本です。

Zenbu de happon desu.
Altogether, they are eight bottles.

25. お金を入れてボタンを押すと切符が出てきますよ。

Okane wo irete botan wo osu to kippu ga dete kimasu yo.
If you put in money and push the button, the ticket will emerge and come, for sure.

26. ストーブを点けて暖かくしましょうか。

Sutoobu wo tsukete atatakaku shimashou ka.
Shall I turn on the heater and make it warm?

27. ええ、お願いします。

Ee, onegai shimasu.
Yeah, please do.

28. ドアを閉める。

Doa wo shimeru.
I will close the door.

29. パスポートを拝見できますか。

Pasupooto wo haiken dekimasu ka.
Is it possible to look humbly at your passport?

30. きれいなテーブルクロスですね。

Kirei na teeburukurosu desu ne.
It's a pretty tablecloth, huh.

31. メキシコの友達が送ってくれたんですよ。

Mekishiko no tomodachi ga okutte kuretan desu yo.
A Mexican friend sent and gave it, for sure.

32. それでお礼の手紙を書こうと思っています。

Sore de orei no tegami wo kakou to omotte imasu.
For that reason, I shall write a letter of thanks, I'm thinking.

33. 押入れが閉まらない。

Oshiire ga shimaranai.
The closet won't close.

34. 男の人が電気を点けました。

Otoko no hito ga denki wo tsukemashita.
The man turned on the light.

35. 部屋を暖かくします。

Heya wo atatakaku shimasu.
I'll make the room warm.

36. 電気が点いています。

Denki ga tsuite imasu.
The light is on.

Chapter 22

New Kanji in this Chapter

#250 川	#255 泳	#499 渡	#54 覚	#139 橋
#287 働	#486 供	#489 夜	#135 横	#235 女

1. この川を泳いで渡れるかどう か今度泳いでみます。

Kono kawa wo oyoide watareru ka douka kondo oyoide mimasu.
On this river swimming, whether I can cross or not, this time, I will swim and see.

2. もうひらがなを覚えてしまい ましたか。

Mou hiragana wo oboete shimaimashita ka.
Already, did you completely memorize hiragana?

3. 橋本さんは毎日何時間寝ます か。

Hashimoto-san wa mainichi nanjikan nemasu ka.
As for Hashimoto, every day, how many hours does he sleep?

4. いつまで働きますか。

Itsu made hatarakimasu ka.
Until when will you labor?

5. 子供が生まれるまで。

Kodomo ga umareru made.
Until the child is born.

6. いつまで日本語を勉強します か。

Itsu made nihongo wo benkyou shimasu ka.
Until when will you study Japanese?

7. 漢字をたくさん覚えるまで。

Kanji wo takusan oboeru made.
Until kanji, a lot, I memorize.

8. あっ、あぶない！子供が川を 泳いで渡ろうとしています。

A, abunai! Kodomo ga kawa wo oyoide watarou to shite imasu.
Ah, danger. A child, swimming on the river, is trying to cross.

9. 朝8時から夜10時まで仕事 をしています。

Asa hachiji kara yoru juuji made shigoto wo shite imasu.
From 8 in the morning until 10 at night, I am working.

10. 働き過ぎて疲れませんか。

Hataraki sugite tsukaremasen ka.
Because you labor too much, don't you tire?

11. この川はきれいですか。

Kono kawa wa kirei desu ka.
Is this river clean?

12. いいえ、きれいじゃない。

Iie, kirei ja nai.
No, it isn't clean.

13. プールの横でなわとびをしている女の子は花子ちゃんです。

Puuru no yoko de nawatobi wo shite iru onna no ko wa hanako-chan desu.
The girl beside the pool skipping rope is little Hanako.

14. ひらがなをもう覚えてしまいました。

Hiragana wo mou oboete shimaimashita.
I already memorized hiragana completely.

15. これからは川を泳いで渡ったりしません。

Kore kara wa kawa wo oyoide watattari shimasen.
As for from now, on the river swimming, crossing, etc., I will not do.

16. 橋田さんはもう一度寿司屋へ行った。

Hashida-san wa mou ichido sushiya e itta.
Hashida went to the sushi place once again.

17. 夜なので今度はすいていた。

Yoru na node kondo wa suite ita.
Because it is (or was) night, as for this time, it was uncrowded.

18. 女の人が電話の横にいます。

Onna no hito ga denwa no yoko ni imasu.
A woman exists next to the phone.

19. 一時間働いてどのくらいのお金がもらえますか。

Ichijikan hataraite, dono kurai no okane ga moraemasu ka.
Laboring one hour, about how much money can she receive?

20. 電話は机の横です。

Denwa wa tsukue no yoko desu.
As for the telephone, it's beside the desk.

21. 女の人が電気を点けます。

Onna no hito ga denki wo tsukemasu.
The woman will turn on the light.

22. 夜遅く電話をしないでください。

Yoru osoku denwa wo shinai de kudasai.
Late at night, please don't do a phone call.

23. 橋を渡る。

Hashi wo wataru.
I cross the bridge.

24. 子供は川で泳いでいます。

Kodomo wa kawa de oyoide imasu.
The children are swimming in the river.

Chapter 23

New Kanji in this Chapter

# 72 猫	# 402 易	# 522 夏	# 410 問	# 454 題
# 278 暑	# 311 窓	# 553 変	# 507 寒	# 116 旅

1. 机の下に何がいますか。

Tsukue no shita ni nani ga imasu ka.
At under the desk, what exists?

2. 猫がいます。

Neko ga imasu.
A cat exists.

3. 日本語は易しいですか。

Nihongo wa yasashii desu ka.
As for the Japanese language, is it easy?

4. 今年の夏にどんなことをした
いですか。

Kotoshi no natsu ni donna koto wo shitai
desu ka.
At this year's summer, what kinds of
things would you like to do?

5. そんな難しい問題、できっこ
ない。

Sonna muzukashii mondai, dekikkonai.
That kind of difficult problem, I can never
do. (-kkonai = never can do, when used
after a potential verb stem)

6. 明日はおそらく暑いでしょ
う。

Ashita wa osoraku atsui deshou.
As for tomorrow, it's very likely it will be
hot, probably.

7. 窓が開かない。

Mado ga akanai.
The window will not open.

8. 箱に猫を入れる。

Hako ni neko wo ireru.
I will put the cat in the box.

9. このテストの問題は全部すぐ
分かりましたよ。

Kono tesuto no mondai wa zenbu sugu
wakarimashita yo.
As for this test's problems, I soon
understood all of them, for sure.

10. そうですか。あなたには易
し過ぎましたね。

Sou desu ka. Anata ni wa
yasashisugimashita ne.
Is that so? As for to you, it was too easy,
huh.

11. 日本語の勉強はどうです
か。

Nihongo no benkyou wa dou desu ka.
As for Japanese study, how is it?

12. トムさんは易しいって言ってたけど私には大変です。

Tomu-san wa yasashii tte itteta kedo watashi ni wa taihen desu.
As for Tom, it's easy, he was saying, but as for me, it's terrible.

13. それは子供でさえできる問題だ。

Sore wa kodomo de sae dekiru mondai da.
As for that, a child even to be able to do problem it is. (sae, or de sae, = "even")

14. 寒い時、窓を閉めます。

Samui toki, mado wo shimemasu.
When it's cold, I close the window.

15. その問題はほっておいてください。

Sono mondai wa hotteoite kudasai.
As for that problem, please leave it alone.

16. 電車が込んで大変です。

Densha ga konde, taihen desu.
Because the train gets crowded, it's terrible.

17. あの猫は木の近くにいます。

Ano neko wa ki no chikaku ni imasu.
That cat over there exists at the tree's closely. (i.e., it's close to the tree)

18. 車が多くてうるさいんです。

Kuruma ga ookute, urusain desu.
Because there are many cars, it's noisy.

19. 日本語は易しくありません。

Nihongo wa yasashiku arimasen.
The Japanese language isn't easy.

20. 日本の夏は暑くて大変です。

Nihon no natsu wa atsukute taihen desu.
Since Japanese summers are hot, it's terrible.

21. どんなスポーツをしたいですか。

Donna supootsu wo shitai desu ka.
What kinds of sports would you like to do?

22. どこに旅行したいですか。

Doko ni ryokou shitai desu ka.
Where would you like to travel?

23. 夏休みは何週間ですか。

Natsu yasumi wa nanshuukan desu ka.
How many weeks duration is summer vacation?

24. 暑いので窓を開けてください。

Atsui node mado wo akete kudasai.
Since it's hot, please open the window.

25. 道子さんのクラスには、何が好きな人が多いですか。

Michiko-san no kurasu ni wa, nani ga suki na hito ga ooi desu ka.
As for in Michiko's class, what liking people are numerous?

26. 旅行が好きな人が多いです。

Ryokou ga suki na hito ga ooi desu.
Travel-liking people are numerous.

27. ちょっと寒くなりましたね。

Chotto samuku narimashita ne.
It became a little cold, huh.

28. その窓を閉めて下さいませんか。

Sono mado wo shimete kudasaimasen ka.
Won't you close that window and give?

29. 公園はとても寒かった。

Kouen wa totemo samukatta.
As for the park, it was very cold.

30. 森さんは今旅行しているから来るはずがありません。

Mori-san wa ima ryokou shite iru kara, kuru hazu ga arimasen.
Since Mori is traveling now, it's impossible that he will come.

Chapter 24

New Kanji in this Chapter

#392 古	#213 寺	#273 神	#473 色	#431 信
#102 刀	#547 危	#196 険	#227 緑	#134 竹

1. 京都ってどんな所ですか。

Kyouto tte, donna tokoro desu ka.
As for the one called Kyoto, what kind of place is it?

2. 古いお寺や神社がたくさんある所ですよ。

Furui otera ya jinja ga takusan aru tokoro desu yo.
Old temples and shrines, etc., many exist place it is, for sure.

3. 人々は色々な神を信じている。

Hitobito wa iroiro na kami wo shinjite iru.
As for people, they are believing in various gods.

4. あの刀は 鋭 いから気をつけてください。
<ruby>するど</ruby>

Ano katana wa surudoi kara ki wo tsukete kudasai.
As for that sword, since sharp, please be careful.

5. 神社への山道は狭くて危険だ。

Jinja e no yamamichi wa semakute kiken da.
As for the mountain road that leads to the shrine, it's narrow and dangerous.

6. お寺の後ろには険しい山があり緑の竹も多い。

Otera no ushiro ni wa kewashii yama ga ari midori no take mo ooi.
As for at behind the temple, there is a steep mountain, and green bamboo also is numerous.

7. アイロンが欲しいんですが、どんな物がありますか。

Airon ga hoshiin desu ga, donna mono ga arimasu ka
I desire an iron, but what kind of things exist?

8. はい、色々あります。

Hai, iroiro arimasu.
Yes. Various exist.

9. 古いお寺がたくさんある。

Furui otera ga takusan aru.
A lot of old temples exist.

10. その女の子の目の色は緑です。

Sono onna no ko no me no iro wa midori desu.
That girl's eyes' color is green.

11. 私はあなたを信じています。

Watashi wa anata wo shinjite imasu.
As for me, I'm believing you. (i.e., I believe you)

12. この本は古くありません。

Kono hon wa furuku arimasen
This book isn't old.

13. この川で泳ぐのは危ない。

Kono kawa de oyogu no wa abunai.
As for to swim in this river, dangerous.

14. 信じられない。

Shinjirarenai.
I can't believe it.

15. 新しい家を見せます。

Atarashii ie wo misemasu.
I will show the new house.

16. 竹田さんは明日お寺に行くそうだ。

Takeda-san wa ashita otera ni iku sou da.
Takeda will go to the honorable temple tomorrow, reportedly.

17. この古い刀はあまり切れません。

Kono furui katana wa amari kiremasen.
As for this old sword, it hardly cuts.

18. あの川は危険です。

Ano kawa wa kiken desu.
As for that river over there, it's dangerous.

19. あの女の人のドレスは緑色です。

Ano onna no hito no doresu wa midori iro desu.
As for that over there's woman's dress, it's green.

20. 古い刀について勉強しています。

Furui katana ni tsuite benkyou shite imasu.
I am studying regarding old swords.

21. 山に竹の子がたくさんありますよ。

Yama ni takenoko ga takusan arimasu yo.
On the mountain, there are a lot of bamboo shoots, for sure.

Chapter 25

New Kanji in this Chapter

# 179 五	# 3 三	# 2 二	# 111 九	# 15 八	# 17 六
# 6 四	# 20 七	# 47 百	# 22 千	# 113 万	# 318 億

1. ゼロ。

Zero, or rei.
Zero. (two different ways to say zero)

2. 五。 一。 三。

Go. Ichi. San.
Five. One. Three.

3. 二。 九。

Ni. Ku, or kyuu.
Two. Nine. (two different ways to say nine)

4. 八。 六。 四。

Hachi. Roku. Yon, or shi.
Eight. Six. Four. (two different ways to say four)

5. 十 。 七。

Juu. Nana, or shichi.
Ten. Seven. (two different ways to say seven)

6. 十一。 十二。

Juuichi. Juuni.
Eleven. Twelve.

7. 十九。

Juuku, or juukyuu.
Nineteen. (two different ways to say nineteen)

8. 二十。 三十。

Nijuu. Sanjuu.
Twenty. Thirty.

9. 四十。

Yonjuu, or shijuu.
Forty. (two different ways to say forty)

10. 五十。 六十。 八十。

Go-juu. Roku-juu. Hachi-juu.
Fifty. Sixty. Eighty.

11. 七十。

Shichijuu, or nanajuu.
Seventy. (two different ways to say seventy)

12. 九十。 百。 百一。 百十一。

Kyuujuu. Hyaku. Hyakuichi. Hyakujuuichi.
90. 100. 101. 111.

13. 二百。 三百。 四百。 五百。
Nihyaku. Sanbyaku.
Yonhyaku. Gohyaku.
200. 300. 400. 500.

14. 六百。 七百。 八百。 九百。
Roppyaku. Nanahyaku.
Happyaku. Kyuuhyaku.
600. 700. 800. 900.

15. 千。 千一。 千百十一。
Sen. Senichi. Sen hyaku juuichi.
1,000. 1,001. 1,111.

16. 二千。 二千二百二十二。
三千。
Nisen. Nisen nihyaku nijuuni. Sanzen.
2,000. 2,222. 3,000.

17. 四千。 五千。 六千。 七千。
Yonsen. Gosen.
Rokusen. Nanasen.
4,000. 5,000. 6,000. 7,000.

18. 八千。 九千。 一万。 二万。
Hassen. Kyuusen.
Ichiman. Niman.
8,000. 9,000. 10,000. 20,000.

19. 三万三千三百三十三。
Sanman sanzen sanbyaku sanjuusan.
33,333.

20. 十万。
Juuman.
100,000.

21. 四十四万四千四百四十四。
Yonjuu yonman yonsen yonhyaku
yonjuu yon.
444,444.

22. 百万。 一千万。 一億。
Hyakuman. Issenman. Ichioku.
1,000,000. 10,000,000. 100,000,000.

23. 十億。 百億。
Juuoku. Hyakuoku.
One billion. Ten billion.

24. 一本。 二本。
Ippon. Nihon.
One bottle. Two bottles.

25. 三本。 四本。 五本。
Sanbon. Yonhon. Gohon.
Three bottles. Four bottles. Five bottles.

26. 六本。 七本。 八本。
Roppon, or rokuhon. Shichihon, or
nanahon. Happon, or hachihon.
Six bottles. Seven bottles.
Eight bottles.

27. 九本。 十本。 何本？
Kyuuhon. Juppon, or jippon. Nanbon?,
or nanhon?
Nine bottles. Ten bottles. How many
bottles?

28. 一つ。 二つ。 三つ。 四つ。
Hitotsu. Futatsu. Mittsu. Yottsu.
One object. Two objects. Three objects.
Four objects.

29. 五つ。六つ。七つ。八つ。

Itsutsu. Muttsu. Nanatsu. Yattsu.
Five objects. Six objects. Seven objects.
Eight objects.

30. 九つ。十。いくつ？

Kokonotsu. Too. Ikutsu?
Nine objects. Ten objects. How many
objects?

31. 三本飲みました。

Sanbon nomimashita.
I drank three bottles.

32. 昨日寿司をいくつ食べました
か。

Kinou sushi wo ikutsu tabemashita ka.
Yesterday, sushi, how many did you eat?

33. トロを三つとエビを五つ食べ
ました。

Toro wo mittsu to ebi wo itsutsu
tabemashita.
I ate 3 fatty tuna and 5 shrimp.

34. グレイスさんは十ぐらい食べ
ました。

Gureisu-san wa juu gurai tabemashita.
As for Grace, she ate about 10.

35. 一人。二人。三人。四人。

Hitori. Futari. Sannin. Yonin.
One person. Two people. Three people.
Four people.

36. 五人。十人。千人。何人？

Gonin. Juunin. Sennin. Nannin?
Five people. Ten people. 1,000 people.
How many people?

37. ビール三本ください。

Biiru sanbon kudasai.
Beer three bottles, please.

38. ビール二本あります。

Biiru nihon arimasu.
Beer two bottles exist.

39. 1990年。

Sen kyuuhyaku kyuujuu nen.
1990.

40. 平成二年
へいせい

Heisei ni nen.
The 2nd year of the Heisei era. (1990)

41. 一月。二月。三月。四月。

Ichigatsu. Nigatsu. Sangatsu. Shigatsu.
January. February. March. April.

42. 五月。六月。七月。八月。

Gogatsu. Rokugatsu. Shichigatsu, or
nanagatsu. Hachigatsu.
May. June. July. August.

43. 九月。十月。十一月。
十二月。

Kugatsu. Juugatsu. Juuichigatsu.
Juunigatsu.
September. October. November.
December.

44. 何月？

Nangatsu?
What month? (nangetsu, *not* OK; nantsuki, *not* OK)

45. 何年？ 何日？

Nannen? Nannichi?
What year? (nantoshi, not OK) What day?

46. 一日。 二日。 三日。 四日。

Tsuitachi. Futsuka. Mikka. Yokka.
1st of the month. 2nd of the month. 3rd of the month. 4th of the month.

47. 五日。 六日。 七日。 八日。

Itsuka. Muika. Nanoka. Youka.
5th of the month. 6th of the month. 7th of the month. 8th of the month.

48. 九日。 十日。
十一日。 十二日。

Kokonoka. Tooka. Juu ichi nichi. Juu ni nichi.
9th of the month. 10th of the month. 11th of the month. 12th of the month.

49. 十四日。 二十日。
二十四日。

Juu yokka. Hatsuka. Nijuu yokka.
14th of the month. 20th of the month. 24th of the month.

50. 子供の日はいつですか。

Kodomo no hi wa itsu desu ka.
When is Children's Day?

51. 5月5日です。

Gogatsu itsuka desu.
It's May 5th.

52. この日本語の本はあまり新し
くありません。

Kono nihongo no hon wa amari atarashiku arimasen.
This Japanese language book isn't very new.

Chapter 26

New Kanji in this Chapter

#131 村	#43 英	#574 飛	#137 機	#373 北
#397 肉	#545 野	#121 菜	#408 歩	#98 頼

1. 木村さんは毎日何時間、英語 の勉強をしますか。

Kimura-san wa mainichi nanjikan, eigo no benkyou wo shimasu ka.
As for Kimura, every day, how many hours does he do English's study?

2. デイビッドさんは飛行機の中 で本を読んでいませんでし た。

Deibiddo-san wa hikouki no naka de hon wo yonde imasen deshita.
As for David, at the plane's inside, he was not reading a book.

3. あなた、北村さん達がいらっ しゃいましたよ。

Anata, kitamura-san tachi ga irasshaimashita yo.
Darling, the Kitamuras honorably came, for sure.

4. 飛行機の食事は何でしたか。

Hikouki no shokuji wa nan deshita ka.
As for the plane's meal, what was it?

5. 肉と野菜でした。

Niku to yasai deshita.
It was meat and vegetables.

6. 6時40分までに上野駅に来て ください。

Rokuji yonjuppun made ni ueno eki ni kite kudasai.
Please come to Ueno Station by 6:40.

7. 少し歩きましょうか。

Sukoshi arukimashou ka.
Shall we walk a little?

8. 北村さんはアンドリューさん に何を頼みましたか。

Kitamura-san wa andoryuu-san ni nani wo tanomimashita ka.
What did Kitamura request of Andrew?

9. レポートを今日中に仕上げる ことを頼みました。

Repooto wo kyou juu ni shiageru koto wo tanomimashita.
He requested that he finish the report by the end of today.

10. 誰が飛行機の中で寝ました か。

Dare ga hikouki no naka de nemashita ka.
Who slept inside the plane?

11. デイビッドさんです。

Deibiddo-san desu.
It's David.

12. 肉ばかりじゃなくて野菜も食べないといけませんよ。

Niku bakari ja nakute yasai mo tabenai to ikemasen yo.
It isn't only meat, and you must eat vegetables also, for sure.

13. 北村さんは黒田さんにタバコを買うように頼みました。

Kitamura-san wa kuroda-san ni tabako wo kau you ni tanomimashita.
As for Kitamura, he asked Kuroda to buy cigarettes.

14. この英語の先生は分かりやすい。

Kono eigo no sensei wa wakariyasui.
As for this English teacher, she is easy to understand.

15. 上田さんはあのバラの花をくれるでしょうか。

Ueda-san wa ano bara no hana wo kureru deshou ka.
Will Ueda probably give that rose flower over there to us?

16. くれるかどうか分からないけれど頼んでみます。

Kureru ka douka wakaranai keredo tanonde mimasu.
Whether he will give it I don't know, but I'll request it and see.

17. ブリアンナさんと野村さんはおしゃべりをしながら歩きました。

Burianna-san to nomura-san wa oshaberi wo shi nagara, arukimashita.
As for Brianna and Nomura, while doing chattering, they walked.

18. 英字新聞は読みません。

Eiji shinbun wa yomimasen.
As for an English newspaper, I don't read one.

19. 私は英語もスペイン語も日本語も分かります。

Watashi wa eigo mo supeingo mo nihongo mo wakarimasu.
As for me, I understand English also, Spanish also, Japanese also.

20. 病院では静かに歩きましょう。

Byouin de wa shizuka ni arukimashou.
As for in the hospital, let's walk quietly.

21. 手紙が書きたい。

Tegami ga kakitai
I want to write a letter. (tegami wo, also OK)

22. ここの肉や野菜がとてもおいしい。

Koko no niku ya yasai ga totemo oishii.
As for here's (i.e., this place's) meat, vegetables, etc., they are very delicious.

23. 明日休みたいんですが。

Ashita yasumitain desu ga...
Tomorrow, I'd like to rest, but... (i.e., I'd like to be off)

24. 本を書きたくない。

Hon wo kakitakunai.
I don't want to write a book.

25. 寿司を食べたいです。

Sushi wo tabetai desu.
I want to eat sushi.

26. 飲み物は何がいいですか。

Nomimono wa nani ga ii desu ka.
As for drinks, what is good?

27. 今日は暖かいからビールが飲みたいですね。

Kyou wa atatakai kara biiru ga nomitai desu ne.
As for today, since it's warm, I want to drink beer, huh.

28. 私もビールがいいです。

Watashi mo biiru ga ii desu.
I also, beer is good. (i.e., I'll also have beer)

29. すみません。ビールを三本。

Sumimasen. Biiru wo sanbon.
Excuse me. Beer, three bottles.

30. それからトロを二つとエビを一つお願いします。

Sore kara toro wo futatsu to ebi wo hitotsu onegai shimasu.
And then, fatty tuna, two items, and shrimp, one item, I beg.

Chapter 27

New Kanji in this Chapter

# 160 夕	# 465 酒	# 586 忙	# 50 母	# 163 外
# 170 国	# 244 妹	# 143 父	# 529 弟	# 482 作

1. 夕食は何を食べますか。

Yuushoku wa nani wo tabemasu ka.
As for dinner, what will they eat?

2. 胃の具合が悪いんでしょう？

I no guai ga waruin deshou?
The stomach's condition is bad probably?

3. お酒を飲むのを止めたらどうですか。

Osake wo nomu no wo yametara dou desu ka.
If you stop to drink honorable sake (i.e., stop drinking it), how is that?

4. 好きだからいくら具合が悪くてもなかなか止められないんですよ。

Suki dakara ikura guai ga warukutemo nakanaka yamerarenain desu yo.
Since I like, how much the condition is bad even though, readily I cannot stop, for sure.

5. 昨日は忙しかったですか。

Kinou wa isogashikatta desu ka.
As for yesterday, was it busy?

6. あなたのお母さんは来年の夏、外国に旅行しますか。

Anata no okaasan wa rainen no natsu, gaikoku ni ryokou shimasu ka.
Will your mother travel to a foreign country next year's summer?

7. 外国の旅行の方が安いと思っています。

Gaikoku no ryokou no hou ga yasui to omotte imasu.
She thinks that foreign countries' travel is cheaper.

8. 妹はケーキを買ってくれました。

Imouto wa keeki wo katte kuremashita.
As for younger sister, she bought a cake and gave (to me).

9. もしもし。今日は会議で遅くなるから晩ご飯はうちで食べないからね。

Moshimoshi. Kyou wa kaigi de osoku naru kara bangohan wa uchi de tabenai kara ne.
Hello, as for today, since the meeting will become late, as for supper, at home, since I will not eat, huh.

10. お母さん、お父さん、今日は会議で遅くなるから晩ご飯はうちで食べないって。

Okaasan, otousan, kyou wa kaigi de osoku naru kara bangohan wa uchi de tabenai tte.
Mother, Father, as for today, since the meeting will become late, as for supper, at home, he will not eat, reportedly.

11. トーマスさんはビールとお酒を飲みました。

Toomasu-san wa biiru to osake wo nomimashita.
Thomas drank beer and honorable sake.

12. 弟はスーパーマンになりたいと思っています。

Otouto wa suupaaman ni naritai to omotte imasu.
As for the little brother, he is thinking that he wants to become superman.

13. お母さんが子供にクッキーを作ってあげる。

Okaasan ga kodomo ni kukkii wo tsukutte ageru.
Honorable mother, for the child, will make and give cookies.

14. なぜ明日学校に来ないんですか。

Naze ashita gakkou ni konain desu ka.
Why will you not come to school tomorrow?

15. 国から父が来るんです。

Kuni kara chichi ga kurun desu.
My father is coming from the hometown.

16. 夕べはお酒を飲み過ぎました。

Yuube wa osake wo nomisugimashita.
As for last night, I drank too much honorable sake.

17. 父が私にセーターを買ってくれました。

Chichi ga watashi ni seetaa wo katte kuremashita.
My father, for me, bought and gave a sweater.

18. 妹は父にセーターを買ってもらいました。

Imouto wa chichi ni seetaa wo katte moraimashita.
As for younger sister, by my father, a sweater he bought and she received.

19. これ、私が作ったクッキーですが、どうぞ。

Kore, watashi ga tsukutta kukkii desu ga, douzo.
These are cookies I made, but go ahead.

20. 妹のせいで学校に遅れた。

Imouto no sei de gakkou ni okureta.
Due to little sister's fault, I was delayed to school.

21. 犬が外に出た。

Inu ga soto ni deta.
The dog went to outside.

22. 弟はドイツの会社の社員で4年前からドイツに行っています。

Otouto wa doitsu no kaisha no shain de yonen mae kara doitsu ni itte imasu.
Since my younger brother is a German company's employee, since four years ago, he went to Germany and exists.

23. 仕事は面白いですか。

Shigoto wa omoshiroi desu ka.
Is the work interesting?

24. 空港は込んでいますが、道はすいています。

Kuukou wa konde imasu ga, michi wa suite imasu.
The airport is being crowded, but the streets are being uncrowded.

25. 寿司屋に行きましょうか。

Sushiya ni ikimashou ka.
Shall we go to a sushi store?

26. 夕べは寒かったですか。

Yuube wa samukatta desu ka.
Was last night cold?

27. これは弟さんが昨日買った本です。

Kore wa, otouto-san ga kinou katta hon desu.
As for this, it's a book that your little brother bought yesterday.

28. 土田さんは今週と来週とどちらが忙しいですか。

Tsuchida-san wa konshuu to raishuu to, dochira ga isogashii desu ka.
As for Tsuchida, this week vs. next week, which is busier?

29. 私の父はお酒を作っていた。

Watashi no chichi wa osake wo tsukutte ita.
As for my father, he was making honorable sake.

30. 仕事は面白いですがとても忙しいです。

Shigoto wa omoshiroi desu ga, totemo isogashii desu.
Work is interesting, but it's very busy.

31. 毎年たくさんの外国人が京都に行きます。

Mainen takusan no gaikokujin ga kyouto ni ikimasu.
Every year, a lot of foreigners go to Kyoto. (it's also OK to pronounce this maitoshi, instead of mainen)

Chapter 28

New Kanji in this Chapter

# 315 息	# 202 集	# 316 娘	# 534 歌	# 573 形
# 575 並	# 270 位	# 569 置	# 360 遊	# 567 皿

1. 息子は切手を集めるのが大好きです。

Musuko wa kitte wo atsumeru no ga daisuki desu.
As for the son (i.e., my son), he loves to collect stamps.

2. 娘さん、アルバイトが忙しいんだって。

Musume-san, arubaito ga isogashiin datte.
The honorable daughter (i.e., your daughter), the part-time work is busy, reportedly.

3. 歌を歌う。

Uta wo utau.
I will sing a song

4. かわいい人形が並んでいるわね。

Kawaii ningyou ga narande iru wa ne.
Some cute dolls are lined up, huh.

5. 私が集めているのよ。

Watashi ga atsumete iru no yo.
I am collecting, for sure.

6. なんだ五位か。がっかりしちゃった。

Nanda, go i ka. Gakkari shichatta.
What do you mean, 5th place? I got completely disappointed. (shichatta = shite shimaimashita)

7. 中村さんの息子さんはよく勉強していたそうです。

Nakamura-san no musuko-san wa yoku benkyou shite ita sou desu.
As for Nakamura's honorable son, reportedly he was studying often.

8. 日本の車とアメリカの車は同じですか、違いますか。

Nihon no kuruma to amerika no kuruma wa onaji desu ka, chigaimasu ka.
As for Japanese cars and American cars, are they the same, are they different?

9. 形はほとんど同じですがハンドルの位置が違います。

Katachi wa hotondo onaji desu ga handoru no ichi ga chigaimasu.
As for the shape, it's almost the same, but the steering wheel's position is different.

10. 娘が人形と遊んでいる。

Musume ga ningyou to asonde iru.
The daughter (i.e., my daughter) is playing with a doll.

11. テーブルの上にコップとお皿を並べてください。

Teeburu no ue ni koppu to osara wo narabete kudasai.
Please line up the cups and honorable plates on top of the table.

12. 勉強をしてから遊びます。

Benkyou wo shite kara asobimasu.
After I study, I'll play.

13. 娘と息子が三人ずついます。

Musume to musuko ga sannin zutsu imasu.
Daughters and sons, three each exist. (i.e., I have three of each)

14. 時間があったらうちに遊びに来てください。

Jikan ga attara uchi ni asobi ni kite kudasai.
If there is time, please come to the home for the purpose of play.

15. ブラウンさん達は何位になりましたか。

Buraun-san tachi wa nan i ni narimashita ka.
As for the Brown group, to what place did it develop?

16. 三位になりました。

San i ni narimashita.
To third place it developed.

17. ジョーンズさんも奥さんも切手を集めるのが大好きです。

Joonzu-san mo okusan mo kitte wo atsumeru no ga daisuki desu.
Jones also, his wife also, love collecting stamps.

18. コップとお皿をもう並べたわよ。

Koppu to osara wo mou narabeta wa yo.
The cups and plates were already lined up by someone, for sure.

19. ここは前は公園でした。

Koko wa mae wa kouen deshita.
As for here, as for before, it was a park.

20. とても静かでした。

Totemo shizuka deshita.
It was very quiet.

21. こんなにうるさくありませんでした。

Konna ni urusaku arimasen deshita.
It wasn't noisy like this.

22. ここに置いておいたバッグを取られたようなんです。

Koko ni oite oita baggu wo torareta you nan desu.
The was-placed-at-here-in-advance bag was taken on me, apparently.

23. えっ、大変だ。

E! Taihen da.
Eh! It's terrible.

24. お皿を並べる。

Osara wo naraberu.
I line up the dishes.

25. 小さいプールで泳ぎます。

Chiisai puuru de oyogimasu.
I swim in a small pool.

26. 私はその歌のタイトルをどうしても思い出せなかった。

Watashi wa sono uta no taitoru wo doushitemo omoidasenakatta.
As for me, that song's title, somehow or other, I could not remember.

27. 白いお皿を五枚出してくださいませんか。

Shiroi osara wo gomai dashite kudasaimasenka.
Won't you take out five white plates and give? (i.e., won't you do it for me?)

28. おかしいなぁ。机の上に置いておいたのに、ないんだよ。

Okashii naa. Tsukue no ue ni oite oita noni, nain da yo.
Strange. I placed it on the desk in advance, in spite of the fact that it doesn't exist, for sure.

29. 地下鉄は不便なので、バスで行きました。

Chikatetsu wa fuben na node, basu de ikimashita.
Since the subways are inconvenient, he went by bus.

30. 息子はこの歌が大好きです。

Musuko wa kono uta ga daisuki desu.
As for the son, he loves this song.

Chapter 29

New Kanji in this Chapter

#207 午	#331 半	#167 住	#158 消	#366 踊
#251 水	#443 火	#343 去	#24 又	

1. 3時頃、成田空港へ行きます。
Sanji goro, narita kuukou e ikimasu.
About 3:00, I will go to Narita airport.

2. 明日の午後4時にアンソニーさんに会います。
Ashita no gogo yoji ni ansonii-san ni aimasu.
At tomorrow's 4:00 p.m., I will meet Anthony.

3. ちょうど1時。
Choudo ichiji.
Exactly 1:00.

4. 3時15分。
Sanji juugofun.
3:15.

5. 3時15分過ぎ。
Sanji juugofun sugi.
15 minutes following 3:00.

6. 午前5時27分。
Gozen goji nijuunanafun.
5:27 a.m.

7. 8時30分。
Hachiji sanjuppun.
8:30. (sanjippun, also OK)

8. 8時半。
Hachiji han.
Half past 8:00.

9. 15時45分。
Juugoji yonjuu gofun.
15:45. (3:45 p.m.)

10. 午後3時45分。
Gogo sanji yonjuu gofun.
3:45 p.m.

11. 狭いアパートに住んでいる。
Semai apaato ni sunde iru.
I live in a small or narrow apartment.

12. 光が消えない。
Hikari ga kienai.
The light doesn't go out.

13. スキーよりもディスコで踊る方が好きです。

Sukii yori mo disuko de odoru hou ga suki desu.
Compared to skiing, I prefer dancing in a disco.

14. 午後 4 時 15 分前。

Gogo yoji juugofun mae.
15 minutes before 4:00 p.m.

15. バスで 35 分かかります。

Basu de sanjuu gofun kakarimasu.
By bus, it takes 35 minutes.

16. 時間はどのくらいかかりますか。

Jikan wa dono kurai kakarimasu ka.
As for time, about how much does it take?

17. 1 時間半ぐらいです。

Ichijikan han gurai desu.
It's about 1 ½ hours.

18. 水曜日。 金曜日。
日曜日。何曜日？

Suiyoubi. Kinyoubi.
Nichiyoubi. Nanyoubi?
Wednesday. Friday.
Sunday. What day of the week?

19. 木曜日。火曜日。土曜日。
月曜日。

Mokuyoubi. Kayoubi. Doyoubi.
Getsuyoubi.
Thursday. Tuesday. Saturday. Monday.

20. 私は毎朝、花に水をやります。

Watashi wa maiasa hana ni mizu wo yarimasu.
As for me, every morning, to the flowers I give water.

21. 三月十日は何曜日ですか。

San gatsu tooka wa nan youbi desu ka.
What day of the week is March 10th?

22. 土曜日です。

Doyoubi desu.
It's Saturday.

23. おととい。今日。昨日。

Ototoi. Kyou. Kinou.
The day before yesterday. Today. Yesterday.

24. 明日。あさって。

Ashita, or asu, or myounichi. Asatte.
Tomorrow. The day after tomorrow.

25. 先週。来週。今週。

Senshuu. Raishuu. Konshuu.
Last week. Next week. This week.

26. 先月。

Sengetsu.
Last month. (sengatsu, not OK)

27. 今月。

Kongetsu.
This month. (kongatsu, not OK)

28. 来月。

Raigetsu.
Next month. (raigatsu, not OK)

29. おととし。去年。今年。来年。

Ototoshi. Kyonen. Kotoshi. Rainen.
The year before last. Last year. This year. Next year.

30. おととい、寿司屋に行きました。

Ototoi sushiya ni ikimashita.
We went to a sushi bar the day before yesterday.

31. 今度の土曜日も又行きます。

Kondo no doyoubi mo mata ikimasu.
We are going again this coming Saturday as well.

32. 電気が消してあります。

Denki ga keshite arimasu.
The light has been turned off by someone.

33. この前の日曜日にディズニーランドに行きました。

Kono mae no nichiyoubi ni dizuniirando ni ikimashita.
We went to Disneyland last Sunday.

34. 来月の十四日に又行きます。

Raigetsu no juuyokka ni mata ikimasu.
We are going to go again on the 14th of next month.

35. 今日は何月何日何曜日ですか。

Kyou wa nan gatsu nan nichi nan youbi desu ka.
What month, day and day of the week is it today?

36. 1時間半ぐらい踊りました。

Ichiji kan han gurai odorimashita.
I danced for about an hour and a half.

37. それじゃ、少し疲れましたね。

Sore ja, sukoshi tsukaremashita ne.
In that case, you got a little tired, huh.

38. 水を買わなかった。

Mizu wo kawanakatta.
I didn't buy water.

39. 去年の八月に来日したんですか。

Kyonen no hachigatsu ni rainichi shitan desu ka.
Did you come to Japan at last year's August?

40. じゃあ、かれこれ1年日本にいるという訳ですね。

Jaa, karekore ichinen nihon ni iru to iu wake desu ne.
Well, about one year you exist in Japan (quote) to-say reason it is, huh. (i.e., therefore you've been here about a year)

41. 又、込んでいるかもしれないので、火曜日は早くうちを出ましょう。

Mata, konde iru kamoshirenai node, kayoubi wa, hayaku uchi wo demashou.
Again, since it might be crowded, as for Tuesday, let's leave home early.

42. 火を消してください。

Hi wo keshite kudasai.
Please extinguish the fire.

43. 去年まで六本木に住んでいました。

Kyonen made roppongi ni sunde imashita.
I was living in Roppongi until last year.

44. どんなことをしますか。

Donna koto wo shimasu ka.
What kind of thing do they do?

45. 歌を歌ったり踊ったりゲームをしたりします。

Uta wo utattari odottari geemu wo shitari shimasu.
Sing songs, etc., dance, etc., do games, etc., they do.

46. あの人はメキシコに住んだことがあります。

Ano hito wa mekishiko ni sunda koto ga arimasu.
That person over there has lived in Mexico.

47. 男の人が電気を消しています。

Otoko no hito ga denki wo keshite imasu.
The man is turning off the light.

Chapter 30

New Kanji in this Chapter

# 371 彼	# 461 若	# 421 元	# 312 急	# 364 用
# 317 意	# 245 味	# 323 知	# 297 登	# 337 海

1. 彼女は若くありません。

Kanojo wa wakaku arimasen.
She isn't young.

2. 手紙にとても元気だと書きました。

Tegami ni totemo genki da to kakimashita.
I wrote to the letter (i.e., in the letter) that I'm very healthy.

3. すみません。急に用事ができてテニスができなくなったんですよ。

Sumimasen. Kyuu ni youji ga dekite tenisu ga dekinakunattan desu yo.
Excuse me. Suddenly, since an errand got ready, I became unable to do tennis, for sure.

4. この漢字の意味を知っていますか。

Kono kanji no imi wo shitte imasu ka.
Are you knowing the meaning of this kanji?

5. さぁ、私はちょっと...

Saa, watashi wa chotto...
Well, as for me, a little bit...

6. あの人は若いのに色々なことを知っています。

Ano hito wa wakai noni, iroiro na koto wo shitte imasu.
That person over there, even though young, is knowing various things.

7. 彼は元気じゃありませんでした。

Kare wa genki ja arimasen deshita.
He was not healthy.

8. 山登りに行けないってなぜですか。

Yama nobori ni ikenai tte naze desu ka.
As for the one called not able to go for the purpose of mountain climb, why is it? (i.e., why can't you go?)

9. 病気で寝ているんです。

Byouki de nete irun desu.
Because of illness, I'm sleeping.

10. 先生、意見を言ってもいいで
すか。

Sensei, iken wo itte mo ii desu ka.
Teacher, is it OK if I say an opinion?

11. あの険しい道を登るのは、若
い人でも大変だ。

Ano kewashii michi wo noboru no wa,
wakai hito demo taihen da.
As for to climb that steep road over there,
even though young people, it's terrible.

12. 元気を出してください。

Genki wo dashite kudasai.
Please put forth health. (i.e., keep your
chin up)

13. 山本さんを知ってますか。

Yamamoto-san wo shittemasu ka.
Do you know Yamamoto? (shortened for
speech)

14. 今日はここで失礼します。急
いでいますので。

Kyou wa koko de shitsurei shimasu.
Isoide imasu node.
As for today, at this moment, I'll commit
a discourtesy. Because I'm hurrying.
(koko de = right now)

15. すみません。マフラーを見せ
てください。

Sumimasen. Mafuraa wo misete kudasai.
Excuse me, please show me a scarf.

16. 地味なのはありますが...

Jimi na no wa arimasu ga...
A plain one exists, but...

17. 山の上まで登ったら遠くの海
が見えました。

Yama no ue made nobottara tooku no
umi ga miemashita.
When I climbed until the top of the
mountain, the far-away ocean was
visible.

18. 彼は来週旅行に行くのに、ま
だ用意をしていません。

Kare wa raishuu ryokou ni iku noni,
mada youi wo shite imasen.
As for him, even though next week he is
going on a trip, he still isn't doing
preparations.

19. 夏の旅行は海へ行った人より
山へ行った人の方が多いです
か。

Natsu no ryokou wa umi e itta hito yori
yama e itta hito no hou ga ooi desu ka.
As for summer's travel, compared to the
people who went to the ocean, are the
people who went to the mountains more
numerous?

20. 急いでコピーします。

Isoide kopii shimasu.
I'll copy it hurriedly.

21. マリアさんはお寿司が好きじ
ゃありません。

Maria-san wa osushi ga suki ja arimasen.
As for Maria, she doesn't like honorable
sushi.

22. どんな味がするんですか。

Donna aji ga surun desu ka.
What kind of flavor does it do? (i.e., how does it taste?)

23. 今日は暑いですね。

Kyou wa atsui desu ne.
Today is hot, huh.

24. 私は北海道から来たので東京の夏は暑すぎる。

Watashi wa hokkaidou kara kita node toukyou no natsu wa atsusugiru.
As for me, since I came from Hokkaido, Tokyo summers are too hot.

25. この申し込み用紙にお名前とご住所をお書きになってください。

Kono moushikomi youshi ni onamae to gojuusho wo okaki ni natte kudasai.
On this application form, please honorably write the honorable name and honorable address.

26. 花は机の上にあります。

Hana wa tsukue no ue ni arimasu.
As for flowers, they exist on top of the desk.

27. 机の下に何がありますか。

Tsukue no shita ni nani ga arimasu ka.
At below the desk, what exists?

28. 箱とバッグがあります。

Hako to baggu ga arimasu.
A box and a bag exist.

29. 机の上に何がありますか。

Tsukue no ue ni nani ga arimasu ka.
On top of the desk, what exists?

30. 本とノートがあります。

Hon to nooto ga arimasu.
A book and a notebook exist.

31. 私はお寿司が好きです。

Watashi wa osushi ga suki desu.
As for me, I like honorable sushi.

32. 日本語が分かりません。

Nihongo ga wakarimasen.
I don't understand the Japanese language.

33. 学校で勉強した方がいいですよ。

Gakkou de benkyou shita hou ga ii desu yo.
You'd better study at a school, for sure.

Chapter 31

New Kanji in this Chapter

#456 左	#579 両	#383 親	#457 右	#82 曲
#490 側	#306 心	#466 配	#81 角	#203 進

1. 花屋の左に何がありますか。

Hanaya no hidari ni nani ga arimasu ka.
At the flower shop's left, what exists?

2. ニューヨークの両親に毎月電話を掛けることにしています。

Nyuuyooku no ryoushin ni maitsuki denwa wo kakeru koto ni shite imasu.
My routine is to call on the phone to the New York parents every month.

3. 50メートルぐらい行って右に曲がると左側に病院が見えます。

Go juu meetoru gurai itte migi ni magaru to hidari gawa ni byouin ga miemasu.
When you go about 50 meters and turn right, on the left side a hospital will be visible.

4. ご心配かけて申し訳ございせん。

Goshinpai kakete moushiwake gozaimasen.
Causing honorable worry, there's no excuse. (i.e., I'm sorry to cause worry)

5. 左側と右側を良く見てください。

Hidarigawa to migigawa wo yoku mite kudasai.
On the left side and the right side, please look well.

6. その前にあります。

Sono mae ni arimasu.
It exists in front of that.

7. 右手を上げなさい。

Migi te wo agenasai.
Raise the right hand.

8. 二つ目の角を左に曲がって三つ目のビルです。

Futatsume no kado wo hidari ni magatte mittsume no biru desu.
You turn left on the second corner, and it's the third building.

9. 進さんが歌っています。

Susumu-san ga utatte imasu.
Susumu is singing.

10. 机の右に窓があります。

Tsukue no migi ni mado ga arimasu.
At the desk's right side, a window exists.

11. この先の橋を渡って行くと左側に銀行があります。

Kono saki no hashi wo watatte iku to hidarigawa ni ginkou ga arimasu.
If you cross and go over this bridge ahead, there is a bank on the left side.

12. 来月の社員旅行、いらっしゃらないんですか。

Raigetsu no shain ryokou irassharanain desu ka.
Next month's company employee trip, will you not honorably go?

13. 行かないと言う訳ではないんだが、あまり気が進まなくてね。

Ikanai to iu wake de wa nain da ga, amari ki ga susumanakute ne.
Not go, reason it isn't, but not very much, since feeling doesn't advance, huh. (i.e., it isn't that I won't go, but I'm not very enthusiastic)

14. あの角を右に曲がるとガソリンスタンドがあります。

Ano kado wo migi ni magaru to gasorin sutando ga arimasu.
When you turn right on that corner over there, there is a gas station.

15. ニューヨークの両親は私が電話を掛けるまで心配していました。

Nyuuyooku no ryoushin wa watashi ga denwa wo kakeru made shinpai shite imashita.
As for the New York parents, until I call on the phone, they were being worried.

16. 公園の左に大きい建物があります。

Kouen no hidari ni ookii tatemono ga arimasu.
On the park's left side, big buildings exist.

17. 曲がり角を左に進んでください。

Magari kado wo hidari ni susunde kudasai.
On the curve of the corner, please advance to the left.

18. アメリカで大雨が降ったそうですね。

Amerika de ooame ga futta sou desu ne.
In America, a heavy rain fell, reportedly, huh.

19. ええ、ちょっと心配でね、両親に電話を掛けようと思っています。

Ee, chotto shinpai de ne, ryoushin ni denwa wo kakeyou to omotte imasu.
Yeah, since a little worry, huh, I shall call on the phone to the parents, I'm thinking.

Chapter 32

New Kanji in this Chapter

#504 池	#210 産	#332 業	#27 卒	#286 動
#55 自	#73 由	#132 付	#439 説	#458 石

1. 今、池田産業の社員です。

Ima, ikeda sangyou no shain desu.
Now I'm an employee of Ikeda Industries.

2. いつまで日本にいますか。

Itsu made nihon ni imasu ka.
Until when will you exist in Japan?

3. 大学を卒業するまでいます。

Daigaku wo sotsugyou suru made imasu.
Until I graduate the university, I will exist.

4. そのアパートは新しいですか。

Sono apaato wa atarashii desu ka.
Is that apartment new?

5. 新しいかどうか分からないから不動産屋に聞いてみます。

Atarashii ka douka wakaranai kara, fudousanya ni kiite mimasu.
Since I don't know whether it's new or not, I'll ask the real estate store (i.e., agent) and see.

6. 机を動かす。

Tsukue wo ugokasu.
I will move the desk.

7. 池田さんはドイツ語が分かると思いますか。

Ikeda-san wa doitsugo ga wakaru to omoimasu ka.
Do you think that Ikeda understands German?

8. ドイツの大学を出たんだから分かるはずです。

Doitsu no daigaku wo detan dakara, wakaru hazu desu.
Since he graduated a German university, he ought to understand it.

9. 自分が子供を持って、初めて親の有り難みが分かる。

Jibun ga kodomo wo motte, hajimete oya no arigatami ga wakaru.
Oneself child having, for the first time parent's value one understands.

10. メリーランド大学ビジネススクールの卒業生です。

Meriirando daigaku bijinesu sukuuru no sotsugyou sei desu.
It's a graduate of Maryland University business school. (i.e., I'm a graduate of that school)

11. ミシガン大学では何を勉強しましたか。

Mishigan daigaku de wa nani wo benkyou shimashita ka.
As for at Michigan University, what did you study?

12. 東洋学です。

Touyougaku desu.
It's Eastern studies.

13. このおもちゃの自動車は電池で動く。

Kono omocha no jidousha wa denchi de ugoku.
This toy car moves by batteries.

14. 前は田中産業の社員でした。

Mae wa tanaka sangyou no shain deshita.
As for before, I was an employee of Tanaka Industries.

15. あの店ではコーヒーを自由に飲ませてくれるらしいよ。

Ano mise de wa koohii wo jiyuu ni nomasete kureru rashii yo.
As for at that store over there, coffee freely they let you drink and give to our in-group, it seems, for sure.

16. カリフォルニア大学を卒業しました。

Kariforunia daigaku wo sotsugyou shimashita.
I graduated the University of California.

17. リボンを付けましょうか。

Ribon wo tsukemashou ka.
Shall I attach a ribbon?

18. はい、お願いします。プレゼントなので。

Hai onegai shimasu. Purezento na node.
Yes, please do. Because it's a present.

19. 日本語で説明ができますか。

Nihongo de setsumei ga dekimasu ka.
Will you be able to explain it in Japanese?

20. 小林ですが石川さんをお願いします。

Kobayashi desu ga ishikawa-san wo onegaishimasu.
This is Kobayashi, but I beg Ishikawa. (i.e., may I speak to him?)

21. いつ頃お帰りになりますか。

Itsu goro okaeri ni narimasu ka.
About when will he honorably return?

22. 5時までには帰ると思いますが、何かお言付けがありますか。

Goji made ni wa kaeru to omoimasu ga, nanika okotozuke ga arimasu ka.
As for by 5:00, I think he will return, but is there anything message?

23. 又、その頃お電話します。

Mata sono koro odenwa shimasu.
Again about that time, I will do a humble phone call.

24. では、失礼します。

Dewa, shitsurei shimasu.
Well, I will commit a discourtesy. (i.e., "good-bye," on the phone)

25. 石川さんに理由を聞かれたけれど、説明しにくかった。

Ishikawa-san ni riyuu wo kikareta keredo, setsumei shi nikukatta.
By Ishikawa the reason was asked on me, but it was difficult to do explanation.

26. 食事に気を付けて病気にならないようにしないといけませんよ。

Shokuji ni ki wo tsukete byouki ni naranai you ni shinai to ikemasen yo.
Being careful to meals, you must make an effort to not become sick, for sure.

27. それだけの理由で悪いことが起こる。

Sore dake no riyuu de warui koto ga okoru.
Of that only's reason, bad things happen. (i.e., just because of that, bad things can occur)

28. 石田さんに手紙を出しました。

Ishida-san ni tegami wo dashimashita.
To Ishida I sent a letter.

29. 説明ができるかどうか分からないけれどやってみます。

Setsumei ga dekiru ka douka wakaranai keredo, yatte mimasu.
Whether I can explain it I don't know, but I'll do it and see.

30. 日本の小説を読んだことがありますか。

Nihon no shousetsu wo yonda koto ga arimasu ka.
Have you ever read a Japan's novel?

31. 面白いですよ。一度読んでみてください。

Omoshiroi desu yo. Ichido yonde mite kudasai
It's interesting, for sure. Please try reading once and see.

Chapter 33

New Kanji in this Chapter

#231 結	#141 構	#4 回	#229 練	#472 習
#578 授	#540 始	#226 続	#527 復	#570 直

1. お酒をどうぞ。

Osake wo douzo.
Honorable sake, go ahead. (i.e., have some sake)

2. いいえ、結構です。

Iie, kekkou desu.
No, it's fine (i.e., no thank you).

3. 新しい漢字を十回ずつ書いて練習する。

Atarashii kanji wo jukkai zutsu kaite renshuu suru.
Writing new kanji 10 times each, I practice.

4. 上手になりましたね。

Jouzu ni narimashita ne.
You became skilled, huh.

5. 小さい時ピアノを習っていました。

Chiisai toki piano wo naratte imashita.
When I was small, I was learning piano.

6. 会議は一週間に一回、水曜日の午前中にあります。

Kaigi wa isshuukan ni ikkai, suiyoubi no gozenchuu ni arimasu.
As for the meeting, one time per week, on during a Wednesday morning, it exists.

7. 授業を始める。

Jugyou wo hajimeru.
I will start the class.

8. 日本語の勉強を続ける。

Nihongo no benkyou wo tsuzukeru.
I will continue Japanese study.

9. 日本語のテストがあります。その前にどんなことをしておきますか。

Nihongo no tesuto ga arimasu. Sono mae ni donna koto wo shite okimasu ka.
A Japanese language test exists. At before that, what kinds of things will you do in advance?

10. テキストを復習しておきます。

Tekisuto wo fukushuu shite okimasu.
I will review the textbook in advance.

11. テープを聞いておきます。

Teepu wo kiite okimasu.
I will listen to the tapes in advance.

12. 漢字を勉強しておきます。

Kanji wo benkyou shite okimasu.
I will study kanji in advance.

13. サラリーマンですから月一回しかゴルフに行けません。

Sarariiman desu kara tsuki ikkai shika gorufu ni ikemasen.
Since I'm a salaryman, except for once per month only I cannot go for the purpose of golf.

14. もう会議を始めますよ。

Mou kaigi wo hajimemasu yo.
Already, someone will start the meeting, for sure.

15. 毎日よく練習しました。

Mainichi yoku renshuu shimashita.
I practiced frequently every day.

16. ダニエルさんには復習をする時間があまりありません。

Danieru-san ni wa fukushuu wo suru jikan ga amari arimasen.
As for to Daniel, to-do-review time hardly exists.

17. 会社は今、困難に直面している。

Kaisha wa ima, kon'nan ni chokumen shite iru.
As for the company, now, to difficulty it is facing.

18. パンフレットにはどんなことが書いてありますか。

Panfuretto ni wa donna koto ga kaite arimasu ka.
As for to the pamphlet, what kind of thing is written?

19. 曜日や授業料について書いてあります。

Youbi ya jugyouryou ni tsuite kaite arimasu.
Concerning the days of the week, the tuition, etc., are written.

20. 映画が始まらない。

Eiga ga hajimaranai.
The movie doesn't start.

21. 直子さんは話さなかった。

Naoko-san wa hanasanakatta.
Naoko didn't talk.

22. 会議をいつしましょうか。木曜日でよろしいですか。

Kaigi wo itsu shimashou ka. Mokuyoubi de yoroshii desu ka.
The meeting, when shall we do? Will Thursday be all right?

23. ええ、それで結構です。

Ee, sore de kekkou desu.
Yeah, that will be fine.

24. 円高は続くでしょうか。

Endaka wa tsuzuku deshou ka.
As for the strong yen, will it probably continue?

25. じゃ、又今度にします。

Ja, mata kondo ni shimasu.
Well, again, at next time, I'll do it.

26. この時計を直して欲しいんですがいつできますか。

Kono tokei wo naoshite hoshiin desu ga, itsu dekimasu ka.
I desire you to repair this clock, but when will it be ready?

27. そうですね。今ちょっと忙しいから...

Sou desu ne. Ima chotto isogashii kara...
That's so, huh. Since now, a little bit busy...

28. 三日後ならできますよ。

Mikka go nara dekimasu yo.
In the case of after three days, it will be ready, for sure. (mikka ato, also OK)

29. ジョシュアさんは仕事がなかなか終わらなかったので日本語の授業に遅れました。

Joshua-san wa shigoto ga nakanaka owaranakatta node, nihongo no jugyou ni okuremashita.
As for Joshua, since the work didn't finish readily, he was delayed to Japanese language class.

30. もう一ついかがですか。

Mou hitotsu ikaga desu ka.
Another one, how is it? (i.e., do you want another piece?, e.g., of candy)

31. いいえ、もう結構です。

Iie, mou kekkoo desu.
No, I'm already fine.

32. 毎日続けて練習すれば覚えられます。

Mainichi tsuzukete renshuu sureba oboeraremasu.
Every day continuing, if you do practice, you will be able to memorize.

33. 本を読んでます。

Hon wo yondemasu.
He is reading a book. (shortened for speech)

34. 日本語のクラスの前にいつも復習しておきます。

Nihongo no kurasu no mae ni itsumo fukushuu shite okimasu.
At before Japanese class, I always do review.

35. 石田さんが来たら会議を始めましょう。

Ishida-san ga kitara kaigi wo hajimemashou.
When Ishida comes, let's start the meeting.

Chapter 34

New Kanji in this Chapter

#328 番	#470 号	#187 教	#345 伝	#447 赤
#136 様	#155 青	#511 科	#505 他	#444 灰

1. 電話番号は何番ですか。

Denwa bangou wa nanban desu ka.
As for the phone number, what number is it?

2. 教授のうちにはキャデラックとベンツがあって、お手伝いさんも二人います。

Kyouju no uchi ni wa kyaderakku to bentsu ga atte, otetsudai-san mo futari imasu.
As for at the professor's home, a Cadillac and a Benz exist, and two honorable maids also exist.

3. 赤信号で止まる。

Aka shingou de tomaru.
I stop for the red light.

4. 小林から電話があったとお伝えください。

Kobayashi kara denwa ga atta to otsutae kudasai.
Please honorably report that there was a phone call from Kobayashi

5. そちら様の電話番号は？

Sochira sama no denwa bangou wa?
As for that very honorable side's phone number?

6. 03-3251-0479 です。

Zero san no san ni go ichi no zero yon nana kyuu desu.
It's 03-3251-0479.

7. お伝えします。

Otsutae shimasu.
I will humbly report. (i.e., I will convey the message)

8. では、よろしくお願いします。

Dewa, yoroshiku onegai shimasu.
Well, I beg you well. (i.e., please convey my message)

9. 日本料理では何が一番好きですか。

Nihon ryouri de wa nani ga ichiban suki desu ka.
As for of Japanese cooking, what do you like best?

10. 私はお寿司が一番好きです。

Watashi wa osushi ga ichiban suki desu.
As for me, I like honorable sushi the best.

11. 赤ちゃんが生まれる。

Akachan ga umareru.
The baby will be born.

12. 白いシーツを見せてくださ
い。

Shiroi shiitsu wo misete kudasai.
Please show me some white sheets.

13. 青いのはありますが、白いの
はありません。

Aoi no wa arimasu ga, shiroi no wa
arimasen.
Blue ones exist, but white ones don't
exist.

14. 来年の一月までにこの教科書
の勉強は全部終わりますか。

Rainen no ichigatsu made ni kono
kyoukasho no benkyou wa zenbu
owarimasu ka.
By next year's January, will the study of
this textbook completely finish?

15. まだ開いていないですね。

Mada aite inai desu ne.
It still isn't open, huh.

16. 他の店に行きましょう。

Hoka no mise ni ikimashou.
Let's go to another store.

17. あのう、あなたのうちの電話
番号を教えてください。

Anou, anata no uchi no denwa bangou
wo oshiete kudasai.
Say, please teach me your home phone
number. (i.e., tell me)

18. あの、課長、お客様がいらっ
しゃいました。

Ano, kachou, okyakusama ga
irasshaimashita.
Say, Section Manager, a very honorable
customer honorably came.

19. 今、ネクタイは赤いのと青い
のはありますが、他の色はな
いんです。

Ima, nekutai wa akai no to aoi no wa
arimasu ga, hoka no iro wa nain desu.
Now, as for neckties, we have red ones
and blue ones, but other colors don't
exist.

20. その火事は全ての村を灰にし
てしまった。

Sono kaji wa subete no mura wo hai ni
shite shimatta.
As for that fire, it completely turned the
entire village to ashes.

21. この道はだめだ。

Kono michi wa dame da.
As for this street, it's bad.

22. 他の道を通りましょう。

Hoka no michi wo toorimashou.
Let's pass by on another street.

23. 午前六時に起きます。

Gozen rokuji ni okimasu.
I get up at 6 a.m.

24. 石川さんは何時にうちを出ま
すか。

Ishikawa-san wa nanji ni uchi wo
demasu ka.
As for Ishikawa, at what time does she
leave the home?

25. 昨晩のテレビは面白かったで
   すか。

Sakuban no terebi wa omoshirokatta desu ka.
Was last night's TV interesting?

26. 私の父は青と灰色のネクタイ
   を持っている。

Watashi no chichi wa ao to haiiro no nekutai wo motte iru.
My father has a blue and grey necktie.

27. ちょっと疲れました。

Chotto tsukaremashita.
I got a little tired.

28. 少し休んだ方がいいですよ。

Sukoshi yasunda hou ga ii desu yo.
It would be better to rest a while, for sure.

29. では又、後ほどお電話しま
   す。

Dewa mata, nochihodo odenwa shimasu.
Well, again, more in the future, I will do a humble phone call.

30. 手伝いましょうか。

Tetsudaimashou ka.
Shall I help?

31. すみません。一人ではできな
   いんです。

Sumimasen. Hitori de wa dekinain desu.
Excuse me. As for by myself, I can't do it.

32. 私は科学の先生が好きだ。

Watashi wa kagaku no sensei ga suki da.
As for me, I like the science teacher.

33. 月野様とおっしゃる方がいら
   っしゃいました。

Tsukino-sama to ossharu kata ga irasshaimashita.
A person whom they honorably call very honorable Mr. Tsukino honorably came.

34. そこの灰皿を取っていただけ
   ますか。

Soko no haizara wo totte itadakemasu ka.
Can you pass that place's ashtray and I humbly receive?

35. 部屋は空いています。

Heya wa aite imasu
The room is unoccupied.

36. この教科書はとても分かりや
   すい。

Kono kyoukasho wa totemo wakariyasui.
As for this textbook, it's very easy to understand.

Chapter 35

New Kanji in this Chapter

#387 辞	#476 引	#539 治	#453 越	#533 歯
#325 医	#276 者	#310 忘	#485 借	#333 僕

1. 難しい漢字を知っているんですね。

Muzukashii kanji wo shitte irun desu ne.
You are knowing some difficult kanji, huh.

2. 辞書を引いたんです。

Jisho wo hiitan desu.
I consulted on a dictionary

3. 五日間しか休めないなんてがっかりしました。

Itsukakan shika yasumenai nante gakkari shimashita.
Except for 5 days' duration only, I cannot rest, such a thing! I got disappointed!

4. もっと休みたかったら会社を辞めるしかありませんね。

Motto yasumitakattara kaisha wo yameru shika arimasen ne.
If you want to vacation more, except to resign the company only, doesn't exist, huh.

5. 病気がまだ治らない。

Byouki ga mada naoranai.
The illness still doesn't heal.

6. 和光は三越デパートの前にあります。

Wakou wa mitsukoshi depaato no mae ni arimasu.
Wakou exists in front of Mitsukoshi department store.

7. いつ引っ越ししましたか。

Itsu hikkoshi shimashita ka.
When did you do moving?

8. 4ヶ月前に引っ越ししました。

Yonkagetsu mae ni hikkoshi shimashita.
I did moving at 4 months ago.

9. 歯医者さんは毎日何時に起きますか

Haishasan wa mainichi nanji ni okimasu ka.
As for the dentist, every day, at what time does she get up?

10. これは日本語の辞書です。

Kore wa nihongo no jisho desu.
This is a Japanese language's dictionary.

11. いつまで会社を休みますか。

Itsu made kaisha wo yasumimasu ka.
Until when will you rest the company?
(i.e., take time off)

12. 病気が治るまで会社を休みます。

Byouki ga naoru made kaisha wo yasumimasu.
Until the illness heals, I will rest the company.

13. 歯が痛い。

Ha ga itai.
The tooth hurts.

14. 本を忘れました。

Hon wo wasuremashita.
I forgot a book.

15. 友達に借りた方がいいですよ。

Tomodachi ni karita hou ga ii desu yo.
You'd better borrow from a friend.

16. お医者さんが薬で病気を治してくれた。

Oishasan ga kusuri de byouki wo naoshite kureta.
The doctor healed the illness with medicine and gave.

17. 黒田さん、僕にもハンバーガーを買ってきて欲しいんだけど。

Kuroda-san, boku ni mo hanbaagaa wo katte kite hoshiin dakedo...
Kuroda, for me as well, I desire you to buy a hamburger and come, but...

18. ええ、いいですよ。野村さんもいかが？

Ee, ii desu yo. Nomura-san mo ikaga?
Yeah, it's good, for sure. Nomura also, how...?

19. そうだな。僕にも買ってきてよ。

Sou da na. Boku ni mo katte kite yo.
That's so. For me also, buy and come, for sure.

20. 部屋がきれいだったら借ります。

Heya ga kirei dattara, karimasu.
If the room is clean, I'll rent it.

21. 道が込んでいます。

Michi ga konde imasu.
The streets are crowded.

22. 電車で行った方がいいですよ。

Densha de itta hou ga ii desu yo.
It would be better to go by train.

23. いいカメラですねぇ。僕もそんなカメラが欲しいなぁ。

Ii kamera desu nee. Boku mo sonna kamera ga hoshii naa.
It's a good camera, huh. I also desire such a camera.

24. そうですか。私はもう使わないから欲しければ持っていってもいいですよ。

Sou desu ka. Watashi wa mou tsukawanai kara, hoshikereba, motte itte mo ii desu yo.
Is that so? As for me, since I no longer use it, if you desire it, it's OK if you take it away, for sure.

25. いつ引っ越しますか。

Itsu hikkoshimasu ka.
When will you move?

26. 僕は花に水をやるのを忘れてしまった。

Boku wa hana ni mizu wo yaru no wo wasurete shimatta.
As for me, I completely forgot to give water to the flowers.

27. 歯医者さんは9時までに来るはずでしたが、なかなか来ませんでした。

Haisha-san wa kuji made ni kuru hazu deshita ga, nakanaka kimasen deshita.
The dentist was supposed to come by 9:00, but she didn't come readily.

28. 薬を飲んだ方がいいですよ。

Kusuri wo nonda hou ga ii desu yo.
It would be better to take medicine.

29. 明日テストがあります。

Ashita tesuto ga arimasu.
Tomorrow a test exists.

30. すぐ勉強した方がいいですよ。

Sugu benkyou shita hou ga ii desu yo.
It would be better to study soon.

31. 2週間後に引っ越します。

Nishuukan go ni hikkoshimasu.
I will move in two weeks. (nishuukan ato ni, also OK as a reading of this kanji)

32. 何をしに行きますか。

Nani wo shi ni ikimasu ka.
For the purpose of doing what, will he go?

33. 本を借りに行きます。

Hon wo kari ni ikimasu.
He will go for the purpose of borrowing a book.

34. 忘れないでください。

Wasurenai de kudasai.
Please don't forget.

Chapter 36

New Kanji in this Chapter

#240 婚	#42 最	#30 久	#285 転	#509 乗
#449 足	#517 勤	#560 招	#249 式	#428 呼

1. あなたの両親はいつ結婚しましたか。

Anata no ryoushin wa itsu kekkon shimashita ka.
When did your parents get married?

2. 最近、疲れているみたいだけど、無理をしないで。

Saikin, tsukarete iru mitai dakedo, muri wo shinai de.
Recently, it's being tired, apparently, but don't do the impossible. (i.e., don't overdo it)

3. うん、今週は久しぶりに休みが取れそうなんだ。

Un, konshuu wa hisashiburi ni yasumi ga toresou nan da.
Yeah, as for this week, at after a long time of absence, it seems that I can take a vacation.

4. 何度も転んでやっと自転車に乗れるようになりました。

Nandomo koronde yatto jitensha ni noreru you ni narimashita.
Falling many times, finally, I got to the point that I was able to ride a bicycle.

5. 足が長い人です。

Ashi ga nagai hito desu.
He's a person with long legs.

6. 今、新聞社に勤めています。

Ima shinbunsha ni tsutomete imasu.
Now I am employed at a newspaper company.

7. テニスをするのは久しぶりなんですよ。

Tenisu wo suru no wa hisashiburi nan desu yo.
As for to do tennis, it's after a long time of absence, for sure.

8. 最近、ちょっと足が痛いんです。

Saikin, chotto ashi ga itain desu.
Recently, a little, the leg hurts.

9. それで会社に歩いて行かない方がいいと思っているんですよ。

Sore de kaisha ni aruite ikanai hou ga ii to omotte irun desu yo.
For that reason, it would be better *not* to go to the company walking, I'm thinking, for sure.

10. アンソニーさんが転んだところです。

Ansonii-san ga koronda tokoro desu.
Anthony has just fallen over.

11. 久しぶりに隣の奥さんが私達をパーティーに招待してくれました。

Hisashiburi ni tonari no okusan ga watashitachi wo paatii ni shoutai shite kuremashita.
After a long time, the neighbor's honorable wife invited us to a party and gave.

12. 日本の結婚式は300万円かかります。

Nihon no kekkonshiki wa sanbyakuman'en kakarimasu.
A Japanese wedding costs 3 million yen.

13. 医者を呼ぶほど気分が悪いんですか。

Isha wo yobu hodo kibun ga waruin desu ka.
To the degree that you will call a doctor, is the feeling bad? (i.e., do you feel bad enough to call a doctor?)

14. 今度大阪に転勤することになったんですよ。

Kondo oosaka ni tenkin suru koto ni nattan desu yo.
Next time, it was scheduled that I will transfer to Osaka, for sure.

15. じゃ、これからはなかなか会えなくなりますね。

Ja, kore kara wa nakanaka aenakunarimasu ne.
Well, as for from now, readily it will become unable to meet, huh.

16. 結婚式に招かれたけれど、何を着ていったら良いか分からない。

Kekkonshiki ni manekareta keredo, nani wo kite ittara yoi ka wakaranai.
To a wedding ceremony I was invited on, but what if I wear and go good (question), I don't understand. (i.e., I don't know what to wear)

17. ニコラスさんの最初の日の仕事はどうでしたか。

Nikorasu-san no saisho no hi no shigoto wa dou deshita ka.
As for Nicholas's first day's work, how was it?

18. 3度も乗りかえます。

Sando mo norikaemasu.
I transfer all of 3 times.

19. 2時間もかかります。

Nijikan mo kakarimasu.
It takes 2 full hours.

20. 犬を車に乗せる。

Inu wo kuruma ni noseru.
I will put the dog in the car.

21. 直子さんの結婚式はいつか聞いていますか。

Naoko-san no kekkonshiki wa itsu ka kiite imasu ka.
As for Naoko's wedding, when (question) are you hearing?

22. 銀行に勤めてます。

Ginkou ni tsutometemasu.
She is being employed at a bank.
(shortened for speech)

23. 駅は近いですが、車で行きますか。

Eki wa chikai desu ga, kuruma de ikimasu ka.
As for the station, it's close, but will you go by car?

24. ええ、近くても車で行きます。

Ee, chikakutemo, kuruma de ikimasu.
Yeah, even though close, I will go by car.

25. そうですか。じゃ、タクシーを呼びましょう。

Sou desu ka. Ja, takushii wo yobimashou.
Is that so? Well, let's call a taxi.

26. お寿司は好きじゃありませんか。

Osushi wa suki ja arimasen ka.
As for honorable sushi, don't you like it?

27. はい、好きじゃありません。

Hai, suki ja arimasen.
Yes, I don't like it. (when agreeing to a negative question, Japanese people tend to answer "yes" rather than "no")

28. 犬は四本足である。

Inu wa yonhon ashi de aru.
As for a dog, four legs exist. (i.e., a dog has four legs)

29. エミリーさん、日曜日はいつも何をしますか。

Emirii-san, nichiyoubi wa itsumo nani wo shimasu ka.
Emily, as for Sundays, always, what do you do?

30. ゆっくり寝ます。

Yukkuri nemasu.
I sleep leisurely.

31. 彼女は私達を夕食に招いた。

Kanojo wa watashitachi wo yuushoku ni maneita.
As for her, she invited us to dinner.

32. すぐ呼んで来ます。

Sugu yonde kimasu.
Soon I will call and come. (i.e., I'll summon him and return)

Chapter 37

New Kanji in this Chapter

#80 魚	#266 音	#520 楽	#488 件	#403 場
#544 予	#225 約	#561 別	#218 特	#455 定

1. 飛行機の食事は肉でした。

Hikouki no shokuji wa niku deshita.
The airplane's meal was meat.

2. 魚じゃありませんでした。

Sakana ja arimasen deshita.
It was not fish.

3. どんな音楽を聞きたいですか。

Donna ongaku wo kikitai desu ka.
What kind of music do you want to listen to?

4. すみません。今勉強しているんです。

Sumimasen. Ima benkyou shite irun desu.
Excuse me, I'm studying now.

5. ラジオの音を小さくしてくださいませんか。

Rajio no oto wo chiisaku shite kudasaimasen ka.
Won't you please make the radio's sound small and give?

6. 昨日のパーティーはとても楽しかったです。

Kinou no paati wa totemo tanoshikatta desu.
As for yesterday's party, it was very pleasant.

7. 大切な用件があるんだ。

Taisetsu na youken ga arun da.
An important business matter exists.

8. スキー場ではもうスキーができますか。

Sukii jou de wa mou sukii ga dekimasu ka.
As for at the ski area, can you already ski?

9. ええ、もう少し雪が降ればスキーができるようになります。

Ee, mou sukoshi yuki ga fureba, sukii ga dekiru you ni narimasu.
Yeah, if it snows a little more, then it will get to the point that skiing can be done.

37-102

10. この魚は新しいから刺身(さしみ)にしましょう。

Kono sakana wa atarashii kara sashimi ni shimashou.
As for this fish, since it's fresh, let's make sashimi out of it.

11. ホテルを予約しておいたらどうですか。

Hoteru wo yoyaku shite oitara dou desu ka.
How is it if you reserve the hotel in advance?

12. 外国にクリスマスカードを送る場合は遅くても十二月十日までに出してください。

Gaikoku ni kurisumasu kaado wo okuru baai wa osokutemo juunigatsu tooka made ni dashite kudasai.
To foreign countries, as for Christmas cards to send cases, at the very latest, by December 10th, please send.

13. 私達は音楽を聞きながら食事をしました。

Watashitachi wa ongaku wo kiki nagara, shokuji wo shimashita.
As for us, while listening to music, we did a meal.

14. 日曜日は何をしますか。

Nichiyoubi wa nani wo shimasu ka.
As for Sunday, what will you do?

15. 別に何もしません。

Betsu ni nani mo shimasen.
In particular, I will not do anything.

16. 特に予定はありません。

Toku ni yotei wa arimasen.
In particular, plans do not exist.

17. 危険な場所に行こうとする彼を、みんなが引き止めた。

Kiken na basho ni ikou to suru kare wo, minna ga hikitometa.
On the to-a-dangerous-place-he-will-try-to-go him, everyone detained.

18. この件について、コメントが欲しいんですが。

Kono ken ni tsuite, komento ga hoshiin desu ga...
Regarding this matter, I desire comments (i.e., your comments), but...

19. インタビューは明日午前10時に予定されている。

Intabyuu wa asu gozen juuji ni yotei sarete iru.
As for the interview, tomorrow at 10 a.m., it is being scheduled on. (i.e., it's scheduled for 10 a.m.)

20. 猫は別として動物は好きだ。

Neko wa betsu to shite doubutsu wa suki da.
As for cats, apart from, as for animals, I like them. (i.e., I don't like cats, but I like other animals)

21. ホテルを予約しておかない方がいいですよ。

Hoteru wo yoyaku shite okanai hou ga ii desu yo.
It would be better to *not* reserve the hotel in advance, for sure.

22. 日本語の勉強は難しいです。でも、とても楽しいです。

Nihongo no benkyou wa muzukashii desu. Demo, totemo tanoshii desu.
As for Japanese language study, it's difficult. But it's very pleasant.

23. 飛行機は込むから3ヶ月前に予約しておいた方がいいですよ。

Hikouki wa komu kara sanka getsu mae ni yoyaku shite oita hou ga ii desu yo.
Since the planes will get crowded, it would be better to make the reservation at three months in advance, for sure.

24. 石田さん、彼女と別れたらしいよ。

Ishida-san, kanojo to wakareta rashii yo.
Ishida, with her (i.e., his girlfriend), he separated apparently, for sure.

25. 信じられない！

Shinjirarenai!
I can't believe it!

26. どうしてその魚を食べませんでしたか。

Doushite sono sakana wo tabemasen deshita ka.
Why didn't you eat that fish?

27. 私は音楽、特にクラシック音楽が好きだ。

Watashi wa ongaku, toku ni kurashikku ongaku ga suki da.
As for me, music, in particular classical music, I like.

28. 僕はガールフレンドと一緒にスキーに行く予定です。

Boku wa gaarufurendo to issho ni sukii ni iku yotei desu.
As for me, with the girlfriend, together, it's a go-for-the-purpose-of-skiing plan.

29. 今日は楽しいなぁ。

Kyou wa tanoshii naa.
As for today, pleasant!

30. この件についてあなたと話をしたいのですが。

Kono ken ni tsuite anata to hanashi wo shitai no desu ga...
Regarding this matter, with you, I would like to do conversation, but...

31. 今年の夏は特に暑かった。

Kotoshi no natsu wa toku ni atsukatta.
As for this summer, it was especially hot.

Chapter 38

New Kanji in this Chapter

#124 体	#441 調	#479 風	#7 呂	#65 熱
#477 張	#407 珍	#552 代	#362 辺	#591 払

1. 高橋さんは大体 15 分待ちます。

Takahashi-san wa daitai juu go fun machimasu.
Takahashi generally waits 15 minutes.

2. ペンギンはアフリカに住んでいますか。

Pengin wa afurika ni sunde imasu ka.
Do penguins live in Africa?

3. アフリカに住んでいるかどうか分からないから本で調べてみます。

Afurika ni sunde iru ka douka wakaranai kara hon de shirabete mimasu.
Since I don't know whether they live in Africa, I will check from a book and see.

4. このお風呂は熱すぎます。

Kono ofuro wa atsusugimasu.
This honorable bath is too hot.

5. ハナさんは窓を開けました。

Hana-san wa mado wo akemashita.
Hannah opened the window.

6. 風で窓が開きました。

Kaze de mado ga akimashita.
By the wind, the window opened.

7. ニコラスさんは出張に一人で行きますか。

Nikorasu-san wa shutchou ni hitori de ikimasu ka.
As for Nicholas, to the business trip, will he go alone?

8. いいえ、奥さんも一緒に行きます。

Iie, okusan mo issho ni ikimasu.
No, his wife also together will go.

9. 珍しい花がある。

Mezurashii hana ga aru.
A rare flower exists.

10. お風呂に入らない。

Ofuro ni hairanai.
I won't get into the bath.

11. お体の調子はいかがですか。

Okarada no choushi wa ikaga desu ka.
As for the condition of the honorable body, how is it?

12. ええ、頭が痛くて熱があるようなんです。

Ee, atama ga itakute netsu ga aru you nan desu.
Yeah, the head hurts, and fever exists, it appears.

13. そんなに具合が悪いんだったら、出張は野村さんにでも代わってもらったら？

Sonna ni guai ga waruin dattara, shutchou wa nomura-san ni demo kawatte morattara?
So much, if the condition is bad, as for the business trip, if to Nomura or someone it will exchange and you receive? (i.e., if he could take your place?)

14. 田辺さんは電気代をどこで払えばいいと言いましたか。

Tanabe-san wa denkidai wo doko de haraeba ii to iimashita ka.
As for Tanabe, where if you pay the electricity cost will be good, did she say?

15. 近くの銀行で払えばいいと言いました。

Chikaku no ginkou de haraeba ii to iimashita.
At the nearby bank, if you pay it will be good, she said.

16. 彼の電話番号を調べた。

Kare no denwa bango wo shirabeta.
I checked (i.e., looked up) his telephone number.

17. この辺がこんなに静かなのは、珍しいんじゃありませんか。

Kono hen ga konna ni shizuka na no wa, mezurashiin ja arimasen ka.
This area, as for to be this quiet, isn't it unusual?

18. もしお風呂が熱すぎたら水を入れてください。

Moshi ofuro ga atsusugitara mizu wo irete kudasai.
Supposing the honorable bath is too hot, please add water.

19. お金を払ったのに品物をくれません。

Okane wo haratta noni shinamono wo kuremasen.
Even though I paid money, they don't give me the merchandise.

20. 渡辺さんは先週ホンコンへ行ったと聞きましたが。

Watanabe-san wa senshuu honkon e itta to kikimashita ga...
As for Watanabe, last week he went to Hong Kong I heard, but...

21. 困ったなぁ。明日の会議に出られなくなっちゃった。

Komatta naa. Ashita no kaigi ni derarenakunatchatta.
Inconvenienced. I completely became unable to attend tomorrow's meeting.

22. じゃ、誰かに代わってもらえば？

Ja, dareka ni kawatte moraeba?
Well, to someone, if it exchanges and you receive?

23. 私は結婚しています。

Watashi wa kekkon shite imasu.
As for me, I'm married.

24. 彼が早起きするなんて珍しい。

Kare ga hayaoki suru nante mezurashii.
He, to do early arising, such a thing, unusual.

25. ライアンさんは出張の計画書を書きました。

Raian-san wa shutchou no keikakusho wo kakimashita.
As for Ryan, he wrote the business trip's written itinerary.

26. ウイリヤムさんは寿司が好きですか。

Uiriamu-san wa sushi ga suki desu ka.
As for William, does he like sushi?

27. ああ、中村さん。こんにちは。

Aa, nakamura-san. Konnichi wa.
Ah, Nakamura. Hello.

28. カードで払ってもいいでしょうか。

Kaado de haratte mo ii deshou ka.
Is it probably OK if I pay with a card?

29. 両親が心配しているから、ちょっとホテルで電話をしたいんですが。

Ryoushin ga shinpai shite iru kara, chotto hoteru de denwa wo shitain desu ga...
Because the parents are worried, for a moment, I'd like to do a phone call at the hotel, but...

30. じゃ、すぐホテルに帰りましょう。

Ja, sugu hoteru ni kaerimashou
Well, let's return to the hotel soon.

31. アメリカでは夏休みは大体どのくらい取れますか。

Amerika de wa natsu yasumi wa daitai dono kurai toremasu ka.
As for in America, as for summer vacation, usually, about how much can one take?

32. 一ヶ月ぐらいです。

Ikkagetsu gurai desu.
It's about one month.

Chapter 39

New Kanji in this Chapter

# 212 茶	# 605 残	# 342 荷	# 247 紅	# 299 冷
# 305 館	# 11 立	# 314 念	# 354 運	# 356 返

1. 今、このお茶を飲んじゃう。

Ima kono ocha wo non jau.
I will now finish drinking this tea. (non jau = contracted form of nonde shimau)

2. 花田さん、今日は少し残業して欲しいんだけど。

Hanada-san, kyou wa sukoshi zangyou shite hoshiin dakedo...
Hanada, as for today, I desire you to do a little overtime work, but...

3. 田辺さん、荷物をたくさんお持ちですねぇ。

Tanabe-san, nimotsu wo takusan omochi desu nee.
Tanabe, you are honorably carrying luggage, a lot, huh.

4. 一つお持ちしましょうか。

Hitotsu omochi shimashou ka?
One thing shall I humbly carry?

5. 紅茶が冷めますよ。

Koucha ga samemasu yo.
The black tea will cool off, for sure.

6. 熱いうちに飲んでください。

Atsui uchi ni nonde kudasai.
While still hot, please drink.

7. スープが冷たくなりましたね。

Suupu ga tsumetaku narimashita ne.
The soup became cold, huh.

8. じゃ、少し暖かくしましょう。

Ja, sukoshi atatakaku shimashou.
Well, let's make it a little warm.

9. 映画館が込んでいたので映画を立って見ました。

Eigakan ga konde ita node eiga wo tatte mimashita.
Since the movie theater was crowded, I watched the movie standing up.

10. コーヒーがよろしいですか、それとも紅茶がよろしいですか。

Koohii ga yoroshii desu ka. Soretomo koucha ga yoroshii desu ka.
Is coffee good? Or is black tea good?

11. 石田さん、テニスに行きましょうか。

Ishida-san, tenisu ni ikimashou ka.
Ishida, shall we go for the purpose of tennis?

12. 残念ですが、ちょっと用があって。

Zannen desu ga, chotto you ga atte...
It's too bad, but a little, a job exists and...

13. 食べてばかりいないで少し運動した方がいいですよ。

Tabete bakari inai de sukoshi undou shita hou ga ii desu yo.
Eating only not being, it would be better to do a little exercise, for sure.

14. 私はコーヒーは何でもいいが、紅茶にはこだわっている。

Watashi wa koohii wa nandemo ii ga, koucha ni wa kodawatte iru.
As for me, as for coffee, anything good, but as for to black tea, I am being particular.

15. 疲れたでしょう。冷たいジュースでもいかがですか。

Tsukareta deshou. Tsumetai juusu demo ikaga desu ka.
You got tired probably. How would cold juice or something be?

16. 辞書を貸してくださいね。

Jisho wo kashite kudasai ne.
Please lend me the dictionary, huh.

17. 明日お返ししますから。

Ashita okaeshi shimasu kara.
Since tomorrow I will humbly return it.

18. すみません。この荷物を運んでもらいたいんですけど。

Sumimasen. Kono nimotsu wo hakonde moraitain desu kedo...
Excuse me. I would like you to carry this luggage and I receive, but...

19. ブラウンさんは運動会で何に出ますか。

Buraun-san wa undoukai de nani ni demasu ka.
As for Brown, at the sports tournament, to what will he go out? (i.e., what sport will he play?)

20. リレーに出ます。

Riree ni demasu.
He will go out to the relay.

21. 図書館に行って本を返して来てください。

Toshokan e itte hon wo kaeshite kite kudasai.
Please go to the library, return the books and come.

22. お茶とコーヒーと紅茶ではどれが一番好きですか。

Ocha to koohii to koucha de wa dore ga ichiban suki desu ka.
As for of honorable tea, coffee and black tea, which do you like best?

23. どれも好きではありません。

Dore mo suki dewa arimasen.
I don't like none of them.

24. 十時まで残業できる？

Juuji made zangyou dekiru?
Can you do overtime work until 10:00?

25. ドアを開けると荷物を持った男の人が立っていました。

Doa wo akeru to nimotsu wo motta otoko no hito ga tatte imashita.
When I open the door, a luggage-carried man was standing.

26. 人が映画館の前で並んでいる。

Hito ga eigakan no mae de narande iru.
The people are lining up in front of the movie theater.

27. 楽しみにしていたのに残念だなぁ。

Tanoshimi ni shite ita noni zannen da naa.
In spite of the fact that to enjoyment I was doing (i.e., I was looking forward to it), it's too bad.

28. 林にきれいな花が目立つ。

Hayashi ni kirei na hana ga medatsu.
In the grove, pretty flowers stand out.

29. 図書館に行くんだけど返す本、ある？

Toshokan ni ikun dakedo kaesu hon, aru?
I will go to the library, but are there any to-take-back books?

30. 今この本を読んじゃうから。

Ima kono hon wo yon jau kara.
Because I will now read this book completely, i.e. finish it.

31. 残念ながら今日は会社に行けません。

Zannen nagara kyou wa kaisha ni ikemasen.
While too bad (i.e., regrettably), as for today, I cannot go to the company.

Chapter 40

New Kanji in this Chapter

# 205 牛	# 186 乳	# 222 低	# 40 声	# 107 力
# 526 落	# 95 顔	# 423 洗	# 246 工	# 201 濯

1. 牛乳は飲みません。

Gyunyuu wa nomimasen.
As for cow's milk, I don't drink it.

2. 赤ちゃんがお乳を欲しがっている。

Akachan ga ochichi wo hoshigatte iru.
The baby seems to be wanting honorable milk.

3. 低い声で歌った。

Hikui koe de utatta.
She sang in a low voice.

4. 最近の子供達の体力は低下している。

Saikin no kodomotachi no tairyoku wa teika shite iru.
As for recent's children's stamina, it is decreasing.

5. 本が机から落ちた。

Hon ga tsukue kara ochita.
The book fell from the desk.

6. 父は僕の顔を洗ってくれました。

Chichi wa boku no kao wo aratte kuremashita.
As for my father, he washed my face and gave.

7. あの声はダニエルさんのようですね。

Ano koe wa danieru-san no you desu ne.
As for that voice over there, it seems to be Daniel, huh.

8. 私の力で、できることは何でもやります。

Watashi no chikara de, dekiru koto wa nandemo yarimasu.
Of my power, as for able to do thing, I will do anything. (i.e., I will do everything in my power)

9. うちの牛は全く乳がでない。

Uchi no ushi wa mattaku chichi ga denai.
As for the home's cow, completely, milk doesn't come out.

10. 工員は何時頃朝ご飯を食べますか。

Kouin wa nanji goro asagohan wo tabemasu ka.
As for the factory worker, about what time does he eat breakfast?

11. 洗濯は地下でします。

Sentaku wa chika de shimasu.
As for the laundry, we do it in the basement.

12. みんなにはっきり聞こえるように大きな声で話してください。

Minna ni hakkiri kikoeru you ni ookii na koe de hanashite kudasai.
To everyone, clearly, in order to be audible, please talk with a big voice.

13. せっけんで手を洗ったよ。

Sekken de te wo aratta yo.
I washed the hands with soap, for sure.

14. マンションにエアコンを取り付ける工事をしている。

Manshon ni eakon wo toritsukeru kouji wo shite iru.
To the condominiums, on air conditioning, to-install construction is being done by someone.

15. もう洗濯をしてしまいました。

Mou sentaku wo shite shimaimashita.
I already completely did the laundry.

16. 顔を洗っているところです。

Kao wo aratte iru tokoro desu.
He's in the process of washing the face.

17. 工事中です。中に入ってはいけません。

Kouji-chuu desu. Naka ni haitte wa ikemasen.
It's under construction. You may not enter to inside.

18. 日曜日は洗濯をしたり、買い物に出かけたりします。

Nichiyoubi wa sentaku wo shitari, kaimono ni dekaketari shimasu.
As for Sundays, do laundry, etc., go out for the purpose of shopping, etc., I do.

19. 今朝、牛乳を飲んだとたんに気持ちが悪くなった。

Kesa, gyuunyuu wo nonda totan ni kimochi ga warukunatta.
This morning, I drank cow's milk, as soon as, the feeling became bad.

20. りんごを落とす。

Ringo wo otosu.
I will drop (or knock down) an apple.

21. 花田さんは困っているようです。

Hanada-san wa komatte iru you desu.
As for Hanada, it seems like being inconvenienced.

22. 昨日会った人はサンタクロースのような顔をしていました。

Kinou atta hito wa santakuroosu no you na kao wo shite imashita.
The person I met yesterday had (or was wearing) a face like Santa Claus.

23. いい天気なので公園へ行きましょう。

Ii tenki na node kouen e ikimashou.
Since it's good weather, let's go to the park.

24. ここのお寿司はおいしいから、ここで食べましょう。

Koko no osushi wa oishii kara, koko de tabemashou.
As for here's honorable sushi, since delicious, let's eat here.

25. どうして遅れましたか。

Doushite okuremashita ka.
Why were you delayed?

26. すみません。道が込んでいたので。

Sumimasen. Michi ga konde ita node.
Excuse me. Because the streets were crowded.

27. みんなで力を出して働こう。

Minna de chikara wo dashite hatarakou.
All together, let's put out power and labor. (i.e., let's work hard together)

28. ヘリコプターが、とても低く飛んでいる。

Herikoputaa ga totemo hikuku tonde iru.
The helicopter is flying very low.

29. りんごが落ちる。

Ringo ga ochiru.
An apple will fall.

Chapter 41

New Kanji in this Chapter

#152 背	#546 柔	#352 選	#558 投	#563 倒
#256 浴	#568 冊	#590 打	#519 努	#587 果

1. 背の低い柔道の選手は背の高い選手を投げ倒した。

Se no hikui juudou no senshu wa se no takai senshu wo nagetaoshita.
As for the short judo athlete, he threw the tall athlete down.

2. 今日は朝、起きてから何をしましたか。

Kyou wa asa, okite kara nani wo shimashita ka.
As for today, morning, after getting up, what did you do?

3. シャワーを浴びてコーヒーを飲んで新聞を読んでからうちを出ました。

Shawaa wo abite koohii wo nonde shinbun wo yonde kara uchi wo demashita.
After I took a shower, drank coffee, and read the newspaper, I left home.

4. 彼は毎月 20 冊もの本を読む。

Kare wa maitsuki nijussatsu mo no hon wo yomu.
As for him, every month, he reads as many as twenty books.

5. タイプを打とうとしている。

Taipu wo utou to shite iru.
She is trying to type.

6. この牛肉は柔らかい。

Kono gyuuniku wa yawarakai.
This beef is tender.

7. 私に柔道を教えてください。

Watashi ni juudou wo oshiete kudasai.
Please teach me judo.

8. ここにある三つの物の中からどれか一つを選んでください。

Koko ni aru mittsu no mono no naka kara doreka hitotsu wo erande kudasai.
From the at-here-existing three things, please choose one of them, one thing.

9. ボールを投げて犬に取って来させています。

Booru wo nagete inu ni totte kosasete imasu.
The ball throwing, to the dog he is making get and come.

10. 努力しよう。

Doryoku shiyou.
Let's do effort. (i.e., let's try hard)

11. 背中を真っ直ぐにしてください。

Senaka wo massugu ni shite kudasai.
Please make the back of the body straight. (i.e., straighten up)

12. 彼は、病気で倒れてしまった。

Kare wa byouki de taorete shimatta.
As for him, due to illness, he fell completely. (i.e., he collapsed)

13. 時々運動して体力を落とさないように努めている。

Tokidoki undou shite tairyoku wo otosanai you ni tsutomete iru.
Sometimes doing exercise, I am making an effort not to drop stamina.

14. 打った、取った、投げた。

Utta, totta, nageta.
Hitting, catching, throwing! (all three verbs are in the exclamatory tense)

15. ちょっとシャワーを浴びた。

Chotto shawaa wo abita.
I took a quick shower.

16. 本を何冊か貸してあげましょう。

Hon wo nansatsuka kashite agemashou.
Books, some volumes I shall lend and give to you. (i.e., I will lend you some books)

17. 水野さんをお願いします。

Mizuno-san wo onegai shimasu.
I beg Mizuno. (i.e., I'd like to speak to her)

18. 水野さんは今タイプを打っています。

Mizuno-san wa ima taipu wo utte imasu.
As for Mizuno, now, she is typing.

19. じゃ又後で、電話します。

Ja mata ato de, denwa shimasu.
Well, again, of later, I will do a phone call.

20. スーパーに行くなら果物を買ってきてね。

Suupaa ni iku nara, kudamono wo katte kite ne.
In the case of to go to the supermarket, buy fruit and come, huh.

21. 背広を着ています。

Sebiro wo kite imasu.
I am wearing a business suit.

22. 思いがけない結果になった。

Omoigakenai kekka ni natta.
Unexpected results developed.

23. お待たせしました。

Omatase shimashita.
I'm sorry to have kept you waiting.

24. サラさんはシャワーを浴びていますがすぐ来ます。

Sara-san wa shawaa wo abite imasu ga, sugu kimasu.
As for Sarah, she is taking a shower, but she will come soon.

25. そうですか。じゃ、バーで待ちましょう。

Sou desu ka. Ja, baa de machimashou.
Is that so? Well, let's wait at the bar.

26. 読みたい本があったらどれでも一冊選んでください。

Yomitai hon ga attara doredemo issatsu erande kudasai.
If there is a book you want to read, any of them, one volume, please choose.

27. 面倒なことをお願いして大変申し訳ございません。

Mendou na koto wo onegaishite taihen moushiwake gozaimasen.
Since I beg a troublesome thing, terrible, there's no excuse.

28. 大学を一番に卒業できたのは、日々の努力の結果にほかならない。

Daigaku wo ichiban ni sotsugyou dekita no wa, hibi no doryoku no kekka ni hoka naranai.
As for was able to accomplish university graduation as number one, every day's effort's results is nothing but. (i.e., it's due to nothing but daily effort)

Chapter 42

New Kanji in this Chapter

#309 恥	#238 要	#307 必	#602 船	#537 吹
#581 袋	#138 械	#497 座	#496 席	#518 務

1. 私はみんなの前で恥をかいた。

Watashi wa minna no mae de haji wo kaita.
As for me, in front of everyone, I was put to shame.

2. じゃ、要りません。

Jaa, irimasen
Well, I don't need it.

3. 私はみんなにジロジロ見られてとても恥ずかしかった。

Watashi wa minna ni jirojiro mirarete totemo hazukashikatta.
As for me, by everyone I was stared at, and I was very embarrassed.

4. そんな必要はありません。

Sonna hitsuyou wa arimasen.
That kind of necessity doesn't exist.
(i.e., such a thing is not necessary)

5. 船に乗る前、風はどうでしたか。

Fune ni noru mae, kaze wa dou deshita ka.
Before to get on the boat, as for the wind, how was it?

6. 強く吹いていました。

Tsuyoku fuite imashita.
It was blowing strongly.

7. 昨日、日本語のテープを聞きましたか。

Kinou nihongo no teepu wo kikimashita ka.
Yesterday, did you listen to the Japanese language tape?

8. 彼は手袋をしていたようだ。

Kare wa tebukuro wo shite ita you da.
As for him, he was wearing gloves, it appears.

9. すみません。この仕事、今日中にはできないんですが。

Sumimasen. Kono shigoto, kyoujuuni wa dekinain desu ga...
Excuse me. This work, as for by the end of today, cannot be accomplished, but...

10. じゃ、今日中でなくてもいいです。

Ja, kyoujuu de nakute mo ii desu.
Well, of by the end of today, it isn't necessary.

11. 明日は必ず終わるようにして
ください。

Ashita wa kanarazu owaru you ni shite
kudasai ne.
As for tomorrow, certainly, please make
an effort to finish, huh.

12. 機械を止める。

Kikai wo tomeru.
I will stop the machine.

13. 今日は冷たい風が吹いて寒い
一日でした。

Kyou wa tsumetai kaze ga fuite samui
ichinichi deshita.
As for today, a cold wind blew, and it
was a cold all-day.

14. その袋に果物が入っている
よ。

Sono fukuro ni kudamono ga haitte iru
yo.
In that bag, fruit is being entered, for
sure. (i.e., the bag contains fruit)

15. 船を降りた後、銀座で食事を
しました。

Fune wo orita ato, ginza de shokuji wo
shimashita.
After we got down the boat, we did a
meal in Ginza.

16. どうぞお掛けください。

Douzo okake kudasai.
Go ahead, please honorably sit. (implies
that the person will sit on a chair or sofa)

17. お座りください。

Osuwari kudasai.
Please honorably sit. (implies that the
person will sit on a zabuton)

18. 私はフルートを吹いたが、
あまり上手ではなかったので
恥ずかしかった。

Watashi wa furuuto wo fuita ga, amari
jouzu de wa nakatta node hazukashikatta.
As for me, I played the flute, but since I
wasn't very skillful, I got embarrassed.

19. あさって駅で新幹線の座席を
予約してきます。

Asatte eki de shinkansen no zaseki wo
yoyaku shite kimasu.
The day after tomorrow, at the station, I
will reserve seats for the bullet train and
come.

20. 事務員は何時にうちに帰りま
すか。

Jimuin wa nanji ni uchi ni kaerimasu ka.
As for the office worker, at what time
does he return to the home?

21. もしもし。石田ですが北村さ
んをお願いします。

Moshimoshi. Ishida desu ga kitamura-
san wo onegai shimasu.
Hello (on the phone). It's Ishida, but I
beg Kitamura. (i.e., I'd like to speak to
him)

22. 申し訳ございませんが、北村
は今、席を外しております。

Moushiwake gozaimasen ga, kitamura
wa ima, seki wo hazushite orimasu.
There's no excuse, but Kitamura now is
disconnected from his seat.

23. はい、失礼いたしました。

Hai, shitsurei itashimashita.
Yes, I humbly did a discourtesy. (i.e., good-bye)

24. その時、機械のモーターが急に止まった。

Sono toki, kikai no mootaa ga kyuu ni tomatta.
Then the machine's motor suddenly stopped.

25. あの、私達の結婚式に出席していただきたいんですが。

Ano, watashitachi no kekkon shiki ni shusseki shite itadakitain desu ga...
Say, to our wedding, we would like you to attend and us to receive humbly, but...

26. 事務の前田さんです。

Jimu no maeda-san desu.
It's the office's Maeda.

27. 船は三時に出ました。

Fune wa sanji ni demashita.
The ship left at 3:00.

28. これは特に若者向けにデザインされている。

Kore wa toku ni wakamono muke ni dezain sarete iru.
As for this, in particular, for young people it is designed on. (i.e., it's particularly designed for them)

29. この機械を使う時には、手袋が必要です。

Kono kikai wo tsukau toki ni wa, tebukuro ga hitsuyou desu.
As for at the time you use this machine, gloves are necessary.

30. 着物を着ているのは誰ですか。

Kimono wo kite iru no wa dare desu ka.
As for the kimono-wearing one, who is it?

31. 本日の司会を務める木村です。

Honjitsu no shikai wo tsutomeru kimura desu.
It's today's on master of ceremonies will-discharge-my-duties Kimura. (i.e., I'm Kimura, and I will be the master of ceremonies today)

Chapter 43

New Kanji in this Chapter

# 577 受	# 379 際	# 33 昔	# 436 試	# 382 験
# 528 優	# 149 勝	# 228 線	# 388 南	# 326 米

1. この間お願いしました件はいかがでしょうか。

Kono aida onegai shimashita ken wa ikaga deshou ka.
The other day, as for the we-humbly-begged matter, how is it probably?

2. お引き受け願えますでしょうか。

Ohikiuke negaemasu deshou ka.
Are we able to beg honorable taking charge, probably?

3. これは実際にあったことです。

Kore wa jissai ni atta koto desu.
As for this, truly, it-existed thing it is.
(i.e., this really happened)

4. 思いがけず昔の友達に会った。

Omoigakezu mukashi no tomodachi ni atta.
Unexpectedly, I met an old times' friend.

5. 試験に受かったんですすって。良かったですね。

Shiken ni ukattan desutte. Yokatta desu ne.
To the exam you passed, reportedly. (woman's speech) It was good huh.

6. 優勝してください。

Yuushou shite kudasai.
Please do victory.

7. 成田空港は国際線の空港です。

Narita kuukou wa kokusai sen no kuukou desu.
Narita Airport is an international airlines' airport.

8. この車を試してみてください。

Kono kuruma wo tameshite mite kudasai.
Please test this car and see.

9. 羽田空港は国内線の空港です。

Haneda kuukou wa kokunai sen no kuukou desu.
Haneda Airport is a domestic airlines' airport.

10. 羽田は東京の南にあります。

Haneda wa toukyou no minami ni arimasu.
Haneda exists south of Tokyo.

11. 品川からモノレールで 30 分ぐらいかかります。

Shinagawa kara monoreeru de sanjuppun gurai kakarimasu.
From Shinagawa, by monorail, it takes about 30 minutes.

12. とても近いです。

Totemo chikai desu.
It's very close.

13. 便利です。

Benri desu.
It's convenient.

14. この地方は昔からお米を作っています。

Kono chihou wa mukashi kara okome wo tsukutte imasu.
As for this region, since ancient times, they are producing honorable rice.

15. 白い線の内側に下がってお待ちください。

Shiroi sen no uchigawa ni sagatte omachi kudasai.
To the white line's interior, step back and please honorably wait. (i.e., wait behind the white line)

16. 明日は試験があるからよく復習しておいてください。

Ashita wa shiken ga aru kara yoku fukushuu shite oite kudasai.
As for tomorrow, since a test exists, please do a thorough review in advance.

17. 実際に会ってみないことには、いい人かどうか分からない。

Jissai ni atte minai koto ni wa, ii hito ka douka wakaranai.
Unless I truly meet and see, whether a good person or not, I do not understand.
(koto ni wa, used after a negative plain verb, = unless)

18. 優勝おめでとうございます。

Yuushou omedetou gozaimasu.
Victory, congratulations.

19. 鹿児島というのはどこにあるんですか。

Kagoshima to iu no wa doko ni arun desu ka.
As for the one called Kagoshima, where does it exist?

20. 九州の一番南にありますよ。

Kyuushuu no ichiban minami ni arimasu yo.
It exists at Kyushu's farthest south, for sure.

21. 優さんは空港で待っていなかった。

Yuu-san wa kuukou de matte inakatta.
Yuu wasn't waiting at the airport.

22. 日本は、サッカーでは、南米の国にあまり勝てない。

Nihon wa, sakkaa de wa, nanbei no kuni ni amari katenai.
As for Japan, as for of soccer, to South America's countries, it can hardly win.

23. 試験の結果はどのように知らせてもらえますか。

Shiken no kekka wa dono you ni shirasete moraemasu ka.
As for the result of the test, in what way can she be informed and receive?

24. ウイリヤムさんは受付の人に何を渡しましたか。

Uiriamu-san wa uketsuke no hito ni nani wo watashimashita ka.
As for William, to the reception person, what did he hand?

25. 金太郎という人を知っていますか。

Kintarou to iu hito wo shitte imasu ka.
Are you knowing the person named Kintarou?

26. 日本の昔話に出てくる男の子で、とても強い男の子なんですよ。

Nihon no mukashi banashi ni dete kuru otoko no ko de, totemo tsuyoi otoko no ko nan desu yo.
He's a boy who emerges and comes in a Japanese fairy tale, and he's a very strong boy, for sure.

27. 優さんが来ない。

Yuu-san ga konai.
Yuu will not come.

28. 日本人は主に米を食べる。

Nihonjin wa omo ni kome wo taberu.
As for Japanese people, they eat mainly rice.

29. 赤いワンピースを着ているのは誰ですか。

Akai wanpiisu wo kite iru no wa dare desu ka.
As for the red-frock-wearing one, who is it?

30. 上田さんの奥さんです。

Ueda-san no okusan desu.
It's Ueda's wife.

31. 早く寝た方がいいですよ。

Hayaku neta hou ga ii desu yo.
It would be better to sleep early.

Chapter 44

New Kanji in this Chapter

#322 歳	#28 卵	#395 個	#446 焼	#224 経
#259 済	#64 堂	#70 町	#376 眠	#550 記

1. 36歳になりました。

Sanjuu roku sai ni narimashita.
He became 36 years old.

2. フライパンで卵を二個焼きます。

Furaipan de tamago wo niko yakimasu.
In the frying pan, I will fry two eggs.

3. 日本語の勉強を始めたばかりでまだ二ヶ月しか経っていません。

Nihongo no benkyou wo hajimeta bakari de mada nikagetsu shika tatte imasen.
I began Japanese study a while ago, and still except for only two months are not elapsing. (i.e., 2 months haven't elapsed)

4. 大学で経済と日本語を勉強しました。

Daigaku de, keizai to nihongo wo benkyou shimashita.
At university, I studied economics and the Japanese language.

5. 誰かに手伝ってもらうといいですよ。

Dareka ni tetsudatte morau to ii desu yo.
By someone if they help and you receive, it's good, for sure.

6. 仕事を済ませておかなければなりません。

Shigoto wo sumasete okanakereba narimasen.
Work must be finished (by someone) in advance.

7. 公会堂はこの道の先にあります。

Koukaidou wa kono michi no saki ni arimasu.
As for the public hall, it's at the end of this street.

8. 町を歩き回った。

Machi wo arukimawatta.
I walked around the town.

9. 若い内に色々な事を経験しておきたいと思っています。

Wakai uchi ni iroiro na koto wo keiken shite okitai to omotte imasu.
While still young, various things I want to experience in advance, I'm thinking.

10. 昨日はすき焼きを食べました。

Kinou wa sukiyaki wo tabemashita.
As for yesterday, I ate sukiyaki.

11. 残りの5個を送ってください。

Nokori no goko wo okutte kudasai.
Please send the remaining five units.

12. 食堂はどこですか。

Shokudou wa doko desu ka.
As for the cafeteria, where is it?

13. 1940年に生まれたから、76歳のはずです。

Sen kyuuhyaku yonjuu nen ni umareta kara, nanajuu rokusai no hazu desu.
Since she was born in 1940, she should be 76 years old.

14. その古い家は焼けて灰になった。

Sono furui ie wa yakete hai ni natta.
As for that old house, it burned and became ashes.

15. ぐっすり眠った。

Gussuri nemutta.
I slept soundly.

16. 休みを取りたいんですが仕事が忙しくて、なかなか...

Yasumi wo toritain desu ga shigoto ga isogashikute, nakanaka...
I would like to take vacation, but since work is busy, readily...

17. 休日出勤をして仕事を早く済ませた方がいいですよ。

Kyuujitsu shukkin wo shite shigoto wo hayaku sumaseta hou ga ii desu yo.
It would be better to do holiday work attendance and finish the work early, for sure.

18. お母さんはいつも卵焼きを作ってくれます。

Okaasan wa itsumo tamagoyaki wo tsukutte kuremasu.
As for honorable mother, she always prepares rolled omelettes and gives.

19. 町の公会堂は人でいっぱいだ。

Machi no koukaidou wa hito de ippai da.
As for the town's public hall, it is full of people.

20. 申込書にご記入ください。

Moushikomisho ni go kinyuu kudasai.
Please honorably fill in the application form.

21. 今22歳です。

Ima nijuu nisai desu.
Now I'm 22 years old.

22. 先生の話を聞いているうちに眠くなってきた。

Sensei no hanashi wo kiite iru uchi ni nemukunatte kita.
As I am listening to the teacher's speech, it became sleepy and came. (i.e., I got sleepy)

23. 私の朝食はトーストとコーヒーとゆで卵一個です。

Watashi no choushoku wa toosuto to koohii to yudetamago ikko desu.
As for my breakfast, it's toast, coffee and one boiled egg.

24. 東京の町を見物しに行きます。

Toukyo no machi wo kenbutsu shi ni ikimasu.
He will go for the purpose of sightseeing Tokyo's town.

25. 土田さんの日記。

Tsuchida-san no nikki.
Tsuchida's diary.

26. 寿司屋へ行った。

Sushiya e itta.
I went to a sushi place.

27. アレクサンダーさんもグレイスさんもお寿司が好きだからだ。

Arekusandaa-san mo gureisu-san mo osushi ga suki dakara da.
It's because Alexander also, Grace also, like honorable sushi.

28. たくさん食べた。

Takusan tabeta.
We ate a lot.

29. ビールも飲んだ。

Biiru mo nonda.
We also drank beer.

30. 両親が心配しているので電話を掛けた。

Ryoushin ga shinpai shite iru node denwa wo kaketa.
Because the parents are worried, we called on the phone.

31. 新聞の記事には、時々でたらめなものがある。

Shinbun no kiji ni wa, tokidoki detarame na mono ga aru.
As for to newspapers' articles, sometimes nonsensical things exist.

32. 今日は眠いです。

Kyou wa nemui desu.
As for today, I'm sleepy.

Chapter 45

New Kanji in this Chapter

#523 愛	#144 交	#394 故	#257 温	#156 情
#386 報	#151 育	#252 泉	#429 告	#234 冬

1. 愛子さんは何も食べなかった。

Aiko-san wa nanimo tabenakatta.
Aiko didn't eat anything.

2. 交通事故でけがをしたんですって。

Koutsuu jiko de kega wo shitan desutte.
By a traffic accident, you did an injury reportedly. (woman's speech)

3. 早く良くなってくださいね。

Hayaku yoku natte kudasai ne.
Please become well soon, huh.

4. はい、有難うございます。

Hai. Arigatou gozaimasu.
Yes, thank you a lot.

5. 温度が下がった。

Ondo ga sagatta.
The temperature went down.

6. アンドリューさんはまだ日本語のニュースや交通情報を聞き取ることができません。

Andoryuu-san wa mada nihongo no nyuusu ya koutsuu jouhou wo kikitoru koto ga dekimasen.
As for Andrew, still, to listen/take Japanese language news, traffic information, etc., can't be done.

7. 人の名前が思い出せないなんて、本当に情けない。

Hito no namae ga omoidasenai nante, hontou ni nasakenai.
People's names are unable to remember, such a thing, truly regrettable.

8. ところで、飛行機の食事は何でしたか。

Tokoro de, hikouki no shokuji wa nan deshita ka.
By the way, what was the airplane's meal?

9. 肉でしたか、魚でしたか。

Niku deshita ka, sakana deshita ka.
Was it meat, was it fish?

10. 肉と野菜でした。

Niku to yasai deshita.
It was meat and vegetables.

11. 親が愛情を込めて子を育てる。

Oya ga aijou wo komete ko wo sodateru.
Parents, putting love into, they raise children. (i.e., parents put love into raising children)

12. 温泉に入ります。

Onsen ni hairimasu.
I will enter a hot spring.

13. 息子が交通事故にあったので、これから病院にいかなけりゃならないんです。

Musuko ga koutsuu jiko ni atta node, kore kara byouin ni ikanakerya naranain desu.
The son, since to a traffic accident he met, from now, I must go to the hospital.

14. 報告書は3時までにできますか。

Houkokusho wa sanji made ni dekimasu ka.
As for the report, will it accomplish by 3:00?

15. 他の仕事を2時までしますから...

Hoka no shigoto wo niji made shimasu kara...
Since I'll do other work until 2:00... (i.e., I won't be able to do it)

16. この泉の水はおいしいです。

Kono izumi no mizu wa, oishii desu.
As for this spring's water, it's delicious.

17. 天気予報によると今年の冬は寒いそうです。

Tenki yohou ni yoru to kotoshi no fuyu wa samui sou desu.
According to the weather report, this year's winter will be cold, reportedly.

18. 彼女はおじいさんに育てられた。

Kanojo wa ojiisan ni sodaterareta.
As for her, she was brought up by the grandfather.

19. 遅れてごめんなさい。待った？

Okurete gomen nasai. Matta?
Because I am delayed, forgive me. Did you wait?

20. ううん、そんなに。どうしたの。

Uun. Sonna ni. Doushita no?
No. That much. How did it do? (i.e., what happened?)

21. 事故のために道が込んでいたものだから。

Jiko no tame ni, michi ga konde ita mono dakara.
For the sake of an accident, since the-streets-were-being-crowded thing.

22. ジョナサンさんは広告を見ながら漢字の勉強をします。

Jonasan-san wa koukoku wo mi nagara kanji no benkyou wo shimasu.
As for Jonathan, while he looks at advertisements, he does kanji's study.

23. 冬のプールの水は温かい方が
いいです。

Fuyu no puuru no mizu wa atatakai hou ga ii desu.
As for winter's pool's water, warm is better.

24. 課長がエマさんに報告書を作
らせた。

Kachou ga ema-san ni houkokusho wo tsukuraseta.
The section manager made Emma create a written report.

25. 彼女は親の愛情のもとで幸せ
に育った。

Kanojo wa oya no aijou no moto de shiawase ni sodatta.
As for her, on the basis of parent's love, she was brought up happily.

26. 愛子さんは道子さんと違う時
計をしています。

Aiko-san wa michiko-san to chigau tokei wo shite imasu.
As for Aiko, she is wearing a watch that is different from Michiko.

27. 国に帰る前に旅行がしたいん
ですが、どこへ行ったらいい
でしょうね。

Kuni ni kaeru mae ni ryokou ga shitain desu ga, doko e ittara ii deshou ne?.
At before I return to the country (i.e., my country), I would like to travel, but where if I go will probably be good, huh?

28. 旅行に行くなら北海道はどう
ですか。

Ryokou ni iku nara hokkaidou wa dou desu ka.
In the case of to go for travel, as for Hokkaido, how is it?

29. 温泉がたくさんありますよ。

Onsen ga takusan arimasu yo.
Hot springs, a lot, exist, for sure.

30. 今年の冬は寒いんだそうで
す。

Kotoshi no fuyu wa samuin da sou desu.
As for this year's winter, it will reportedly be cold.

31. 夕食は魚がいいですね。

Yuushoku wa sakana ga ii desu ne.
As for dinner, fish is good, huh.

Chapter 46

New Kanji in this Chapter

# 451 徒	# 601 以	# 487 化	# 180 決	# 168 注
# 75 戻	# 536 次	# 491 宿	# 25 文	# 192 喫

1. この生徒の熱は 37 度以下だから、心配はありません。

Kono seito no netsu wa sanjuu shichido ika dakara, shinpai wa arimasen.
Since this student's temperature is less than 37 degrees, as for worry, it doesn't exist. (OK to substitute nanado for shichido)

2. 日本は最近アメリカ化されるようになった。

Nihon wa saikin amerikaka sareru you ni natta.
As for Japan, recently, Americanization to be done on, it got to that point. (i.e., Japan became Americanized)

3. 夏休みはどこに行きますか。

Natsu yasumi wa doko ni ikimasu ka.
As for summer vacation, where will you go?

4. どこに行くかまだ決めていません。

Doko ni iku ka mada kimete imasen.
Where to I will go (question) still I am not arranging.

5. 私がどんなに注意しても言うことを聞かない。

Watashi ga donna ni chuui shite mo iu koto wo kikanai.
I, whatever kind of caution I do, you do not hear the to-say thing.

6. 生徒達が来るんじゃないでしょうか。

Seitotachi ga kurun ja nai deshou ka.
The students will come, isn't it, probably?

7. 土田さんはどうして寿司屋へ戻りましたか。

Tsuchida-san wa doushite sushiya e modorimashita ka.
As for Tsuchida, why did he return to the sushi place?

8. この道を真っ直ぐに行って次の信号の手前にあります。

Kono michi wo massugu ni itte tsugi no shingou no temae ni arimasu.
You go straight on this street, and it exists on this side of the following stoplight.

9. 新宿のレストランで注文した焼き肉はとても柔らかかったです。

Shinjuku no resutoran de chuumon shita yakiniku wa totemo yawarakakatta desu.
The broiled meat that I ordered at a Shinjuku's restaurant was very soft.

10. あそこの喫茶店でコーヒーでも飲もう。

Asoko no kissaten de koohii demo nomou.
At that over there place's coffeeshop, let's drink coffee or something.

11. 日にちを決めなくてはいけません。

Hinichi wo kimenakutewa ikemasen.
We have to arrange the date.

12. アメリカの文化は日本の文化と違います。

Amerika no bunka wa nihon no bunka to chigaimasu.
As forAmerican culture, with Japanese culture, it differs.

13. 宿題は明日までだから今日中にしておきます。

Shukudai wa ashita made dakara kyou juu ni shite okimasu.
Since the homework is until tomorrow (i.e., it's due by tomorrow), I will do it in advance sometime today.

14. すみませんが次のバスは何分に来るでしょうか。

Sumimasen ga tsugi no basu wa nan pun ni kuru deshou ka.
Excuse me, but as for the following bus, at what time precisely will it probably come?

15. 後5分ぐらいで来ると思いますよ。

Ato gofun gurai de kuru to omoimasu yo.
I think it will come of (i.e., in) about five minutes later, for sure.

16. 喫茶店でウェイターにコーヒーをこぼされたんです。

Kissaten de ueitaa ni koohii wo kobosaretan desu.
At the coffee house, by the waiter, coffee was spilled on me.

17. 決めた以上やるしかない。

Kimeta ijou yaru shika nai.
Arranged, beyond that, except for to do only doesn't exist. (i.e., once we've arranged things, there's nothing left but to do it)

18. 奥さんはショッピングに行ったきり戻って来ません。

Okusan wa shoppingu ni itta kiri modotte kimasen.
As for the honorable wife, since she went for the purpose of shopping, she doesn't return and come.

19. 宿題をしてから寝ます。

Shukudai wo shite kara nemasu.
After I do the homework, I'll sleep.

20. 生徒達は日本語の先生に作文を書かされました。

Seitotachi wa nihongo no sensei ni sakubun wo kakasaremashita.
As for the students, by the Japanese language teacher, they were made to write a composition.

21. 先生にもっと字をきれいに書くように注意されたので練習しようと思います。

Sensei ni motto ji wo kirei ni kaku you ni chuui sareta node renshuu shiyou to omoimasu.
By the teacher, since more to write characters cleanly a caution was done on me, I shall practice I think.

22. 以前はここに古い寺がありましたが、今は喫茶店などになっています。

Izen wa koko ni furui tera ga arimashita ga, ima wa kissaten nado ni natte imasu.
A long time ago, an old temple existed here, but now coffee shops and so forth are becoming.

23. 私は化学の先生が好きです。

Watashi wa kagaku no sensei ga suki desu.
As for me, I like the chemistry teacher.

24. 宿題はどうしましたか。

Shukudai wa dou shimashita ka.
As for the homework, how did it do? (i.e., what happened?)

25. すみません。忘れました。この次は忘れないようにします。

Sumimasen. Wasuremashita. Kono tsugi wa wasurenai you ni shimasu.
Excuse me. I forgot. As for this following, I will make an effort not to forget.

26. 旅行先で取られたスーツケースを取り戻した。

Ryokousaki de torareta suutsukeesu wo torimodoshita.
The at-the-destination-of-the-trip was-taken-on-me suitcase I got back.

Chapter 47

New Kanji in this Chapter

# 241 姉	# 500 岸	# 595 拾	# 284 重	# 289 軽
# 542 世	# 69 界	# 556 島	# 71 留	# 214 守

1. 姉は 10 分以内に行きますから海岸で待っていてください。

Ane wa juppun inai ni ikimasu kara kaigan de matte ite kudasai.
Since my older sister will go within ten minutes, please be waiting at the beach.

2. 彼はボールを拾った。

Kare wa booru wo hirotta.
As for him, he picked up the ball.

3. このスーツケースは重いですね。

Kono suutsukeesu wa omoi desu ne.
This suitcase is heavy, huh.

4. じゃ、本を出して軽くしましょう。

Ja, hon wo dashite karuku shimashou.
Well, taking out the books, let's make it light.

5. 世界で一番長い橋はどこにありますか。

Sekai de ichiban nagai hashi wa doko ni arimasu ka.
Where is the longest bridge in the world?

6. 島田さんは多分来るでしょう。

Shimada-san wa tabun kuru deshou.
As for Shimada, she will probably come probably.

7. 重いでしょう。お持ちしましょう。

Omoi deshou. Omochi shimashou.
It's probably heavy. I shall humbly hold/carry.

8. 有難う。一人じゃとても持てなくて困っていたところなんですよ。

Arigatou. Hitori ja totemo motenakute komatte ita tokoro nan desu yo.
Thank you. As for of one person, since very much unable to hold/carry, it's a was-being-inconvenienced moment, for sure. (ja = de wa)

9. お皿を洗った後は、重ねて置いておく。

Osara wo aratta ato wa, kasanete oite oku.
As for after honorable plates were washed, we pile them up and place them in advance.

10. 私が留守の間、姉が犬の世話をしてくれた。

Watashi ga rusu no aida, ane ga inu no sewa wo shite kureta.
I, absence's interval, older sister did the dog's care and gave. (i.e., she took care of the dog for me while I was absent)

11. このナイフは軽いし良く切れます。

Kono naifu wa karui shi yoku kiremasu.
This knife is light and cuts well. (shi implies an explanation, i.e., this is why I like it)

12. ボートは岸へ打ち上げられた。

Booto wa kishi e uchiagerareta.
As for the boat, to the beach it was cast ashore on.

13. 中村さんの息子さんはアメリカの高校に留学することになりました。

Nakamura-san no musuko-san wa amerika no koukou ni ryuugaku suru koto ni narimashita.
As for Nakamura's honorable son, he was scheduled to do study abroad to an American high school.

14. この授業を受けるに際して、次のことを守ってください。

Kono jugyou wo ukeru ni saishite, tsugi no koto wo mamotte kudasai.
Take this class, at the time of (i.e., at the time you take it), please observe the following things.

15. お世話になった先生がいらっしゃる同窓会だから、行かない訳にはいかない。

Osewa ni natta sensei ga irassharu dousoukai dakara, ikanai wake ni wa ikanai.
Since it's the honorable-care-developed teacher-will-honorably-go class reunion, not go, I can't possibly do. (i.e., I have to attend)

16. 私の姉は毎朝シャワーを浴びます。

Watashi no ane wa maiasa shawaa wo abimasu.
As for my older sister, every morning, she takes a shower.

17. 世界には四つの海洋がある。

Sekai ni wa yottsu no kaiyou ga aru.
There are four oceans in the world.

18. アンソニーさんはなぜ中島さんに二回目の電話を掛けたのですか。

Ansonii-san wa naze nakashima-san ni nikai me no denwa wo kaketa no desu ka.
As for Anthony, why to Nakashima did he make the 2nd phone call?

19. 一回目は中島さんが会議中で話せなかったからです。

Ikkaime wa nakashima-san ga kaigichuu de hanasenakatta kara desu.
As for the first time, it's because Nakashima, because in a meeting, could not talk.

20. 渡辺さんは留守ですが…

Watanabe-san wa rusu desu ga...
Watanabe is absent, but...

21. 駅前でタクシーを拾った。

Eki mae de takushii wo hirotta.
In front of the station I picked up (i.e., caught) a taxi.

22. エベレストは世界で一番高い山です。

Eberesuto wa sekai de ichiban takai yama desu.
As for Everest, of the world, it's the tallest mountain.

23. このバッグは軽いし大きいから便利です。

Kono baggu wa karui shi ookii kara benri desu.
This bag is light and, since it's big, it's convenient.

24. 私はニュージャージーの小さな町で生まれました。

Watashi wa nyuujaajii no chiisana machi de umaremashita.
As for me, I was born in a New Jersey's small town.

25. 十歳までそこにいました。

Jussai made soko ni imashita.
Until 10-years-old I existed there. (jissai made, also OK)

26. 十一歳の時ニューヨークへ行きました。

Juuissai no toki nyuuyooku e ikimashita.
11-year-old's time, I went to New York.

27. そして、ニューヨークの学校へ行きました。

Soshite, nyuuyooku no gakkou e ikimashita.
And then I went to a New York's school.

28. 私は学校がとても好きでした。

Watashi wa gakkou ga totemo suki deshita.
As for me, I liked school a lot.

29. その島は子供にとって楽園だ。

Sono shima wa kodomo ni totte rakuen da.
As for that island, from the point of view of children, it's a paradise.

30. 道で百円玉を拾った。

Michi de hyakuen dama wo hirotta.
I picked up a 100-yen coin in the street.

Chapter 48

New Kanji in this Chapter

# 159 散	# 353 連	# 543 葉	# 571 値	# 559 段
# 530 第	# 85 貿	# 230 絡	# 295 答	# 598 階

1. 犬を散歩に連れていってやり
ました。

Inu wo sanpo ni tsurete itte yarimashita.
I took the dog along for the purpose of a walk and gave.

2. 言葉が分からないとき、辞書
で調べます。

Kotoba ga wakaranai toki jisho de shirabemasu.
When I don't understand a word, I check the dictionary.

3. 値段が高いのにおいしくあり
ません。

Nedan ga takai noni oishiku arimasen.
In spite of the fact that the price is high, it isn't delicious.

4. 会議はどこでしますか。

Kaigi wa doko de shimasu ka.
As for the meeting, where will they do it?

5. 大阪の第一貿易でします。
   （おおさか）

Oosaka no dai ichi boueki de shimasu.
They will do it at Osaka's Number One Trade.

6. 会議が終わって席に戻ると、
次のようなメモが置いてあり
ました。

Kaigi ga owatte seki ni modoru to, tsugi no you na memo ga oite arimashita.
The meeting finished, and when I returned to the seat, the following appearing memo was being placed.

7. 連絡メモだった。

Renraku memo datta.
It was a contact memo.

8. 部長とよく話してから返事を
すると答えました。

Buchou to yoku hanashite kara henji wo suru to kotaemashita.
After I talk with the division manager well, I will do a reply, he replied.

9. 犬が部屋を散らかした。

Inu ga heya wo chirakashita.
The dog messed up the room.

10. 第五課を復習しましょう。

Daigo ka wo fukushuu shimashou.
Let's review Lesson 5.

11. 値段を下げてください。

Nedan wo sagete kudasai.
Please lower the price.

12. すみません。明日は９時に山川貿易で月野さんに会うことになっていますので...

Sumimasen. Ashita wa kuji ni yamakawa boueki de tsukino-san ni au koto ni natte imasu node...
Excuse me. Because, as for tomorrow, at 9:00, at Yamakawa Trade, I'm scheduled to meet Tsukino....

13. 連絡が遅れてすみませんでした。

Renraku ga okurete sumimasen deshita.
Because communication is delayed, excuse me for what I did.

14. このエレベーターは今動いていませんね。

Kono erebeetaa wa ima ugoite imasen ne.
This elevator isn't moving now, huh.

15. 階段を登りましょう。

Kaidan wo noborimashou.
Let's climb the stairs.

16. 木々は葉をつけ始めた。

Kigi wa ha wo tsukehajimeta.
The trees began to come into leaf.

17. 問題の答えは別の紙に書きなさい。

Mondai no kotae wa betsu no kami ni kakinasai.
As for the problem's answer, to the separate paper, write.

18. 山川貿易の電話番号が分からないんですが。

Yamakawa boueki no denwa bangou ga wakaranain desu ga...
I don't know/understand Yamakawa Trade's phone number, but...

19. 向こうのお寿司は日本のと同じですか。

Mukou no osushi wa nihon no to onaji desu ka.
Is the other side's honorable sushi the same as the Japanese?

20. ええ、味はほとんど同じですけど、値段はもっと安いですよ。

Ee. Aji wa hotondo onaji desu kedo, nedan wa motto yasui desu yo.
Yeah. As for the flavor, it's almost the same, but as for the price, it's more cheap, for sure.

21. 子供の部屋は散らかっている。

Kodomo no heya wa chirakatte iru.
The children's room is messy.

22. エレベーターで五階まで行ってください。

Erebeetaa de gokai made itte kudasai.
By the elevator, please go to the 5th floor.

23. 第一貿易の人はジェイコブさんに何を頼みましたか。

Dai ichi boueki no hito wa jeikobu-san ni nani wo tanomimashita ka.
As for the Number One Trade's people, what did they request of Jacob?

24. 第一貿易の人の言葉で答えなさい。

Dai ichi boueki no hito no kotoba de kotaenasai.
Reply with the Number One Trade's people's words.

25. 真さんに散歩に連れていってもらいました。

Makoto-san ni sanpo ni tsurete itte moraimashita.
By Makoto, for the purpose of a walk, he took me along, and I received.

26. 階段から落ちました。

Kaidan kara ochimashita.
I fell down from the stairs.

27. ちゃんと連絡してくれないと困るなあ。

Chanto renraku shite kurenai to komaru naa.
Properly, if you don't do communication and give, I get inconvenienced.

Chapter 49

New Kanji in this Chapter

# 589 菓	# 425 売	# 204 準	# 367 備	# 468 写
# 419 君	# 469 考	# 298 発	# 541 甘	# 450 走

1. オリビアさんはコーヒーを飲んでお菓子を食べました。

Oribia-san wa koohii wo nonde okashi wo tabemashita.
As for Olivia, she drank coffee and ate sweets.

2. トマトは夏の野菜ですよね。

Tomato wa natsu no yasai desu yo ne.
Tomatoes are summer vegetables, for sure, huh.

3. ええ、でも一年中、店で売っていますよ。

Ee, demo ichinen juu mise de utte imasu yo.
Yeah, but all year long they are selling them in stores, for sure.

4. 十月の会議の準備で忙しいので毎日残業をしなくちゃならないんです。

Juugatsu no kaigi no junbi de isogashii node mainichi zangyou wo shinakucha naranain desu.
Because of the October meeting's preparations, since we are busy, every day, I must do overtime. (nakucha = nakutewa)

5. 弟は公務員で妹は写真家です。

Otouto wa koumuin de imouto wa shashinka desu.
Little brother is a public employee, and little sister is a photographer.

6. 誰があのチョコレートをもらったんですか。

Dare ga ano chokoreeto wo morattan desu ka.
Who received that chocolate over there?

7. 田中君がもらったんです。

Tanaka-kun ga morattan desu.
Young man Tanaka received it.

8. 運動会の準備では良くやってくれましたね。

Undoukai no junbi de wa yoku yatte kuremashita ne.
As for of the sports tournament's preparation, you did well and gave to us, huh.

9. ケーキはまだありますか。

Keeki wa mada arimasu ka.
As for cake, does it still exist?

10. いいえ、売れてしまいました。

Iie, urete shimaimashita.
No, it was able to be sold completely.

11. 夏休みに何をしようかと今考えているところです。

Natsu yasumi ni nani wo shiyou ka to ima kangaete iru tokoro desu.
In summer vacation, what I shall do (question) now, I'm the process of thinking.

12. 渡辺君、転勤するんだって。

Watanabe-kun, tenkin surun datte.
Young man Watanabe is going to transfer, reportedly.

13. うん、僕も聞いた。それでニューヨークに行くんだって。

Un, boku mo kiita. Sore de nyuuyooku ni ikun datte.
Yeah, I also heard it. Consequently, he will go to New York, reportedly.

14. アイスクリームを売っている所です。

Aisukuriimu wo utte iru tokoro desu.
It's a place where ice cream is being sold.

15. 山口君、病気だそうです。

Yamaguchi-kun byouki da sou desu.
Young man Yamaguchi is sick, reportedly.

16. ええ、私も聞きました。それで入院するんだそうです。

Ee, watashi mo kikimashita. Sore de nyuuin surun da sou desu.
Yeah, I also heard it. Consequently, he is going to be hospitalized, reportedly.

17. ブラジルに行く準備ができて後は飛行機に乗るだけです。

Burajiru ni iku junbi ga dekite ato wa hikouki ni noru dake desu.
Since the preparations to go to Brazil accomplish, as for later, it's only to board the plane.

18. 彼はあまり発言をしない。無口な人だ。

Kare wa amari hatsugen wo shinai. Mukuchi na hito da.
As for him, not very much, statements he doesn't do. He's a taciturn person.

19. 真一君からどんな物をもらいましたか。

Shin'ichi-kun kara donna mono wo moraimashita ka.
What kind of thing did he receive from young Shin'ichi?

20. 札幌の雪祭りの写真はどれですか。

Sapporo no yukimatsuri no shashin wa dore desu ka.
As for Sapporo's snow festival's photograph, which is it?

21. 来年、引っ越しをするので準備を始めなくてはいけないと思っているんですよ。

Rainen, hikkoshi wo suru node junbi wo hajimenakute wa ikenai to omotte irun desu yo.
Next year, since I will do moving, I must begin preparation, I'm thinking, for sure.

22. まだ、始めなくてもいいんじゃありませんか。

Mada, hajimenakute mo iin ja arimasen ka.
Still, isn't it unnecessary to begin?

23. 来年になってからでも間に合いますよ。

Rainen ni natte kara demo maniaimasu yo.
After next year develops even, you will be in time, for sure.

24. デイビッドさんは日本語学校に入ることにしましたか。

Deibiddo-san wa nihongo gakkou ni hairu koto ni shimashita ka.
Did David decide to enter the Japanese language school?

25. いいえ、家に帰って考えてみることにしました。

Iie, ie ni kaette kangaete miru koto ni shimashita.
No, he returned to the house and decided to think and see.

26. このケーキは私には甘すぎます。

Kono keeki wa watashi ni wa amasugimasu.
This cake, as for for me, is too sweet.

27. 駅まで走って行きました。

Eki made hashitte ikimashita.
We went running until the station.

28. その件については私にも考えがあります。

Sono ken ni tsuite wa watashi ni mo kangae ga arimasu.
As for regarding that matter, to me also, thinking exists. (i.e., I have some ideas about it)

29. 私に意見を言わせてください。

Watashi ni iken wo iwasete kudasai.
To me, please let say an opinion.

30. どうぞ。言いたいことがあったら何でも言ってください。

Douzo. Iitai koto ga attara nandemo itte kudasai.
Go ahead. If want-to-say thing exists, please say anything.

31. 来週ヨーロッパに出発することになっています。

Raishuu yooroppa ni shuppatsu suru koto ni natte imasu.
Next week, I'm scheduled to leave for Europe.

32. 私は走るのも泳ぐのもダンスをするのも好きです。

Watashi wa hashiru no mo oyogu no mo
dansu wo suru no mo suki desu.
As for me, I like running also, swimming
also, dancing also.

33. ねぇ、昨日もらったお菓子はどこ？

Nee, kinou moratta okashi wa doko.
Hey, as for the sweets we received
yesterday, where?

34. ああ、あれは子供達が食べてしまったけれど、カステラが買ってあります。

Aa, are wa kodomotachi ga tabete
shimatta keredo, kasutera ga katte
arimasu.
Ah, as for that over there, the kids ate it
completely, but sponge cake is bought
and exists.

35. 写真は 1839 年にフランスで発明されました。

Shashin wa sen happyaku san juu kyuu
nen ni furansu de hatsumei saremashita.
As for photography, in 1839, in France, it
was invented.

36. 甘い物が何もないから何か買ってきましょう。

Amai mono ga nanimo nai kara nanika
katte kimashou.
Since sweet thing nothing doesn't exist,
let's buy something and come.

37. 何でもいいですよ。

Nan demo ii desu yo.
Anything is good, for sure.

38. 友達が待っているので走って行きました。

Tomodachi ga matte iru node hashitte
ikimashita.
Since the friend is waiting, I went
running.

39. 日本のお菓子は甘いです。

Nihon no okashi wa amai desu.
Japanese candy is sweet.

Chapter 50

New Kanji in this Chapter

# 580 製	# 290 乾	# 375 民	# 274 祝	# 265 震
# 606 球	# 515 涼	# 445 秋	# 242 市	# 584 舞

1. 新製品のカメラを6万円で売りたいんですけどどうでしょう？

Shin seihin no kamera wo rokuman'en de uritain desu kedo dou deshou?
The new product's camera, for 60,000 yen, I would like to sell, but how is it probably?

2. 6万円では売れないと思います。

Rokuman'en de wa urenai to omoimasu.
As for for 60,000 yen, you cannot sell, I think.

3. 4万円ぐらいなら売れるかもしれませんね。

Yon man'en gurai nara ureru kamoshiremasen ne.
In the case of about 40,000 yen, you might be able to sell, huh.

4. アンソニーさんは中島さんに、どんなことを頼みましたか。

Ansonii-san wa nakashima-san ni, donna koto wo tanomimashita ka.
As for Anthony, to Nakashima, what sort of thing did he request?

5. 自分の会社の製品について説明するために会ってもらうことです。

Jibun no kaisha no seihin ni tsuite setsumei suru tame ni atte morau koto desu.
Regarding his own company's product, in order to explain, it's the to-meet-and-receive thing. (i.e., Anthony asked Nakashima to meet in order for Anthony to explain his company's products)

6. シャツはまだ乾いていない。

Shatsu wa mada kawaite inai.
As for the shirts, they are still not being dry. (i.e., they aren't dry)

7. 直子さんは何が欲しいと言いましたか。

Naoko-san wa nani ga hoshii to iimashita ka.
As for Naoko, what does she desire she said?

8. 電気製品です。

Denki seihin desu.
It's electric appliances.

9. 今日は国民の祝日です。

Kyou wa kokumin no shukujitsu desu.
As for today, it's a citizens' national holiday (i.e., a national holiday).

10. この前の地震、ひどかったですね。

Kono mae no jishin, hidokatta desu ne.
The earthquake of before this was awful, huh.

11. 実は日曜日の野球の切符を二枚もらったんですけど僕は急に都合が悪くなったんです。

Jitsu wa nichiyoubi no yakyuu no kippu wo nimai morattan desu kedo boku wa kyuuni tsugou ga warukunattan desu.
The fact is, I received two Sunday baseball tickets but, as for me, suddenly the circumstances became bad.

12. 良かったら、奥さんと一緒にいかがですか。

Yokattara, okusan to issho ni ikaga desu ka.
If good, with your wife together, how is it?

13. 暑い夏が終わって涼しい秋になりました。

Atsui natsu ga owatte suzushii aki ni narimashita.
The hot summer finished, and it became the cool autumn.

14. 東京は治安のいい都市だ。

Toukyou wa chian no ii toshi da.
As for Tokyo, it's a safety-is-good city.

15. 空気が乾いています。

Kuuki ga kawaite imasu.
The air is dry.

16. 石田さんの結婚祝いを買いますから、一人につき 1,000 円ずつ集めます。

Ishida-san no kekkon iwai wo kaimasu kara, hitori ni tsuki sen'en zutsu atsumemasu.
Since we will buy Ishida's wedding present, per one person, 1000 yen apiece, we will collect.

17. あの国の市民はよく地震に見舞われる。

Ano kuni no shimin wa yoku jishin ni mimawareru.
As for that over there country's citizens, often by earthquakes they undergo. (i.e., earthquakes happen to them)

18. 部屋の中の方が外より涼しい。

Heya no naka no hou ga soto yori suzushii.
Inside the room, compared to outside, it's cooler.

19. その新しい製品は、東京をはじめ、全国の主な都市で売られている。

Sono atarashii seihin wa, toukyou wo hajime, zenkoku no omo na toshi de urarete iru.
As for that new merchandise, Tokyo including, in the whole country's main cities it is being sold on.

20. 新聞に昨日地震があったと書いてありました。

Shinbun ni kinou jishin ga atta to kaite arimashita.
In the newspaper, yesterday there was an earthquake, it was written.

21. 夏、仕事をする部屋は涼しい方がいいです。

Natsu, shigoto wo suru heya wa suzushii hou ga ii desu.
Summer, as for the to-do-work room, cool is better.

22. 乾電池が切れた。

Kandenchi ga kireta.
The dry cell battery ran out.

23. アレクサスさんは野球を見たことがありません。

Arekusasu-san wa yakyuu wo mita koto ga arimasen.
Alexis has never watched baseball.

24. 入院している友達のお見舞いに行かなくちゃならない。

Nyuuin shite iru tomodachi no omimai ni ikanakucha naranai.
I have to go for the purpose of a being-hospitalized friend's honorable visit.

25. 秋になって寒くなったらコートを着ます。

Aki ni natte samuku nattara kooto wo kimasu.
When autumn becomes, and it becomes cold, I wear a coat.

26. このお皿は結婚祝いのプレゼントにどうでしょうか。

Kono osara wa kekkon iwai no purezento ni dou deshou ka.
As for this honorable plate, to a marriage celebration's present, how is it probably?

27. 明日からあさってにかけて、台風が近づきますので、関東地方は強い風と雨に見舞われるでしょう。

Ashita kara asatte ni kakete, taifuu ga chikazukimasu node, kantou chihou wa tsuyoi kaze to ame ni mimawareru deshou.
From tomorrow extending into the day after tomorrow, since a typhoon will approach, as for the Kantou region, by strong wind and rain it will be struck, probably.

28. どうして昨日会社を休んだんですか。

Doushite kinou kaisha wo yasundan desu ka.
Why did you rest the company yesterday? (i.e., why didn't you go to work?)

29. 家内が病気だったんです。

Kanai ga byouki dattan desu.
The wife was sick.

30. 何でそんなに勉強するんですか。

Nande sonna ni benkyou surun desu ka.
How come you study so much?

31. 明日テストがあるからです。

Ashita testo ga aru kara desu.
It's because there's a test tomorrow.

32. どうして遅れたんですか。

Doushite okuretan desu ka.
Why were you delayed?

33. 道が込んでいたんです。

Michi ga konde itan desu.
The streets were crowded.

34. アッシュリーさんは日曜日に田辺さんと野球を見ることにしました。

Asshurii-san wa nichiyoubi ni tanabe-san to yakyuu wo miru koto ni shimashita.
As for Ashley, she decided to watch baseball on Sunday with Tanabe.

35. 東京は面白いです。けれども物価が高いですね。

Toukyou wa omoshiroi desu. Keredomo bukka ga takai desu ne.
Tokyo is interesting. But the prices are high, huh.

36. 10時まで待ちました。しかし、お姉さんは来ませんでした。

Juuji made machimashita. Shikashi, oneesan wa kimasen deshita.
I waited until 10:00. However, as for your honorable older sister, she didn't come.

37. 秋に音楽ホールで市民のためのコンサートがある。

Aki ni ongaku hooru de shimin no tame no konsaato ga aru.
In Autumn, at the music hall, for the sake of the townspeople, a concert exists.

38. 見ましたけれど面白くなかったです。

Mimashita keredo omoshirokunakatta desu.
I watched it, but it wasn't interesting.

39. 部屋は広いですが...

Heya wa hiroi desu ga...
The room is spacious but...

40. これは誰の車ですか。

Kore wa dare no kuruma desu ka.
As for this, whose car is it?

41. 私のです。昨日買ったんです。

Watashi no desu. Kinou kattan desu.
It's mine. I bought it yesterday.

Chapter 51

New Kanji in this Chapter

#320 区	#557 役	#359 速	#37 晴	#427 吸
#150 服	#562 割	#21 宅	#174 正	#506 春

1. 区役所に行ってから会社に来ます。

Kuyakusho ni itte kara kaisha ni kimasu.
After I go to the ward office, I will come to the company.

2. 電車はバスより速いです。

Densha wa basu yori hayai desu.
The trains are faster than the buses.

3. 午前中雨が降りますが、午後は晴れるでしょう。

Gozenchuu ame ga furimasu ga, gogo wa hareru deshou.
Throughout the morning, it will rain, but, as for the afternoon, it will probably clear up.

4. 今タバコを吸ってはいけないことになっているんですね。

Ima tabako wo sutte wa ikenai koto ni natte irun desu ne.
Now it is scheduled that one must not smoke tobacco, huh. (i.e., we aren't supposed to smoke now)

5. 洋服をハンガーに掛ける。

Youfuku wo hangaa ni kakeru.
I will hang the Western clothes on a hanger.

6. 僕は人の役に立つ仕事がしたいです。

Boku wa hito no yaku ni tatsu shigoto ga shitai desu.
As for me, people's to-be-useful work I would like to do.

7. すみません。お皿を割ってしまったんです。

Sumimasen. Osara wo watte shimattan desu.
Excuse me. I completely broke an honorable plate.

8. 気にしないでください。

Ki ni shinai de kudasai.
Please don't do to spirit. (i.e., don't be concerned)

9. 区役所で住所と名前とパスポートの番号を紙に書いて出しました。

Kuyakusho de juusho to namae to pasupooto no bangou wo kami ni kaite dashimashita.
At the ward office, he wrote the address and name and passport number to paper and put it out. (i.e., turned it in)

10. パスポートを見せて、少し待ちました。

Pasupooto wo misete, sukoshi machimashita.
He showed his passport and waited a little.

11. 割引切符についてどこで聞けばいいですか。

Waribiki kippu ni tsuite doko de kikeba ii desu ka.
Concerning discount tickets, at where if you ask is good?

12. 駅のみどりの窓口です。

Eki no midori no madoguchi desu.
It's the station's green ticket window.

13. お宅はどちらですか。

Otaku wa dochira desu ka.
Where is the honorable home?

14. タバコを吸う女の人はタバコを吸わない女の人より何人少ないですか。

Tabako wo suu onna no hito wa, tabako wo suwanai onna no hito yori nan nin sukunai desu ka.
Women who smoke tobacco, compared to women who don't smoke tobacco, are how many people fewer?

15. 天気予報で明日は晴れるって言っていました。

Tenki yohou de ashita wa hareru tte itte imashita.
From the weather report they were saying tomorrow will be sunny.

16. 正男さんは一人で来ていますか。

Masao-san wa hitori de kite imasu ka.
Is Masao being come by himself?

17. ジェイムズさんは昨日区役所に行ったかもしれません。

Jeimuzu-san wa kinou kuyakusho ni itta kamoshiremasen.
James might have gone to the ward office yesterday.

18. 見込みのある若い人を育てるのがベテラン社員の役割だ。

Mikomi no aru wakai hito wo sodateru no ga beteran shain no yakuwari da.
On prospects exist young people, to bring up thing, it's the veteran company employees' role.

19. 先生と学生は帽子と洋服と靴下が違います。

Sensei to gakusei wa boushi to youfuku to kutsushita ga chigaimasu.
As for teacher and student, hat and Western clothes and socks are different.

20. お宅のまわりは静かですか。

Otaku no mawari wa shizuka desu ka.
Are the honorable home's surroundings quiet?

21. ええ、静かなのでいい所ですよ。

Ee, shizuka na node ii tokoro desu yo.
Yeah, since it's quiet, it's a good place, for sure.

22. いいえ、車が多くてうるさい
です。

Iie, kuruma ga ookute urusai desu.
No, since there are a lot of cars, it's
noisy.

23. 山下さんのお宅ですか。

Yamashita-san no otaku desu ka.
Is it the Yamashita residence?

24. いいえ、違いますけど。

Iie, chigaimasu kedo...
No, it's different, but...

25. あ、どうも失礼しました。

A, doumo shitsurei shimashita.
Ah, I'm sorry for committing a
discourtesy.

26. 私も来年の春休みに3週間ぐ
らいヨーロッパへ行きたいと
思って、アルバイトを始めま
した。

Watashi mo rainen no haru yasumi ni
sanshuukan gurai yorooppa e ikitai to
omotte, arubaito wo hajimemashita.
Since I also, at next year's spring
vacation, for about 3 weeks, want to go
to Europe, I think, I started a part-time
job.

27. 車と電車とどちらが速いです
か。

Kuruma to densha to dochira ga hayai
desu ka.
Car vs. train, which is faster?

28. やっぱり、電車の方が速いで
しょう。

Yappari, densha no hou ga hayai deshou.
When you think about it, the train is
probably faster.

29. 道が込みますから。

Michi ga komimasu kara.
Because the streets get crowded.

30. 春なのに暖かくなりません。

Haru na noni atatakaku narimasen.
Even though it's spring, it doesn't
become warm.

31. 明日晴れたらいいですね。

Ashita haretara ii desu ne.
Tomorrow, it would be nice if it got
sunny, huh.

32. 大阪へは新幹線より飛行機の
方が1時間速いです。

Oosaka e wa shinkansen yori hikouki no
hou ga ichijikan hayai desu.
As for to Osaka, compared to the bullet
train, the airplane is one hour faster.

33. 正しいのはどちらですか。

Tadashii no wa dochira desu ka.
As for the correct one, which is it?

34. タバコを吸いたいんですが。

Tabako wo suitain desu ga...
I would like to smoke tobacco, but...

35. ここは狭いし小さい子供がいるので...

Koko wa semai shi chiisai kodomo ga iru node...
As for here, it's narrow or tight, and because a small child exists...

36. 正子さんは直子さんと同じ洋服を着ています。

Masako-san wa naoko-san to onaji youfuku wo kite imasu.
As for Masako, she is wearing Western clothes that are the same as Naoko.

37. 3週間ぐらい行きたいと思っています。

Sanshuukan gurai ikitai to omotte imasu.
She thinks that she would like to go for about three weeks.

38. 来年の春休みに行きたいと思っています。

Rainen no haruyasumi ni ikitai to omotte imasu.
She thinks that she would like to go at next year's spring vacation.

39. 春子さんは子供が好きだから、小学校の先生になりたいと思っています。

Haruko-san wa kodomo ga suki dakara, shougakkou no sensei ni naritai to omotte imasu.
As for Haruko, since she likes children, she would like to become an elementary school teacher, she is thinking.

40. 体に悪いからタバコを吸わない方がいいですよ。

Karada ni warui kara, tabako wo suwanai hou ga ii desu yo.
Since it's bad for the body, it's better not to smoke tobacco, for sure.

Chapter 52

New Kanji in this Chapter

#115 族	#12 泣	#223 絵	#164 死	#120 案
#45 的	#420 兄	#599 喜	#341 伺	#462 存

1. 家族は二人ですが、部屋は九つあります。

Kazoku wa futari desu ga, heya wa kokonotsu arimasu.
As for the family, it's two people, but there are nine rooms.

2. それじゃ、広すぎるでしょう。

Sore jaa, hirosugiru deshou.
In that case, it's probably too spacious.

3. 赤ちゃんに泣かれた。

Akachan ni nakareta.
We got cried on by the baby.

4. 英語の絵本をあげましょうか。

Eigo no ehon wo agemashou ka.
Shall we give him an English picture book?

5. 父が死にそうなんです。

Chichi ga shini sou nan desu.
My father will die, it appears.

6. その案については引き受けないものでもないが、もう少し具体的に聞かせて欲しい。

Sono an ni tsuite wa hikiukenai mono demo nai ga, mou sukoshi gutaiteki ni kikasete hoshii.
As for regarding that proposal, not to undertake not necessarily, but a little more specifically to make hear I desire. (i.e., I won't necessarily *not* undertake the proposal, but I desire you to inform me more specifically)

7. お兄さんはどこにいらっしゃいますか。

Onii-san wa doko ni irasshaimasu ka.
As for your older brother, where does he honorably exist?

9. 兄ですか。兄なら公園に行っているはずですけど。

Ani desu ka. Ani nara kouen ni itte iru hazu desu kedo...
Is it my older brother? In the case of my older brother, he should have gone to and be existing at the park, but...

10. ピカソの絵は高いですよ。

Pikaso no e wa takai desu yo.
Picasso pictures are expensive, for sure.

11. どんなに高くても欲しいんです。

Donna ni takakutemo hoshiin desu.
Whatever kind of expensive even though, I desire it.

12. ご案内します。

Goannai shimasu.
I will do humble guidance.

13. いくら強い男でも親が死んだときには、泣くでしょう。

Ikura tsuyoi otoko demo oya ga shinda toki ni wa, naku deshou.
How much strong male even though, as for at the parent-died time, he will cry probably.

14. 喜んで伺います。

Yorokonde ukagaimasu.
I'll visit you delightedly. (i.e., with pleasure)

15. 夕べは大変でしたね。

Yuube wa taihen deshita ne.
As for last night, it was terrible, huh.

16. ええ、赤ちゃんに泣かれて眠れませんでした。

Ee, akachan ni nakarete nemuremasen deshita.
Yeah, by the baby he cried on me, and I couldn't sleep.

17. 友達と家族的なお付き合いをさせていただいております。

Tomodachi to kazokuteki na otsukiai wo sasete itadaite orimasu.
With the friends, family-like humble relationships they let me do, and I am humbly receiving.

18. 兄がこの辞書はいいと言っていましたよ。

Ani ga kono jisho wa ii to itte imashita yo.
My older brother was saying that this dictionary is good, for sure.

19. 明日の会議のことを社長はご存じですか。

Ashita no kaigi no koto wo shachou wa gozonji desu ka.
Tomorrow's meeting's things, as for the president, does he honorably know?

20. 駅の前に誰か案内の人が立っているといいんですが。

Eki no mae ni dareka annai no hito ga tatte iru to iin desu ga...
At in front of the station, if someone guidance's person will be standing, it's good, but... (i.e., it would be good if someone could be giving directions)

21. じゃ、ジョシュア君が何か手伝いたいと言っていたから彼に立たせましょう。

Ja, joshua-kun ga nanika tetsudaitai to itte ita kara kare ni tatasemashou.
Well, young man Joshua, since something wants to help he was saying, to him, let's make stand.

22. 渡辺さんは部屋に掛けてある
絵を買いました。

Watanabe-san wa heya ni kakete aru e
wo kaimashita.
As for Watanabe, he bought the picture
that has been hung and exists in the
room.

23. あの会社の山本さんをご存じ
ですか。

Ano kaisha no yamamoto-san wo gozonji
desu ka.
Are you honorably knowing that
company over there's Yamamoto?

24. ちょっと伺いますが、桜ヶ
丘三丁目五番地はこの辺です
か。

Chotto ukagaimasu ga, sakuragaoka san
choume go banchi wa kono hen desu ka.
I will ask for a second, but as for
Sakuragaoka 3 choume 5 banchi, is it this
area?

25. 山田さんはなぜ切手をもらっ
て喜びましたか。

Yamada-san wa naze kitte wo moratte
yorokobimashita ka.
As for Yamada, why did she receive the
stamps and get delighted?

26. 家族の中で一番背が高いのは
僕です。

Kazoku no naka de ichiban se ga takai no
wa boku desu.
Among the family (i.e., my family) the
tallest one is I.

27. 兄にお金をもらうくらいな
ら、死んだ方がいい。

Ani ni okane wo morau kurai nara,
shinda hou ga ii.
By my older brother to receive money
approximately case, it would be better to
die. (i.e., it would be better to die than to
get money from him)

28. この道を真っ直ぐ行けば、目
的地に着きます。

Kono michi wo massugu ikeba,
mokutekichi ni tsukimasu.
On this way, if you go straight, to the
destination you will arrive.

29. 赤ちゃんが泣いた。

Akachan ga naita.
The baby cried.

30. 子供達をディズニーランドに
連れていったら喜ぶと思いま
すよ。

Kodomotachi wo dizuniirando ni tsurete
ittara yorokobu to omoimasu yo.
If you take the children to Disneyland,
they will get delighted I think, for sure.

31. 社長にお会いしたいので明日
そちらにお伺いしたいと存じ
ます。

Shachou ni oai shitai node ashita sochira
ni oukagai shitai to zonjimasu.
Since I would like to humbly meet the
president, tomorrow, to that way I would
like to humbly visit, I humbly think.

32. 1 年。1 ヶ月。2 ヶ月。
3 ヶ月。

Ichinen. Ikka getsu. Nika getsu.
Sanka getsu.
One year. One month. Two months.
Three months.

33. 4 ヶ月。5 ヶ月。6 ヶ月。
7 ヶ月。

Yonka getsu. Goka getsu. Rokka getsu.
Nanaka getsu.
Four months. Five months. Six months.
Seven months.

34. 8 ヶ月。9 ヶ月。10 ヶ月。

Hakka getsu, or hachika getsu. Kyuuka
getsu. Jukka getsu, or jikka getsu.
Eight months. Nine months.
Ten months.

35. 14 ヶ月。20 ヶ月。

Juuyonka getsu.
Nijukka getsu, or nijikka getsu.
Fourteen months. Twenty months.

36. 10 週間。20 週間。

Jusshuukan, or jisshukan.
Nijusshuukan, or nijisshukan.
Ten weeks. Twenty weeks.

37. 何年？何ヶ月？

Nan nen? Nanka getsu?
How many years, or which year? How
many months?

38. 何週間？何日？

Nanshuukan? Nan nichi?
How many weeks? How many days, or
which day?

39. 三日間の旅行に行きます。

Mikkakan no ryokou ni ikimasu.
I'm going for the purpose of a three-day
duration's trip.

Chapter 53

New Kanji in this Chapter

#492 係	#600 嬉	#258 薄	#181 片	#185 厚
#26 支	#268 暗	#483 任	#404 湯	#264 雲

1. 島田さんはデパートでエレベーター係りをしています。

Shimada-san wa, depaato de erebeetaa kakari wo shite imasu.
As for Shimada, she is doing elevator duty (i.e., operating an elevator) in a department store.

2. ご結婚おめでとう。

Gokekkon omedetou.
Congratulations on the honorable marriage.

3. 有難う。今日ほど嬉しい日はありません。

Arigatou. Kyou hodo ureshii hi wa arimasen.
Thank you. Compared to today, more pleasing days don't exist.

4. この本は薄いですが片方のは厚いです。

Kono hon wa usui desu ga katahou no wa atsui desu.
As for this book, it's thin, but as for the other one, it's thick.

5. すみません。電話代をお支払いしたいんですが、ここでよろしいでしょうか。

Sumimasen. Denwa dai wo oshiharai shitain desu ga, koko de yoroshii deshou ka.
Excuse me. I would like to humbly pay the phone cost, but is at here probably good?

6. この部屋は暗いですね。

Kono heya wa kurai desu ne.
This room is dark, huh.

7. そこのスタンドを点けて明るくした方がいいですね。

Soko no sutando wo tsukete akaruku shita hou ga ii desu ne.
It would be better if you turned on that place's standing light and brightened it, huh.

8. 私はあなたに全てを任せることにしました。

Watashi wa anata ni subete wo makaseru koto ni shimashita.
As for me, to you everything I decided to entrust.

9. 温泉のお湯がぬるかった。

Onsen no oyu ga nurukatta.
The hot spring's hot water was lukewarm.

10. 厚子さんの話では今年の冬は
寒いそうです。

Atsuko-san no hanashi de wa kotoshi no fuyu wa samui sou desu.
As for from Atsuko's speech, this year's winter will be cold, reportedly. (i.e., that's what she said)

11. コーヒーは薄いのが好きです。

Koohii wa usui no ga suki desu.
As for coffee, the thin one is liked. (i.e., I like weak coffee)

12. 係員は今、昼ご飯を食べています。

Kakariin wa ima hirugohan wo tabete imasu.
As for the person in charge, now she is eating lunch.

13. 部屋を片付けたら机の下に千円が落ちていました。

Heya wo katazuketara tsukue no shita ni sen'en ga ochite imashita.
When I straightened up the room, under the desk, 1,000 yen was fallen.

14. 空には一片の雲もなかった。

Sora ni wa ippen no kumo mo nakatta.
As for in the sky, not even one piece of cloud existed.

15. この花を下さるんですか。

Kono hana wo kudasarun desu ka.
Will you give these flowers to me?

16. まぁ、嬉しい。

Maa. Ureshii.
My. Pleased. (maa is woman's speech)

17. もう暗くなりましたから、そろそろ失礼します。

Mou kuraku narimashita kara, sorosoro shitsurei shimasu.
Since it already became dark, gradually I'll commit a discourtesy. (i.e., I'd better get going)

18. 今日は暖かいのにどうしたんですか。

Kyou wa atatakai noni doushitan desu ka.
As for today, even though warm, how did it do? (i.e., what happened?)

19. そんなに厚いセーターを着て。

Sonna ni atsui seetaa wo kite...
That sort of thick sweater you're wearing...

20. ええ、ちょっと寒気がするんですよ。

Ee, chotto samuke ga surun desu yo.
Yeah, a little bit, a chill does, for sure.

21. 月が雲の後ろから顔を出した。

Tsuki ga kumo no ushiro kara kao wo dashita.
The moon put out its face from behind the clouds. (i.e., it came out)

22. 係の人達に日にちと場所を連絡しなくてはなりません。

Kakari no hitotachi ni hinichi to basho wo renraku shinakute wa narimasen.
To the people in charge, they must communicate the date and place.

23. お湯にはジョシュアさんが先に入った。

Oyu ni wa joshua-san ga saki ni haitta.
As for to the hot water, Joshua entered first.

24. 急に空が夜のように暗くなって雨が降ってきた。

Kyuu ni sora ga yoru no you ni kuraku natte ame ga futte kita.
Suddenly the sky like night became dark, and it started to rain.

25. ウイリヤムさんは何の会議に出ますか。

Uiriamu-san wa nan no kaigi ni demasu ka.
As for William, what sort of meeting will he attend?

26. アメリカに支社を出す件についての会議です。

Amerika ni shisha wo dasu ken ni tsuite no kaigi desu.
It's a meeting regarding the matter of putting out a branch office to America.

27. この仕事を片づけないうちは、出かけられない。

Kono shigoto wo katazukenai uchi wa dekakerarenai.
As for while we do not straighten up this work, we cannot depart.

28. コーヒーをお湯で薄めた。

Koohii wo oyu de usumeta.
I diluted the coffee with hot water.

29. 仕事がたくさん残っていて、今日も又、残業なんですよ。

Shigoto ga takusan nokotte ite, kyou mo mata, zangyou nan desu yo.
Work, a lot, is being remaining, and today also again, it's overtime, for sure.

30. 少しは部下に任せたら？

Sukoshi wa buka ni makasetara?
As for a little bit, if you entrust to subordinates?

31. 一人で何もかもしようと思わない方がいいですよ。

Hitori de nanimokamo shiyou to omowanai hou ga ii desu yo.
By yourself, it's better not to think that you shall do everything, for sure.

32. 空に薄い雲が見えます。

Sora ni usui kumo ga miemasu.
In the sky, thin clouds are visible.

33. 明日が休みなのは、嬉しいです。

Ashita ga yasumi na no wa ureshii desu.
As for tomorrow-is-vacation, it's pleasing.

34. 自動引き落としにすれば便利だと言いました。

Jidou hikiotoshi ni sureba benri da to iimashita.
If she chooses automatic withdrawal, it will be convenient, he said.

35. 主任は新しい車を買いました。

Shunin wa atarashii kuruma wo kaimashita.
As for the foreman, he bought a new car.

36. 野球のチケットがあるんですが、私はあまり好きじゃないのでどうぞ。

Yakyuu no chiketto ga arun desu ga, watashi wa amari suki ja nai node, douzo.
Baseball's tickets exist, but as for me, because I don't like it much, go ahead (i.e., take them).

37. 17日のと 18日のがあります。

Juu shichi nichi no to juu hachi nichi no ga arimasu.
There are some for the 17th and some for the 18th.

38. 17日に大阪に行くから、18日のでいいな。

おおさか

Juu shichi nichi ni oosaka ni iku kara, juu hachi nichi no de ii na.
Since I'm going to Osaka on the 17th, I'll be good with the ones for the 18th.

39. 会議をしたいんですが、十日でいいですか。

Kaigi wo shitain desu ga, tooka de ii desu ka.
I'd like to do a meeting, but is the 10th all right?

40. 飲み物は何がいいですか。

Nomimono wa nani ga ii desu ka.
As for drinks, what is good?

41. すき焼きでいいですか。

Sukiyaki de ii desu ka.
Would sukiyaki be all right?

42. 土曜日は仕事なんですが、日曜日なら都合がいいです。

Doyoubi wa shigoto nan desu ga, nichiyoubi nara tsugou ga ii desu.
As for Saturdays, it's work, but in the case of Sunday, circumstances are good.

43. これ、いくらですか。

Kore, ikura desu ka.
This, how much is it?

44. 千円でございます。

Sen'en de gozaimasu.
It's 1000 yen. (humble speech)

45. このペンは四本で二百円です。

Kono pen wa yonhon de nihyaku en desu.
As for these pens, of four, they are 200 yen.

46. 三年間、日本の銀行で働いて今度ニューヨークの支店に転勤することになりました。

San nen kan, nihon no ginkou de hataraite kondo nyuuyooku no shiten ni tenkin suru koto ni narimashita.
Three years duration, I labor at a Japanese bank, and this time, to a New York's branch store I was scheduled to transfer.

Chapter 54

New Kanji in this Chapter

#91 資	#86 質	#344 法	#417 律	#378 途
#99 束	#60 塩	#319 怒	#531 沸	#597 皆

1. 白い資料はどこに置いてあり
   ましたか。

   Shiroi shiryou wa doko ni oite arimashita ka.
   As for the white literature, where was it placed?

2. 先生が忙しかったので質問を
   することができませんでし
   た。

   Sensei ga isogashikatta node shitsumon wo suru koto ga dekimasen deshita.
   Since the teacher was busy, I couldn't do a question.

3. 彼女、法律の学位は取れまし
   たか。

   Kanojo, houritsu no gakui wa toremashita ka.
   She, was she able to take a law degree?

4. 家に帰る途中で雨に降られた
   んです。

   Ie ni kaeru tochuu de ame ni furaretan desu.
   To return to the house on the way, by the rain it precipitated on me.

5. 2時の約束だったが友達はな
   かなか来なかった。

   Niji no yakusoku datta ga tomodachi wa nakanaka konakatta.
   It was a 2:00 appointment, but as for the friend, he didn't come readily.

6. あの、ちょっとテーブルの上
   の塩を取って欲しいんだけ
   ど。

   Ano, chotto teeburu no ue no shio wo totte hoshiin dakedo...
   Say, for a moment, I desire you to pass the on-the-table salt, but...

7. ジェイコブさんはなぜ花を買
   ってホテルに行ったのです
   か。

   Jeikobu-san wa naze hana wo katte hoteru ni itta no desu ka.
   As for Jacob, why is it that he bought flowers and went to the hotel?

8. 電話をしなかったのでアッシュリーさんがちょっと怒っていたからです。

Denwa wo shinakatta node asshurii-san ga chotto okotte ita kara desu.
It's because, since he didn't do a phone call, Ashley was being a little mad.

9. 土田さんはお茶を入れる前にお湯を沸かします。

Tsuchida-san wa ocha wo ireru mae ni oyu wo wakashimasu.
As for Tsuchida, at before making honorable tea, she boils hot water.

10. 友達に成田からうちに来る方法を知らせなければなりません。

Tomodachi ni narita kara uchi ni kuru houhou wo shirasenakereba narimasen.
To the friend, the from-Narita-to-the-home to-come method you must inform.

11. 彼女はいつも約束の時間に遅れるので困ります。

Kanojo wa itsumo yakusoku no jikan ni okureru node, komarimasu.
As for her, because always to the appointment's time she gets delayed, I get inconvenienced.

12. 黒田さんはコピーした資料をどこに置きましたか。

Kuroda-san wa kopii shita shiryou wo doko ni okimashita ka.
As for Kuroda, at where did she place the copied literature?

13. ジョナサンさんはいつ雨に降られましたか。

Jonasan-san wa itsu ame ni furaremashita ka.
As for Jonathan, when, by the rain, did it precipitate on him?

14. 日本語学校から帰る途中です。

Nihongo gakkou kara kaeru tochuu desu.
It's the return from Japanese school on the way.

15. この店には品質が良く手頃な値段の品物が多くある。

Kono mise ni wa hinshitsu ga yoku tegoro na nedan no shinamono ga ooku aru.
As for in this store, product-quality-is-good affordable prices' merchandise numerously exists.

16. 旅行に行く行かないにかかわらず、皆さん説明だけはお聞きになってください。

Ryokou ni iku ikanai ni kakawarazu, minasan setsumei dake wa okiki ni natte kudasai.
To go for the purpose of travel, not go, regardless, honorable everyone, explanation at least, please honorably listen.

17. 法律は守らなければなりません。

Houritsu wa mamoranakereba narimasen.
As for the law, we must observe it (i.e., follow it).

18. 弟が私のケーキを食べました。

Otouto ga watashi no keeki wo tabemashita.
Little brother ate my cake.

19. 私は弟にケーキを食べられて怒りました。

Watashi wa otouto ni keeki wo taberarete okorimashita.
As for me, by little brother, cake was eaten on me, and I got mad.

20. 約束の時間が変わったとお伝えください。

Yakusoku no jikan ga kawatta to otsutae kudasai.
Please honorably report that the appointment time changed.

21. 資料を十枚ずつコピーしてください。

Shiryou wo juumai zutsu kopii shite kudasai.
The literature, 10 sheets each, please do copying.

22. お湯が沸いたよ。

Oyu ga waita yo.
The honorable hot water is boiling, for sure. (i.e., the water is hot enough for a bath, not literally boiling)

23. 皆様、今日は私達のために送別会を開いてくださってどうも有難うございます。

Minasama, kyou wa watashitachi no tame ni soubetsukai wo hiraite kudasatte, doumo arigatou gozaimasu.
Very honorable everyone, as for today, for the purpose of us, since a farewell party opening and giving, thank you very much.

24. この一年間、楽しい事や困った事が色々ありましたが...

Kono ichinenkan, tanoshii koto ya komatta koto ga iroiro arimashita ga...
This one year period, pleasant things, etc., inconvenienced things, various existed, but...

25. その法律は議会を通過した。

Sono houritsu wa gikai wo tsuuka shita.
As for that law, it went through the Diet.

26. ちょっと、味をみてください。

Chotto aji wo mite kudasai.
Please taste for a second.

27. しょっぱい！塩を入れ過ぎたんじゃありませんか。

Shoppai! Shio wo iresugitan ja arimasen ka.
Salty! Didn't you put in too much salt?

28. うん、もう怒ったぞ。

Un, mou, okotta zo.
Oh, already I got angry. (zo = man's word used for emphasis)

29. 大学教授はその店員に質問しました。

Daigaku kyouju wa sono tenin ni shitsumon shimashita.
The university professor asked that sales clerk a question.

30. 夕方家を出て駅に向かうと、帰宅途中の父とすれ違った。

Yuugata ie wo dete eki ni mukau to, kitaku tochuu no chichi to surechigatta.
Evening, leaving the house, when I head to the station, with returning-home on-the-way's father I passed by going in the opposite direction.

31. 皆様に大変親切にしていただいて本当に幸せです。

Minasama ni taihen shinsetsu ni shite itadaite hontou ni shiawase desu.
To very honorable everyone, extremely, to kindness you do, and we humbly receive, and truly it's happiness.

32. お湯を沸かして塩と野菜を入れて、柔らかくなるまで待ちましょう。

Oyu wo wakashite shio to yasai wo irete, yawarakaku naru made machimashou.
Hot water boiling, inserting salt and vegetables, until they become soft, let's wait.

33. アンソニーの日記。

Ansonii no nikki.
Anthony's diary.

34. 日曜日にハナさんと野球を見に行った。

Nichiyoubi ni hana-san to yakyuu wo mi ni itta.
On Sunday, with Hannah, we went in order to see baseball.

35. 中で売っているビールは高いから、どこかでカンビールを買って行った方がいいですね。

Naka de utte iru biiru wa takai kara, dokoka de kanbiiru wo katte itta hou ga ii desu ne.
Since the beer being sold inside expensive, at somewhere it would be better to buy canned beer and go, huh.

36. これは親切なアドバイスだった。

Kore wa shinsetsu na adobaisu datta.
This was kind advice.

Chapter 55

New Kanji in this Chapter

# 119 末	# 269 倍	# 409 門	# 594 捨	# 83 貝
# 237 妻	# 74 届	# 548 包	# 576 普	# 110 勢

1. ところでマーティンさん、今度の週末は何か予定がありますか。

Tokoro de maatin-san, kondo no shuumatsu wa nanika yotei ga arimasu ka.
By the way, Martin, as for next weekend, do anything plans exist?

2. 土曜日はテニスをするつもりですが、日曜日は別に何もありませんが。

Doyoubi wa tenisu wo surutsumori desu ga, nichiyoubi wa betsu ni nani mo arimasen ga...
As for Saturday, I plan to play tennis, but as for Sunday, there is nothing in particular, but...

3. すき焼きを食べたいんですが末広へはどう行ったらいいですか。

Sukiyaki wo tabetain desu ga suehiro e wa dou ittara ii desu ka.
I would like to eat sukiyaki, but as for to Suehiro, how when you go is good? (Suehiro = name of a restaurant in Tokyo)

4. 晴海通りを真っ直ぐ行くと三つ目の角に左内があります。

Harumi doori wo massugu iku to mittsume no kado ni sanai ga arimasu.
If you go straight on Harumi street, at the 3rd corner Sanai exists. (Sanai = name of a building in Ginza)

5. 彼は私の倍食べた。

Kare wa watashi no bai tabeta.
As for him, he ate my double. (i.e., he ate twice as much as I did)

6. 誰かが門の所に立っている。

Dareka ga mon no tokoro ni tatte iru.
Someone at the gate's place is standing.

7. 三越デパートもありますからすぐ分かりますよ。

Mitsukoshi depaato mo arimasu kara sugu wakarimasu yo.
Since Mitsukoshi department store also exists, you will soon understand, for sure.

8. ここにゴミを捨ててはいけません。

Koko ni gomi wo sutete wa ikemasen.
You must not throw garbage here.

9. 毎日、くたくたに疲れて週末は寝るだけなんですよ。

Mainichi, kuta kuta ni tsukarete shuumatsu wa neru dake nan desu yo.
Every day, since I get dead tired, as for the weekend, it's only to sleep, for sure.

10. ちょっと胃が痛いんです。

Chotto i ga itain desu.
A little, the stomach hurts.

11. それはきっと夕べ、貝を食べ過ぎたからですよ。

Sore wa kitto yuube, kai wo tabesugita kara desu yo.
As for that, certainly, last night, it's because you ate too much shellfish, for sure.

12. 顔色が悪いですよ。

Kao iro ga warui desu yo.
The face color is bad, for sure. (i.e., you don't look very healthy)

13. 門の前に車を止めないで下さいませんか。

Mon no mae ni kuruma wo tomenai de kudasaimasen ka.
Won't you not park the car in front of the gate and give?

14. 毎朝妻がネクタイを結んでくれます。

Maiasa tsuma ga nekutai wo musunde kuremasu.
Every morning the wife ties the necktie and gives. (i.e., she ties it for me)

15. 明日中に届くように小包を速達で出します。

Asujuu ni todoku you ni kozutsumi wo sokutatsu de dashimasu.
Sometime tomorrow, so as to arrive, I will send the package by express delivery.

16. 島の海岸できれいな貝を拾った。

Shima no kaigan de kirei na kai wo hirotta.
On the island's beach, I picked up a pretty shell.

17. 普通北へ行けば行くほど涼しくなりますよ。

Futsuu kita e ikeba iku hodo suzushiku narimasu yo.
Generally, if you go to north go, it becomes cool, for sure. (i.e., the more you go north, the cooler it gets)

18. 日本で一番大勢の人がするスポーツは野球とサッカーです。

Nihon de ichiban oozei no hito ga suru supootsu wa yakyuu to sakkaa desu.
In Japan, as for sports that the most numerous people do, they are baseball and soccer.

19. 奥さん、女優さんみたいにきれいですね。

Okusan, joyuu-san mitai ni kirei desu ne.
The honorable wife, like a Miss Actress it's pretty huh. (i.e., she's beautiful like an actress)

20. いやぁ、とんでもないです。妻ももう年ですよ。

Iyaa, tondemonai desu. Tsuma mo mou toshi desu yo.
Nah, it's not at all. The wife also, already it's elderly, for sure. (toshi is short for toshiyori)

21. 家に帰ると小包が届いていました。

Ie ni kaeru to kozutsumi ga todoite imashita.
When I return to the house, a package was arrived.

22. ゴミをこんな所に捨てちゃだめよ。

Gomi wo konna tokoro ni sutecha dame yo.
Garbage, to this kind of place, as for throwing, bad, for sure. (sutecha = sutete wa = as for throwing)

23. 特急の方が普通より速いです。

Tokkyuu no hoo ga futsuu yori hayai desu.
The special express, compared to the local train, is fast.

24. 銀行の前に人が大勢集まっていますね。

Ginkou no mae ni hito ga oozei atsumatte imasu ne.
At the bank's front, people, many, are gathering, huh.

25. 門の前の階段から貝が落ちてきた。

Mon no mae no kaidan kara kai ga ochite kita.
From the stairs in front of the gate, the seashell fell and came.

26. 何をして過ごすんですか。

Nani wo shite sugosun desu ka.
What will you do and spend?

27. いや、ゆっくり寝るだけですよ。

Iya, yukkuri neru dake desu yo.
Nah, it's only to sleep leisurely, for sure.

28. 普段、忙しいものですから。

Fudan, isogashii mono desu kara.
Usually, since it's busy things.

29. 10セントの10倍は1ドルである。

Jussento no juu bai wa ichi doru de aru.
As for ten cents' ten times, one dollar exists. (i.e., ten dimes are equal to one dollar)

30. ゴミを捨てるな。

Gomi wo suteru na.
Don't throw garbage. (na = "do not," used by men or seen on signs)

31. 妻と子供が二人います。

Tsuma to kodomo ga futari imasu.
A wife and two children exist. (i.e., I have a wife and two kids)

32. 京都には一年中大勢の人が来ます。

Kyouto ni wa ichinen juu oozei no hito ga kimasu.
As for to Kyoto, all year long numerous people come.

33. サマンサさんは船便で小包を
出します。

Samansa-san wa funabin de kozutsumi
wo dashimasu.
As for Samantha, she will send the
package by ship mail.

34. 次にスペースキーを押すと漢
字になります。

Tsugi ni supeesu kii wo osu to kanji ni
narimasu.
Next, if you press the spacebar, it
becomes kanji.

35. F1 キーを押すと倍角になり
ます。

Efu ichi kii wo osu to baikaku ni
narimasu.
If you press the F1 key, it becomes
double-size font. (bai = double amount;
baikaku = double size font)

36. F2 キーを押すとあみかけに
なります。

Efu ni kii wo osu to amikake ni
narimasu.
If you press the F2 key, it becomes font
shading. (ami = netting)

37. 注意: 倍角とあみかけの両方
をするときは、 F1 キーを押
して倍角にしてから、F2 キー
を押してください。

Chuui: Baikaku to amikake no ryouhou
wo suru toki wa, efu ichi kii wo oshite
baikaku ni shite kara, efu ni kii wo oshite
kudasai.
Attention: As for the time when you do
both double font and font shading, push
the F1 key, and after you change to
double font, please push the F2 key.

38. ウイリヤムさんが会社に行っ
ている間にアメリカの両親か
ら小包が届きました。

Uiriamu-san ga kaisha ni itte iru aida ni
amerika no ryoushin kara kozutsumi ga
todokimashita.
While William is going to the company,
a package arrived from the American
parents.

Chapter 56

New Kanji in this Chapter

# 495 庭	# 582 表	# 108 助	# 117 放	# 128 枝
# 358 迎	# 97 類	# 220 細	# 565 刻	# 555 鳥

1. 広くてりっぱな庭ですね。

Hirokute rippa na niwa desu ne.
It's a spacious and splendid garden, huh.

2. 公園みたいですね。

Kouen mitai desu ne.
It's like a park, huh.

3. この紙はどちらが表だか見分けがつかない。

Kono kami wa dochira ga omote da ka miwake ga tsukanai.
As for this paper, which is the front side (question) I do not determine. (i.e., I can't tell which is the front side)

4. 昨日の会議では、良いアイデアが次々に発表された。

Kinou no kaigi de wa, yoi aidea ga tsugitsugi ni happyou sareta.
As for yesterday's meeting, good ideas, one after the other, were presented on. (i.e., were presented)

5. あなたは仕事と家庭とどちらの方が大切ですか。

Anata wa shigoto to katei to dochira no hou ga taisetsu desu ka.
As for you, work and home/family and, which one is more important?

6. 子供が助けられました。

Kodomo ga tasukeraremashita.
The child was rescued on (i.e., he was rescued by someone).

7. 放送時間になりました。ラジオを点けてください。

Housou jikan ni narimashita. Rajio wo tsukete kudasai.
The broadcast time became. Turn on the radio please.

8. 刀で木の枝を切った。

Katana de ki no eda wo kitta.
With a sword, he cut the tree's branch.

9. お客様を温かく迎える。

Okyakusama wo atatakaku mukaeru.
Very honorable guests are met/welcomed warmly.

10. もう少し軽いのが欲しいんですけど。

Mou sukoshi karui no ga hoshiin desu kedo...
I desire a little lighter one, but...

11. 北村課長は書類をチェックし
てくれましたか。

Kitamura kachou wa shorui wo chiekku shite kuremashita ka.
As for section manager Kitamura, did he check the documents and give to us?

12. はい、漢字の間違いも直して
下さいました。

Hai, kanji no machigai mo naoshite kudasaimashita.
Yes, he corrected the kanji mistakes also and gave to us.

13. 野菜を細かく刻んで、スープ
に入れる。

Yasai wo komakaku kizande, suupu ni ireru.
Dicing vegetables in a detailed way, we put them into the soup.

14. この辞書を借りてもいいでし
ょうか。

Kono jisho wo karite mo ii deshou ka.
Would it probably be OK if I borrow this dictionary?

15. ええ、もちろん。明日まで使
っていても構いませんよ。

Ee, mochiron. Ashita made tsukatte ite mo kamaimasen yo.
Yeah, of course. It doesn't matter if you are using it until tomorrow, for sure.

16. 有難う。助かります。

Arigatou. Tasukarimasu.
Thank you. I will be rescued.

17. 毎日、日本語のラジオ放送を
聞いたのでニュースを聞き取
れるようになりました。

Mainichi nihongo no rajio housou wo kiita node nyuusu wo kikitoreru you ni narimashita.
Since every day I listened to Japanese language radio broadcasts, I got to the point that I was able to hear/take news.

18. ほら、けがをした鳥が飛ぼ
うとしている。

Hora, kega wo shita tori ga tobou to shite iru.
Look, the injured bird is trying to fly.

19. この点を見るために、下の表
を見なさい。

Kono ten wo miru tame ni, shita no hyou wo minasai.
In order to see this point, look at the table below.

20. 夜遅く友達に来られて困りま
した。

Yoru osoku tomodachi ni korarete komarimashita.
Late at night, by the friend, he came (against my wishes), and I got inconvenienced.

21. 引っ越しの時、友達に来ても
らって助かりました。

Hikkoshi no toki, tomodachi ni kite moratte tasukarimashita.
The move's time, by the friend he came, and I received and was rescued.

22. あそこの木の枝に止まってい
るのは何という鳥ですか。

Asoko no ki no eda ni tomatte iru no wa
nan to iu tori desu ka.
As for the one that is stopped on that
over there place's tree's branch, what to-
call bird is it? (i.e., what is it called?)

23. この書類、どうしたらいい
かしら。

Kono shorui, dou shitara ii kashira.
These documents, how if I do will be
good, I wonder.

24. 庭の手入れはいつもダニエル
さんがなさるんですか。

Niwa no teire wa itsumo danieru-san ga
nasarun desu ka.
As for the garden's care, always, does
Daniel honorably do?

25. ええ、ブリアンナがするとき
もありますが、たいていは僕
が一人でやります。

Ee, burianna ga suru toki mo arimasu ga,
taitei wa boku ga hitori de yarimasu.
Yeah, Brianna-to-do time also exists, but
as for usually, I by myself do.

26. すみません。電話を掛けるの
でお金を細かくしてもらいた
いんですけど。

Sumimasen. Denwa wo kakeru node,
okane wo komakaku shite moraitain desu
kedo...
Excuse me, since I will call on the phone,
I would like you to make money small or
detailed and me to receive, but...

27. 友達を空港まで迎えにいかな
くてはならない。

Tomodachi wo kuukou made mukae ni
ikanakute wa naranai.
The friend, until the airport, in order to
meet/receive, I have to go.

28. 私を押し上げてくれれば枝
に手が届くと思うけど。

Watashi wo oshiagete kurereba eda ni te
ga todoku to omou kedo...
If you boost me up and give, the hand
(i.e., my hand) will reach the branch, I
think, but...

29. バスが遅れたために遅刻しま
した。

Basu ga okureta tame ni chikoku
shimashita.
As a result of the bus was delayed, I got
tardy.

30. 来月からフランス語を勉強す
るつもりです。

Raigetsu kara furansugo wo benkyou
surutsumori desu.
From next month, I plan to study French.

31. 部長は書類の書き方を教えて
下さいました。

Buchou wa shorui no kaki kata wo
oshiete kudasaimashita.
As for the section manager, he showed
the documents' method of writing and
gave to me.

32. 小鳥は空に放されました。

Kotori wa sora ni hanasaremashita.
As for little birds, to the sky, they were
set free (by someone).

33. 日本では夏によくそうめんを食べるんですよ。

Nihon de wa natsu ni yoku soumen wo taberun desu yo.
As for in Japan, in summer, frequently we eat soumen, for sure.

34. そうめんってどんな物ですか。

Soumen tte donna mono desu ka.
As for the one called soumen, what kind of thing is it?

35. そうめんはうどんのような食べ物でうどんより細いんですよ。

Soumen wa udon no you na tabemono de udon yori hosoin desu yo.
As for soumen, it's a food like udon, and compared to udon, it's thin, for sure.

36. 又、遅刻したの？

Mata, chikoku shita no?
Again, did you get tardy?

37. もっと早く起きなきゃだめでしょう。

Motto hayaku oki nakya dame deshou.
You must get up earlier, probably.
(nakya = nakereba = nakerya)

38. 京都駅に着いたら広田さんが迎えに来ていました。

Kyouto eki ni tsuitara hirota-san ga mukae ni kite imashita.
When I arrived at Kyoto station, Hirota, for the purpose of meet/receive, came and was.

39. もう少し安いのがいいんですけど...

Mou sukoshi yasui no ga iin desu kedo...
A little cheaper one would be good, but...

40. 寿司を食べたことがありますか。

Sushi wo tabeta koto ga arimasu ka.
Have you ever eaten sushi?

41. いいえ、まだ食べたことはありません。

Iie, mada tabeta koto wa arimasen.
No, I haven't eaten it yet.

Chapter 57

New Kanji in this Chapter

# 604 寄	# 57 耳	# 62 室	# 463 怖	# 475 触
# 191 太	# 79 隅	# 384 辛	# 61 増	# 92 慣

1. このスポーツは若い人は言う
までもなく、お年寄りにも楽
しんでいただけます。

Kono supootsu wa wakai hito wa iu
made mo naku, otoshiyori ni mo
tanoshinde itadakemasu.
As for this sport, as for young people,
needless to say, to honorable elderly also,
they will enjoy and we can humbly
receive. (iu made mo naku = "to say so
far also is not," i.e., "not necessary"; this
means "needless to say")

2. 彼が寄付をしていると知っ
て、見直した。

Kare ga kifu wo shite iru to shitte,
minaoshita.
Since I know that he is doing donations, I
corrected the view. (i.e., I reconsidered
my opinion of him)

3. 音が聞こえないように両手で
耳をふさぐ。

Oto ga kikoenai you ni ryoute de mimi
wo fusagu.
In order not to hear the noise, I block my
ears with both hands.

4. 野田君、ちょっと会議室に来
て欲しいんだけど。

Noda-kun, chotto kaigi shitsu ni kite
hoshiin dakedo...
Young man Noda, for a moment, I desire
you to come to the meeting room, but...

5. はい、かしこまりました。

Hai, kashikomarimashita.
Yes, understood. (humble speech)

6. お宅の犬、怖かったので触ら
なかった。

Otaku no inu, kowakatta node
sawaranakatta.
Since the honorable home's dog was
scary, I didn't touch him.

7. 去年買った服が着られなくな
ったんですよ。

Kyonen katta fuku ga kirarenakunattan
desu yo.
The clothes bought last year became
unable to wear, for sure.

8. へえ、そんなに太ったんです
か。

Hee. Sonna ni futtotan desu ka.
Really. Did you get that fat?

9. いすを部屋の隅へ運んだ。

Isu wo heya no sumi e hakonda.
I carried the chair to the corner of the room.

10. 彼は辛い人生を送った。

Kare wa tsurai jinsei wo okutta.
He lived a bitter life. (i.e., a difficult life)

11. 耳がかぶれています。

Mimi ga kaburete imasu.
The ear is having an infection (or inflammation).

12. 先月は野菜の値段が高くなったので、食料品代が増えた。

Sengetsu wa yasai no nedan ga takakunatta node, shokuryou hindai ga fueta.
As for last month, since the price of vegetables increased, the cost of groceries increased.

13. ジョーンズさんが会うのは山本部長で太っている人です。

Joonzu-san ga au no wa yamamoto buchou de futotte iru hito desu.
As for the one that Jones will meet, he is Division Manager Yamamoto and is a fat person.

14. ブラウンさんが会うのは野田課長でやせている人です。

Buraun-san ga au no wa noda kachou de yasete iru hito desu.
As for the one that Brown will meet, he is Section Manager Noda and is a thin person.

15. 彼は旅行に慣れているので、荷物の準備など手際がいい。

Kare wa ryokou ni narete iru node, nimotsu no junbi nado tegiwa ga ii.
As for him, since he is being used to travel, luggage's preparation, etc., skill is good.

16. 登山の楽しみは山のすがすがしい空気に触れることだ。

Tozan no tanoshimi wa yama no sugasugashii kuuki ni fureru koto da.
As for mountain climbing's pleasure, to mountain's refreshing air to-experience thing it is.

17. 最近3キロも太っちゃった。やせなくちゃ。

Saikin san kiro mo futocchatta. Yasenakucha.
Recently, all of 3 kilos, I fattened completely. I must thin down. (yasenakucha = shortened version of yasenakute wa ikemasen)

18. 知人が増えれば増えるほど、それだけ会う時間が少なくなる。

Chijin ga fuereba fueru hodo, sore dake au jikan ga sukunaku naru.
The more acquaintances increase, that only, to meet time becomes few. (i.e., the more people you know, for that reason alone, you have less time to see them) (sore dake de, also OK)

19. 会議室を予約しておかなくてはいけません。

Kaigi shitsu wo yoyaku shite okanakute wa ikemasen.
She must reserve the meeting room in advance.

20. 耳がかゆいのです。

Mimi ga kayui no desu.
The ears itch.

21. 庭の隅に大きな木がありま
す。

Niwa no sumi ni ookina ki ga arimasu.
In the garden's corner, there is a big tree.

22. お金があるのに寄付をしない
なんて、あの人はけちだ。

Okane ga aru noni kifu wo shinai nante,
ano hito wa kechi da.
In spite of the fact that money exists, he
doesn't do a donation, such a thing, as
for that person over there, he's stingy.

23. 洋子、熱が高くてすごく辛そ
うだ。

Youko, netsu ga takakute sugoku
tsurasou da.
Yoko, the fever is high, and super bitter
it seems.

24. このカレーは辛くないから子
供向きだ。

Kono karee wa karakunai kara kodomo
muki da.
As for this curry, since not spicy, it's
children suitability. (i.e., suitable for
children)

25. 失業者が増えたと言っても、
１パーセントに過ぎない。

Shitsugyou sha ga fueta to itte mo,
ippaasento ni suginai.
Unemployed people increased, even
though they say, to 1% it doesn't exceed.

26. 木曜日の午後、会議室は空い
ていますか。

Mokuyoubi no gogo, kaigi shitsu wa aite
imasu ka.
Thursday afternoon, are meeting rooms
available?

27. キャー！怖い！

Kyaa! Kowai!
Kyaa! Scared! (kyaa = sound made
when surprised)

28. ウィルソンさんは新入社員な
のでボーナスは0.8ヶ月分し
かもらえないからがっかりし
ています。

Uiruson-san wa shinnyuu shain na node
boonasu wa rei ten hachikagetsu bun
shika moraenai kara gakkari shite imasu.
As for Wilson, since he is a new
employee, as for the bonus, since except
for 0.8 month's portion only he cannot
receive, he is being disappointed.

29. アメリカではボーナスを休み
でもらうこともできますが日
本にはそういう習慣がない。

Amerika de wa boonasu wo yasumi de
morau koto mo dekimasu ga nihon ni wa
sou iu shuukan ga nai.
As for in America, bonus-to-receive-in-
vacation-thing is also possible, but as for
in Japan, that said custom doesn't exist.

30. バーバラさんはもう日本料理を食べるのに慣れています。

Baabara-san wa mou nihon ryouri wo taberu noni narete imasu.
As for Barbara, already, while eating Japanese cuisine, she is being used to it.

31. 少女は教室の隅で泣いていた。

Shoujo wa kyoushitsu no sumi de naite ita.
The little girl was crying in the inside corner of the classroom.

32. 犬が走って近づいてきたので怖かった。

Inu ga hashitte chikazuite kita node kowakatta.
Since the dog runs and approaches and came, it was frightening.

33. （触って見て）熱があるようだ。

(sawatte mite) Netsu ga aru you da.
(feeling and seeing) It appears a fever exists.

34. このシーツは白くて大きいです。

Kono shiitsu wa shirokute ookii desu.
As for these sheets, they are white and big.

35. どうして地下鉄で行かない方がいいのですか。

Doushite chikatetsu de ikanai hou ga ii no desu ka.
Why is it better not to go by subway?

36. 今度の日曜日はどうするつもりですか。

Kondo no nichiyoubi wa dou surutsumori desu ka.
As for this Sunday, how are you planning to do it? (i.e., what are you planning to do?)

37. ドイツ語は勉強したことがありますが、フランス語はありません。

Doitsugo wa benkyou shita koto ga arimasu ga, furansugo wa arimasen.
As for German, I've studied it, but as for French, I haven't.

38. 1月1日。元日。

Ichigatsu tsuitachi. Ganjitsu.
January 1st. New Year's Day.

Chapter 58

New Kanji in this Chapter

# 199 笑	# 48 星	# 572 県	# 175 政	# 145 郊	# 9 虫
# 84 贈	# 165 夢	# 516 景	# 442 研	# 112 究	

1. 彼は笑われた。

Kare wa warawareta.
He was laughed at.

2. 星がたくさん見えますね。

Hoshi ga takusan miemasu ne.
Stars, many are visible, huh.

3. 明日も天気が良さそうです
ね。

Ashita mo tenki ga yosa sou desu ne.
Tomorrow also the weather seems to be good, huh.

4. 長野県で生まれました。

Nagano ken de umaremashita.
I was born in Nagano prefecture.

5. あの政治家は東京の郊外に住
んでいる。

Ano seijika wa toukyou no kougai ni sunde iru.
That politician over there lives in the suburbs of Tokyo.

6. 歯がズキズキするんです。

Ha ga zukizuki surun desu.
The tooth does throbbing.

7. きっと虫歯ですよ。

Kitto mushiba desu yo.
Surely, it's a decayed tooth, for sure.

8. 歯医者さんに行った方がいい
ですよ。

Haishasan ni itta hou ga ii desu yo.
It would be better to go to Mr. Dentist, for sure.

9. 結婚のお祝いに、これをお贈
りします。

Kekkon no oiwai ni, kore wo o okuri shimasu.
For a humble wedding gift, I humbly give this. (the giver is speaking to the recipient)

10. 星さんは嬉しいそうです。

Hoshi-san wa ureshi sou desu.
As for Hoshi, pleased it seems.

11. この子のポケットには虫やら
ガムやらいろんな物が入って
いる。

Kono ko no poketto ni wa mushi yara gamu yara ironna mono ga haitte iru.
As for to this child's pockets, insects, etc., gum, etc., various things are being entered.

12. 政治家になる夢が正夢となっ
た。

Seijika ni naru yume ga masayume
tonatta.
The to-become-a-politican dream became
a prophetic dream. (i.e., it came true)

13. 落語家が客を笑わせていま
す。

Rakugoka ga kyaku wo warawasete
imasu.
The comic storyteller is making the
customer laugh.

14. 夜中、海岸から景色が良く
て億の星が見えた。

Yonaka, kaigan kara keshiki ga yokute
oku no hoshi ga mieta.
The dead of night, from the beach, the
view is good, and 100 million stars were
visible.

15. 研究が中止って、どういうこ
とですか。

Kenkyuu ga chuushi tte, dou iu koto desu
ka.
Research cancellation (quote), how to
say thing is it? (i.e., why are you saying
the research is cancelled?)

16. 実行しなければ、ただの夢で
しかない。

Jikkou shinakereba, tada no yume de
shikanai.
If you don't do implementation, except
for of-only's dream, it's nothing. (i.e.,
it's only a dream)

17. 郊外の景色のいい住宅地に住
みたい。

Kougai no keshiki no ii juutakuchi ni
sumitai.
In a suburb's view-is-good residential
district, I would like to live.

18. 千葉県では生徒達が研究のた
め虫を取り、袋に入れて持ち
帰る。

Chiba ken de wa seitotachi ga kenkyuu
no tame mushi wo tori, fukuro ni irete
mochikaeru.
As for in Chiba Prefecture, the students,
for the sake of research, take insects, put
them into bags and take them back. (i.e.,
take them home)

19. 森さんは学者と言うよりはむ
しろ政治家です。

Mori-san wa gakusha to iu yori wa
mushiro seijika desu.
As for Mori, not so much a scholar as
he's a politician.

20. 私は遠い郊外からわざわざ通
勤しなくてはいけない。

Watashi wa tooi kougai kara wazawaza
tsuukin shinakutewa ikenai.
As for me, I have to commute expressly
from a distant suburb.

21. 食事の後、旅館の外に出て星
を見ていたら大きなくしゃみ
が出た。

Shokuji no ato, ryokan no soto ni dete
hoshi wo mite itara ookina kushami ga
deta.
After the meal, we went out to the
Japanese inn's outside, and when we
were looking at stars, a big sneeze
emerged.

22. 黒田さんに薬をもらって早く寝ることにした。

Kuroda-san ni kusuri wo moratte hayaku neru koto ni shita.
From Kuroda I received medicine, and I decided to sleep early.

23. 明日は又、元気になれそうな気がする。

Ashita wa mata, genki ni nare sou na ki ga suru.
As for tomorrow, again, to health I'll be able to become, it appears, I have a feeling.

24. 小川さんは人に笑われるのも構わず、自分の研究を続けた。

Ogawa-san wa hito ni warawareru no mo kamawazu, jibun no kenkyuu wo tsuzuketa.
As for Ogawa, by people laughed on thing even not minding, himself's research he continued.

25. 姉の夢は広島県の緑が多い、景色のいい日本風の家に住むことだ。

Ane no yume wa hiroshima ken no midori ga ooi, keshiki no ii nihonfuu no ie ni sumu koto da.
As for older sister's dream, it is Hiroshima prefecture's green-is-numerous views-are-good Japanese style house to-live-in thing. (i.e., she wants to live in a Japanese style house in Hiroshima prefecture, where there's a lot of greenery, and the views are good)

26. ミラーさん、お中元はもう贈りましたか。

Miraa-san, ochuugen wa mou okurimashita ka.
Miller, as for the mid-year gift, did you already send it?

27. お中元というのは何ですか。

Ochuugen to iu no wa nan desu ka.
As for the one called ochuugen, what is it?

28. お中元というのはお世話になった人に送る贈り物のことですよ。

Ochuugen to iu no wa osewa ni natta hito ni okuru okurimono no koto desu yo.
As for the one called ochuugen, a to-send-to-people-who-developed-care gift's thing it is, for sure.

29. 彼女は笑った。

Kanojo wa waratta.
She laughed.

Chapter 59

New Kanji in this Chapter

#46 泊	#56 首	#467 汚	#585 亡	#525 路
#272 祖	#471 弱	#106 召	#193 咲	#393 苦

1. 橋本さんは宿はどうすればいいと言っていますか。

Hashimoto-san wa yado wa dou sureba ii to itte imasu ka.
As for Hashimoto, as for lodging, how if to do will be good, is she saying?

2. 橋本さんの家に泊まればいいと言っています。

Hashimoto-san no ie ni tomareba ii to itte imasu.
If one stays at Hashimoto's house, it's good, she is saying.

3. 手首が痛い。

Tekubi ga itai.
The wrist hurts.

4. その汚い犬を台所に入れないでください。

Sono kitanai inu wo daidokoro ni irenai de kudasai.
Please don't put that dirty dog in the kitchen.

5. 私の父は若くして亡くなった。

Watashi no chichi wa wakaku shite nakunatta.
As for my father, he died young.

6. 明日は日曜日だからきっと道路が込んでいますよ。

Asu wa nichiyoubi dakara kitto douro ga konde imasu yo.
As for tomorrow, since it's Sunday, surely the roads will be being crowded, for sure.

7. 行くのを止めたらどう？

Iku no wo yametara dou?
If you give up on going, how? (i.e., maybe you shouldn't go)

8. いいえ、込んでいても行きます。

Iie, konde itemo ikimasu.
No, even though being crowded, I will go.

9. それなら、朝早く出かけた方がいいですよ。

Sore nara, asa hayaku dekaketa hou ga ii desu yo.
In that case, early morning, it would be better to leave, for sure.

10. 私の祖父は幸せそうです。

Watashi no sofu wa shiawase sou desu.
As for my grandfather, he appears happy.

11. 彼の呼吸は次第に弱くなった。

Kare no kokyuu wa shidai ni yowaku natta.
As for his breathing, it gradually became weak.

12. これは私が作ったクッキーなんですよ。召し上がってみてください。

Kore wa watashi ga tsukutta kukkii nan desu yo. Meshiagatte mite kudasai.
As for this, it's an I-made cookie, for sure. Please honorably eat and see.

13. 花が咲いたかと思ったら、もう散り始めた。

Hana ga saita ka to omottara, mou chirihajimeta.
The flowers blossomed (question quote) if I think (i.e., they blossomed a moment ago), already they are starting to scatter.

14. 祖父が亡くなって三年になります。

Sofu ga nakunatte san nen ni narimasu.
Since Grandfather died, it will become three years. (i.e., it is three years)

15. 苦しそうですね。

Kurushisou desu ne.
It appears to be tight, huh. (referring to a tight feeling in the chest, etc.)

16. すぐ病院に行きましょう。

Sugu byouin ni ikimashou.
Soon let's go to the hospital.

17. 明日から旅行に行かれるんですってね。

Ashita kara ryokou ni ikarerun desu tte ne.
From tomorrow, you will honorably go for the purpose of travel, reportedly, huh.

18. 旅行と言っても一晩泊まるに過ぎないんですよ。

Ryokou to ittemo hitoban tomaru ni suginain desu yo.
"Travel" saying even though, one night to stay it doesn't exceed, for sure.

19. お風呂はちょっと熱いかもしれません。

Ofuro wa chotto atsui kamoshiremasen.
As for the honorable bath, a little hot it might be.

20. 熱かったら水を入れてくださいね。

Atsukattara mizu wo irete kudasai ne.
If it's hot, please add water, huh.

21. 熱くてもいいですよ。

Atsukutemo ii desu yo.
Even though hot, it's OK, for sure.

22. そうですか。外国の方は熱い
お風呂は苦手だと聞いていた
ものですから。

Sou desu ka. Gaikoku no kata wa atsui ofuro wa nigate da to kiite ita mono desu kara.
Is that so? As for foreign countries' people, as for hot honorable baths, since "it's a weakness" I was hearing thing it is. (mono implies "because" in this sentence)

23. 医者の苦しさが、経験のない
人に分かるものか。

Isha no kurushisa ga, keiken no nai hito ni wakaru mono ka.
A doctor's pain, experience-doesn't-exist person to, to understand thing (question). (i.e., a person who hasn't experienced a doctor's stress will never understand it; mono ka = never)

24. 弱い方に味方する。

Yowai hou ni mikata suru.
I support the weaker side.

25. あの人は首が長い。

Ano hito wa kubi ga nagai.
As for that person, the neck is long.

26. 道路のそばに色々な花が咲い
ている。

Douro no soba ni iroiro na hana ga saite iru.
At the road's proximity, various flowers are blooming.

27. 洋服が汚れてますね。

Youfuku ga yogoretemasu ne.
The Western clothes are being soiled, huh. (i.e., they are soiled, shortened for speech)

28. 私達は東京のホテルに泊まっ
た。

Watashitachi wa toukyou no hoteru ni tomatta.
As for us, we stayed at a hotel in Tokyo.

29. 夕飯はいつも何時頃召し上が
りますか。

Yuuhan wa itsumo nanji goro meshiagarimasu ka.
As for the evening meal, always about what time do you honorably eat?

30. 道路を作る計画を実行するの
は難しいだろう。

Douro wo tsukuru keikaku wo jikkou suru no wa muzukashii daroo.
The to-create-a-road plan, as for to-implement thing, it will probably be difficult.

31. 山下さんが昨日亡くなったそ
うです。

Yamashita-san ga kinou nakunatta sou desu.
Yamashita died yesterday, reportedly.

32. 祖母が急に死んだという知ら
せがあった。

Sobo ga kyuu ni shinda to iu shirase ga atta.
My grandmother suddenly died (quote) to-say notification existed. (i.e., I learned that she died suddenly)

33. 足首にけがをした。

Ashikubi ni kega wo shita.
I did an injury to the ankle.

34. このケーキ、よろしかったら
もう一つ召し上がりません
か。

Kono keeki, yoroshikattara mou hitotsu
meshiagarimasen ka.
If this cake is good, won't you honorably
eat one more?

35. その猫は体が弱くなり、水を
飲む力も無くなって死んでし
まった。

Sono neko wa karada ga yowakunari,
mizu wo nomu chikara mo nakunatte
shinde shimatta.
As for that cat, the body becomes weak,
and water-to-drink force also disappears,
and it died completely.

36. 彼は服が汚れるのも構わず、
犬と遊んだ。

Kare wa fuku ga yogoreru no mo
kamawazu, inu to asonda.
As for him, the-clothes-will-get-dirty
thing even not minding, he played with
the dog.

37. 赤やら青やら、いろんな色の
花が咲いている。

Aka yara ao yara, ironna iro no hana ga
saite iru.
Red, etc., blue, etc., various colors'
flowers are blossoming.

38. 電車の中の日本人のマナーは
いいですか。

Densha no naka no nihon jin no manaa
wa ii desu ka.
As for inside-the-trains' Japanese
people's manners, are they good?

39. 道子さんの話。

Michiko-san no hanashi.
Michiko's story

40. 私のクラスには旅行の好きな
人が多いです。

Watashi no kurasu ni wa ryokou no suki
na hito ga ooi desu.
As for in my class, the travel-liking
people are numerous.

41. 外国へ行ったことがある人も
たくさんいます。

Gaikoku e itta koto ga aru hito mo
takusan imasu.
There are also a lot of people who have
been to foreign countries.

42. 日本の乗り物やホテルは高い
から、外国へ行った方が安い
と正男君が言っていました
が、本当でしょうか。

Nihon no norimono ya hoteru wa takai
kara, gaikoku e itta hou ga yasui to
masao-kun ga itte imashita ga, hontou
deshou ka.
Since Japanese transportation, hotels,
etc., are expensive, to go to foreign
countries is cheaper, Masao-kun was
saying, but is it probably true?

Chapter 60

New Kanji in this Chapter

# 209 性	# 288 輸	# 219 糸	# 406 参	# 66 士
# 126 磨	# 260 活	# 296 容	# 464 西	# 87 負

1. 田中さんはなぜロボットを作ったのですか。

Tanaka-san wa naze robotto wo tsukutta no desu ka.
As for Tanaka, why did he make a robot?

2. 会社の女性にお茶を入れてもらえなくなったからです。

Kaisha no josei ni ocha wo irete moraenakunatta kara desu.
By the company's women, since make tea and it became unable to receive it is.

3. アンソニーさんの会社は、なぜ工業用ロボットを中島さんの会社で輸出してもらいたいと思っているのですか。

Ansonii-san-no kaisha wa naze kougyou you robotto wo nakashima-san no kaisha de yushutsu shite moraitai to omotte iru no desu ka.
As for Anthony's company, why, industrial use robots, by Nakashima's company they want to export and receive, they are thinking?

4. 中島さんの会社ではヨーロッパの会社との取り引きが多いからです。

Nakashima-san no kaisha de wa yooroppa no kaisha to no torihiki ga ooi kara desu.
It's because, as for at Nakashima's company, with Europe's companies, business deals are numerous.

5. 私達は赤い糸で結ばれていたのよ。

Watashitachi wa akai ito de musubarete ita no yo.
As for us, by a red thread we were being bound on, for sure. (i.e., we were destined to get married)

6. 日本はアメリカから米を輸入し始めた。

Nihon wa amerika kara kome wo yunyuu shihajimeta.
As for Japan, it began to import rice from America.

7. 部長、パーティにいらっしゃいますか。

Buchou, paatii ni irasshaimasu ka.
Division Manager, to the party will you honorably come?

8. 私も参ります。

Watashi mo mairimasu.
I also will humbly go.

9. 私達はお互い同士、親切にすべきだ。

Watashitachi wa otagai doushi, shinsetsu ni subeki da.
As for us, to each other, we should be kind. (subeki = suru beki)

10. お客さんが来るから、窓ガラスを磨きましょう。

Okyakusan ga kuru kara, mado garasu wo migakimashou.
Since the honorable customer will come, let's brush the window glass. (i.e., let's wash the windows)

11. あのカタログを持ってきてください。

Ano katarogu wo motte kite kudasai.
Please bring that catalogue over there.

12. はい、持って参ります。

Hai, motte mairimasu.
Yes, I will bring humbly.

13. ロボットが田中さんにお茶を入れないで女性にコーヒーやジュースを飲ませている。

Robotto ga Tanaka-san ni ocha wo irenai de josei ni koohii ya juusu wo nomasete iru.
The robot, to Tanaka, tea not making, to women, coffee and juice, etc., he is making drink.

14. どんなに働いても生活は楽になりません。

Donna ni hataraitemo seikatsu wa raku ni narimasen.
What kind of to labor even though, as for life, to comfort it does not become.

15. ジェーンさんの話の内容がほとんど聞き取れなかった。

Jeen-san no hanashi no naiyou ga hotondo kikitorenakatta.
Jane's talk's content almost could not be listened/taken. (i.e., I could hardly follow what she said)

16. 西村さんはさっき帰りました。

Nishimura-san wa sakki kaerimashita.
As for Nishimura, just now he returned.

17. 日本のチームは試合に負けた。

Nihon no chiimu wa shiai ni maketa.
The Japanese team lost the game.

18. アンソニーさんの会社では工業用ロボットをどこに輸出したいと思っているのですか。

Ansonii-san-no kaisha de wa kougyou you robotto wo doko ni yushutsu shitai to omotte iru no desu ka.
As for at Anthony's company, industrial use robots, to where do they want to export, are they thinking?

19. ヨーロッパに輸出したいと思っています。

Yooroppa ni yushutsu shitai to omotte imasu.
To Europe they want to export, they are thinking.

20. お客さんに：部長は会議に出ておりますので終わったらすぐ参ります。

Okyakusan ni: buchou wa kaigi ni dete orimasu node owattara sugu mairimasu.
To the honorable Mr. Customer: as for the division manager, since he is humbly attending a meeting, when it finishes, he will soon humbly come.

21. 父は自分の車をピカピカに光るまで磨いた。

Chichi wa jibun no kuruma wo pikapika ni hikaru made migaita.
As for my father, he polished his car until it shone in a sparkling way.

22. 長い糸はからまりやすい。

Nagai ito wa karamariyasui.
A long thread is easily entangled.

23. 野菜を中心とした食生活をする。

Yasai wo chuushin to shita shokuseikatsu wo suru.
On vegetables center, was in the capacity of, eating habits I do. (i.e., my diet is centered on vegetables)

24. 私達は隣同士です。

Watashitachi wa tonari doushi desu.
We are next-door neighbors.

25. これはメニューに書かれてあった内容と違っています。

Kore wa menyuu ni kakarete atta naiyou to chigatte imasu.
As for this, to the menu is written on and existed content with is being different. (i.e., the food is different from what was written on the menu)

26. 西村さんは女の人みたいなしゃべり方をする。

Nishimura-san wa onna no hito mitai na shaberi kata wo suru.
As for Nishimura, a woman-appearing talk method he does. (i.e., he imitates a woman's speech)

27. 野球の試合に負けた。

Yakyuu no shiai ni maketa.
I lost to the baseball's game.

28. 歯を毎日磨きます。

Ha wo mainichi migakimasu.
I brush the teeth every day.

29. 彼は学士号を持っている。

Kare wa gakushigou wo motte iru.
As for him, he has a bachelor's degree.

30. このクラスはとても活気がある。

Kono kurasu wa totemo kakki ga aru.
As for this class, very much liveliness exists.

31. 彼は西日本を中心に活動している。

Kare wa nishi nihon wo chuushin ni katsudou shite iru.
As for him, on western-Japan-centered-around he is doing activity. (i.e., his work is centered in western Japan)

32. 彼は重いリュックサックを
    背負って山に出かけた。

Kare wa omoi ryukkusakku wo seotte yama ni dekaketa.
As for him, carrying a heavy knapsack on his back, he left to the mountain.

33. 針^{はり}と糸を持っていません
    か。

Hari to ito wo motte imasen ka.
Don't you have a needle and thread?

34. 私の課は男性７人と女性４人
    です。

Watashi no ka wa dansei shichinin to josei yonin desu.
As for my section, it's seven men and four women.

35. さすがに学者だけあって彼は
    その問いに容易に答えた。

Sasuga ni gakusha dake atte kare wa sono toi ni youi ni kotaeta.
As expected, since a scholar, as for him, to that question he answered easily.

36. 音楽を聞いている人やマンガ
    を読んでいる人がいます。

Ongaku wo kiite iru hito ya manga wo yonde iru hito ga imasu.
There are people listening to music, people reading comics, etc.

37. 空港には銀行やレストランな
    どがあります。

Kuukou ni wa ginkou ya resutoran nado ga arimasu.
As for at the airport, there are banks, restaurants, etc.

38. シーツとかアイロンとか、
    色々な物を買いました。

Shiitsu toka airon toka, iroiro na mono wo kaimashita.
Sheets, etc., an iron, etc., I bought various things.

39. どんな所へ行きたいですか。

Donna tokoro e ikitai desu ka.
What kind of place would you like to go to?

40. そうですね。温泉があってあ
    まり遠くない所、たとえば
    箱根^{はこね}や伊豆^{いず}へ行きたいです。

Sou desu ne. Onsen ga atte amari tookunai tokoro, tatoeba hakone ya izu e ikitai desu.
Let me see. Hot springs exist and not-too-far place, for example, to Hakone, Izu, etc., I'd like to go.

Chapter 61

New Kanji in this Chapter

#374 将	#381 駐	#551 替	#554 換

1. 自分の過去と将来をよく考えます。

Jibun no kako to shourai wo yoku kangaemasu.
On myself's past and future I often think.

2. 彼女は空き地に駐車した。

Kanojo wa akichi ni chuusha shita.
As for her, in a vacant lot, she parked.

3. 一日中着替えないでパジャマのままだなんて、だらしない。

Ichinichijuu kigaenai de pajama no mama da nante, darashinai.
All day long, not changing clothes, it's pajama's state, such a thing, sloppy.

4. 六本木に行きたい人は恵比寿_{えびす}で日比谷線_{ひびやせん}に乗り換えます。

Roppongi ni ikitai hito wa ebisu de hibiyasen ni norikaemasu.
As for people who want to go to Roppongi, at Ebisu they transfer to Hibiyasen.

5. 日本の将来がどうなるか、とても不安に思う。

Nihon no shourai ga dou naru ka, totemo fuan ni omou.
Japan's future, how it will develop (question), I think very uneasily.

6. ここに駐車するつもりです。

Koko ni chuusha surutsumori desu.
I plan to park here.

7. ああ、パソコンがフリーズしちゃった。

Aa, pasokon ga furiizu shichatta.
Ah, the personal computer froze completely.

8. 買い換えた方がいいんじゃない？

Kaikaeta hou ga iin ja nai?
It would be better to buy a replacement, isn't it?

9. ジョンソンさん、仕事はどうでしたか。

Jonson-san, shigoto wa dou deshita ka.
Johnson, as for the work, how was it?

10. 最初の日だからちょっと疲れました。

Saisho no hi dakara chotto tsukaremashita.
Since it's my first day, I got a little tired.

11. でも面白かったですよ。

Demo omoshirokatta desu yo.
But it was interesting, for sure.

12. オフィスの人はどうですか。

Ofisu no hito wa dou desu ka.
As for the office's people, how are they?

13. ええ、みんな親切で明るい人達でした。

Ee, minna shinsetsu de akarui hitotachi deshita.
Yeah, all of them were kind and cheerful people.

14. それは良かったですね。

Sore wa yokatta desu ne.
As for that, it was good, huh.

15. それに若くてきれいな女の人がたくさんいますね。

Sore ni wakakute kireina onna no hito ga takusan imasu ne.
Besides, young and pretty women, a lot exist, huh.

16. ところで明日は休みですね。

Tokoro de ashita wa yasumi desu ne.
By the way, as for tomorrow, it's vacation huh.

17. ええ、銀座のデパートへ行きます。

Ee, ginza no depaato e ikimasu.
Yeah, I will go to a Ginza's department store.

18. アパートへ引っ越すので色々な物が要るんですよ。

Apaato e hikkosu node, iroiro na mono ga irun desu yo.
Since we will move to an apartment, various things are needed, for sure.

19. アメリカから持ってこなかったんですね。

Amerika kara motte konakattan desu ne.
You didn't bring them from America, huh.

20. その…持ってきたんですが、テイラーが新しいのを欲しがっているものですから。

Sono... motte kitan desu ga, teiraa ga atarashii no wo hoshigatte iru mono desu kara.
That... we did bring, but since Taylor new ones seems to be wanting thing it is.
(sono in this sentence means "well..."; mono in this sentence means something like "because")

21. 将来、科学者になるため努力しています。

Shourai, kagakusha ni naru tame doryoku shite imasu.
In the future, for the sake of to become a scientist, I am making effort. (i.e., I'm trying to become a scientist in the future)

22. この白いシーツが欲しいんですが、もっと大きいサイズのはありませんか。

Kono shiroi shiitsu ga hoshiin desu ga, motto ookii saizu no wa arimasen ka.
I desire these white sheets, but as for a larger size, doesn't it exist?

23. 大きいのですね。

Ookii no desu ne.
It's a big one, huh. (i.e., it's a big one you want)

24. 少々お待ちください。

Shoushou omachi kudasai.
Please honorably wait a moment.

25. これが一番大きいサイズなんです。

Kore ga ichiban ookii saizu nan desu.
This is the largest size. (nan is to soften the sentence; it's OK to omit it)

26. そうですか。じゃ、結構です。

Sou desu ka. Ja, kekkou desu.
Is that so? Well, it's fine. (this means that he will *not* buy the sheets)

27. 新宿の銀行でお金を両替しました。

Shinjuku no ginkou de okane wo ryougae shimashita.
At a Shinjuku bank, I exchanged some money.

28. この人形、もっと大きいのと取り替えてください。

Kono ningyou, motto ookii no to torikaete kudasai.
This doll, with (or for) a larger one, please exchange.

29. 次の駅でお乗り換えください。

Tsugi no eki de onorikae kudasai.
At the next station, please honorably transfer.

30. 広い駐車場に車を止めた。

Hiroi chuushajou ni kuruma wo tometa.
In the spacious parking lot, I parked the car.

31. そのアイロンはいくらですか。

Sono airon wa, ikura desu ka.
As for that iron, how much is it?

32. 1万5千円です。

Ichiman gosen'en desu.
It's 15,000 yen.

33. ちょっと高いですね。

Chotto takai desu ne.
It's a little expensive, huh.

34. もう少し安くて軽いのはありませんか。

Mou sukoshi yasukute karui no wa arimasen ka.
As for a little more cheap and light ones, don't they exist?

35. それではこんなのはいかがですか。

Sore de wa konna no wa ikaga desu ka.
Well then, as for this type, how is it?

36. お値段はあまり高くありません。

Onedan wa amari takaku arimasen.
The humble price isn't very expensive.

37. じゃ、これで結構です。

Ja, kore de kekkou desu.
Well, with this is fine. (this means that he will buy it)

38. はい、有難うございます。

Hai. Arigatou gozaimasu.
Yes. Thank you a lot.

39. このりんごはいくらですか。

Kono ringo wa ikura desu ka.
As for this apple, how much is it? (i.e., how much does it cost?)

40. 一つ千円です。

Hitotsu sen'en desu
It's 1000 yen each.

41. ちょっと高いね。こっちの
は？

Chotto takai ne. Kotchi no wa?
It's a little expensive, huh. As for this way's one?

42. それは一つ百五十円です。

Sore wa hitotsu hyaku go juu en desu.
As for that, one, it's 150 yen. (i.e., it's 150 yen apiece)

43. じゃ、それを五つください。
それからミカンを一山くださ
い。

Ja, sore wo itsutsu kudasai. Sore kara mikan wo hitoyama kudasai.
Well, those, five please. (i.e., please give me five) And then, tangerines, a pile please. (yama = a counter for piles or heaps)

44. 有難うございます。全部で千
円です。

Arigatou gozaimasu. Zenbu de sen'en desu.
Thank you a lot. Altogether, it's 1,000 yen.

Part Two: Additional Practice

No new kanji are introduced in Part Two of the Reader. Please continue reading in order to gain more experience with the 608 target kanji that were introduced in Part One.

Chapter 62

1. 明日はどうしても都合がつかない。

Asu wa doushitemo tsugou ga tsukanai.
As for tomorrow, one way or the other, circumstances are not available. (i.e., I'm booked up)

2. 引き出しを閉める。

Hikidashi wo shimeru.
I will close the drawer.

3. 電気を点ける。

Denki wo tsukeru.
I will turn on the light.

4. 二年生は部屋を出た。

Ninensei wa heya wo deta.
The second-year students left the room.

5. 靴を変えない。

Kutsu wo kaenai.
I won't change the shoes.

6. 何も変わらない。

Nanimo kawaranai.
Nothing changes.

7. 飛行機に乗らない。

Hikouki ni noranai.
I won't ride in the airplane.

8. 赤ちゃんを寝かす。

Akachan wo nekasu.
I will put the baby to bed.

9. いつも午後九時に寝る。

Itsumo gogo kuji ni neru.
I always go to bed at 9 p.m.

10. 思いきって留学することにした。

Omoikitte ryuugaku suru koto ni shita.
Cutting off thought (i.e., taking the plunge), I decided to do foreign study.

11. ろうそくを消す。

Rousoku wo kesu.
I will put out the candle.

12. ストーブを点けてください。

Sutoobu wo tsukete kudasai.
Please turn on the space heater.

13. 窓が開いていますね。

Mado ga aite imasu ne.
The window is open, huh.

14. ええ、暑いから開けてあるん
です。

Ee, atsui kara akete arun desu.
Yeah, because it's hot, it has been opened by someone.

15. 窓が閉まっています。

Mado ga shimatte imasu.
The window is closed.

16. コップとお皿はもう出ています
か。

Koppu to osara wa mou dete imasu ka.
As for the honorable cups and plates, are they already out?

17. ええ、出してありますよ。

Ee, dashite arimasu yo.
Yeah, they've been put out by someone, for sure.

18. ストーブが点いていますね。
消しましょうか。

Sutoobu ga tsuite imasu ne.
Keshimashou ka.
The space heater is on, huh. Shall I turn it off?

19. いいえ、消さないでくださ
い。部屋が寒いから点けてい
るんです。

Iie, kesanai de kudasai. Heya ga samui kara, tsukete irun desu.
No, please don't turn it off. Because the room is cold, it is being turned on.

20. 電気も点いていますよ。

Denki mo tsuite imasu yo.
The lights are also on, for sure.

21. ああ、電気は消してくださ
い。

Aa, denki wa keshite kudasai.
Ah, as for the lights, please turn them off.

22. 窓が開いていますね。閉めま
すか。

Mado ga aite imasu ne. Shimemasu ka.
The window is open, right. Will I close it? (i.e., shall I close it?)

23. 少し空気が悪いから開けてい
るんです。

Sukoshi kuuki ga warui kara akete irun desu.
A little, because the air is bad, it is being opened.

24. もう四時になりましたか。

Mou yoji ni narimashita ka.
Did it already become 4:00?

25. いいえ、まだ四時になりませ
ん。

Iie, mada yoji ni narimasen.
No, it still doesn't become 4:00.

26. トイレットペーパーを買いま
したか。

Toiretto peepaa wo kaimashita ka.
Did you buy toilet paper?

27. いいえ、まだ買っていません。

Iie, mada katte imasen.
No, I still am not buying. (i.e., I haven't bought)

28. もう行きましたか。

Mou ikimashita ka.
Did you already go?

29. いいえ、まだ行っていません。

Iie, mada itte imasen.
No, I still am not going. (i.e., I haven't gone)

30. 子供がお菓子を食べてしまいました。

Kodomo ga okashi wo tabete shimaimashita.
The child ate the sweets completely.

31. 今この本を読んでしまうからちょっと待っていてください。

Ima kono hon wo yonde shimau kara chotto matte ite kudasai.
Since I will now finish reading this book, please be waiting for a moment.

32. 手紙はもう書いちゃいました。

Tegami wa mou kai chai mashita.
As for the letter, I already finished writing it. (chau = a contraction of te shimau)

33. もう出ましょうか。

Mou demashou ka.
Shall we leave already? (in this sentence, mou = now or soon)

34. ちょっと待ってて。

Chotto matte te.
Be waiting for a moment. (shortened for speech)

35. お皿を洗ってしまうから。

Osara wo aratte shimau kara.
Because I will completely wash the honorable plates. (i.e., the dishes)

36. ミカンをたくさんもらいました。

Mikan wo takusan moraimashita.
I got a lot of mandarin oranges.

37. じゃ、ジュースにして飲みましょう。

Ja, juusu ni shite nomimashou.
Well, let's turn them into juice and drink them.

38. 暑いですね。窓を開けましょうか。

Atsui desu ne. Mado wo akemashou ka.
It's hot, huh. Shall I open the window?

39. ええ、お願いします。

Ee, onegai shimasu.
Yeah, please do.

40. わたしはサッカーと野球と
ラグビーが好きです。

Watashi wa sakka to yakyuu to ragubii
ga suki desu.
As for me, I like soccer, baseball and
rugby.

41. そのバッグを持ちましょう
か。

Sono baggu wo mochimashou ka.
Shall I hold that bag? (i.e., shall I carry
it?)

42. 駅まで車で送りましょう
か。

Eki made kuruma de okurimashou ka.
Shall I see you off by car until the
station?

43. いいえ、結構です。歩きます
から。

Iie, kekkou desu. Arukimasu kara.
No, it's fine. Because I will walk.

44. 英語で説明しましょうか。

Eigo de setsumei shimashou ka.
Shall I explain it in English?

45. はい、お願いします。日本語
はあまり分かりませんので。

Hai, onegai shimasu. Nihongo wa amari
wakarimasen node.
Yes, please do. Because, as for Japanese,
I hardly don't understand.

46. フォークを持ってきましょう
か。

Fooku wo motte kimashou ka.
Shall I bring a fork?

47. いいえ、結構です。

Iie, kekkou desu.
No, it's fine.

48. 最近、運動不足なんですよ。

Saikin, undou busoku nan desu yo.
Recently, it's not enough exercise, for
sure.

49. それで毎日会社に歩いて行こ
うと思っているんですよ。

Sore de mainichi kaisha ni aruite ikou to
omotte irun desu yo.
For that reason, every day, I shall go to
the company walking, I'm thinking, for
sure.

50. エベレストと富士山とどちら
の方が高いですか。

Eberesuto to fujisan to dochira no hou ga
takai desu ka.
Everest vs. Mt. Fuji, which is higher?

51. エベレストの方が、ずっと高
いです。

Eberesuto no hou ga zutto takai desu.
Everest is much higher.

52. 昨日の帰り、雨に降られたで
しょう。

Kinou no kaeri, ame ni furareta deshou.
Yesterday's return, by the rain you got
precipitated on probably.

53. それが、家に着いたかと思う
と降り出したのよ。

Sore ga, ie ni tsuita ka to omou to
furidashita no yo.
That, to the house I arrived, as soon as, it
precipitated/put out, for sure.

54. 遠いから電車で行ったら？

Tooi kara densha de ittara?
Since far, if you go by train?

55. 電車で行っても一時間はかか
ると思いますよ。

Densha de ittemo ichijikan wa kakaru to
omoimasu yo.
Even though I go by train, as for one-
hour duration it will take, I think, for
sure.

****

56. もう四時半になりますが息子
はまだ学校から帰りません。

Mou yojihan ni narimasu ga musuko wa
mada gakkou kara kaerimasen.
Already it will become half past 4, but,
as for the son, he still doesn't return from
school.

57. 息子の部屋を見てください。

Musuko no heya wo mite kudasai.
Please look at the son's room.

58. 靴下やボールなどが散らかっ
ています。

Kutsushita ya booru nado ga chirakatte
imasu.
Socks, balls, etc., are messy.

59. 部屋の電気は消してあります
が、机の上の電気は消してあ
りません。

Heya no denki wa keshite arimasu ga,
tsukue no ue no denki wa keshite
arimasen.
The room light is turned off by someone,
but the light on top of the desk is not
turned off by anyone.

60. それにドアも窓も閉めてあり
ません。

Sore ni doa mo mado mo shimete
arimasen.
Moreover, the door also, the window
also, are not closed (by anyone).

61. CDはきれいに並べてありま
すが、机の上の本はきれいに
並べてありません。

Shiidii wa kirei ni narabete arimasu ga,
tsukue no ue no hon wa kirei ni narabete
arimasen.
The CD's are neatly lined up (by
someone), but the books on top of the
desk are not neatly lined up (by anyone).

62. その紙に「散らかさない」と
書いてあります。

Sono kami ni "chirakasanai" to kaite
arimasu.
To that paper, "I won't make a mess" is
written.

Chapter 63

1. タイラーさんの日記。

   Tairaa-san no nikki.
   Tyler's diary.

2. 今日はローレンと一緒に銀座のデパートに行った。

   Kyou wa rooren to issho ni ginza no depaato ni itta.
   As for today, with Lauren, together, we went to a Ginza's department store.

3. 大きくてきれいなデパートだった。

   Ookikute kireina depaato datta.
   It was a large and pretty department store.

4. それに店員も親切だった。

   Sore ni tenin mo shinsetsu datta.
   Besides, the clerks also were kind.

5. けれども、値段は高かった。

   Keredomo, nedan wa takakatta.
   However, as for the prices, they were high.

6. ローレンは一万一千円の日本製のアイロンを買った。

   Rooren wa ichiman issen'en no nihonsei no airon wo katta.
   As for Lauren, she bought an 11,000-yen Japanese-made iron.

7. もう少し大きいのが良かったが、ローレンが気に入ったのだから仕方がない。

   Mou sukoshi ookii no ga yokatta ga, rooren ga ki ni itta no dakara shikata ga nai.
   A little larger one was good, but because Lauren was pleased, it can't be helped.
   (入った could also be pronounced haitta, but not in this context)

8. 帰りに小さい店があったので僕も入った。

   Kaeri ni chiisai mise ga atta node boku mo haitta.
   At the return, because a small store existed, I also entered.

9. 狭いところに人がたくさんいたので込んでいた。

   Semai tokoro ni hito ga takusan ita node konde ita.
   In a tight place, because people, a lot, existed, it was crowded.

10. 店員はあまり親切ではなかったが、すごく安かった。

    Tenin wa amari shinsetsu dewa nakatta ga, sugoku yasukatta.
    The clerks were not very kind, but it was super cheap.

    ****

11. 明日は港区の区役所に行くつもりなんですが。

    Ashita wa minatoku no kuyakusho ni ikutsumori nan desu ga...
    As for tomorrow, I'm planning to Minato ward's ward office, but...

12. 場所を知っていますか。

Basho wo shitte imasu ka.
Are you knowing the place?

13. 行ったことがありますか。

Itta koto ga arimasu ka.
Have you ever gone?

14. いいえ、ないんです。

Iie, nain desu.
No, I haven't.

15. 明日は土曜日だから 12 時までですよ。

Ashita wa douyobi dakara juuni ji made desu yo.
As for tomorrow, since it's Saturday, it's until 12:00, for sure.

16. 込んでいるかもしれませんよ。

Konde iru kamoshiremasen yo.
It might be crowded, for sure.

17. だいぶ待つでしょうか。

Daibu matsu deshou ka.
Greatly, will I probably wait?

18. 待つでしょうから早くうちを出た方がいいですよ。

Matsu deshou kara hayaku uchi wo deta hou ga ii desu yo.
Since you will wait probably, it would be better to leave home early, for sure

19. ところで乗り物は地下鉄がいいでしょうか、それともバスがいいでしょうか。

Tokoro de norimono wa chikatetsu ga ii deshou ka, soretomo basu ga ii deshou ka.
By the way, as for transportation, would the subway probably be good, or would the bus probably be good?

20. 地下鉄では行かない方がいいでしょう。

Chikatetsu de wa ikanai hou ga ii deshou.
As for by subway, not to go would probably be better.

21. 地下鉄は少し不便なんですよ。

Chikatetsu wa sukoshi fuben nan desu yo.
The subway is a little inconvenient, for sure.

22. 駅を出てから歩いて 10 分ぐらいかかります。

Eki wo dete kara aruite jippun gurai kakarimasu.
After leaving the station, it will take about 10 minutes walking.

****

23. 区役所に行きましたか。

Kuyakusho ni ikimashita ka.
Did you go to the ward office?

24. それが...実はまだなんです。

Sore ga... jitsu wa mada nan desu.
That, to tell the truth, not yet.

25. 行ったんですが、とても込んでいたので、できなかったんです。

Ittan desu ga, totemo konde ita node, dekinakatta desu.
I went, but since it was very crowded, I couldn't do it.

26. 家を何時に出たんですか。

Ie wo nanji ni detan desu ka.
At what time did you leave the house?

27. それが、9時に出るつもりだったんですが、雨が降っていたので止むまで待って、10時頃出たんです。

Sore ga, kuji ni derutsumori dattan desu ga, ame ga futte ita node yamu made matte, juuji goro detan desu.
That, I planned to leave at 9:00, but since it was raining, I wait until it will stop, and I left about 10:00.

28. それで区役所には何時に着きましたか。

Sore de kuyakusho ni wa nanji ni tsukimashita ka.
And then, as for to the ward office, at what time did you arrive?

29. 11時過ぎだったんです。

Juu ichi ji sugi dattan desu.
It was following 11:00.

30. ですから、来週の土曜日にもう一度行くつもりです。

Desu kara, raishuu no doyoubi ni mou ichido ikutsumori desu.
Therefore, on next week's Saturday, I plan to go one more time.

31. 来週の土曜日は祝日ですよ。

Raishuu no doyoubi wa shukujitsu desu yo.
Next week's Saturday is a national holiday, for sure.

32. 知りませんでした。

Shirimasen deshita.
I didn't know.

33. 困ったなぁ。

Komatta naa.
Inconvenienced.

34. 明日の朝、会社を休んで行った方がいいですよ。

Ashita no asa, kaisha wo yasunde itta hou ga ii desu yo.
Tomorrow morning, it would be better to take time off from the company and go, for sure.

35. それじゃ、朝、区役所に行ってから会社に来ます。

Sore ja, asa, kuyakusho ni itte kara kaisha ni kimasu.
In that case, morning, after going to the ward office, I'll come to the company.

36. ジョンさんはなぜ火曜日に区役所に行ったのですか。

Jon-san wa naze kayoubi ni kuyakusho ni itta no desu ka.
As for John, why, on Tuesday, did he go to the ward office?

****

37. お先に失礼します。

Osaki ni shitsurei shimasu.
To humble ahead, I'll commit a discourtesy. (i.e., I'll go first)

38. お疲れ様でした。

Otsukare sama deshita.
Thanks for your honorable fatigue. (i.e., thanks for your hard work)

39. ウイリヤムズさんは何で帰りますか。

Uiriamuzu-san wa nani de kaerimasu ka.
As for Williams, by what will he return?

40. 私は地下鉄です。

Watashi wa chikatetsu desu.
As for me, it's the subway.

41. ところで六本木のお宅はどうですか。

Tokoro de roppongi no otaku wa dou desu ka.
By the way, as for Roppongi's honorable home, how is it?

42. 便利ですが、あの辺は夜も車が多くてうるさいんですよ。

Benri desu ga, ano hen wa yoru mo kuruma ga ookute urusain desu yo.
It's convenient, but since, as for that place over there, even at night the cars are numerous, it's loud, for sure.

43. それに通勤の電車は込んで大変でしょう。

Sore ni tsuukin no densha wa konde taihen deshou.
Moreover, since the commuter's trains get crowded, they're probably terrible.

44. ええ、本当に。

Ee, hontou ni.
Yeah, truly.

45. 4ヶ月前に浦和へ引っ越したんですよ。

Yonkagetsu mae ni urawa e hikkoshitan desu yo.
At four months ago, I moved to Urawa, for sure.

46. 前より遠いんですか。

Mae yori tooin desu ka.
Is it far compared to before?

47. ええ、だいぶ遠いです。

Ee, daibu tooi desu.
Yeah, it's quite far.

48. 三度も乗り換えるから二時間近くかかります。

Sando mo norikaeru kara nijikan chikaku kakarimasu.
Since I transfer all of three times, it takes close to two hours

49. えっ！ 二時間も？

E! Nijikan mo?
Eh! Two whole hours?

50. 大変ですね。

Taihen desu ne.
It's terrible, huh.

51. 行きと帰りとどちらが込みますか。

Iki to kaeri to dochira ga komimasu ka.
Going vs. returning, which gets more crowded?

52. 行きの方がひどいと思います。

Iki no hou ga hidoi to omoimasu.
Going is more awful I think.

53. 寿司と天ぷらとどっちが好き？

Sushi to tenpura to dotchi ga suki?
Sushi vs. tempura, which do you like better?

54. どちらも好き。

Dochira mo suki.
I like both.

55. 横浜は大きいですか。

Yokohama wa ookii desu ka.
Is Yokohama big?

56. ええ、でも東京や大阪ほど大きくありません。

Ee, demo toukyou ya oosaka hodo ookiku arimasen.
Yeah, but compared to Tokyo, Osaka, etc., it isn't big.

57. ちょっとその日は都合が悪いんです。

Chotto sono hi wa tsugou ga waruin desu.
A little bit, as for that day, the circumstances are bad.

58. 日を変えて下さいませんか。

Hi wo kaete kudasaimasenka.
Won't you change the day and give?

59. 朝食。昼食。夕食。

Choushoku. Chuushoku. Yuushoku.
Breakfast. Lunch. Dinner.

60. 道子さんはいすに座れました。

Michiko-san wa isu ni suwaremashita.
As for Michiko, she was able to sit on a chair.

61. 高橋さんは来るでしょう。

Takahashi-san wa kuru deshou.
As for Takahashi, he will come probably.

62. お待たせしました。石川です。

Omatase shimashita. Ishikawa desu.
I'm sorry to have kept you waiting. It's Ishikawa.

Chapter 64

1. へー、日本では電車の中で大学生やサラリーマンがマンガを読んでいると聞きましたが、本当なんですねぇ。

Hee. Nihon de wa densha no naka de daigakusei ya sarariiman ga manga wo yonde iru to kikimashita ga, hontou nan desu nee.
Hey. As for in Japan, inside the trains, college students and salarymen, etc., are reading comics, I heard, but it's true, huh.

2. イヤホンで音楽を聞きながら、新聞を読んでいる人もいますね。

Iyahon de ongaku wo kiki nagara, shinbun wo yonde iru hito mo imasu ne.
While listening to music with earphones, there are also newspaper-reading people, huh.

3. 私は広告を見ながら、漢字やカタカナを勉強していますけど。

Watashi wa koukoku wo mi nagara, kanji ya katakana wo benkyou shite imasu kedo...
As for me, while I look at advertisements, I'm studying kanji and katakana, etc., but...

4. ああ、ウイリヤムズさんは勉強家ですね。

Aa, Uiriamuzu-san wa benkyouka desu ne.
Ah, as for Williams, it's a diligent student, huh.

5. 知らない言葉がたくさんあって難しいですね。

Shiranai kotoba ga takusan atte muzukashii desu ne.
Since words that I don't know, a lot exist, it's difficult, huh.

6. でも、日本語の教科書ほどじゃありませんよ。

Demo, nihongo no kyoukasho hodo ja arimasen yo.
But it's not as much as a Japanese language textbook, for sure.

****

7. 電車の中で本を読んでいる人です。

Densha no naka de hon wo yonde iru hito desu.
It's a person who is reading a book inside a train.

8. ローレンさんが買ったアイロンは1万1千円でした。

Rooren-san ga katta airon wa ichiman issen'en deshita.
The iron Lauren bought was 11,000 yen.

9. その辞書は小さくて便利です。

Sono jisho wa chiisakute benri desu.
That dictionary is small and convenient.

10. 電車と車とどちらの方が速いですか。

Densha to kuruma to dochira no hou ga hayai desu ka.
Train vs. car, which is faster?

11. 車より電車の方が速いです。

Kuruma yori densha no hou ga hayai desu.
Compared to a car, the train is faster.

12. 三日前に日本に来ました。

Mikka mae ni nihon ni kimashita.
I came to Japan at three days ago.

13. バスで行くより車で行く方がちょっと速いです。

Basu de iku yori kuruma de iku hou ga chotto hayai desu.
Compared to to go by bus, to go by car is a little faster.

****

14. 遅れてすみません。

Okurete sumimasen.
Since I get delayed, excuse me.

15. 構いませんよ。お仕事がなかなか終わらなかったんでしょう。

Kamaimasen yo. Oshigoto ga nakanaka owaranakattan deshou.
It doesn't matter, for sure. The honorable work didn't finish readily probably.

16. いえ、実はそうじゃないんです。

Ie, jitsu wa sou ja nain desu.
No, to tell the truth, it isn't so.

17. 電車の中でね、日本語のテープを聞いているうちに乗り越してしまったんです。

Densha no naka de ne, nihongo no teepu wo kiite iru uchi ni norikoshite shimattan desu.
Inside the train, huh, while I am still listening to a Japanese language tape, I completely missed my stop.

18. 乗り越すぐらいはいいけど、テープを聞きながら道を歩くと危ないから気を付けてくださいね。

Norikosu gurai wa ii kedo, teepu wo kiki nagara michi wo aruku to abunai kara ki wo tsukete kudasai ne.
As for to miss the stop approximately, good, but since while to listen to tapes if you walk on the street it's dangerous, please be careful, huh.

19. はい、気を付けます。

Hai, ki wo tsukemasu.
Yes, I will be careful.

20. 予習、復習の時間がなかなか取れないものですから。

Yoshuu fukushuu no jikan ga nakanaka torenai mono desu kara.
Since study ahead/review's time is a not readily able to take thing.

21. 今度から遅れないようにします。

Kondo kara okurenai you ni shimasu.
From next time, I'll see to it that I'm not delayed.

****

22. 先生、聞き取りがなかなか上手にならないんですがどうしたらいいでしょうか。

Sensei, kikitori ga nakanaka jouzu ni naranain desu ga, dou shitara ii deshou ka.
Teacher, the listen/take will not become skillful readily, but how if I do will probably be good?

23. そうですね。デイビスさんはテレビかラジオを持っていますか。

Sou desu ne. Deibisu-san wa terebi ka rajio wo motte imasu ka.
Let's see. Does Davis have a TV or a radio?

24. はい、テレビもラジオも持っています。

Hai, terebi mo rajio mo motte imasu.
Yes, I have a TV also, a radio also.

25. でも、仕事が忙しくてなかなかテレビもゆっくり見られません。

Demo, shigoto ga isogashikute nakanaka terebi mo yukkuri miraremasen.
But since work is busy, readily, I can't leisurely watch even TV.

26. でも、ラジオなら通勤の途中の電車の中でも聞けるでしょう。

Demo, rajio nara tsuukin no tochuu no densha no naka de mo kikeru deshou.
But in the case of a radio, even inside the commuter's on-the-way's train, you can listen probably.

27. 聞けますが、ラジオを聞くだけで、日本語が上手になりますか。

Kikemasu ga, rajio wo kiku dake de, nihongo ga jouzu ni narimasu ka.
I can listen, but only by to listen to radio, will the Japanese become skillful?

28. ええ、もちろん。毎日聞いているうちにニュースも分かるようになりますよ。

Ee, mochiron. Mainichi kiite iru uchi ni nyuusu mo wakaru you ni narimasu yo.
Yeah, of course. Every day, while still being listening, even the news will come to understand, for sure.

29. でも、ニュースや交通情報は速すぎてとても聞き取ることができません。

Demo nyuusu ya koutsuu jouhou wa hayasugite totemo kikitoru koto ga dekimasen.
But since the news, the traffic information, etc., are too fast, to listen/take a lot won't be possible.

30. 最初は天気予報が聞きとれればいいですよ。

Saisho wa tenki yohou ga kikitorereba ii desu yo.
As for the beginning, if you are able to listen/take the weather report, then it will be good, for sure.

31. そのうちだんだん耳が慣れてくるでしょうから心配は要りませんよ。

Sono uchi dandan mimi ga narete kuru deshou kara shinpai wa irimasen yo.
Before long, gradually, since the ear will probably get used to it and come, worry isn't needed, for sure.

****

32. お帰りなさい。遅かったわね。

Okaerinasai. Osokatta wa ne.
Welcome home. It was late, huh.

33. 10時には帰ると言ってたのにもう11時よ。

Juuji ni wa kaeru to itteta noni mou juu ichiji yo.
As for at 10:00, in spite of you were saying you will return, already 11:00, for sure.

34. うん、途中で事故があってね。

Un, tochuu de jiko ga atte ne.
Yeah, on the way, since there is an accident, and... huh.

35. 電車が遅れたんだよ。

Densha ga okuretan da yo.
The train was delayed, for sure.

36. そう言えば、さっき、テレビのニュースで事故のため電車が止まっているって言ってたわ。

Sou ieba, sakki, terebi no nyuusu de jiko no tame densha ga tomatte iru tte itteta wa.
If one says, then (i.e., that reminds me), earlier, on the TV news, due to an accident, the trains are stopping, they were saying.

37. アレクサスは毎日ゆっくりテレビを見る時間があっていいね。

Arekusasu wa mainichi yukkuri terebi wo miru jikan ga atte ii ne.
Because as for Alexis, every day, leisurely to watch television time exists, good, huh.

38. クリストファーさんは日本語の聞き取りが上手です。

Kurisutofaa-san wa nihongo no kikitori ga jouzu desu.
As for Christopher, Japanese language's listen/taking is skillful.

39. アレクサスさんはテレビを見
たら日本語が上手になると思
っています。

Arekusasu-san wa terebi wo mitara
nihongo ga jouzu ni naru to omotte
imasu.
As for Alexis, if she watches TV, the
Japanese will become skillful, she is
thinking.

****

40. コアラだからオーストラリア
の切手ですか。

Koara dakara oosutoraria no kitte desu
ka.
Since there's a koala bear, is it an
Australian stamp?

41. ええ、友達にもらったんで
す。

Ee, tomodachi ni morattan desu.
Yeah, I received it from a friend.

42. 3枚あるから1枚あげましょ
う。

San mai aru kara ichimai agemashou.
Since three exist, I shall give you one.
(referring to stamps)

43. 下さるんですか。嬉しいわ。

Kudasarun desu ka. Ureshii wa.
Will you honorably give? Pleased!

44. 息子が切手を集めているんで
すよ。

Musuko ga kitte wo atsumete irun desu
yo.
The son is collecting stamps, for sure.

45. 珍しい外国の切手を見るのは
楽しいですね。

Mezurashii gaikoku no kitte wo miru no
wa tanoshii desu ne.
As for to see unusual foreign countries'
stamps, it's pleasant, huh.

46. 他にも色々ありますよ。

Hoka ni mo iroiro arimasu yo.
Others also, various exist, for sure.

47. パンダの切手や珍しい魚の切
手もありますから、これもあ
げましょう。

Panda no kitte ya mezurashii sakana no
kitte mo arimasu kara, kore mo
agemashou.
Since panda stamps and unusual fish
stamps, etc., also exist, I shall give you
this one too.

48. きっと息子が喜びますわ。

Kitto musuko ga yorokobimasu wa.
Surely the son will get delighted.

Chapter 65

1. そこにあるのはご家族の写真ですか。

Soko ni aru no wa gokazoku no shashin desu ka.
As for the one that is there, is it a picture of the honorable family?

2. ええ、アメリカにいる家族の写真です。

Ee, Amerika ni iru kazoku no shashin desu.
Yeah, it's a picture of the family that exists in America.

3. 真ん中が母で、その後ろに立っているのが妹です。

Mannaka ga haha de, sono ushiro ni tatte iru no ga imouto desu.
Middle is my mother, and the at-that-behind-standing one is my younger sister.

4. 妹さんの隣にいるのがご主人ですか。

Imouto-san no tonari ni iru no ga goshujin desu ka.
The one that exists beside your younger sister, is it the honorable husband?

5. 市役所に勤めているんですよ。

Shiyakusho ni tsutomete irun desu yo.
He's employed at a city office, for sure.

6. お子さんは3人ですね。

Okosan wa sannin desu ne.
As for honorable children, it's three people, huh.

7. 一番下のお子さんはおいくつですか。

Ichiban shita no okosan wa oikutsu desu ka.
How honorably old is the youngest honorable child?

8. 来月六つになると言ってました。

Raigetsu muttsu ni naru to ittemashita.
They were saying he will become six next month.

9. じゃ、もうすぐ学校ですね。

Ja, mou sugu gakkou desu ne.
Well, pretty soon it's school, huh.

10. 今年小学校に入ります。

Kotoshi shougakkou ni hairimasu.
He will enter elementary school this year.

****

11. これ、少しですけど...どうぞ。

Kore sukoshi desu kedo... douzo.
This, it's a little, but go ahead.

12. わあ、大きなミカンですね。

Waa, ookina mikan desu ne.
Wow, it's big mandarin oranges, huh.

13. 家内も私も大好きなんです。

Kanai mo watashi mo daisuki nan desu.
My wife also, I also, love them.

14. 兄が両親と一緒に作っているんですよ。

Ani ga ryoushin to issho ni tsukutte irun desu yo.
My older brother, together with my parents, is growing them, for sure.

15. お兄さんがご両親と一緒にねえ。

Onii-san ga goryoushin to issho ni nee.
Your older brother, with your parents together, huh.

16. ご家族はみんな静岡ですか。

Gokazoku wa minna shizuoka desu ka.
As for your family, are they all Shizuoka? (i.e., are they all there?)

17. 姉は結婚して大阪に住んでいます。

Ane wa kekkon shite oosaka ni sunde imasu.
As for my older sister, she got married and lives in Osaka.

****

18. 子供は大きくなります。

Kodomo wa ookiku narimasu.
Children become big. (i.e., they grow up)

19. 今五つです。来月六つになります。

Ima itsutsu desu. Raigetsu muttsu ni narimasu.
He's five now. Next month he will become six.

20. 日本語の勉強が面白くなりました。

Nihongo no benkyou ga omoshiroku narimashita.
Japanese study became interesting.

21. 日本語が上手になったから日本に行きたくなりました。

Nihongo ga jouzu ni natta kara nihon ni ikitaku narimashita.
Since the Japanese became skillful, it developed that I want to go to Japan.

22. 何になりたいですか。

Nan ni naritai desu ka.
What do they want to become?

23. 真さんはマンガが上手だからマンガ家になりたいと思っています。

Makoto-san wa manga ga jouzu dakara mangaka ni naritai to omotte imasu.
As for Makoto, since he is skillful at comics, he would like to become a cartoonist, he is thinking.

24. 道子さんは色々な国へ行きたいから、スチュワーデスになりたいと思っています。

Michiko-san wa iroiro na kuni e ikitai kara, suchuwaadesu ni naritai to omotte imasu.
As for Michiko, since she wants to go to various countries, she would like to become a stewardess, she is thinking.

25. 午前中ずっと日本語を勉強していました。

Gozenchuu zutto nihongo wo benkyou shite imashita.
Throughout the morning, all the way through, I was studying Japanese.

26. 弟は今ドイツに行っています。

Otouto wa ima doitsu ni itte imasu.
As for my younger brother, now, he went to Germany and is there.

27. 昨日マディソンさんが買ったのは何？

Kinou madison-san ga katta no wa nani?
Yesterday, as for the one Madison bought, what? (i.e., what was it that she bought yesterday?)

28. 漢字を覚えるのは大変です。

Kanji wo oboeru no wa taihen desu.
As for to memorize kanji, it's terrible.

29. 山下さんが昨日うちに来たことを知っていますか。

Yamashita-san ga kinou uchi ni kita koto wo shitte imasu ka.
Are you knowing that Yamashita yesterday came to the home?

30. 歯医者さんが部屋を出るのを見ました。

Haishasan ga heya wo deru no wo mimashita.
I saw the dentist leave the room.

31. 走るのと泳ぐのが好きです。

Hashiru no to oyogu no ga suki desu.
I like running and swimming.

32. プレゼントの箱がありますか。

Purezento no hako ga arimasu ka.
Is there a present's box? (i.e., a box for the present)

33. 家内の京子です。

Kanai no kyouko desu.
It's my wife, Kyouko.

34. 英語の手紙はまだ読んだことがありません。

Eigo no tegami wa mada yonda koto ga arimasen.
As for an English language letter, I still have never read one.

35. ドイツ語の手紙はまだもらったことがありません。

Doitsugo no tegami wa mada moratta koto ga arimasen.
As for a German language letter, I still have never received one.

36. あなたの国では結婚する人にどんな物をあげますか。

Anata no kuni de wa kekkon suru hito ni donna mono wo agemasu ka.
As for in your country, to do-marriage people, what kind of things do you give?

****

37. 田中さんのうちの前に1時間ぐらい前から、赤いスポーツカーが止まっています。

Tanaka-san no uchi no mae ni ichijikan gurai mae kara, akai supootsukaa ga tomatte imasu.
In front of Tanaka's home, since about an hour before, a red sports car is parked.

38. あれは弟の正男さんの車です。

Are wa otouto no masao-san no kuruma desu.
That over there is younger brother Masao's car.

39. 正男さんが家族と一緒に来ているんでしょう。

Masao-san ga kazoku to issho ni kite irun deshou.
Masao, together with the family, is come and is here probably.

40. 田中さんの奥さんは台所で料理をしています。

Tanaka-san no okusan wa daidokoro de ryouri wo shite imasu.
As for Tanaka's wife, she is doing some cooking in the kitchen.

41. 白いエプロンは誰にもらいましたか。

Shiroi epuron wa dare ni moraimashita ka.
As for the white apron, from whom did he receive it?

42. 赤い車はいつから止まっていますか。

Akai kuruma wa itsu kara tomatte imasu ka.
As for the red car, since when is it being parked?

****

43. どうぞお上がりください。

Douzo oagari kudasai.
Go ahead, please honorably rise. (i.e., please come in)

44. 失礼します。

Shitsurei shimasu.
I will commit a discourtesy. (i.e., I'm sorry to bother you)

45. りっぱなお宅ですね。

Rippa na otaku desu ne.
It's a splendid honorable home, huh.

46. お茶でもいかがですか。

Ocha demo ikaga desu ka.
Honorable tea, at least, how is it?

47. お菓子もどうぞ。

Okashi mo douzo.
Sweets as well, go ahead.

48. 甘くておいしいですね。

Amakute oishii desu ne.
It's sweet and delicious, huh.

49. 家の中をご案内しましょうか。

Ie no naka wo go annai shimashou ka.
Shall I do a humble tour of the inside of the house?

50. あら、どうも。日本の家を見るのは初めてなんですよ。

Ara, doumo. Nihon no ie wo miru no wa hajimete nan desu yo.
Wow, thanks. As for to see a Japanese house, it's the first time, for sure.

51. 散らかっていますけど、どうぞ。

Chirakatte imasu kedo, douzo.
It's messy, but go ahead.

52. ここが食堂です。

Koko ga shokudou desu.
Here is the dining room.

53. きれいな絵が掛かっていますね。

Kirei na e ga kakate imasu ne.
A pretty picture is hanging, huh.

54. 恥ずかしいんですが、僕がかいたんですよ。

Hazukashiin desu ga, boku ga kaitan desu yo.
It's embarrassing, but I painted it, for sure.

55. えっ、本当ですか。お上手ですね。

E, hontou desu ka. Ojouzu desu ne.
Eh, is that true? You're honorably skillful, huh.

56. さあ、二階へ行きましょうか。

Saa, nikai e ikimashou ka.
Well, shall we go to the second floor?

57. ここが息子の部屋です。

Koko ga musuko no heya desu.
Here it's the son's room.

58. あれ、又電気が点けてある。

Are, mata denki ga tsukete aru.
Hey, again, the light has been turned on by someone.

59. おや、ギターが置いてありますね。

Oya, gitaa ga oite arimasu ne.
Hey. (to express surprise, doubt, etc.) A guitar is placed by someone, huh.

60. CDもたくさん並んでいますね。

Shiidii mo takusan narande imasu ne.
CD's also, a lot are lined up, huh.

61. 息子は音楽が大好きなんですよ。

Musuko wa ongaku ga daisuki nan desu yo.
As for the son, he loves music, for sure.

Chapter 66

1. 山川貿易の月野と申しますが課長の北村さんいらっしゃいますか。

Yamakawa boueki no tsukino to moushimasu ga kachou no kitamura-san irasshaimasu ka.
I am humbly called Yamakawa Trading's Tsukino, but does Section Manager's Kitamura honorably exist?

2. 黒田さん、その電話の横の資料を三部ずつ急いでコピーしておいて。

Kuroda-san, sono denwa no yoko no shiryou wo sanbu zutsu isoide kopii shite oite.
Kuroda, the literature beside that phone, three apiece, hurriedly, do copies in advance. ("bu" is a counter used for magazines and brochures)

3. 山川貿易の月野さんがいらっしゃるから。

Yamakawa boueki no tsukino-san ga irassharu kara.
Because Tsukino of Yamakawa Trading will honorably come.

4. この青いのですか。

Kono aoi no desu ka.
Is it this blue one?

5. いや、その白いの。

Iya, sono shiroi no.
Nah, that white one.

6. それから、大阪支社の報告は？

Sore kara, oosaka shisha no houkoku wa?
And then, as for the Osaka branch office report?

7. あ、そこのキャビネットの二番目の引き出しに入っていますよ。

A, soko no kyabinetto no niban me no hikidashi ni haitte imasu yo.
Ah, it is being entered in that place's cabinet's second drawer, for sure. ("me" is used as a counter for ordinal numbers in a series)

8. じゃ、これも頼むよ。

Ja, kore mo tanomu yo.
Well, this also I request, for sure.

9. コピーは僕の机の上に置いておいて。

Kopii wa boku no tsukue no ue ni oite oite.
As for the copies, put them on top of my desk in advance. (the 1st oite comes from oku = to place; the 2nd oite from oku = to do in advance)

10. 2時までにできる？

Niji made ni dekiru?
Can you do it by 2:00?

11. はい、急いでします。

Hai, isoide shimasu.
Yes, I'll do hurriedly.

****

12. 私、山川貿易の月野と申します。

Watakushi, yamakawa boueki no tsukino to moushimasu.
I am humbly called Yamakawa Trading's Tsukino.

13. 初めまして。

Hajimemashite.
Pleased to meet you.

14. 「月野洋」と読むんですか。

"Tsukino you" to yomun desu ka.
Do you read it as "Tsukino you"?

15. いや、「洋」と書いて「ひろし」と読むんです。

Iya, "you" to kaite "hiroshi" to yomun desu.
Nah, you write it as "you," and you read it as "Hiroshi."

16. なるほど。日本人の名前は難しいですね。

Naruhodo. Nihonjin no namae wa muzukashii desu ne.
I see. Japanese people's names are difficult, huh.

17. 誰が誰に電話を掛けましたか。

Dare ga dare ni denwa wo kakemashita ka.
Who, to whom, called on the phone?

18. 月野さんとデイビスさんは前に会ったことがありますか。

Tsukino-san to deibisu-san wa mae ni atta koto ga arimasu ka.
Have Tsukino and Davis met at before?

****

19. 会長。社長。

Kaichou. Shachou.
Chairman of the board.
Company president.

20. 部長。課長。係長。主任。

Buchou. Kachou. Kakarichou. Shunin.
Division manager. Section manager. Assistant manager. Foreman, or person in charge.

21. 少しずつ入れてください。

Sukoshi zutsu irete kudasai.
Please insert, or add, a little at a time.

22. いくつもらいましたか。

Ikutsu moraimashita ka.
How many did he receive?

23. 全部で二つもらいました。

Zenbu de futatsu moraimashita.
Altogether he received two.

24. お子さんは何人ですか。

Okosan wa nannin desu ka.
As for honorable children, how many people is it?

25. 女の子と男の子が二人ずつい
ます。

Onna no ko to otoko no ko ga futari zutsu imasu.
Girls and boys, two each exist.

26. お寿司は何を食べましたか。

Osushi wa nani wo tabemashita ka.
As for honorable sushi, what did you eat?

27. トロとエビを三つずつ食べま
した。

Toro to ebi wo mittsu zutsu tabemashita.
Fatty tuna and shrimp, three apiece I ate.

28. 全部で六つ食べました。

Zenbu de muttsu tabemashita.
Altogether I ate six.

29. 会議があるから資料をコピー
しておきましょう。

Kaigi ga aru kara shiryou wo kopii shite okimashou.
Since a meeting exists, let's copy the literature in advance.

30. 全部で 20 枚です。

Zenbu de nijuumai desu.
Altogether, it's 20 sheets.

****

31. お客さんが来ます。何をして
おきますか。

Okyaku-san ga kimasu. Nani wo shite okimasu ka.
Honorable guests will come. What will they do in advance?

32. 真一は部屋を片付けておきま
す。

Shin'ichi wa heya wo katatzukete okimasu.
Shin'ichi will straighten up the room in advance.

33. お母さんは料理をしておきま
す。

Okaasan wa ryouri wo shite okimasu.
Honorable Mother will do some cooking in advance.

34. 旅行をします。その前にどん
なことをしておきますか。

Ryokou wo shimasu. Sono mae ni donna koto wo shite okimasu ka.
I will travel. At before that, what kinds of things will I do in advance?

35. スーツケースに荷物を入れて
おきます。

Suutsukeesu ni nimotsu wo irete okimasu.
I will put baggage in the suitcase in advance.

36. ホテルを予約しておきます。

Hoteru wo yoyaku shite okimasu.
I will reserve a hotel in advance.

37. 切符を買っておきます。

Kippu wo katte okimasu.
I will buy a ticket in advance.

38. 結婚します。その前にどんな
ことをしておきますか。

Kekkon shimasu. Sono mae ni donna koto wo shite okimasu ka.
I will marry. At before that, what kinds of things will I do in advance?

39. 部屋を借りておきます。

Heya wo karite okimasu.
I will rent a room in advance.

40. 家具を買っておきます。

Kagu wo katte okimasu.
I will buy furniture in advance.

****

41. 電車に乗って行きましょう。

Densha ni notte ikimashou.
Riding by train, let's go. (i.e., let's go riding by train)

42. 寝ぼうしたのであわててうち
を出ました。

Neboushita node awatete uchi wo demashita.
Since I overslept, I left home in a frenzy.

43. 時間がないからタクシーに乗
って行きましょう。

Jikan ga nai kara takushii ni notte ikimashou.
Since there isn't time, let's go riding in a taxi.

44. 学校から家まで歩いて帰りま
すか。

Gakkou kara ie made aruite kaerimasu ka.
Do you return from school until the house walking?

45. いいえ、電車に乗って帰りま
す。

Iie, densha ni notte kaerimasu.
No, I return riding a train.

46. 日本語はどうやって覚えます
か。

Nihongo wa dou yatte oboemasu ka.
As for Japanese, how doing do you memorize it?

47. テープを聞いて覚えます。

Teepu wo kiite oboemasu.
I memorize listening to tapes.

48. ウエッブさんはどうやってカ
タカナを勉強しますか。

Uebbu-san wa douyatte katakana wo benkyou shimasu ka.
As for Webb, how doing does he study katakana?

49. 電車の中の広告を見て勉強し
ます。

Densha no naka no koukoku wo mite benkyou shimasu.
He studies looking at inside-the-train's ads.

50. 来週テストがありますから、
それまでにこの漢字を覚えた
いんです。

Raishuu tesuto ga arimasu kara, sore made ni kono kanji wo oboetain desu.
Since a test exists next week, by then, I want to memorize these kanji.

51. すみません。急いでいるんで
すがこのシャツ、あさってま
でにできますか。

Sumimasen. Isoide irun desu ga kono shatsu asatte made ni dekimasu ka.
Excuse me. I'm hurrying, but will these shirts accomplish by the day after tomorrow? (i.e., will they be ready?)

52. あさってですね。はい、で
きますよ。

Asatte desu ne. Hai, dekimasu yo.
It's the day after tomorrow, huh. Yes, they will accomplish, for sure. (i.e., they'll be done)

53. 私が行くまで待っていてくだ
さいね。

Watashi ga iku made matte ite kudasai ne.
Until I go, please be waiting, huh.

54. 急いで2時までに行きますか
ら。

Isoide niji made ni ikimasu kara.
Because I'll go hurriedly by 2:00.

55. あさってから夏休みですか
ら、仕事を明日までに終わり
たいと思います。

Asatte kara natsuyasumi desu kara, shigoto wo ashita made ni owaritai to omoimasu.
Since summer vacation is from the day after tomorrow, I'd like the work to finish by tomorrow, I think.

56. この犬、どうしたの？

Kono inu, doushita no?
This dog, how did it do? (i.e., what's wrong?)

57. 元気がないですね。

Genki ga nai desu ne.
Health doesn't exist, huh.

58. 危なかった。遅刻すると思っ
たよ。

Abunakatta. Chikoku suru to omotta yo.
It was dangerous. I will be tardy, I thought, for sure.

59. ギリギリ間に合ったね。

Girigiri maniatta ne.
At the last moment you were on time, huh.

60. よく練習したのでやっとでき
るようになりました。

Yoku renshuu shita node yatto dekiru you ni narimashita.
Since I did practice often, at last I got to the point that I was able.

61. 子供に薬を飲ませたんです
が、なかなか熱が下がらない
んですよ。

Kodomo ni kusuri wo nomasetan desu ga, nakanaka netsu ga sagaranain desu yo.
To the child, I made drink medicine, but readily, the fever doesn't go down, for sure.

Chapter 67

1. はい、上田でございます。

Hai, ueda de gozaimasu.
Yes, this is Ueda. (answering the phone)

2. 木村は席を外しております
が。

Kimura wa seki wo hazushite orimasu ga...
Kimura is leaving the seat humbly, but...

3. 森は外出中ですが...

Mori wa gaishutsu chuu desu ga...
Mori is in the middle of going out, but...

4. 島田は会議中ですが...

Shimada wa kaigi chuu desu ga...
Shimada is in the middle of a meeting, but...

5. 高橋は出かけておりますが...

Takahashi wa dekakete orimasu ga...
Takahashi is departing humbly, but...

6. 山口はまだ帰りませんが...

Yamaguchi wa mada kaerimasen ga...
Yamaguchi still doesn't return, but...

7. 何かお言付けがありますか。

Nanika okotozuke ga arimasu ka.
Is there anything honorable message?

8. いいえ、結構です。

Iie, kekkou desu.
No, it's fine.

9. 真一さんは道子さんにお酒を
飲ませました。

Shin'ichi-san wa michiko-san ni osake wo nomasemashita.
As for Shin'ichi, he made Michiko drink honorable sake.

10. 森田さんをお願いします。

Morita-san wo onegaishimasu.
May I speak to Morita?

11. 森田はただいま出かけており
ますが...

Morita wa tadaima dekakete orimasu ga...
As for Morita, right this moment he is being departed humbly, but...

12. じゃ、帰ったらミラーから電
話があったとお伝えくださ
い。

Ja, kaettara miraa kara denwa ga atta to otsutae kudasai.
Well, when he returns, please report that there was a phone call from Miller.

****

13. 田辺さんは遅いですね。

Tanabe-san wa osoi desu ne.
As for Tanabe, he's late, huh.

14. 場所が分からないのかもしれませんねぇ。

Basho ga wakaranai no kamoshiremasen nee.
He might not know/understand the place, huh.

15. ちゃんと伝えたから知ってるはずですがねぇ。

Chanto tsutaeta kara shitteru hazu desu ga nee.
Since I reported precisely, he should be knowing, but... huh.

16. メモと一緒に地図も渡したし...

Memo to issho ni chizu mo watashita shi...
A memo and together also a map I handed and...

****

17. 遅くなりました。

Osoku narimashita.
I became late.

18. 日比谷からタクシーに乗ったんだけど道がひどく込んでねぇ。

Hibiya kara takushii ni nottan dakedo michi ga hidoku konde nee.
From Hibiya, I rode in a taxi, but streets awfully crowded, huh.

19. 今日は金曜日ですからねぇ。

Kyou wa kinyoubi desu kara nee.
Because today is Friday, huh.

20. じゃ、そろそろ始めましょうか。

Jaa sorosoro hajimemashou ka.
Well, shall we start it gradually?

21. あれ、花田さんは来ないの？

Are, hanada-san wa konai no?
Hey, as for Hanada, won't she come?

22. 少し遅くなるけど来るはずです。

Sukoshi osoku naru kedo kuru hazu desu.
She'll become a little late, but she's supposed to come.

23. それから広報課の池田さんも仕事が早く終わったら来ると言ってました。

Sore kara kouhouka no ikeda-san mo shigoto ga hayaku owattara kuru to ittemashita.
And then, the Public Relations Section's Ikeda also, if the work finishes early, he will come, he was saying.

****

24. 今度皆さんと一緒に働くことになりました。

Kondo minasan to issho ni hataraku koto ni narimashita.
This time, together with honorable everyone, it was scheduled that I will labor.

25. 一ヶ月前にニューヨークから来ました。

Ikka getsu mae ni nyuuyooku kara kimashita.
At one month ago, I came from New York.

26. アメリカでは銀行に勤めていましたが、大学で日本語を少し習ったし...

Amerika de wa ginkou ni tsutomete imashita ga, daigaku de nihongo wo sukoshi naratta shi.
As for in America, I was employed in a bank, but in college I learned a little Japanese and...

27. 時間があったら旅行もしたいと思っています。

Jikan ga attara ryokou mo shitai to omotte imasu.
If there is time, travel also I'd like to do, I'm thinking.

28. 家族は妻と二人です。

Kazoku wa tsuma to futari desu.
As for the family, with the wife it's two people.

29. どうぞよろしくお願いします。

Douzo yoroshiku onegai shimasu.
Go ahead, be good to me.

****

30. この近くにいい店があるんです。

Kono chikaku ni ii mise ga arun desu.
At this closely, a good store exists. (i.e., nearby there's a good bar)

31. そうですね。せっかくですが今日はビールも飲んだし、お酒も飲んだから、気分が少し...

Sou desu nee. Sekkaku desu ga kyou wa biiru mo nonda shi, osake mo nonda kara, kibun ga sukoshi...
Let me see. It's kind of you, but as for today, since I also drank beer and also drank honorable sake, the health-related feeling is a little...

32. そうですか。少し飲み過ぎたんですね。

Sou desu ka. Sukoshi nomisugitan desu ne.
Is that so? A little, you drank too much, huh.

33. ええ、今日は早く帰ることにします。

Ee, kyou wa hayaku kaeru koto ni shimasu.
Yeah, as for today, I decide to return early.

34. そうですね。残念ですがそうしましょう。

Sou desu ne. Zannen desu ga, sou shimashou.
That's so huh. That's too bad, but let's do so.

****

35. 田辺さんは地図とメモを持っていました。

Tanabe-san wa chizu to memo wo motte imashita.
Tanabe was having a map and a memo.

36. 田辺さんは電車が込んで遅れました。

Tanabe-san wa densha ga konde okuremashita.
As for Tanabe, because the train gets crowded, he was delayed.

37. ブラウンさんはニューヨークから二ヶ月前に来ました。

Buraun-san wa nyuuyooku kara nikagetsu mae ni kimashita.
Brown came from New York at two months ago.

38. テイラーさんは日本の会社で日本語を勉強しました。

Teiraa-san wa nihon no kaisha de nihongo wo benkyou shimashita.
Taylor studied Japanese at a Japanese company.

39. アンダーソンさんには子供はいません。

Andaason-san ni wa kodomo wa imasen.
As for to the Andersons, there are no children.

40. ジャクソンさんは今いい気分です。

Jakuson-san wa ima ii kibun desu.
As for Jackson, now it's good health-related feeling.

41. ホワイトさんはこれからみんなと近くの店に行きます。

Howaito-san wa kore kara minna to chikaku no mise ni ikimasu.
As for White, from now, with everyone, he will go to closely's store. (i.e., the one nearby)

42. この店のコーヒーはおいしいはずです。

Kono mise no koohii wa oishii hazu desu.
This shop's coffee ought to be delicious.

43. 木村さんはまだ仕事をしているから、来ないはずです。

Kimura-san wa mada shigoto wo shite iru kara, konai hazu desu.
Since Kimura is still working, I expect him not to come.

44. 島田さんは遅いですねぇ。

Shimada-san wa osoi desu nee.
Shimada is late, huh.

45. 田辺さんはもう出かけましたか。

Tanabe-san wa mou dekakemashita ka.
Did Tanabe depart already?

46. 田辺さんの車があるからまだ出かけていないはずです。

Tanabe-san no kuruma ga aru kara mada dekakete inai hazu desu.
Since Tanabe's car exists, he should still not be departed.

47. チンさんは何人でしょうか。

Chin-san wa nani jin deshou ka.
What nationality is Chin, probably?

48. ペキンから来たと言っていたから、中国人のはずです。

Pekin kara kita to itte ita kara, chugokujin no hazu desu.
Since he was saying that he came from Beijing, he ought to be a Chinese person.

49. 田辺さんはバスで来ますか。

Tanabe-san wa basu de kimasu ka.
Will Tanabe come by bus?

50. いや、地下鉄の駅からタクシーで来るはずですよ。

Iya, chikatetsu no eki kara takushii de kuru hazu desu yo.
Nah, from the subway station, he ought to come by taxi, for sure.

51. 地図を持っているから場所を知っているはずです。

Chizu wo motte iru kara basho wo shitte iru hazu desu.
Since she is having a map, she ought to be knowing the place.

52. 病気だから今日は来ないはずです。

Byouki dakara kyou wa konai hazu desu.
Since she's sick, as for today, I expect her not to come.

53. 土曜日だから銀行は休みのはずです。

Doyoubi dakara ginkou wa yasumi no hazu desu.
Since it's Saturday, the banks ought to be holiday. (i.e., closed)

54. 明りが点いているから、誰かいるはずです。

Akari ga tsuite iru kara, dareka iru hazu desu.
Since the lamp is on, someone ought to exist.

55. ああ、良かった。ここは開いている。

Aa, yokatta. Koko wa aite iru.
Ah, it was good. (i.e., it is good) As for here, it's open.

56. 他の人が使っています。少し待ちましょう。

Hoka no hito ga tsukatte imasu. Sukoshi machimashou.
Another person is using it. Let's wait a bit.

57. 今、会議をしているんですね。

Ima kaigi wo shite irun desu ne.
Now a meeting is being done by someone, huh. (i.e, being held)

58. 又、後で来ましょう。

Mata ato de kimashou.
Again, of later, let's come. (i.e., let's come again later)

Chapter 68

1. バーゲンセールだから安いはずです。

Baagenseeru dakara yasui hazu desu.
Since it's a bargain sale, it should be cheap.

2. 渡辺さんはパーティーに来るでしょうか。

Watanabe-san wa paatii ni kuru deshou ka.
Will Watanabe probably come to the party?

3. 多分来るだろうと思います。

Tabun kuru darou to omoimasu.
Probably he will probably come, I think.

4. 飲み物は何にしますか。

Nomimono wa nan ni shimasu ka.
As for drinks, what will you choose?
(nani ni shimasu, also OK)

5. 暑いからビールにしましょうか。

Atsui kara biiru ni shimashou ka.
Since it's hot, shall I choose beer?

6. 来年からフランス語を勉強することにしました。

Rainen kara furansugo wo benkyou suru koto ni shimashita.
I decided to study French starting next year.

7. 会議は10時に始めることにします。

Kaigi wa juuji ni hajimeru koto ni shimasu.
As for the meeting, I decide to start it at 10:00.

8. 電車に乗るときは広告を見ながら漢字の勉強をすることにしています。

Densha ni noru toki wa koukoku wo mi nagara kanji no benkyou wo suru koto ni shite imasu.
As for to-ride-the-train time, while I look at advertisements, my routine is to do kanji's study.

9. 会議は10時から始めることになりました。

Kaigi wa juuji kara hajimeru koto ni narimashita.
As for the meeting, it was scheduled that someone will start it from 10:00.

10. デパートは今日は休みですよ。

Depaato wa kyou wa yasumi desu yo.
As for the department stores, today is a holiday, for sure.

11. じゃ、明日行くことにします。

Ja, ashita iku koto ni shimasu.
Well, I will decide to go tomorrow.

12. 昼ご飯はいつもサンドイッチ
を食べることにしています。

Hirugohan wa itsumo sandoicchi wo
taberu koto ni shite imasu.
As for lunch, I am always deciding to eat
a sandwich.

13. 疲れたので今日はもう、うち
に帰ることにする。

Tsukareta node kyou wa mou, uchi ni
kaeru koto ni suru.
Because I got tired, as for today, already
I will decide to return to home.

14. では、話の続きは明日にしま
しょう。

Dewa, hanashi no tsuzuki wa ashita ni
shimashou.
Well, as for the continuation of the
conversation, let's do it tomorrow.

****

15. 山口さんは朝9時に会議に出
ることになっています。

Yamaguchi-san wa asa kuji ni kaigi ni
deru koto ni natte imasu.
Yamaguchi is scheduled to attend the
meeting at 9:00 in the morning.

16. 山口さんは10時半に読売新
聞社の人に会うことになって
います。

Yamaguchi-san wa juuji han ni yomiuri
shinbunsha no hito ni au koto ni natte
imasu.
Yamaguchi is scheduled to meet a person
from the Yomiuri newspaper company at
half past nine.

17. 1時に文法社に行って4時半
に会社に戻ることになってい
ます。

Ichiji ni bunpou sha ni itte yoji han ni
kaisha ni modoru koto ni natte imasu.
At 1:00, he will go to the Bunpou
company, and at half past 4, he's
scheduled to return to the company.

18. 3時から会議があって、7時
に朝日社の水野さんと会うこ
とになっています。

Sanji kara kaigi ga atte, shichiji ni asahi
sha no mizuno-san to au koto ni natte
imasu.
From 3:00 there's a meeting, and at 7:00
he is scheduled to meet with Mizuno
from Asahi company.

****

19. ダイヤのネックレスは私には
高すぎます。

Daiya no nekkuresu wa watashi ni wa
takasugimasu.
The diamond necklace, as for to me, is
too expensive.

20. このシャツは大き過ぎます。

Kono shatsu wa ookisugimasu.
This shirt is too big.

21. 今、箱にりんごが三つ入って
います。

Ima hako ni ringo ga mittsu haitte imasu.
Now, in the box, apples, three are being
entered.

22. 今、箱にりんごが一つも入っ
ていません。

Ima hako ni ringo ga hitotsu mo haitte
imasen.
Now, in the box, not even one apple is
being entered.

23. 明日テニスに行くときお金を忘れないでね。

Ashita tenisu ni iku toki okane wo wasurenai de ne.
Tomorrow, when we go for the purpose of tennis, don't forget the money, huh.

24. あまり遅く帰ってくるなよ。

Amari osoku kaette kuru na yo.
Don't return and come very late, for sure. (na = don't do, used by men)

25. 赤ちゃんがいるのでタバコを吸わないでいただけませんか。

Akachan ga iru node tabako wo suwanai de itadakemasen ka.
Because a baby exists, can you not not-smoke tobacco and I receive?

26. 日本語の新聞は難しくてなかなか読めませんでしたが、最近は少し読めるようになりました。

Nihongo no shinbun wa muzukashikute, nakanaka yomemasen deshita ga, saikin wa, sukoshi yomeru you ni narimashita.
As for Japanese language newspapers, since difficult, readily I could not read, but as for recently, a little, it got to the point that I was able to read.

27. 寿司が好きでよく寿司屋へ行きます。

Sushi ga suki de yoku sushiya e ikimasu.
Since I like sushi, I often go to a sushi place.

28. 病気で学校を休みました。

Byouki de, gakkou wo yasumimashita.
Since I was sick, I missed school.

29. 飲み物は何がいいですか。コーヒーがいいですか、紅茶がいいですか。

Nomimono wa nani ga ii desu ka.
Koohii ga ii desu ka, kocha ga ii desu ka.
As for drinks, what is good? Is coffee good, is black tea good?

30. 今日は暑いからアイスコーヒーがいいですね。

Kyou wa atsui kara aisu koohii ga ii desu ne.
Since today is hot, iced coffee is good, huh.

31. 食事は何がいいですか。

Shokuji wa nani ga ii desu ka.
As for a meal, what is good?

32. 明日は10時に行きましょうか。

Ashita wa juuji ni ikimashou ka.
As for tomorrow, shall we go at 10:00?

33. いいえ、それでは遅すぎます。9時までに来てください。

Iie, sore de wa ososugimasu. Kuji made ni kite kudasai.
No, in that case, it's too late. Please come by 9:00.

34. 暑かったら窓を開けてください。

Atsukattara mado wo akete kudasai.
If it's hot, please open the window.

35. おいしい寿司だったら食べます。

Oishii sushi dattara tabemasu.
If it's delicious sushi, I'll eat it.

36. 石田さんも一緒に来たら良かったですね。

Ishida-san mo issho ni kitara yokatta desu ne.
If Ishida also together had come, it was good, huh.

37. もし道が込んでいたら電車で行きます。

Moshi michi ga konde itara densha de ikimasu.
If the street is being crowded, I'll go by train.

38. もしも百万円あったらダイヤを買います。

Moshimo hyaku man en attara daiya wo kaimasu.
If 1 million yen exist, I'll buy a diamond.

39. もし明日雨が降ったらうちで本を読みます。

Moshi ashita ame ga futtara uchi de hon wo yomimasu.
If it rains tomorrow, I'll read a book at home.

40. もし部屋が寒かったらストーブを点けてください。

Moshi heya ga samukattara sutoobu wo tsukete kudasai.
If the room is cold, please turn on the space heater.

41. 日本語が上手になったらガイドになりたいです。

Nihongo ga jouzu ni nattara gaido ni naritai desu.
When the Japanaese becomes skillful, I would like to become a guide.

42. 電車の中には新聞を読んでいる人もいるし、寝ている人もいます。

Densha no naka ni wa shinbun wo yonde iru hito mo iru shi, nete iru hito mo imasu.
As for inside the train, people who are reading newspapers also exist, and people who are sleeping also exist.

43. 明日テニスをしませんか。

Ashita tenisu wo shimasen ka.
Tomorrow, won't you play tennis?

44. そうですね。でも明日は映画も見たいし...

Sou desu nee. Demo ashita wa eiga mo mitai shi...
Let me see. But as for tomorrow, I also want to see a movie, and so therefore...

45. そのアパートは駅から遠いし狭いから、あまり良くありません。

Sono apaato wa eki kara tooi shi semai kara, amari yoku arimasen.
That apartment is far from the station and, because it's small, it isn't very good.

46. このナイフは軽いし良く切れるしそれに安いんです。

Kono naifu wa karui shi yoku kireru shi sore ni yasuin desu.
As for this knife, it's light, and it cuts well and, moreover, it's cheap.

47. 地下鉄は速いし便利だからよく乗ります。

Chikatetsu wa hayai shi benri dakara yoku norimasu.
The subways are fast and, because they're convenient, I ride them often.

48. お菓子を小さく切ってください。

Okashi wo chiisaku kitte kudasai.
Please cut the sweets small (i.e. into small pieces).

49. あのレストランはおいしいし安いからいつも込んでいます。

Ano resutoran wa oishii shi yasui kara itsumo konde imasu.
That restaurant over there is delicious and, because it's cheap, it's always crowded.

50. 日光は近いし有名だから一度行ったらどうですか。

Nikkou wa chikai shi yuumei dakara ichido ittara dou desu ka.
Nikkou is close and, since it's famous, if you go once, how would it be?

51. もう 12 時になりましたね。

Mou juuniji ni narimashita ne.
It already became 12:00, huh.

52. 急いで行きましょう。

Isoide ikimashou.
Let's go hurriedly.

53. 字は大きく書いてください。

Ji wa ookiku kaite kudasai.
As for the characters, please write them large.

54. 今度の旅行にはアンドリューさんは行かないようですよ。

Kondo no ryokou ni wa andoryuu-san wa ikanai you desu yo.
As for to this next trip, as for Andrew, it seems he will not go, for sure.

55. 何か間違いでもしたんでしょうか。

Nanika machigai demo shitan deshou ka.
Something mistake at least did I do probably?

Chapter 69

1. ジェイコブさんが帰りの電車の中で思ったこと。

Jeikobu-san ga kaeri no densha no naka de omotta koto.
Jacob, inside the return's train thought/ felt thing.

2. 公園で桜の花を見ながらお酒を飲むのは初めてだった。

Kouen de sakura no hana wo mi nagara osake wo nomu no wa hajimete datta.
In a park, while looking at cherry blossoms, as for to drink honorable sake, it was the first time.

3. 夜だから寒いだろうと思っていたがそうでもなかった。

Yoru dakara samui darou to omotte ita ga, sou demo nakatta.
Since it is night, I was thinking it will probably be cold, but it wasn't so at all.

4. 私はちょっと飲み過ぎた。

Watashi wa chotto nomi sugita.
As for me, I drank a little too much.

5. 青い顔でうちに帰ったらオリビアは心配するだろう。

Aoi kao de uchi ni kaettara oribia wa shinpai suru darou.
With a blue face, if I return home, as for Olivia, she will probably do worry. (aoi kao = blue face, i.e., looking sick)

6. でも赤い顔で帰ったら怒るかもしれないし...

Demo akai kao de kaettara okoru kamoshirenai shi...
But if I return with a red face, she might get angry and... (akai kao = red face, i.e., looking drunk)

7. そうだ、途中でコーヒーを飲んで帰ることにしよう。

Sou da, tochuu de koohii wo nonde kaeru koto ni shiyou.
That's so. (i.e., I got an idea) On the way, I shall decide to drink coffee and return.

8. ジェイコブさんは今とても気分がいい。

Jeikobu-san wa ima totemo kibun ga ii.
As for Jacob, now, very much the health-related feeling is good.

****

9. ちょっと小包を出しに行ってきます。

Chotto kozutsumi wo dashi ni itte kimasu.
For a moment, I will go for the purpose of sending a package and return.

10. すみませんけど、ついでに切手とはがきを買ってきてくれませんか。

Sumimasen kedo, tsuide ni kitte to hagaki wo katte kite kuremasen ka.
Excuse me, but while you're at it, won't you buy some stamps and postcards and come and give?

11. はい、いいですよ。どのくらい買ってきましょうか。

Hai, ii desu yo. Dono kurai katte kimashou ka.
Yes, it's good, for sure. About how many shall I buy and come?

12. 62円の切手を300枚とはがきを100枚、お願いします。

Roku juu ni en no kitte wo sanbyakumai to hagaki wo hyakumai, onegai shimasu.
62-yen stamps, 300, and postcards, 100, if you please.

13. なるべく早く帰ってきます。

Narubeku hayaku kaette kimasu.
I will return and come as quickly as possible.

****

14. この小包お願いします。

Kono kozutsumi onegai shimasu.
This package if you please.

15. 船便ですか。

Funabin desu ka.
Is it ship mail?

16. 船便ではアメリカまでどのくらいかかりますか。

Funabin de wa amerika made dono kurai kakarimasu ka.
As for by ship mail, until America, about how long will it take?

17. 3週間ぐらいで届きますか。

San shuukan gurai de todokimasu ka.
Will it arrive in about three weeks?

18. 普通は届きますが、今込んでいるから3週間で届くかどうか分かりませんよ。

Futsuu wa todokimasu ga, ima konde iru kara sanshuukan de todoku ka douka wakarimasen yo.
As for ordinarily it will arive, but since it's crowded now, I don't know/understand whether it will arrive in three weeks, for sure.

19. それからお金を送りたいんですが、何番の窓口へ行ったらいいんでしょうか。

Sore kara okane wo okuritain desu ga, nanban no madoguchi e ittara iin deshou ka.
And then, I'd like to send money, but to what number service window, if I go, will it probably be good?

****

20. 駅の前に新しいレストランができましたよ。

Eki no mae ni atarashii resutoran ga dekimashita yo.
In front of the station, a new restaurant was accomplished, for sure.

21. 今度一緒に食べに行ってみましょう。

Kondo issho ni tabe ni itte mimashou.
Next time, together, for the purpose of to eat, let's go and see.

22. 一緒に映画を見に行きません
か。

Issho ni eiga wo mi ni ikimasen ka.
Won't you go together to see a movie?

23. 日本へは何をしに来たのです
か。

Nihon e wa nani wo shi ni kita no desu
ka.
As for to Japan, what did you come to
do?

24. 日本語を勉強しに来ました。

Nihongo wo benkyou shi ni kimashita.
I came to study Japanese.

25. あの人に道を聞いてみましょ
う。

Ano hito ni michi wo kiite mimashou.
Let's ask that person over there the way
and see.

26. 海に泳ぎに行きます。

Umi ni oyogi ni ikimasu.
To the ocean, he will go for the purpose
of swimming.

27. 魚を買って来ます。

Sakana wo katte kimasu.
I will buy some fish and come.

28. 辞書を引けば分かると思いま
すよ。

Jisho wo hikeba wakaru to omoimasu yo.
If you consult on a dictionary, then you
will understand, I think, for sure.

29. 病院へ行って薬をもらって来
てください。

Byouin e itte kusuri wo moratte kite
kudasai.
Please go to the hospital, receive the
medicine and come.

30. 銀行へ行ってお金を下ろして
来てください。

Ginkou e itte okane wo oroshite kite
kudasai.
Please go to the bank, withdraw some
money and come.

31. 明日、成田空港に行ってき
ます。

Ashita narita kuukou ni itte kimasu.
Tomorrow I will go to Narita airport and
come.

32. 昨日は動物園でパンダの赤ち
ゃんを見てきました。

Kinou wa doubutsuen de panda no
akachan wo mite kimashita.
As for yesterday, at the zoo, I saw the
panda baby and came.

33. さっき新聞屋さんがお金を取
りに来ました。

Sakki shinbunya-san ga okane wo tori ni
kimashita.
Previously, Mr. Newspaper Store came
for the purpose of getting money.

34. 明日、図書館で本を借りてき
ます。

Ashita toshokan de hon wo karite
kimasu.
Tomorrow I will borrow books at the
library and come.

35. いつかお宅に行きたいんですが。

Itsuka otaku ni ikitain desu ga...
Sometime, I'd like to go to the honorable home (i.e., your home), but...

36. 火曜日でなかったらいつでもいいですよ。

Kayoubi de nakattara itsudemo ii desu yo.
If it isn't a Tuesday, anytime is good, for sure.

37. 火曜日はいつもダンスを習いに行っているんです。

Kayoubi wa itsumo dansu wo narai ni itte irun desu.
As for Tuesdays, I'm always going for the purpose of learning dancing.

38. ああ、それで火曜日はいつもうちにいないんですね。

Aa, sore de kayoubi wa itsumo uchi ni inain desu ne.
Ah, for that reason, as for Tuesdays, always you are not at home, huh.

39. 今日誰かあなたのうちに来ますか。

Kyou dareka anata no uchi ni kimasu ka.
Today will someone come to your home?
(dareka ga, also OK)

40. いいえ、誰も来ません。

Iie, daremo kimasen.
No, no one will come.

41. 日本語しか分からなかったら外国に行ったとき困りませんか。

Nihongo shika wakaranakattara gaikoku ni itta toki komarimasen ka.
If except for Japanese only you don't understand, the time you went to a foreign country (after going), will you not get inconvenienced?

42. この前の日曜日はどこかへ行きましたか。

Kono mae no nichiyoubi wa dokoka e ikimashita ka.
As for this past Sunday, did you go somewhere?

43. いいえ、どこにも行きませんでした。

Iie, doko ni mo ikimasen deshita.
No, I didn't go to nowhere.

44. 日曜日はどこも込んでいますから。

Nichiyoubi wa dokomo konde imasu kara.
Because, as for Sunday, everywhere is crowded.

45. 隣の部屋に誰かいますか。

Tonari no heya ni dareka imasu ka.
Is someone in the room next door?

46. 誰もいませんでしたよ。

Daremo imasen deshita yo.
No one was there, for sure.

47. 地下鉄はいつもこんなに込んでいるんですか。

Chikatetsu wa itsumo konna ni konde irun desu ka.
Are the subways always this crowded?

48. いいえ、朝と夕方だけです。

Iie, asa to yuugata dake desu.
No, it's only morning and evening.

49. 寿司や天ぷらは食べますか。

Sushi ya tenpura wa tabemasu ka.
As for sushi, tempura, etc., do you eat them?

50. ええ、どちらも好きだからよく食べますよ。

Ee, dochira mo suki dakara yoku tabemasu yo.
Yeah, since I like either of them, I eat them often, for sure.

51. 今度の旅行はどこに行きましょうか。

Kondo no ryokou wa doko ni ikimashou ka.
As for the next trip, where shall we go?

52. 私はどこでもいいですよ。

Watashi wa dokodemo ii desu yo.
As for me, anywhere is good, for sure.

53. 北海道に行ったことがありますか。

Hokkaidou ni itta koto ga arimasu ka.
Have you gone to Hokkaido?

54. いいえ、でもいつか行きたいと思っています。

Iie, demo itsuka ikitai to omotte imasu.
No, but sometime I would like to go, I'm thinking.

55. お母さん、このケーキ食べてもいい?

Okaasan, kono keeki tabete mo ii?
Mother, OK if I eat this cake?

56. だめよ。お客様に出すんだから。

Dame yo. Okyakusama ni dasun dakara.
Bad, for sure. Since I will put it out to very honorable guests.

57. その切手は誰がくれたんですか。

Sono kitte wa dare ga kuretan desu ka.
As for that stamp, who gave it to you?

58. 弟がくれました。

Otouto ga kuremashita.
My younger brother gave it to me.

59. 新しいのは一つもありません。

Atarashii no wa hitotsu mo arimasen.
As for new ones, not even one exists.

Chapter 70

1. 明日天気が良くなるかどうか分かりません。

Ashita tenki ga yoku naru ka douka wakarimasen.
Tomorrow I don't know whether the weather will become good.

2. 上田さんは来ますか。

Ueda-san wa kimasu ka.
Will Ueda come?

3. 来るかどうか分からないから電話で聞いてみます。

Kuru ka douka wakaranai kara denwa de kiite mimasu.
Since I don't know whether he will come, I will ask by telephone and see.

4. その箱に何か入っていますか。

Sono hako ni nanika haitte imasu ka.
In that box, is something entered?

5. 何が入っているかどうか分からないから開けてみます。

Nani ga haitte iru ka douka wakaranai kara, akete mimasu.
Since I don't know whether something is being entered in it, I will open it and see.

6. 土田さんは今度の木曜日は都合がいいですか。

Tsuchida-san wa kondo no mokuyoubi wa tsugou ga ii desu ka.
As for Tsuchida, as for next Thursday, are the circumstances good?

7. 都合がいいかどうか分からないから聞いてみます。

Tsugou ga ii ka douka wakaranai kara, kiite mimasu.
Since I don't know whether the circumstances are good, I will ask and see.

8. 歯医者さんは部屋にいますか。

Haisha-san wa heya ni imasu ka.
Is the dentist in the room?

9. 部屋にいるかどうか分からないから見てみます。

Heya ni iru ka douka wakaranai kara mite mimasu.
Since I don't know whether he's in the room, I will look and see.

10. この頃はアメリカでもお寿司をよく食べるそうですね。

Kono goro wa amerika de mo osushi wo yoku taberu sou desu ne.
As for nowadays, in America also, reportedly they eat honorable sushi often, huh.

11. 夕べは遅く帰りました。

Yuube wa osoku kaerimashita.
As for last night, you returned late.

12. 区役所はまだ開いています
か。

Kuyakusho wa mada aite imasu ka.
Is the ward office still open?

13. 開いているかどうか分からな
いけれど行ってみます。

Aite iru ka douka wakarani keredo itte
mimasu.
Whether it is open I don't know, but I'll
go and see.

14. その魚はおいしいですか。

Sono sakana wa oishii desu ka.
Is that fish delicious?

15. おいしいかどうか分からない
けれど食べてみます。

Oishii ka douka wakaranai keredo tabete
mimasu.
Whether it's delicious I don't know, but
I'll eat it and see.

16. 今日は火曜日だからゴミを出
しちゃいけませんよ。

Kyou wa kayoubi dakara gomi wo
dashicha ikemasen yo.
Since today is Tuesday, you must not
throw out garbage, for sure. (dashite wa
= dashicha = as for throwing)

17. あら、このセーター、水で洗
っちゃだめなんだわ。

Ara, kono seetaa, mizu de aratcha dame
nan da wa.
Hey, this sweater, in water, it's bad to
wash. (aratcha = aratte wa = as for
washing)

18. 日本では会社の人達が一緒に
旅行をするそうですね。

Nihon de wa kaisha no hitotachi ga issho
ni ryokou wo suru sou desu ne.
As for in Japan, company's people
reportedly travel together, huh.

19. 一年に何回ぐらいするんです
か。

Ichinen ni nankai gurai surun desu ka.
In a year, about how many times do they
do?

20. 年に二回することもあります
が、たいていは一回ですね。

Nen ni nikai suru koto mo arimasu ga,
taitei wa ikkai desu ne.
In a year, to-do-two-times thing also
exists, but as for usually, it's one time
huh.

21. 道子さんは真一さんにお酒を
飲ませられました。

Michiko-san wa shin'ichi-san ni osake
wo nomaseraremashita.
As for Michiko, she was forced to drink
honorable sake by Shin'ichi.

22. 面白い話をしてみんなを笑わ
せる。

Omoshiroi hanashi wo shite minna wo
warawaseru.
Doing a funny talk, everyone is made to
laugh.

****

23. あの赤いワンピースを着ている方はどなたですか。

Ano akai wanpiisu wo kite iru kata wa donata desu ka.
Who is that red-frock-wearing person over there?

24. ああ、あれは土田さんの奥さんです。

Aa, are wa tsuchida-san no okusan desu.
Ah, that over there is Mr. Tsuchida's wife.

25. あちらの着物の方は？

Achira no kimono no kata wa?
As for that way over there's kimono person?

26. 事務の前田さんじゃありませんか。

Jimu no maeda-san ja arimasen ka.
Isn't it the office's Maeda?

27. パーティーの時はいつも和服だから。

Paatii no toki wa itsumo wafuku dakara.
Since as for party times, it's always Japanese clothes.

28. あっ、本当だ。ちっとも分からなかった。

A, hontou da. Chittomo wakaranakatta.
Ah, that's true, I didn't know/understand her at all. (i.e., I didn't recognize her)

29. おや、山下さんがいませんねえ。

Oya, yamashita-san ga imasen nee.
Expression of mild surprise. Yamashita doesn't exist, huh.

30. きっとまだ会社でしょう。

Kitto mada kaisha deshou.
Surely, still it's the company, probably. (i.e., he's at the company)

31. 今日中に大阪支社に送る報告書があるって言ってましたから。

Kyou juu ni oosaka shisha ni okuru houkokusho ga aru tte ittemashita kara.
Because they were saying, by the end of today, to the Osaka branch office, a to-send written report exists. (aru tte = aru to)

32. ああ、昨日も一日中ずっとやっていましたね。

Aa, kinou mo ichinichijuu zutto yatte imashita ne.
Ah, yesterday also, all day, all the way through, he was doing it, huh.

33. あれはトムソンさんの奥さんでしょう。

Are wa tomuson-san no okusan deshou.
As for that over there, it's probably Thompson's wife.

34. 土田さんの奥さんは着物を着ている。

Tsuchida-san no okusan wa kimono wo kite iru.
As for Tsuchida's wife, she is wearing a kimono.

35. 会社の人はみんなパーティーに来ている。

Kaisha no hito wa minna paatii ni kite iru.
As for the company people, they are all come to the party.

36. 山下さんはどうしてパーティーに来ていないのですか。

Yamashita-san wa doushite paatii ni kite inai no desu ka.
As for Yamashita, why is he not being come to the party?

37. まだ会社で仕事をしているからです。

Mada kaisha de shigoto wo shite iru kara desu.
It's because he's still doing work at the company.

38. イザベラさんはパーティが終わったら花田さんと寿司屋へ行きますか。

Izabera-san wa paatii ga owattara hanada-san to sushiya e ikimasu ka.
As for Isabella, when the party finishes, will she go to a sushi place with Hanada?

39. いいえ、でもいつか行くでしょう。

Iie, demo itsuka iku deshou.
No, but sometime she will probably go.

****

40. バーバラさんは日本料理では何が一番好きですか。

Baabara-san wa nihon ryouri de wa nani ga ichiban suki desu ka.
As for Barbara, as for of Japanese cooking, what does she like best?

41. お寿司が一番好きです。

Osushi ga ichiban suki desu.
She likes honorable sushi best.

42. ハワイに行ったとき、水着を買いました。

Hawai ni itta toki mizugi wo kaimashita.
When I went to Hawaii (after going), I bought a swimsuit.

43. 部屋がもっと静かな時に話をしましょう。

Heya ga motto shizuka na toki ni hanashi wo shimashou.
At the-room-is-more-quiet time, let's do talking.

44. 学生の時フランス語を勉強しました。

Gakusei no toki furansugo wo benkyou shimashita.
The student's time, I studied French.

45. お客さんが来るときには部屋をきれいにしておきます。

Okyakusan ga kuru toki ni wa heya wo kirei ni shite okimasu.
As for at when an honorable guest comes, I make the room clean in advance.

46. 分からない時は先生に聞いて
    ください。

Wakaranai toki wa sensei ni kiite kudasai.
As for when you don't understand, please ask the teacher.

47. 夜、寝るとき、おやすみなさ
    いと言う。

Yoru, neru toki, oyasuminasai to iu.
Night, when one goes to sleep, one says "good night."

48. 部屋に入るとき、失礼します
    と言う。

Heya ni hairu toki, shitsurei shimasu to iu.
When one enters a room, one says "I will commit a discourtesy."

49. お客さんが来たとき、良くい
    らっしゃいましたと言う。

Okyakusan ga kita toki, yoku irasshaimashita to iu.
When an honorable guest came, one says "welcome."

50. 昼、人に会ったとき、こんに
    ちはと言う。

Hiru, hito ni atta toki, konnichi wa to iu.
Noon, when one met a person, one says "hello."

51. 夜、人に会ったとき、こんば
    んはと言う。

Yoru, hito ni atta toki, konban wa to iu.
Night, when one met a person, one says "good evening."

52. ご飯を食べるとき、いただき
    ますと言う。

Gohan wo taberu toki, itadakimasu to iu.
When one eats rice, one says "I will receive."

53. 病気で休むとき、会社に電話
    をします。

Byouki de yasumu toki, kaisha ni denwa wo shimasu.
The time one rests because of illness, one does a phone call to the company.

54. 十歳の男の子が一番マンガを
    多く読んでいます。

Jussai no otokonoko ga ichiban manga wo ooku yonde imasu.
Ten-year-old boys are reading comics the most numerously.

55. 男の子と女の子では男の子の
    方がよくマンガを読んでいま
    す。

Otokonoko to onnanoko de wa otokonoko no hou ga yoku manga wo yonde imasu.
As for among boys and girls, boys are reading comics more frequently.

56. 大きくなるとマンガを読まな
    くなっています。

Ookiku naru to manga wo yomanaku natte imasu.
If one becomes big, not-reading-comics is becoming.

Chapter 71

1. 昨日は一日中雨が降っていました。

Kinou wa ichinichijuu ame ga futte imashita.
As for yesterday, all day long it was raining.

2. 今年は夏中、海で働きました。

Kotoshi wa natsu juu, umi de hatarakimashita.
As for this year, all summer long I labored at the ocean.

3. ハワイはいつも暖かくていいですね。

Hawai wa itsumo atatakakute ii desu ne.
As for Hawaii it's always warm and good, huh.

4. ええ、一年中、夏と同じですよ。

Ee, ichinen juu, natsu to onaji desu yo.
Yeah, all year long it's the same as summer, for sure.

5. もう午後8時だからスーパーは閉まっていますね。

Mou gogo hachiji dakara suupaa wa shimatte imasu ne.
Since it's already 8 p.m., supermarkets are closed, huh.

6. ええ、でもコンビニは一晩中開いていますよ。

Ee, demo konbini wa hitoban juu aite imasu yo.
Yeah, but convenience stores are open all night long, for sure.

7. いや、疲れました。今日は一日中忙しかったんです。

Iya, tsukaremashita. Kyou wa ichinichi juu isogashikattan desu.
Wow, I got tired. As for today, all day long, I was busy.

8. 夏中ビアガーデンでアルバイトをするつもりです。

Natsu juu bia gaaden de arubaito wo surutsumori desu.
All summer long, I plan to do part-time work in a beer garden.

9. 速達で送ったから今日中に着きますよ。

Sokutatsu de okutta kara kyou juu ni tsukimasu.
Since I sent it by express, it will arrive sometime today, for sure.

10. 今年中に結婚したいですね。

Kotoshi chuu ni kekkon shitai desu ne.
Sometime this year, I want to get married, huh.

11. 明日は銀行が休みだから今日中に行っておきます。

Ashita wa ginkou ga yasumi dakara kyou juu ni itte okimasu.
As for tomorrow, since the bank will be on holiday, I will go in advance sometime today.

12. 来週は忙しいから今週中にやっておきましょう。

Raishuu wa isogashii kara konshuu chuu ni yatte okimashou.
As for next week, since busy, let's do in advance sometime this week.

13. 来年はオーストラリアに帰るから今年中に京都に行っておきます。

Rainen wa oosutoraria ni kaeru kara kotoshi juu ni kyouto ni itte okimasu.
As for next year, since I will return to Australia, I will go to Kyoto in advance sometime this year.

14. ジムさんはダニエルさんと違う洋服を着ています。

Jimu-san wa danieru-san to chigau youfuku wo kite imasu.
As for Jim, he is wearing Western clothes that are different from Daniel.

15. 雪子さんは直子さんと違うハンドバッグを持っています

Yukiko-san wa naoko-san to chigau handobaggu wo motte imasu.
As for Yukiko, she has a handbag that is different from Naoko.

16. 時計を外します。

Tokei wo hazushimasu.
I will take off the watch.

17. めがねを掛けます。

Megane wo kakemasu.
I will put on glasses.

18. 土田さんはまだ会社で仕事をしています。

Tsuchida-san wa mada kaisha de shigoto wo shite imasu.
As for Tsuchida, he is still working at the company.

19. これはもう使いませんか。

Kore wa mou tsukaimasen ka.
As for this, won't you use it anymore?

20. いいえ、まだ使いますよ。捨てないでください。

Iie, mada tsukaimasu yo. Sutenai de kudasai.
No, I will still use it, for sure. Please don't throw it away.

21. まだ寒いですか。

Mada samui desu ka.
Is it still cold?

22. いいえ、もう寒くありません。

Iie, mou samuku arimasen.
No, it's no longer cold.

23. 私はイザベラハリスと申します。

Watashi wa izabera harisu to moushimasu.
As for me, I am humbly called Isabella Harris.

24. 国はアメリカです。

Kuni wa amerika desu.
The country (i.e., my country) is America.

25. まだ雨が降っていますか。

Mada ame ga futte imasu ka.
Is it still raining?

26. いいえ、もう降っていません。

Iie, mou futte imasen.
No, it isn't precipitating any more.

27. 島田さん、結婚するんですって。

Shimada-san, kekkon surun desu tte.
As for Shimada, they were saying that he will get married. (woman's speech)

28. ええ、私も聞いたわ。

Ee, watashi mo kiita wa.
Yeah, I also heard it. (woman's speech)

29. それで会社を辞めるんですって。

Sore de kaisha wo yamerun desu tte.
For that reason, he will resign the company, reportedly.

30. 広田さんから結婚式は来月の五日だって聞きました。

Hirota-san kara kekkon shiki wa raigetsu no itsuka da tte kikimashita.
From Hirota, I heard that, as for the wedding, it's the 5th of next month.

31. 野村さん、仕事が終わらないんですって。

Nomura-san, shigoto ga owaranain desu tte.
Nomura, the work will not finish, reportedly. (woman's speech)

32. ええ、私も聞いたわ。それでパーティに行かないんですって。

Ee, watashi mo kiita wa. Sore de paati ni ikanain desu tte.
Yeah, I also heard it. Consequently, he will not go to the party, reportedly. (woman's speech)

33. 日本料理では何が一番好きですか。

Nihon ryouri de wa nani ga ichiban suki desu ka.
As for of Japanese cooking, what do you like the best?

34. すき焼きが一番好きです。

Sukiyaki ga ichiban suki desu.
I like sukiyaki the best.

35. 日本料理は全部好きです。

Nihon ryouri wa zenbu suki desu.
As for Japanese cooking, I like it all.

36. 東京では何月が一番暑いですか。

Toukyou de wa nan gatsu ga ichiban atsui desu ka.
As for of Tokyo, what month is the hottest?

37. 八月が一番暑いです。

Hachigatsu ga ichiban atsui desu.
August is the hottest.

38. 一月が一番寒いです。

Ichigatsu ga ichiban samui desu.
January is the coldest.

39. 東京で一番雨が多いのは何月ですか。

Toukyou de ichiban ame ga ooi no wa
nangatsu desu ka.
Of Tokyo, as for the one with the most
numerous rain, which month is it?

40. 九月です。

Kugatsu desu.
It's September.

41. 東京で一番雨が少ないのは何月ですか。

Toukyou de ichiban ame ga sukunai no
wa nangatsu desu ka.
Of Tokyo, as for the one with the least
rain, which month is it?

42. 一月です。

Ichigatsu desu.
It's January.

43. 一月と五月と十月では何月が一番雨が多いですか。

Ichigatsu to gogatsu to juugatsu de wa
nangatsu ga ichiban ame ga ooi desu ka.
As for among January and May and
October, which month is the most
numerous rain?

44. 十月が一番雨が多いです。

Juugatsu ga ichi ban ame ga ooi desu.
October is the most numerous rain.

45. その本、そんなに面白いの？

Sono hon, sonna ni omoshiroi no?
That book, so much interesting?

46. ええ、これほど面白い本は読んだことがありません。

Ee, kore hodo omoshiroi hon wa yonda
koto ga arimasen.
Yeah, compared to this, as for a more
interesting book, I have never read.

47. 味はどうですか。

Aji wa dou desu ka.
As for the flavor, how is it?

48. ええ、これほどおいしい物は食べたことがありません。

Ee, kore hodo oishii mono wa tabeta koto
ga arimasen.
Yeah, compared to this, as for more
delicious things, I have not eaten.

49. エベレストはそんなに高い山なんですか。

Eberesto wa sonna ni takai yama nan
desu ka.
As for Everest, is it such a tall mountain?

50. ええ、エベレストほど高い山はありません。

Ee, eberesto hodo takai yama wa
arimasen.
Yeah, compared to Everest, taller
mountains don't exist.

51. 暑いですねぇ。

Atsui desu nee.
It's hot, huh.

52. 本当に。一年中で八月ほど暑い月はありません。

Hontou ni. Ichinenjuu de hachigatsu
hodo atsui tsuki wa arimasen.
That's for sure. Of throughout the year,
compared to August, hotter months don't
exist.

53. お手伝いしましょうか。

Otetsudai shimashou ka.
Shall I humbly do help?

54. 有難う。あなたほど親切な人
はいません。

Arigatou. Anata hodo shinsetsu na hito
wa imasen.
Thank you. Compared to you, kinder
people don't exist.

55. ボーナスは多くても二ヵ月分
しか出ないでしょう。

Boonasu wa ookutemo nikagetsu bun
shika denai deshou.
As for bonuses, at the very most, except
for a two-month portion only, they will
probably not come out.

56. 日本の会社ではお正月の休み
は長くても十日間ぐらいで
す。

Nihon no kaisha de wa oshougatsu no
yasumi wa nagakutemo tooka kan gurai
desu.
As for at Japanese companies, as for the
New Year's vacation, at the very longest,
it's about 10 days' duration.

57. あの靴なら安くても五千円ぐ
らいで買えますよ。

Ano kutsu nara yasukutemo gosen'en
gurai de kaemasu yo.
In the case of those shoes over there, at
the very least expensive, for about 5,000
yen, you can buy, for sure.

****

58. ねずみのお父さんが娘のちゅ
う子に聞きました。

Nezumi no otousan ga musume no
chuuko ni kikimashita.
The mouse's father asked the daughter's
Little Squeak. (i.e., his daughter)

59. ちゅう子は誰と結婚したい？

Chuuko wa dare to kekkon shitai?
As for Little Squeak, with whom does
she want to marry?

60. 世界で一番強い人と結婚した
いわ。

Sekai de ichiban tsuyoi hito to kekkon
shitai wa.
Of the world, the strongest person, I want
to marry with.

61. 雲さん、あなたほど強い方は
世界にいません。

Kumo-san, anata hodo tsuyoi kata wa
sekai ni imasen.
Mr. Cloud, compared to you, stronger
people in the world don't exist.

62. 私は風ほど強くありませんと
雲は言いました。

Watashi wa kaze hodo tsuyoku arimasen
to kumo wa iimashita.
As for me, compared to the wind, I am
not strong, said the cloud.

Chapter 72

1. ちょっと伺いますが桜ヶ丘<ruby>桜<rt>さくら</rt></ruby><ruby>ヶ丘<rt>が おか</rt></ruby>三丁目<ruby>三丁目<rt>ちょうめ</rt></ruby>はどう行くんでしょうか。

   Chotto ukagaimasu ga sakuragaoka san choume wa dou ikun deshou ka.
   I will ask for a second, but as for Sakuragaoka 3 Choume, how do you probably go?

2. この道を300メートルぐらい行くと左側にガソリンスタンドがあります。

   Kono michi wo sanbyaku meetoru gurai iku to hidari gawa ni gasorin sutando ga arimasu.
   If you go about 300 meters on this street, on the left side there is a gas station.

3. その角を左に曲がって、しばらく行くと広い通りに出ます。

   Sono kado wo hidari ni magatte, shibaraku iku to hiroi toori ni demasu.
   Turning that corner to the left, if you go for awhile, you will come out to a wide street.

4. その向こうが三丁目<ruby>三丁目<rt>ちょうめ</rt></ruby>です。

   Sono mukou ga san choume desu.
   That far (side) is 3 Choume.

5. ガソリンスタンドの角を左に曲がって広い通りの向こうですね。

   Gasorin sutando no kado wo hidari ni magatte hiroi toori no mukou desu ne.
   On the gas station's corner, turning left, it's the wide street's far side, huh.

   ****

6. 遅くなりまして...

   Osoku narimashite...
   I became late and...

7. 男の人に聞いてみたらかえって分からなくなってしまったんですよ。

   Otoko no hito ni kiite mitara kaette wakaranaku natte shimattan desu yo.
   When I ask a man and see, changing (i.e., contrary to expectations), it became completely unable to understand, for sure.

8. それは大変でしたね。

   Sore wa taihen deshita ne.
   That was terrible huh.

9. 最近よく降りますねぇ。

   Saikin yoku furimasu nee.
   Recently it precipitates often, huh.

10. ところで息子さんが留学生の試験に受かったそうですね。

    Tokoro de musuko-san ga ryuugakusei no shiken ni ukatta sou desu ne.
    By the way, the honorable son passed to the foreign student's exam, reportedly, huh.

11. 難しかったんでしょうね。

Muzukashikattan deshou ne.
It was probably difficult huh.

12. さあ、遊んでばかりいたけど。

Saa, asonde bakari ita kedo...
Well, playing only he was, but...

13. でもアメリカの大学は入ってから大変だそうですね。

Demo amerika no daigaku wa haitte kara taihen da sou desu ne.
But American universities, after entering, are terrible, reportedly, huh.

14. ちょっと心配なんですよ。

Chotto shinpai nan desu yo.
A little, it's worry, for sure.

15. 中村さんの家はすぐ分かりましたか。

Nakamura-san no ie wa sugu wakarimashita ka.
As for Nakamura's house, did he understand it soon? (i.e., was he able to find it readily?)

****

16. ジェイムズが日本で働くことになったとき、私は日本語があまり分からなかったし、日本の事は少ししか知らなかったので、とても心配でした。

Jeimuzu ga nihon de hataraku koto ni natta toki, watashi wa nihongo ga amari wakaranakatta shi, nihon no koto wa sukoshi shika shiranakatta node, totemo shinpai deshita.
James, in-Japan-was-scheduled-to-labor time, as for me, the Japanese language, almost I did not understand, and as for Japan's things, since except for only a little I did not know, it was very much worry.

17. それで日本に来る前に、日本語の本や日本について書いてある本を買って勉強しました。

Sore de nihon ni kuru mae ni, nihongo no hon ya nihon ni tsuite kaite aru hon wo katte benkyou shimashita.
For that reason, at before-to-come-to-Japan, Japanese language books, etc., regarding Japan written-and-exist books I bought and studied.

18. でも、本で勉強するのと、本当に経験するのとは、ずいぶん違いますね。

Demo, hon de benkyou suru no to, hontou ni keiken suru no to wa, zuibun chigaimasu ne.
But, to do study from books and as for truly to do experience and, extremely, they are different huh.

19. 成田空港に着いてみると何も分からなかったので困りました。

Narita kuukou ni tsuite miru to nanimo wakaranakatta node komarimashita.
When I arrived at Narita airport and saw, since I didn't understand anything, I got inconvenienced.

20. 私がアメリカで勉強した日本語は日本の人が話す日本語とは違うのかしらと思いました。

Watashi ga amerika de benkyou shita nihongo wa nihon no hito ga hanasu nihongo to wa chigau no kashira to omoimashita.
I, in America, as for studied-Japanese, as for Japan's-people-speak-Japanese and, different I wonder, I thought.

21. でも、皆様に教えていただいたり、日本語学校で勉強したりしました。

Demo, minasama ni oshiete itadaitari, nihongo gakkou de benkyou shitari shimashita.
But, by very honorable everyone, you taught and I humbly received, etc., at Japanese language school I studied, etc., I did.

22. 一人で買い物に行ったり地下鉄に乗ったりすることができるようになりました。

Hitori de kaimono ni ittari chikatetsu ni nottari suru koto ga dekiru you ni narimashita.
By myself, to go for the purpose of shopping, etc., to board the subway, etc., to be able to do, it came to that point.

23. 大阪へ行ってからも皆様のご親切は決して忘れません。

Oosaka e itte kara mo minasama no goshinsetsu wa kesshite wasuremasen.
After going to Osaka also, as for very honorable everyone's honorable kindness, never, I will not forget.

24. 大阪へいらっしゃるときはぜひご連絡ください。

Oosaka e irassharu toki wa zehi gorenraku kudasai.
As for the time when you honorably come to Osaka, without fail, honorable communication please.

25. 又、お目にかかれるのを楽しみにしております。

Mata, ome ni kakareru no wo tanoshimi ni shite orimasu.
Again, to humble-eyes-it-is-able-to-cost thing, I will be looking forward on humbly. (i.e., I will be looking forward to being able to meet you)

26. その時までどうぞお元気で。

Sono toki made douzo ogenki de.
Until that time, go ahead with honorable health.

****

27. 真さんだけが休んでいる。

Makoto-san dake ga yasunde iru.
Only Makoto is being off.

28. この前の日曜日、ディズニーランドに行ったが、人ばかりで面白くなかった。

Kono mae no nichiyoubi, dizuniirando ni itta ga, hito bakari de omoshirokunakatta.
Last Sunday I went to Disneyland, but because it was nothing but people, it wasn't fun.

29. 真さんは食べてばかりいて花
子さんを手伝いません。

Makoto-san wa tabete bakari ite hanako-
san wo tetsudaimasen.
Makoto is only eating, and he doesn't
help Hanako.

30. 子供達は遊んでばかりでちっ
とも勉強しないんですよ。

Kodomotachi wa asonde bakari de
chittomo benkyou shinain desu yo.
As for the children, since only playing,
they don't study at all, for sure.

31. 上田さん、昨日のお昼は何を
食べましたか。

Ueda-san kinou no ohiru wa nani wo
tabemashita ka.
Ueda, as for yesterday's honorable noon,
what did he eat?

32. カレーと一緒に何か他の物も
食べているんですか。

Karee to issho ni nanika hoka no mono
mo tabete irun desu ka.
Together with curry, is he eating
something other thing also?

33. 何人かまだ会社に残って仕事
をしていますか。

Nanninka mada kaisha ni nokotte shigoto
wo shite imasu ka.
Are some people still staying behind at
the company and doing work?

34. いいえ、小川さんだけです。

Iie, ogawa-san dake desu.
No, it's just Ogawa.

35. 他の人達はもう帰ったはずで
す。

Hoka no hitotachi wa mou kaetta hazu
desu.
As for other people, they should already
returned.

36. 小川さんはいつも残業ばかり
していますねぇ。

Ogawa-san wa itsumo zangyou bakari
shite imasu nee.
As for Ogawa, always, he is doing
overtime work only, huh.

37. そんなに忙しいんでしょう
か。

Sonna ni isogashiin deshou ka.
Is he probably that busy?

38. 朝から寒かったのにセーター
を持ってきませんでした 。

Asa kara samukatta noni seetaa wo motte
kimasen deshita.
Even though it was cold since morning, I
didn't bring a sweater.

39. あの人は学生なのにちっとも
勉強をしません。

Ano hito wa gakusei na noni chittomo
benkyou wo shimasen.
As for that person over there, even
though he's a student, he doesn't study at
all.

40. 手紙が届いているはずなのに
返事がきません。

Tegami ga todoite iru hazu na noni henji
ga kimasen.
Even though the letter should be being
arrived, an answer doesn't come.

41. 病気なのに会社を休みません。

Byouki na noni kaisha wo yasumimasen.
Although he's sick, he doesn't take off from the company.

42. お花見に行ったのに花はもう散っていました。

Ohanami ni itta noni hana wa mou chitte imashita.
Even though I went for honorable flower viewing, as for the blossoms, they already were fallen.

43. 電話で行くと言っておいたのにソフィアさんは留守でした。

Denwa de iku to itte oita noni sofia-san wa rusu deshita.
On the phone, even though she said in advance that she will go, Sophia was absent.

44. 走ったのに電車に間に合いませんでした。

Hashitta noni densha ni maniaimasen deshita.
Even though I ran, I wasn't on time for the train.

45. 厚子さんは女なのに男のように話します。

Atsuko-san wa onna na noni otoko no you ni hanashimasu.
As for Atsuko, even though she's a female, she speaks like a male.

46. ウエッブさん、すてきなセーターですね。

Uebbu-san, suteki na seetaa desu ne.
Webb, it's a lovely sweater, huh.

47. アメリカの母が送ってくれた。

Amerika no haha ga okutte kureta.
My American mother sent it and gave it.

48. 一番目に日本人の好きな仕事はエンジニアです。

Ichiban me ni nihon jin no suki na shigoto wa enjinia desu.
In the first place, the job that Japanese people like is engineer.

49. 二番目に日本人の好きな仕事はパイロットです。

Niban me ni nihon jin no suki na shigoto wa pairotto desu.
In the second place, the job that Japanese people like is pilot.

Chapter 73

1. ロビンソンさんはウセインボルトみたいに速く走ります。

Robinson-san wa usein boruto mitai ni hayaku hashirimasu.
Robinson, like Usain Bolt, runs fast.

2. 十一月なのに今日は春のように暖かいです。

Juuichigatsu na noni kyou wa haru no you ni atatakai desu.
Even though it's November, today, like spring, is warm.

3. 暑くなったから窓を開けてもいい？

Atsukunatta kara mado wo akete mo ii?
Since it became hot, is it OK to open the windows?

4. 春になると暖かくなります。

Haru ni naru to atatakaku narimasu.
When it becomes spring, it becomes warm.

5. 雨が止んだらハイキングに行きましょう。

Ame ga yandara haikingu ni ikimashou.
When the rain stops, let's go hiking.

6. タバコを吸ったらだめですよ。

Tabako wo suttara dame desu yo.
When you smoke tobacco, it's bad, for sure.

7. このボタンを押すと火が消えます。

Kono botan wo osu to hi ga kiemasu.
When one pushes this button, the fire goes out.

8. ここに立つとドアが開きます。

Koko ni tatsu to doa ga akimasu.
When one stands here, the door opens.

9. ここにテレフォンカードを入れると電話ができます。

Koko ni terehon kaado wo ireru to denwa ga dekimasu.
When one inserts a telephone card here, the phone can be done. (i.e., can be used)

10. このキーを押すと字が大きくなります。

Kono kii wo osu to ji ga ookiku narimasu.
When one pushes this key, the character becomes big.

11. 夏になると泳ぎたくなります。

Natsu ni naru to oyogitaku narimasu.
When it becomes summer, wanting to swim will become.

12. 電車を降りると橋本さんが待っていました。

Densha wo oriru to hashimoto-san ga matte imashita.
When I get off the train, Hashimoto was waiting.

13. 銀行に行ったらもう閉まっていました。

Ginkou ni ittara mou shimatte imashita.
When I went to the bank, it was already closed.

14. アリッサさんに電話をしたら留守でした。

Arissa-san ni denwa wo shitara rusu deshita.
When I did a phone call to Alyssa, she was absent.

15. 夕方、魚屋へ行ったらさんまを安く売っていました。

Yuugata, sakanaya e ittara sanma wo yasuku utte imashita.
Evening, when I went to the fish store, they were selling Pacific saury cheaply.

16. うちのそばまで来るとピアノの音が聞こえました。

Uchi no soba made kuru to piano no oto ga kikoemashita.
When one comes until close to the home, piano sound was audible.

17. 渋谷駅で電車を降りて北口に出ます。

Shibuya eki de densha wo orite kitaguchi ni demasu.
You get off the train at Shibuya station and leave by the north exit.

18. そして公園通りを代々木公園の方へ真っ直ぐ行くと左側にNHKホールがあります。

Soshite kouen doori wo yoyogi kouen no hou e massugu iku to hidarigawa ni enu eichi kei hooru ga arimasu.
Then on Park street, in the direction of Yoyogi Park, when you go straight, on the left side NHK Hall exists.

19. この道をしばらく行くと教会があります。

Kono michi wo shibaraku iku to kyoukai ga arimasu.
If you go on this street for awhile, there is a church.

20. 信号の先。

Shingou no saki.
Ahead of (i.e., past) the stoplight.

21. この先。

Kono saki.
Further on (ahead of here).

22. 信号の手前。

Shingou no temae.
Before the stoplight.

23. この先の信号の手前。

Kono saki no shingou no temae.
Before this stoplight ahead.

24. 病院の方。

Byouin no hou.
In the direction of the hospital.

25. その角を曲がるとあります。

Sono kado wo magaru to arimasu.
If you turn on that corner, it exists.

26. あのう、三越デパートへはどう行ったらいいですか。

Anou, mitsukoshi depaato e wa dou ittara ii desu ka.
Say, as for to Mitsukoshi department store, how when you go is good?

27. この通りを渡って真っ直ぐ行ってください。

Kono toori wo watatte massugu itte kudasai.
Cross this street and go straight, please.

28. 五つ目の角に三和銀行があります。

Itsutsume no kado ni sanwa ginkou ga arimasu.
At the 5th corner, Sanwa Bank exists.

29. その角を左に曲がっていくと左側にありますよ。

Sono kado wo hidari ni magatte iku to hidarigawa ni arimasu yo.
If you turn left and go on that corner, it exists on the left side, for sure.

30. この通りを渡って五つ目の角を左ですね。

Kono toori wo watatte itsutsume no kado wo hidari desu ne.
I cross this street, and it's left on the 5th corner, huh.

31. それから和光へはどう行ったらいいでしょうか。

Sore kara wakou e wa dou ittara ii deshou ka.
And then, as for to Wakou, how when you go is probably good?

32. その角を右に曲がって一つ目の角に松坂屋デパートがあります。

Sono kado wo migi ni magatte hitotsume no kado ni matsuzakaya depaato ga arimasu.
You turn right on that corner, and at the first corner Matsuzakaya department store exists.

33. そこを左に曲がって行くと右側にありますよ。

Soko wo hidari ni magatte iku to migigawa ni arimasu yo.
If you turn left and go on that place, it exists on the right side, for sure.

34. すみません。今度の日曜日は何日ですか。

Sumimasen. Kondo no nichiyoubi wa nan nichi desu ka.
Excuse me. What day is next Sunday?

35. 28日ですよ。

Nijuu hachi nichi desu yo.
It's the 28th, for sure.

36. 夜、遅くまで起きていない方がいいと思うよ。

Yoru osoku made okite inai hou ga ii to omou yo.
Until late at night, not being awake is better, I think, for sure.

37. 山田さんにこの仕事を頼んだらどうですか。

Yamada-san ni kono shigoto wo tanondara dou desu ka.
How is it if you request this work to Yamada?

38. 山田さんにこの仕事を頼まない方がいいですよ。

Yamada-san ni kono shigoto wo tanomanai hou ga ii desu yo.
It would be better not to request this work to Yamada, for sure.

39. ソフィアさんに会いに行った方がいいですよ。

Sofia-san ni ai ni itta hou ga ii desu yo.
It would be better to go in order to meet Sophia, for sure.

40. 京都について知りたいんですが。

Kyouto ni tsuite shiritain desu ga...
I would like to know about Kyoto, but...

41. 図書館で調べたらいいですよ。

Toshokan de shirabetara ii desu yo.
If you check in the library, it's good, for sure.

42. あれ！ 道が分からなくなりましたよ。

Are! Michi ga wakaranaku narimashita yo.
Hey! It developed that I don't know/understand the way, for sure.

43. あの店で聞いてみたらどうですか。

Ano mise de kiite mitara dou desu ka.
If you ask and see at that store over there, how is that?

44. 日本の寿司はおいしいですか。

Nihon no sushi wa oishii desu ka.
Is Japanese sushi delicious?

45. ええ、おいしいですよ。 一度食べてみたらどうですか。

Ee, oishii desu yo. Ichido tabete mitara dou desu ka.
Yeah, it's delicious, for sure. If you eat it once to see, how is that?

46. 野村君に手伝ってもらって急いでまとめてください。

Nomura-kun ni tetsudatte moratte isoide matomete kudasai.
To young man Nomura help and receive, and conclude it in a hurry please.

47. 明日の会議で発表することになっているから、今日中に仕上げてくれますか。

Ashita no kaigi de happyou suru koto ni natte iru kara, kyou juu ni shiagete kuremasu ka.
Since I am scheduled to give a presentation at tomorrow's meeting, by the end of today, will you finish it and give?

48. 黒田さん、この書類をコピーしてもらいたいんだけど。

Kuroda-san, kono shorui wo kopii shite moraitain dakedo...
Kuroda, I would like you to copy this document and I receive, but...

49. 明日、朝8時に駅の前に来て
もらいたいんだけど。

Ashita, asa hachiji ni eki no mae ni kite
moraitain dakedo...
Tomorrow, morning, at 8:00, I would
like you to come to the front of the
station and I receive, but...

50. エリザベスさんという人を知
っていますか。

Erizabesu-san to iu hito wo shitte imasu
ka.
Are you knowing the person called
Elizabeth?

51. ジョンさんの奥さんで明るく
てとてもいい人ですよ。

Jon-san no okusan de akarukute totemo ii
hito desu yo.
She's John's wife, and she's cheerful, and
she's a very good person, for sure.

52. 直子さんはちょっと話しにく
い人ですよ。

Naoko-san wa chotto hanashinikui hito
desu yo.
As for Naoko, it's a-little-difficult-to-talk
person, for sure. (i.e., she's a little
difficult to talk to)

53. 病気の間、何も食べられま
せんでした。

Byouki no aida, nanimo taberaremasen
deshita.
The sickness interval, I could not eat
anything. (i.e., I couldn't eat anything
while sick)

54. 遅くなったので友達に車で送
ってもらった。

Osoku natta node tomodachi ni kuruma
de okutte moratta.
Since I became late, by the friend, by car,
he saw me off, and I received.

55. 部長、この書類にサインをし
ていただきたいんですが。

Buchou, kono shorui ni sain wo shite
itadakitain desu ga...
Division Manager, I would like for you
to sign to this document and I humbly
receive, but...

56. 悪いけど、今ちょっと。

Warui kedo, ima chotto...
Bad, but now, a little bit... (i.e., I can't
do it)

57. 買い物に行ってきてちょうだ
い。

Kaimono ni itte kite choudai.
Please go for the purpose of shopping
and come. (speaking to a child)

58. 今友達と遊んでいるんだよ。

Ima tomodachi to asonde irun da yo.
Now, with the friend, I'm playing, for
sure.

Chapter 74

1. あのう、黒田さん、今課長さ
んを北村って言ったでしょ
う？

Anou, kuroda-san, ima kachousan wo
"kitamura" tte itta deshou ?
Say, Kuroda, now you called Mr. Section
Manager "Kitamura," probably? ("tte" =
variant of quotation marker "to")

2. どうして北村さんって言わな
いんですか。

Doushite kitamura-san tte iwanain desu
ka.
Why do you not call him Kitamura san?

3. ちょっと教えてくれません
か。

Chotto oshiete kuremasen ka.
For a moment won't you teach and give?

4. 外の人に言うときには自分の
会社の人達には「さん」を付
けないのよ。

Soto no hito ni iu toki ni wa jibun no
kaisha no hitotachi ni wa "san" wo
tsukenai no yo.
As for at the time when I say to an
outside person, as for to my own
company's people, I don't attach "san,"
for sure.

5. でも普通は「黒田さん、お電
話です」って言うでしょう？

Demo futsuu wa "kuroda-san odenwa
desu" tte iu deshou?
But as for usually, I say "Kuroda san, it's
an honorable phone call" probably?

6. そうね。どう説明したらいい
か。

Sou ne. Dou setsumei shitara ii ka.
So, huh. (i.e., that's so) How if I
explained would be good?

7. ちょっと難しいんだけど会社
の中にも内と外があって...

Chotto muzukashiin dakedo kaisha no
naka ni mo uchi to soto ga atte...
It's a little difficult, but at inside the
company also, in-group and outside exist,
and...

8. そういうことをどこかで教え
てくれないかなぁ。

Sou iu koto wo dokoka de oshiete
kurenai kanaa.
I wonder if at someplace they won't teach
and give that sort of thing.

9. 私も教えてあげるけど、東京
には日本語学校がたくさんあ
るから、仕事の後で通ってみ
たら？

Watashi mo oshiete ageru kedo, toukyou
ni wa nihongo gakkou ga takusan aru
kara, shigoto no ato de kayotte mitara?
I also will teach and give, but as for in
Tokyo, since there are a lot of Japanese
language schools, after work, if you
could commute and see?

****

10. お話中すみません。

Ohanashi chuu sumimasen.
In the middle of honorable conversation, excuse me.

11. 事務員：何でしょうか。

Jimuin: Nan deshou ka.
Office person: What is it probably?

12. 日本語の会話のクラスについて教えてもらいたいんですが。

Nihongo no kaiwa no kurasu ni tsuite oshiete moraitain desu ga...
Regarding Japanese language's conversation's class, I would like you to teach and me to receive, but...

13. はい、えーと、プライベートのクラスとグループのクラスがありますけど。

Hai. Eeto, puraibeeto no kurasu to guruupu no kurasu ga arimasu kedo...
Yes. Uh, there are private classes and group classes, but...

14. そうですか。グループのクラスは何人ですか。

Sou desu ka. Guruupu no kurasu wa nannin desu ka.
Is that so? As for the group classes, how many people is it?

15. クラスによって違いますが大体10人ぐらいです。

Kurasu ni yotte chigaimasu ga daitai juunin gurai desu.
According to the class, it differs, but generally it's about 10 people.

16. 曜日や授業料についてはこちらのパンフレットに書いてあります。

Youbi ya jugyouryou ni tsuite wa kochira no panfuretto ni kaite arimasu.
As for regarding the days of the week, the tuition, etc., they're written to this way's pamphlet.

17. （パンフレットを読みながら）なるほど。

(panfuretto wo yomi nagara) Naruhodo.
(as she reads the pamphlet) I see.

18. じゃ、うちに帰って考えてみます。

Ja, uchi ni kaette kangaete mimasu.
Well, I will return home and think and see.

19. 決まったらもう一度来ます。

Kimattara mou ichido kimasu.
When it arranges, one more time I will come.

20. はい、お待ちしています。

Hai. Omachi shite imasu.
Yes. I will be doing humble waiting.

****

21. 電話が掛かってきたとき北村
さんはいましたか。

Denwa ga kakatte kita toki kitamura-san wa imashita ka.
The time the phone called and came, as for Kitamura, did he exist?

22. 黒田さんは電話で北村課長の
ことを何と言いましたか。

Kuroda-san wa denwa de kitamura kachou no koto wo nan to iimashita ka.
As for Kuroda, on the phone, what did she call Section Manager Kitamura's thing?

23. 北村と言いました。

Kitamura to iimashita.
She called him Kitamura.

24. それはどうしてですか。

Sore wa doushite desu ka.
As for that, why is it?

25. 北村さんが自分の会社の人だ
からです。

Kitamura-san ga jibun no kaisha no hito dakara desu.
It's because Kitamura is her own company's person.

26. 黒田さんはグレイスさんにど
うしたらいいと言いました
か。

Kuroda-san wa gureisu-san ni dou shitara ii to iimashita ka.
As for Kuroda, to Grace, how if to do is good did she say?

27. 仕事の後、日本語学校に通っ
てみたらいいと言いました。

Shigoto no ato nihongo gakkou ni kayotte mitara ii to iimashita.
After work, if she commutes to a Japanese language school and sees, good, she said.

****

28. お仕事中申し訳ありません
が、駅に行く道を教えて下さ
いませんか。

Oshigoto chuu moushiwake arimasen ga, eki ni iku michi wo oshiete kudasaimasen ka.
In the middle of honorable work, there's no excuse, but won't you show the way to go to the station and give?

29. ええ、いいですよ。この先
の角を右に曲がると駅です
よ。

Ee, ii desu yo. Kono saki no kado wo migi ni magaru to eki desu yo.
Yeah, it's good, for sure. On this corner ahead, if you turn right, it's the station, for sure.

30. 今日は忙しくてこの仕事はと
ってもできません。

Kyou wa isogashikute kono shigoto wa tottemo dekimasen.
As for today, since I'm busy, as for this work, it is extremely unable to do.

31. じゃ、明日することにした
ら？

Ja, ashita suru koto ni shitara?
Well, if you decide to do it tomorrow?

32. 明日は雨が降るそうですよ。

Ashita wa ame ga furu sou desu yo.
As for tomorrow, it will rain, reportedly, for sure.

33. じゃ、明日は海に行かない方がいいんじゃない？

Ja, ashita wa umi ni ikanai hou ga iin ja nai?
Well, as for tomorrow, wouldn't it be better not to go to the ocean?

34. 花田さんが黒田さんにサンドイッチを買ってきてあげました。

Hanada-san ga kuroda-san ni sandoitchi wo katte kite agemashita.
Miss Hanada, for Miss Kuroda, bought a sandwich, came and gave.

35. テイラーさん、時計は見つかりましたか。

Teiraa-san, tokei wa mitsukarimashita ka.
Taylor, as for the watch, was it found?

36. ええ、島田さんが見つけてくれました。

Ee, shimada-san ga mitsukete kuremashita.
Yeah, Shimada found it and gave. (i.e., found it for me)

37. それは良かったですね。

Sore wa yokatta desu ne.
That was good, huh.

38. 駅までの道が分かりました。

Eki made no michi ga wakarimashita.
I knew/understood the way of until the station.

39. おまわりさんが教えてくれました。

Omawarisan ga oshiete kuremashita.
A policeman showed and gave me.

40. 仕事が終わりましたか。

Shigoto ga owarimashita ka.
Did the work finish?

41. 田辺さんが手伝ってくれました。

Tanabe-san ga tetsudatte kuremashita.
Tanabe helped and gave me.

42. お父さん、この本を買って。

Otousan, kono hon wo katte.
Father, buy this book.

43. 息子に本を買ってやった。

Musuko ni hon wo katte yatta.
For the son I bought and gave the book.

44. 父に本を買ってもらった。

Chichi ni hon wo katte moratta.
By my father, the book was bought and received.

45. 母が病気で寝ているので大き
い音を出さないで欲しいんで
すが。

Haha ga byouki de nete iru node ookii
oto wo dasanai de hoshiin desu ga...
Since Mother is sleeping due to illness, I
desire that you do not put out big sounds,
but...

46. 転んだ人は足を強く打ちま
した。

Koronda hito wa ashi wo tsuyoku
uchimashita.
As for the person who fell over, she hit
the leg strongly.

****

47. サマンサさん、元気になって
良かったですね。

Samansa-san, genki ni natte yokatta desu
ne.
Samantha, since health developed, it was
good, huh.

48. 病気の時ご主人は何かしてく
れましたか。

Byouki no toki goshujin wa nanika shite
kuremashita ka.
The sickness time, as for your husband,
did he do something and give to our in-
group?

49. ええ、洗濯をしてくれまし
た。

Ee, sentaku wo shite kuremashita.
Yeah, he did laundry and gave to me.

50. 買い物をしてきてくれまし
た。

Kaimono wo shite kite kuremashita.
He did shopping, came and gave to me.

51. お医者さんに電話をしてくれ
ました。

Oishasan ni denwa wo shite kuremashita.
He did a phone call to the honorable Mr.
Doctor and gave to me.

52. 食事も作ってあげたよ。

Shokuji mo tsukutte ageta yo.
I created a meal also and gave, for sure.

53. 薬ももらってきてあげたよ。

Kusuri mo moratte kite ageta yo.
I received medicine also, came and gave,
for sure.

54. 熱も計ってあげたよ。

Netsu mo hakatte ageta yo.
I measured the fever also and gave, for
sure.

Chapter 75

1. ウイリヤムズ君、ちょっと。

Uiriamuzu-kun, chotto...
Young man Williams, just a moment...

2. あのね、来週の金曜日に大阪
に行って欲しいんだけど。

Ano ne, raishuu no kinyoubi ni oosaka ni
itte hoshiin dakedo...
Say there, on next week's Friday, I desire
you to go to Osaka, but...

3. 大阪のうちの子会社を知って
いるね。

Oosaka no uchi no kogaisha wo shitte iru
ne.
You are knowing Osaka's in-group's
subsidiary company, huh.

4. はい、第一貿易という会社で
すね。

Hai. Dai ichi boueki to iu kaisha desu
ne.
Yes. It's the Number One Trade called
company, huh.

5. そう、そこの会議に出席して
欲しいんだ。

Sou. Soko no kaigi ni shusseki shite
hoshiin da.
Right. I desire you to attend that place's
meeting.

6. はあ、何の会議でしょうか。

Haa. Nan no kaigi deshou ka.
Ah, yes. What sort of meeting is it
probably?

7. アメリカへ支社を出す件につ
いての会議なんだ。

Amerika e shisha wo dasu ken ni tsuite
no kaigi nan da.
It's a meeting regarding the matter of
putting out a branch office to America.

8. 何か書類を持っていきます
か。

Nanika shorui wo motte ikimasu ka.
Something documents will I take?

9. いや、ファックスで送ったか
らいいよ。

Iya, fakkusu de okutta kara ii yo.
Nah, because I sent them by fax, good,
for sure.

10. その日のうちに帰らなくても
いいですか。

Sono hi no uchi ni kaeranakute mo ii
desu ka.
While it's still that day, is it OK if I don't
return?

11. ちょうど金曜日だから土日にかけて京都と奈良でも見物してきたらいいよ。

Choudo kinyoubi dakara donichi ni kakete kyouto to nara demo kenbutsu shite kitara ii yo.
Since it happens to be Friday, spending to Saturday/Sunday, if you sightsee at least Kyoto and Nara and come, good, for sure. (donichi = Saturday and Sunday)

12. 報告はファックスで送っておいて。

Houkoku wa fakkusu de okutte oite.
As for the report, send it by fax in advance.

13. あのう、家内を連れていってもいいですか。

Anou, kanai wo tsurete itte mo ii desu ka.
Say, is it OK if I take the wife?

14. 家内も私もまだ日本国内を旅行していないので一緒に行きたいです。

Kanai mo watashi mo mada nihon kokunai wo ryokou shite inai node issho ni ikitai desu.
Since the wife also, I also, still not doing travel on Japan domestic, I would like to go together.

****

15. あのう、課長、出張の計画書を見ていただきたいんですが。

Anou, kachou, shutchou no keikakusho wo mite itadakitain desu ga...
Say, Section Manager, I would like you to look at the written itinerary for the business trip and I receive, but...

16. あ、悪いけど、客が来たので後にしてもらいたいんだ。

A, warui kedo, kyaku ga kita node ato ni moraitain da.
Ah, bad, but since a customer came, at later I would like you to do and I receive.

17. はい、じゃ又、後で来ます。

Hai. Ja mata, ato de kimasu.
Yes. Well, again, of later, I will come.

****

18. あのう、ウイリヤムズさん、京都に行くんですって。

Anou, uiriamuzu-san, kyouto ni ikun desu tte.
Say, Williams, you're going to Kyoto reportedly.

19. ええ、大阪の出張の帰りに寄るつもりなんです。

Ee, oosaka no shutchou no kaeri ni yorutsumori nan desu.
Yeah, at the Osaka's business trip's return, I plan to stop by.

20. ちょっと、お願いしてもいいかしら。

Chotto onegaishite mo ii kashira.
A little, doing begging is OK, I wonder.

21. ええ、何ですか。

Ee. Nan desu ka.
Yeah. What is it?

22. 京都の八つ橋というお菓子を
買ってきてもらいたいの。

Kyouto no yatsuhashi to iu okashi wo
katte kite moraitai no.
I would like you to buy and come and me
to receive Kyoto's yatsuhashi-called
sweets.

23. うちの母が大好きなのよ。

Uchi no haha ga daisuki na no yo.
My in-group's mother loves them, for
sure.

****

24. ああ、ウイリヤムズ君。さっ
きの出張の計画書の件だけ
ど、手が空いたから持ってき
て。

Aa, uiriamuzu-kun. Sakki no shutchou
no keikakusho no ken dakedo, te ga aita
kara motte kite.
Ah, young man Williams. It's the of-
previous business trip's written
itinerary's matter, but since my hand
became vacant (i.e., I became free), bring
it.

25. 今、見てしまうから。

Ima, mite shimau kara.
Now, since I will finish looking at it.

****

26. 北村課長はジョセフさんにど
こに行って欲しいと言ってい
ますか。

Kitamura kachou wa josefu-san ni doko
ni itte hoshii to itte imasu ka.
As for Section Manager Kitamura, to
Joseph, where is he saying he desires him
going?

27. ジョセフさんは何か書類を持
っていきますか。

Josefu-san wa nanika shorui wo motte
ikimasu ka.
As for Joseph, will he take something
documents?

28. 何も持っていきません。

Nanimo motte ikimasen.
He will take nothing.

29. 北村課長は今、忙しいので後
でジョセフさんの所へ行きま
す。

Kitamura kachou wa ima, isogashii node
ato de josefu-san no tokoro e ikimasu.
As for Section Manager Kitamura, now,
since he's busy, of later he will go to
Joseph's place.

30. ジョセフさんは黒田さんに京
都のお菓子を買って帰ること
になりました。

Josefu-san wa kuroda-san ni kyouto no
okashi wo katte kaeru koto ni
narimashita.
As for Joseph, for Kuroda, he was
scheduled to buy Kyoto's sweets and
return.

31. 黒田さんは八つ橋が大好きで
す。

Kuroda-san wa yatsuhashi ga daisuki
desu.
Kuroda loves yatsuhashi.

****

32. うちの課長、遅刻をするとすごくうるさいんです。

Uchi no kachou, chikoku wo suru to sugoku urusain desu.
The in-group's section manager, if one is tardy, is super noisy. (i.e., he complains awfully)

33. 遅刻をしないで欲しい。

Chikoku wo shinai de hoshii.
I desire that you not be tardy.

34. もっと残業をしてもらいたい。

Motto zangyou wo shite moraitai.
I would like you to do more overtime and I receive.

35. 字をきれいに書いてもらいたい。

Ji wo kirei ni kaite moraitai.
I would like you to write characters cleanly and I receive.

****

36. すみません。カメラのシャッターを押していただきたいんですが。

Sumimasen. Kamera no shattaa wo oshite itadakitain desu ga...
Excuse me. I would like you to push the camera shutter and I receive, but...

37. サンシャインビルというビルを知っていますか。

Sanshain biru to iu biru wo shitte imasu ka.
Are you knowing the building called the Sunshine building?

38. 東京で二番目に高いビルですよ。

Toukyou de nibanme ni takai biru desu yo.
Of Tokyo, it's the second tallest building, for sure.

39. カーネーションという花を知っていますか。

Kaaneeshon to iu hana wo shitte imasu ka.
Are you knowing the flower called carnation?

40. どんな花ですか。

Donna hana desu ka.
What sort of flower is it?

41. 母の日にお母さんにプレゼントする花で赤や白の物がありますよ。

Haha no hi ni okaasan ni purezento suru hana de aka ya shiro no mono ga arimasu yo.
On Mother's Day, it's a do-present-to-Mother flower, and there are red and white, etc. things, for sure.

42. せっかく京都に行くんだから、金閣寺でも見物してきたら？

Sekkaku kyouto ni ikun dakara, kinkakuji demo kenbutsu shite kitara?
With much trouble, since you're going to Kyoto, if you could sightsee Kinkakuji at least and come?

43. 天気がいいから散歩でもして来ようかな。

Tenki ga ii kara, sanpo demo shite koyou kana.
Since the weather is good, I wonder if I shall do walking or something and come.

44. ローレンさんが来るまでトランプでもしていましょう。

Rooren-san ga kuru made toranpu demo shite imashou.
Until Lauren comes, let's be playing cards or something.

45. 今度の日曜日は車で箱根にでも行きませんか。

Kondo no nichiyoubi wa kuruma de hakone ni demo ikimasen ka.
As for next Sunday, will we not go to Hakone or somewhere by car?

46. 今日、お宅に行ってもよろしいでしょうか。

Kyou, otaku ni itte mo yoroshii deshou ka.
Today would it probably be all right if I go to the honorable home?

47. ちょっと、母が病気なので。

Chotto, haha ga byouki na node.
A little bit, because Mother is sick. (i.e., please don't come)

48. これ、もう捨ててもよろしいですか。

Kore, mou sutete mo yoroshii desu ka.
This, already, is it all right if I throw it away?

49. いや、捨てないでください。

Iya, sutenai de kudasai.
Nah, don't throw it away please.

50. ちょっと、調べたいことがあるから。

Chotto shirabetai koto ga aru kara.
A little bit, because want-to-check thing exists.

51. 5時前に帰ってもよろしいでしょうか。

Go ji mae ni kaette mo yoroshii deshou ka.
Is it probably all right if I return before 5:00?

52. ああ、構いませんよ。どうぞ。

Aa. Kamaimasen yo. Douzo.
Ah, it doesn't matter, for sure. Go ahead.

53. 子供にりんごを取らせています。

Kodomo ni ringo wo torasete imasu.
To the child, he is making take the apple.

Chapter 76

1. 仕事が終わってから京都見物
   をする予定だったので、アッ
   シュリーと二人で東京を出発
   した。

   Shigoto ga owatte kara kyouto kenbutsu
   wo suru yotei datta node, asshurii to
   futari de toukyou wo shuppatsu shita.
   After work finished, because it was a do-
   sightsee-Kyoto plan, with Ashley, of
   two people, we departed from Tokyo.

2. 私の仕事が終わるまで一人で
   京都を見物するといって、ア
   ッシュリーは途中の京都駅で
   新幹線を降りた。

   Watashi no shigoto ga owaru made hitori
   de kyouto wo kenbutsu suru to itte,
   asshuri wa tochuu no kyouto eki de
   shinkansen wo orita.
   Until my work will finish, by herself,
   saying she will sightsee Kyoto, Ashley,
   at the on-the-way Kyoto station, got off
   the bullet train.

3. 新大阪駅には第一貿易の人が
   二人、迎えにきてくれてい
   た。

   Shin oosaka eki ni wa dai ichi boueki no
   hito ga futari, mukae ni kite kurete ita.
   As for at the New Osaka station, Number
   One Trade people, two people, in order
   to meet/receive, came, gave and were.

4. 会社は駅から近かった。

   Kaisha wa eki kara chikakatta.
   As for the company, from the station it
   was close.

5. アメリカに支社を出す件につ
   いての話が早く終わったの
   で、他のことについても話し
   合った。

   Amerika ni shisha wo dasu ken ni tsuite
   no hanashiai ga hayaku owatta node,
   hoka no koto ni tsuite mo hanashiatta.
   Since the discussion regarding the matter
   of putting out a branch office to America
   finished early, we discussed regarding
   other things also.

6. 10時頃、大阪駅からアッシュ
   リーに電話した。

   Juuji goro, oosaka eki kara asshurii ni
   denwa shita.
   About 10:00, from the Osaka station, I
   did a phone call to Ashley.

7. アッシュリーはちょっと怒っ
   ていた。

   Asshurii wa chotto okotte ita.
   Ashley was a little mad.

8. もっと早く電話して欲しかっ
たと言った。

Motto hayaku denwa shite hoshikatta to
itta.
I desired you to do a phone call earlier,
she said.

9. それで花を買って急いでホテ
ルへ行った。

Sore de hana wo katte isoide hoteru e
itta.
For that reason, I bought flowers and
went hurrying to the hotel.

10. アッシュリーさんはジェイコ
ブさんにどんなことを頼みま
したか。

Asshurii-san wa jeikobu-san ni donna
koto wo tanomimashita ka.
As for Ashley, what sort of thing did she
request of Jacob?

11. 仕事が終わったらホテルに電
話をすることを頼みました。

Shigoto ga owattara hoteru ni denwa wo
suru koto wo tanomimashita.
When the work finished, she asked him
to do a phone call to the hotel.

****

12. 暗くなってきたから電気を点
けてもいいかしら？

Kurakunatte kita kara denki wo tsukete
mo ii kashira?
Since it became dark and came (i.e., it
started to get dark), is it OK to turn on
the light I wonder?

13. 他に席が空いていないのでこ
こに座ってもいいですか。

Hoka ni seki ga aite inai node koko ni
suwatte mo ii desu ka.
Since differently a seat is not open (i.e., a
different seat is not open), is it OK if I sit
here?

14. あの、すみません。友達が来
ることになっていますので...

Ano, sumimasen. Tomodachi ga kuru
koto ni natte imasu node...
Say, excuse me. Because a friend is
scheduled to come...

15. 遅れてすみません。

Okurete sumimasen.
Since I get delayed, excuse me.

16. 会議がなかなか終わらなかっ
たものですから。

Kaigi ga nakanaka owaranakatta mono
desu kara.
Because the meeting was a not readily
ended thing.

17. ああ、そうですか。構いませ
んよ。

Aa, sou desu ka. Kamaimasen yo.
Ah, is that so? It doesn't matter, for sure.

18. 駅の近くまで車で行きました
が道がとても込んでいまし
た。

Eki no chikaku made kuruma de
ikimashita ga michi ga totemo konde
imashita.
Until the station's closely, I went by car,
but the street was very crowded.

19. 約束した時間より 1 時間も遅れました。

Yakusoku shita jikan yori, ichijikan mo okuremashita.
Compared to the hour I did the appointment, I was as much as one hour delayed.

20. 遅れてごめんなさい。 道がとても込んでいたので。

Okurete gomen nasai. Michi ga totemo konde ita node.
Since I got delayed, forgive me. Because the streets were very crowded.

21. そう、あまり遅いからもう来ないかと思ったよ。

****

Sou. Amari osoi kara mou konai ka to omotta yo.
Is that so? Since very late, will no longer come (question) I thought, for sure.

22. 火曜日に小田さんのうちでパーティをします。

Kayoubi ni oda-san no uchi de paati wo shimasu.
On Tuesday, we will do a party at Oda's home.

23. 前田さんも行くつもりでしたが、急に大阪に出張することになりました。

Maeda-san mo ikutsumori deshita ga, kyuu ni oosaka ni shutchou suru koto ni narimashita.
Maeda also was planning to go, but suddenly he was scheduled to do a business trip to Osaka.

24. 申し訳ないんですが、パーティに行けなくなってしまいました。

Moushiwake nain desu ga, paatii ni ikenaku natte shimaimashita.
There's no excuse, but it completely became unable to go to the party.

25. 急に大阪に出張することになったものですから。

****

Kyuu ni oosaka ni shutchou suru koto ni natta mono desu kara.
Suddenly since to-Osaka-do-business-trip-was-scheduled thing it is.

26. 小林さんは水野さんと 3 時に会う約束をしていました。

Kobayashi-san wa mizuno-san to sanji ni au yakusoku wo shite imashita.
As for Kobayashi, with Mizuno, an at-3:00-to-meet appointment, he was doing.

27. でも会議が長くなって 3 時には会えませんでした。

Demo kaigi ga nagaku natte sanji ni wa aemasen deshita.
But since a meeting becomes long, as for at 3:00, he was not able to meet.

28. 水野さんは帰ってしまいました。

Mizuno-san wa kaette shimaimashita.
As for Mizuno, he completely returned.

29. もしもし、小林ですが先ほど
   は申し訳ありませんでした。

Moshimoshi, kobayashi desu ga saki hodo wa moushiwake arimasen deshita.
Hello. It's Kobayashi, but as for a little while ago, there was no excuse.

30. 会議が長くなってしまったも
   のですから。

Kaigi ga nagakunatte shimatta mono desu kara.
Since it's a meeting-became-completely-long thing.

31. ああ、そうですか。では又、
   今度よろしくお願いします。
                    ****

Aa, sou desu ka. Dewa, mata kondo yoroshiku onegai shimasu.
Ah, is that so? Well, again next time, please be good to me.

32. 山本さんは竹田さんから借り
   た書類にコーヒーをこぼしま
   した。

Yamamoto-san wa takeda-san kara karita shorui ni koohii wo koboshimashita.
As for Yamamoto, to a document borrowed from Takeda, he spilled coffee.

33. 申し訳ございません。書類に
   コーヒーをこぼしてしまいま
   した。

Moushiwake gozaimasen. Shorui ni koohii wo koboshite shimaimashita.
There's no excuse. To the document, I completely spilled coffee.

34. 困るねぇ。もっと気を付けて
   くださいよ。
                    ****

Komaru nee. Motto ki wo tsukete kudasai yo.
I will be inconvenienced, huh. Please be more careful, for sure.

35. 図書館から本を3冊借りまし
   たが忙しくて読む時間があり
   ませんでした。

Toshokan kara hon wo sansatsu karimashita ga isogashikute yomu jikan ga arimasen deshita.
From the library, I borrowed three books, but since I am busy, there was no reading time.

36. 返すのが遅くなってすみませ
   ん。

Kaesu no ga osoku natte sumimasen.
Since returning them became late, excuse me.

37. 忙しくて読む時間がなかった
   ものですから。

Isogashikute yomu jikan ga nakatta mono desu kara.
I'm busy, and it's since reading time didn't exist thing.

38. そうでしたか。じゃ、仕方が
   ないですね。

Sou deshita ka. Ja, shikata ga nai desu ne.
Was that so? Well, it can't be helped, huh.

39. でもこれからは気を付けてく
ださいよ。

Demo kore kara wa ki wo tsukete
kudasai yo.
But as for from now, please be careful,
for sure.

****

40. 夜はテレビを見たりレコード
を聞いたりして過ごします。

Yoru wa terebi wo mitari rekoodo wo
kiitari shite sugoshimasu.
As for evenings, watch TV, etc., listen to
records, etc., I do and spend.

41. 小さい子供がいるのでここで
野球をしたりしてはいけませ
ん。

Chiisai kodomo ga iru node koko de
yakyuu wo shitari shite wa ikemasen.
Because small children exist, at here, do
baseball, etc., you mustn't do.

42. 毎朝日本の新聞を読んでいま
すか。

Maiasa nihon no shinbun wo yonde
imasu ka.
Every morning, are you reading a
newspaper of Japan?

43. いいえ、読んだり読まなかっ
たりです。

Iie, yondari yomanakattari desu.
No, sometimes I read, sometimes I don't
read.

44. 洋服を作ったり犬を連れて散
歩に行ったりします。

Youfuku wo tsukuttari inu wo tsurete
sanpo ni ittari shimasu.
Make Western clothes, etc., take dogs
along and go for the purpose of a walk,
etc., they do.

45. 食べ過ぎたり飲み過ぎたりす
ると病気になりますよ。

Tabesugitari nomisugitari suru to byouki
ni narimasu yo.
If you eat too much, etc., drink too much,
etc., do, it will develop sickness, for sure.

46. ホテルを予約したり洋服をバ
ッグに入れたりして旅行の準
備をします。

Hoteru wo yoyaku shitari youfuku wo
baggu ni iretari shite ryokou no junbi wo
shimasu.
Reserve a hotel, etc., put Western clothes
in a bag, etc., doing, I will do travel
preparations.

47. 仕事が大変な間はテレビは見
られません。

Shigoto ga taihen na aida wa terebi wa
miraremasen.
As for work-terrible interval, as for TV, I
cannot watch. (i.e., I can't watch TV
when I'm busy at work)

48. あの画家はとても正直です。

Ano gaka wa totemo shoujiki desu.
That artist is very honest.

49. 僕はその日出張なんです
よ。

Boku wa sono hi shutchou nan desu yo.
As for me, that day it is a business trip,
for sure.

Chapter 77

1. テレビを見たりテープを聞いたりして日本語の勉強をしています。

Terebi wo mitari teepu wo kiitari shite nihongo no benkyou wo shite imasu.
Watch TV, etc., listen to tapes, etc. doing, I'm doing Japanese language's study.

2. 日曜日にはいつもゴルフに行きますか。

Nichiyoubi ni wa itsumo gorufu ni ikimasu ka.
As for on Sunday, do you always go for the purpose of golf?

3. 行ったり行かなかったりです。

Ittari ikanakattari desu.
Sometimes I go, sometimes I don't go.

4. 仕事が忙しい時には行きません。

Shigoto ga isogashii toki ni wa ikimasen.
As for at the time when work is busy, I don't go.

5. 毎晩テレビを見るんですか。

Maiban terebi wo mirun desu ka.
Every night, do you watch TV?

6. 見たり見なかったりです。

Mitari minakattari desu.
Sometimes I watch, sometimes I don't watch.

7. 日本では野菜は一年中高いですか。

Nihon de wa yasai wa ichinenjuu takai desu ka.
As for in Japan, as for vegetables, are they expensive throughout the year?

8. 高かったり安かったりです。

Takakattari yasukattari desu.
Sometimes they're expensive, sometimes they're cheap.

9. 夏は大体安いですよ。

Natsu wa daitai yasui desu yo.
As for summer, generally they're cheap, for sure.

10. スペイン語ができたら一度メキシコへ行ってみたいです。

Supeingo ga dekitara, ichido mekishiko e itte mitai desu.
If I could do Spanish, one time I would like to go to Mexico and see.

11. 子供の時は泳ぐことができませんでした。

Kodomo no toki wa oyogu koto ga dekimasen deshita.
As for the child time, I could not swim.

12. ジョセフさんは日本語で手紙を書くことができるんですよ。

Josefu-san wa nihongo de tegami wo kaku koto ga dekirun desu yo.
As for Joseph, in Japanese he can write a letter, for sure.

13. サラさんは何でも食べられますので、どうぞ心配しないでください。

Sara-san wa nandemo taberaremasu node, douzo shinpai shinai de kudasai.
Since, as for Sarah, she can eat anything, go ahead, please don't worry.

14. ここから富士山が良く見えますよ。

Koko kara fujisan ga yoku miemasu yo.
From here, Mt. Fuji can be seen well, for sure.

15. 隣の部屋のラジオの音が聞こえますか。

Tonari no heya no rajio no oto ga kikoemasu ka.
Is the next-door room's radio sound audible?

16. 電話が掛けられる。

Denwa ga kakerareru.
It's possible to call on the phone.

17. プールで泳ぐことができます。

Puuru de oyogu koto ga dekimasu.
One can swim in the pool.

18. ボートに乗れます。

Booto ni noremasu.
One can ride in a boat.

19. バストイレが使えます。

Basu toire ga tsukaemasu.
One can use a bath/toilet.

20. 山登りができます。

Yama nobori ga dekimasu.
One can do mountain climb.

21. フランス料理が食べられます。

Furansu ryouri ga taberaremasu.
One can eat French cuisine.

22. ホテルでは部屋のお風呂の他に温泉に入れます。

Hoteru de wa heya no ofuro no hoka ni onsen ni hairemasu.
As for at the hotel, in addition to the room's honorable bath, one can enter a hot spring.

23. 日本では六月になるとよく雨が降るようになります。

Nihon de wa rokugatsu ni naru to yoku ame ga furu you ni narimasu.
As for in Japan, when June becomes, it gets to the point that it often rains.

24. 店がきれいになってからたく
さんのお客さんが来るように
なりました。

Mise ga kirei ni natte kara takusan no okyakusan ga kuru you ni narimashita.
Since the store becomes pretty, it got to the point that lots of honorable customers come.

25. 日本語の新聞が読めるように
なりたいです。

Nihongo no shinbun ga yomeru you ni naritai desu.
I would like to get to the point that I can read a Japanese language newspaper.

26. 練習しているうちにスケート
ができるようになりました。

Renshuu shite iru uchi ni sukeeto ga dekiru you ni narimashita.
While still being doing practice, it got to the point that I was able to skate.

27. 夏休み中プールに通ったので
500メートル泳ぐことができ
るようになりました。

Natsuyasumi chuu puuru ni kayotta node go hyaku meetoru oyogu koto ga dekiru you ni narimashita.
Throughout summer vacation, since I commuted to a pool, I got to the point that I was able to swim 500 meters.

28. 毎日練習したので漢字が上手
に書けるようになりました。

Mainichi renshuu shita node kanji ga jouzu ni kakeru you ni narimashita.
Because every day I practiced, I got to the point that I was able to write kanji skillfully.

29. 日本人の友達に教えてもらっ
て日本の歌が歌えるようにな
りました。

Nihonjin no tomodachi ni oshiete moratte nihon no uta ga utaeru you ni narimashita.
By a Japanese person's friend teaching and I receiving, I got to the point that I was able to sing Japan's songs.

30. もっと漢字を覚えるようにし
ます。

Motto kanji wo oboeru you ni shimasu.
I'll make an effort to memorize more kanji.

31. 帰りが遅い時は電話をして
ね。

Kaeri ga osoi toki wa, denwa wo shite ne.
As for the return-is-late time, do a phone call, huh.

32. うん、電話を掛けるようにす
るよ。

Un, denwa wo kakeru you ni suru yo.
Yeah, I will make an effort to call on the phone, for sure.

33. 又、遅れましたね。

Mata okuremashita ne.
Again, you were delayed huh.

34. すみません。明日は遅れない
ようにします。

Sumimasen. Ashita wa okurenai you ni shimasu.
Excuse me. As for tomorrow, I will make an effort not to be delayed.

35. 学生のうちによく勉強してお
きなさい。

Gakusei no uchi ni yoku benkyou shite okinasai.
While you are still a student, study in advance often.

36. 学生の間にいろんな所を旅行
するつもりです。

Gakusei no aida ni ironna tokoro wo ryokou surutsumori desu.
While I'm a student, I plan to travel on various places.

37. どうぞ、熱いうちに食べてく
ださい。

Douzo, atsui uchi ni tabete kudasai.
Go ahead, while it's still hot, eat please.

38. スープが冷めないうちに飲ん
でください。

Suupu ga samenai uchi ni nonde kudasai.
While the soup still doesn't get cold, please drink.

39. 雨が降らないうちに帰った方
がいいと思うからこれで失礼
します。

Ame ga furanai uchi ni kaetta hou ga ii to omou kara kore de shitsurei shimasu.
Since, while it still doesn't rain, I think it would be better to return, from now I will commit a discourtesy. (i.e., I will leave)

40. 雨が止んでいる間に買い物に
行ってきましょう。

Ame ga yande iru aida ni kaimono ni itte kimashou.
While the rain is stopping, let's go for shopping and come.

41. 来年から値段が上がります。

Rainen kara nedan ga agarimasu.
From next year, prices will rise.

42. 安いうちに買っておいた方が
いいですよ。

Yasui uchi ni katte oita hou ga ii desu yo.
While still cheap, it would be better to buy in advance, for sure.

43. 音楽を聞いているうちに踊り
たくなってきました。

Ongaku wo kiite iru uchi ni odoritakunatte kimashita.
While still is listening to music, it became wanting to dance and came.

44. 暗くならないうちに散歩に行
ってきましょう。

Kurakunaranai uchi ni sanpo ni itte kimashou.
While it still doesn't become dark, let's go for a walk and come.

45. マリースミスさんは漢字がど
のくらい読めますか。

Marii sumisu-san wa kanji ga dono kurai yomemasu ka.
As for Mary Smith, about how many kanji can she read?

46. 試験の結果はいつ頃分かりま
すか。

Shiken no kekka wa itsu goro wakarimasu ka.
As for the result of the test, about when will she know/understand?

47. いい友達がたくさんできて幸せです。

Ii tomodachi ga takusan dekite shiawase desu.
Because many good friends are possible, it's happiness.

48. あっ！びっくりした。急に犬が飛び出して来るんだもの。

A! Bikkuri shita. Kyuu ni inu ga tobidashite kurun da mono.
Ah! I got surprised. Suddenly a dog jumps out and will come thing.

****

49. 花田さん、夏休みはどうするんですか。

Hanada san, natsuyasumi wa dou surun desu ka.
Hanada, as for summer vacation, how will you do?

50. 鹿児島ってどこですか。

Kagoshima tte doko desu ka.
As for the one called Kagoshima, where is it?

51. 九州の一番南にある県よ。

Kyuushuu no ichiban minami ni aru ken yo.
Kyushu's at-farthest-south-it-exists prefecture, for sure.

52. 桜島という火山があるわ。

Sakurajima to iu kazan ga aru wa.
The Sakurajima-called volcano exists.

53. ああ、一度テレビで見たことがあります。

Aa, ichido terebi de mita koto ga arimasu.
Ah, one time on TV I have seen it.

54. 本物を見てみたいなぁ。

Honmono wo mite mitai naa.
I would like to see the real one and see.

55. いつか奥さんと遊びに来て。いい所よ。

Itsuka okusan to asobi ni kite. Ii tokoro yo.
Sometime with the wife for the purpose of play, come. Good place, for sure.

56. ニコラスさんは何を見てみたいと言っていますか。

Nikorasu-san wa nani wo mite mitai to itte imasu ka.
As for Nicholas, what would he like to see and see, is he saying?

57. 本物の桜島を見てみたいと言っています。

Honmono no sakurajima wo mite mitai to itte imasu.
He is saying that he would like to see and see the real Sakurajima.

Chapter 78

1. 今年の四月に課長になりました。

Kotoshi no shigatsu ni kachou ni narimashita.
At this year's April, I became section manager.

2. 初めはとても嬉しかったのですがこの頃はちょっと。

Hajime wa totemo ureshikatta no desu ga kono goro wa chotto...
As for the beginning, I was very pleased, but as for these days, a little bit...

3. 課長になってから前より残業が多くなりました。

Kachou ni natte kara mae yori zangyou ga ooku narimashita.
Since I become section manager, compared to before, overtime became numerous.

4. 部下が仕事をしているのに私だけ先に帰れませんから。

Buka ga shigoto wo shite iru noni watashi dake saki ni kaeremasen kara.
Since, in spite of the fact that subordinates are working, I alone cannot return before others.

5. ちっとも疲れが取れません。

Chittomo tsukare ga toremasen.
Not at all, I can't take the fatigue out of myself.

6. 最近、夜も眠れないんです。

Saikin, yoru mo nemurenain desu.
Recently, even night I cannot sleep.

7. ベッドに入ってから2時間も3時間も眠れないことが多いんです。

Beddo ni haitte kara nijikan mo sanjikan mo nemurenai koto ga ooin desu.
After getting into bed, as much as two hours, as much as three hours, unable-to-sleep thing is numerous.

8. それで朝早く起きられませんし朝食もあまり食べられません。

Sore de asa hayaku okiraremasen shi choushoku mo amari taberaremasen.
For that reason, early in the morning, I can't get up, and even breakfast I can hardly eat.

9. 新聞もあまり読めないんです。

Shinbun mo amari yomenai desu.
Even the newspaper I can hardly read.

10. 読むと頭が痛くなって。

Yomu to atama ga itaku natte...
If I read, the head becomes painful, and...

11. 会社に行くのが辛くなりました。

****

Kaisha ni iku no ga tsuraku narimashita.
To go to the company became bitter.

12. 山田さんはとても真面目な方だと思います。

Yamada-san wa totemo majime na kata da to omoimasu.
As for Yamada, he is a sincere person, I think.

13. でも、人間は一人で何もかもすることはできません。

Demo, ningen wa hitori de nanimokamo suru koto wa dekimasen.
But humans, by themselves, as for to do everything, they are unable.

14. 部下に仕事を任せることも必要です。

Buka ni shigoto wo makaseru koto mo hitsuyou desu.
To the subordinates, to entrust work thing is also necessary.

15. そして、休みの日にはスポーツをしたり散歩をしたりいい音楽を聞いたりしてください。

Soshite, yasumi no hi ni wa supootsu wo shitari sanpo wo shitari ii ongaku wo kiitari shite kudasai.
And then, as for on vacation days, do sports, etc., do walking, etc., listen to good music, etc, do please.

16. そのうちにリラックスできるようになります。

****

Sono uchi ni rirakkusu dekiru you ni narimasu.
Before long, you will get to the point that you are able to relax.

17. 山田さんが疲れるのはどうしてですか。

Yamada-san ga tsukareru no wa doushite desu ka.
As for Yamada will tire thing, why is it?

18. 課長になってから前より残業が増えたり休みの日も仕事のことを色々考えて、ゆっくり休めないからです。

Kachou ni natte kara mae yori zangyou ga fuetari yasumi no hi mo shigoto no koto wo iroiro kangaete, yukkuri yasumenai kara desu.
Since he became section manager, compared to before, overtime work increased, etc., even vacation days he thinks about various work things, and he cannot rest leisurely, it's because.

19. 山田さんは休みの日にはどんなことを考えていますか。

Yamada-san wa yasumi no hi ni wa donna koto wo kangaete imasu ka.
As for Yamada, as for on vacation days, what kind of things is he thinking?

20. 課長の仕事がちゃんとできる
だろうか、部下をうまくコン
トロールできるだろうかなど
と考えています。

Kacho no shigoto ga chanto dekiru darou
ka, buka wo umaku kontorooru dekiru
darou ka nado to kangaete imasu.
Will the section manager's work probably
properly accomplish, on the
subordinates, skillfully will the control
probably accomplish, etc., he is thinking.

21. そのために山田さんはどうな
りましたか。

Sono tame ni yamada-san wa dou
narimashita ka.
As a result of that, as for Yamada, how
did it develop?

22. 夜眠れなかったり、朝早く起
きれなかったり、朝食もあま
り食べられなかったり、新聞
を読むと頭が痛くなったりす
るようになりました。

Yoru nemurenakattari, asa hayaku
okirenakattari, choushoku mo amari
taberarenakattari, shinbun wo yomu to
atama ga itakunattari suru you ni
narimashita.
Night unable to sleep, etc., morning
unable to get up early, etc., even
breakfast hardly able to eat, etc., if he
reads the newspaper, head becomes
painful, etc., to do, it got to this point.

****

23. 僕は3週間ぐらい休みが欲し
いなぁ。

Boku wa sanshuukan gurai yasumi ga
hoshii naa.
As for me, I desire about a three-week
vacation.

24. ボーナスを休みでもらえない
んですか。

Boonasu wo yasumi de moraenain desu
ka.
Can't I receive the bonus as vacation?

25. ええ、日本ではボーナスはお
金でもらうのよ。

Ee, nihon de wa boonasu wa okane de
morau no yo.
Yeah, as for in Japan, as for bonuses, we
receive them in money, for sure.

26. 一週間だけか夏休みは。

Isshuukan dake ka, natsuyasumi wa.
Only one week (question), as for summer
vacation.

27. やっぱり働き過ぎなんじゃな
い、日本人は。

Yappari hatarakisugi nan ja nai, nihonjin
wa.
When you think about it, too much labor,
isn't it, as for Japanese people?

28 そうね。私もそう思うわ。

Sou ne. Watashi mo sou omou wa.
True huh. I also think so.

29. アメリカではどのくらい休む
の？

Amerika de wa dono kurai yasumu no?
As for in America, about how long do
they rest?

30. 人によるけど大体一ヶ月ぐら
いかな。

Hito ni yoru kedo daitai ikka getsu gurai
kana.
It will depend to the person, but usually
about one month, I wonder.

31. えっ、1ヶ月も。いいわね
え。

E, ikkagetsu mo. Ii wa nee.
Eh, as much as one month. Good, huh.

32. ニコラスさんは自分がもらう
ボーナスを、多いと言ってい
ますか、少ないと言っていま
すか。

Nikorasu-san wa jibun ga morau boonasu
wo, ooi to itte imasu ka, sukunai to itte
imasu ka.
As for Nicholas, the himself-will-receive
bonus is numerous, is he saying, is few,
is he saying?

33. 少ないと言っています

Sukunai to itte imasu.
It's few, he is saying. (i.e., it's a little)

****

34. 直子さんと結婚することにな
ったんですって。

Naoko-san to kekkon suru koto ni nattan
desu tte.
With Naoko, it was scheduled to marry,
reportedly. (woman's speech)

35. ずいぶん楽しそうでしたよ。

Zuibun tanoshi sou deshita yo.
Extremely pleasant it seemed, for sure.
(i.e., she looked very happy)

36. ジェイムズさんは京都に行っ
たけど雨が降ってつまらなか
ったと言っていました。

Jeimuzu-san wa kyouto ni itta kedo ame
ga futte tsumaranakatta to itte imashita.
As for James, he went to Kyoto, but
since it rained, it was boring, he was
saying.

37. 今年のベースアップは0.7パ
ーセントだそうですよ。

Kotoshi no beesuappu wa rei ten nana
paasento da sou desu yo.
As for this year's raise of the wage base,
it is 0.7%, reportedly, for sure.

38. 何だ0.7パーセントしかない
んですか。

Nanda, rei ten nana paasento shika nain
desu ka.
What do you mean? Except for 0.7%
only, it's nothing?

39. 良く勉強しましたね。テスト
は百点でしたよ。

Yoku benkyou shimashita ne. Tesuto wa
hyaku ten deshita yo.
You studied well, huh. As for the test, it
was 100 points, for sure.

40. えっ！ 本当ですか。嬉しい
なぁ。90点しか取れないと思
っていました。

E! Hontou desu ka. Ureshii naa.
Kyuujutten shika torenai to omotte
imashita.
Eh, is that true. Pleased! Except for 90
points only I cannot take, I was thinking.

41. 前田さんと結婚するので一ヶ
月休みが欲しいんですが。

Maeda-san to kekkon suru node
ikkagetsu yasumi ga hoshiin desu ga...
Because I will marry with Maeda, I
desire one month vacation, but...

42. 一ヶ月も？ 直子さんの仕事
を誰に頼んだらいいかなぁ。

Ikkagetsu mo? Naoko-san no shigoto wo
dare ni tanondara ii kanaa.
All of one month? Naoko's work, to
whom if I request will be good, I wonder.

43. 直子さんは嬉しそうです。

Naoko-san wa ureshii sou desu.
As for Naoko, pleased it seems.

44. 池田さんはがっかりしていま
す。

Ikeda-san wa gakkari shite imasu.
As for Ikeda, he is being disappointed.

45. 返事を出さないうちに、又次
の手紙が来てしまいました。

Henji wo dasanai uchi ni, mata tsugi no
tegami ga kite shimaimashita.
While the reply still is not sent, again the
following letter came completely (i.e.,
came anyway).

46. 水野さん、ニコニコして、ず
いぶん嬉しそうですねぇ。何
かあったんですか。

Mizuno-san, nikoniko shite, zuibun
ureshi sou desu nee. Nanika attan desu
ka.
Mizuno, doing a smile, is extremely
pleased it seems, huh. Did something
exist? (i.e., did something happen?)

47. ええ、ボーナスを六ヶ月分も
もらったんだそうですよ。

Ee, boonasu wo rokkagetsu bun mo
morattan da sou desu yo.
Yeah, he received as much as a six-
month part bonus reportedly, for sure.

48. 僕は二ヶ月分しかもらえない
んですよ。

Boku wa nikkagetsu bun shika
moraenain desu yo.
As for me, except for a two-month part
only, I cannot receive, for sure.

Chapter 79

1. あぁ、楽しかった、友達が来てくれて。

Aa, tanoshikatta, tomodachi ga kite kurete...
Ah, it was pleasant. The friend coming and giving...

2. あの店にはこれしかなかったんですよ。

Ano mise ni wa kore shika nakattan desu yo.
As for in that store over there, except for this only, it didn't exist, for sure. (i.e., this is the only kind they had)

3. 仕方がないですね。じゃ、これで結構です。

Shikata ga nai desu ne. Ja, kore de kekkou desu.
It can't be helped, huh. Well, with this is fine.

4. 夏休みは何日取れるんですか。

Natsuyasumi wa nannichi torerun desu ka.
As for summer vacation, how many days can you take?

5. それが一週間しか取れないんですよ。

Sore ga isshuukan shika torenain desu yo.
That, except for one week only, I cannot take, for sure.

6. 東京から京都まで新幹線でどのくらいかかるんですか。

Toukyou kara kyouto made shinkansen de dono kurai kakarun desu ka.
From Tokyo to Kyoto, by bullet train, about how long will it take?

7. 2時間45分しかからないんですよ。

Nijikan yonjuu gofun shika kakaranain desu yo.
Except for 2 hours and 45 minutes only, it doesn't take, for sure.

8. 私は社宅に住んでいますから二万円しかかかりません。

Watashi wa shataku ni sunde imasu kara niman'en shika kakarimasen.
As for me, since I'm living in company housing, except for 20,000 yen only, it doesn't cost.

9. 楽しいショーですねぇ。終わりまで後、何時間ありますか。

Tanoshii shou desu nee. Owari made ato, nanjikan arimasu ka.
It's a pleasant show, huh. Until the end, remaining, how many hours exist?

10. 後20分で終わりですよ。

Ato nijuppun de owari desu yo.
Remaining, in 20 minutes (i.e., in another 20 minutes), the end is, for sure.

11. 後20分しかないんですか。
残念だなぁ。

Ato nijippun shika nain desu ka. Zannen da naa.
Except for remaining 20 minutes only, doesn't it exist? That's too bad.

12. あなたの会社には英語を話せる人がたくさんいるんでしょう？

Anata no kaisha ni wa eigo wo hanaseru hito ga takusan irun deshou?
As for at your company, able-to-speak-English people, a lot, exist probably?

13. それが二、三人しかいないんですよ。

Sore ga nisan nin shika inain desu yo.
That, except for two/three people only, they don't exist, for sure.

14. 食事をして行きたいんだけど、君、お金を持ってる？

Shokuji wo shite ikitain dakedo, kimi, okane wo motteru?
I would like to do a meal and go, but you, are you having money?

15. 今千円しか持っていないけど。

Ima sen'en shika motte inai kedo...
Now, except for 1,000 yen only, I am not having, but...

16. なんだ、それだけしかないのか。

Nanda, sore dake shika nai no ka.
What do you mean? Except for that only, doesn't it exist?

17. じゃ、食事をしないでうちに帰ろう。

Ja, shokuji wo shinai de uchi ni kaerou.
Well, not doing a meal, let's return to home.

18. お母さん、友達が五人来るんだけどお菓子、買ってある？

Okaasan, tomodachi ga gonin kurun dakedo okashi, katte aru?
Mother, five friends will come, but sweets, are they bought and exist?

19. えっ、五人も。ケーキを三つしか買ってないのよ。

E! Gonin mo. Keeki wo mittsu shika katte nai no yo.
Eh. All of five people. Except for cakes three only, they are not bought and do not exist, for sure.

20. 困ったわねぇ。

Komatta wa nee.
Inconvenienced, huh.

21. このバッグはあの店しか売ってないそうですよ。

Kono baggu wa ano mise shika utte nai sou desu yo.
As for this bag, except for that store over there only, they are not selling, reportedly, for sure.

22. じゃ、欲しかったらあの店に
買いに行くしかないわね。

Ja, hoshikattara ano mise ni kai ni iku
shika nai wa ne.
Well, if you desire it, except to go for the
purpose of buying to that store over there
only, it doesn't exist, huh.

23. あの映画は今日までだそうで
すよ。

Ano eiga wa kyou made da sou desu yo.
As for that movie over there, it's until
today, reportedly, for sure.

24. そうですか。じゃ、雨が降っ
ているけど今日見に行くしか
ないですね。

Sou desu ka. Jaa, ame ga futte iru kedo
kyou mi ni iku shika nai desu ne.
Is that so? Well, it's raining, but today
except for to go for the purpose of
seeing, it doesn't exist, huh.

25. ホンコンというのはどんな
所ですか。

Honkon to iu no wa donna tokoro desu
ka.
As for the one called Hong Kong, what
kind of place is it?

26. あの建物の中に入っちゃだめ
だよ。

Ano tatemono no naka ni haitcha dame
da yo.
To that over there's building's inside, as
for entering, it's bad, for sure.

27. だめってどうしてですか。

Dame tte doushite desu ka.
As for the one called bad, why is it?
(i.e., why do you say bad?)

28. 工事中で危ないからだよ。

Kouji chuu de abunai kara da yo.
Since under construction, since
dangerous it is, for sure.

29. 会社の社長って誰ですか。

Kaisha no shachou tte dare desu ka.
As for the one called the company's
president, who is it?

30. 中山さんです。

Nakayama-san desu.
It's Nakayama.

31. 夏休みっていつですか。

Natsuyasumi tte itsu desu ka.
As for the one called summer vacation,
when is it?

32. 七月二十日から九月五日まで
ですよ。

Shichigatsu hatsuka kara kugatsu itsuka
made desu yo.
From July 20th until September 5th it is,
for sure.

33. 私は山は好きですが、海はあ
まり好きじゃないんですよ。

Watashi wa yama wa suki desu ga, umi
wa amari suki ja nain desu yo.
As for me, as for mountains, I like them,
but as for the ocean, I don't like it much,
for sure.

34. 好きじゃないってどうしてですか。

Suki ja nai tte doushite desu ka.
As for the one called I don't like, why is it?

35. だって泳げないんです。

Datte oyogenain desu.
Because I can't swim.

36. 人が泳いでいるのを見ているだけじゃつまらないですから。

Hito ga oyoide iru no wo mite iru dake ja tsumaranai desu kara.
As for of only to be looking at people-are-swimming thing, since it's boring.

37. 誰に聞いたらいいか教えてください。

Dare ni kiitara ii ka oshiete kudasai.
To whom if I ask good (question), please teach.

38. 来週のパーティには何人来ますか。

Raishuu no paatii ni wa nannin kimasu ka.
As for to next week's party, how many will come?

39. 何人来るか聞いていません。

Nannin kuru ka kiite imasen.
How many will come (question) I'm not hearing.

40. 誰が来ないか早く調べておいた方がいいですよ。

Dare ga konai ka hayaku shirabete oita hou ga ii desu yo.
Who won't come (question), early, it would be better to check in advance, for sure.

41. 花田さんにどこへ行くつもりか聞きました。

Hanada-san ni doko e ikutsumori ka kikimashita.
By Hanada, to where they are planning to go (question), I heard.

42. 駅で何時間並んだかもう忘れてしまいました。

Eki de nanjikan naranda ka mou wasurete shimaimashita.
At the station, how many hours I lined up (question), already I completely forgot.

43. 大阪はどこにあるかこの地図で教えてください。

Oosaka wa doko ni aru ka kono chizu de oshiete kudasai.
As for Osaka, where it exists (question), with this map, please teach.

44. 明日のパーティーに誰が来るか知りません。

Ashita no paatii ni dare ga kuru ka, shirimasen.
To tomorrow's party, who will come (question), I don't know.

45. ホテルを予約できたか黒田さんに聞いてみます。

Hoteru wo yoyaku dekita ka kuroda-san ni kiite mimasu.
To reserve the hotel was possible (question), I will ask Kuroda and see.

46. 小川さんは何をしているか木村さんだったら知っているでしょう。

Ogawa-san wa nani wo shite iru ka kimura-san dattara shitte iru deshou.
As for Ogawa, what he is doing (question), if it were Kimura, she will be knowing probably.

47. 会社の社長は誰か知っていますか。

Kaisha no shachou wa dare ka shitte imasu ka.
As for the company's president, who (question) are you knowing?

48. なぜ山登りに行けないのか知っていますか。

Naze yama nobori ni ikenai no ka shitte imasu ka.
Why for the purpose of mountain climb, can't he go? Are you knowing?

49. ジョンさんは黒田さんのために京都のお土産を買ってきました。

Jon-san wa kuroda-san no tame ni kyouto no omiyage wo katte kimashita.
As for John, for the sake of Kuroda, he bought a Kyoto souvenir and came.

50. 会議に出るために来週大阪へ出張することになりました。

Kaigi ni deru tame ni raishuu oosaka e shutchou suru koto ni narimashita.
For the sake of to attend a meeting, next week I was scheduled to do a business trip to Osaka.

51. フランス語を覚えるためにはやはりフランスに留学した方がいいでしょうね。

Furansugo wo oboeru tame ni wa yahari furansu ni ryuugaku shita hou ga ii deshou ne.
As for for the sake of to memorize French, when you think about it, it would probably be better to do a foreign study to France, huh.

52. 誰でも読めるように字をきれいに書いてください。

Daredemo yomeru you ni ji wo kirei ni kaite kudasai.
So that any of them can read, please write characters cleanly.

53. 明日からしばらく留守にします。

Asu kara shibaraku rusu ni shimasu.
From tomorrow, for awhile, I will be absent.

54. 荷物が着いたら受け取っておいてください。

Nimotsu ga tsuitara uketotte oite kudasai.
If luggage arrives, please receive in advance.

Chapter 80

1. 私にも分かるようにもっと易しく説明してください。

Watashi ni mo wakaru you ni motto yasashiku setsumei shite kudasai.
In such a way that by me also will understand, more easily do explanation please.

2. 言葉の意味を調べるために辞書を引く。

Kotoba no imi wo shiraberu tame ni jisho wo hiku.
In order to check the meaning of words, I consult a dictionary.

3. 新幹線に乗るために東京駅へ行く。

Shinkansen ni noru tame ni toukyou eki e iku.
In order to board a bullet train, I go to Tokyo Station.

4. 分からないところを教えてもらうために先生の部屋に行く。

Wakaranai tokoro wo oshiete morau tame ni sensei no heya ni iku.
In order to teach and receive the part that I don't understand, I go to the teacher's room.

5. 書類を早くきれいに書くためにコンピューターを使う。

Shorui wo hayaku kirei ni kaku tame ni konpyuutaa wo tsukau.
In order to quickly, neatly write documents, I use a computer.

6. 家族旅行に行くために休みを取る。

Kazoku ryokou ni iku tame ni yasumi wo toru.
In order to go for the purpose of family travel, I will take vacation.

7. アメリカから来た友達に会うために新宿のホテルへ行きました。

Amerika kara kita tomodachi ni au tame ni shinjuku no hoteru e ikimashita.
In order to meet the came-from-America friend, I went to a Shinjuku hotel.

8. 授業に遅れないようにもう少し早く家を出ることにします。

Jugyou ni okurenai you ni mou sukoshi hayaku ie wo deru koto ni shimasu.
So as to not be delayed to class, I will decide to leave the house a little earlier.

9. このパンフレットは外国人にも読めるように英語やフランス語などで書いてあります。

Kono panfuretto wa gaikokujin ni mo yomeru you ni eigo ya furansugo nado de kaite arimasu.
As for this pamphlet, so that also by foreigners they can read, it is written in English and French, etc.

10. 子供が喜ぶようにお菓子をた
くさん買っておきました。

Kodomo ga yorokobu you ni okashi wo
takusan katte okimashita.
So that children will get delighted,
sweets, a lot, I bought in advance.

11. 病気が早く治るように薬を飲
んで寝ます。

Byouki ga hayaku naoru you ni kusuri
wo nonde nemasu.
So that the illness will quickly heal, I
will drink medicine and sleep.

12. 日本人も最近はだいぶ夏休み
を取るようになりました。

Nihonjin mo saikin wa daibu
natsuyasumi wo toru you ni narimashita.
Japanese people also, as for recently,
very much got to the point that they will
take summer vacation.

13. 愛子さんはなぜ札幌の雪祭り
の写真を見ていますか。

Aiko-san wa naze sapporo no
yukimatsuri no shashin wo mite imasu
ka.
As for Aiko, why is she looking at
Sapporo's snow festival's photos?

14. 愛子さんが旅行の予約をする
ため。

Aiko-san ga ryokou no yoyaku wo suru
tame.
For the sake of Aiko will do travel
reservations.

15. 去年の雪祭りを思い出したか
ら。

Kyonen no yukimatsuri wo omoidashita
kara.
Because she remembered last year's
snow festival.

****

16. おや、どうしたんですか、そ
のけがは。

Oya, doushitan desu ka, sono kega wa.
Hey. (to express surprise or doubt) How
did it do, as for that injury? (i.e., what
happened?)

17. 天気がいいから自転車で駅ま
で行こうと思ったんです。

Tenki ga ii kara jitensha de eki made
ikou to omottan desu.
Since the weather is good, by bicycle,
until the station I shall go, I thought.

18. そして、うちの近くの角を曲
がろうとしたとき転んだんで
す。

Soshite, uchi no chikaku no kado wo
magarou to shita toki korondan desu.
And then, the time when I tried to turn
the corner near the home, I fell over.

19. ああ、そうですか。気を付け
てくださいね。

Aa, sou desu ka. Ki wo tsukete kudasai
ne.
Ah, is that so? Please be careful huh.

20. それにもうすぐ社内運動会で
しょう？

Sore ni mou sugu shanai undou kai
deshou?
Besides, pretty soon it's probably the
inside-the-company sports tournament?

21. ブラウンさんにもリレーに出てもらおうと思っていますから。

Buraun-san ni mo riree ni dete moraou to omotte imasu kara.
By Brown also, to the relay race you will go out, and I shall receive, since I'm thinking.

22. ええ、えーと運動会はいつでしたっけ。

Ee. Eeto, undou kai wa itsu deshitakke.
Yeah. Uh, as for the sports tournament, when was it again?

23. 今月の 18 日ですよ。

Kongetsu no juuhachinichi desu yo.
It's the 18th of this month, for sure.

24. ところで雨が降ったらどうなるんですか。

Tokoro de ame ga futtara dou narun desu ka.
By the way, if it rains, how will it develop? (i.e., what will you do?)

25. 降らなければいいですね。

Furanakereba ii desu ne.
If it doesn't precipitate, then it's good huh.

****

26. 花田くん、リレーはもう始まってる。

Hanada-kun, riree wa mou hajimatteru?
Young woman Hanada, as for the relay, already is it starting?

27. ええ、ちょうど今、田辺さんが走っているところです。

Ee. Choodo ima tanabe-san ga hashitte iru tokoro desu.
Yeah. Just now Tanabe is in the process of running.

28. 黒田君やブラウン君はまだ？

Kuroda-kun ya Buraun-kun wa mada?
As for young woman Kuroda and young man Brown, etc, not yet?

29. 田辺さんの次に誰が走りますか。

Tanabe-san no tsugi ni dare ga hashirimasu ka.
At following Tanabe, who will run?

30. 黒田さんです。

Kuroda-san desu.
It's Kuroda.

31. 黒田さんがこれから走るところです。

Kuroda-san ga kore kara hashiru tokoro desu.
Kuroda, from now, is just about to run.

32. 今、田辺さんが黒田さんにバトンを渡していますよ。

Ima, tanabe-san ga kuroda-san ni baton wo watashite imasu yo.
Now Tanabe, to Kuroda, is handing the baton, for sure.

33. 次はブラウンさんですよ。

Tsugi wa Buraun-san desu yo.
As for the following, it's Brown, for sure.

34. 黒田さんがブラウンさんにバトンを渡そうとしたとき転ぶ。

Kuroda-san ga Buraun-san ni baton wo watasou to shita toki korobu.
Kuroda, the time when she was trying to hand the baton to Brown, falls over.

35. あっ、黒田さんが転んだ。黒田さん、しっかり！

Aa, kuroda-san ga koronda. Kuroda san, shikkari!
Ah, Kuroda is falling over. (exclamatory tense) Kuroda, get hold of yourself!

36. あ、ブラウン君が助けてバトンを取った。

A, buraun-kun ga tasukete baton wo totta.
Ah, young man Brown rescues and is taking the baton.

37. 走れ、走れ！

Hashire! Hashire!
Run! Run! (imperative tense)

38. ブラウン君、速いなぁ。

Buraun-kun, hayai naa.
Young man Brown, fast!

39. バトンを渡そうとしたとき転んで足を強く打ったそうです。

Baton wo watasou to shita toki koronde ashi wo tsuyoku utta sou desu.
The time she tried to hand the baton, falling over, she hit the leg strongly, reportedly.

40. そう、大変だったね。

Sou, taihen datta ne.
I see. It was terrible huh.

41. ブラウンさん達は運動会の後、何をしますか。

Buraun-san tachi wa undoukai no ato, nani wo shimasu ka.
As for the Brown group, after the sports tournament, what will they do?

42. ビールを飲みに行きます。

Biiru wo nomi ni ikimasu.
They will go for the purpose of drinking beer.

****

43. もう6時だ。さぁ、起きようか。

Mou rokuji da. Saa, okiyou ka.
Already it's 6:00. Well, shall I get up?

44. もうお寿司はいいですか。

Mou osushi wa ii desu ka.
Already, as for honorable sushi, is it good? (i.e., have you had enough?)

45. じゃ、残りは僕が食べることにしましょう。

Ja, nokori wa boku ga taberu koto ni shimashou.
Well, as for the remainder, I shall decide to eat it.

46. 明日は早く起きようと思います。

Ashita wa hayaku okiyou to omoimasu.
As for tomorrow, I shall get up early, I think.

47. 一緒に映画でも見ようと思って、ソフィアさんに電話をしました。

Issho ni eiga demo miyou to omotte, sofia-san ni denwa wo shimashita.
Thinking that together we shall watch a movie or something, I did a phone call to Sophia.

48. 来年の夏イギリスに行こうと思っています。

Rainen no natsu igirisu ni ikou to omotte imasu.
Next year's summer, I shall go to England, I'm thinking.

49. この本を今日中に読もうと思っています。

Kono hon wo kyou juu ni yomou to omotte imasu.
This book, sometime today, I shall read, I'm thinking.

50. あのベンチに座ろうと思います。

Ano benchi ni suwarou to omoimasu.
I shall sit on that bench over there, I think.

51. 10時に会議を始めようと思います。

Juu ji ni kaigi wo hajimeyou to omoimasu.
At 10:00, I shall start the meeting, I think.

52. あの店でコーヒーを飲もうと思っています。

Ano mise de koohii wo nomou to omotte imasu.
I shall drink coffee at that shop over there, I'm thinking.

53. 電話を掛けようとしたら十円玉がなかったんです。

Denwa wo kakeyou to shitara juu en dama ga nakattan desu.
When I tried to call on the phone, there was no 10-yen coin.

54. ジュースを飲もうとしてこぼしてしまいました。

Juusu wo nomou to shite koboshite shimaimashita.
Trying to drink juice, I spilled it completely.

55. それから先は神に頼むばかりだった。

Sore kara saki wa kami ni tanomu bakari datta.
Beyond that, as for the future, it was only to request to God. (i.e., she could only ask God)

56. 彼は経験がない割に良くやる。

Kare wa keiken ga nai wari ni yoku yaru.
As for him, experience doesn't exist relatively, he does well. (i.e., considering that he doesn't have experience, he does well)

Chapter 81

1. 電話を掛けようとしている。

   Denwa wo kakeyou to shite iru.
   He is trying to call on the phone.

2. 買い物に出かけようとしている。

   Kaimono ni dekakeyou to shite iru.
   She is trying to leave for the purpose of shopping.

3. レコードを掛けようとしている。

   Rekoodo wo kakeyou to shite iru.
   He is trying to hang the record. (i.e., to play it)

4. 魚を切ろうとしている。

   Sakana wo kirou to shite iru.
   He is trying to cut the fish.

5. あっ、黒田さんが転んだ。

   A, kuroda-san ga koronda.
   Ah, Kuroda is falling over!

6. 毎朝早く起きようとしているんですがなかなか起きられないんです。

   Maiasa hayaku okiyou to shite irun desu ga nakanaka okirarenain desu.
   Every morning, I'm trying to get up early, but I cannot get up readily.

7. 朝早く起きるとそんなに気持ちがいいんですか。

   Asa hayaku okiru to sonna ni kimochi ga iin desu ka.
   If you get up early in the morning, is the feeling that good?

8. じゃ、私も一度、朝早く起きてみます。

   Ja, watashi mo ichido, asa hayaku okite mimasu.
   Well, I also, one time, will get up early in the morning and see.

9. 明日、日本語の試験があるので今その勉強をしているところです。

   Ashita, nihongo no shiken ga aru node ima sono benkyou wo shite iru tokoro desu.
   Since tomorrow a Japanese language test exists, now I'm in the middle of doing that study.

10. 父は今お風呂に入ったところなんです。

    Chichi wa ima ofuro ni haitta tokoro nan desu.
    As for my father, now, into the honorable bath, he has just entered.

11. 30分後に、又電話をしていただけませんか。

    Sanjuppun go ni, mata denwa wo shite itadakemasenka.
    At after 30 minutes, again, can you not do a phone call and we humbly receive?

12. 今お風呂から上がったところ
    です。

Ima ofuro kara agatta tokoro desu.
Now, from the honorable bath he has just finished rising.

13. 少々お待ちください。

Shoushou omachi kudasai.
Please wait a moment. Very polite.

14. 買い物に行こうと思っている
    ところに野田さんが来まし
    た。

Kaimono ni ikou to omotte iru tokoro ni noda-san ga kimashita.
At I am in the process of thinking/feeling that I shall go for the purpose of shopping, Noda came.

15. 父は帰ってきたばかりでまだ
    食事をしていません。

Chichi wa kaette kita bakari de mada shokuji wo shite imasen.
As for my father, he has returned and come a while ago, and still he isn't doing a meal. (i.e., he hasn't eaten)

16. ボールを打つところです。

Booru wo utsu tokoro desu.
He's on the verge of hitting the ball.

17. 火を点けるところです。

Hi wo tsukeru tokoro desu.
She's on the verge of lighting a fire.

18. バトンを渡すところです。

Baton wo watasu tokoro desu.
He's on the verge of handing the baton.

19. プールに飛び込もうとしてい
    る。

Puuru ni tobikomou to shite iru.
He is trying to jump into the pool.

20. 電車に乗るところです。

Densha ni noru tokoro desu.
He's on the verge of boarding a train.

21. これから山に登るところで
    す。

Kore kara yama ni noboru tokoro desu.
From now, he's on the verge of climbing to the mountain.

22. 川のそばで休んでいるところ
    です。

Kawa no soba de yasunde iru tokoro desu.
At close to the river, he's in the process of resting.

23. 川の水を飲んでいるところで
    す。

Kawa no mizu wo nonde iru tokoro desu.
He's in the process of drinking the river's water.

24. 車が左に曲がろうとしてい
    る。

Kuruma ga hidari ni magarou to shite iru.
The car is trying to turn left.

25. もうすぐ、富士山が見えるは
ずなんですけどねぇ。

Mou sugu, fujisan ga mieru hazu nan
desu kedo nee.
Pretty soon, Mt. Fuji should be visible,
but, huh.

26. あっ、見えました、見えました。

A, miemashita, miemashita.
Ah, it's visible, it's visible!

27. 書類をこの机の上に置いたはずなんだけどなぁ。

Shorui wo kono tsukue no ue ni oita hazu
nan da kedo naa.
The documents should have been placed
on this desk, but...

28. あっ、あった、あった。

A, atta, atta.
Ah, here they are, here they are!

29. 打った。ホームランです。

Utta. Hoomu ran desu.
He's hitting! It's a home run.

30. あ、ランナー、走った。

Aa, rannaa, hashitta.
Ah, the runner is running!

31. 1時までに駅に行けば水野さんに会えますよ。

Ichi ji made ni eki ni ikeba mizuno-san ni
aemasu yo.
If you go to the station by 1:00, then you
can meet Mizuno, for sure.

32. もし、安ければその机を買います。

Moshi, yasukereba sono tsukue wo
kaimasu.
If, if it's cheap, then I will buy that desk.

33. 安くなければ買いません。

Yasukunakereba kaimasen.
If it isn't cheap, then I won't buy.

34. もし、明日晴れればディズニーランドに行きます。

Moshi, ashita harereba dizuniirando ni
ikimasu.
If, if tomorrow is sunny, then we will go
to Disneyland.

35. 真さんが来たら会議を始めましょう。

Makoto-san ga kitara kaigi wo
hajimemashou.
When Makoto comes, let's start the
meeting.

36. 渡辺さんが来れば会議がうまくいくでしょう。

Watanabe-san ga kureba kaigi ga umaku
iku deshou.
If Watanabe comes, then the meeting will
probably go well.

37. もし、京都に行ったらお土産を買って来てください。

Moshi, kyouto ni ittara omiyage wo katte
kite kudasai.
If, if you go to Kyoto, please buy a
souvenir and come.

38. お客さん、ミカンはどうですか。

Okyakusan, mikan wa dou desu ka.
Mr. Honorable Customer, as for the mandarin oranges, how are they?

39. 安くしますから買ってくださいよ。

Yasuku shimasu kara katte kudasai yo.
Since I will make them cheap, please buy them, for sure.

40. そうですね。安ければ買ってもいいけど。

Sou desu ne. Yasukereba katte mo ii kedo...
Let me see. If they are cheap, then it's OK to buy, but...

41. 明日一緒にピクニックに行きませんか。

Ashita issho ni pikunikku ni ikimasen ka.
Tomorrow, together, won't you go for the purpose of a picnic?

42. そうですね。天気がよければ行ってもいいですよ。

Sou desu ne. Tenki ga yokereba, itte mo ii desu yo.
Let me see. If the weather is good, it's OK to go, for sure.

43. ここから駅まで何分ぐらいですか。

Koko kara eki made nanpun gurai desu ka.
From here, until the station, about how many minutes is it?

44. 歩くと遠いですが車で行けば10分ぐらいです。

Aruku to tooi desu ga kuruma de ikeba juppun gurai desu.
If you walk, it's far, but if you go by car, then it's about 10 minutes.

45. 明日映画を見に行きませんか。

Ashita eiga wo mi ni ikimasen ka.
Tomorrow will you not go for the purpose of seeing a movie?

46. ええ、でも込んでるでしょう？

Ee, demo konderu deshou?
Yeah, but will it be crowded probably?

47. すいていれば行ってもいいけど...

Suite ireba itte mo ii kedo...
If it's being empty (i.e., uncrowded), it will be OK to go, but...

48. 京都に着いたら電話をしてください。

Kyouto ni tsuitara denwa wo shite kudasai.
When you arrive in Kyoto, please do a phone call.

49. 9時に家を出れば間に合いますよ。

Kuji ni ie wo dereba maniaimasu yo.
If you leave the house at 9:00, then you will be on time, for sure.

50. 暑ければ窓を開けてもいいで
すよ。

Atsukereba mado wo akete mo ii desu
yo.
If it's hot, then it's OK to open the
window, for sure.

51. 野田さんに会ったらこの手紙
を渡してください。

Noda-san ni attara kono tegami wo
watashite kudasai.
If you meet Noda, please hand this letter
to him.

52. 今度の仕事は大変ですね。

Kondo no shigoto wa taihen desu ne.
As for the next work, it's terrible huh.

53. 野球の試合では優勝してくだ
さい。

Yakyuu no shiai de wa yuushou shite
kudasai.
As for at the baseball game, please do
victory.

54. どうぞお大事に。

Douzo odaiji ni.
Go ahead, take care. (said to a sick
person)

55. テストの点が悪かったんです
か。

Tesuto no ten ga warukattan desu ka.
Was the test's mark bad?

56. 心配しないでください。

Shinpai shinai de kudasai.
Please don't do worry.

57. 気を落とさないでください。

Ki wo otosanai de kudasai.
Please don't drop your spirit. (i.e., don't
get discouraged)

58. 洗えばきれいになりますから
気にしないでください。

Araeba kirei ni narimasu kara ki ni shinai
de kudasai.
Since, if I wash it, it will become clean,
please don't do to spirit (i.e., don't
worry).

59. ノアさんは運動会の準備のた
めに先週の日曜日に会社に出
ました。

Noa-san wa undoukai no junbi no tame
ni senshuu no nichiyoubi ni kaisha ni
demashita.
As for Noah, for the purpose of the sports
tournament's preparation, on last week's
Sunday, he went out to the company.

60. それで、その代わりに来週の
火曜日に代休を取りたいと思
っています。

Sore de, sono kawari ni raishuu no
kayoubi ni daikyuu wo toritai to omotte
imasu.
And then, to that exchange (i.e., in place
of that), on next week's Tuesday he
wants to take compensatory time, he is
thinking.

61. その日は家にいるつもりで
す。

Sono hi wa ie ni irutsumori desu.
As for that day, he plans to be at the
house.

Chapter 82

1. あの、これ、どこで払えばいいんですか。
Ano, kore, doko de haraeba iin desu ka.
Say, this, where if I pay, then it will be good? (referring to an invoice)

2. 電気代ですか？ ああ、電気の料金ですか。
Denkidai desu ka? Aa, denki no ryoukin desu ka.
Is it the electricity cost? Ah, is it the electricity's fee?

3. 近くの銀行で払えばいいんですよ。
Chikaku no ginkou de haraeba iin desu yo.
If you pay at a nearby bank, then it will be good, for sure.

4. 駅前にある銀行ならどこでもいいですよ。
Eki mae ni aru ginkou nara dokodemo ii desu yo.
In the case of exist-in-front-of-the-station banks, anywhere is good, for sure.

5. 銀行に行くと案内の人がいますから、その人に聞けば分かりますよ。
Ginkou ni iku to annai no hito ga imasu kara, sono hito ni kikeba wakarimasu yo.
If you go to the bank, since a guidance person will exist, if you ask that person, then you will understand, for sure.

6. そうですか。銀行は3時までですよね。
Sou desu ka. Ginkou wa sanji made desu yo ne.
Is that so? As for the banks, they are until 3:00, for sure, huh.

7. 間に合うでしょうか。
Maniau deshou ka.
Will I probably be on time?

8. ええ、今行けば間に会いますよ。
Ee, ima ikeba maniaimasu yo.
Yeah, if you go now, then you will be on time, for sure.

9. でも、来月の八日までに払えばいいんでしょう？
Demo, raigetsu no youka made ni haraeba iin deshou?
But by the 8th of next month, if you pay, then it will be good probably?

10. 明日ゆっくりいらっしゃれば。
Ashita yukkuri irasshareba...
Tomorrow, leisurely, if you will honorably go...

11. 明日なら私も行きますし。
Ashita nara watashi mo ikimasu shi...
In the case of tomorrow, I also will go, and...

12. 有難うございます。でも明日
はちょっと用があるものです
から。

Arigatou gozaimasu. Demo ashita wa
chotto you ga aru mono desu kara.
Thank you a lot. But as for tomorrow, a
little bit, since it's an errand-exists thing.

****

13. あの、電気代を払いたいんで
すが、どうしたらいいんでし
ょう？

Ano, denkidai wo haraitain desu ga, dou
shitara iin deshou?
Say, I would like to pay the electricity
cost, but how if I do is good, probably?

14. 係員：電気代ですか。

Kakari in: denkidai desu ka.
Person in charge: is it the electricity
cost?

15. 電気代の方はこちらの窓口で
す。

Denkidai no kata wa kochira no
madoguchi desu.
As for the electricity cost's people, it's
this way's service window.

16. このボックスのカードをお取
りください。

Kono bokkusu no kaado wo otori
kudasai.
Please honorably take this box's card.

17. ずいぶん待つんですね。

Zuibun matsun desu ne.
I will wait extremely, huh.

18. そうですね。月末はいつも込
むんですよ。

Sou desu ne. Getsumatsu wa itsumo
komun desu yo.
It's so, huh. As for the end of the month,
always it gets crowded, for sure.

19. 毎月こうだと大変ですね。

Maitsuki kou da to taihen desu ne.
If it's like this every month, it's terrible,
huh.

20. ええ、あの、お客様はこちら
の銀行に口座をお持ちです
か。

Ee. Ano, okyakusama wa kochira no
ginkou ni kouza wo omochi desu ka.
Yeah. Say, as for the very honorable
customer, to this way's bank, do you
honorably hold a savings account?

21. ええ、主人のですけど。

Ee, shujin no desu kedo...
Yeah, it's my husband's, but...

22. それなら、口座からの自動引
き落としにすると便利です
よ。

Sore nara, kouza kara no jidou hikiotoshi
ni suru to benri desu yo.
In that case, if you choose from-the-
savings-account's automatic withdrawal,
it's convenient, for sure.

23. 自動引き落としって何です
か。

Jidou hikiotoshi tte nan desu ka.
As for the one called automatic withdrawal, what is it?

24. 口座から自動的に毎月の電気
代を払うんです。

Kouza kara jidouteki ni maitsuki no denkidai wo haraun desu.
From the savings account, automatically, every month's electricity cost you pay.

****

25. 銀行はもうお済みになりまし
たか。

Ginkou wa mou osumi ni narimashita?
As for the bank, already, did you honorably finish?

26. ええ、銀行の人が親切に教え
てくれました。

Ee, ginkou no hito ga shinsetsu ni oshiete kuremashita.
Yeah, the bank person kindly taught and gave.

27. それで来月から自動引き落と
しにすることにしました。

Sore de raigetsu kara jidou hikiotoshi ni suru koto ni shimashita.
For that reason, from next month, I chose to choose automatic withdrawal.

28. ああ、自動引き落としなら便
利でいいですね。

Aa, jidou hikiotoshi nara benri de ii desu ne.
Ah, in the case of automatic withdrawal, because it's convenient, it's good, huh.

****

29. アリッサさんは田辺さんと一
緒に銀行に行くことにしまし
たか。

Arissa-san wa tanabe-san to issho ni ginkou ni iku koto ni shimashita ka.
As for Alyssaa, with Tanabe, together, did she decide to go to the bank?

30. いいえ、一人で行くことにし
ました。

Iie. Hitori de iku koto ni shimashita.
No, she decided to go by herself.

31. アリッサさんはこれから毎月
銀行に電気代を払いに行くつ
もりですか。

Arissa-san wa kore kara maitsuki ginkou ni denkidai wo harai ni ikutsumori desu ka.
As for Alyssa, from now, every month, to the bank, for the purpose of paying the electricity cost, does she plan to go?

32. いいえ、自動引き落としにす
ることにしました。

Iie, jidou hikiotoshi ni suru koto ni shimashita.
No, she decided to decide on automatic withdrawal.

33. アリッサさんは田辺さんに何
をしてあげましたか。

Arissa-san wa tanabe-san ni nani wo shite agemashita ka.
As for Alyssa, to Tanabe, what did she do and give?

34. 荷物を持ってあげました。

Nimotsu wo motte agemashita.
She held (i.e., carried) the baggage and gave.

****

35. 池田産業はアメリカに工場を
作ろうとしている。

Ikeda sangyou wa amerika ni koujou wo tsukurou to shite iru.
As for Ikeda industries, to America, a factory they are trying to make.

36. 会社が買おうとしている土地
について。

Kaisha ga kaou to shite iru tochi ni tsuite.
Regarding the land the company is trying to buy.

37. サンフランシスコから南に
50キロぐらいの所にある。

Sanfuranshisuko kara minami ni gojukkiro gurai no tokoro ni aru.
From San Francisco to the south, at about 50 kilometers' place it exists.

38. 広さは5エーカー。

Hirosa wa go eekaa.
As for area, 5 acres.

39. 土地を売りたがっていない人
はスミスさんです。

Tochi wo uritagatte inai hito wa sumisu-san desu.
As for the person who doesn't appear to be wanting to sell the land, it's Smith.

40. アメリカに作る工場につい
て。

Amerika ni tsukuru koujou ni tsuite.
Regarding the to-America-to-make factory.

41. 工場で働く人は最初は80人
です。

Koujou de hataraku hito wa saisho wa hachijuunin desu.
As for people who will labor at the factory, as for the beginning, it's 80 people.

42. 工場のそばにプールとテニス
コートを作るつもりだ。

Koujou no soba ni puuru to tenisukooto wo tsukurutsumori da.
To the factory's nearby, they plan to make a pool and a tennis court.

43. 最初の工場長は日本人にする
つもりだ。

Saisho no koujouchou wa nihonjin ni surutsumori da.
As for the beginning's factory manager, they plan to decide on a Japanese person.

****

44. 土曜日はマディソンと買い物
に行かなくてはならないの
で、できたら金曜日がいいん
ですが。

Doyoubi wa madison to kaimono ni ikanakutewa naranai node dekitara kinyoubi ga iin desu ga...
As for Saturday, with Madison, since I have to go for the purpose of shopping, if it's possible, Friday would be good, but...

45. そうですか。じゃ、金曜日に しましょう。

Sou desu ka. Ja, kinyoubi ni shimashou.
Is that so? Well, on Friday, let's do.

46. 何時にしましょうか。

Nanji ni shimashou ka.
At what time shall we do?

47. そうですね。5時半頃はどう ですか。

Sou desu ne. Gojihan goro wa dou desu ka.
That's so huh. (i.e., let me see) As for about half past 5, how is it?

48. じゃ、鳥せんの店の前で会い ましょう。

Ja, torisen no mise no mae de aimashou.
Well, let's meet at Torisen's store's front.

49. あの、鳥せんってどこにある んですか。

Ano, torisen tte doko ni arun desu ka.
Say, as for the one called Torisen, where does it exist?

50. ああ、場所が分からないんで すか。

Aa, basho ga wakaranain desu ka.
Ah, don't you understand the place?

51. じゃ、地図を見せますから ね。

Jaa, chizu wo misemasu kara ne.
Well, since I will show a map, huh.

52. ほら、駅を出てからこの角を 右に曲がればいいんですよ。

Hora, eki wo dete kara kono kado wo migi ni magareba iin desu yo.
Look, after you leave the station, if you turn right on this corner, it will be good, for sure.

53. そこなら前に行ったことがあ りますよ。

Soko nara mae ni itta koto ga arimasu yo.
In the case of that place, to in-front, I have gone, for sure.

54. 焼き鳥のおいしい店でしょ う?

Yakitori no oishii mise deshou?
It's probably a yakitori's delicious store?

55. じゃ、そこに5時半までに来 てくださいね。

Ja, soko ni gojihan made ni kite kudasai ne.
Well, to that place, by half past 5, please come, huh.

Chapter 83

1. すみません。この書類なんで
すがどうしたらいいんです
か。

Sumimasen. Kono shorui nan desu ga
dou shitara iin desu ka.
Excuse me. It's these documents, but
how if I do is good?

2. ああ、それは部長のサインを
もらえばいいんですよ。

Aa, sore wa buchou no sain wo moraeba
iin desu yo.
Ah, as for those, if you receive the
division manager's signature, it will be
good, for sure.

3. 地下鉄の切符を買いたいんで
すが、どうすればいいです
か。

Chikatetsu no kippu wo kaitain desu ga
dou sureba ii desu ka.
I would like to buy a subway ticket, but
how if I do is good?

4. ここにお金を入れて、このボ
タンを押せばいいですよ。

Koko ni okane wo irete, kono botan wo
oseba ii desu yo.
You insert money here, and if you push
this button, it's good, for sure.

5. 切符が出てきますから。

Kippu ga dete kimasu kara.
Because the ticket emerges and comes.

6. 東京駅からヒルトンホテルへ
行く方法が分からないんです
が。

Toukyou eki kara hiruton hoteru e iku
houhou ga wakaranain desu ga...
The from Tokyo Station to the Hilton
Hotel to-go method I don't
know/understand, but...

7. ホテルに電話をしてみればい
いですよ。

Hoteru ni denwa wo shite mireba ii desu
yo.
If you do a phone call to the hotel and
see, it's good, for sure.

8. 東京駅からタクシーに乗った
らいいですよ。

Toukyou eki kara takushii ni nottara ii
desu yo.
From Tokyo Station, if you ride in a taxi,
it's good, for sure.

9. 地下鉄で赤坂まで行くといい
ですよ。

Chikatetsu de akasaka made iku to ii
desu yo.
By subway, if you go until Akasaka, it's
good, for sure.

10. 日本語が上手になりたいんで
すが。

Nihongo ga jouzu ni naritain desu ga...
I would like the Japanese to become skillful, but...

11. 日本語学校に行くといいです
よ。

Nihongo gakkou ni iku to ii desu yo.
If you go to Japanese language school, it's good, for sure.

12. 日本語のニュースを毎日聞い
たらいいですよ。

Nihongo no nyuusu wo mainichi kiitara ii desu yo.
If you listen to Japanese language news every day, it's good, for sure.

13. 子供の頃何になりたいと思っ
ていましたか。

Kodomo no koro nani ni naritai to omotte imashita ka.
The child's approximate time, what do you want to become, you were thinking?

14. この機械の使い方を知りたい
んですけど。

Kono kikai no tsukai kata wo shiritain desu kedo...
I would like to know this machine's use way, but...

15. 山本さんに聞くといいです
よ。

Yamamoto-san ni kiku to ii desu yo.
If you ask Yamamoto, it's good, for sure.

16. 機械の説明書を読むといいで
すよ。

Kikai no setsumeisho wo yomu to ii desu yo.
If you read the machine's explanation sheet, it's good, for sure.

17. 日本の大学に入りたいんで
す。

Nihon no daigaku ni hairitain desu.
I would like to enter a Japanese university.

18. どんな大学があるか知りたい
んですが。

Donna daigaku ga aru ka shiritain desu ga...
What kind of universities exist (question) I would like to know, but...

19. 図書館で調べてみたらいいで
すよ。

Toshokan de shirabete mitara ii desu yo.
If you check at a library and see, it's good, for sure.

20. この部屋は少し暑いですね。

Kono heya wa sukoshi atsui desu ne.
As for this room, it's a little hot, huh.

21. 暑いならそこの窓を開けても
いいですよ。

Atsui nara, soko no mado wo akete mo ii desu yo.
In case it's hot, it's OK to open that place's window, for sure.

22. この仕事、来週の月曜日までにできますか。

Kono shigoto, raishuu no getsuyoubi made ni dekimasu ka.
This work, will it be ready by next week's Monday?

23. 月曜日ですか。月曜日は無理ですね。

Getsuyoubi desu ka. Getsuyoubi wa muri desu ne.
Is it Monday? As for Monday, it's impossible, huh.

24. 水曜日までならできますが。

Suiyoubi made nara dekimasu ga...
In the case of until Wednesday, it will accomplish, but...

25. 山に行きたいんだけど、どこがいいでしょうかね。

Yama ni ikitain dakedo, doko ga ii deshou ka ne.
I'd like to go to the mountains, but where is probably good (question), huh?

26. 山に行くなら富士山がいいですよ。

Yama ni iku nara fujisan ga ii desu yo.
In the case of to go to the mountains, Mt. Fuji is good, for sure.

27. 温泉に行きたいんだけど、どこかいい所を教えてくれませんか。

Onsen ni ikitain dakedo, dokoka ii tokoro wo oshiete kuremasen ka.
I'd like to go to a hot spring, but somewhere good place, won't you teach and give?

28. 温泉なら箱根がいいですよ。

Onsen nara hakone ga ii desu yo.
In the case of hot springs, Hakone is good, for sure.

29. 寒いわね。

Samui wa ne.
Cold, huh.

30. 寒いならストーブを点ければ？

Samui nara sutoobu wo tsukereba?
In the case of cold, if you turn on the heater?

31. 明日は雨が降るそうですよ。

Ashita wa ame ga furu sou desu yo.
As for tomorrow, it will rain, reportedly, for sure.

32. 雨が降るならゴルフに行くのは止めようかな。

Ame ga furu nara gorufu ni iku no wa yameyou kana.
In the case of it will rain, as for I-will-go-for-golf thing, I shall stop, I wonder.

33. 東京貿易の社長に会いたいんですが会って下さるでしょうか。

Toukyou boueki no shachou ni aitain desu ga atte kudasaru deshou ka.
I would like to meet Tokyo Trading's president, but will he probably meet and give?

34. 社長は無理だと思います。

Shachou wa muri da to omoimasu.
As for the president, it's impossible, I think.

35. 部長なら会って下さると思いますけど。

Buchou nara atte kudasaru to omoimasu kedo...
In the case of the division manager, he will meet and give, I think, but...

36. 今あなたが読んでいる本を買いたいんですが、駅前の本屋さんで買えるでしょうか。

Ima anata ga yonde iru hon wo kaitain desu ga, eki mae no honyasan de kaeru deshou ka.
Now I would like to buy the book you are reading, but at the Mr. Bookstore of the station front, can I probably buy?

37. 駅前の本屋にはないと思いますよ。

Eki mae no honya ni wa nai to omoimasu yo.
As for at the station front's bookstore, not, I think, for sure.

38. もっと大きい本屋ならあると思いますが。

Motto ookii honya nara aru to omoimasu ga...
In the case of a larger bookstore, it exists, I think, but...

39. ここに住所を漢字で書いてください。

Koko ni juusho wo kanji de kaite kudasai.
Please write the address in kanji at here.

40. え、漢字でですか。困ったなあ。

E, kanji de desu ka. Komatta naa.
Eh, is it in kanji? Inconvenienced.

41. ひらがななら書けるんですが。

Hiragana nara kakerun desu ga...
In the case of hiragana, I can write, but...

42. それでは失礼いたします。

Sore de wa, shitsurei itashimasu.
Well then, I will commit a discourtesy. (i.e., I will leave)

43. あら、もうお帰りですか。

Ara, mou okaeri desu ka.
My goodness, are you already honorably returning? (i.e., are you leaving?)

44. あの店で食事をしませんか。

Ano mise de shokuji wo shimasen ka.
Will we not do a meal at that store over there?

45. いやぁ、さっき食事をしたばかりなんですよ。

Iyaa, sakki shokuji wo shita bakari nan desu yo.
Nah, previously I just did a meal a while ago, for sure.

46. 社長は毎日2時のニュースを
お聞きになります。

Shachou wa mainichi niji no nyuusu wo
okiki ni narimasu.
As for the president, every day he
honorably listens to the 2:00 news.

47. 今朝は何時にお出かけになり
ましたか。

Kesa wa nanji ni odekake ni narimashita
ka.
As for this morning, at what time did you
honorably depart?

48. やぁ、疲れました。車に乗り
たいですね。

Yaa, tsukaremashita. Kuruma ni noritai
desu ne.
Hey, I got tired. I would like to ride in a
car, huh.

49. 会社の旅行で箱根の温泉に行
きました。

Kaisha no ryokou de hakone no onsen ni
ikimashita.
For company's travel, we went to
Hakone's hot spring.

50. この旅行で温泉がとても好き
になりました。

Kono ryokou de onsen ga totemo suki ni
narimashita.
On this trip, hot springs' very-much-
liking developed.

51. 日本にいる間、週に3回日
本語学校で勉強しました。

Nihon ni iru aida, shuu ni sankai nihongo
gakkou de benkyou shimashita.
During to be in Japan, three times a
week, at Japanese language school, I
studied.

52. いつか又、日本に帰ってきた
いと思っています。

Itsuka mata, nihon ni kaette kitai to
omotte imasu.
Sometime again, to Japan I would like to
return and come, I am thinking.

53. メアリーさんは今、何歳です
か。

Mearii-san wa ima, nansai desu ka.
As for Mary, now, how many years is it?
(i.e., how old is she?)

54. 25歳です。

Nijuu go sai desu.
She is 25 years old.

55. 空が暗くなってきましたね。

Sora ga kuraku natte kimashita ne.
The sky became dark and came, huh.

56. ええ、今にも雨が降りそうで
すね。

Ee, ima ni mo ame ga furi sou desu ne.
Yeah, any minute now, it will rain
apparently huh.

57. 声が聞こえませんね。

Koe ga kikoemasen ne.
A voice is not audible, huh.

Chapter 84

1. もしもし、先生はおいでになりますか。

Moshimoshi, sensei wa oide ni narimasu ka.
Hello, as for teacher, is he there?

2. 先生の奥さん：いいえ、おりません。

Sensei no okusan: Iie, orimasen.
Teacher's wife: No, he doesn't exist.

3. 何時頃お帰りになりますか。

Nanji goro okaeri ni narimasu ka.
About what time will he honorably return?

4. 今日は8時頃には帰ると言っていましたが。

Kyou wa hachiji goro ni wa kaeru to itte imashita ga...
As for today, as for at about 8:00, he will return, he was saying, but...

5. そうですか。じゃ、又、その頃お電話します。

Sou desu ka. Ja, mata sono koro odenwa shimasu.
Is that so? Well, again about that time, I will humbly do a phone call.

****

6. グレイステイラー様。

Gureisu teiraa sama.
Very honorable Grace Taylor. (used to open a letter)

7. 9月に入ったのに毎日暑い日が続きますね。

Kugatsu ni haitta noni mainichi atsui hi ga tsuzukimasu ne.
In spite of the fact that we entered in September, every day hot days continue, huh.

8. グレイスさん、お元気ですか。

Gureisu-san, ogenki desu ka.
Grace, is it honorable health? (i.e., how are you?)

9. 先週グレイスさんからのお手紙を受け取りました。

Senshuu gureisu-san kara no otegami wo uketorimashita.
Last week, I received/took a from-Grace honorable letter.

10. 十月の初めにジェイコブさんとこちらにいらっしゃるそうですね。

Juugatsu no hajime ni jeikobu-san to kochira ni irassharu sou desu ne.
At the beginning of October, with Jacob, to this way you will honorably come, reportedly, huh.

11. 大変嬉しく思います。

Taihen ureshiku omoimasu.
Extremely pleasingly I think/feel. (i.e., I'm very pleased)

12. 長野に来るには JR 線で来る方法と車で来る方法とがあります。

Nagano ni kuru ni wa jei aaru sen de kuru houhou to kuruma de kuru houhou to ga arimasu.
As for to come to Nagano, to come by JR line method and to come by car method and, exist. ("to" is used twice to indicate an exhaustive list)

13. JR 線で来れば速くて便利です。

Jei aaru sen de kureba hayakute benri desu.
If you come by the JR line, it's fast and convenient.

14. 特急に乗れば 3 時間、急行に乗れば 4 時間と少しで着きます。

Tokkyuu ni noreba sanjikan, kyuukou ni noreba yojikan to sukoshi de tsukimasu.
If you ride on special express, three hours duration, if you ride on express, in four hours duration and a little you will arrive.

15. 自由席じゃ座れないかもしれません。

Jiyuuseki ja suwarenai kamoshiremasen.
As for of nonreserved seats, you cannot sit, it might be. (ja = de wa)

16. JR 線で来るときは割引切符を利用するといいですよ。

Jei aaru sen de kuru toki wa waribiki kippu wo riyou suru to ii desu yo.
As for the come-by-JR-line time, if you use a discount ticket, it's good, for sure.

17. 車も便利ですが道路がとても込むので止めておいた方がいいでしょう。

Kuruma mo benri desu ga douro ga totemo komu node yamete oita hou ga ii deshou.
A car also is convenient, but since the roads will get very crowded, it would probably be better to give up in advance.

18. 宿の件ですが私の家に泊まればいいですよ。

Yado no ken desu ga watashi no ie ni tomareba ii desu yo.
It's a lodging matter, but if you stay at my house, it's good, for sure.

19. ホテルや旅館は高いし秋の旅行シーズンでとても込んでいますから。

Hoteru ya ryokan wa takai shi aki no ryokou shiizun de totemo konde imasu kara.
As for hotels, Japanese inns, etc., they are expensive, and because of the fall's travel season, since they are very crowded.

20. ではお二人にお会いできる日を楽しみにしております。

Dewa ofutari ni oai dekiru hi wo tanoshimi ni shite orimasu.
Well, to the honorable-two-people able-to-honorably-meet day, I am looking forward on.

21. 橋本さんは長野まで行くために何を使えばいいと言っていますか。

Hashimoto-san wa nagano made iku tame ni nani wo tsukaeba ii to itte imasu ka.
As for Hashimoto, in order to go until Nagano, if you use what, then it will be good, is she saying?

22. 橋本さんはいつグレイスさん達に会えますか。

Hashimoto-san wa itsu gureisu-san tachi ni aemasu ka.
As for Hashimoto, when will she be able to meet the Grace group?

23. 十月の初めに会えます。

Juugatsu no hajime ni aemasu.
She will be able to meet at the beginning of October.

****

24. タクシーに大事な書類を忘れてしまった。

Takushii ni daiji na shorui wo wasurete shimatta.
In the taxi, he completely forgot important documents.

25. 前田さんはどこに電話をすればいいと言いましたか。

Maeda-san wa doko ni denwa wo sureba ii to iimashita ka.
As for Maeda, to where if one does a phone call, it will be good, he said?

26. タクシー近代化センターに電話すればいいと言いました。

Takushii kindaika sentaa ni denwa sureba ii to iimashita.
If one does a phone call to the Taxi Modernization Center, it's good, he said. (kindai = modern; ka = "-ize")

27. お客さんが来るので、ビールを冷やしてあります。

Okyakusan ga kuru node, biiru wo hiyashite arimasu.
Since the honorable Mr. Customer will come, beer is being chilled by someone and exists.

28. その電車は駅に止まらないで通り過ぎました。

Sono densha wa eki ni tomaranai de toori sugimashita.
As for that train, not stopping at the station, it went past.

29. 最近、小川君に会いましたか。

Saikin ogawa-kun ni aimashita ka.
Recently did you meet young man Ogawa?

30. いいえ、先生はお会いになりましたか。

Iie, sensei wa oai ni narimashita ka.
No, as for teacher, did you honorably meet him?

31. 黒田さんに京都のお菓子を買ってくるように頼まれました。

Kuroda-san ni kyouto no okashi wo katte kuru you ni tanomaremashita.
By Kuroda, I was asked to buy Kyoto's sweets and come.

32. 母にいつも部屋をきれいにす
るように言われるけど、なか
なかできません。

Haha ni itsumo heya wo kirei ni suru you
ni iwareru kedo, nakanaka dekimasen.
By my mother, always make the room
clean she says on me, but readily I cannot
do.

33. 5時に区役所に行ったら、明
日又来るように言われまし
た。

Goji ni kuyakusho ni ittara, ashita mata
kuru you ni iwaremashita.
At 5:00, when I went to the ward office,
"tomorrow again come" was said on me.

34. お茶をどうぞ。何かご用があ
りましたらこちらのお電話で
どうぞ。

Ocha wo douzo. Nanika goyou ga
arimashitara kochira no odenwa de
douzo.
Have some tea. If there is anything
honorable errand, with this here's
humble telephone, go ahead.

35. 東京はまだ暑いけど箱根は涼
しいですね。

Toukyou wa mada atsui kedo hakone wa
suzushii desu ne.
As for Tokyo, still hot, but as for
Hakone, it's cool, huh.

36. 本当にそうですね。

Hontou ni sou desu ne.
Truly, it's so, huh.

37. ところで食事をする前に温泉
に入りませんか。

Tokoro de shokuji wo suru mae ni, onsen
ni hairimasen ka.
By the way, at before to do a meal, will
we not enter a hot spring?

****

38. 熱そうですね。

Atsu sou desu ne.
It looks hot, huh.

39. 僕は熱いお風呂はだめなんで
すよ。

Boku wa atsui ofuro wa dame nan desu
yo.
As for me, as for hot honorable baths,
they are bad, for sure.

40. じゃ、僕がお先に。

Ja, boku ga osaki ni.
Well, me first.

41. あぁ、いい気持ち。

Aa, ii kimochi.
Ah, good feeling.

42. 熱いですか。

Atsui desu ka.
Is it hot?

43. ええ、僕にはちょっと熱すぎ
ますね。

Ee, boku ni wa chotto atsusugimasu ne.
Yeah, as for to me, it gets a little too hot,
huh.

44. そうですか。じゃ、少し水を入れましょう。

Sou desu ka. Ja, sukoshi mizu wo iremashou.
Is that so? Well, a little, let's put in water.

45. 入れ過ぎるとぬるくなるから。

Iresugiru to nuruku naru kara.
Since, if we put in too much, it will become lukewarm.

46. そうですね。まだちょっと熱いけど、このくらい熱い方が体にいいような気がします。

Sou desu ne. Mada chotto atsui kedo, kono kurai atsui hou ga karada ni ii you na ki ga shimasu.
Let me see. Still a little hot, but about this much hot, for the body is better, it appears, I have a feeling.

47. ああ、よく飲んだ。

Aa, yoku nonda.
Ah, I drank well. (i.e., I had plenty to drink)

48. やっぱり温泉に入った後で飲むビールはおいしいですねえ。

Yappari onsen ni haitta ato de nomu biiru wa oishii desu nee.
When you think about it, after you entered a hot spring, as for beer that one drinks, it's delicious huh.

49. ええ、みんな楽しそうでしたね。

Ee, minna tanoshisou deshita ne.
Yeah, everyone, it seemed pleasant, huh. (i.e., everyone seemed to be enjoying themselves)

****

50. ちょっと寒気がします。

Chotto samuke ga shimasu.
A little, a chill does. (i.e., I have a chill)

51. それに少し熱もあるようです。

Sore ni sukoshi netsu mo aru you desu.
Besides, a little fever also seems to exist.

52. 部屋に帰りましょう。

Heya ni kaerimashou.
Let's return to the room.

53. 部屋の中は暖かいから。

Heya no naka wa atatakai kara.
Because, as for the insides of the rooms, warm.

54. 旅館の人に用があるときは電話を使う。

Ryokan no hito ni you ga aru toki wa denwa wo tsukau.
To the Japanese inn's person, as for an errand exists time, you use a phone. (i.e., you call him)

Chapter 85

1. 寒いですね。温泉に入って温まりましょう。

Samui desu ne. Onsen ni haitte atatamarimashou.
It's cold, huh. Let's get in the hot spring and warm up.

2. 客： 今日は外は風が強くて寒いけれど、部屋の中は暖かいですね。

Kyaku: Kyou wa soto wa kaze ga tsuyokute samui keredo, heya no naka wa atatakai desu ne.
Customer: As for today, as for outside, the wind is strong and cold, but as for the inside of the room, it's warm, huh.

3. もう少し温度を低くしてくれませんか。

Mou sukoshi ondo wo hikuku shite kuremasen ka.
A little more, won't you make the temperature low and give?

4. ボーイ：はい、今下げます。

Booi: Hai, ima sagemasu.
Busboy: Yes, now I will lower it.

5. あのう、窓を少し開けましょうか。

Anou, mado wo sukoshi akemashou ka.
Say, shall I open the window a little?

6. 冷たい空気が入ってくれば、すぐ涼しくなりますから。

Tsumetai kuuki ga haitte kureba sugu suzushiku narimasu kara.
Since, if the cold air enters and comes, soon it will become cool.

7. 有難う。先ず温泉に入りたいんだけど、ここの温泉は熱いですか。

Arigatou. Mazu onsen ni hairitain dakedo, koko no onsen wa atsui desu ka.
Thank you. First I would like to enter the hot spring, but is this place's hot spring hot?

8. 32度ぐらいでぬるいのでホテルで少し温めています。

Sanjuuni do gurai de nurui node hoteru de sukoshi atatamete imasu.
Since it's about 32 degrees and lukewarm, by the hotel, a little bit they are warming it.

9. そうですか。風呂から出てきたら冷たいビールをお願いします。

Sou desu ka. Furo kara dete kitara tsumetai biiru wo onegaishimasu.
Is that so? When I emerge and come from the bath, a cold beer, if you please.

****

10. 熱いうちに食べましょう。

Atsui uchi ni tabemashou.
While still hot, let's eat.

11. コーヒーを入れるときのお湯の温度は熱い方がいいです。

Koohii wo ireru toki no oyu no ondo wa atsui hou ga ii desu.
As for to-make-coffee time's hot water's temperature, hot is better.

12. 夏に飲むスープは冷たい方がいいです。

Natsu ni nomu suupu wa tsumetai hou ga ii desu.
In summer, as for soup that one drinks, cold is better.

13. お風呂のお湯は熱い方がいいです。

Ofuro no oyu wa atsui hou ga ii desu.
As for the honorable bath's hot water, hot is better.

14. ビールは冷たい方がいいです。

Biiru wa tsumetai hou ga ii desu.
As for beer, cold is better.

15. ワインはあまり冷たくない方がいいです。

Wain wa amari tsumetaku nai hou ga ii desu.
As for wine, not very cold is better.

16. 海で泳ぐときの気温は暑い方がいいです。

Umi de oyogu toki no kion wa atsui hou ga ii desu.
As for to-swim-in-the-ocean time's air temperature, hot is better.

17. 山登りをするときの気温は涼しい方がいいです。

Yamanobori wo suru toki no kion wa suzushii hou ga ii desu.
As for to-do-mountain-climb time's air temperature, cool is better.

18. 黒田さんはプレゼントをもらって嬉しそうでした。

Kuroda-san wa purezento wo moratte, ureshi sou deshita.
As for Kuroda, she received a present and appeared pleased.

19. わぁ、おいしそうなケーキ。

Waa, oishisou na keeki.
Wow, delicious appearing cake.

20. 三つぐらい食べられそう。

Mittsu gurai taberare sou.
I can eat about three, it appears.

21. あの本は面白そうじゃありません。

Ano hon wa omoshiro sou ja arimasen.
As for that book over there, it doesn't appear to be interesting.

22. あの本は面白くなさそうです。

Ano hon wa omoshiroku nasa sou desu.
As for that book over there, it appears to be not interesting.

23. 今日は雨は降りそうにありません。

Kyou wa ame wa furisou ni arimasen.
As for today, as for rain, appear-to-precipitate does not exist.

24. 午後から雨が降るようです。

Gogo kara ame ga furu you desu.
From the afternoon, it seems that it will rain.

25. 天気予報でそう言っていましたよ。

Tenki yohou de sou itte imashita yo.
From the weather report, they were saying so, for sure.

26. 熱が下がってしまいました。

Netsu ga sagatte shimaimashita.
The fever went down completely.

27. もう3時のようですね。

Mou sanji no you desu ne.
Already it seems to be 3:00, huh.

28. あの店には行ったことはないんですが、おいしいらしいですよ。

Ano mise ni wa itta koto wa nain desu ga, oishii rashii desu yo.
As for to that store over there, I have never gone, but it appears to be delicious, for sure.

29. もうすっかり元気です。

Mou sukkari genki desu.
Already I'm thoroughly healthy.

30. 見ただけで熱がありそうだ。

Mita dake de netsu ga ari sou da.
From only saw, it appears a fever exists. (i.e., based on seeing only)

31. おいしそうな料理ですね。

Oishisou na ryouri desu ne.
It's delicious-appearing cuisine, huh.

32. 今度の魚は大きそうです。

Kondo no sakana wa ooki sou desu.
As for this time's fish, it appears to be big.

33. 難しそうな本ですね。

Muzukashi sou na hon desu ne.
It's a difficult-appearing book, huh.

34. あっ、本が落ちそう。

A! Hon ga ochisou.
Ah. It appears the book will fall.

35. 大変。会社に遅れそう。

Taihen. Kaisha ni okuresou.
Terrible. To the company, it appears I will get delayed.

36. 北村さんは病気らしいわ。

Kitamura-san wa byouki rashii wa.
As for Kitamura, sick, it appears.

37. テイラーさんはどこかに出かけているらしいな。

Teiraa-san wa dokoka ni dekakete iru rashii na.
As for Taylor, to somewhere she is being departed, it seems.

38. 事故があったらしい。

Jiko ga atta rashii.
An accident existed, it appears.

39. 高橋さんは今度の旅行に行きますか。

Takahashi-san wa kondo no ryokou ni ikimasu ka.
As for Takahashi, will he go on the next trip?

40. 彼女は人目も構わず泣いた。

Kanojo wa hitome mo kamawazu naita.
As for her, public gaze even not minding, she cried.

41. レコードをお掛けしましょうか。

Rekoodo wo okake shimashou ka.
Shall I humbly hang a record?

42. 車の本をお見せしましょうか。

Kuruma no hon wo omise shimashou ka.
Shall I humbly show a car book?

43. パソコン、空いてる？

Pasokon aiteru?
Is the computer being open? (i.e., available)

44. 部長がお使いです。

Buchou ga otsukai desu.
The division manager is honorably using.

45. あなた、お客様がお帰りですよ。

Anata, okyakusama ga okaeri desu yo.
Darling, the very honorable customer is honorably returning, for sure.

46. ここにお名前とご住所をお書きください。

Koko ni onamae to gojuushou wo okaki kudasai.
Please honorably write your honorable name and honorable address here.

47. お返事は手紙でお知らせ下さいませんか。

Ohenji wa tegami de oshirase kudasaimasenka.
As for the honorable reply, by letter, won't you honorably inform and give?

48. コンサートは6時半からです。

Konsaato wa rokuji han kara desu.
As for the concert, it's from half past six.

49. 後30分ほどロビーでお待ちください。

Ato sanjuppun hodo robii de omachi kudasai.
After about 30 minutes, please honorably wait in the lobby.

50. ホテルのボーイがお客さんに：ご用の時はこちらの電話をお使いください。

Hoteru no booi ga okyakusan ni: goyou no toki wa kochira no denwa wo otsukai kudasai.
The hotel's bellboy to the honorable customer: as for the honorable errand time, please honorably use this way's phone.

51. お客さんが店員に：ちょっと寒いんです。

Okyakusan ga tenin ni: Chotto samuin desu.
Honorable customer to clerk: It's a little cold.

52. エアコンを止めて下さいませんか。

Eakon wo tomete kudasaimasenka.
Won't you stop the air conditioner and give?

53. 寒いですね。そこの店で熱いコーヒーを飲みましょう。

Samui desu ne. Soko no mise de atsui koohii wo nomimashou.
It's cold huh. At that place's store, let's drink hot coffee.

54. 暖かいうちにスープをどうぞ。

Atatakai uchi ni suupu wo douzo.
While still warm, go ahead with the soup.

55. 有難う。あれ、少しぬるくなっていますね。

Arigatou. Are, sukoshi nurukunatte imasu ne.
Thank you. Hey, a little bit, it is becoming lukewarm, huh.

56. あ、すみません。すぐ温めます。

A, sumimasen. Sugu atatamemasu.
Ah, excuse me. Soon I will warm it.

57. 思いやりがなくて冷たい人です。

Omoiyari ga nakute tsumetai hito desu.
Empathy doesn't exist, and it's a cold person.

58. そのお茶は熱いですから少し冷まして飲んでください。

Sono ocha wa atsui desu kara sukoshi samashite nonde kudasai.
As for that honorable tea, since it is hot, a little bit, please cool it (i.e., let it cool) and drink.

59. 冷たいビールをどうぞ。

Tsumetai biiru wo douzo.
Cold beer, go ahead.

60. ああ、おいしい。良く冷えていますね。

Aa, oishii. Yoku hiete imasu ne.
Ah, delicious. It's being well chilled, huh.

61. 台風のため、今日の大学の授業は全て休校になった。

Taifuu no tame, kyou no daigaku no jugyou wa subete kyuukou ni natta.
Due to the typhoon, as for today's university's classes, all, to school closing became. (i.e, they were all suspended)

Chapter 86

1. 今日は社員旅行で箱根に来た。

Kyou wa shain ryokou de hakone ni kita.
As for today, for an employee trip, we came to Hakone.

2. 天気予報では降ると言っていたんだけれど。

Tenki yohou de wa furu to itte itan da keredo...
As for from the weather report, it will precipitate they were saying, but...

3. 旅館に行く前にみんなで山に登った。

Ryokan ni iku mae ni minna de yama ni nobotta.
At before to go to the Japanese inn, of everyone, we climbed to a mountain.

4. みんな元気に登っていたが北村課長はずいぶん疲れているようだった。

Minna genki ni nobotte ita ga kitamura kachou wa zuibun tsukarete iru you datta.
Everyone, energetically was climbing, but as for Section Manager Kitamura, he is extremely being tired, it appeared.

5. 土田部長に聞いたんだけど、最近課長は残業が多いらしいわよ、と黒田さんが言った。

Tsuchida buchou ni kiitan dakedo, saikin kachou wa zangyou ga ooi rashii wa yo to kuroda-san ga itta.
She asked Division Manager Tsuchida, but recently, as for the section manager, overtime is numerous, it appears, for sure, Kuroda said.

6. 旅館に着いて温泉に入ったら北村課長の疲れも取れたらしい。

Ryokan ni tsuite onsen ni haittara kitamura kachou no tsukare mo toreta rashii.
We arrived at the Japanese inn, and when we entered the hot spring, Section Manager Kitamura's fatigue also he was able to take out of himself, it appears.

7. ビールをおいしそうに飲んでいた。

Biiru wo oishi sou ni nonde ita.
Beer, like delicious, he was drinking. (i.e., he drank like it was delicious)

8. 食事をしながらカラオケが始まった。

Shokuji wo shi nagara karaoke ga hajimatta.
While we do a meal, karaoke began.

9. 池田さんは歌がとても好きなようだ。

Ikeda-san wa uta ga totemo suki na you da.
As for Ikeda, he likes songs a lot, apparently.

****

10. 先週は船で浅草から浜離宮ま
で行きました。

Senshuu wa fune de asakusa kara
hamarikyuu made ikimashita.
As for last week, by boat, from Asakusa
we went until Hamarikyuu.
(Hamarikyuu = a park in Tokyo, next to
the Sumida River)

11. 船から房総半島が良く見えま
した。

Fune kara bousouhantou ga yoku
miemashita.
From the boat, Bousou Hantou could be
seen well. (Bousou Hanto = the Boso
peninsula across Tokyo Bay from Tokyo)

12. 行く前に電話で予約をしてお
きました。

Iku mae ni denwa de yoyaku wo shite
okimashita.
At before to go, by telephone, I made a
reservation in advance.

13. レストランはとても込んでい
たので、予約をしておいて良
かったと思いました。

Resutoran wa totemo konde ita node,
yoyaku wo shite oite yokatta to
omoimashita.
As for the restaurant, since it was very
crowded, since I make a reservation in
advance, it was good, I thought.

14. 食事の後、有楽町で映画を見
ました。

Shokuji no ato, yuurakuchou de eiga wo
mimashita.
After the meal, at Yuurakuchou, we saw
a movie.

15. 映画が始まる1時間前からた
くさんの人が並んでいまし
た。

Eiga ga hajimaru ichijikan mae kara
takusan no hito ga narande imashita.
The movie will start, from one hour
before, a lot of people were lined up.

16. 映画を見た後、喫茶店でお茶
を飲みながら話をしました。

Eiga wo mita ato, kissaten de ocha wo
nomi nagara hanashi wo shimashita.
After we watched the movie, at a coffee
house, while drinking honorable tea, we
did talking.

17. レストランはどうでしたか。
すぐ食事ができましたか。

Resutoran wa dou deshita ka. Sugu
shokuji ga dekimashita ka.
As for the restaurant, how was it. Soon,
was the meal possible?

18. とても込んでいました。でも
予約をしておいたのですぐ食
事ができました。

Totemo konde imashita. Demo yoyaku
wo shite oita node sugu shokuji ga
dekimashita.
It was very crowded. But since he made
the reservation in advance, soon the meal
was possible.

****

19. トーマスさん、今度の土曜日
にうちに遊びに来ませんか。

Toomasu-san, kondo no doyoubi ni uchi
ni asobi ni kimasen ka.
Thomas, on this next Saturday, won't
you come to the home to play?

20. 有難うございます。でも今度
の土曜日は仕事でゴルフに行
かなくちゃならないんです。

Arigatou gozaimasu. Demo kondo no
doyoubi wa shigoto de gorufu ni
ikanakucha naranain desu.
Thank you a lot. But as for this next
Saturday, for work, I have to go for the
purpose of golf.

21. そうですか。残念ですね。じ
ゃ又、今度。

Sou desu ka. Zannen desu ne. Ja mata,
kondo.
Is that so? It's too bad, huh. Well, again
next time.

22. 切手を30枚買ってくるよう
に頼まれたんです。

Kitte wo sanjuu mai katte kuru you ni
tanomaretan desu.
I was requested to buy 30 stamps and
come.

23. どうしても明日までにこのレ
ポートを書かなければならな
いんです。

Doushitemo ashita made ni kono repooto
wo kakanakereba naranain desu.
One way or another, by tomorrow, I must
write this report.

24. 多分心配しているだろうから
ニューヨークのご両親にはも
っと電話をしなくてはだめで
すよ。

Tabun shinpai shite iru darou kara,
nyuuyooku no goryoushin ni wa motto
denwa wo shinakute wa dame desu yo.
Since probably they are probably being
worried, as for to the New York's
honorable parents, you must do more
phone calls, for sure.

25. 日本語のレッスンを受けなく
ちゃならない。

Nihongo no ressun wo ukenakucha
naranai.
I have to receive a Japanese lesson.

26. 友達の子供に英語を教えない
といけない。

Tomodachi no kodomo ni eigo wo
oshienai to ikenai.
I have to teach English to a friend's
child.

27. 新しいコンピューターの使い
方を習わなくてはいけない。

Atarashii konpyuutaa no tsukai kata wo
narawanakute wa ikenai.
I have to learn the use method of a new
computer.

28. 家内の手伝いをしなくちゃい
けない。

Kanai no tetsudai wo shinakucha ikenai.
I have to do wife's help. (i.e., help the
wife)

29. 明日、福岡に出張することに
なりました。

Asu, fukuoka ni shutchou suru koto ni narimashita.
Tomorrow, to Fukuoka, I was scheduled to do a business trip.

30. 課長、福岡での仕事は何ですか。

Kachou, fukuoka de no shigoto wa nan desu ka.
Section Manager, as for the at-Fukuoka's work, what is it?

31. 仕事の説明を聞いておかなくてはなりません。

Shigoto no setsumei wo kiite okanakute wa narimasen.
He must listen to the work's explanation in advance.

32. 予約をお願いします。

Yoyaku wo onegai shimasu.
I beg reservations. (i.e., please make reservations)

33. 飛行機やホテルを予約しておかないといけません。

Hikouki ya hoteru wo yoyaku shite okanai to ikemasen.
She must reserve the plane, the hotel, etc. in advance.

34. 会議の資料を用意しておかなくてはいけません。

Kaigi no shiryou wo youi shite okanakute wa ikemasen.
He must prepare the meeting's literature in advance.

35. いつにするか決めなくてはいけません。

Itsu ni suru ka kimenakutewa ikemasen.
At when to do (question) we must arrange.

36. 会社に休みの届けを出しておかなくてはなりません。

Kaisha ni yasumi no todoke wo dashite okanakute wa narimasen.
To the company, vacation's notification must be sent in advance.

37. 病気の時はゆっくり休まなくては。

Byouki no toki wa yukkuri yasumanakute wa.
As for the sickness's time (i.e., the time when you are sick), you must leisurely rest. (shortened for speech; ikemasen, ikenai, narimasen, naranai, & dame desu can be omitted when saying "one must")

38. 明日はゴルフだから早く起きないと。

Ashita wa gorufu dakara hayaku okinai to.
As for tomorrow, since it's golf, I must get up early. (shortened for speech)

39. （車の止まる音を聞いて）あっ、社長が着いたようですね。

(kuruma no tomaru oto wo kiite) A, shachou ga tsuita you desu ne.
(hearing the car's to-stop noise) Ah, the president arrived, it appears, huh.

40. 兄に母と一緒に住んでもらいたかったけれど、兄は仕事でイギリスへ行ってしまいました。

Ani ni haha to issho ni sunde moraitakatta keredo, ani wa shigoto de igirisu e itte shimaimashita.
To older brother, with my mother together dwelling I desired, but as for older brother, for work, he went to England completely.

41. （部屋の中から外を見て）外は寒そうですね。

(heya no naka kara soto wo mite) Soto wa samu sou desu ne.
(from inside the room, looking at outside) As for outside, it appears cold, huh.

42. あの人が石田さんらしい。

Ano hito ga ishida-san rashii.
That person over there appears to be Ishida.

43. すみません。又後で。電車が出そうなんです。

Sumimasen. Mata ato de. Densha ga de sou nan desu.
Excuse me. Again, of later. (i.e., I'll be in touch later) The train will leave, apparently.

44. 雨でも運動会をするらしい。

Ame demo undoukai wo suru rashii.
Even rain, they will do the sports tournament, it appears.

45. 十一月二十日です。

Juuichi gatsu hatsuka desu.
It's November 20th.

46. 前田さんはそこの電話番号を知っていましたか。

Maeda-san wa soko no denwa bangou wo shitte imashita ka.
As for Maeda, was he knowing that place's telephone number?

47. いいえ、知っていませんでした。

Iie, shitte imasen deshita.
No, he was not knowing.

48. 電話番号が分からない時はどうすればいいですか。

Denwa bangou ga wakaranai toki wa dou sureba ii desu ka.
As for the time you don't know/ understand a phone number, how if you do is good?

49. NTT の 104 で聞けばいいです。

NTT no ichi zero yon de kikeba ii desu.
If you ask of NTT's 104, it's good.

50. 飲み放題の店に行きましょう。

Nomihoudai no mise ni ikimashou.
Let's go to an all-you-can-drink shop.

Chapter 87

1. あの、お願いします。

Ano, onegai shimasu.
Say, I beg you. (i.e., can you help me?)

2. 受付：はい、どうなさいましたか。

Uketsuke: Hai, dou nasaimashita ka.
Reception: Yes, how did you honorably do? (i.e., what's wrong?)

3. ちょっと頭が痛くて少し熱があるようなんです。

Chotto atama ga itakute sukoshi netsu ga aru you nan desu.
A little bit, the head hurts, and a little fever appears to exist.

4. この病院は初めてですか。

Kono byouin wa hajimete desu ka.
As for this hospital, is it the first time?

5. ええ。

Ee.
Yeah.

6. はい。じゃ、名前を呼ばれるまでそこのいすに掛けていてください。

Hai. Ja, namae wo yobareru made soko no isu ni kakete ite kudasai.
Yes, well, until the name is called, on that place's chair, be sitting please.

7. それから、待っている間に熱を計っておいてくださいね。

Sore kara, matte iru aida ni netsu wo hakatte oite kudasai ne.
And then, while being waiting, please measure the fever in advance, huh.

8. はい。体温計。

Hai. Taionkei.
Yes. Thermometer. (i.e., here's a thermometer)

9. 医者：どうしました？

Isha: Dou shimashita.
Doctor: How did it do? (i.e., what's wrong?)

10. ちょっと頭が痛くて熱があるんです。

Chotto atama ga itakute netsu ga arun desu.
A little, the head hurts and fever exists.

11. それに体もだるいんです。

Sore ni karada mo daruin desu.
Moreover, the body also is lethargic.

12. 体温計を見せてください。

Taionkei wo misete kudasai.
Show the thermometer please.

13. うん。なるほど。38度もある。

Un. Naruhodo. Sanjuuhachi do mo aru.
Well. I see. As much as 38 degrees exist.

14. はい。大きく息を吸って。

Hai. Ookiku iki wo sutte.
Yes. Suck the breath deeply.

15. はい。結構です。

Hai. Kekkou desu.
Yes. It's fine. (i.e., that's enough.)

16. 今までに大きな病気をしたことがありますか。

Ima made ni ookina byouki wo shita koto ga arimasu ka.
By now, have you ever done a big illness?

17. いいえ、別に。

Iie, betsu ni.
No, not particularly.

18. 二、三日ゆっくり休まなくちゃいけませんね。

Ni san nichi yukkuri yasumanaku cha ikemasen ne.
Two/three days, leisurely you must rest, huh.

19. あさって、大事な会議があるんでその前に会議の資料を作らなくてはいけませんし...

Asatte, daiji na kaigi ga arun de sono mae ni kaigi no shiryou wo tsukuranakute wa ikemasen shi...
The day after tomorrow, an important meeting exists, and at before that, I have to make meeting literature, and...

20. そうですか。じゃ、会社は休まなくてもいいけど、早くうちに帰って寝るようにしてください。

Sou desu ka. Ja, kaisha wa yasumanakute mo ii kedo, hayaku uchi ni kaette neru you ni shite kudasai.
Is that so? Well, as for the company, it's all right if you don't rest, but returning early to home, see to it to sleep, please.

21. 無理をしてはいけませんよ。

Muri wo shite wa ikemasen yo.
You must not do the impossible, for sure. (i.e., don't over-exert yourself)

22. それから熱が下がるまでお風呂に入ってはいけませんよ。

Sore kara netsu ga sagaru made ofuro ni haitte wa ikemasen yo.
And then, until the fever goes down, you must not get into the honorable bath, for sure.

23. そして食欲がなくてもきちんと食べなくちゃだめですよ。

Soshite shokuyoku ga nakutemo kichinto tabenakucha dame desu yo.
And then, even if the appetite is not, properly you must eat, for sure.

24. それじゃ、薬を三日分出しておきましょう。

Sore ja, kusuri wo mikkabun dashite okimashou.
Well then, medicine, three days' quantity, I shall put out in advance.

25. じゃ、二、三日様子をみて熱が下がらないようでしたら又来てください。

Ja, nisan nichi yousu wo mite netsu ga sagaranai you deshitara mata kite kudasai.
Well, two/three days, watching the condition, if it's the fever doesn't appear to go down, again please come.

26. ジョセフアンダーソンさん、はい、お薬です。

Josefu andaason-san, hai, okusuri desu.
Joseph Anderson, yes, it's honorable medicine.

27. 三日分入っています。

Mikka bun haitte imasu.
A three-day supply is entered.

28. はい、分かりました。で、おいくらですか。

Hai, wakarimashita. De, oikura desu ka.
Yes, understood. And then, how honorable much is it?

29. はい、2300円。どうも有難うございました。

Hai, nisen sanbyaku en. Doumo arigatou gozaimashita.
Yes, 2300 yen. Thank you very much for what you did.

30. お大事に。

Odaiji ni.
Take care. (said to a sick person)

****

31. ジョセフさんは待っている間に何をしましたか。

Josefu-san wa matte iru aida ni nani wo shimashita ka.
As for Joseph, while waiting, what did he do?

32. 熱を計りました。

Netsu wo hakarimashita.
He measured the fever.

33. ジョセフさんはなぜゆっくり休めないのですか。

Josefu-san wa naze yukkuri yasumenai no desu ka.
As for Joseph, why is he unable to rest leisurely?

34. 会議の資料を作らなくてはいけないからです。

Kaigi no shiryou wo tsukuranakute wa ikenai kara desu.
It's because he has to make a meeting's literature.

35. お医者さんはジョセフさんにどんなことをしてはいけないと言いましたか。

Oishasan wa josefu-san ni donna koto wo shite wa ikenai to iimashita ka.
As for the honorable doctor, to Joseph, what kind of thing must he not do, he said?

36. お風呂に入ったりシャワーを浴びたりしてはいけないと言いました。

Ofuro ni haittari shawaa wo abitari shite wa ikenai to iimashita.
Enter to an honorable bath, etc., take a shower, etc., he must not do, he said.

37. ジョセフさんは薬を何日分もらいましたか。

Josefu-san wa kusuri wo nannichi bun moraimashita ka.
As for Joseph, medicine, how many day's supply did he receive?

38. 三日分もらいました。

Mikka bun moraimashita.
Three days' supply he received.

****

39. 明日は8時までに来なければいけませんか。

Ashita wa hachiji made ni konakereba ikemasen ka.
As for tomorrow, do I have to come by 8:00?

40. 無理だったら8時までに来なくてもいいですよ。

Muri dattara hachiji made ni konakute mo ii desu yo.
If it's impossible, you don't have to come by 8:00, for sure.

41. 無理に8時までに来ることはありませんよ。

Muri ni hachiji made ni kuru koto wa arimasen yo.
Straining, you don't have to come by 8:00, for sure. (i.e., if it's difficult, you don't have to come)

42. 部屋がちょっと暗いようですが。

Heya ga chotto kurai you desu ga...
The room seems to be a little dark, but...

43. もっと明るい方が良くありませんか。

Motto akarui hou ga yoku arimasen ka.
Isn't more bright better?

44. いいえ、そんなに明るくなくても構いませんよ。

Iie, sonna ni akarukunakute mo kamaimasen yo.
No, that kind of not-brightness doesn't matter, for sure.

45. すみません。今青いシーツは置いてないんです。

Sumimasen. Ima aoi shiitsu wa oite nain desu.
Excuse me. Now, as for blue sheets, they are not placed. (i.e., we don't have any)

46. そうですか。じゃ、青いのでなくてもいいですよ。

Sou desu ka. Ja, aoi no de nakute mo ii desu yo.
Is that so? Well, with-blue-ones-not is good, for sure. (i.e., blue ones aren't necessary)

47. 明日の会議にはどうしても出なくちゃならないんですよ。

Ashita no kaigi ni wa doushitemo denakucha naranain desu yo.
As for to tomorrow's meeting, one way or another, I must attend, for sure.

48. 無理に出なくてもいいんじゃないですか。

Muri ni denakute mo iin ja nai desu ka.
Straining, isn't it all right not to attend?

49. この報告書は明日までに作らなくてはいけませんか。

Kono houkokusho wa asu made ni tsukuranakute wa ikemasen ka.
As for this report, by tomorrow do I have to make it?

50. いいえ、あさってまでに作ってもらえばいいですよ。

Iie, asatte made ni tsukutte moraeba ii desu yo.
No, by the day after tomorrow, if you make it and I receive, it will be good, for sure.

51. 食事は一日に三度きちんと食べてください。

Shokuji wa ichinichi ni sando kichinto tabete kudasai.
As for meals, three times per day, properly eat please.

52. オフィスの古いタイプライターは使いにくくて、誰も使いません。

Ofisu no furui taipuraitaa wa tsukai nikukute, dare mo tsukaimasen.
As for the office's old typewriter, since difficult to use, no one uses it.

53. 黒田さんは喜んでいます。

Kuroda-san wa yorokonde imasu.
As for Kuroda, she is being delighted.

****

54. アメリカの本社には週に一度火曜日にレポートを送ることになっていますが。

Amerika no honsha ni wa shuu ni ichido kayoubi ni repooto wo okuru koto ni natte imasu ga,
As for to the American head office, once per week, on Tuesday, a report is being scheduled to be sent, but...

55. 今週は報告することが多かったので月曜日から一日おきに送りました。

Konshuu wa houkoku suru koto ga ookatta node getsuyoubi kara ichinichi oki ni okurimashita.
As for this week, since to-report thing was numerous, since Monday, every other day, we sent them.

56. 来週からは又、いつもの通りです。

Raishuu kara wa mata, itsumo no toori desu.
As for from next week, again, it's the always street. (i.e., it's the as-usual way of doing)

57. いつもの通りなら何日にレポートを送りますか。

Itsumo no toori nara nan nichi ni repooto wo okurimasu ka.
In the case of the as-usual way of doing, on what days do we send the report?

Chapter 88

1. 頭がガンガンする。

Atama ga gangan suru.
The head does a splitting pain.

2. 歯がズキズキする。

Ha ga zukizuki suru.
The tooth does throbbing.

3. 気分が悪い。

Kibun ga warui.
The health-related feeling is bad.

4. ちょっと頭が痛いんです。

Chotto atama ga itain desu.
A little bit, the head hurts.

5. 胃がキリキリするんです。

I ga kirikiri surun desu.
The stomach does sharp pain.

6. 首がズキズキするんです。

Kubi ga zukizuki surun desu.
The neck does throbbing.

7. 頭が痛くて寒気がするんです。

Atama ga itakute samuke ga surun desu.
The head hurts, and a chill does.

8. 熱があってめまいがするんです。

Netsu ga atte memai ga surun desu.
Fever exists, and dizziness does.

9. 胃が痛くて食欲がないんです。

I ga itakute shokuyoku ga nain desu.
The stomach hurts, and the appetite doesn't exist.

10. 元気がないですね。

Genki ga nai desu ne.
Health doesn't exist, huh.

11. あっ、危ない。どうしたんですか。

A! Abunai. Dou shitan desu ka.
Ah. Danger. How did it do? (i.e., what's wrong?)

12. 何だか顔も青いようですよ。

Nandaka kao mo aoi you desu yo.
What is it? The face is also seemingly blue, for sure.

13. じゃ、車を止めて外に出ましょう。

Ja, kuruma wo tomete soto ni demashou.
Well, stopping the car, let's go outside.

14. 早く帰って休んだ方がいいですよ。

Hayaku kaette yasunda hou ga ii desu yo.
It would be better to return early and rest, for sure.

15. ええ、少し熱があるみたいなんです。

Ee, sukoshi netsu ga aru mitai nan desu.
Yeah, a little fever exists, it appears.

16. あっ、痛た。

A, itata.
Ah, it hurts. (exclamatory tense)

17. 熱があって体がだるいんです。

Netsu ga atte karada ga daruin desu.
A fever exists, and the body is lethargic.

18. 食欲がないみたいですね。

Shokuyoku ga nai mitai desu ne.
The appetite doesn't exist, it appears, huh.

19. 目が痛いんです。

Me ga itain desu.
The eyes hurt.

20. 目の使い過ぎですね。

Me no tsukai sugi desu ne.
It's the eyes' excessive use, huh.

21. 頭が痛いそうですが、どんな風に痛みますか。

Atama ga itai sou desu ga donna fuu ni itamimasu ka.
The head hurts reportedly, but to what kind of way does it hurt?

****

22. ジュリーさんの仕事は何ですか。

Jurii-san no shigoto wa nan desu ka.
As for Julie's work, what is it?

23. テレビの英語ニュースのアナウンサーです。

Terebi no eigo nyuusu no anaunsaa desu.
She's television's English news' announcer.

24. ジュリーさんはなぜ6時半に家を出なくてはならないのですか。

Jurii-san wa naze rokuji han ni ie wo denakute wa naranai no desu ka.
As for Julie, why, at half past 6, must she leave the house?

25. 放送の前に打ち合わせがあるからです。

Housou no mae ni uchiawase ga aru kara desu.
It's because, at before the broadcast, a planning meeting exists.

26. ジュリーさんはなぜ疲れるのですか。

Jurii-san wa naze tsukareru no desu ka.
As for Julie, why does she tire?

27. 二つ答えなさい。

Futatsu kotaenasai.
Reply two times. (i.e., give two reasons)

28. 朝、早く起きなくてはならないし、放送中は間違えないようにしなくてはいけないからです。

Asa hayaku okinakute wa naranai shi, housou chuu wa machigaenai you ni shinakute wa ikenai kara desu.
It's because she has to get up early in the morning, and as for during the broadcast, she has to make an effort not to mistake.

****

29. 初めてスキーをする人は私の所に来てください。

Hajimete sukii wo suru hito wa watashi no tokoro ni kite kudasai.
As for beginning-to-do-ski people, please come to my place.

30. レッスンは一日に三回、三時間ずつやっています。

Ressun wa ichinichi ni sankai, sanjikan zutsu yatte imasu.
As for lessons, three times per day, three hours each, I am doing.

31. 私はいつも社長と一緒にいます。

Watashi wa itsumo shachou to issho ni imasu.
As for me, always I am together with the president.

32. 社長のスケジュールは全部私が決めるんですよ。

Shachou no sukejuuru wa zenbu watashi ga kimerun desu yo.
As for the president's schedule, everything, I arrange, for sure.

33. 社長のプライバシーを守らなければなりません。

Shachou no puraibashii wo mamoranakereba narimasen.
I have to defend the president's privacy.

34. 私は一日中外で働いています。

Watashi wa ichinichijuu soto de hataraite imasu.
As for me, all day long I am laboring outside.

35. お客さんを乗せて色々な所に行くので道を良く知っていなければなりません。

Okyakusan wo nosete iroiro na tokoro ni iku node michi wo yoku shitte inakereba narimasen.
Loading honorable customers, since I go to various places, I must be knowing the streets well.

36. 交通事故を起こさないように気を付けて運転しています。

Koutsuu jiko wo okosanai you ni ki wo tsukete unten shite imasu.
In such a way as to not cause a traffic accident, being careful, I am doing driving.

37. 私は白い服を着て働いています。

Watashi wa shiroi fuku wo kite hataraite imasu.
As for me, wearing white clothes, I am laboring.

38. どんなに疲れているときでも
笑顔と優しさを忘れないよう
にしています。

Donna ni tsukarete iru toki demo egao to
yasashisa wo wasurenai you ni shite
imasu.
What kind of being-tired time even, I am
making an effort not to forget a smiling
face and gentleness.

39. 病人は体の弱い人達ですから
ね。

Byounin wa karada no yowai hitotachi
desu kara ne.
As for sick people, since bodies-are-
weak people they are, huh.

****

40. 一体何それ？ 気持ち悪い。

Ittai nani sore? Kimochi warui.
What, that? (i.e., what on earth is it?;
ittai is used for emphasis) The feeling is
bad. (i.e., I feel uneasy, seeing this)

41. 昨日やけどしちゃって。

Kinou yakedo shichatte...
Yesterday a burn I do completely, and...

42. ストーブを点けたのは渡辺さ
んの奥さんです。

Sutoobu wo tsuketa no wa watanabe-san
no okusan desu.
The one who turned on the heater is
Watanabe's wife.

43. エマさんは前に日本の家を見
たことがあります。

Ema-san wa mae ni nihon no ie wo mita
koto ga arimasu.
As for Emma, at before, she has looked
at a Japanese house.

44. 隣のステレオがうるさいわ
ね。

Tonari no sutereo ga urusai wa ne.
The neighboring stereo is noisy, huh.

45. 隣の子に音を小さくするよう
に言ってくる。

Tonari no ko ni oto wo chiisaku suru you
ni itte kuru.
To the neighboring child, I will say to
make the sound small and come.

46. 子供が料理を手伝ってくれて
います。

Kodomo ga ryouri wo tetsudatte kurete
imasu.
The child (i.e., my child), on the cuisine,
is helping and giving.

47. 私は一日に一回犬を散歩させ
ています。

Watashi wa ichinichi ni ikkai inu wo
sanpo sasete imasu.
As for me, once a day, the dog I am
making do a walk.

Chapter 89

1. ライアン君達は遅いね。

Raian-kuntachi wa osoi ne.
As for the young man Ryan group, late, huh.

2. きっと東京の道が込んでいるんですよ。

Kitto toukyou no michi ga konde irun desu yo.
Surely, Tokyo streets are crowded, for sure.

3. あそこに泉があるらしいね。

Asoko ni izumi ga aru rashii ne.
At over there, a spring apparently exists, huh.

4. あそこでライアン君の車を待つことにしよう。

Asoko de raian-kun no kuruma wo matsu koto ni shiyou.
At over there, let's decide to wait for young man Ryan's car.

5. 車を降りて水を飲む。

Kuruma wo orite mizu wo nomu.
She gets down from the car and drinks the water.

6. さすがに富士山の水ね。

Sasuga ni fujisan no mizu ne.
As expected, Mt. Fuji's water, huh.

7. 冷たくておいしいわ。

Tsumetakute oishii wa.
Cold and delicious.

8. ここに、この水は日本の名水の一つに選ばれたと書いてあるよ。

Koko ni, kono mizu wa nihon no meisui no hitotsu ni erabareta to kaite aru yo.
To here, as for this water, it was chosen to one of the Japanese famous waters, it is written, for sure.

9. 僕も飲んでみようか。

Boku mo nonde miyou ka.
I also, shall I drink and see?

10. こんなにおいしい水が東京でも飲めたらいいのに。

Konna ni oishii mizu ga toukyou demo nometara ii noni.
This kind of delicious water, Tokyo even, if we are able to drink, good, if only. (i.e, if only we were able to drink it)

11. 帰りにこの水を持って帰りましょうね。

Kaeri ni kono mizu wo motte kaerimashou ne.
At the return, let's hold this water and return, huh.

12. 持って帰ってお隣の前田さん
にもあげたらいいね。

Motte kaette otonari no maeda-san ni mo
agetara ii ne.
Holding and returning, to the honorable
neighbor's Maeda also, if we give, good,
huh.

13. お二人とも茶の湯の先生だか
らきっと喜んでもらえるよ。

Ofutari tomo chanoyu no sensei dakara
kitto yorokonde moraeru yo.
The honorable both of them, since they
are tea ceremony teachers, surely they
will get delighted, and we can receive,
for sure.

14. それにしてもあの人達は遅い
わね。

＊＊＊＊＊＊＊＊

Sore ni shite mo ano hitotachi wa osoi
wa ne.
Even so, as for those people over there,
late, huh.

15. 遅くなってすみません。

Osoku natte sumimasen.
Since we became late, excuse us.

16. 今日は月末だから込んだんで
しょう。

Kyou wa getsumatsu dakara kondan
deshou.
As for today, since it's the end of the
month, it probably got crowded.

17. ええ。それにおまわりさん
に車を止められたわねぇ、ラ
イアン。

Ee. Sore ni omawarisan ni kuruma o
tomerareta wa nee, raian.
Yeah. Moreover, by a policeman the car
was stopped on us, huh, Ryan.

18. あんな静かな所でおまわりさ
んに見られているなんて思い
ませんでしたわ。

Anna shizuka na tokoro de omawarisan
ni mirarete iru nante omoimasen deshita
wa.
In that over there kind of quiet place, to
be being watched by a policeman, such a
thing, I did not think.

19. あなたももっと気を付ければ
良かったのに。

Anata mo motto ki wo tsukereba yokatta
noni.
You also, if you are more careful, it was
good, if only. (i.e., if only you had been
more careful)

20. 私達がまだ日本の交通事情を
知らないから仕方がないけれ
ど、これからは気を付けるよ
うに言われました。

＊＊＊＊＊＊＊＊

Watashitachi ga mada nihon no koutsuu
jijou wo shiranai kara shikata ga nai
keredo, korekara wa ki wo tsukeru you ni
iwaremashita.
Since we still don't know Japanese
traffic facts, it can't be helped, but as for
from now, "be careful," he said on us.

21. ほら、いつか旅館で出された
食事みたいだわ。

Hora, itsuka ryokan de dasareta shokuji
mitai da wa.
See, it's like the once-at-a-Japanese-inn
we-were-served meal.

22. 奥さんがお作りになったんですか。

Okusan ga otsukuri ni nattan desu ka.
Did the honorable wife honorably make it?

23. こちらはあなた方の分ですよ。

Kochira wa anatagata no bun desu yo.
As for this way, it's you honorable people's portion, for sure.

24. 召し上がってみてください。

Meshiagatte mite kudasai.
Please eat and see.

25. わあ、僕達の分もですか。

Waa, bokutachi no bun mo desu ka.
Wow, is it our portion also? (i.e., is there some for us too?)

26. どうも有難うございます。

Doumo arigatou gozaimasu.
Thank you very much.

****

27. 中村さんも料理をすることがあるんですか。

Nakamura-san mo ryouri wo suru koto ga arun desu ka.
Nakamura also, does to-do-cuisine thing exist?

28. この間僕が作った魚の料理ね、隣の猫に食べられたようだね。

Kono aida boku ga tsukutta sakana no ryouri ne, tonari no neko ni taberareta you da ne.
The other day, the fish cuisine I made, huh, by the neighbor cat it got eaten on me, it appears, huh.

29. あなた、あんな真っ黒になった魚は猫でも食べませんよ。

Anata, anna makkuro ni natta sakana wa neko demo tabemasen yo.
Darling, as for that over there sort of became-jet-black fish, even the cat will not eat, for sure.

30. 私が捨てちゃいました。

Watashi ga sute chaimashita.
I threw it away completely.

****

31. ライアンさんはどうしておまわりさんに車を止められたのですか。

Raian-san wa doushite omawarisan ni kuruma wo tomerareta no desu ka.
As for Ryan, why, by the policeman, did the car get stopped on him?

32. スピードを出し過ぎたからです。

Supiido wo dashi sugita kara desu.
It's because he put out the speed too much.

33. 中村さんが作った魚の料理はどうなりましたか。

Nakamura-san ga tsukutta sakana no ryouri wa dou narimashita ka.
As for the Nakamura-made fish cuisine, how did it develop?

34. 奥さんが捨ててしまいました。

Okusan ga sutete shimaimashita.
The honorable wife threw it away completely.

****

35. アンディさんがビルさんの手紙を読んだ。

Andi-san ga biru-san no tegami wo yonda.
Andy read Bill's letter.

36. ビルさんはアンディさんに手紙を読まれた。

Biru-san wa andi-san ni tegami wo yomareta.
As for Bill, he had the letter read on him by Andy.

37. 雪子さんに花をプレゼントして喜ばれました。

Yukiko-san ni hana wo purezento shite yorokobaremashita.
To Yukiko, flowers, I made a present, and she got delighted on me.

38. この本はたくさんの人に読まれています。

Kono hon wa takusan no hito ni yomarete imasu.
As for this book, by a lot of people it is being read.

39. 来週、直子さんの結婚式を行います。

Raishuu naoko-san no kekkon shiki wo okonaimasu.
Next week, someone will hold Naoko's wedding. (compare 行きます = I will go)

40. 直子さんの結婚式が来週行われます。

Naoko-san no kekkon shiki ga raishuu okonawaremasu.
Naoko's wedding, next week, will be held.

41. ファックスはどこのオフィスでも使われています。

Fakkusu wa doko no ofisu demo tsukawarete imasu.
As for fax, in any place's office it is being used.

42. オリンピックは４年に一回開かれます。

Orinpikku wa yonen ni ikkai hirakaremasu.
As for the Olympics, one time every four years, it will be opened.

43. タイラーさんにカップが渡されました。

Tairaa-san ni kappu ga watasaremashita.
To Tyler, the cup got handed.

44. 母に友達から来た手紙を読まれてしまいました。

Haha ni tomodachi kara kita tegami wo yomarete shimaimashita.
By my mother, the came-from-the-friend letter was read on me completely. (a negative event)

45. 友達から来た手紙を母に読んでもらいました。

Tomodachi kara kita tegami wo haha ni yonde moraimashita.
The came-from-the-friend letter, by my mother, she read, and I received. (a positive event)

46. 私達の話を誰かに聞かれたみたいです。

Watashitachi no hanashi wo dareka ni kikareta mitai desu.
Our conversation, by someone, was heard on us it seems.

47. みんなが私をジロジロ見ました。

Minna ga watashi wo jirojiro mimashita.
Everyone stared at me.

48. 弟は母に朝早く起こされて眠いようです。

Otouto wa haha ni asa hayaku okosarete nemui you desu.
As for little brother, by my mother he is awakened early morning, and he looks sleepy.

49. 背の高い人に前に座られて映画がよく見えませんでした。

Se no takai hito ni mae ni suwararete eiga ga yoku miemasen deshita.
By a tall person sits in front on me, and I could not see the movie well.

50. お母さんに本を読んでもらっています。

Okaasan ni hon wo yonde moratte imasu.
By the honorable mother, she is reading a book, and he is receiving.

51. 風に帽子を飛ばされました。

Kaze ni boushi wo tobasaremashita.
By the wind, the hat was sent flying on me.

52. コンピューターの使い方を教えてもらっています。

Konpyuutaa no tsukai kata wo oshiete moratte imasu.
The computer's use method she is teaching, and he is receiving.

53. もしもし、北村さんはお留守ですか。

Moshimoshi, kitamura-san wa orusu desu ka.
Hello (on the phone). As for Kitamura, is he honorably absent?

54. では後で電話をいただきたいんですが。

Dewa ato de denwa wo itadakitain desu ga...
Well, of later I would like to humbly receive a phone call, but...

55. 帰りましたら電話をするようにお伝えします。

Kaerimashitara denwa wo suru you ni otsutae shimasu.
When he returns, to do a phone call I will humbly tell.

Chapter 90

1. ご飯ができたけどお父さんは
   まだお風呂かしら。

   Gohan ga dekita kedo otousan wa mada
   ofuro kashira.
   The rice got ready, but as for honorable
   Father, still honorable bath, I wonder.

2. じゃ、お父さんに早くお風呂
   から出るように言ってくる
   ね。

   Ja, otousan ni hayaku ofuro kara deru
   you ni itte kuru ne.
   Well, to honorable Father, quickly to
   emerge from the honorable bath, I will
   say and come, huh.

3. ジョン君の報告書はまだか
   な。

   Jon-kun no houkokusho wa mada kana.
   As for young man John's report, still, I
   wonder.

4. 今日中に欲しいんだけど。

   Kyoujuuni hoshiin dakedo...
   By the end of today I desire, but...

5. じゃ、ジョン君に早く仕上げ
   るように言っておきます。

   Ja, jon-kun ni hayaku shiageru you ni itte
   okimasu.
   Well, to young man John, to finish early
   I will say in advance.

6. すみません。こんなアイロン
   はどこで売っているか、教え
   てもらえませんか。

   Sumimasen. Konna airon wa doko de
   utte iru ka, oshiete moraemasen ka.
   Excuse me. As for this kind of iron,
   where they are selling (question), can
   you not teach and I receive?

7. もっと早くお医者さんにみて
   もらえば良かったのに。

   Motto hayaku oishasan ni mite moraeba
   yokatta noni.
   More early by the honorable doctor if he
   looks and you receive, it was good, if
   only.

8. スピードを出さなければ良か
   ったのに。

   Supiido wo dasanakereba yokatta noni.
   If you don't put out speed, it was good, if
   only.

9. おまわりさんに車を止められ
   てしまった。

   Omawarisan ni kuruma wo tomerarete
   shimatta.
   By the policeman the car was stopped on
   me completely.

10. ああ、もっとゆっくり走れば
    良かった。

    Aa, motto yukkuri hashireba yokatta.
    Ah, more slowly if I ran it was good.
    (i.e., if I drove)

11. あんなにスピードを出すんじ
ゃなかった。

Anna ni supiido wo dasun ja nakatta.
That over there kind of to put out speed
thing it was not. (i.e., I shouldn't have
gone so fast)

12. 子供達をディズニーランドに
連れて行くつもりだったの
に。

Kodomotachi wo dizuniirando ni tsurete
ikutsumori datta noni.
The children, to Disneyland I was
planning to take, too bad.

13. 明日は朝早く起きなきゃなら
ないから今晩はもう寝ます。

Ashita wa asa hayaku okinakya naranai
kara konban wa mou nemasu.
As for tomorrow, since I have to get up
early in the morning, as for tonight,
already I will sleep.

14. 信号を良く見ればいいのに。

Shingou wo yoku mireba ii noni.
If he looks at the stoplight well, good, if
only.

15. 車で来れば良かったのに。

Kuruma de kureba yokatta noni.
If he comes by car, it was good, if only.

16. 子供も連れて行けばいいの
に。

Kodomo mo tsurete ikeba ii noni.
The child also, if she takes along, good,
if only.

17. 宿題をしてくれるロボットが
いればいいのに。

Shukudai wo shite kureru robotto ga
ireba ii noni.
If a homework do and give robot exists,
good, if only.

18. もっと大きい魚だったら良か
ったのに。

Motto ookii sakana dattara yokatta noni.
If it's a bigger fish, it was good, if only.

19. 土田部長とゴルフに行くは
ずだったのに。

Tsuchida buchou to gorufu ni iku hazu
datta noni.
With Division Manager Tsuchida, I was
supposed to go for the purpose of golf,
too bad.

20. 休みを取って京都に行くはず
だったのに。

Yasumi wo totte kyouto ni iku hazu datta
noni.
Taking vacation, I was supposed to go to
Kyoto, too bad.

****

21. ジョナサンさんの日記。

Jonasan-san no nikki.
Jonathan's diary.

22. 日本語学校から帰る途中、雨
に降られた。

Nihongo gakkou kara kaeru tochuu, ame
ni furareta.
From Japanese language school to return
on the way, by the rain, it precipitated on
me.

23. 大した雨ではないので、その
まま歩いて行った、ずっとま
わりの人からジロジロ見られ
ていたような気がする。

****

Taishita ame de wa nai node, sono mama
aruite itta, zutto mawari no hito kara
jirojiro mirarete ita you na ki ga suru.
Since it isn't a great rain, that manner I
was walking, all the way, by the
surrounding's people, were staring on
me, it seems, I have a feeling.

24. もうあの映画をごらんになり
ましたか。

Mou ano eiga wo goran ni narimashita
ka.
Did you already honorably see that
movie over there?

25. 毎晩、何時頃お休みになりま
すか。

Maiban, nanji goro oyasumi ni narimasu
ka.
Every night, about what time do you
honorably rest?

26. なるべく早く休むようにいた
しております。

Narubeku hayaku yasumu you ni itashite
orimasu.
As early as possible, I am humbly
making an effort to rest.

27. 部長はパーティにいらっしゃ
るかな。

Buchou wa paatii ni irassharu kana.
As for Division Manager, to the party,
will you honorably go, I wonder?

28. ああ、行くよ。君は？

Aa, iku yo. Kimi wa?
Ah, I will go, for sure. As for you?

29. そう。社長もいらっしゃるそ
うだよ。

Sou. Shachou mo irassharu sou da yo.
So. (i.e., yes) The president also will
honorably come reportedly, for sure.

30. 石川さんは来られましたか。

Ishikawa-san wa koraremashita ka.
As for Ishikawa, did he honorably come?

31. 今夜はどこで食事をなさいま
すか。

****

Konya wa doko de shokuji wo nasaimasu
ka.
As for this evening, where will you
honorably do a meal?

32. 土田部長、クラーク会長が日
本にいらっしゃったそうです
ね。ご存じですか。

Tsuchida buchou, kuraaku kaichou ga
nihon ni irasshatta sou desu ne. Gozonji
desu ka.
Division Manager Tsuchida, Board
Chairman Clark honorably came to
Japan, reportedly, huh. Do you
honorably know him?

33. クラーク会長にはお子さんは
何人いらっしゃいますか。

Kuraaku kaichou ni wa okosan wa nan nin irasshaimasu ka.
As for to Board Chairman Clark, as for honorable children, how many honorably exist?

34. 部長はクラーク会長がお酒を
たくさん召し上がるのをご存
じでしたか。

Buchou wa kuraaku kaichou ga osake wo takusan meshiagaru no wo gozonji deshita ka.
As for the division manager, Board Chairman Clark, honorable sake will honorably drink a lot, did he honorably know?

35. 部長はアメリカに出張したと
きクラーク会長とお会いにな
ったそうですね。

Buchou wa amerika ni shutchou shita toki kuraaku kaichou to oai ni natta sou desu ne.
As for the division manager, the time when he did a business trip to America, he honorably met with Board Chairman Clark, reportedly, huh.

36. クラーク会長が来週、部長に
会いたいとおっしゃっていま
した。

Kuraaku kaichou ga raishuu, buchou ni aitai to oshatte imashita
Board Chairman Clark, next week, would like to meet the division manager, he was honorably saying.

37. クラーク会長は部長に会える
かどうか心配していらっしゃ
いましたよ。

Kuraaku kaichou wa buchou ni aeru ka douka shinpai shite irasshaimashita yo.
As for Board Chairman Clark, whether he will be able to meet the division manager, he was worried honorably, for sure.

38. クラーク会長に電話をしてく
れましたか。

Kuraaku kaichou ni denwa wo shite kuremashita ka.
To Board Chairman Clark, did you do a phone call and give to me?

39. はい、外出中でいらっしゃい
ませんでした。

Hai, gaishutsu chuu de irasshaimasen deshita.
Yes, since in the middle of going out, he didn't honorably exist.

40. 又、後で電話をいたします。

Mata, ato de denwa wo itashimasu.
Again, of later, I will humbly do a phone call.

41. クラーク会長にうちの会社に
来ていただけそうですか。

Kuraaku kaichou ni uchi no kaisha ni kite itadake sou desu ka.
By Board Chairman Clark, to the in-group's company, will he come and we be able to humbly receive, it seems?

****

42. あれ、雨が降ってる。

Are, ame ga futteru.
Hey, it's raining.

43. さっきまで晴れそうだったの
に。

Sakki made hare sou datta noni.
Until a while ago, it looked like it would
be sunny, too bad.

44. ノアさん、社長が社長室に来
るようにとおっしゃっていま
すよ。

Noa-san, shachou ga shachou shitsu ni
kuru you ni to osshatte imasu yo.
Noah, the president, "come to the
president's room," he is honorably
saying, for sure.

45. 日本では土曜日でも子供達は
学校に行きます。

Nihon de wa doyoubi demo kodomotachi
wa gakkou ni ikimasu.
As for in Japan, even Saturday, as for
children, they go to school.

46. 外国語を習うときは下手でも
たくさんしゃべった方がいい
んですよ。

Gaikokugo wo narau toki wa heta demo
takusan shabetta hou ga iin desu yo.
As for to-learn-a-foreign-language time,
even if unskillful, it's better to chatter
many (i.e., a lot), for sure.

47. 仕事が忙しくても月に一度は
映画を見にいきます。

Shigoto ga isogashikutemo tsuki ni
ichido wa eiga wo mi ni ikimasu.
Even though work is busy, as for once a
month, I go for the purpose of seeing a
movie.

48. あの人にドイツ語で話しかけ
ても分からないでしょう。

Ano hito ni doitsugo de hanashikaketemo
wakaranai deshou.
To that person over there, even if you
address him in German, he will not
understand probably.

49. たとえ雨が降っても運動会は
行います。

Tatoe ame ga futtemo undoukai wa
okonaimasu.
Supposing, even if it rains, as for the
sports tournament, we will hold it.

50. どんなに寒くても私はストー
ブを点けません。

Donna ni samukutemo watashi wa
sutoobu wo tsukemasen.
Whatever kind of cold, as for me, I don't
turn on the space heater.

51. あのバイキングのレストラン
は食べ放題です。

Ano baikingu no resutoran wa
tabehoudai desu.
That Viking restaurant over there is all-
you-can-eat.

52. この映画は子供向けに製作さ
れた。

Kono eiga wa kodomo muke ni seisaku
sareta.
As for this movie, children intended for,
it was produced on. (i.e., it was
produced for kids)

Chapter 91

1. もしもし、お待たせいたしました。

Moshimoshi. Omatase itashimashita.
Hello. I humbly made you wait. (i.e., I'm sorry to have kept you waiting)

2. 中島でございます。

Nakashima de gozaimasu.
It's Nakashima. (i.e., I'm Nakashima)

3. 先日、見本市でお目にかかった池田産業のロビンソンでございます。

Senjitsu, mihon'ichi de ome ni kakatta ikeda sangyou no robinson de gozaimasu.
The other day, at the sample show I humbly met, it is Ikeda Industries' Robinson.

4. あ、あの時はお世話になりました。

A, ano toki wa osewa ni narimashita.
Ah, as for that time over there, honorable care developed. (i.e., thank you for your help)

5. 先ほどお電話をいただきましたそうで。

Sakihodo odenwa wo itadakimashita sou de...
A little while ago, I humbly received an honorable phone call, reportedly, and...

6. 会議中で大変失礼いたしました。

Kaigi chuu de taihen shitsurei itashimashita.
Since in the middle of a meeting, terrible, I humbly did a discourtesy.

7. いいえ、お忙しいところを申し訳ございません。

Iie. Oisogashii tokoro wo, moushiwake gozaimasen.
No. On an honorably busy moment, there's no excuse.

8. 早速ですが先日ごらんいただいた、わが社の製品について、もう少しご説明したいと思いまして。

Sassoku desu ga senjitsu goran itadaita, wagasha no seihin ni tsuite, mou sukoshi, go setsumei shitai to omoimashite...
It's sudden, but the other day an honorable look I humbly received, regarding our company's products, a little bit more, I would like to humbly explain, I think, and...

9. ご都合がよろしかったらお伺いしたいのですが。

Go tsugou ga yoroshikattara oukagai shitai no desu ga...
If the honorable cirumstances are good, I would like to do a humble visit, but...

10. そうですね。実は明日から
九州に出張することになっ
ております。
きゅうしゅう

Sou desu ne. Jitsu wa asu kara kyuushuu ni shutchou suru koto ni natte orimasu. That's so huh. To tell the truth, from tomorrow, to Kyushu, I am humbly scheduled to do a business trip.

11. 木曜日には帰って参りますの
で、金曜日の午後ならお会い
できると思いますが、一時半
ではいかがでしょうか。

Mokuyoubi ni wa kaette mairimasu node, kinyoubi no gogo nara oai dekiru to omoimasu ga ichijihan de wa ikaga deshou ka. As for on Thursday, since I will return and humbly come, in the case of Friday afternoon, I can humbly meet, I think, but as for of half past one, how is it probably?

12. はい、それで結構です。

Hai, sore de kekkou desu. Yes, with that it's fine.

13. では一時半にそちらに伺いま
す。

De wa ichijihan ni sochira ni ukagaimasu. Well, at half past one, I will visit to that way.

14. あ、ちょっとお待ちくださ
い。

A, chotto omachi kudasai. Ah, please honorably wait a moment.

15. 一時半は他の予定が入ってお
りました。

Ichijihan wa hoka no yotei ga haitte orimashita. As for half past one, another plan was being entered humbly.

16. 忘れないようにメモをしてお
いたのにうっかりしていまし
た。

Wasurenai you ni memo wo shite oita noni ukkari shite imashita. In order not to forget, even though I did a memo in advance, I was doing carelessly. (i.e., it slipped my mind)

17. 申し訳ありませんが、3時に
していただけませんでしょう
か。

Moushiwake arimasen ga sanji ni shite itadakemasen deshou ka. There's no excuse, but at 3:00 will you do, and am I not able to humbly receive probably?

18. はい、では3時にお伺いいた
します。

Hai, de wa sanji ni oukagai itashimasu. Yes, well, at 3:00, I will humbly visit.

****

19. 先日はお電話で失礼いたしま
した。

Senjitsu wa odenwa de shitsurei itashimashita. As for the other day, by humble phone, I did a discourtesy. (i.e., I called you)

20. あの、部長の土田からもよろ
しくとのことでございます。

Ano, buchou no tsuchida kara mo
yoroshiku tono koto de gozaimasu.
Say, from the division manager's
Tsuchida also, regards-I-hear thing it is.
(i.e., he said to say hello)

21. 課長さんとは昔からのお知り
合いだそうですね。

Kachou-san to wa mukashi kara no
oshiriai da sou desu ne.
As for with Mr. Section Manager, since-
old-times' honorable acquaintance he is,
reportedly, huh. (addressing the section
manager)

22. 女性社員がお茶を持ってく
る。

Josei shain ga ocha wo motte kuru.
A woman company employee brings
honorable tea.

23. 失礼いたします。どうぞ。

Shitsurei itashimasu. Douzo.
I will humbly do a discourtesy. Go
ahead.

24. すみません。どうぞお構いな
く。

Sumimasen. Douzo okamainaku.
Excuse me. Go ahead not honorably
minding. (i.e., don't bother about me)

25. ところで、工業用ロボットの
件ですが、わが社ではアメリ
カだけでなく、ヨーロッパの
方にも進出したいと考えてお
ります。

Tokoro de, kougyou you robotto no ken
desu ga, wagasha de wa amerika dake de
naku, yorooppa no hou ni mo shinshutsu
shitai to kangaete orimasu.
By the way, it's the industrial use robot's
matter, but as for at our company, not in
America only, to Europe's direction also,
we want to advance, we are humbly
thinking.

26. こちらではヨーロッパの会社
との取り引きが多いと伺いま
したので、ぜひわが社の製品
も輸出していただければと思
いまして。

Kochira de wa yorooppa no kaisha to no
torihiki ga ooi to ukagaimashita node,
zehi wagasha no seihin mo yushutsu
shite itadakereba to omoimashite...
As for at this way, since we heard that
with-Europe's companies' business deals
are numerous, by all means, our
company's products also, if export and
we are able to humbly receive, we think,
and...

27. お宅でしたら、少なくても年
に 500 台は売っていただける
のではないかと思うのです
が、いかがでしょうか。

Otaku deshitara, sukunakute mo nen ni
gohyaku dai wa utte itadakeru no de wa
nai ka to omou no desu ga, ikaga deshou
ka.
If it's honorable you, at least, as for 500
units per year, you sell and we are able to
receive thing, isn't it (question), I think,
but how is it probably?

28. ヨーロッパに合わせて、モデルのチェンジもできますのでよろしくお願いいたします。

Yooroppa ni awasete, moderu no chenji mo dekimasu node yoroshiku onegai itashimasu.
To Europe fitting, model's changes also, since we are able to do, I beg you well humbly.

29. 結構なお話だと思いますが、私の考えだけではすぐにお返事できません。

Kekkou na ohanashi da to omoimasu ga, watakushi no kangae dake de wa sugu ni ohenji dekimasen.
I think it's a fine honorable speech, but as for only from my thinking, immediately, a humble reply can't be done.

30. 部長ともよく話しまして近いうちにご連絡いたします。

Buchou to mo yoku hanashimashite chikai uchi ni go renraku itashimasu.
With the division manager also I will talk well, and while still close, I will do humble communication. (i.e., I'll do it soon)

31. よろしくお願いいたします。

Yoroshiku onegai itashimasu.
I beg you well.

32. アンソニーさんはいつ中島さんと会うことになりましたか。

Ansonii-san wa itsu nakashima-san to au koto ni narimashita ka.
As for Anthony, when was he scheduled to meet with Nakashima?

33. 金曜日の3時です。

Kinyoubi no sanji desu.
It's Friday's 3:00.

****

34. お客さんに：部長は隣の部屋におりますからそちらにいらしてください。

Okyakusan ni: Buchou wa tonari no heya ni orimasu kara sochira ni irashite kudasai.
To the honorable Mr. Customer: As for the division manager, since he is humbly in the next room, please honorably go to that way.

35. 仕事は遅くても午後8時には終わるでしょう。

Shigoto wa osokutemo gogo hachiji ni wa owaru deshou.
As for the work, at the very latest, as for at 8 p.m., it will probably finish.

36. 冬のボーナスは多くても3.5ヶ月分ぐらいじゃないかと思います。

Fuyu no boonasu wa ookutemo san ten go kagetsu bun gurai ja nai ka to omoimasu.
As for the winter's bonus, at the very most, about 3.5 month's portion, isn't it (question), I think.

37. エミリーさんはお茶を出したのに飲まなかったんです。

Emirii-san wa ocha wo dashita noni nomanakattan desu.
As for Emily, in spite of I put out honorable tea, she did not drink.

38. その辞書は高くても買った方がいいですよ。

Sono jisho wa takakutemo katta hou ga ii desu yo.
As for that dictionary, even though expensive, it would be better to buy, for sure.

39. 今、道が込んでいるからタクシーで行っても間に合わないでしょう。

Ima, michi ga konde iru kara takushii de ittemo maniawanai deshou.
Now, since the streets are being crowded, even if you go by taxi, you will probably not be on time.

40. 今から大事な会議があるので、いくら疲れていても帰れないんですよ。

Ima kara daiji na kaigi ga aru node ikura tsukarete itemo kaerenain desu yo.
From now, since an important meeting exists, how much I am being tired even though, I am not able to return, for sure.

41. お金がないんでしょう？

Okane ga nain deshou?
Money doesn't exist probably?

42. ご両親に借りたらどうですか。

Go ryoushin ni karitara dou desu ka.
If you borrow from the honorable parents, how is it?

43. 両親は今、旅行中なのでお金を借りたくても借りられないんですよ。

Ryoushin wa ima, ryokouchuu na node okane wo karitakutemo karirarenain desu yo.
As for the parents, now, since they are in the middle of travel, even though I want to borrow money, I cannot borrow, for sure.

44. 明日は雨が降るかもしれませんよ。

Ashita wa ame ga furu kamoshiremasen yo.
As for tomorrow, it will rain, it might be, for sure.

45. 雨が降ったらどうしますか。

Ame ga futtara dou shimasu ka.
If it rains, how will you do?

46. 行くのを止めたら？

Iku no wo yametara?
To go, if you stop?

47. ええ、雨が降っても行きます。

Ee, ame ga futtemo ikimasu.
Yeah, even though it will rain, I will go.

48. 学生は先生にその本を読むように言われました。

Gakusei wa sensei ni sono hon wo yomu you ni iwaremashita.
As for the student, by the teacher, to read that book was said on him.

Chapter 92

1. キャシーに：こちらは僕の祖母です。

   Kyashii ni: Kochira wa boku no sobo desu.
   To Kathy: As for this way, it's my grandmother.

2. こちらが父、母、それに兄です。

   Kochira ga chichi, haha, sore ni ani desu.
   This way, it's father, mother, moreover older brother.

3. 初めまして。どうぞよろしく。

   Hajimemashite. Douzo yoroshiku.
   Pleased to meet you. Please be good to me.

4. 皆：こちらこそ。よくいらっしゃいました。

   Minna: Kochira koso. Yoku irasshaimashita.
   Everyone: The pleasure is ours. Well honorably came (i.e., welcome).

5. お元気そうですね。

   Ogenki sou desu ne.
   Honorably healthy appearing it is, huh. (referring to the grandmother)

6. お母さんは何かお仕事をなさっているんですか。

   Okaasan wa nanika oshigoto wo nasatte irun desu ka.
   As for honorable Mother, are you honorably doing something honorable work?

7. 大学で英語を教えているんですよ。

   Daigaku de eigo wo oshiete irun desu yo.
   At a university, I am teaching English, for sure.

8. キャシーさんは今どこに住んでいらっしゃるんですか。

   Kyashii-san wa ima doko ni sunde irassharun desu ka.
   As for Kathy, now, where are you living honorably?

9. 六本木に住んでいます。

   Roppongi ni sunde imasu.
   I am living in Roppongi.

10. 幸一とはどこで知り合ったんですか。

    Kouichi to wa doko de shiriattan desu ka.
    As for with Kouichi, where did you get acquainted?

11. 六本木のディスコです。

    Roppongi no disuko desu.
    It's a Roppongi's disco.

12. ところでお父さんはどんなお仕事をなさっているんですか。

Tokoro de otousan wa donna oshigoto wo nasatte irun desu ka.
By the way, as for honorable father, what kind of honorable work are you honorably doing?

13. 山川貿易に勤めているんですよ。

Yamakawa boueki ni tsutomete irun desu yo.
At Yamakawa Trade, I am being employed, for sure.

14. キャシーさんはアメリカのどこでお生まれになったんですか。

Kyashii-san wa amerika no doko de oumare ni nattan desu ka.
As for Kathy, America's at where were you honorably born?

15. ニューヨークで生まれました。

Nyuuyooku de umaremashita.
I was born in New York.

16. キャシーさんは日本語が上手ですね。

Kyashii-san wa nihongo ga jouzu desu ne.
As for Kathy, Japanese is skillful, huh.

17. どこで勉強なさったんですか。

Doko de benkyou nasattan desu ka.
At where did you honorably do study?

18. イリノイ大学で勉強しました。

Irinoi daigaku de benkyou shimashita.
At Illinois University I studied.

19. お兄さんはお仕事で外国にいらっしゃることがあるんですか。

Oniisan wa oshigoto de gaikoku ni irassharu koto ga arun desu ka.
As for older brother, for honorable work, does to-foreign-countries-honorably-go thing exist?

20. ええ、時々ありますよ。

Ee. Tokidoki arimasu yo.
Yeah. Sometimes it exists, for sure.

21. キャシーさんはいつまで日本にいらっしゃるんですか。

Kyashii-san wa itsu made nihon ni irassharun desu ka.
As for Kathy, until when will you honorably exist in Japan?

22. 来年の三月までいます。

Rainen no sangatsu made imasu.
I will exist until next year's March.

23. お兄さんはアメリカへ出張する予定はないんですか。

Oniisan wa amerika e shutchou suru yotei wa nain desu ka.
As for big brother, as for to-America to-do-business-trip plans, do they not exist?

24. ありますよ。来年の四月に行く予定です。

Arimasu yo. Rainen no shigatsu ni iku yotei desu.
They exist, for sure. At next year's April, it's a to-go plan.

25. 向こうでお会いできるといいですね。

Mukou de oai dekiru to ii desu ne.
At the far side, if I am able to humbly meet, it's good, huh.

****

26. 先日はお忙しいところをお会いいただきましてどうも有難うございました。

Senjitsu wa oisogashii tokoro wo oai itadakimashite doumo arigatou gozaimashita.
As for the other day, on an honorably busy moment, I humbly received a humble encounter, and thank you very much for what you did.

27. さて、当日お願いいたしました件ですが当社ではぜひともヨーロッパへ市場を広げたいと考えておりますのでどうぞよろしくお願い申し上げます。

Sate, toujitsu onegai itashimashita ken desu ga tousha de wa zehitomo yooroppa e shijou wo hirogetai to kangaete orimasu node douzo yoroshiku onegai moushiagemasu.
Now then, the designated day, it's the "begged humbly" matter, but as for at the designated company, by all means, to Europe the market we want to expand, since we are thinking humbly, go ahead, be good to us, we beg humbly.

28. 当社の工業用ロボットはアメリカでの売り上げも増えており、その品質には自信を持っております。

Tousha no kougyou you robotto wa amerika de no uriage mo fuete ori, sono hinshitsu ni wa jishin wo motte orimasu.
As for the designated company's industrial use robots, in-America's gross sales are also increasing humbly, and as for to that product quality, we are humbly having self-confidence.

29. なお、先日お届けいたしました英文の資料の他に、ドイツ語とフランス語の資料も作りましたので、お送りいたします。

Nao, senjitsu otodoke itashimashita eibun no shiryou no hoka ni, doitsugo to furansugo no shiryou mo tsukurimashita node, o okuri itashimasu.
Moreover, the other day, in addition to the humbly sent English text's literature, since we produced German and French literature also, we will send humbly.

30. ヨーロッパの会社への説明の
時にお使いください。

        ****

Yooroppa no kaisha e no setsumei no toki ni otsukai kudasai.
At the to-Europe's companies' explanation's time, please honorably use.

31. これは誰が誰に出した手紙で
すか。

Kore wa dare ga dare ni dashita tegami desu ka.
As for this, who, to whom, sent letter is it?

32. アンソニーさんが山川貿易の
中島さんに出した物です。

Ansonii-san ga yamakawa boueki no nakashima-san ni dashita mono desu.
It's an Anthony-to-Yamakawa-Trade's-Nakashima-sent thing.

33. 何を送ると書いてあります
か。

Nani wo okuru to kaite arimasu ka.
What will he send, is written?

34. ドイツ語とフランス語の資料
を送ると書いてあります。

Doitsugo to furansugo no shiryou wo okuru to kaite arimasu.
He will send German and French literature, it is written.

35. なぜドイツ語とフランス語の
資料も作ったのでしょうか。

Naze doitsugo to furansugo no shiryou mo tsukutta no deshou ka.
Why, German and French literature also, did they probably make?

36. ヨーロッパの会社への説明に
使ってもらうためです。

        ****

Yooroppa no kaisha e no setsumei ni tsukatte morau tame desu.
For the sake of to Europe's companies' explanation, for the purpose of to use and they will receive it is.

37. 今夜は帰りが遅くなるから先
に寝てください。

Konya wa kaeri ga osoku naru kara saki ni nete kudasai.
As for this evening, since the return will become late, at before me, please sleep.

38. いいえ、遅くても起きて待っ
ていますよ。

Iie, osokutemo okite matte imasu yo.
No, even though late, I will be awake and waiting, for sure.

39. そう、じゃ、できるだけ早く
帰るようにします。

Sou. Ja, dekiru dake hayaku kaeru you ni shimasu.
So. Well, I will make an effort to return as early as possible.

40. あれ、子供がビールを飲んで
る。

Are. Kodomo ga biiru wo nonderu.
Hey. The child is drinking beer.

41. ええ、ドイツでは子供でもビールを飲むんですよ。

Ee, doitsu de wa kodomo demo biiru wo nomun desu yo.
Yeah, as for in Germany, even though a child, they drink beer, for sure.

42. 品物がない場合もあります。

Shinamono ga nai baai mo arimasu.
Merchandise doesn't exist cases also exist.

43. 駅までは遠いですよ。タクシーで行けば？

Eki made wa tooi desu yo. Takushii de ikeba?
As for until the station, it's far, for sure. If you go by taxi?

44. 遠くても歩いていきます。

Tookutemo aruite ikimasu.
Even though far, I will go walking.

45. この字、日本人なら読めるんでしょう？

Kono ji, nihonjin nara yomerun deshou?
These characters, in case of Japanese people, can they probably read?

46. いや、こんな字は日本人でも読めませんよ。

Iya, konna ji wa nihonjin demo yomemasen yo.
Nah, as for this kind of character, even though Japanese people, they cannot read, for sure.

47. ミッキーマウスは有名なんですね。

Mikkii mausu wa yuumei nan desu ne.
As for Mickey Mouse, he is famous, huh.

48. ええ、小さい子供でも知っていますよ。

Ee, chiisai kodomo demo shitte imasu yo.
Yeah, even though small children, they are knowing, for sure.

49. ボーナスは少なくても二ヶ月分は欲しいですね。

Boonasu wa sukunakutemo nikagetsu bun wa hoshii desu ne.
As for bonuses, at the very least, as for a two-month portion, I desire, huh.

50. この漢字は昨日習ったのにもう忘れてしまいました。

Kono kanji wa kinou naratta noni mou wasurete shimaimashita.
As for this kanji, even though I learned it yesterday, already I forgot completely.

51. この漢字は何回練習しても上手に書けません。

Kono kanji wa nankai renshuu shitemo jouzu ni kakemasen.
As for this kanji, many times I practice even though, I cannot write skillfully.

Chapter 93

1. もうすぐ直子さんが結婚されるでしょう。

Mou sugu naoko-san ga kekkon sareru deshou.
Pretty soon, Naoko will honorably do marriage probably.

2. 結婚祝いはどんな物がいいと思う、黒田さん？

Kekkon iwai wa donna mono ga ii to omou, kuroda-san?
As for a wedding gift, what kind of thing is good, do you think, Kuroda?

3. そうね。直子さんに聞かずに決めてしまうのは。

Sou ne. Naoko-san ni kika zuni kimete shimau no wa...
So huh. To Naoko not asking, we will arrange completely...

4. じゃ、直子さんに何が欲しいか聞いてみましょう。

Ja, naoko-san ni nani ga hoshii ka kiite mimashou.
Well, to Naoko, what does she desire (question) let's ask and see.

5. じゃ、私が直子さんに言って選んでもらいましょう。

Ja, watashi ga naoko-san ni itte erande moraimashou.
Well, I, to Naoko will say, and she will choose, and we shall receive.

****

6. あの、直子さんの結婚祝いのことですけど。

Ano, naoko-san no kekkon iwai no koto desu kedo...
Say, it's Naoko wedding present's thing, but...

7. 直子さんはできたら電気製品が欲しいそうです。

Naoko-san wa dekitara denki seihin ga hoshii sou desu.
As for Naoko, if it can be done, an electric product she desires, reportedly.

8. 電子レンジはもう買ってあって、後アイロンとトースターがないんですって。

Denshi renji wa mou katte atte, ato airon to toosutaa ga nain desu tte.
As for a microwave, already it is bought and exists, and the rest, an iron and a toaster, don't exist, reportedly.

9. カタログを見せる。

Katarogu wo miseru.
She shows a catalogue.

10. これが気に入ったわ。

Kore ga ki ni itta wa.
This is pleasing me.

11. （笑いながら）あなたが結婚するときにはこれをあげましょうね。

(warai nagara) Anata ga kekkon suru toki ni wa kore wo agemashou ne.
(while laughing) As for at the time *you* will get married, we shall give this, huh.

12. 直子さんは下さるならこちらがいいっておっしゃってたわ。

Naoko-san wa kudasaru nara kochira ga ii tte oshatteta wa.
As for Naoko, in the case of you will honorably give, this way is good, she was honorably saying.

13. じゃ、僕の友人に電気屋をしているのがいるから彼に持って来させよう。

Ja, boku no yuujin ni denkiya wo shite iru no ga iru kara kare ni motte kosaseyou.
Well, among my friends, since electric-store-doing one exists, to him I shall make him bring.

14. 先ず、電話をしてこの品物があるかどうか聞いてみなくてはね。

Mazu, denwa wo shite kono shinamono ga aru ka douka kiite minakutewa ne.
First, I will do a phone call and this merchandise, whether it exists or not, I must ask and see, huh.

15. 品物によってはないこともあるそうだから。

Shinamono ni yotte wa nai koto mo aru sou dakara.
As for depending on the merchandise, since not-existing thing also exists, reportedly. (i.e., sometimes they don't have it)

16. このし紙にみんなの名前を書いて送りましょう。

Kono noshigami ni minna no namae wo kaite okurimashou.
To this wrapper, let's write everyone's name and send.

17. 係長さんから、どうぞ。

Kakarichou-san kara, douzo.
From (i.e., starting with) Mr. Assistant Manager, go ahead.

18. 僕は字が下手だから困るな。

Boku wa ji ga heta dakara komaru na.
As for me, since characters are unskillful, I will be inconvenienced.

19. 誰か書いてくれないかな。

Dareka kaite kurenai kana.
Will someone not write and give, I wonder?

20. こう言うときにはいつも家内に書かせることにしているんだよ。

Kou iu toki ni wa itsumo kanai ni kakaseru koto ni shite irun da yo.
As for at like-this-said times, always to the wife to make write I am deciding, for sure.

21. 字なら黒田さんにお願いする
のが一番よ。

Ji nara kuroda-san ni onegai suru no ga
ichiban yo.
In the case of characters, to Kuroda, to
do humble begging thing, number one,
for sure. (i.e., it's best to ask Kuroda)

22. 黒田さんは字がきれいだか
ら。

Kuroda-san wa ji ga kirei dakara.
As for Kuroda, since characters are
pretty.

23. 僕の名前もお願いします。

Boku no namae mo onegai shimasu.
My name also I beg.

24. いつも私が書かされることに
なっちゃうわね。

Itsumo watashi ga kakasareru koto ni
natchau wa ne.
Always I am made to write is scheduled
completely, huh.

25. 黒田さんがみんなの名前を書
いてしまう。

Kuroda-san ga minna no namae wo kaite
shimau.
Kuroda writes everyone's names
completely.

26. これ、誰が直子さんのうちに
持っていくの？

Kore, dare ga naoko-san no uchi ni motte
iku no?
This, who will take to Naoko's home?

27. 宅配便に頼もう。

Takuhaibin ni tanomou.
Let's request to a home delivery service.

28. 宅配便なら、遅くともあさっ
てまでには届くだろう。

Takuhaibin nara, osokutomo asatte made
ni wa todoku darou.
In the case of a home delivery service, at
the latest, as for by the day after
tomorrow, it will be delivered probably.

29. じゃ、私が頼んできます。

Ja, watashi ga tanonde kimasu.
Well, I will request and come.

****

30. ジェイムズさん達は直子さん
の結婚祝いの品物を決める前
にどうすることにしました
か。

Jeimuzu-san tachi wa naoko-san no
kekkon iwai no shinamono wo kimeru
mae ni dou suru koto ni shimashita ka.
As for the James group, at before to
arrange Naoko's wedding present's
merchandise, how to do did they decide?

31. 直子さんに何が欲しいか聞い
てみることにしました。

Naoko-san ni nani ga hoshii ka kiite miru
koto ni shimashita.
To Naoko, what she desires (question)
they decided to ask and see.

32. 結婚祝いのお金は誰が一番多
く出すことになりましたか。

Kekkon iwai no okane wa dare ga,
ichiban ooku dasu koto ni narimashita ka.
As for the wedding present's money,
who was scheduled to put out the most
numerously?

33. 田辺係長です。

Tanabe kakarichou desu.
It's assistant manager Tanabe.

34. 結婚祝いの品物はどこの店で買うことになりましたか。

Kekkon iwai no shinamono wa doko no mise de kau koto ni narimashita ka.
As for the wedding gift's merchandise, at where's store was it scheduled to buy?

35. 田辺係長の友達の店で買うことになりました。

Tanabe kakarichou no tomodachi no mise de kau koto ni narimashita.
It was scheduled to buy at assistant manager Tanabe's friend's store.

36. どうして黒田さんがのし紙にみんなの名前を書いたのですか。

Doushite kuroda-san ga noshigami ni minna no namae wo kaita no desu ka.
Why did Kuroda write everyone's names to the wrapper?

37. 黒田さんは字がきれいだからです。

Kuroda-san wa ji ga kirei dakara desu.
As for Kuroda, it's because the characters are pretty.

38. 結婚祝いの品物はどうやって直子さんに届けられますか。

Kekkon iwai no shinamono wa douyatte naoko-san ni todokeraremasu ka.
As for the wedding gift's merchandise, how doing, to Naoko will it be delivered?

39. 宅配便で直子さんのうちに届けられます。

Takuhaibin de naoko-san no uchi ni todokeraremasu.
By home delivery service, to Naoko's home it will be delivered.

****

40. 学生達に勉強させるための静かな部屋があるといいんですが。

Gakuseitachi ni benkyou saseru tame no shizuka na heya ga aru to iin desu ga...
To students, if a for-the-purpose-of-to-make-study quiet room exists, it's good, but...

41. 子供達がそんなにその映画を見たがっているんなら見にいかせたら？

Kodomotachi ga sonna ni sono eiga wo mitagatte irun nara mi ni ikasetara?
The children, so much that movie appear wanting to see case, if we let them go for the purpose of seeing?

42. おかずが多すぎて全部はとても食べられません。

Okazu ga oosugite zenbu wa totemo taberaremasen.
Since side dishes are too numerous, as for all, very much unable to eat.

43. 残してもいいですか。

Nokoshitemo ii desu ka.
Is it all right if I leave behind?

44. 残ったら犬に食べさせるから構いませんよ。

Nokottara inu ni tabesaseru kara kamaimasen yo.
If it is left behind, since to the dog I will make eat, it doesn't matter, for sure.

****

45. うちでは真一にたくさんのものを習わせています。

Uchi de wa shin'ichi ni takusan no mono wo narawasete imasu.
As for at the home, to Shin'ichi, a lot of things I am making him learn.

46. バイオリン、水泳、そろばん、英会話、それに書道を習わせています。

Baiorin, suiei, soroban, eikaiwa, sore ni shodou wo narawasete imasu.
Violin, swimming, abacus, English conversation, moreover calligraphy I am making him learn.

47. 日曜日には少年野球チームで野球をさせていますけれどね。

Nichiyoubi ni wa shounen yakyuu chiimu de yakyuu wo sasete imasu keredo ne.
As for on Sunday, by the boy baseball team, I am making him do baseball, but, huh.

48. うちはなにも習わせていませんが毎日一つずつうちの手伝いをさせています。

Uchi wa nanimo narawasete imasen ga mainichi hitotsu zutsu uchi no tetsudai wo sasete imasu.
As for home, I am not making her learn anything, but every day, one each, the home's help I am making her do.

49. 水曜日はお使いに行かせます。

Suiyoubi wa otsukai ni ikasemasu.
As for Wednesday, I make her go for the purpose of honorable errands.

50. 木曜日は犬の散歩をさせます。

Mokuyoubi wa inu no sanpo wo sasemasu.
As for Thursday, I make her do the dog's walk.

51. 土曜日は庭の手入れをさせます。

Doyoubi wa niwa no teire wo sasemasu.
As for Saturday, I make her do the garden's care.

52. 日曜日は手伝いをさせないで一日中外で遊ばせます。

Nichiyoubi wa tetsudai wo sasenai de ichinichi juu soto de asobasemasu.
As for Sunday, not making her do help, all day long, I let her play outside.

53. まあ、うちも少しは手伝わせた方がいいかしら。

Maa, uchi mo sukoshi wa tetsudawaseta hou ga ii kashira.
My, home also, as for a little, it would be better to make him help, I wonder.

Chapter 94

1. お母さんが赤ちゃんにミルク
を飲ませています。

Okaasan ga akachan ni miruku wo
nomasete imasu.
Honorable mother to the baby is making
drink milk.

2. 先生は子供達に話を聞かせて
います。

Sensei wa kodomotachi ni hanashi wo
kikasete imasu.
As for the teacher, to the children, she is
making them hear the story.

3. 3時頃に又お電話をさせてい
ただきます。

Sanji goro ni mata odenwa wo sasete
itadakimasu.
At about 3:00, again, you will let me do a
humble phone call, and I will receive.
(this is very polite speech)

4. あまり残業をさせないでくだ
さい。

Amari zangyou wo sasenai de kudasai.
Very much, overtime don't make me do,
please.

5. カナダへ出張ですか。いいで
すね。

Kanada e shutchou desu ka. Ii desu ne.
Is it a to-Canada business trip? It's good,
huh.

6. ぜひ、私に行かせてくださ
い。

Zehi, watashi ni ikasete kudasai.
Without fail, to me, let me go please.

7. 君なら英語もできるし、じ
ゃ、君に行ってもらうことに
しようか。

Kimi nara eigo mo dekiru shi, ja, kimi ni
itte morau koto ni shiyou ka.
In the case of you, you can do English
also and, well, to you, to go and I
receive, shall I decide?

8. 家内が病気なので早く帰らせ
ていただきたいんですが。

Kanai ga byouki na node hayaku
kaerasete itadakitain desu ga...
The wife, since it's illness, early let me
return, and I would like to receive, but...

9. それは心配だね。

Sore wa shinpai da ne.
As for that, it's worry, huh.

10. 構わないから早く帰ってあげ
なさい。

Kamawanai kara hayaku kaette agenasai.
Since it doesn't matter, early return and
give. (i.e., return for her)

11. お母さん、私、ピアノが習いたいの。

Okaasan, watashi, piano ga naraitai no.
Mother, I want to learn piano.

12. お願いだから習わせて？

Onegai dakara narawasete?
Since it's humble begging, let me learn?

13. そんなに習いたいならしょうがないわね。

Sonna ni naraitai nara shou ga nai wa ne.
In the case that you want to learn so much, it can't be helped, huh.

14. 習いに行ってもいいわ。

Narai ni itte mo ii wa.
It's OK to go for the purpose of learning.

15. 今日の食事代は私に払わせてください。

Kyou no shokuji dai wa watashi ni harawasete kudasai.
As for today's meal cost, to me, let me pay, please.

16. アルバイトのお金が入ったんですよ。

Arubaito no okane ga haittan desu yo.
Part-time work's money came in, for sure.

17. 僕は花子さんと結婚したいんです。

Boku wa hanako-san to kekkon shitain desu.
As for me, with Hanako, I want to marry.

18. 今度の日曜日に花子さんのお父さんに会って花子さんと結婚させて下さるようにお願いするつもりです。

Kondo no nichiyoubi ni hanako-san no otousan ni atte hanako-san to kekkon sasete kudasaru you ni onegai surutsumori desu.
On this Sunday, I will meet Hanako's father, and with Hanako to let marry and give, I plan to humbly beg.

19. 遅くまで残業させないでください。

Osoku made zangyou sasenai de kudasai.
Please don't make me do overtime work until late.

20. お酒を無理に飲ませないでください。

Osake wo muri ni nomasenai de kudasai.
Please don't make me drink sake by force.

21. 男の社員の手伝いばかりさせないでください。

Otoko no shain no tetsudai bakari sasenai de kudasai.
Please don't make me do male company employee's help only.

22. 愛子さんは色々な手伝いをさせられています。

Aiko-san wa iroiro na tetsudai wo saserarete imasu.
As for Aiko, various helps, she is being made to do.

23. お母さんは子供に野菜を食べさせています。

Okaasan wa kodomo ni yasai wo tabesasete imasu.
As for honorable mother, to the child, she is making him eat vegetables.

24. 課長は花田さんにお茶を入れさせています。

Kachou wa hanada-san ni ocha wo iresasete imasu.
As for the section manager, to Hanada, he is making her make honorable tea.

25. お茶を入れさせないでください。

Ocha wo iresasenai de kudasai.
Please don't make me make tea.

26. お母さんが子供を買い物に行かせています。

Okaasan ga kodomo wo kaimono ni ikasete imasu.
Honorable mother, on the child, for the purpose of shopping, she is making him go.

27. 朝ご飯を食べないで学校に来ました。

Asagohan wo tabenai de gakkou ni kimashita.
Not eating breakfast, I came to school.

28. 昨日は会社に行かずに家で寝ていました。

Kinou wa kaisha ni ika zuni ie de nete imashita.
As for yesterday, not going to the company, I was sleeping at the house.

29. 父は三日間うちに帰らずに会社で仕事をしていました。

Chichi wa mikka kan uchi ni kaera zuni kaisha de shigoto wo shite imashita.
As for my father, three days' duration, not returning to home, at the company, he was doing work.

30. 今夜はうちでテレビを見ないで会議の報告書を書きます。

Konya wa uchi de terebi wo minai de kaigi no houkokusho wo kakimasu.
As for this evening, at the home, not watching TV, I will write a meeting's report.

31. 店でこの服を着てみずに買って帰ったら小さ過ぎました。

Mise de kono fuku wo kite mi zuni katte kaettara chiisa sugimashita.
At the store, not wearing and seeing this clothing, when I bought and returned, it was too small.

32. 眠そうですね。

Nemu sou desu ne.
You look sleepy huh.

33. ええ、今日テストがあるので、夕べ寝ないで勉強したんですよ。

Ee. Kyou tesuto ga aru node yuube nenai de benkyou shitan desu yo.
Yeah. Today, since a test exists, last night, not sleeping, I studied, for sure.

34. 寒そうですね。

Samusou desu ne.
You look cold, huh.

35. ええ、コートを着ずに来てしまったんですよ。

Ee. Kooto wo ki zuni kite shimattan desu yo.
Yeah. Not wearing a coat, I came completely, for sure.

36. ガスの火を消さないで出てきたわ。

Gasu no hi wo kesanai de dete kita wa.
Not turning off the gas's fire, I went out and came.

37. バスに乗らずに走ってきたんです。

Basu ni nora zuni hashitte kitan desu.
Not boarding the bus, I ran and came.

38. 部長のサインをもらわずにきたんですか。

Buchou no sain wo morawa zuni kitan desu ka.
Without receiving the division manager's signature, did you come?

39. もう一度行ってもらってきてください。

Mou ichido itte moratte kite kudasai.
One more time, go, receive and come please.

40. 社長は昼休みには社長室にいらっしゃいますか。

Shachou wa hiru yasumi ni wa shachou shitsu ni irasshaimasu ka.
As for the president, as for at the noon break, does he honorably exist in the president's room?

41. 今日は天気もいいし部屋にはいらっしゃらないかもしれませんね。

Kyou wa tenki mo ii shi heya ni wa irassharanai kamoshiremasen ne.
As for today, the weather also is good and, as for in the room, not to honorably exist, he might be, huh.

42. 急に会議に呼び出されることがあるので資料はいつも用意してあります。

Kyuu ni kaigi ni yobidasareru koto ga aru node shiryou wa itsumo youi shite arimasu.
Suddenly, since to-be-summoned-to-a-meeting thing exists, as for literature, it is always prepared.

43. 朝、食事をしないで出かけることがあります。

Asa, shokuji wo shinai de dekakeru koto ga arimasu.
Mornings, not doing a meal, to-depart thing exists. (i.e., sometimes I don't eat breakfast)

44. この店はいつもこんなにうるさいんですか。

Kono mise wa itsumo konna ni urusain desu ka.
As for this store, always, is it this noisy?

45. いいえ、静かな時もあるんで
すけどねぇ。

Iie, shizuka na toki mo arun desu kedo
nee.
No, quiet times also exist, but, huh.

46. 花田さんはパーティにはたい
ていドレスを着て出ますが、
たまに着物の場合もありま
す。

Hanada-san wa paatii ni wa taitei doresu
wo kite demasu ga, tama ni kimono no
baai mo arimasu.
As for Hanada, as for to parties, usually,
a dress she wears and goes out, but
occasionally kimono's cases also exist.

47. 日本語のニュースが分かりま
すか。

Nihongo no nyuusu ga wakarimasu ka.
Do you understand Japanese language's
news?

48. 時々、分からないときもあり
ますが、大体分かるようにな
りましたよ。

Tokidoki, wakaranai toki mo arimasu ga,
daitai wakaru you ni narimashita yo.
Sometimes not-understand times also
exist, but generally it got to the point that
I understand, for sure.

49. この店はいつもすいていてい
いですね。

Kono mise wa itsumo suite ite ii desu ne.
As for this store, since always being
empty, it's good, huh.

50. ええ、でもたまに込んでいる
こともあるんですよ。

Ee, demo tama ni konde iru koto mo arun
desu yo.
Yeah, but occasionally being crowded
thing also exists, for sure.

51. おいしい！ これ、奥さんが
お作りになったんですか。

Oishii! Kore, okusan ga otsukuri ni
nattan desu ka.
Delicious! This, did the wife honorably
make?

52. いいえ、主人なんですよ。

Iie. Shujin nan desu yo.
No, it's my husband, for sure.

54. 主人もたまには料理をするこ
とがあるんですよ。

Shujin mo tama ni wa ryouri wo suru
koto ga arun desu yo.
My husband also, as for occasionally, do-
cuisine thing exists, for sure.

53. 朝ご飯にはいつもパンを食べ
ていらっしゃるんですか。

Asagohan ni wa itsumo pan wo tabete
irassharun desu ka.
As for at breakfast, always, are you
eating bread honorably?

54. パンの場合もありますし、ご
飯の場合もありますよ。

Pan no baai mo arimasu shi, gohan no
baai mo arimasu yo.
Bread's cases also exist, and rice's cases
also exist, for sure.

Chapter 95

1. 部長は毎日、会社に車で来ていらっしゃるんですか。

Buchou wa mainichi, kaisha ni kuruma de kite irassharun desu ka.
As for the division manager, every day, to the company by car is he coming honorably?

2. 車の時もありますが、普通は電車でいらっしゃいますよ。

Kuruma no toki mo arimasu ga, futsuu wa densha de irasshaimasu yo.
The car's times also exist, but as for usually, he honorably comes by train, for sure.

3. でも今日は大きな荷物を運ばなければならないっておっしゃっていたから、多分車で来ていらっしゃるでしょう。

Demo kyou wa ookina nimotsu wo hakobanakereba naranai tte osshatte ita kara, tabun kuruma de kite irassharu deshou.
But as for today, since large luggage he must carry he was honorably saying, probably he is coming honorably by car, probably.

4. あの店へ行けばその薬が買えますか。

Ano mise e ikeba sono kusuri ga kaemasu ka.
If I go to that store over there, can I buy that medicine?

5. ええ、多分買えるだろうと思いますが、時々ないことがあるそうですから...

Ee, tabun kaeru darou to omoimasu ga, tokidoki nai koto ga aru sou desu kara...
Yeah, probably you can buy probably I think, but sometimes, since not-exist thing exists reportedly...

6. 電話であるかどうか聞いてから行った方がいいですよ。

Denwa de aru ka douka kiite kara itta hou ga ii desu yo.
After asking by telephone whether or not it exists, it would be better to go, for sure.

7. ローレンさん、ご主人はいつも帰りが遅いんですか。

Rooren-san, goshujin wa itsumo kaeri ga osoin desu ka.
Lauren, as for your husband, always is the return late?

8. ええ、たまに早く帰ってくることもあるんですけどね。

Ee. Tama ni hayaku kaette kuru koto mo arun desu kedo ne.
Yeah. Occasionally early-return-and-come thing also exists, but, huh.

9. 今日は急いでしなければなら
ない仕事がないようでしたか
ら、多分早く帰ってくるでし
ょう。

Kyou wa isoide shinakereba naranai
shigoto ga nai you deshita kara, tabun
hayaku kaette kuru deshou.
As for today, since hurriedly-must-do
work doesn't exist, it appeared, probably
he will return and come early, probably.

****

10. 田中さんはお茶が大好きでい
つもお茶を飲まずにはいられ
ない。

Tanaka-san wa ocha ga daisuki de itsumo
ocha wo noma zuni wa irarenai.
As for Tanaka, since he loves tea,
always, as for without drinking tea, he
cannot be.

11. いつも会社の女性にお茶を入
れてもらっていたが…

Itsumo kaisha no josei ni ocha wo irete
moratte ita ga...
Always, by the company's women, tea
they were making, and he was receiving,
but...

12. ある日とうとう「私達にお茶
ばかりをいれさせないでくだ
さい」と言われてしまった。

Aru hi toutou "watashitachi ni, ocha
bakari wo iresasenai de kudasai" to
iwarete shimatta.
One day, at last, "To us, tea only, please
do not make us make," they said on him
completely.

13. そこで田中さんは自分にお茶
をいれさせるロボットを作る
ことにした。

Soko de tanaka-san wa jibun ni ocha wo
iresaseru robotto wo tsukuru koto ni
shita.
At that place (i.e., at that time), as for
Tanaka, to himself (i.e., for himself), a
to-cause-to-make-tea robot he decided to
make.

14. 言葉も話せた方がいいと思っ
て言葉も話せるように作っ
た。

Kotoba mo hanaseta hou ga ii to omotte
kotoba mo hanaseru you ni tsukutta.
Thinking it would be better to be able to
speak words also, words also to be able
to speak, in such a way he made it.

15. 二ヶ月後ロボットが出来上が
った。

Nikagetsu go robotto ga dekiagatta.
Two months later, a robot became ready.

16. まだ、言葉の使い方は上手で
はない。

Mada, kotoba no tsukai kata wa jouzu de
wa nai.
Still, as for the word's use method, it
isn't skillful.

17. とてもかわいい男の子の顔を
しているので「ロボちゃん」
と呼ばれて会社の人気者にな
った。

Totemo kawaii otoko no ko no kao wo
shite iru node "robochan" to yobarete
kaisha no ninkimono ni natta.
Since a very cute boy's face it is wearing,
Robo-chan it was called, and it became a
company's celebrity.

18. 女性達はもう自分でコーヒー
を入れずにロボちゃんに任せ
るようになってしまった。

Josei tachi wa mou jibun de koohii wo
ire zuni robochan ni makaseru you ni
natte shimatta.
As for the women, already of themselves
not making coffee (i.e., no longer making
it themselves), to Robochan, in such a
way as to entrust it became completely.

19. ロボちゃん、私、コーヒーの
ブラックが欲しいわ。

Robochan, watashi, koohii no burakku ga
hoshii wa.
Robochan, I, coffee's black desire.

20. ロボちゃん、私、冷たいジュ
ースがいいわ。

Robochan, watashi, tsumetai juusu ga ii
wa.
Robochan, I, cold juice, good.

21. はい、お持ちします。

Hai, omochi shimasu.
Yes, I will humbly hold. (i.e., I will
humbly bring)

22. 今度は正しく言えた。

Kondo wa tadashiku ieta.
As for this time, he was able to say it
correctly.

23. そこに、外出していた田中さ
んが帰ってきた。

Soko ni, gaishutsu shite ita tanaka-san ga
kaette kita.
At that place (i.e., at that moment) was-
being-gone-out Tanaka returned and
came.

24. おーい、ロボちゃん、お茶。

Ooi, robochan, ocha.
Hey you, Robochan, tea.

25. 今、かわいいレディー達にコ
ーヒーやジュースを飲ませて
いるから後にしてください。

Ima, kawaii redii tachi ni koohii ya juusu
wo nomasete iru kara ato ni shite
kudasai.
Now, to cute ladies, since I am making
them drink coffee, juice, etc., at later
please do.

26. 何！お前の主人はこの僕な
んだぞ。

Nani! Omae no shujin wa kono boku
nan da zo.
What! As for your master, it's this "I."
(zo is used for emphasis by males)

27. 何のためにお前を作ったと思
っているんだ。

Nan no tame ni omae wo tsukutta to
omotte irun da.
For what purpose I made you, he is
thinking.

28. 田中さんはカンカンに怒って
こう思った。

Tanaka-san wa kankan ni okotte kou omotta.
As for Tanaka, he gets furious, and he thought this way.

29. やっぱりあいつを男に作るん
じゃなかった。

Yappari aitsu wo otoko ni tsukurun ja nakatta.
When you think about it, on that damn fellow over there, to-a-male-to-make thing it wasn't. (i.e., I shouldn't have made him a male)

30. 田中さんが作ったロボットは
どんなロボットでしたか。

Tanaka-san ga tsukutta robotto wa donna robotto deshita ka.
As for the Tanaka-made robot, what kind of robot was it?

31. お茶を入れてくれるロボット
で言葉も話せます。

Ocha wo irete kureru robotto de kotoba mo hanasemasu.
A to-make-tea-and-give robot, and words also it can speak.

****

32. 土田部長はクリストファーさ
んにどんな仕事をさせたいと
思っていますか。

Tsuchida buchou wa kurisutofaa-san ni donna shigoto wo sasetai to omotte imasu ka.
As for Division Manager Tsuchida, to Christopher, what kind of work would he (i.e., Christopher) like to be made to do, is he thinking?

33. 石川産業との取り引きの仕事
をさせたいと思っています。

Ishikawa sangyou to no torihiki no shigoto wo sasetai to omotte imasu.
A with-Ishikawa-industries business deal's work he wants to be made to do, he is thinking.

34. 北村課長が今度の仕事をクリ
ストファーさんにやらせても
いいんじゃないかと思ったの
はなぜですか。

Kitamura kachou ga kondo no shigoto wo kurisutofaa-san ni yarasete mo iin ja nai ka to omotta no wa naze desu ka.
Section Manager Kitamura, the next work to Christopher to make do is all right, isn't it (question), as for he thought thing, why is it?

35. クリストファーさんが山川貿
易との取り引きをうまくやっ
たからです。

Kurisutofaa-san ga yamakawa boueki to no torihiki wo umaku yatta kara desu.
It's because Christopher, the with-Yamakawa-Trade's business deal, he did cleverly.

36. クリストファーさんは今度の
仕事のためにどんなことをし
なければなりませんか。

Kurisufotaa-san wa kondo no shigoto no tame ni donna koto wo shinakereba narimasen ka.
As for Christopher, for the purpose of the next work, what kind of thing must he do?

37. 今までよりも多くの残業や出張をしなければなりません。

Ima made yori mo ooku no zangyou ya shutchou wo shinakereba narimasen.
Compared to until now, numerous overtime and business trips, etc. he must do.

38. クリストファーさんは今度の仕事を一人でしますか。

Kurisufotaa-san wa kondo no shigoto wo hitori de shimasu ka.
As for Christopher, the next work, will he do it by himself?

39. いいえ、野村さんと一緒にします。

Iie, nomura-san to issho ni shimasu.
No, with Nomura, together, he will do.

****

40. この薬を6時間おきに飲んでください。

Kono kusuri wo rokuji kan oki ni nonde kudasai.
This medicine, every six hours' duration, please take it.

41. 私の友達は二年おきに新しい車を買うんですよ。

Watashi no tomodachi wa ninen oki ni atarashii kuruma wo kaun desu yo.
As for my friend, every two years, he buys a new car, for sure.

42. 弟はデパートに勤めているので年に四回ぐらいヨーロッパに出張します。

Otouto wa depaato ni tsutomete iru node nen ni yonkai gurai yooroppa ni shutchou shimasu.
As for the younger brother, since he is employed in a department store, about four times per year, he does a business trip to Europe.

43. その作家は私に彼の最近作を一冊贈ってくれた。

Sono sakka wa watashi ni kare no saikin saku wo issatsu okutte kureta.
As for that author, to me, he gave one volume of his recent work and gave. (i.e., he gave it for me)

44. 辞書を買わないことには外国語の勉強は始められない。

Jisho wo kawanai koto ni wa gaikokugo no benkyou wa hajimerarenai.
Unless you buy a dictionary, as for foreign language's study, you cannot begin.

45. その男性は60歳を越えているに違いない。髪が白髪だから。

Sono dansei wa rokujussai wo koete iru ni chigainai. Kami ga shiraga dakara.
As for that man, he is exceeding 60 years undoubtedly. It's since the hair is grey hair. (i.e., he must be over 60, since his hair is grey) (we could substitute haku-hatsu for shiraga here; both are spelled 白髪, but hakuhatsu is more bookish)

Chapter 96

1. エミリーさん、もう引っ越しの準備はできましたか。

   Emirii-san, mou hikkoshi no junbi wa dekimashita ka.
   Emily, already, as for the move's preparations, did they accomplish?

2. ええ、やっと済みました。

   Ee, yatto sumimashita.
   Yeah, finally they finished.

3. それにしても一年の間にずいぶん色々な物が増えていた。

   Sore ni shitemo ichinen no aida ni zuibun iroiro na mono ga fuete ita.
   Even so, during one year, extremely, various things were increasing.

4. 私も部屋が狭いから、なるべく物を買わないようにしているんですけど、いつの間にか増えてしまうんですよね。

   Watashi mo heya ga semai kara, narubeku mono wo kawanai you ni shite irun desu kedo, itsu no manika fuete shimaun desu yo ne.
   I also, since the room is tight, as much as possible, I'm making an effort not to buy things, but before you realize it, they increase completely, for sure, huh.

5. 私達が日本に来て最初に困ったことは借りた家に家具が付いていなかったことです。

   Watashitachi ga nihon ni kite saisho ni komatta koto wa karita ie ni kagu ga tsuite inakatta koto desu.
   We, coming to Japan, at first, as for got-inconvenienced thing, to the rented house it's furniture-was-not-being-attached thing.

6. 何から何まで買わなければなりませんでした。

   Nani kara nani made kawanakereba narimasen deshita.
   From A to Z, we had to buy.

7. ずいぶん色々な物を買わされましたよ。

   Zuibun iroiro na mono wo kawasaremashita yo.
   Extremely, various things I was made to buy, for sure.

8. 今、買った物を見てみると本当に必要だった物は少ないね。

   Ima, katta mono wo mite miru to hontou ni hitsuyou datta mono wa sukunai ne.
   Now, if I look and see purchased things, as for truly were-necessary things, few, huh.

9. 私も転勤の度に古い物は捨てて、引っ越し先で新しく買うことにしているんですよ。

   Watashi mo tenkin no tabi ni furui mono wa sutete, hikkoshi saki de atarashiku kau koto ni shite irun desu yo.
   I also, at transfer's occasions, as for old things discarding, at the moving destination newly to buy I am deciding, for sure.

10. その方が安上がりなんです。

Sono hou ga yasuagari nan desu.
That way it's cheaper.

11. それでまだ使える物が捨てられてるんですね。

Sore de mada tsukaeru mono ga suterareterun desu ne.
For that reason, still usable things are being discarded, huh.

12. 私の知っている学生は結構いい物を拾ってきて便利に使っていますよ。

Watashi no shitte iru gakusei wa kekkou ii mono wo hirotte kite benri ni tsukatte imasu yo.
As for I-being-knowing students, quite good things they are picking up and coming and conveniently using, for sure.

13. ところで運送会社にはもう頼みましたか。

Tokoro de unsougaisha ni wa mou tanomimashita ka.
By the way, as for to the shipping company, already, did you request?

14. ええ、来週の土曜日に運んでくれることになっています。

Ee, raishuu no doyoubi ni hakonde kureru koto ni natte imasu.
Yeah, at next week's Saturday to-carry-and-give is being scheduled.

15. うんと手伝わされるんじゃないかと思っていましたが、運送会社の人が全部やってくれるんだそうで安心しましたよ。

Unto tetsudawasarerun ja nai ka to omotte imashita ga, unsougaisha no hito ga zenbu yatte kurerun da sou de anshin shimashita yo.
Greatly I will be made to help, isn't it (question) I was thinking, but the moving company's person, since everything he will do and give, reportedly, I did relief, for sure.

****

16. ジャクソンさん、一年会社で仕事をしてみて何が一番大変でした？

Jakuson-san, ichinen kaisha de shigoto wo shite mite nani ga ichiban taihen deshita?
Jackson, one year at the company doing work and seeing, what was the most terrible?

17. そうですね。係長さんの難しい字を読まされたことかな。

Sou desu ne. Kakarichou-san no muzukashii ji wo yomasareta koto kana.
That's so, huh. Mr. Assistant Manager's difficult characters I was made to read thing, I wonder.

18. 黒田さんにはよく助けてもらいましたね。

Kuroda-san ni wa yoku tasukete moraimashita ne.
As for by Kuroda, often she rescued and I received, huh.

19. そう、私も係長の字には泣かされているわ。

Sou. Watashi mo kakarichou no ji ni wa nakasarete iru wa.
So. I also, as for by Assistant Manager's characters, am being made to cry.

20. 全く読めない字が並んでいる
    んだから。

Mattaku yomenai ji ga narande irun
dakara.
Since utterly unable-to-read characters
are lined up.

21. 読めない字が並んでいると言
    うのはちょっと言い過ぎじゃ
    ない？

Yomenai ji ga narande iru to iu no wa
chotto iisugi ja nai?
As for the one called "unable-to-read
characters are lined up," a little
exaggeration, isn't it?

22. そんなに読めないって言われ
    るんなら僕もこれからはパソ
    コンを使うことにしようか
    な。

Sonna ni yomenai tte iwarerun nara boku
mo kore kara wa pasokon wo tsukau koto
ni shiyou kana.
So much unable to read they say on me
case, I also, as for from now, shall decide
to use a computer, I wonder.

23. もっと早くパソコンの練習を
    してもらえたら良かったな
    あ。

Motto hayaku pasokon no renshuu wo
shite moraetara yokatta naa.
More early computer's practice do, and if
I was able to receive, it was good.

****

24. ええ、皆さん、ご存じのよう
    に、ジャクソンさんがこの
    度、大阪支社に転勤されるこ
    とになりました。

Ee, minasan, gozonji no you ni, jakuson-
san ga kono tabi, oosaka shisha ni tenkin
sareru koto ni narimashita.
Eh, honorable everyone, as you
honorably know, Jackson, this occasion,
to the Osaka branch office to-do-transfer-
on-him was scheduled.

25. それでは、ジャクソンさん、
    お願いします。

Sore de wa, jakuson-san, onegai shimasu.
Well then, Jackson, I beg you.

26. はい、あの、本日は私達のた
    めに、このようなすばらしい
    パーティを開いていただきま
    してどうも有難うございま
    す。

Hai. Ano, honjitsu wa watashitachi no
tame ni kono you na subarashii paatii wo
hiraite itadakimashite doumo arigatou
gozaimasu.
Yes. Say, as for today, for the purpose of
us, like this, a wonderful party opening
and humbly receiving, thank you very
much.

27. この一年色々なことがありま
    したが無事にここまで来られ
    ました。

Kono ichinen iroiro na koto ga
arimashita ga buji ni koko made
koraremashita.
This one year, various things existed, but
safely until here we were able to come.

28. 大阪に参りましても皆様のご親切は決して忘れません。

（おおさか）

****

Oosaka ni mairimashitemo minasama no goshinsetsu wa kesshite wasuremasen.
To Osaka we humbly go, even though, as for very honorable everyone's honorable kindness, we will never forget.

29. ジェイムズさん達が日本に来て最初に困ったことは何でしたか。

Jeimuzu-san tachi ga nihon ni kite saisho ni komatta koto wa nan deshita ka.
The James group, coming to Japan, at the beginning, as for got-inconvenienced thing, what was it?

30. 借りた家に家具が付いていなかったことです。

Karita ie ni kagu ga tsuite inakatta koto desu.
At the rented house, furniture-was-not-being-attached thing it is.

31. 田辺さんは転勤の度に古い物を持っていきますか。

Tanabe-san wa tenkin no tabi ni furui mono wo motte ikimasu ka.
As for Tanabe, at transfer's occasion, does he take old things?

32. 引っ越し先で新しく買うことにしています。

Hikkoshi saki de atarashiku kau koto ni shite imasu.
At the moving destination, newly to buy he is deciding.

33. 運送会社はいつエミリーさん達の荷物を運んでくれることになっていますか。

Unsougaisha wa itsu emirii-san tachi no nimotsu wo hakonde kureru koto ni natte imasu ka.
As for the moving company, when is the Emily group's luggage-carry-and-give thing being scheduled?

34. 来週の土曜日に運んでくれることになっています。

Raishuu no doyoubi ni hakonde kureru koto ni natte imasu.
At next week's Saturday, carry-and-give is being scheduled.

35. ジェイムズさんが会社で一番困ったことは何でしたか。

Jeimuzu-san ga kaisha de ichiban komatta koto wa nan deshita ka.
James, at the company, as for the most inconvenienced thing, what was it?

36. 田辺さんの下手な字を読まされたことです。

Tanabe-san no heta na ji wo yomasareta koto desu.
It's Tanabe's unskillful characters he was made to read thing.

37. 田辺さんはパソコンの使い方を習いたがっていますか。

****

Tanabe-san wa pasokon no tsukai kata wo naraitagatte imasu ka.
As for Tanabe, the computer's use method, does he appear wanting to learn?

38. 今晩は家内に早く帰ると言ってしまったんですが。

Konban wa kanai ni hayaku kaeru to itte shimattan desu ga...
As for tonight, to the wife, "early I will return," I said completely, but...

39. そうか。じゃ、会議室で話そうか。

Sou ka. Ja, kaigi shitsu de hanasou ka.
Is that so? Well, in the meeting room shall we talk?

40. それが急だけど今月の末までに大阪に行って欲しいんだ。

Sore ga kyuu dakedo kongetsu no sue made ni oosaka ni itte hoshiin da.
That, it's sudden, but by this month's end, to-Osaka-to-go I desire.

41. えっ、それじゃ後二週間しかありませんね。

E! Sore ja ato nishuukan shika arimasen ne.
Eh! In that case, except for only two weeks more, they don't exist, huh.

42. 初めの予定ではもう少し後になっていましたが。

Hajime no yotei de wa mou sukoshi ato ni natte imashita ga...
As for of-the-beginning's plan, a little more at later it was being scheduled, but...

43. 予定より早くなってしまったけれど、これも仕事だから仕方がないだろう。

Yotei yori hayaku natte shimatta keredo, kore mo shigoto dakara shikata ga nai darou.
Compared to the plan, it became early completely, but since this also is work, it can't be helped, probably.

44. 東京での仕事はだいたい覚えてもらったし...

Toukyou de no shigoto wa daitai oboete moratta shi...
As for at Tokyo's work, generally, you memorized, and I received, and...

45. サンフランシスコ支社の件で大阪では早く来て欲しいそうなんだよ。

Sanfuranshisuko shisha no ken de oosaka de wa hayaku kite hoshii sou nan da yo.
Due to San Francisco branch office's matter, as for at Osaka, early coming they desire, reportedly, for sure.

46. すぐ、転勤の用意を始めます。

Sugu, tenkin no youi wo hajimemasu.
Soon, transfer's preparation I will begin.

Chapter 97

1. あなたは色々な所に転勤させられるのは構いませんか。

Anata wa iroiro na tokoro ni tenkin saserareru no wa kamaimasen ka.
As for you, at various moments, as for you are made to do transfer, does it not matter?

2. 構わないと言った人はなぜですか。

Kamawanai to itta hito wa naze desu ka.
As for they said it doesn't matter people, why is it?

3. 奥さんが行きたくないと言ったらどうしますか。

Okusan ga ikitakunai to ittara dou shimasu ka.
The honorable wife, if she says she doesn't want to go, how will you do?

4. 日本の会社では転勤は会社員にとってとても大切です。

Nihon no kaisha de wa tenkin wa kaishain ni totte totemo taisetsu desu.
As for at Japanese companies, as for transfer, by the company employee taking, it's very important.

****

5. エミリーさんと田辺さんの奥さんが話しています。

Emiri-san to tanabe-san no okusan ga hanashite imasu.
Emily and Tanabe's honorable wife are talking.

6. ジェイムズさんが転勤で大阪（おおさか）に行くことになりましたが、エミリーさんは大阪（おおさか）へはあまり行きたくありません。

Jeimuzu-san ga tenkin de oosaka ni iku koto ni narimashita ga, emirii-san wa oosaka e wa amari ikitaku arimasen.
James, by transfer, was scheduled to go to Osaka but, as for Emily, as for to Osaka, she doesn't want to go very much.

7. エミリーさん、今度大阪（おおさか）へ転勤するんですって。

Emirii-san, kondo oosaka e tenkin surun desutte.
Emily, this time you will transfer to Osaka reportedly.

8. 引っ越しの準備で大変でしょう。

Hikkoshi no junbi de taihen deshou.
Because of moving's preparation, it's terrible probably.

9. 何かお手伝いしましょうか。

Nanika otetsudai shimashou ka.
Something shall I do humble help?

10. 有難うございます。でも、運送会社の人が全部やってくれるので心配しないでください。

Arigatou gozaimasu. Demo, unsougaisha no hito ga zenbu yatte kureru node shinpai shinai de kudasai.
Thank you a lot. But the moving company's person, since everything he will do and give, please don't worry.

11. あまり嬉しそうじゃありませんね。

Amari ureshisou ja arimasen ne.
Not very pleased appearing it isn't, huh.

12. ええ、実は本当はあまり大阪へは行きたくないんです。

Ee. Jitsu wa hontou wa amari oosaka e wa ikitakunain desu.
Yeah, the fact is, as for the truth, not very much, as for to Osaka, I don't want to go.

13. でも、転勤だから...

Demo, tenkin dakara...
But, since it's a transfer...

14. ええ、それは分かっているんですが東京へ来てまだ一年しか経っていないし、せっかく皆さんとお友達に慣れたのに...

Ee, sore wa wakatte irun desu ga toukyou e kite mada ichinen shika tatte inai shi, sekkaku minasan to otomodachi ni nareta noni...
Yeah, as for that, I am understanding, but to Tokyo coming, still except for only one year not elapsing, and with much trouble, with honorable everyone, to honorable friends I got used to, even though...

15. いつでも東京に遊びに来られるじゃありませんか。

Itsudemo toukyou ni asobi ni korareru ja arimasen ka.
Anytime, to Tokyo, for the purpose of play, you are able to come, isn't it?

16. そうですね。大阪に行っても時々、東京に遊びに来ますね。

Sou desu ne. Oosaka ni ittemo tokidoki, toukyou ni asobi ni kimasu ne.
That's so huh. Even if I go to Osaka, sometimes to Tokyo, for the purpose of play, I will come, huh.

17. 又、二人で買い物に行ったり映画を見に行ったりしましょうね。

Mata, futari de kaimono ni ittari eiga wo mi ni ittari shimashou ne.
Again, of two people, go for the purpose of shopping, etc., go for the purpose of to see movies, etc., we shall do, huh.

18. それから時々、お手紙をくださいね。

Sore kara tokidoki, otegami wo kudasai ne.
And then, sometimes, honorable letter, please, huh.

19. ええ、まだ日本語の手紙は上手に書けないんですが...

Ee. Mada nihongo no tegami wa jouzu ni kakenain desu ga...
Yeah. Still, as for Japanese language letters, skillfully I cannot write, but...

20. 勉強だと思って月に一回は書くようにします。

Benkyou da to omotte tsuki ni ikkai wa kaku you ni shimasu.
It's study, I think and, as for once a month, I will make an effort to write.

21. お話をしたら少し元気が出てきました。

Ohanashi wo shitara sukoshi genki ga dete kimashita.
When I did humble conversation, a little, health emerged and came.

****

22. いつ引っ越しますか。

Itsu hikkoshi shimasu ka.
When will you do moving?

23. 三月はどこの会社でも転勤が多いので忙しいから...

Sangatsu wa doko no kaisha demo tenkin ga ooi node isogashii kara...
As for March, at any place's company, since transfers are numerous, since we are busy...

24. 早く引っ越しの日を決めてもらいたい。

Hayaku hikkoshi no hi wo kimete moraitai.
Early, the move's day arrange, and I would like to receive.

25. 引っ越しは三月の月末の土曜日です。

Hikkoshi wa sangatsu no getsumatsu no doyoubi desu.
As for the move, it's March's end-of-month's Saturday.

26. どこへ引っ越しますか。

Doko e hikkoshi shimasu ka.
To where will you do moving?

27. 大阪へ引っ越しします。

Oosaka e hikkoshi shimasu.
We will do moving to Osaka.

28. 荷物はどのぐらいありますか。

Nimotsu wa dono gurai arimasu ka.
As for luggage, about how much exists?

29. 大阪に持って行きたい物を見せる。

Oosaka ni motte ikitai mono wo miseru.
She shows the to-Osaka want-to-take things.

30. 台所用品、洋服、ジェイムズの机、タンス、パソコンなど。

Daidokoro youhin, youfuku, jeimuzu no tsukue, tansu, pasokon nado.
Kitchen equipment, Western clothes, James's desk, a dresser, the personal computer, etc.

31. 引っ越しのタイプを説明して
どちらのタイプがいいか決め
てもらってください。

Hikkoshi no taipu wo setsumei shite
dochira no taipu ga ii ka kimete moratte
kudasai.
Moving's types I will explain, and which
type is good (question) arrange, and I
will receive, please.

32. タイプ A。荷物を運ぶのもパ
ッキングするのも全部運送会
社がします。

Taipu A. Nimotsu wo hakobu no mo
pakkingu wo suru no mo zenbu
unsougaisha ga shimasu.
Type A. To carry luggage also, to do
packing also, the moving company will
do everything.

33. 料金は高いですが安全で便利
です。

Ryoukin wa takai desu ga anzen de benri
desu.
As for the fee, it's expensive, but it's safe
and convenient.

34. タイプ B。荷物を運ぶだけで
パッキングはお客様がしま
す。

Taipu B. Nimotsu wo hakobu dake de
pakkingu wa okyakusama ga shimasu.
Type B. To carry luggage only, and as
for packing, the very honorable customer
will do.

35. 料金はタイプ A より安いで
す。

Ryoukin wa taipu A yori yasui desu.
As for the fee, compared to type A, it's
cheap.

36. 自分でパッキングするのは大
変だから全部運送会社の人に
頼みましょう。

Jibun de pakkingu suru no wa taihen
dakara zenbu unsougaisha no hito ni
tanomimashou.
By myself, as for to do packing, since it's
terrible, everything, to the moving
company's person, I shall request.

37. パッキングは引っ越しの前の
日にします。

Pakkingu wa hikkoshi no mae no hi ni
shimasu.
As for packing, on the move's before's
day (i.e., on the day before the move) I
will do.

38. その時は誰か家にいて欲しい
んです。

Sono toki wa dareka ie ni ite hoshiin
desu.
As for that time, someone being in the
house I desire.

39. パッキングの日には自分が家
にいるつもりです。

Pakkingu no hi ni wa jibun ga ie ni
irutsumori desu.
As for on the packing's day, myself, plan
to be in the house.

****

40. 何か冷たい飲み物でもいただ
けませんか。

Nanika tsumetai nomimono demo
itadakemasenka.
Something cold drink at least can I not
humbly receive?

41. 会議はもう終わりましたか。

Kaigi wa mou owarimashita ka.
As for the meeting, already did it finish?

42. 私は明日の会議に出席するつもりです。

Watashi wa ashita no kaigi ni shusseki surutsumori desu.
As for me, to tomorrow's meeting, I plan to attend.

43. お風呂に入ろうとしたところに電話が掛かってきました。

Ofuro ni hairou to shita tokoro ni denwa ga kakatte kimashita.
At I was trying to enter the honorable bath, the phone rang and came.

44. 彼は学生なのに勉強をしないでアルバイトばかりしています。

Kare wa gakusei na noni benkyou wo shinai de arubaito bakari shite imasu.
As for him, although he's a student, not studying, he is only doing part-time work.

45. サンフランシスコに支社を作る準備をするためにアメリカに出張することになりました。

Sanfuranshisuko ni shisha wo tsukuru junbi wo suru tame ni amerika ni shutchou suru koto ni narimashita.
To San Francisco, branch-office-to-create preparations, for the purpose of to do, I was scheduled to do a business trip to America.

46. 課長はいつも部下の人達にしっかり働くようにと言っています。

Kachou wa itsumo buka no hitotachi ni shikkari hataraku you ni to itte imasu.
As for the section manager, always, to subordinate's people, strongly to labor, he is saying.

47. ヨーロッパでもこの製品がよく売れるようにモデルチェンジをしました。

Yooroppa de mo kono seihin ga yoku ureru you ni moderu chenji wo shimashita.
In Europe also, this product, in such a way as to be able to sell well, we did model changes.

48. ご飯を食べながらテレビを見るのは良くないですよ。

Gohan wo tabe nagara terebi wo miru no wa yokunai desu yo.
While eating rice, as for to watch TV, it's not good, for sure.

49. せっかくマディソンさんの家に行ったのに彼女は出かけていて会えなかった。

Sekkaku madison-san no ie ni itta noni kanojo wa dekakete ite aenakatta.
With much trouble, even though I went to Madison's house, as for her, she is being departed, and we could not meet.

Chapter 98

1. 料金のことで、ちょっとお伺いしたいんですが。

   Ryoukin no koto de, chotto oukagai shitain desu ga...
   Of the fee's thing, for a moment, I would like to humbly inquire, but...

2. 田村さんの茶色の背広は柔らかくてカッコイイです。

   Tamura-san no chairo no sebiro wa yawarakakute kakko ii desu.
   Tamura's brown suit is soft and attractive.

3. 和田さんは宿題を終えたところです。

   Wada-san wa shukudai wo oeta tokoro desu.
   As for Wada, she has just finished the homework.

4. 熱があると言っていたからアンドリューさんは多分、今日のゴルフには来ないでしょう。

   Netsu ga aru to itte ita kara andoryuu-san wa tabun, kyou no gorufu ni wa konai deshou.
   Since he was saying that fever exists, as for Andrew, probably, as for to today's golf, he will not come, probably.

5. この仕事はあさってまでにはきっと仕上げますから安心してください。

   Kono shigoto wa asatte made ni wa kitto shiagemasu kara anshin shite kudasai.
   As for this work, as for by the day after tomorrow, since I will surely finish, please do relief.

6. もっと良く働くロボットは作れないんですか。

   Motto yoku hataraku robotto wa tsukurenain desu ka.
   As for a better to-labor robot, can you not make it?

7. 心配したとおりですね。

   Shinpai shita toori desu ne.
   It's did-worry way, huh. (i.e., this is what I worried about)

8. 小田さんはやっぱり来ませんでした。

   Oda-san wa yappari kimasen deshita.
   As for Oda, after all, he did not come.

9. 毎日、何時頃シャワーを浴びるんですか。

   Mainichi, nanji goro shawaa wo abirun desu ka.
   Every day, about what time do you take a shower?

10. 私は朝、起きてからシャワーを浴びるんですよ。

    Watashi wa asa, okite kara shawaa wo abirun desu yo.
    As for me, morning, after I get up, I take a shower, for sure.

11. 夜、電気なしで本を読むことができません。

Yoru, denki nashi de hon wo yomu koto ga dekimasen.
Night, without electricity, I cannot read a book.

12. 授業は分かりやすいです。

Jugyou wa wakariyasui desu.
As for the lesson, it's easy to understand.

13. この音楽は聞きにくいです。

Kono ongaku wa kikinikui desu.
This music is difficult to hear.

14. 予約するために前もって電話してもいいです。

Yoyaku suru tame ni maemotte denwa shite mo ii desu.
In order to make a reservation, in advance, it's OK to do a phone call.

15. 野田ですが明日の夜七時頃二人の席がありますか。

Noda desu ga asu no yoru shichiji goro futari no seki ga arimasu ka.
It's Noda, but tomorrow's evening, about 7:00, are there seats for two people?

16. 山を下った。

Yama wo kudatta.
He went down the mountain.

17. 手伝っていただけたら有難いです。

Tetsudatte itadaketara arigatai desu.
If you help, and I am able to humbly receive, it's grateful. (i.e., I would be grateful)

18. こんなところに靴下がぬぎっぱなし。

Konna tokoro ni kutsushita ga nugippanashi.
In this kind of place, socks are taken off and left. (i.e., the action is unfinished)

19. 歩道に割れ目がある。

Hodou ni wareme ga aru.
There's a crack in the sidewalk.

20. 遅れていた時計を正しい時間に合わせた。

Okurete ita tokei wo tadashii jikan ni awaseta.
The was-being-delayed watch, to the correct time I adjusted.

21. 薬は体に悪い場合がある。

Kusuri wa karada ni warui baai ga aru.
As for medicine, to the body, bad cases exist. (i.e., sometimes medicine is dangerous)

22. 家族は支え合って生きていくべきだ。

Kazoku wa sasae atte ikite iku beki da.
As for the family, we must support each other and live and go (i.e., keep living).

23. 無理だと彼はまわりに聞こえないほどの声で言った。

Muri da to kare wa mawari ni kikoenai hodo no koe de itta.
It's impossible (quote), as for him, to the surroundings in a to-the-degree-inaudible voice, he said.

24. 道にあった小石につまずいて
転んでしまった。

Michi ni atta koishi ni tsumazuite
koronde shimatta.
To the existed-on-the-street small stone, I
tripped and fell over completely.

25. このシャツはボタンが取れて
いるから着られない。

Kono shatsu wa botan ga torete iru kara
kirarenai.
As for this shirt, since the button is being
come off, I can't wear it.

26. 事故のため電車の運行を見合
わせている。

Jiko no tame densha no unkou wo
miawasete iru.
Due to the accident, they are postponing
the train's operation.

27. 目の前を黒い猫が横切った。

Me no mae wo kuroi neko ga yokogitta.
On the eyes' front (i.e., before my eyes),
a black cat cut across.

28. 長生きしてください。

Naga iki shite kudasai.
Please live long.

29. 間もなく大阪に着きます。

Mamonaku oosaka ni tsukimasu.
Before long we will arrive to Osaka.

30. ベッドの上で猫がおしっこし
ました。

Beddo no ue de neko ga oshikko
shimashita.
The cat urinated on top of the bed.

31. 日本では地方によって気温が
違いますね。

Nihon de wa chihou ni yotte kion ga
chigaimasu ne.
As for in Japan, depending to the region,
the air temperature differs, huh.

32. 彼はいつも勤務時間に遅れて
来ますね。

Kare wa itsumo kinmu jikan ni okurete
kimasu ne.
As for him, always to the service hour he
gets delayed and comes, huh. (i.e., he's
late to work)

33. 注意するだけはしたんです
が、ちっとも聞かないんです
よ。

Chuui suru dake wa shitan desu ga,
chittomo kikanain desu yo.
To do a caution as much as one can, I did
but, not at all, he doesn't listen, for sure.

34. いつお会いしてもお若いです
ね。

Itsu oai shite mo owakai desu ne.
When I humbly meet, no matter how, it's
honorably young, huh. (i.e., you are
young)

35. とんでもない。この頃は何で
も忘れがちになって困ってい
ます。

Tondemonai. Kono goro wa nandemo
wasuregachi ni natte komatte imasu.
Not at all. As for these days, since
anything-forget tendency becomes, I am
being inconvenienced. (i.e., I'm starting
to forget everything)

36. 寒いから厚いセーターを着て
います。

Samui kara atsui seetaa wo kite imasu.
Since it's cold, I'm wearing a thick
sweater.

37. 今、勤務中です。

Ima, kinmu chuu desu.
Now he is on duty.

38. 内田さんご兄弟は、お兄さん
は言うまでもなく、弟さんも
いい方ですね。

Uchidasan gokyoudai wa, oniisan wa iu
made mo naku, otoutosan mo ii kata desu
ne.
As for the Uchida honorable brothers, as
for older brother, needless to say,
younger brother also, they are good
honorable people, huh.

39. そうなんですよ。あのご兄弟
は子供の時から頭が良くて人
気者でした。

Sou nan desu yo. Ano gokyoudai wa
kodomo no toki kara atama ga yokute
ninkimono deshita.
That's so, for sure. As for those
honorable brothers over there, since the
child's time, heads are good, and it was
popular people.

40. 台風でも来なかったら、試合
は中止しません。

Taifuu demo konakattara, shiai wa
chuushi shimasen.
If a typhoon or something doesn't come,
as for the game, we will not cancel it.

41. 空が暗くなったかと思った
ら、雨が降り出した。

Sora ga kuraku natta ka to omottara, ame
ga furidashita.
The sky became dark, as soon as, rain
fell/put out.

42. ベッドに入ったかと思った
ら、もう眠ってしまった。

Beddo ni haitta ka to omottara, mou
nemutte shimatta.
He entered the bed, as soon as, already
he slept completely.

43. 両親が頭がいいと、子供も頭
がいいんでしょう。

Ryoushin ga atama ga ii to, kodomo mo
atama ga iin deshou.
If parents' heads are good (i.e., smart),
children also, heads are good, probably.

44. 必ずしもそうとは言えないよ
うですよ。

Kanarazu shimo sou to wa ienai you desu
yo.
Not necessarily, as for the one called sou,
we cannot say, it seems, for sure. (i.e.,
we can't know if what you said is true)

45. あの国には物売りの子供がた
くさんいたでしょう。

Ano kuni ni wa monouri no kodomo ga
takusan ita deshou.
As for in that country over there, a lot of
street peddlers' children existed
probably.

46. 町の中でね、小学校にも行っていないような小さな子供が花を売っていたの。

Machi no naka de ne, shougakkou ni mo itte inai you na chiisana kodomo ga hana wo utte ita no.
Inside the town, huh, even to primary school not going, it appears, small children were selling flowers.

47. 見かねてついお金をあげてしまったのよ。

Mikanete tsui okane wo agete shimatta no yo.
Since being unable to look, in spite of myself, I gave money completely, for sure.

48. 遅いはね、林さん。もしかしたら来ないんじゃない。

Osoi wa ne, hayashi-san. Moshikashitara konain ja nai.
Late, huh, Hayashi. Maybe she won't come, isn't it?

49. この前に行ったマンション、お買いになるんですか。

Kono mae ni itta manshon, okai ni narun desu ka.
This previously-went-to condominium, will you honorably buy?

50. 値段によっては買わないこともないんですが。

Nedan ni yotte wa kawanai koto mo nain desu ga...
As for depending to the price, to buy thing is possible, but... (nai koto mo nai = possibly)

51. 高橋さんと前田さん、結婚しそうですか。

Takahashi-san to maeda-san, kekkon shisou desu ka.
Takahashi and Maeda, does it appear that they will marry?

52. 高橋さんの気持ち次第で、結婚しないこともないような気がしますけど。

Takahashi-san no kimochi shidai de, kekkon shinai koto mo nai you na ki ga shimasu kedo...
Depending on Takahashi's feelings, they will possibly marry, it appears, I have a feeling, but...

53. 窓が開けっぱなしよ。

Mado ga akeppanashi yo.
The window is opened/left, for sure.

54. 雨が降ってきたから閉めてちょうだい。

Ame ga futte kita kara shimete choudai.
Since the rain falls and is coming, please close. (speaking to a child)

55. 後は空港へ行きさえすればいいんだ。

Ato wa kuukou e iki sae sureba iin da.
As for later, to the airport going only, if we do, it's good. (i.e., all we have to do later is go to the airport)

56. 暗くなるにつれて、気温がだんだん下がっていった。

Kuraku naru ni tsurete, kion ga dandan sagatte itta.
It becomes dark, accordingly, the air temperature gradually declined and went.

Chapter 99

1. 学校から帰って来たかと思うと、子供はもう出かけてしまった。

Gakkou kara kaette kita ka to omou to, kodomo wa mou dekakete shimatta.
From school returned and came, as soon as, as for the children, they already departed completely.

2. タクシーに乗ったら、かえって遅くなった。

Takushii ni nottara kaette osoku natta.
When we boarded a taxi, contrary to expectations, we became late.

3. もうすぐお客様がお着きになりますよ。

Mou sugu okyakusama ga otsuki ni narimasu yo.
Pretty soon the very honorable customers will honorably arrive, for sure.

4. 大変だ。のんびりお茶など飲んではいられない。

Taihen da. Nonbiri ocha nado nonde wa irarenai.
It's terrible. Peacefully, tea, etc., as for drinking, we cannot be.

5. 朝、目が覚めて初めて、外が雪なのに気がついた。

Asa me ga samete hajimete, soto ga yuki na noni ki ga tsuita.
Morning, the eyes waking, for the first time, even though outside is snow, feeling arrived. (i.e., even though outside was snow, when I woke up, I first noticed it)

6. 林田さんをご存じですか。

Hayashida-san wo gozonji desu ka.
Do you honorably know Hayashida?

7. ええ、山本さんを通じて一度お会いしたことがあるんですよ。

Ee, yamamoto-san wo tsuujite ichido oai shita koto ga arun desu yo.
Yeah, on Yamamoto communicating, one time I have humbly met, for sure.

8. あの人は誰が何と言おうとも、決して聞かない。

Ano hito wa dare ga nan to iou tomo, kesshite kikanai.
As for that person over there, who, what shall say, no matter, she never listens.

9. 他の人が行こうと行くまいと、私は行くつもりだ。

Hoka no hito ga ikou to ikumai to, watashi wa ikutsumori da.
Other person, if shall go, if not go, as for me, I plan to go. (ikumai = another way to say ikanai, but ikumai implies "probably won't" or "don't want to" go)

10. 彼女は歌手になろうと、歌の
勉強をしている。

Kanojo wa kashu ni narou to, uta no benkyou wo shite iru.
As for her, to a singer she shall become (i.e., she wants to become), and she is doing song's study. ("narou to" is an abbreviation of "narou to omou" = "thinks she shall become," or "wants to become")

11. この作品を仕上げるのに、
１ヶ月かかった。

Kono sakuhin wo shiageru noni, ikkagetsu kakatta.
For the purpose of to finish this work of literature, it took one month.

12. 高飛び込みの選手は高い台の
上からプールに飛び込んだ。

Takatobikomi no senshu wa takai dai no ue kara puuru ni tobikonda.
As for the high dive's athlete, from the top of a high stand, he dove to the pool.

13. 受験生はいっせいに試験に取
りかかった。

Jukensei wa issei ni shiken ni torikakatta.
As for the test-taking people, all together, to the test they started.

14. 電車の中で眠ってしまい、
駅を乗り越した。

Densha no naka de nemutte shimai, eki wo norikoshita.
I am sleeping completely inside the train, and I missed the station.

15. 飛行機の中で隣の席の女性に
話しかけて、親しくなった。

Hikouki no naka de tonari no seki no josei ni hanashikakete, shitashikunatta.
At inside the airplane, to the neighbor's seat's woman I addressed, and it became friendly.

16. 家を出た後、忘れ物に気がつ
いて引き返した。

Ie wo deta ato, wasuremono ni ki ga tsuite hikikaeshita.
After I left the house, to forgotten items I become aware, and I turned back.

17. もうすぐ来る夏休みが待ち
遠しい。

Mou sugu kuru natsuyasumi ga machidooshii.
The pretty-soon-will-come summer vacation is being looked forward to.

18. 次から次へと客が来て、あわ
ただしい一日だった。

Tsugi kara tsugi e to kyaku ga kite, awatadashii ichinichi datta.
Following from, following to with, customers come (i.e., they came one after the other), and it was a hasty all-day.

19. 行進曲は、どれも好き。

Koushin kyoku wa doremo suki.
As for march songs (i.e., marching songs), I like all of them.

20. 年をとっても、おしゃれな服
を着たい。

Toshi wo tottemo, oshare na fuku wo kitai.
Even though I take years (i.e., get old), I want to wear stylish clothes.

21. 一人で海外旅行をしたとき、言葉も分からなくて心細かった。

Hitori de kaigai ryokou wo shita toki, kotoba mo wakaranakute kokorobosokatta.
By myself I did overseas travel time (i.e., at the time I did it), since words even I do not understand, I got downhearted.

22. 彼はどんな頼みごとも引き受けてくれる頼もしい人だ。

Kare wa donna tanomi goto mo hikiukete kureru tanomoshii hito da.
As for him, what kind of request-thing even he undertakes and gives, reliable person it is. (i.e., whatever request he agrees to undertake, he's reliable)

23. 銀行から借りた資金で何とか会社を立ち上げた。

Ginkou kara karita shikin de nantoka kaisha wo tachiageta.
With capital borrowed from a bank, somehow or other I started a company.

24. 明日から旅行なのにまだ準備していないなんて、のんきな人だ。

Asu kara ryokou na noni mada junbi shite inai nante, nonki na hito da.
From tomorrow, even though it's travel, still he isn't doing preparations, such a thing, it's a carefree person.

25. 隣の奥さんはいつも明るく話しかけてくれる。

Tonari no okusan wa itsumo akaruku hanashikakete kureru.
As for the neighbor's honorable wife (i.e., the woman next door), she always cheerfully addresses and gives.

26. 山村で私は生まれました。

Sanson de watashi wa umaremashita
I was born in a mountain village.

27. 彼の日本語の上達は目覚しい。

Kare no nihongo no joutatsu wa mezamashii.
As for his Japanese language's improvement, outstanding.

28. サンドイッチ一つでは物足りない。もっと食べよう。

Sandoicchi hitotsu de wa monotarinai. Motto tabeyou.
As for of one sandwich, unsatisfied. Let's eat more.

29. スタートの合図で、選手達は走り始めた。

Sutaato no aizu de, senshutachi wa hashirihajimeta.
Of the start's signal, as for the athletes, they began to run.

30. 漢字はたくさんあって、いくら覚えてもきりがない。

Kanji wa takusan atte, ikura oboete mo kiri ga nai.
As for kanji, a lot exist, and how much one memorizes, even though, limit doesn't exist. (i.e., there's no end to them)

31. 忙しいから読書ができないと
言うのは、口実に過ぎない。

Isogashii kara dokusho ga dekinai to iu
no wa, koujitsu ni suginai.
Since busy, reading cannot be done
(quote), as for to-say thing, to an excuse
it doesn't exceed. (i.e., it's only an
excuse to say you don't read because
you're busy)

32. 私がミスをしたと彼は言うの
だが、全く心当たりがない。

Watashi ga misu wo shita to kare wa iu
no da ga, mattaku kokoroatari ga nai.
I did a miss (i.e., a mistake) (quote), as
for him, he says, but utterly a clue
doesn't exist. (i.e., I have no idea what
mistake I allegedly made)

33. 新入社員に仕事の心構えについ
いて話をした。

Shinnyu shain ni shigoto no
kokorogamae ni tsuite hanashi wo shita.
To new-enter employees, regarding
work's mental attitude, I did a talk.

34. おいしい料理を作るにはコツ
がある。

Oishii ryouri wo tsukuru ni wa kotsu ga
aru.
As for for the sake of to make delicious
cuisine, a knack exists.

35. 最近は息子の好みに合わせ
て、肉料理をたくさん作って
いる。

Saikin wa musuko no konomi ni awasete,
niku ryouri wo takusan tsukutte iru.
As for recently, harmonizing to the son's
taste, meat cuisine, a lot, I am making.

36. 大学卒業生の大半が、国内外
へ卒業旅行に行くそうだ。

Daigaku sotsugyou sei no taihan ga,
kokunaigai e sotsugyou ryokou ni iku
sou da.
The university graduate people's
majority, to domestic/foreign for the
purpose of graduation travel will go
reportedly. (i.e., the graduates will do
graduation travel either domestically or
internationally, reportedly)

37. あんぽんたんは少しバカと言
う意味です。

Anpontan wa sukoshi baka to iu imi
desu.
As for a simpleton, a-little-bit-stupid to-
call meaning it is. (i.e., it means
someone who is a little bit stupid)

38. 大学に入学するための手続き
をした。

Daigaku ni nyuugaku suru tame no
tetsuzuki wo shita.
To university, enrollment to do, for the
sake of, procedure I did.

39. 他人の悪口を言うと、自分も
言われることになる。

Ta'nin no waruguchi wo iu to, jibun mo
iwareru koto ni naru.
If one says other people's slander, one's
self also to-be-said-on thing will become.

40. 日本は安全な国だと言われて
いる。

Nihon wa anzen na kuni da to iwarete iru.
As for Japan, it's a safe country, they are saying on it.

41. 無理なスケジュールを立てて
も実行できない。

Muri na sukejuuru wo tatete mo jikkou dekinai.
Although you put up an unreasonable schedule, you cannot implement.

42. 気に入った仕事をしている彼
が、会社を辞める訳がない。

Ki ni itta shigoto wo shite iru kare ga, kaisha wo yameru wake ga nai.
It-is-pleasing work is doing him, on the company to resign reason doesn't exist. (i.e., it's unthinkable that the guy who's enjoying the work would resign the company)

43. 子供の頃アメリカに住んでい
ました。

Kodomo no koro amerika ni sunde imashita.
The child's time, I lived in America.

44. 道理で英語が話せる訳です
ね。

Douri de eigo ga hanaseru wake desu ne.
No wonder you can speak English, reason it is, huh. (i.e., therefore it's no wonder that you can speak English)

45. 親に無理に頼んで授業料を出
してもらったのだから、今勉
強を止める訳にはいかない。

Oya ni muri ni tanonde jugyouryou wo dashite moratta no dakara, ima benkyou wo yameru wake ni wa ikanai.
To the parents, forcibly requesting, since tuition they put out and I received, now to quit study, I can't possibly do.

46. 子供の頃、遅くまでテレビ
を見ないように親に何回言わ
れたことか。

Kodomo no koro, osoku made terebi wo minai you ni oya ni nankai iwareta koto ka.
The child's approximate time, until late, make an effort not to watch TV, by the parents, how many times they said on me thing (question). ("nankai... koto ka" is a way to exclaim "how many times!")

47. 課長から電話があり、10時頃
こちらに着くということで
す。

Kachou kara denwa ga ari, juuji goro kochira ni tsuku to iu koto desu.
From the section manager a phone call exists, and around 10:00 to this way he will arrive (quote) to-say thing it is. (i.e., reportedly, he'll get here around 10:00)

48. 今後のことを考えると、頭が
痛いよ。

Kongo no koto wo kangaeru to, atama ga itai yo.
On hereafter's things, if I think, the head hurts, for sure. (i.e., thinking about the future makes me worry)

Chapter 100

1. このボタンを押すと機械が作動します。

Kono botan wo osu to kikai ga sadou shimasu.
If you push this button, the machine will operate.

2. そのチーズは牛乳から作られている。

Sono chiizu wa gyuunyuu kara tsukurarete iru.
As for that cheese, from cow's milk it is being made on.

3. 竹が風でざわめいている。

Take ga kaze de zawameite iru.
The bamboo, by the wind, is rustling.

4. 公園には大勢の人がいて散歩をしたり話をしたりしています。

Kouen ni wa oozei no hito ga ite sanpo wo shitari hanashi wo shitari shite imasu.
As for in the park, a lot of people are, and they do walking, etc., they do talking, etc., they are doing.

5. 先生、ちょっとお伺いしたいんですが、お時間ありますか。

Sensei, chotto oukagai shitain desu ga, ojikan arimasu ka.
Teacher, for a moment I would like to humbly inquire, but does honorable time exist?

6. 困ったときはいつでも言ってください。お手伝いしますので。

Komatta toki wa itsudemo itte kudasai. Otetsudai shimasu node.
As for the time you were inconvenienced, whenever, please say. Since I will do humble help.

7. そう言ってくれると有難いです。

Sou itte kureru to arigatai desu.
If in that way you say and give, it's grateful. (i.e., I'm happy to hear it)

8. たくさんの人が祝ってくれて、有難かったよ。

Takusan no hito ga iwatte kurete, arigatakatta yo.
Since many people are celebrating and giving to me, it was grateful, for sure. (i.e., I was grateful)

9. 田中さんが連絡はもっと早めに欲しいって。

Tanaka-san ga renraku wa motto hayame ni hoshii tte.
Tanaka, as for communication, more as early as possible, he desires, reportedly. (i.e., he wants you to get in touch earlier.)

10. 早いものだ、もう来日して
1年経った。

Hayai mono da, mou rainichi shite ichinen tatta.
Fast thing it is, already, visiting Japan, one year elapsed. (hayai mono da = time really flies; mono da is used to express emotion)

11. 子供の頃は、暗くなるまで友達と外で遊んだものだ。

Kodomo no koro wa, kuraku naru made tomodachi to soto de asonda mono da.
As for the child's approximate time, until it becomes dark, with the friends in outside, I played thing it is. (here, mono da expresses nostalgia)

12. 電車が遅れたものだから、遅刻してしまいました。

Densha ga okureta mono dakara, chikoku shite shimaimashita.
Since the train was delayed, I got tardy completely. ("mono dakara" and "mono desu ka" can be used to mean "since")

13. お先に失礼します。病院へ行かなければならないものですから。

Osaki ni shitsurei shimasu. Byouin e ikanakereba naranai mono desu kara.
To humble ahead I will commit a discourtesy. (i.e., I will leave before you) Since I must go to the hospital.

14. この店は土曜日以外は開いています。

Kono mise wa doyoubi igai wa aite imasu.
As for this store, except on Saturdays, it's open.

15. 間違えたら、消しゴムできれいに消してください。

Machigaetara, keshigomu de kirei ni keshite kudasai.
If you mistake, with an eraser cleanly erase, please.

16. 好きな方を選んでください。

Suki na hou wo erande kudasai.
Please choose the one you like more.

17. 先週は一週間のうち四日も休んでしまった。

Senshuu wa isshuukan no uchi yokka mo yasunde shimatta.
As for last week, among one week's duration, all of four days I rested completely.

18. 夜中に何度も目が覚めました。

Yonaka ni nandomo me ga samemashita.
At the dead of night, many times I woke up.

19. 9月も半ばを過ぎると、夏の暑さが少し和らいでくる。

Kugatsu mo nakaba o sugiru to, natsu no atsusa ga sukoshi yawaraide kuru.
When on September's middle it exceeds, the summer's heat a little will soften and come. (i.e., it will start to cool down) (mo = no, in this sentence, i.e., it's a possessive particle)

20. 味も悪いし、サービスも最
    低。あんな店、二度と行くも
    のですか。

Aji mo warui shi, saabisu mo saitei.
Anna mise, nido to iku mono desu ka.
Taste also bad, and service also the
worst. That over there kind of store, two
times with to go, thing it is (question).
(i.e., I will never go to that kind of
restaurant again) (mono desu ka = never)

21. 新しいパソコンソフトを買っ
    たものの、使いこなせるかど
    うか自信がない。

Atarashii pasokon sofuto wo katta
monono, tsukaikonaseru ka douka jishin
ga nai.
I bought new personal computer
software, even though to be able to
master, whether or not, self-confidence
doesn't exist. (monono = even though)

22. あの学生は漢字が書けないも
    のの、日本語の会話は十分で
    きる。

Ano gakusei wa kanji ga kakenai
monono, nihongo no kaiwa wa juubun
dekiru.
As for that student over there, even
though he cannot write kanji, as for
Japanese language's conversation, he can
do enough.

23. 海外旅行、行けるものなら行
    きたいが、今は無理だ。

Kaigai ryokou, ikeru mono nara ikitai ga,
ima wa muri da.
Overseas travel, able to go thing
supposing, I would like to go, but as for
now, it's impossible.

24. 父は自分の思い通りにしたい
    人だ。

Chichi wa jibun no omoi doori ni shitai
hito da.
As for my father, to himself's think-way
wants-to-do person he is. (i.e., he likes
to do things his way)

25. 家から駅まで約300メートル
    です。

Ie kara eki made yaku sanbyaku meetoru
desu.
From the house until the station, it's
approximately 300 meters.

26. 彼にゴルフのことで話しかけ
    ようものなら、何時間でも話
    し続けて止まらない。

Kare ni gorufu no koto de
hanashikakeyou mono nara, nanjikan
demo hanashi tsuzukete tomaranai.
To him, of golf's thing you shall address,
thing supposing, many hours even,
continuing to talk, he will not stop.

27. 工場を建てる計画が中止にな
    った。

Koujou wo tateru keikaku ga chuushi ni
natta.
The factory-will-construct plan, to
cancellation became.

28. この薬を一週間飲み続けてく
    ださい。

Kono kusuri wo isshuukan
nomitsuzukete kudasai.
This medicine, one week's duration,
please continue drinking.

29. この頃、暑かったり寒かったり、変な天気ですね。

Kono goro, atsukattari samukattari hen na tenki desu ne.
These days, hot, etc., cold, etc., it's strange weather, huh.

30. この本、読み終わったから、貸してあげましょうか。

Kono hon, yomiowatta kara, kashite agemashou ka.
This book, since it finished reading, shall I lend it and give?

31. 食事の支度ができましたよ。

Shokuji no shitaku ga dekimashita yo.
The meal's preparation accomplished, for sure. (i.e., it's ready)

32. 一人も来ないと思っていましたが、五人も来ました。

Hitori mo konai to omotte imashita ga, gonin mo kimashita.
Even one (i.e., one person) will not come, I was thinking, but all of five came.

33. この時代の小説は読みにくい。

Kono jidai no shousetsu wa yominikui.
As for this era's novels, difficult to read.

34. 夏休みは明日で終わります。

Natsuyasumi wa ashita de owarimasu.
As for summer vacation, of tomorrow it will finish. (i.e., it will be over tomorrow)

35. 明日は都合が悪いんです。あさってでもいいですか。

Ashita wa tsugou ga waruin desu. Asatte demo ii desu ka.
As for tomorrow, the circumstances are bad. The day after tomorrow or something, are they good?

36. あんまり時間がないから、走った方がいいですよ。

Anmari jikan ga nai kara, hashitta hou ga ii desu yo.
Since time hardly doesn't exist, it would be better to run, for sure.

37. 私の所に来てください。

Watashi no tokoro ni kite kudasai.
Please come over here.

38. 部長の隣に座っている体の大きい人は奥さんです。

Buchou no tonari ni suwatte iru karada no ookii hito wa okusan desu.
As for the division manager's at-neighbor being-sitting body's-large person, it's the honorable wife. (i.e., the big person sitting next to the division manager is his wife)

39. この頃、パソコンのメールをチェックしていません。

Kono goro, pasokon no meeru wo chekku shite imasen.
These days, I am not checking the personal computer's mail.

40. 暗い空に星が光っている。

Kurai sora ni hoshi ga hikatte iru.
In the dark sky, stars are shining.

41. この番号の通りにボタンを押してください。

Kono bangou no toori ni botan wo oshite kudasai.
To these numbers' way, please push the buttons. (i.e., push the buttons in accordance with these numbers)

42. あの会社は紅茶を生産して、世界中で売っている。

Ano kaisha wa koucha wo seisan shite, sekai juu de utte iru.
As for that company over there, they produce black tea and are selling it throughout the world.

43. 何時にどこで待ち合わせましょうか。

Nanji ni doko de machiawasemashou ka.
At what time, at where, shall we rendezvous?

44. 部長の代わりに来ました。

Buchou no kawari ni kimashita.
I came in place of the division manager.

45. 駅に着いたら電話をください。迎えに行きますから。

Eki ni tsuitara denwa wo kudasai.
Mukae ni ikimasu kara.
When you arrive at the station, please phone. Since I will go for the purpose of meet/welcome.

46. シーツは押入れにしまう。

Shiitsu wa oshiire ni shimau.
As for the sheets, I will put them away to the bedding closet.

47. 私は、甘い物が苦手で、特にチョコレートはだめなんです。

Watashi wa, amai mono ga nigate de, toku ni chokoreeto wa dame nan desu.
As for me, since sweet things are a weak point, in particular, as for chocolate, it's bad.

48. 割れないように、柔らかい紙でクッキーを包んだ。

Warenai you ni, yawarakai kami de kukkii wo tsutsunda.
In such a way that it will not break, with soft paper, I wrapped the cookie.

49. すみませんが、手を洗わせてください。

Sumimasen ga, te wo arawasete kudasai.
Excuse me, but please let me wash my hands.

50. 書けるところだけ書きました。

Kakeru tokoro dake kakimashita.
The able-to-write part only I wrote. (i.e., I only wrote what I could)

51. 散歩中に、捨てられた子猫を見つけた。

Sanpo chuu ni, suterareta koneko wo mitsuketa.
At the middle of the walk, I found a was-thrown-away-on kitten. (i.e., a stray kitten)

Chapter 101

1. 太り過ぎなので、甘い物を止めなければなりません。

Futorisugi na node, amai mono wo yamenakereba narimasen.
Since it's overly fat, I must stop sweet things.

2. 家のすぐそばにコンビニができて、とても便利になった。

Ie no sugu soba ni konbini ga dekite, totemo benri ni natta.
At the house's just near, a convenience store accomplished, and it became very convenient.

3. 夕べ、電気を点けたまま寝てしまった。

Yuube, denki wo tsuketa mama nete shimatta.
Last night, I turned on the light state, I slept completely. (i.e., I went to sleep with the light on)

4. 辞書を使わずに日本語の本を読みたい。

Jisho wo tsukawa zuni nihongo no hon wo yomitai.
Not using a dictionary, I would like to read a Japanese language's book.

5. 味どう？

Aji dou?
Taste, how? (i.e., how is the taste?)

6. ちょっと塩が足りないと思うよ。

Chotto shio ga tarinai to omou yo.
A little, salt is insufficient, I think, for sure.

7. 安心してください。この病気はすぐに治りますよ。

Anshin shite kudasai. Kono byouki wa sugu ni naorimasu yo.
Please do relief. As for this illness, at soon it will heal, for sure.

8. 家を出ようとしたときに、急に雨が降ってきた。

Ie wo deyou to shita toki ni, kyuu ni ame ga futte kita.
At I-tried-to-leave-the-house time, suddenly rain fell and came.

9. 春になって暖かくなったら、両親を呼んでこの町を案内したい。

Haru ni natte atatakaku nattara, ryoushin wo yonde kono machi wo annai shitai.
When spring becomes and it gets warm, I want to call the parents and do guidance on this town.

10. 大きさが違うお皿ですが、値段は同じです。

Ookisa ga chigau osara desu ga, nedan wa onaji desu.
It's sizes-differ honorable plates, but as for the price, it's the same.

11. 猫のしっぽを引っ張るのは止めなさい。

Neko no shippo wo hipparu no wa yamenasai.
As for to pull the cat's tail, stop it.

12. 間もなく電車が参ります。

Mamonaku densha ga mairimasu.
Before long the train will humbly come.

13. 荷物をお届けに参りましたが、お留守でした。

Nimotsu wo otodoke ni mairimashita ga, orusu deshita.
On the luggage, for the purpose of humble delivery, I humbly went, but you were honorably absent.

14. ここは無料で車が止められます。

Koko wa muryou de kuruma ga tomeraremasu.
As for here, free of charge, one is able to park a car.

15. 友達に本を貸してあげたらお礼にお菓子をくれた。

Tomodachi ni hon wo kashite agetara orei ni okashi wo kureta.
When to the friend a book I lent and gave, in gratitude, she gave me honorable sweets.

16. 彼は化学が苦手だ。

Kare wa kagaku ga nigate da.
As for him, chemistry is a weak point.

17. ひらがなも良く読めないのに、漢字が読めるはずがない。

Hiragana mo yoku yomenai noni, kanji ga yomeru hazu ga nai.
While hiragana even he cannot read well, to be able to read kanji, expectation doesn't exist (i.e., we certainly can't expect him to read kanji).

18. 珍しい場所にお連れしましょう。

Mezurashii basho ni otsure shimashou.
I shall humbly take you along to an unusual place.

19. お金を貸してあげるけど、必ず返してね。

Okane wo kashite ageru kedo, kanarazu kaeshite ne.
I will lend and give you money, but certainly give it back, huh.

20. これからそちらに向かいますから、3時までには着くと思います。

Kore kara sochira ni mukaimasu kara, sanji made ni wa tsuku to omoimasu.
From now, since I will head to that way, as for by 3:00, I will arrive, I think.

21. うちの犬は夕方の5時になると散歩に行きたがります。

Uchi no inu wa yuugata no goji ni naru to sanpo ni ikitagarimasu.
As for the home's dog, when the evening's 5:00 becomes, for the purpose of a walk, he appears to want to go.

22. 生徒たちはその新しい英語の
先生にあこがれている。

Seitotachi wa sono atarashii eigo no sensei ni akogarete iru.
As for the students, to that new English teacher, they are longing for. (i.e., they adore her)

23. 主人とは大学の時出会って、
卒業後すぐに結婚しました。

Shujin to wa daigaku no toki deatte, sotsugyou go sugu ni kekkon shimashita.
As for with my husband, the university's time we met, and after graduation immediately we married.

24. 昨日運動し過ぎて、体のあち
こちが痛いです。

Kinou undou shisugite, karada no achikochi ga itai desu.
Yesterday, since I do too much exercise, the body's various places hurt.

25. 落ち着いて話しましょう。

Ochitsuite hanashimashou.
Relax and let's talk.

26. 僕は末っ子で、姉が一人、兄
が二人います。

Boku wa suekko de, ane ga hitori, ani ga futari imasu.
As for me, the youngest child, and older sister one person, older brothers two people exist.

27. この野菜は生で食べられませ
ん。

Kono yasai wa nama de taberaremasen.
As for this vegetable, of raw, you cannot eat. (i.e., you can't eat it raw)

28. ゆでるか焼くかにしてくださ
い。

Yuderu ka yaku ka ni shite kudasai.
Boil or bake or, please decide.

29. 女将さんいますか。

Okamisan imasu ka.
Does the Ms. Hostess (i.e., the landlady or female manager) exist?

30. 発言させていただきます。

Hatsugen sasete itadakimasu.
You let me do a statement, and I will humbly receive. (i.e., with your permission, I will make a statement)

31. 初めてご連絡をさせていただ
きます。

Hajimete gorenraku wo sasete itadakimasu.
For the first time, humble contact you let me do, and I will humbly receive. (said in a business letter when making initial contact)

32. 今日の午後、雨は次第に強く
なるでしょう。

Kyou no gogo, ame wa shidai ni tsuyoku naru deshou.
Today's afternoon, as for rain, gradually it will become strong, probably.

33. 西村さんは仕事が終わっても、なかなか帰ろうとしない。

Nishimura-san wa shigoto ga owattemo, nakanaka kaerou to shinai.
As for Nishimura, work finishes even though, readily he doesn't try to return.

34. 私も一緒に行けば良かった。

Watashi mo issho ni ikeba yokatta.
I also, together, if I go, it was good. (i.e., I should have gone with you)

35. 危なかった。もう少しで事故になるところだった。

Abunakatta. Mou sukoshi de jiko ni naru tokoro datta.
It was dangerous. By a little more to an accident it was on the verge of becoming. (i.e., I almost had an accident)

36. 試験の結果が悪くて、自信を失った。

Shiken no kekka ga warukute, jishin wo ushinatta.
Since the test's results are bad, I lost confidence.

37. 電話くれたらすぐに手伝いに行ったのに、どうして言わなかったの？

Denwa kuretara sugu ni tetsudai ni itta noni, doushite iwanakatta no?
If you give a phone call, immediately for the sake of help I went, if only. Why didn't you say something?

38. あの人と同じクラスなんですが、口をきいたことがありません。

Ano hito to onaji kurasu nan desu ga, kuchi wo kiita koto ga arimasen.
With that person over there, it's a same class, but I have never talked to him.

39. 学校を辞めました。というのは、父が亡くなって働かなければならないからです。

Gakkou wo yamemashita. To iu no wa, chichi ga nakunatte hatarakanakereba naranai kara desu.
I resigned school. Because my father will die (i.e., he died), and it's since I have to labor.

40. この先は道が二つに分かれていますが、どちらの方向に行けばいいですか。

Kono saki wa michi ga futatsu ni wakarete imasu ga, dochira no houkou ni ikeba ii desu ka.
This ahead, the street to two is diverging (i.e., it's splitting into two directions), but to which way's direction if I go will it be good?

41. あ、髪切ったんだね。

A, kami kittan da ne.
Ah, the hair, you cut it, huh.

42. ずいぶんイメージが変わったね。

Zuibun imeeji ga kawatta ne.
Extremely the image changed, huh.

43. 住所を教えてください。

Juusho wo oshiete kudasai.
Please tell me the address.

44. 書道をする者です。

Shodou wo suru mono desu.
It's a (i.e., I'm a) do-calligraphy person.

45. ペンを使用してください。

Pen wo shiyou shite kudasai.
Please use a pen.

46. 私は小学生の頃、おとなしくて友達も少なかったです。

Watashi wa shougakusei no koro, otonashikute tomodachi mo sukunakatta desu.
As for me, the primary school student's approximate time, since quiet or docile, friends even were few.

47. 来年試験を受けます。

Rainen shiken wo ukemasu.
Next year I will take a test.

48. ということは、今年は受けないということですね。

To iu koto wa, kotoshi wa ukenai to iu koto desu ne.
That is to say, as for this year, you will not take it, therefore, huh.

49. 時間があるから、ちょっとその辺をぶらぶらしましょう。

Jikan ga aru kara, chotto sono hen wo burabura shimashou.
Since there is time, for a short time, on that area let's stroll.

50. 犬が人を助けたという物語の映画を見た。

Inu ga hito wo tasuketa to iu monogatari no eiga wo mita.
A dog helped a person (quote) to-say story's movie I watched. (i.e., I watched a movie about a dog who helped a person)

51. サッカーの試合、何時から？

Sakkaa no shiai, nanji kara?
The soccer's game, from what time?

52. もうとっくに始まってるよ。

Mou tokku ni hajimatteru yo.
Already a long time ago it is starting, for sure.

53. 手続きを日本でしなければなりません。

Tetsuzuki wo nihon de shinakereba narimasen.
We must do the procedure in Japan.

54. 車の事故にあったが、大したことがなくて良かった。

Kuruma no jiko ni atta ga, taishita koto ga nakute yokatta.
To a car's accident I met, but since a great thing doesn't exist (i.e., it wasn't serious), it was good.

Chapter 102

1. 息子のケガが軽くて、ほっと しました。

   Musuko no kega ga karukute, hotto shimashita.
   Since the son's injury is light, I did relief.

2. そんなに夜遅く、子供を外出 させるべきではない。

   Sonna ni yoru osoku, kodomo wo gaishutsu saseru beki de wa nai.
   That kind of late at night, to let children go out should not. (i.e., you shouldn't let them go out late)

3. 勉強しないのだから、試験が できる訳がない。

   Benkyou shinai no dakara, shiken ga dekiru wake ga nai.
   Since I do not study, to be able to do the test is not possible.

4. 明日は1年に1回の試験だか ら、休む訳にはいかない。

   Ashita wa ichinen ni ikkai no shiken dakara, yasumu wake ni wa ikanai.
   As for tomorrow, since it's a once-a-year's test, I can't possibly rest (i.e., be absent).

5. 先生に怒られて嬉しい訳がな い。

   Sensei ni okorarete ureshii wake ga nai.
   By the teacher, since he gets angry on me, pleased is not possible.

6. 毎日何回も自分の体重を計る というダイエット方法がある そうです。

   Mainichi nankaimo jibun no taijuu wo hakaru to iu daietto houhou ga aru sou desu.
   Every day, many times to measure oneself's body weight (quote) to-say diet method exists reportedly.

7. 英語は話せないことはないで すが、発音も悪いし下手なん です。

   Eigo wa hanasenai koto wa nai desu ga, hatsuon mo warui shi heta nan desu.
   As for English, not to be able to speak things don't exist (i.e., I can speak some English), but the pronunciation is also bad, and it's unskillful.

8. 彼の知人ですか。

   Kare no chijin desu ka.
   Is it his acquaintance?

9. 卵を半ダース買った。

   Tamago wo handaasu katta.
   I bought half a dozen eggs.

10. 三島さんの不注意で車の事故 が起こった。

    Mishima-san no fuchuui de kuruma no jiko ga okotta.
    Due to Mishima's carelessness, an auto accident occurred.

11. 雪が降るといけないから早く
帰った方がいいですよ。

Yuki ga furu to ikenai kara hayaku kaetta hou ga ii desu yo.
If the snow falls, since bad, it would be better to return early, for sure.

12. 忘れるといけないから、メモ
をしておこう。

Wasureru to ikenai kara, memo wo shite okou.
If I forget, since bad, I shall do a memo in advance.

13. 留学するにあたって、注意す
べきことは何でしょう？

Ryuugaku suru ni atatte, chuui subeki koto wa nan deshou?
Do foreign study, at the time of, as for caution-should-do things (i.e., things to be careful about), what are they, probably?

14. 大人になってもいいことある
よ。

Otona ni nattemo ii koto aru yo.
Even if we become adults, good things will exist (i.e., happen), for sure.

15. 僕が、東大を受けても落ちる
に決まっている。

Boku ga, toudai wo uketemo ochiru ni kimatte iru.
I, even if I apply on Tokyo University, to fail is being arranged. (i.e., I won't be accepted)

16. 本を戻してください。

Hon wo modoshite kudasai.
The book, please put back.

17. 中学から高校の6年間、小川
先生に英語を教わりました。

Chuugaku kara koukou no rokunenkan, ogawa sensei ni eigo wo osowarimashita.
From middle school, high school's 6-year duration (i.e., for 6 years), by Teacher Ogawa I was taught English.

18. 先ず、今日の主なニユースか
らお伝えいたします。

Mazu, kyou no omo na nyuusu kara otsutae itashimasu.
First, from today's main news I will humbly report. (said by a newscaster)

19. 新宿へ行くなら、向こうのホ
ームから東京行きの電車に乗
らないとだめですよ。

Shinjuku e iku nara, mukou no hoomu kara toukyou yuki no densha ni noranai to dame desu yo.
In case you go to Shinjuku, from the other side's platform, to a Tokyo-bound train you must board, for sure.

20. こんなにたくさんの料理、い
くら僕でも食べきれないよ。

Konna ni takusan no ryouri, ikura boku demo tabekirenai yo.
This kind of a lot's cuisine, even if, even though I, cannot finish eating, for sure. (i.e., even I cannot finish it)

21. 今からだと映画に間に合うか
どうか分からないが、とにか
く行ってみよう。

Ima kara da to eiga ni maniau ka dou ka
wakaranai ga, tonikaku itte miyou.
From now, if it is, to the movie we will
be on time, whether or not, I don't
understand, but anyhow, let's go and see.

22. 夕べは、久しぶりに会った高
校時代の友人と、遅くまで楽
しく語り合った。

Yuube wa, hisashiburi ni atta koukou
jidai no yuujin to, osoku made tanoshiku
katariatta.
As for last night, at after a long time of
absence I met, high school era's friend
with, until late, pleasantly we talked
together.

23. 誰か彼の様子を知りません
か。

Dareka kare no yousu wo shirimasen ka.
Does someone not know his condition?

24. それは果たして本当の話だろ
うか。

Sore wa hatashite hontou no hanashi
darou ka.
As for that, really, is it probably a true
talk? (i.e., is it true?)

25. せめて70点は取りたい。

Semete nanajutten wa toritai.
At least, as for 70 points, I want to take.
(said before taking a test)

26. 料理の本に書いてある通りに
作ったのに、おいしくなかっ
た。

Ryouri no hon ni kaite aru toori ni
tsukutta noni, oishikunakatta.
To the cuisine's book, to the is-written
way I created, in spite of the fact that it
wasn't delicious.

27. 音を立ててスープを飲んだ
ら、娘に下品だと言われた。

Oto wo tatete suupu wo nondara,
musume ni gehin da to iwareta.
Making noise when I drink soup, by the
daughter, "it's vulgar," was said on me.

28. さっき雨が降ったかと思った
ら、もう止んでいます。

Sakki ame ga futta ka to omottara, mou
yande imasu.
Previously the rain precipitated (question
quote) if I think (i.e., it rained a moment
ago), already it is stopping.

29. この子は、泣いたと思ったら
もう笑っている。

Kono ko wa, naita to omottara mou
waratte iru.
As for this child, it cried (quote) if I think
(i.e., it cried a moment ago), already it is
laughing.

30. アメリカにいる息子のことが
心配でしょうがない。

Amerika ni iru musuko no koto ga
shinpai de shou ga nai.
The in-America-exists son's thing, since
worry, it can't be helped. (i.e., I'm really
worried about him)

31. 試験の結果が、気になって仕方がない。

Shiken no kekka ga, ki ni natte shikata ga nai.
The test's results, since to feelings it becomes, it can't be helped. (i.e., I'm really worried about it)

32. その映画を見た人はみんな、泣かずにはいられないだろう。

Sono eiga wo mita hito wa minna, nakazuni wa irarenai darou.
As for the people who saw that movie, all, as for not crying, they cannot be, probably.

33. この薬を飲みさえすれば、頭痛はすぐに治りますよ。

Kono kusuri wo nomi sae sureba, zutsuu wa sugu ni naorimasu yo.
This medicine drinking only, if you do, as for the headache, at soon it will heal, for sure.

34. あの人が親切だなんて、とんでもない。

Ano hito ga shinsetsu da nante, tondemonai.
That person over there is kind, such a thing, not at all. (i.e., he isn't kind at all)

35. 英語の手紙など書けません。

Eigo no tegami nado kakemasen.
An English language's letter, such a thing, I cannot write. (i.e., I can never write a letter in English)

36. 5キロは無理かもしれないが、せめて3キロはやせたい。

Go kiro wa muri kamoshirenai ga, semete san kiro wa yasetai.
As for five kilos, impossible it might be, but at least as for three kilos I would like to get thin. (i.e., lose weight)

37. 工事中につき通行止めとなっております。

Koujichuu ni tsuki tsuukoudome tonatte orimasu.
Under construction due to, road closure is humbly becoming.

38. 小田さん、40歳だって。それにしても若く見えるね。

Oda-san, yonjussai da tte. Sore ni shitemo wakaku mieru ne.
Oda, it's 40 years old, reportedly. Even so, she looks young huh.

39. 過去のことを言っても仕方がない。

Kako no koto wo ittemo shikata ga nai.
Even though we speak on the past's thing, it can't be helped. (i.e., it doesn't do any good to talk about it)

40. 土地開発が進むにつれて、緑が少なくなってきた。

Tochi kaihatsu ga susumu ni tsurete, midori ga sukunaku natte kita.
Land development advances accordingly, the green becomes few and is coming. (i.e., greenery is diminishing due to development)

41. この小説は短いので、一日で
読みきれるでしょう。

Kono shousetsu wa mijikai node,
ichinichi de yomikireru deshou.
As for this novel, since it is short, of one
day I will finish reading it, probably.

42. 今日は朝から雪がしきりに降
っている。

Kyou wa asa kara yuki ga shikiri ni futte
iru.
As for today, since the morning, the
snow is constantly falling.

43. この国の人々にとっての一番
の問題は、水が不足している
と言うことだ。

Kono kuni no hitobito ni totte no ichiban
no mondai wa, mizu ga fusoku shite iru
to iu koto da.
This country's people regarding, as for
their number one's problem, water-
doing-insufficiency to-say thing it is.
(i.e., it's a water shortage)

44. 漢字は勉強すればするほど面
白い。

Kanji wa benkyou sureba suru hodo
omoshiroi.
As for kanji, if you do study, do to that
degree, interesting. (i.e., the more you
study kanji, the more interesting they are)

45. その教授は、フランス語がペ
ラペラだそうだね。

Sono kyouju wa, furansugo ga perapera
da sou da ne.
As for that professor, French, it's fluent
(i.e., he's fluent) reportedly, huh.

46. 1000円で買ったのに、次の
日に行ったら900円になって
いた。

Sen'en de katta noni, tsugi no hi ni ittara
kyuu hyaku en ni natte ita.
In spite of the fact that I bought it of
1,000 yen, on the following day, when I
went, it was becoming (i.e., it was) 900
yen.

47. 池田さんは日本人にしては背
が高い。

Ikeda-san wa nihonjin ni shite wa se ga
takai.
As for Ikeda, for a Japanese person, the
height is tall.

48. このお皿を取り替えて欲しい
んです。

Kono osara wo torikaete hoshiin desu.
This plate to exchange I desire. (i.e.,
please exchange this plate)

49. あの人は作家の泉さんだ。

Ano hito wa sakka no izumi-san da.
As for that person, he is Izumi, a writer.

Chapter 103

1. 初めは何も掛けずに食べてください。

Hajime wa nanimo kakezuni tabete kudasai.
As for the beginning, not pouring anything, please eat. (said when telling a person to taste a cake without putting any sauce on it at first)

2. ゲームに熱中していたら、いつの間にか朝になっていた。

Geemu ni netchuu shite itara, itsu no manika asa ni natte ita.
When I was being absorbed to a game, before I realize it, morning was becoming.

3. 来ないにしろ連絡をください。

Konai ni shiro renraku wo kudasai.
Not come, even though, communication please. (i.e., let me know even if you don't come)

4. 優勝できたのは、チームの助けがあったからです。

Yuushou dekita no wa, chiimu no tasuke ga atta kara desu.
As for was-able-to-do-championship thing, it is because the team's support existed.

5. うちに帰ったら、真っ先にシャワーを浴びたい。

Uchi ni kaettara massaki ni shawaa wo abitai.
When I return to home, first of all, I would like to take a shower.

6. その問題については、何も意見はありません。

Sono mondai ni tsuite wa, nanimo iken wa arimasen.
As for concerning that problem, nothing, as for opinions, they don't exist. (i.e., I don't have any opinions)

7. 小川さんの結婚式には、なんとか都合をつけて出席したいと思っています。

Ogawa-san no kekkonshiki ni wa, nantoka tsugou wo tsukete shusseki shitai to omotte imasu.
As for to Ogawa's wedding celebration, somehow arranging I want to attend, I am thinking.

8. 東京駅で思いがけず高校時代の友人に会った。

Toukyou eki de omoigakezu koukou jidai no yuujin ni atta.
In Tokyo station, unexpectedly, I met a high school era's friend.

9. テストが終わったら思い切り遊びたい。

Tesuto ga owattara omoikiri asobitai.
When the test finishes, I want to play with all my heart.

10. 体調が悪いにもかかわらず、
働き続けた。

Taichou ga warui ni mo kakawarazu,
hataraki tsuzuketa.
The physical condition bad, even
regardless, I continued to labor.

11. 足に、子供の頃ケガをしたあ
とが残っている。

Ashi ni, kodomo no koro kega wo shita
ato ga nokotte iru.
To the leg, the child's approximate time,
did-an-injury after-effect is remaining.
(i.e., there's a mark on my leg from a
childhood injury)

12. おおっ、寒い。

Oo, samui.
Oh, cold.

13. 本当だ。もう１枚着た方がい
いな。

Hontou da. Mou ichimai kita hou ga ii
na.
It's true. It would be better to wear one
more layer.

14. 野村さんはいつもおかしなこ
とばかり言う。

Nomura-san wa itsumo okashi na koto
bakari iu.
As for Nomura, always, he only says
funny things.

15. 空車がなかなか来ない。

Kuusha ga nakanaka konai.
A free car (i.e., a free taxi) readily
doesn't come.

16. やっぱりここの寿司が一番だ
よね。

Yappari koko no sushi ga ichiban da yo
ne.
When you think about it, here's sushi is
number one, for sure, huh.

17. そうかな。他にもいい店ある
よ。

Sou kana. Hoka ni mo ii mise aru yo.
So, I wonder. Besides also, good stores
exist, for sure. (i.e., there are other good
restaurants too)

18. あの映画、どうだった？

Ano eiga, dou datta.
That movie over there, how was it?

19. 何て言っていいか分からない
けど、なんか泣けた。

Nante itte ii ka wakaranai kedo, nanka
naketa.
What saying good (question) I do not
understand (i.e., I don't know what to
say), but somehow I could cry.

20. 日本が勝ったよ。

Nihon ga katta yo.
Japan won, for sure.

21. すごく嬉しくて何て言ってい
いか分かりません。

Sugoku ureshikute nante itte ii ka
wakarimasen.
Since super pleased, what saying good
(question) I do not understand. (i.e., I
don't know what to say)

22. あの二人、兄弟なんだって。

Ano futari, kyoudai nan datte.
Those two people over there are siblings
reportedly.

---

23. あそこに立ってる人、もしかして部長？

Asoko ni tatteru hito, moshikashite buchou?
At that place over there being-standing person, maybe the division manager?

24. え！まさか！こんな所にいる訳ないよ。

E! Masaka! Konna tokoro ni iru wake nai yo.
Eh! No way! To exist in this kind of place unthinkable, for sure.

25. 人違いだよ。

Hitochigai da yo.
It's a case of mistaken identity, for sure.

26. 部長は今朝、何であんなに怒ってたの？

Buchou wa kesa, nande anna ni okotteta no?
As for the division manager, this morning, why that over there kind of was being mad? (i.e., why was he so mad?)

27. よくわかんないよ。

Yoku wakannai yo.
I do not understand well, for sure. (i.e., I have no idea)

28. あの二人、又付き合い始めたんだって。

Ano futari, mata tsukiai hajimetan datte.
Those two people over there, again began a relationship, reportedly.

29. 又？訳がわかんないね。

Mata? Wake ga wakannai ne.
Again? Reason I don't understand, huh. (i.e., it doesn't make sense)

30. 課長、言うことがすぐ変わるよね。

Kachou, iu koto ga sugu kawaru yo ne.
The section manager, the to-say thing soon changes, for sure, huh. (i.e., he changes his mind a lot)

31. 本当、訳がわかんないよね。

Hontou, wake ga wakannai yo ne.
True, reason I don't understand, for sure, huh. (i.e., true, it's confusing)

32. もうすぐ出発だけど、準備はできた？

Mou sugu shuppatsu dakedo, junbi wa dekita?
Pretty soon it's departure, but as for preparation, was it accomplished?

33. 宿題、全部できた？

Shukudai, zenbu dekita?
Homework, all got accomplished?

34. いいえ。もう少しかかりそうです。

Iie. Mou sukoshi kakari sou desu.
No. A little more I will spend, apparently. (i.e., it will take a little longer)

35. 工業が発達したのは明治時代以後です。

Kougyou ga hattatsu shita no wa meiji jidai igo desu.
Factories, as for developed thing, it was after the Meiji era. (i.e., they were developed after the Meiji period)

36. 何かにつけて、近所の人には
お世話になっている。

Nanika ni tsukete, kinjo no hito ni wa
osewa ni natte iru.
Something whenever (i.e., whenever
something happens), as for by the
neighborhood's people, honorable care is
becoming. (i.e., they take care of us)

37. 石田さんは、まるで旅館のよ
うな大きい家に住んでいま
す。

Ishida-san wa, maru de ryokan no you na
ookii ie ni sunde imasu.
As for Ishida, no matter how you look at
it, like-a-Japanese-inn big house he is
living in.

38. 途中で止めるなら、むしろし
ない方がいい。

Tochuu de yameru nara, mushiro shinai
hou ga ii.
On the way, to resign, in the case of,
rather not to do would be better. (i.e., if
I'm going to quit half way, it would be
better not to do it)

39. 真面目な彼が休むなんて、何
かあったに違いない。

Majime na kare ga yasumu nante, nanika
atta ni chigainai.
The sincere him will rest, such a thing,
something happened, certainly. (i.e., if
this sincere guy didn't show up,
something must have happened)

40. お昼は、パンなりおにぎりな
り買って食べます。

Ohiru wa, pan nari onigiri nari katte
tabemasu.
As for honorable noon, bread or rice
balls or, I buy and eat. (i.e., I eat either
bread or rice balls for lunch)

41. 本を買うなり借りるなりして
必ず持って来てください。

Hon wo kau nari kariru nari shite
kanarazu motte kite kudasai.
A book, buy or borrow or, do and
certainly bring, please. (i.e., please buy
or borrow a book and bring it)

42. 今年になって一段と物価が上
がりました。

Kotoshi ni natte ichidan to bukka ga
agarimashita.
This year develops, and all the more,
prices increased.

43. これはいったん開けてしまっ
たら、返品はできません。

Kore wa ittan akete shimattara, henpin
wa dekimasen.
As for this, once, if you open it
completely, as for returned goods, it
cannot be done. (i.e., you can't return it)

44. 親が有名人であるばかりに、
いつも注目される。

Oya ga yuumei jin de aru bakari ni,
itsumo chuumoku sareru.
The parents are celebrities, just because,
always attention is done on me. (i.e., I
always get attention)

45. 体が大きいばかりに不便なことが多い。

Karada ga ookii bakari ni fuben na koto ga ooi.
The body is big, just because, inconvenient things are numerous. (i.e., I endure a lot of inconvenience)

46. 試験に落ちちゃった。

Shiken ni ochichatta.
To the exam, I failed completely.

47. 遅れるって、一体どういうことですか。

Okureru tte, ittai dou iu koto desu ka.
Will be delayed (quote), how to say thing is it? (i.e., why on earth are you saying that you will be delayed?; ittai is used for emphasis)

48. 雪で飛行機が飛べないんです。

Yuki de hikouki ga tobenain desu.
Due to snow, the airplane cannot fly.

49. 目が真っ赤ですよ。一体どうしたんですか。

Me ga makka desu yo. Ittai dou shitan desu ka.
The eyes are bright red, for sure. How did it do? (i.e., what on earth happened?)

50. コンタクトレンズが合ってなかったみたいなんです。

Kontakuto renzu ga atte nakatta mitai nan desu.
The contact lenses were not fitting, it seems.

51. 本田だけど、店長いる？

Honda dakedo, tenchou iru?
It's Honda, but does the store manager exist? (i.e., is he here?)

52. 失礼ですが、どちらの本田様ですか。

Shitsurei desu ga, dochira no honda-sama desu ka.
It's discourtesy, but which very honorable Honda is it? (i.e., who are you?)

53. どこに捨てていいか分からないから、ここに置いておく？

Doko ni sutete ii ka wakaranai kara, koko ni oite oku?
To where throwing away, good (question), since I don't understand, at here, place in advance? (i.e., since I don't know where to throw this away, shall I just leave it here?)

54. えっ、いいの？ だめでしょう、ここは。

Ee, ii no? Dame deshoo, koko wa.
Eh, good? It's probably bad, as for here.

Notes about the Kanji Used in this Book

Japanese people often choose *not* to use kanji to write certain words, preferring to use hiragana. The words listed in items 1-14 below are usually written in hiragana, but we have used kanji to write them in this book, so that students may gain more experience in reading all of the target kanji. The word listed in item 15 has an alternative spelling.

1. 難しい muzukashii (difficult) is often written むずかしい.

2. 易しい yasashii (easy) is usually written やさしい.

3. 面白い omoshiroi (interesting) is often written おもしろい.

4. 開く aku (to open, intransitive) is usually written あく; Japanese people usually read 開く as hiraku (to open for business, to unfold, to hold a party or meeting, transitive).

5. 開ける akeru (to open, transitive) is usually written あける; Japanese people usually read 開ける as hirakeru (to improve, to get better).

6. 方がいい hou ga ii (it would be better to) is often written ほうがいい.

7. 無くす nakusu (to lose) is often written なくす.

8. 分かる wakaru (to understand) is often written わかる.

9. 気を付ける ki wo tsukeru (to be careful) is often written 気をつける.

10. 電話を掛ける denwa wo kakeru (to talk on the phone) is often written 電話をかける.

11. 参る mairu (to humbly come or go) is often written まいる.

12. 要る iru (to need) is usually written いる; 要る iru (to need) can be confused with 要する you suru (to need, or to require).

13. 物 mono, when used by itself rather than in compound words, e.g., in phrases like おいしい物 oishii mono (a delicious thing), is often written もの.

14. 点ける tsukeru (to turn on a light or a machine) is usually written つける.

15. 込む komu (to get crowded) is usually spelled 混む when it appears by itself, rather than as part of a compound word. See reference # 357 in the Kanji Catalogue.

How to Read the Listings in the Kanji Catalogue

The listing for 飲 (to drink) is reproduced in the left column for illustration purposes. See the column on the right for explanations of the material found in the different sections of the listing.

399. 飲

PRONUNCIATIONS:
no*mu, in

MEANINGS: to drink or swallow

EXAMPLES: 飲む
nomu = to drink or swallow; 飲食
inshoku = drinking and eating

DESCRIPTION: on the left, 食(べる) taberu (to eat, # 398); on the right, an oil derrick which drinks oil from the ground

CUES: when the Nomads on the moon 食 (eat), they 飲む nomu (drink) oil from the ground and then act Insane

COMPARE: (ご)飯 gohan = meal, cooked rice, # 400

PRONUNCIATIONS: Sometimes pronunciations include asterisks. Only the part of each pronunciation that appears before the asterisk ("no," in this example) is a pronunciation of the kanji itself.

MEANINGS: These are not intended to suggest that the kanji can necessarily be used by itself in Japanese writing. Many kanji, including this one, must be used in combination with other characters.

EXAMPLES: These are words that illustrate the use of this kanji, with their pronunciations and meanings.

DESCRIPTION: In this section, we describe the kanji as an image. 飲 contains two radicals. The radical on the left is 食, which is a kanji in its own right (# 398). Although 食 means "to eat," it isn't used as a word by itself, so we show it as as part of the word 食べる. The reason that we enclose べる in parentheses is to inform you that it isn't really important here. The emphasis is on 食 as a component of 飲.

The radical on the right resembles an oil derrick, in our opinion.

CUES: "Cues" are verbal retrieval cues, or homophones, that match the pronunciations of the kanji. You will find two cues in this sentence: "**No**mads on the moon" and "**In**sane." Please compare these cues to the pronunciations shown in the first section. Note that only the primary cues "**No**" and "**In**," which match the pronunciations of the kanji itself, are shown in bold capitalized text. The secondary cue "moo," which is intended to help you to remember the "mu" sound in the word "nomu," is shown in plain text and may be less noticeable.

The **CUES** section also demonstrates the use of at least one word that contains the kanji under discussion. In this example, that word is "飲む **no**mu." The pronunciation of the kanji is shown in bold underlined text.

COMPARE: In this section we call attention to other kanji that are similar to the kanji under discussion, either because their images are similar, as in this example, or because their pronunciations are the same. The parentheses around ご suggest that ご is *not* the focus of this comparison. Instead, the focus is on 飯.

Kanji Catalogue

Simple Shapes

1. 一

PRONUNCIATIONS: ichi, hito, tsui*tachi

MEANING: one **EXAMPLES:** 一 ichi = one; 一つ hitotsu = one item; 一人 hitori = one person; 一日 tsuitachi = 1st of the month; 一日 ichinichi = one day

CUES: I wrote the number 一 **ichi** (one) on my arm, and my skin became **Itchy**; Hiro**Hito** was 一人 **hito**ri (one person), and he ate 一つの **hito**tsu no (one) **Sweet** apple on 一日 **tsui**tachi (the 1st of the month)

2. 二

PRONUNCIATIONS: ni, futa, futsu, ha*tsuka

MEANING: two **EXAMPLES:** 二 ni = two; 二つ futatsu = two items; 二人 futari = two people; 二日 futsuka = the 2nd of the month, two days; 二十日 hatsuka = the 20th of the month **CUES:** my **Nie**ce is 第二位 dai **ni** i (number two rank) in her class; I bought 二つの **futa**tsu no (two) **F**ull **T**anks of helium and dropped one on my **F**oots (feet) on 二日 **futsu**ka (the 2nd of the month) and the other on my **Ha**ts on 二十日 **ha**tsuka (the 20th of the month)

3. 三

PRONUNCIATIONS: san, mi

MEANING: three

EXAMPLES: 三 san = three; 三つ mittsu = three items; 三日 mikka = 3rd of the month

CUES: **San**ta's hat cost 三ドル **san**doru (three dollars); when my family went to **Meet** him at the mall, he gave us 三つ **mi**ttsu no (three) presents

4. 回

PRONUNCIATIONS: kai, mawa*ru
MEANINGS: times, to rotate **EXAMPLES:** 三回 sankai = three times; 回る mawaru = to rotate **DESCRIPTION:** this looks like a square kite **CUES:** I wash **K**ites in **Ma**donna's **Wa**shing machine and watch them 回る **mawa**ru (rotate) many 回 **kai** (times)

5. 品

PRONUNCIATIONS: pin, shina, hin
MEANINGS: goods, grade, class
EXAMPLES: 返品 henpin = returned goods; 品物 shinamono = merchandise; 品質 hinshitsu = quality
DESCRIPTION: three boxes
CUES: these three **Pin**k boxes contain **Shi**ny **A**rtistic 品物 **shina**mono (goods) for **Hin**dus

6. 四

PRONUNCIATIONS: yon, yo, shi

MEANING: four **EXAMPLES:** 四 yon = four; 四つ yottsu = four items; 四日 yokka = 4th of the month; 四方 shihou = all four directions **DESCRIPTION:** this looks like the floor diagram of a house; it has four sides but is divided into three spaces **CUES:** over **Yon**der, there are 四件の **yon**ken no (four) houses occupied by **Yo**delers, who perform 四つの **yo**ttsu no (four) songs and take care of **Shee**p during all 四季 **shi**ki (four seasons)

7. 呂

PRONUNCIATION: ro **MEANINGS:** spine, backbone **EXAMPLE:** 風呂 furo = bath, bathhouse, bathtub **DESCRIPTION:** this resembles two stacked vertebrae
CUES: when I **Row**, my vertebrae stick out; afterwards I put on my **Ro**be and walk to the 風呂 fu**ro** (bath)

8. 中

PRONUNCIATIONS: chuu, naka, juu **MEANINGS:** inside, middle
EXAMPLES: 散歩中 sanpo chuu = in the middle of a walk; 真ん中 mannaka = middle; 中村 Nakamura = a family name; 一日中 ichinichijuu = all day long
DESCRIPTION: this kanji resembles yakitori (skewered chicken) **CUES:** 中村さん **Naka**mura-san (Mr. Nakamura) **Chews** on some yakitori 中 **naka** (inside) his car parked outside the **Na**tional **Ca**thedral and drinks **Juice COMPARE:** 申(す) mousu = to humbly say, # 10

9. 虫

PRONUNCIATIONS: mushi, chuu
MEANING: insect **EXAMPLES:** 虫 mushi = worm, insect, bug; 害虫 gaichuu = harmful insects **DESCRIPTION:** 中 naka (inside, # 8) with an insect on the ground below **CUES:** I know a **Mushy** song about a 虫 **mushi** (insect) that lies on the ground and tries to go 中 (inside) a house to **Chew** up the furniture

10. 申

PRONUNCIATIONS: mou*su, moushi, shin **MEANING:** to humbly say **EXAMPLES:**
申す mousu = to humbly speak; 申し込む moushikomu = to apply for; 申込書 moushikomisho = application form; 申請する shinsei suru = to apply or request
DESCRIPTION: two lips stitched together

CUES: **Mo**ses 申す **mou**su (speaks humbly) after his lips are stitched together with thread on a **Mor**mon **Shi**p by a **Shin**to priest
COMPARE: 中 naka = inside, middle, # 9

11. 立

PRONUNCIATIONS: ta*tsu, ri*ppa, ritsu, da*tsu **MEANING:** to stand **EXAMPLES:**
立つ tatsu = to stand; 立派 rippa = splendid; 起立 する kiritsu suru = to stand up; 目立つ medatsu = to stand out
DESCRIPTION: a tattletale standing on two shaky legs **CUES:** the **Ta**ttletale 立つ **ta**tsu (stands) and faces his critics, who **Ri**dicule him for wearing **Ritz**y clothes and for driving an old **Da**tsun **NOTE:** a number of kanji pronunciations are understood to include a つ tsu at the end, which means that consonants that follow them are doubled, or "hardened"; for example, in 立派 rippa (splendid), where ri is followed by a consonant, the p is doubled; in contrast, in 起立 kiritsu (to stand up), where there is no consonant following ri, the つ tsu is voiced

12. 泣

PRONUNCIATION: na*ku **MEANING:** to cry
EXAMPLE: 泣く naku = to cry
DESCRIPTION: on the left, a water radical, suggesting a connection with water, like crying; on the right, 立(つ) tatsu (to stand, # 11) **CUE:** when **Na**ncy is cooped up in the house, she 立 (stands) and 泣く **na**ku (cries)

13. 人

PRONUNCIATIONS: hito, nin, jin, ri, na
MEANING: person **EXAMPLES:** 人 hito = person; 人間 ningen = human being; 日本人 nihonjin = Japanese person; 一人 hitori = 1 person; 大人 otona = adult
DESCRIPTION: a symmetrical person with two long legs **CUES:** Hiro**Hito** was a 人 **hito**

(person) with long legs who admired **Nin**jas and who wore **Jean**s when he wanted to look **Rea**lly **Nat**ural **COMPARE:** 入(る) hairu = to enter, #14; 八 hachi = eight, # 15

14. 入

PRONUNCIATIONS: hai*ru, nyuu, i*reru
MEANINGS: to enter, to put into
EXAMPLES: 入る hairu = to enter; 入学 nyuugaku = entering a school; 入れる ireru = to put into
DESCRIPTION: compared to 人 hito (person, # 13), 入 is more asymmetrical, with a line at the top extending to the left
CUES: when I 入る **hai**ru (enter) the house, I say "**Hi Ruth**" before giving her some asymmetrical fruit from **Nyuu**yooku (New York) that was **I**rradiated to kill germs

15. 八

PRONUNCIATIONS: hachi, you*ka, ya*ttsu, ha **MEANING:** eight **EXAMPLES:** 八 hachi = eight; 八日 youka = the 8th of the month, eight days; 八つ yattsu = eight items; 八百 happyaku = eight hundred
DESCRIPTION: 八 resembles the Eiffel tower; in addition, the first two letters of "Eiffel," like the first two letters of the word "eight," are "ei" **CUES:** as we leave to see the Eiffel tower, 八 **hachi** (eight) chicks are **Hatchi**ng from **Y**olks on our **Ya**cht in the **Har**bor **COMPARE:** 人 hito = person, # 13

16. 公

PRONUNCIATIONS: kou, ooyake
MEANING: public **EXAMPLES:** 公園 kouen = park; 公 ooyake = public
DESCRIPTION: at the top, 八 hachi (eight, # 15); at the bottom, the katakana character ム mu (the sound made by a cow)
CUES: in the 公園 **kou**en (park), there are

八 (eight) ム (cows) with thick **Coa**ts, and several **Old Yak**s, for 公の **ooyake** no (public) use

17. 六

PRONUNCIATIONS: roku, mui*ka, mu*ttsu, ro **MEANING:** six **EXAMPLES:** 六人 rokunin = six people; 六日 muika = the 6th of the month, six days; 六つ muttsu = six objects; 六本木 Roppongi = a district in Tokyo **DESCRIPTION:** a mother with a wide skirt **CUES:** confined in the **Locku**p, a mother hen gathers 六 **roku** (six) chicks under her skirt, to keep them away from **Muy** (very, in Spanish) hungry **Moo**nies who might want to **Roa**st them

18. 十

PRONUNCIATIONS: too, juu, ju, ji, tsu
MEANINGS: ten, full **EXAMPLES:** 十 too = 10; 十日 tooka = 10 days, the 10th of the month; 十 juu = 10; 十分 juubun = enough; 十分 juppun, also pronounced jippun, = 10 minutes; 二十日 hatsuka = the 20th of the month **DESCRIPTION:** this looks like a "t" which is the first letter of the word "ten" in English and the word "too" in romaji
CUES: we have 十 **juu** (ten) cans of **To**mato **Jui**ce in the **Jee**p, in a **Tsu**itcase

19. 高

PRONUNCIATIONS: taka*i, kou, daka
MEANINGS: high, tall, expensive
EXAMPLES: 高い takai = high, tall, expensive; 高校 koukou = high school; 最高 saikou = the best; 円高 endaka = rise in the yen's value **DESCRIPTION:** a tower made from tall cans, with a roof on top
CUES: **Ta**ll **Ca**ns have been stacked to create a 高い **taka**i (tall) **Ko**rean tower in **Dakha**, with a roof on top

20. 七

PRONUNCIATIONS: nana, shichi, nano
MEANING: seven **EXAMPLES:** 七つ
nanatsu = seven items; 七時 shichiji = 7:00;
七日 nanoka = 7th of the month, seven days
DESCRIPTION: this is an upside-down 7
CUES: Nancy's **Na**nny gave her 七 **nana**
(seven) bites of **Shee**p **Chee**se for taking a **Na**p
with **No**rma

21. 宅

PRONUNCIATION: taku **MEANINGS:** house,
home **EXAMPLES:** お宅 otaku = your
honorable home; 帰宅 kitaku = the return
home **DESCRIPTION:** at the top, a roof; at
the bottom, 七 shichi (seven, # 20), wearing a
hat **CUE:** in this 宅 **taku** (home), 七 (seven)
Tall people are **Coo**ped up, wearing hats
COMPARE: 民 min = people, # 375

22. 千

PRONUNCIATION: sen, chi*ba, zen
MEANING: thousand **EXAMPLES:** 千 sen =
1,000; 千葉 Chiba = name of a prefecture in
Japan; 三千 sanzen = 3,000
DESCRIPTION: this resembles the katakana
character チ chi, which could stand for cheese
CUES: a **Sen**ator keeps 千 **sen** (1,000) blocks
of **Chee**se at the **Zen** center

23. 手

PRONUNCIATIONS: te, shu, ta, zu
MEANING: hand **EXAMPLES:** 右手 migi te
= right hand; 運転手 untenshu = driver;
下手 heta = unskillful; 上手 jouzu =
skillful **DESCRIPTION:** a hand belonging to
Ted Cruz, with six fingers at the top and a
curved wrist at the bottom **CUES:** when **Te**d
Shooed away a **Ta**rantula in **Zu**rich, I noticed
that his 手 **te** (hand) has six fingers

24. 又

PRONUNCIATION: mata **MEANING:** again
EXAMPLES: 又 mata = again; 又は mata
wa = alternatively **DESCRIPTION:** a simple
table belonging to a matador
CUE: the **Mata**dor liked this table so much
that he bought it 又 **mata** (again)
COMPARE: 文 bun = sentence, # 25

25. 文

PRONUNCIATIONS: mon, bun **MEANINGS:**
sentence, script, culture **EXAMPLES:** 文句
monku = complaint; 文 bun = sentence;
文化 bunka = culture **DESCRIPTION:** an
object, possibly a cultural artifact, on 又
("again," # 24), but this resembles a simple
table **CUES:** a **Mon**k said that Daniel **Boon**e
placed an artifact reflecting his 文化 **bun**ka
(culture) on this 又 (table)

26. 支

PRONUNCIATIONS: shi, sasa, tsuka
MEANINGS: to support; a branch
EXAMPLES: 支社 shisha = branch office;
支店 shiten = branch store; 支持する
shiji suru = to support; 支える sasaeru = to
support; 差し支え sashitsukae = hindrance,
inconvenience, trouble **DESCRIPTION:** at the
top, 士 shi (man, warrior, # 66), which helps
us to pronounce this; at the bottom, 又 mata
("again," # 24), but this resembles springy legs
CUES: according to our sales spread**Shee**ts, the
士 (man) with springy legs who works at our
支社 **shi**sha (branch office) is selling lots of
Salty **Sa**ndwiches, ever since we sent him a
Tsuitcase of **Ca**ffeine
COMPARE: 枝 eda = branch, # 128

27. 卒

PRONUNCIATION: sotsu, so **MEANINGS:** to
end, sudden **EXAMPLES:** 卒業 sotsugyou =

graduation; 卒倒 する sottou suru = to faint or swoon **DESCRIPTION:** a double-breasted kimono, hanging from a hanger **CUES:** **Sot**tish **Su**perman wore a double-breasted kimono to his 卒業 **sotsu**gyou (graduation), where he sang a **So**lo

28. 卵

PRONUNCIATION: tamago **MEANING:** egg
EXAMPLES: 卵 tamago = egg; ゆで卵 yudetamago = boiled egg
DESCRIPTION: two eggs containing yolks
CUE: I will eat these two 卵 **tamago** (eggs) with **Tama**les and **Goa**t cheese

29. 点

PRONUNCIATIONS: tsu, ten **MEANINGS:** spot, dot **EXAMPLES:** 点く tsuku = to ignite or turn on, intransitive; 点ける tsukeru = to ignite or turn on, transitive; 点 ten = score; 百点 hyakuten = 100 points
DESCRIPTION: a portable cannon, which is small enough to be stored in a tsuitcase, on a walking platform **CUES:** a starter removes a cannon from his **Tsu**itcase, aims it at the starting 点 **ten** (dot) and 点ける **tsu**keru (ignites) it to signal the start of a **Ten**nis match

30. 久

PRONUNCIATIONS: kyuu, hisa*shiburi
MEANINGS: long time, lasting **EXAMPLES:**
永久に eikyuu ni = forever, permanently;
久しぶり hisashiburi = after a long time
DESCRIPTION: a cute lady with a ponytail
CUES: this **Cu**te lady asks for his sash, but she has waited until after **His Sa**sh is buried
久しぶり **hisa**shiburi (for a long time)

31. 当

PRONUNCIATIONS: tou, a
MEANINGS: just, right **EXAMPLES:**
本当 hontou = truth; 当然 touzen = naturally, deservedly; 適当 tekitou = suitable; 当社 tousha = our company;

当たり前の atarimae no = right, reasonable, natural; 手当て teate = medical treatment; 突き当たり tsukiatari = T-intersection **DESCRIPTION:** at the top, a switch with three prongs; at the bottom, a tool with three toes for dividing toast
CUES: there is a tool with three **Toe**s which will 当然 **tou**zen (naturally) divide **Toa**st in an 当たり前の **a**tarimae no (reasonable) way, and they are using it at the **A**tari company

Sun

32. 日

PRONUNCIATIONS: hi, nichi, bi, ka, jitsu, you, ni, nou, su, ta, tachi **MEANINGS:** day, sun **EXAMPLES:** 日にち hinichi = date; 一日 ichinichi = one day; 日曜日 nichiyoubi = Sunday; 二日 futsuka = the 2nd day of the month, 2 days; 平日 heijitsu = week day; 今日 kyou = today; 日本 Nihon = Japan; 日光 Nikkou = sunshine, a town and a national park in Japan; 昨日 kinou = yesterday; 明日 asu = tomorrow; 明日 ashita = tomorrow; 一日 tsuitachi = the first day of the month; 明後日 asatte = the day after tomorrow **NOTE:** ichinichi and tsuitachi are both spelled 一日; also, asu and ashita are both spelled 明日 **NOTE:** it isn't practical to divide 明後日 asatte into three component pronunciations; fortunately, this is usually written あさって
DESCRIPTION: a rectangle divided into two halves **CUES:** 日光 **ni**kkou (sunshine) brings **Hea**t to the **Nich**es near the **Bea**ch, where we **Ca**ll on **Jit**tery **Su**perintendants, **Yo**gis and **Ne**anderthals with long **No**ses to **Su**pervise **Ta**xi drivers who are at**Tachi**ng roof signs to their cabs

33. 昔

PRONUNCIATION: mukashi MEANINGS: old days, ancient times EXAMPLE: 昔 mukashi = olden times DESCRIPTION: at the top, bushes; at the bottom, 日 hi (sun, # 32) CUES: nowadays old people fund **Mu**seums with **Cash**, but in 昔 **mukashi** (the olden days), all they had was the 日 (sun) and a couple of bushes

34. 早

PRONUNCIATIONS: haya*i, sou*tai, sa*ssoku MEANING: early EXAMPLES: 早い hayai = early; 早退 soutai = leaving early; 早速 sassoku = immediately, sudden DESCRIPTION: a 日 hi (sun, # 32) on an unstable base; this resembles a spinning top CUES: Prince **Ha**rry's **Ya**cht features a spinning top that was **S**old in **Sa**skatchewan and spins 早い **haya**i (early) in the morning COMPARE: 速(い) hayai = fast, # 359

35. 晩

PRONUNCIATION: ban MEANING: evening EXAMPLE: 今晩 konban = this evening DESCRIPTION: the vertical 日 hi (sun, # 32) on the left is cancelled by the horizontal 日 on sturdy legs on the right, causing things to be dark; there's a fish head on top of the 日 on the right, and there are long banana tree roots below it CUE: we eat fish and **Ban**anas in the 晩 **ban** (evening), when 日 (suns) cancel each other, and it's dark COMPARE: 映画 eiga = movie, # 36

36. 映

PRONUNCIATIONS: utsu*su, ei*ga MEANINGS: to be imaged, to be reflected EXAMPLES: 映す utsusu = to project on a screen, or to be reflected; 映画 eiga = movie DESCRIPTION: these two 日 hi (suns, # 32) do not cancel each other, as they do in 晩 ban (evening, # 35); instead, the 日 on the right is a movie screen on a stand, and the projector utilizes the 日 on the left CUES: by **U**tilizing this 日 (**Su**n) on the left, we can 映す **utsu**su (project) 映画 **ei**ga (movies) about **A**pes onto the screen on the right COMPARE: 英(語) eigo = the English language, # 43

37. 晴

PRONUNCIATIONS: ha*reru, sei*ten, har*umi MEANING: to clear up EXAMPLES: 晴れる hareru = to clear up, to be sunny, to refresh (spirits), to be cleared (of a suspicion); 晴天 seiten = fair weather; 晴海 Harumi = name of a street in Tokyo DESCRIPTION: on the left, 日 hi (sun, # 32); on the right, 青(い) aoi (blue, # 155) CUES: in **Ha**waii, when the weather 晴れる **ha**reru (clears up), we see the 日 (sun) next to a 青 (blue) sky, and we also see **Sa**ils out in the **Har**bor COMPARE: 暗(い) kurai = dark, # 268

38. 暖

PRONUNCIATIONS: atata, dan*bou MEANING: warm (atmosphere) EXAMPLES: 暖かい atatakai = warm (atmosphere); 暖める atatameru = to warm up the atmosphere, transitive; 暖房 danbou = heating, heater DESCRIPTION: on the left, 日 hi (sun, # 32); on the lower right, 友 tomo (friend, # 459), who radiates waves of heat above his head CUES: my 友 (friend) **Ata**turk with a **Tan** radiates heat as he sits in the 暖かい **atata**kai (warm) 日 (sun) and waits for **Dan**'s boy COMPARE: 温(かい) atatakai = warm (objects), # 257; 温(める) atatameru = to warm up an object, such as water, # 257

39. 円

PRONUNCIATIONS: en, maru*i **MEANINGS:** yen, round, circle **EXAMPLES:** 千円 sen'en = 1,000 yen; 円い marui = round

DESCRIPTION: 日 hi (sun, # 32) on its side, with legs **CUES:** 千円 sen'**en** (1,000-yen) coins are 円い **maru**i (round) like the 日 (sun); if they grow legs, they will be able to dance and **En**tertain people who are **Maroo**ned

40. 声

PRONUNCIATIONS: koe, sei **MEANING:** voice **EXAMPLES:** 声 koe = voice; 声援 seien = cheering, support **DESCRIPTION:** at the top, 士 shi (man, warrior, # 66); below that, 日 hi (day, or sun, # 32) on its side, with a handle on the left, resembling a co-ed holding a mask, with openings for her eyes

CUES: the 士 (man)'s girlfriend is a **Co-E**d who wears a mask when they go **Sai**ling; the mask doesn't block her mouth or affect her 声 **koe** (voice)

41. 昨

PRONUNCIATIONS: ki*nou, saku*ban **MEANINGS:** yesterday, previous

EXAMPLES: 昨日 kinou = yesterday; 昨晩 sakuban = last night **DESCRIPTION:** on the left, 日 hi (sun, # 32); on the right, this is said to be a serrated axe, but it resembles a crutch at the top of a ladder

CUES: 昨日 **ki**nou (yesterday) I left my **K**indle and my crutch in a **Sack** out in the attic of the barn and had to climb a ladder under the hot 日 (sun) to retrieve them **COMPARE:** 作(文) sakubun = written composition, # 482

42. 最

PRONUNCIATIONS: sai*sho, motto*mo **MEANING:** the most **EXAMPLES:** 最近 saikin = recently; 最初 saisho = the first;

最高 saikou = the best; 最悪 saiaku = the worst; 最後 saigo = the last; 最も mottomo = the most **DESCRIPTION:** at the top, 日 hi (day, or sun, # 32), but this looks like a large sign on a platform; at the lower left, 耳 mimi (ears); at the lower right, 又 mata ("again"), but this resembles a simple table

CUES: 最近 **sai**kin (recently), when the **Sign** is turned on, I sit at my 又 (table), and my 耳 (ears) can hear the traffic from the **Moto**rway

43. 英

PRONUNCIATION: ei **MEANINGS:** English, excellent **EXAMPLES:** 英語 eigo = the English language; 英雄 eiyuu = hero **DESCRIPTION:** at the top, a plant radical, consisting of a horizontal line intersected by two short verticals, suggesting a connection with plants; in the middle, a horizontal 日 hi (sun, # 32) on legs, which resembles a movie screen on a stand **CUE:** this movie screen shows an 英語 **ei**go (English language) movie about **A**pes and the plants they eat **COMPARE:** 映(画) eiga = movie, # 36

44. 白

PRONUNCIATIONS: shiro*i, haku, shira **MEANING:** white **EXAMPLES:** 白い shiroi = white; 白髪 hakuhatsu = grey or white hair; 白髪 shiraga = grey or white hair **NOTE:** hakuhatsu and shiraga are both spelled 白髪 **DESCRIPTION:** 日 hi (sun, # 32) with a white ray of light emerging from the top **CUES:** a white light from the 日 (sun) shines on white **Shee**p that **Roa**m near the 白い **shiro**i (white) building that is hosting the **Hack**er's convention on a **Shee**p **Ra**nch **COMPARE:** 自(分) jibun = by oneself, on one's own, # 55

408

45. 的

PRONUNCIATIONS: teki, mato MEANINGS: target, having characteristics of EXAMPLES: 目的 mokuteki = purpose, 日本的 nihonteki = having the characteristics of Japan; 自動的な jidouteki na = automatic; 的 mato = target, center of attention

DESCRIPTION: on the left, 白(い) shiroi (white, # 44); on the right, a giant hook

CUES: a giant hook attaches to a 白 (white) Techie with the 目的 moku**teki** (purpose) of dragging him offstage for having stepped on **Ma**'s **Toe**s COMPARE: 約(束) yakusoku = promise, appointment, # 225

46. 泊

PRONUNCIATIONS: haku, to*maru
MEANING: to stay overnight EXAMPLES: 二泊 nihaku = a 2-night stay; 泊まる tomaru = to stay overnight DESCRIPTION: on the left, a water radical (see # 12); on the right, 白(い) shiroi (white, # 44)

CUES: a **Hack** writer will 泊まる **to**maru (spend the night) in a 白 (white) hotel by the water and listen to the croaking of the **Toa**ds

47. 百

PRONUNCIATION: hyaku, byaku[1], pyaku[1]
MEANING: hundred EXAMPLES: 百 hyaku = 100; 三百 sanbyaku = 300; 八百 happyaku = 800 DESCRIPTION: this looks like a hacker's limousine seen from the back, with an antenna CUE: the **Hack**ers own 百 **hyaku** (100) limousines COMPARE: 首 kubi = neck, # 56; 白(い) shiroi = white, # 44; 面(白い) omoshiroi = interesting, # 282

48. 星

PRONUNCIATIONS: hoshi, sei*za
MEANING: star EXAMPLE: 星 hoshi = star; 星座 seiza = constellation DESCRIPTION: 日 hi (sun, # 32) is shining above 生(きる) ikiru (to live, # 208) CUES: a 星 **hoshi** (star) is a 日 (sun) that lives, admired by **Ho**rses and **Shee**p as they eat **Sage** grass

49. 昼

PRONUNCIATION: hiru, chuu*shoku
MEANINGS: daytime, noon EXAMPLES: 昼 hiru = noon; 昼間 hiruma = daytime; 昼食 chuushoku = lunch DESCRIPTION: 日 hi (sun, # 32) under a heavy roof, but 日 resembles a gasoline pump here CUES: since it gets so hot at 昼 **hiru** (noon), the **Heat** has **Ru**ined this gas pump under a heavy roof, where I **Chew** my 昼食 **chuu**shoku (lunch) COMPARE: 午 go = noon, # 207

50. 母

PRONUNCIATIONS: haha, bo, kaa*san
MEANING: mother EXAMPLES: 母 haha = mother; 祖母 sobo = grandmother; お母さん okaasan = honorable mother; お祖母さん obaasan = grandmother

NOTE: it isn't practical to divide the 祖母 baa in obaasan into two component pronunciations, so this syllable must be learned as a combination of the two kanji

DESCRIPTION: a modified 日 hi (day, or sun, # 32), this is said to have originally represented a mother's breasts

CUES: this is a 母 **haha** (mother) who frequently says "**Ha Ha**" and comes from a **Bo**ring town in **Ca**lifornia

---

[1] Alternative pronunciations like these follow the rules of rendaku (see page 515), and we don't always provide separate retrieval cues for them.

Eye

51. 目

PRONUNCIATIONS: me, moku **MEANING:** eye **EXAMPLES:** 目 me = eye; 目上 meue = one's superior; 目的 mokuteki = purpose; 注目 chuumoku = attention **DESCRIPTION:** 日 hi (day, # 32) with an additional horizontal line **CUES:** among the **Me**chanics with big 目 **me** (eyes), the one I saw on **Moku**youbi (Thursday) is the **Mo**st **Coo**l

COMPARE: 耳 mimi = ear, # 57; 木(曜日) mokuyoubi = Thursday, # 118

52. 着

PRONUNCIATIONS: ki*ru, tsu, gi, chaku*seki **MEANINGS:** to arrive, to put clothes on **EXAMPLES:** 着る kiru = to wear clothes; 着物 kimono; 着く tsuku = to arrive; 着ける tsukeru = to wear (accessories); 水着 mizugi = swimsuit; 着席 chakuseki = taking a seat **DESCRIPTION:** at the top, 羊 hitsuji (sheep, not included in this catalogue) which has a head with two horns and two ears, on a body with four legs; in this kanji, 羊 is missing its tail; below 羊, a platform, with a line extending down to the left, suggesting a trailing gown; at the bottom, 目 me (eyes, # 51) belonging to King Rudolph

CUES: **Ki**ng Rudolf's 目 (eyes) widen when he sees this 羊 (sheep), which 着る **ki**ru (wears) a trailing gown; the sheep 着く **tsu**ku (arrives) at the palace with its **Tsu**itcase, followed by some **Gee**se, and it drinks a lot of **Cha**mpagne and **Koo**l-Aid

53. 見

PRONUNCIATIONS: mi*ru, ken **MEANINGS:** to see, to look **EXAMPLES:** 見る miru = to see; 拝見する haiken suru = to humbly look at or see **DESCRIPTION:** 目 me (eye, # 51) on sturdy legs

CUES: this 目 (eye) on sturdy legs 見る **mi**ru (looks) in a **Mi**rror and 見る **mi**ru (sees) **Ken** and Barbie

54. 覚

PRONUNCIATIONS: obo*eru, sa*meru, zama, kaku*go **MEANINGS:** to memorize, realize, wake up **EXAMPLES:** 覚える oboeru = to memorize; 目が覚める me ga sameru = to wake up; 目覚しい mezamashii = outstanding, striking, spectacular; 覚悟する kakugo suru = to be prepared for something unwelcome **DESCRIPTION:** at the top, three old boys on a roof; at the bottom 見(る) miru (to see, # 53)

CUES: three **O**ld **Bo**ys on a roof 覚える **obo**eru (memorize) **Oboe** music; if you 見 (look) up, you can see a **Sa**murai, his **Za**mbian friend **Max**, and **Ka**rl the **Koo**l-Aid vendor

55. 自

PRONUNCIATIONS: ji, mizuka*ra, shi*zen **MEANING:** self **EXAMPLES:** 自分 jibun = by oneself, on one's own; 自ら mizukara = personally, on one's own initiative; 自然 shizen = nature **DESCRIPTION:** 目 me (eyes, # 51), with a tiny "self" standing at the top **CUES:** my 目 (eyes) are good, so I can do **Ji**gsaw puzzles 自分で **ji**bun de (by myself), after giving **Mizu** (water) to the **Ca**t, and feeding the **Shee**p

COMPARE: 白(い) shiroi = white, # 44

56. 首

PRONUNCIATIONS: kubi, shu **MEANINGS:** neck, chief, top **EXAMPLES:** 首 kubi = neck; 首相 shushou = prime minister

DESCRIPTION: in this kanji, 目 me (eye, # 51) can be viewed as a person's body; above the body is a narrow neck; above the neck is a compressed head with two antennae

CUES: a head with antennae, supported by a narrow 首 **kubi** (neck), peers over the wall of its **Cubi**cle and **Shoo**s co-workers away

COMPARE: 百 hyaku = hundred, # 47; 道 michi = street, # 349

57. 耳

PRONUNCIATIONS: mimi, ji*bika

MEANING: ear **EXAMPLES:** 耳 mimi = ear; 耳鼻科 jibika = ENT specialist

DESCRIPTION: 目 me (eyes, # 51) with five additional projections at the corners, some of which look like ear lobes **CUES: Mimi** sits in the **Jee**p, showing off her 耳 **mimi** (ears) which **Mimic**, or resemble, 目 (eyes)

58. 取

PRONUNCIATIONS: to*ru, shu*toku, tori*hiki

MEANING: to take **EXAMPLES:** 取る toru = to take or get; 受け取る uketoru = to receive; 取得する shutoku suru = to acquire; 取引 torihiki = business deal

DESCRIPTION: on the left, 耳 mimi (ear, # 57); on the right 又 mata (again, # 24), which resembles a simple table **CUES:** this 耳 (ear) is going to 取(る) **toru** (take) a **Torp**edo from the 又 (table) and **Shoot** it at a **Tory** **COMPARE:** 恥(ずかしい) hazukashii = embarrassed, shy, ashamed, # 309

Dirt

59. 土

PRONUNCIATIONS: tsuchi, to*chi, mi*yage, do*youbi **MEANING:** dirt **EXAMPLES:** 土田 Tsuchida = family name; 土地 tochi = land; お土産 omiyage = souvenir; 土曜日 doyoubi = Saturday

DESCRIPTION: compared to (兵)士 heishi (soldier, # 66), 土 has shorter arms **CUES:** this kanji points up to the moon, where **Tsu**ki **Chee**se (moon cheese) is as common as 土 **tsuchi** (dirt), and **Toa**ds conduct **Mee**tings under moon **Do**mes

COMPARE: 月 tsuki = moon, # 148

60. 塩

PRONUNCIATIONS: shio, en **MEANING:** salt **EXAMPLES:** 塩 shio = salt; 塩分 enbun = salt content **DESCRIPTION:** on the left, 土 tsuchi (dirt, # 59), suggesting earth where salt is collected via evaporation; at the upper right, a short crutch suspended over a block of salt; at the lower right, 皿 sara (bowl, # 567)

CUES: after we break this 塩 **shio** (salt) block with this **Sho**rt crutch, it trickles into the 皿 (bowl), and we **En**joy eating it **COMPARE:** 温(かい) atatakai = warm (object), # 257

61. 増

PRONUNCIATIONS: fu*eru, zou, ma*su **MEANING:** to increase **EXAMPLES:** 増える fueru = to increase; 倍増する baizou suru = to double; 増す masu = to increase or grow **DESCRIPTION:** on the left, 土 tsuchi (dirt, # 59); at the upper right, this looks like a Cheshire cat's face, with ears above two big square eyes and two big square teeth; at the bottom right, 日 hi (day, or sun, # 32), but this must be the cat's body

CUES: the number of cats living in the 土 (dirt) will 増える **fu**eru (increase) if we give them **Fu**el in the form of cat food, and some may have to be sent to an animal **Zo**ne in **Ma**ssachusetts **COMPARE:** 猫 neko = cat, # 72; 贈(る) okuru = to give a present, # 84; 横 yoko = side, # 135

62. 室

PRONUNCIATION: shitsu **MEANINGS:** room, cellar **EXAMPLE:** 室内 shitsunai = indoors **DESCRIPTION:** at the top, a roof; in the middle, a leg pedaling a bicycle; at the bottom 土 tsuchi (dirt, # 59) **CUE:** I keep my bicycle and my **Sheets** under the roof of my 室 **shitsu** (room), which has a floor of 土 (dirt) **COMPARE:** 屋 ya = store, # 63

63. 屋

PRONUNCIATIONS: ya, oku*jou **MEANINGS:** house, store **EXAMPLES:** 本屋 honya = bookstore; 部屋 heya = room; 屋根 yane = roof; 屋上 okujou = rooftop **DESCRIPTION:** compared to 室 shitsu (room, # 62), this kanji replaces the lightweight roof with a heavy yak-proof double roof, attached to a lean-to **CUES:** since I live in a land of falling yaks, the addition of a heavy **Y**ak-proof 屋根 **ya**ne (roof) and an **Oak** lean-to has allowed me to convert my 室 (room) into a 屋 **ya** (house or store)

64. 堂

PRONUNCIATION: dou **MEANINGS:** hall, grand building **EXAMPLE:** 食堂 shokudou = dining hall **DESCRIPTION:** at the top, a roof decorated with three characters; in the middle, kuchi 口 (mouth, # 426), which resembles a hall; at the bottom, 土 tsuchi (dirt, # 59), suggesting a mound of dirt **CUE:** this 食堂 shoku**dou** (dining hall) in the **Do**minican Republic is built on a mound of 土 (dirt) and decorated with three characters on the roof

65. 熱

PRONUNCIATIONS: atsu*i, netsu, ne **MEANINGS:** hot objects, fever **EXAMPLES:** 熱い atsui = hot (objects); 熱 netsu = fever; 熱心に nesshin ni = enthusiastically

DESCRIPTION: in the upper left, 土 tsuchi (dirt, # 59) appears twice, once on a platform and again below the platform; this suggests items that grow in dirt, like vegetables; in the upper right, 九 kyuu (nine, # 111); at the bottom, a hot fire **CUES:** these 九 (nine) vegetables that are being cooked by a fire **At** **Su**perman's house are 熱い **atsu**i (hot); they will **Net Su**perman a profit when he sells them **Ne**xt door **COMPARE:** 暑(い) atsui = hot atmosphere, # 278; 厚(い) atsui = thick, # 185

Warrior

66. 士

PRONUNCIATIONS: shi **MEANINGS:** man, warrior **EXAMPLES:** 武士 bushi = samurai, warrior; 兵士 heishi = soldier; 紳士 shinshi = gentleman **DESCRIPTION:** compared to 土 tsuchi (dirt, # 59), 士 has a longer horizontal line at the top **CUE:** a 兵士 hei**shi** (soldier) needs long arms in order to catch **Sheep** **COMPARE:** 仕(様) shiyou = means, method, # 67; 使(用) shiyou = use, employment, # 480

67. 仕

PRONUNCIATION: shi, tsuka*eru
MEANINGS: work, service **EXAMPLES:**
仕事 shigoto = work; 仕様 shiyou =
means, method; 仕える tsukaeru = to serve
DESCRIPTION: a man with a slanted hat
standing with a 士 shi (man, warrior, # 66),
which helps us to pronounce this **CUES:** this
man with a slanted hat does 仕事 **shi**goto
(work) for the 士 (man) on the right, washing
his **Shee**ts, and carrying them around in a
Tsuitcase in the **Car COMPARE:** 使(用)
shiyou = use, employment, # 480; 私(用の)
shiyou no = private, # 510

Rice Paddy

68. 田

PRONUNCIATIONS: ta, da, den **MEANINGS:**
rice paddies, field **EXAMPLES:** 田中
Tanaka = family name; 田んぼ tanbo = rice
paddy; 上田 Ueda = family name; 田園
den'en = pastoral, rural **DESCRIPTION:** a
square rice paddy divided into four sections
CUES: 田中さん **ta**naka-san (Mr. Tanaka)
does the **Ta**ngo on a **Da**rk night in **Den**mark at
a 田んぼ **ta**nbo (rice paddy)

69. 界

PRONUNCIATION: kai **MEANING:** world
EXAMPLE: 世界 sekai = the world
DESCRIPTION: at the top, 田(んぼ) tanbo
(rice paddy, # 68), but this resembles a square
kite; at the bottom, an arrow pointing up
CUE: we shoot a **Ki**te up into the sky, where it
will be seen by 世界 se**kai** (the world)

70. 町

PRONUNCIATIONS: chou, machi
MEANING: town **EXAMPLES:** 町名
choumei = town name or street name; 町
machi = town **DESCRIPTION:** on the left,

田(んぼ) tanbo (rice paddy, # 68); on the
right, this J-shaped radical is said to be a nail,
which can be used by certain machines
CUES: a 田 (rice paddy) and a nail can be
seen near a 町 **machi** (town), where they
make rice pudding and the town leaders have
Chosen a new **Machi**ne to nail their pudding
containers shut

71. 留

PRONUNCIATIONS: ryuu*gaku, ru*su,
to*meru **MEANING:** absence **EXAMPLES:**
留学 ryuugaku = foreign study; 留守 rusu
= absence from home; 留める tomeru = to
fasten, button or attach **DESCRIPTION:** at the
top left, a backpack; at the top right, 刀
katana (sword, # 102); at the bottom,
田(んぼ) tanbo (rice paddy, # 68)
CUES: Robert E. **Lee U**ses his 刀 (sword) to
Rule over a 田 (rice paddy) in **To**kyo, but
since he is taking his backpack and leaving for
留学 **ryuu**gaku (foreign study), he will soon
be 留守 **ru**su (absent from home)

72. 猫

PRONUNCIATION: neko **MEANING:** cat
EXAMPLES: 猫 neko = cat; 子猫 koneko =
kitten **DESCRIPTION:** on the left, a woman
contorting her body; on the right, a plant
radical (see # 43) above 田(んぼ) tanbo (rice
paddy, # 68); taken together, the two radicals
on the right look like a Cheshire cat with
prominent eye whiskers at the top, two large
square eyes, two large square teeth and a very
short neck **CUE:** this woman loves her 猫
neko (cat) with a short **Neck** and will contort
herself to please it **COMPARE:** 狭(い)
semai = narrow, # 194; 増(える) fueru = to
increase, # 61; 贈(る) okuru = to give a
present, # 84; 横 yoko = side, # 135

73. 由

PRONUNCIATIONS: yuu, yu **MEANING:** reason **EXAMPLES:** 理由 riyuu = reason; 経由で keiyu de = via, by way of **DESCRIPTION:** at the top, a unit of rice, possibly a metric ton; at the bottom, 田(んぼ) tanbo (rice paddy, # 68) **CUES:** there is a Unit of rice at the top of this 田 (rice paddy), and the 理由 ri**yuu** (reason) is that a **You**th is bringing a truck to take the rice to market

74. 届

PRONUNCIATION: todo*keru **MEANINGS:** to reach, to deliver **EXAMPLES:** 届ける todokeru = to deliver, transitive; 届く todoku = to reach, to be received; 届け todoke = notification **DESCRIPTION:** at the top, a double roof, which could belong to the Tokyo Dome; under the roof, (理)由 riyuu (reason, # 73) **CUE:** the 由 (reason) that I can't 届ける **todo**keru (deliver) the package is that the **To**kyo **Do**me collapsed on me, and I'm stuck under this double roof **COMPARE:** 戻(る) modoru = to return to a place, # 75

75. 戻

PRONUNCIATION: modo*ru **MEANINGS:** to return, revert **EXAMPLES:** 戻る modoru = to return to a place; 戻す modosu = to give something back **DESCRIPTION:** on the left, a lean-to with a double roof, and a layer of snow on top; under the roof, 大(きい) ookii (big, # 188) is a modest doorman **CUE:** the 大 (big) **M**odest **D**oorman and Ruth want to 戻る **modo**ru (return) to their duties, but they're stuck under a double roof with a layer of snow on top **COMPARE:** 届(ける) todokeru = to deliver, # 74

76. 黒

PRONUNCIATIONS: kuro*i, guro[1], koku **MEANINGS:** black **EXAMPLES:** 黒い kuroi = black; 目黒 Meguro = a ward in Tokyo; 黒板 kokuban = blackboard **DESCRIPTION:** a 田(んぼ) tanbo (rice paddy, # 68) on 土 tsuchi (dirt, # 59) with a fire at the bottom **CUES:** since this 田 (rice paddy) is burning, it will turn 黒い **kuro**i (black), and the **Cu**lprit is **Roy**, who tried to put out the flames with a can of **Coke**

77. 画

PRONUNCIATIONS: ga, kaku **MEANINGS:** drawing, painting **EXAMPLES:** 映画 eiga = movie; 漫画 manga = comics; 計画 keikaku = plan **DESCRIPTION:** a 田(んぼ) tanbo (rice paddy, # 68) inside a box, connected to a handle, belonging to Gandalf **CUES:** **Ga**ndalf is making an 映画 ei**ga** (movie) which is set in a 田 (rice paddy), and when he shows us a model of the set, which he keeps in a box with a handle, he **Cack**les about his 計画 kei**kaku** (plans) **COMPARE:** 両(方) ryouhou = both, # 579

78. 理

PRONUNCIATION: ri **MEANINGS:** reason, rational **EXAMPLES:** 理由 riyuu = reason; 料理 ryouri = cooking **DESCRIPTION:** on the left, a reasonable 王 ou (king, not included in this catalogue); on the right, 田(んぼ) tanbo (rice paddy, # 68), above 土 tsuchi (dirt, # 59) **CUE:** this 王 (king), who is a **Rea**sonable guy, has his 理由 **ri**yuu (reasons) for managing his 田 (rice paddy) and 土 (dirt) in the way that he does

79. 隅

PRONUNCIATION: sumi MEANING: inside corner EXAMPLE: 引き出しの隅 hikidashi no sumi = inside corner of a drawer DESCRIPTION: on the left, ß beta from the Greek alphabet, suggesting a Greek citizen named Sumisu (Smith); on the right, 田(んぼ) tanbo (rice paddy, # 68) in a pot, with roots growing below CUE: the roots of this 田 (rice paddy) in a pot are growing more vigorously in the right upper 隅 **sumi** (inside corner), since they are trying to avoid the Greek observer **Sumi**su-san (Mr. Smith)

80. 魚

PRONUNCIATIONS: sakana, zakana[1], uo, gyo MEANING: fish EXAMPLES: 魚 sakana = fish; 小魚 kozakana = small fish; 魚 uo = fish; 金魚 kingyo = goldfish DESCRIPTION: at the top, a fish head; in the middle, 田(んぼ) tanbo (rice paddy, # 68), which looks like scales on a fish; at the bottom, four legs CUES: we have a **S**ack of **Cana**dian 魚 **sakana** (fish) covered with scales that we caught in the **U**ber **O**cean; they each have four legs, and we will use them to make fish **Gyoza**

81. 角

PRONUNCIATIONS: kado, kaku, tsuno MEANING: outside corner EXAMPLES: 角 kado = outside corner; 四角い shikakui = square, rectangular; 角 tsuno = horn, antler, feeler DESCRIPTION: compared to 魚 sakana (fish, # 80), this fish has lost two of its legs CUES: this poor 魚 (fish) lost two legs after getting them caught in a **Car Do**or at a 角 **kado** (corner) near the **Cac**tus farm where he keeps a **Tsu**itcase full of **No**tebooks

82. 曲

PRONUNCIATIONS: ma*garu, kyoku MEANINGS: to bend, musical tune

EXAMPLES: 曲がる magaru = to bend or turn; 曲 kyoku = song, musical composition DESCRIPTION: this six-paddy group of 田(んぼ) tanbo (rice paddies, # 68) has a two-pronged switch at the top, and it resembles a stringed musical instrument CUES: I read an article in a **Ma**gazine about how to 曲がる **ma**garu (bend) this instrument in different directions using the switch at the top, and this allows me to play various 曲 **kyoku** (songs) for the **Kyo**to **Kool**-Aid Club

Money Chest

83. 貝

PRONUNCIATION: kai MEANINGS: shell, shellfish EXAMPLE: 貝 kai = shell DESCRIPTION: a three-drawer money chest belonging to the Kaiser, supported by two legs CUE: the **Kai**ser keeps his 貝 **kai** (shells) in a three-drawer money chest COMPARE: 具 gu = tool, # 100, which is a three-drawer cabinet on a *table* supported by two legs

84. 贈

PRONUNCIATION: oku*ru MEANING: to give a present EXAMPLES: 贈る okuru = to give a present; 贈り物 okurimono = a present DESCRIPTION: on the left, a 貝 kai (shell, money chest, # 83) made from oak; at the upper right, 田(んぼ) tanbo (rice paddy, # 68) with two ears above it, but this resembles a Cheshire cat with two square eyes above two square teeth; at the lower right, 日 hi (sun, # 32), but this must be the cat's body CUE: I will 贈る **oku**ru (give) some cat food from this **Oak** 貝 (money chest) on the left to the cat on the right COMPARE: 送(る) okuru = to send out, # 348; 増(える) fueru = to increase, # 61; 猫 neko = cat, # 72; 横 yoko = side, # 135

85. 貿

PRONUNCIATION: bou*eki **MEANING:** to trade **EXAMPLE:** 貿易 boueki = trade **DESCRIPTION:** a backpack and a 刀 katana (sword, # 102) on top of 貝 kai (shell, money chest, # 83) **CUE:** I have a backpack and a 刀 (sword) on top of my three-drawer 貝 (money chest), and I would like to 貿易する **bou**eki suru (trade) them for a **Bow**ling ball that I saw outside the eki (station) **COMPARE:** 留(守) rusu = absence from home, # 71

86. 質

PRONUNCIATION: shitsu
MEANINGS: contents, quality, to inquire
EXAMPLES: 質問 shitsumon = question; 品質 hinshitsu = product quality
DESCRIPTION: two valuable axe heads on top of 貝 kai (shell, money chest, # 83)
CUES: I bought these two valuable axe heads with money from my three-drawer 貝 (money chest) and was told that they have 品質 hin**shitsu** (product quality), but my 質問 **shitsu**mon (question) is, do you have some **Sheets** that I can wrap them in?

87. 負

PRONUNCIATIONS: fu*sai, o*u, ma
MEANINGS: to lose, to owe, to bear, to be wounded **EXAMPLES:** 負債 fusai = debt; 負う ou = to be indebted to, or to bear responsibility; 負ける makeru = to lose; 負かす makasu = to defeat
DESCRIPTION: a foolish guy keeps a mackerel head, which has no value, on top of his 貝 kai (shell, money chest, # 83)
CUES: the **Fo**ol who **Ow**ns this **Ma**ckerel head accepted it as payment for a 負債 **fu**sai (debt) and 負けた **ma**keta (lost) money

88. 員

PRONUNCIATION: in **MEANINGS:** member of group, official **EXAMPLE:** 会社員 kaishain = company employee
DESCRIPTION: a hat, suggesting membership in a group, on top of 貝 kai (shell, money chest, # 83) **CUE: In**siders are 員 **in** (members), who have three-drawer 貝 (money chests) and wear hats

89. 買

PRONUNCIATIONS: ka*u, bai*bai
MEANING: to buy **EXAMPLES:** 買う kau = to buy; 買い手 kaite = buyer; 売買 baibai = buying and selling **DESCRIPTION:** at the top, three eyes, suggesting an ability to see the prices of things like cars and bikes in the future; at the bottom, 貝 kai (shell, money chest, # 83) **CUES:** my three-drawer 貝 (money chest) has three eyes and can see the future; this allows me to 買う **ka**u (buy) **C**ars and **B**ikes at bargain prices

90. 貸

PRONUNCIATIONS: ka*su, tai **MEANING:** to lend **EXAMPLES:** 貸す kasu = to lend; 賃貸 chintai = lease, rental **DESCRIPTION:** at the upper left, a casual upright guy; at the upper right, a bending person, who looks anxious; at the bottom, 貝 kai (shell, money chest, # 83) **CUES:** the upright stance of the **Ca**sual guy on the left side of this 貝 (money chest) suggests that he 貸す **ka**su (lends) money, perhaps for buying **T**ires, to the bending person on the right **COMPARE:** 借(りる) kariru = to borrow, # 485

91. 資

PRONUNCIATION: shi **MEANINGS:** resources, capital **EXAMPLES:** 資料 shiryou = literature, documents; 資金 shikin = funds, capital **DESCRIPTION:** at the upper left, a water radical (see # 12); at the upper right, an oil derrick (# 534-537); these two radicals may suggest that water is being pumped, rather than oil; at the bottom, 貝 kai (shell, money chest, # 83), which suggests investment capital

CUES: in our three-drawer 貝 (money chest), we keep 資料 **shi**ryou (documents) about the water we pump for the **Shee**p that Pope Leo owns and also about the 資金 **shi**kin (capital) that we invest in our **Shi**nto kindergarten

92. 慣

PRONUNCIATIONS: na*reru, kan **MEANING:** to get used to **EXAMPLES:** 慣れる nareru = to get used to; 習慣 shuukan = customs, habits **DESCRIPTION:** on the left, an man standing erect, who is a narrator; on the upper right, 田(んぼ) tanbo (rice paddy, # 68) with a horizontal line drawn through it, which is said to represent a string of coins; on the lower right, 貝 kai (shell, money chest, # 83) **CUES:** the **Na**rrator 慣れた **na**reta (got used to) the string of coins which, in accordance with his 習慣 shuu**kan** (custom), he keeps on his 貝 (money chest), together with his **Can**dy

COMPARE: 帽(子) boushi = hat, # 243

93. 頭

PRONUNCIATIONS: atama, zu*tsuu, tou **MEANINGS:** head, top, counter for a large animal **EXAMPLES:** 頭 atama = head; 頭痛 zutsuu = headache; 牛五頭 ushi gotou = five cows
DESCRIPTION: on the left, a square head on a stand, covered by a cloth; on the right, 貝 kai (shell, money chest, # 83) with a platform

mounted on top, where the head could fit
CUES: this square 頭 **atama** (head) on the left was removed from his platform on the right for repair after he was **Atta**cked by his **Ma,** at the **Zoo,** for stepping on her **Toe**s, and he is resting on the stand on the left, where he has been covered with a cloth

94. 願

PRONUNCIATIONS: nega*u, gan*bou **MEANINGS:** to wish, a prayer **EXAMPLES:** 願う negau = to wish or beg; 願望 ganbou = wish, longing **DESCRIPTION:** on the left, a lean-to; inside the lean-to, 白(い) shiroi (white, # 44) at the top, and 小(さい) chiisai (small, # 253) at the bottom; on the right, 貝 kai (shell, money chest, # 83) with a platform missing a head, as seen in 頭 atama (head, # 93) **CUES:** losing his head has had a **Nega**tive effect on the 小 (small) 白 (white) guy in the lean-to, and he 願う **nega**u (begs) **Gan**dalf to find it **COMPARE:** 頭 atama = head, # 93; 顔 kao = face, # 95; 頃 koro = approximate time, # 96; (書)類 shorui = documents, # 97; 頼(む) tanomu = to request, # 98

95. 顔

PRONUNCIATIONS: kao, gao[1], gan **MEANING:** face **EXAMPLES:** 顔 kao = face; 笑顔 egao = smiling face; 洗顔 sengan = face washing **DESCRIPTION:** at the upper left, a cow bell; at the lower left, three wrinkles inside a lean-to, suggesting the face of an old cow; on the right, 貝 kai (shell, money chest, # 83) with a platform on top where a face could fit **CUES:** the wrinkles at the lower left belong to the 顔 **kao** (face) of an old **Cow** that wears a cow bell; a **Gang** has removed it from its platform on top of the 貝 (money chest) **COMPARE:** 頭 atama = head, # 93; 願(う) negau = to wish or beg, # 94;

頃 koro = approximate time, # 96; (書)類 shorui = documents, # 97; 頼(む) tanomu = to request, # 98

96. 頃

PRONUNCIATIONS: koro, goro
MEANINGS: about (referring to time)
EXAMPLE: 頃 koro = approximate time, often pronounced goro **DESCRIPTION:** on the left, the katakana character ヒ hi which resembles 七 shichi (seven); on the right, 貝 kai (shell, money chest, # 83) with a platform where a head belongs, but the head is missing, as seen in 頭 atama (head, # 93), suggesting the need for a coroner
CUES: a **Cor**oner is examining the headless guy who was found near the merry-**Go-Ro**und at 七時頃 shichiji **goro** (about 7:00) because he has to conduct an autopsy
COMPARE: 頭 atama = head, # 93; 願(う) negau = to wish or beg, # 94; 顔 kao = face, # 95; (書)類 shorui = documents, # 97; 頼(む) tanomu = to request,# 98

97. 類

PRONUNCIATION: rui **MEANINGS:** sort, variety **EXAMPLES:** 書類 shorui = documents; 衣類 irui = clothes; 種類 shurui = variety **DESCRIPTION:** at the upper left, 米 kome (uncooked rice, # 326); at the lower left, 大(きい) ookii (big, # 188); taken together, these two radicals imply a big rice harvest; on the right, 貝 kai (shell, money chest, # 83) with a platform on top, which looks like Louis XVI without his head
CUE: a 大 (big) harvest of 米 (rice) came in, and we want to show **Louis** some 書類 sho**rui** (documents) about the harvest, but where is his head? **COMPARE:** 頭 atama = head, # 93; 願(う) negau = to wish or beg, # 94; 顔 kao = face, # 95; 頃 koro =

approximate time, # 96; 頼(む) tanomu = to request, # 98

98. 頼

PRONUNCIATIONS: tano*mu, tayo*ru, rai
MEANINGS: trust, request **EXAMPLES:** 頼む tanomu = to request, beg, ask, entrust to; 頼る tayoru = to rely on, depend on; 依頼 irai = request, commission
DESCRIPTION: on the left, (約)束 yakusoku (appointment, # 99), which resembles a tangy orange 木 ki (tree, # 108) that is wearing glasses; on the right, 貝 kai (money chest, # 83), with a platform on top, who keeps some tissue paper in one of her three drawers **CUES:** this is a glasses-wearing **Tangy Orange** tree who 頼む **tano**mu (asks) the platform-topped 貝 (money chest) for tissue paper to clean his glasses, since he 頼る **tayo**ru (depends) on her supply; he will give her some **Tangy Yo**gurt and some **Ri**ce in return
COMPARE: 頭 atama = head, # 93; 願(う) negau = to wish or beg, # 94; 顔 kao = face, # 95; 頃 koro = approximate time, # 96; (書)類 shorui = documents, # 97

99. 束

PRONUNCIATIONS: taba*neru, soku
MEANINGS: bundle, sheaf **EXAMPLES:** 束ねる tabaneru = to bundle; 約束 yakusoku = promise, appointment
DESCRIPTION: a 木 ki (tree, # 118) wearing glasses **CUES:** this is a 木 (tree) who has to wear glasses in order to watch his yak; seeing that the yak is dirty from rolling in **TanBa**rk, he has made a 約束 yaku**soku** (appointment) for some yak **Soak**ing **COMPARE:** 東 higashi = east, # 508; 速(達) sokutatsu = express mail, # 359; 頼(む) tanomu = to request, # 98

Table Cabinet

100. 具

PRONUNCIATION: gu **MEANINGS:** to equip, tool **EXAMPLES:** 道具 dougu = tool; 具体的に gutaiteki ni = concretely; 具合 guai = condition **DESCRIPTION:** unlike 貝 kai (shell, money chest, # 83) and other similar kanji, this consists of a cabinet on a *table* supported by two legs **CUE:** I keep 道具 dou**gu** (tools) in my cabinet on a table, together with the **Goo** that I use to grease them

101. 真

PRONUNCIATIONS: makoto, ma, shin **MEANINGS:** truth, genuine **EXAMPLES:** 真 makoto = truth, sincerity; 真面目な majime na = sincere; 真ん中 mannaka = middle; 真っ直ぐ massugu = straight; 写真 shashin = photograph; 真実 shinjitsu = truth; 真理 shinri = truth **DESCRIPTION:** compared to 具 gu (tool, # 100) which resembles a simple table cabinet, this kanji adds a machine with a shiny antenna at the top **CUES:** this cabinet on a table contains strings for **Ma**'s **Koto** (Japanese harp), and it has a **Ma**chine with a **Shin**y antenna at the top, which delivers 真実の **shin**jitsu no (true) news about 真面目な **ma**jime na (sincere) people

Sword

102. 刀

PRONUNCIATION: katana, tou **MEANINGS:** sword, knife **EXAMPLES:** 刀 katana = sword; 短刀 tantou = dagger **DESCRIPTION:** compared to 力 chikara (force, # 107), 刀 is missing a handle at the top, suggesting a blade without a handle **CUES:** I bought this 刀 **katana** (sword) from a **Cata**logue store in **Na**gasaki in order to cut my

Toenails **COMPARE:** 九 kyuu = nine, # 111; 万 man = ten thousand, # 113; 方 kata = honorable person, # 114

103. 切

PRONUNCIATIONS: ki*ru, gi*ru[1], setsu, sai **MEANINGS:** to cut, serious, earnest **EXAMPLES:** 切る kiru = to cut; 横切る yokogiru = to cut across; 親切 shinsetsu = kind; 大切 taisetsu = important; 一切 issai = everything in affirmative sentences, nothing or never in negative sentences **DESCRIPTION:** on the left, 七 shichi (seven, # 20); on the right, a 刀 katana (sword, # 102), belonging to a friend of King Rudolph **CUES:** it takes 七 (seven) people to 切る **ki**ru (cut) with this big 刀 (sword); when you buy one, **King** Rudolph, who is very 大切 tai**setsu** (important), **Sets U** up with a seller, but you have to **Sign** a contract

104. 初

PRONUNCIATIONS: haji, sho, hatsu*koi **MEANINGS:** for the first time, to begin **EXAMPLES:** 初めて hajimete = for the first time; 最初 saisho = the beginning; 初恋 hatsukoi = first love **DESCRIPTION:** on the left, a happy man named Jimmy Carter, with a thin hat and big lips; on the right 刀 katana (sword, # 102) **CUES:** **Happy Ji**mmy, who has a thin hat and big lips projecting to the right, kisses his 刀 (sword) before his 初めての **haji**mete no (first) battle and **Shows** it to his admirers, after which all of the people remove their **Hats COMPARE:** 始(める) hajimeru = to begin, # 540

105. 分

PRONUNCIATIONS: bun, pun, wa*karu, fun **MEANINGS:** to divide, to understand, minute **EXAMPLES:** 十分 juubun = enough (this can also be read as juppun, or jippun, = 10 minutes); 分かる wakaru = to understand;

分かれる wakareru = to branch off; 五分 gofun = 5 minutes **DESCRIPTION:** at the top, 八 hachi (eight, # 15); at the bottom, a 刀 katana (sword, # 102) belonging to Daniel Boone **CUES:** when Daniel **Boone** lived in the **Pun**jab, he tried to 分かる **wa**karu (understand) a magnet by using a 刀 (sword) to cut it into 八 (eight) parts, which then 分かれた **wa**kareta (separated) from one another; this was **W**acky but **F**un

106. 召

PRONUNCIATION: me*shiagaru **MEANING:** to eat **EXAMPLE:** 召し上がる meshi-agaru = to honorably eat

DESCRIPTION: 刀 katana (sword, # 102) over 口 kuchi (mouth, # 426) **CUE:** a person makes a **Me**ss as he 召し上がる **me**shiagaru (honorably eats) with his 口 (mouth), after cutting his food with his 刀 (sword)

107. 力

PRONUNCIATIONS: chikara, riki*saku, ryoku **MEANINGS:** strength, power, force **EXAMPLES:** 力 chikara = force; 力作 rikisaku = masterpiece; 努力 doryoku = effort **DESCRIPTION:** compared to 九 kyuu (nine, # 111), 力, like the city of Chicago, is in motion to the right; compared to 刀 katana (sword, # 102), 力 has a handle for control **CUES:** in **Chica**go **Ra**mbo showed his motorcycle's 力 **chikara** (force) to **Ri**cky before Pope **Leo Cut** him off with a popemobile **COMPARE:** the katakana character カ ka; 万 man = ten thousand, # 113; 方 kata = honorable person, # 114

108. 助

PRONUNCIATIONS: tasu, jo*shu **MEANING:** to help **EXAMPLES:** 助ける tasukeru = to

help; 助手 joshu = assistant

DESCRIPTION: on the left, a tall 目 me (eyes, # 51); on the right, an even taller 力 chikara (force, # 107)

CUES: good 目 (eyes) and 力 (force) are necessary in order to 助ける **tasu**keru (help) people with their problems, and this **Tall Su**perintendent of schools has both qualities, allowing him to help people like **Joa**n of Arc

109. 男

PRONUNCIATIONS: otoko, dan, o, nan **MEANING:** male **EXAMPLES:** 男の子 otoko no ko = boy; 男性 dansei = man; 正男 Masao = a boy's given name; 長男 chounan = first-born son **DESCRIPTION:** at the top, 田(んぼ) tanbo (rice paddy, # 68); at the bottom, 力 chikara (force, # 107); this kanji appears to be dancing **CUES:** a 男性 **dan**sei (man), who is wearing an **Otto**man-era **Coa**t, demonstrates his 力 (force) by **Dan**cing in a 田 (rice paddy) with its **Ow**ner, **Nan**cy

110. 勢

PRONUNCIATIONS: zei, sei, ikio*i **MEANINGS:** vigor, power **EXAMPLES:** 大勢 oozei = many people; 勢力 seiryoku = power, influence; 勢い ikioi = power, energy **DESCRIPTION:** at the upper left, 土 tsuchi (dirt, # 59) appears twice, once on a platform and again below the platform; this suggests items that grow in dirt, like vegetables; at the upper right, 九 kyuu (nine, # 111); at the bottom, 力 chikara (force, # 107) **CUES:** **Za**ne Grey had the 力 (force) to produce 九 (nine) kinds of **Sa**fe vegetables, providing food for 大勢の oo**zei** no (many) people in the **Icky Oi**l industry **COMPARE:** 熱(い) atsui = hot objects, # 65

111. 九

PRONUNCIATIONS: kyuu, ku, kokono*tsu
MEANING: nine **EXAMPLES:** 九 kyuu =
nine; 九月 kugatsu = September; 九つ
kokonotsu = nine objects
DESCRIPTION: compared to 力 chikara
(force, # 107), 九 kyuu, like Cuba, doesn't
seem as eager to move toward the right
CUES: a **Cu**ban guy with 九 **kyuu** (nine)
Kooky kids eats a lot of **Coconuts** and seems
laid-back **COMPARE:** 刀 katana = sword,
# 102; 万 man = ten thousand, # 113; 方
kata = honorable person, # 114

112. 究

PRONUNCIATION: kyuu **MEANING:** to
investigate thoroughly **EXAMPLES:** 研究
kenkyuu = research; 研究者 kenkyuusha =
researcher **DESCRIPTION:** at the top, a
soaring bird; at the bottom, 九 kyuu (nine,
111), which tells us how to pronounce this
CUES: when the 研究 ken**kyuu** (research) on
Cute kittens was completed, the 九 **Kyuu**
(nine) 研究者 ken**kyuu**sha (researchers)
soared with excitement
COMPARE: 空 sora = sky, # 248

113. 万

PRONUNCIATIONS: ban, man
MEANING: ten thousand **EXAMPLES:** 万事
banji = everything; 二万 niman = 20,000
DESCRIPTION: compared to 力 chikara
(force, # 107), 万 has a flat top; compared to
刀 katana (sword, # 102), 万 has a neck,
allowing its flat top to swivel
CUES: Bankers in **Man**ila use 万 **man**'s flat
top to count 一万円 ichi**man**'en (10,000
yen) bills **COMPARE:** 九 kyuu = nine,
111; 方 kata = honorable person, # 114

114. 方

PRONUNCIATIONS: kata, gata[1], hou
MEANINGS: honorable person, direction,
method **EXAMPLES:** 方 kata = honorable
person; 読み方 yomikata = reading method;
夕方 yuugata = evening; 方がいい hou
ga ii = it would be better **DESCRIPTION:** 万
man (10,000, # 113) wears a flat hat on his
neck, but 方 wears a nicer hat
CUES: the nice hat that this 方 **kata**
(honorable person) is wearing is his 方 **kata**
(method) of impressing people; in a
Catastrophe, you can count on him to **H**old
you tightly
COMPARE: 刀 katana = sword, # 102; 力
chikara = force, # 107; 九 kyuu = nine, # 111

115. 族

PRONUNCIATION: zoku **MEANINGS:**
family, tribe **EXAMPLE:** 家族 kazoku =
family **DESCRIPTION:** on the left, a 方 kata
(honorable person, # 114) named Zooey; on
the right, a crutch held up by her father, an
American Indian chief, who is wearing a war
bonnet **CUES:** this 家族 ka**zoku** (family) of
disabled American Indian 方 (honorable
people) drinks mostly beer, but **Zoo**ey drinks
Kool-Aid **COMPARE:** 旅(行) ryokou = trip,
116; 知(る) shiru = to know, # 323; 短
(い) mijikai = short, # 324; 医(者) isha =
doctor, # 325

116. 旅

PRONUNCIATIONS: ryo, tabi **MEANINGS:**
trip, to travel **EXAMPLES:** 旅行する
ryokou suru = to travel; 旅館 ryokan = a
Japanese inn; 旅 tabi = trip, travel
DESCRIPTION: on the left, a 方 kata
(honorable person, # 114) named Pope Leo;
on the right, compared to 族 zoku (family,
115), the American Indian chief has been

replaced by the legs of a crutch-carrying person, who appears to be stepping out on a journey **CUES:** a 方 (honorable person) named Pope **Leo** and his disabled companion will 旅行する **ryo**kou suru (travel) and are taking the first step on their 旅 **tabi** (trip) with their **Tabby** cat

117. 放

PRONUNCIATIONS: hou, hana*su
MEANINGS: to emit, release **EXAMPLES:** 放送 housou = broadcasting; 食べ放題 tabehoudai = all you can eat; 放す hanasu = to release **DESCRIPTION:** on the left, a 方 kata (honorable person, # 114) named Hopeful Hannah; the bottom half of 方 resembles a small **h**, which helps us to pronounce this; on the right, a person with crossed legs holds Hannah's crutch **CUES:** this **Ho**peful disabled 方 (honorable person) named **Hann**ah wants to 放送する **hou**sou suru (broadcast) information about disabled people, and she will also work to 放す **hana**su (release) all disabled prisoners **COMPARE:** 話(す) hanasu = to talk, # 433; 族 zoku = family, # 115; 旅 tabi = travel, # 116

Tree

118. 木

PRONUNCIATIONS: gi, ki, moku*youbi, boku, ko*noha **MEANINGS:** wood, tree
EXAMPLES: 六本木 roppongi = district in Tokyo; 木の実 kinomi = nut, fruit, berry; 木曜日 mokuyoubi = Thursday; 土木 doboku = public works, civil engineering; 木の葉 konoha = leaf **DESCRIPTION:** a tree with a central trunk and four branches **CUES:** when you return with your **Gui**tar and take out your house **Key**, the 木 **ki** (tree) in the front yard reminds you to buy **More Kool**-Aid but not the **Bo**ring **Kool**-Aid that you got last time, since that's no better than **Co**la

COMPARE: 本 hon = book, # 123; 末 matsu = end, # 119

119. 末

PRONUNCIATIONS: sue, matsu
MEANING: end
EXAMPLES: 末っ子 suekko = youngest child; 週末 shuumatsu = weekend
DESCRIPTION: 木 ki (wood, # 118) with a cross at the top, suggesting a wooden church **CUES:** this church is made of 木 (wood) and doesn't have any furniture; it holds services on **Sue**de **Mats** on 週末 shuu**matsu** (weekends) **COMPARE:** 本 hon = book, # 123

120. 案

PRONUNCIATION: an **MEANINGS:** plan, idea **EXAMPLES:** 案内する annai suru = to show around; 案 an = proposal, idea; 提案 teian = proposal **DESCRIPTION:** at the top, 安(い) yasui, (inexpensive, # 236); at the bottom, a 木 ki (tree, # 118) belonging to Queen Anne **CUE:** Queen **Anne** will 案内する **an**nai suru (show us around) and demonstrate her 案 **an** (proposal) for living in a 安 (inexpensive) way in treetops

121. 菜

PRONUNCIATION: sai **MEANINGS:** vegetable, side dish **EXAMPLES:** 野菜 yasai = vegetable **DESCRIPTION:** at the top, a plant radical (see # 43), suggesting vegetables; in the middle, four lines which could represent a barbecue grate; at the bottom, 木 ki (wood, # 118), suggesting wood **CUE:** during the Vietnam war, people cooked 野菜 ya**sai** (vegetables) over fires fueled by 木 (wood) in **Sai**gon

122. 休
PRONUNCIATIONS: yasu*mu, kyuu
MEANING: rest EXAMPLES: 休む yasumu
= to rest; 休暇 kyuuka = vacation
DESCRIPTION: a man with a slanted hat,
resting against a 木 ki (tree, # 118)
CUES: this man with a slanted hat 休む
yasumu (rests) against a 木 (tree) and drinks
Yak Soup; he's taking a 休暇 **kyuu**ka
(vacation) with his **Cu**te cat
COMPARE: 体 karada = body, # 124

123. 本
PRONUNCIATIONS: hon, moto, pon, bon
MEANINGS: book, a counter for long thin
objects EXAMPLES: 本屋 honya =
bookstore; 四本 yonhon = four bottles;
山本 Yamamoto = a family name; 一本
ippon = one bottle; 何本 nanbon = how many
bottles DESCRIPTION: a 木 ki (tree, # 118)
in Honduras, with a horizontal line across the
lower trunk, which could represent an open
book CUES: the 本 **hon** (book) near the
bottom of this 木 (tree) in **Hon**duras tells the
story of a **Mot**orcycle that ran into a **Pon**y and
broke its **Bon**es
COMPARE: 体 karada = body, # 124

124. 体
PRONUNCIATIONS: karada, tai, tei*sai
MEANING: body EXAMPLES: 体 karada =
body; 身体 shintai = the human body;
体裁 teisai = appearance, looks
DESCRIPTION: on the left, a man with a
slanted hat; on the right, 本 hon (book, # 123)
CUES: a man with a slanted hat wanted to read
a 本 (book) about **Cara**cas' **Da**rk underworld
on a plane, but his 体 **karada** (body) got
Tired, and he fell asleep during **Ta**ke-off
COMPARE: 休(む) yasumu = to rest, # 122

125. 林
PRONUNCIATIONS: hayashi, rin, bayashi
MEANING: grove EXAMPLES: 林 hayashi
= grove; 森林 shinrin = forest; 小林
Kobayashi = a family name DESCRIPTION:
two 木 ki (trees, # 118) CUES: **Hay** is
growing in **Ash**land near this 林 **hayashi**
(grove) of 木 (trees) with **Wr**inkled bark,
where **Ba**ts, **Ya**ks and **She**ep roam

126. 磨
PRONUNCIATION: miga*ku MEANINGS:
grind, polish, scour, brush EXAMPLES:
磨く migaku = to brush; 歯磨き hamigaki
= toothpaste, brushing one's teeth
DESCRIPTION: on the left and top, a lean-to;
inside the lean-to, a picture of a 林 hayashi
(grove, # 125); under this picture, 石 ishi
(stone, # 458), but this resembles a toilet
CUE: some **Mee**k **Ga**kusei (students) 磨く
migaku (brush) their teeth in an outhouse,
where there is a picture of a 林 (grove) over
the toilet

127. 森
PRONUNCIATIONS: mori, shin*rin
MEANING: forest EXAMPLES: 森 mori =
forest; 森林 shinrin = forest
DESCRIPTION: three 木 ki (trees, # 118)
CUES: **Maure**en likes to visit the three 木
(trees) in this 森 **mori** (forest) and worship the
Shintou spirits there

128. 枝
PRONUNCIATION: eda MEANING: branch
EXAMPLES: 枝 eda = branch; 枝豆
edamame = soybeans served in the pod
DESCRIPTION: on the left, an apple 木 ki
(tree, # 118) belonging to an editor; on the
right, 支 shi (branch, # 26), but this looks like
a car jack lifting a branch CUE: a car jack is

lifting a replacement 枝 **eda** (branch) and

lining it up with an existing one on an **Ed**itor's **A**pple 木 (tree) **COMPARE:** 枚 mai = counter for flat thin objects, # 129; (学)校 gakkou = school, # 130

129. 枚

PRONUNCIATION: mai **MEANING:** counter for flat thin objects **EXAMPLE:** 紙を二枚ください kami wo nimai kudasai = please give me two sheets of paper **DESCRIPTION:** on the left, a 木 ki (tree, # 118); on the right, Michael Jackson, a disabled person with crossed legs, is holding up a crutch **CUE:** **Mi**chael, who is disabled, is sitting next to a 木 (tree) and selling paper; he says, "何枚 nan**mai** (how many sheets) do you need?" **COMPARE:** 枝 eda = branch, # 128; (学)校 gakkou = school, # 130

130. 校

PRONUNCIATION: kou **MEANING:** school **EXAMPLE:** 学校 gakkou = school

DESCRIPTION: on the left, 木 ki (tree, # 118); on the right, 交 kou (crossing, # 144), which helps us to pronounce this **CUES:** the 学校 gak**kou** (school) is near a **kou** (crossing), and it's usually **C**old because it's shaded by a 木 (tree)

COMPARE: 枝 eda = branch, # 128; 枚 mai = counter for flat, thin objects, # 129

131. 村

PRONUNCIATIONS: son, mura **MEANING:** village **EXAMPLES:** 村長 sonchou = village mayor; 村 mura = village **DESCRIPTION:** this is a mural showing, on the left, a 木 ki (tree, # 118) and, on the right, a slouching guy, who has dropped a piece of gum on the ground **CUES:** my **Son** painted a **Mura**l which depicts

a 村 **mura** (village), with a 木 (tree) on the left and a slouching guy on the right; the slouching guy has dropped a piece of gum on the ground **COMPARE:** 付(ける) tsukeru = to attach or stick, # 132

132. 付

PRONUNCIATIONS: tsu, zu, fu, tsuke **MEANINGS:** to adhere, to issue **EXAMPLES:** 付ける tsukeru = to attach or stick, transitive; 付く tsuku = to adhere, intransitive; 事付け kotozuke = message; 寄付 kifu = donation; 受付 uketsuke = reception **DESCRIPTION:** on the left, a man with a slanted hat wearing a nice tsuit; on the right, a slouching guy, who has dropped a piece of gum on the ground **CUES:** the man with a slanted hat, who is wearing a nice **Tsu**it, went to **Zu**rich and warned the **Foo**lish slouching guy that the piece of gum might 付く **tsu**ku (adhere) to the guy's shoe or to the man's **Tsu**it**Ke**is (suitcase) **COMPARE:** 村 mura = village, # 131; 符 pu = tag, # 133

133. 符

PRONUNCIATION: pu **MEANING:** tag **EXAMPLE:** 切符 kippu = ticket

DESCRIPTION: at the top, two short 竹 take (bamboo, # 134) which look like clamps; at the bottom, 付く tsuku (to adhere, # 132), which includes a man with a slanted hat named Putin **CUE:** a man with a slanted hat named **Pu**tin clamped some 切符 kip**pu** (tickets) together with 竹 (bamboo) clamps, and now they 付 (adhere) to each other **COMPARE:** 村 mura = village, # 131; 笑(う) warau = to laugh, # 199; 第 dai = order, # 530

134. 竹

PRONUNCIATIONS: take, chiku*rin
MEANING: bamboo **EXAMPLES:** 竹の子 takenoko = bamboo shoot; 竹林 chikurin = bamboo grove **DESCRIPTION:** the two radicals used to write 竹 take (bamboo) are said to be identical, even though the one on the right curves under at the bottom; each of them contains a horizontal line at the top, unlike the radical on the left side of 付 tsu (to adhere, # 132) **CUES:** two cowboys viewed from the side, each with his hat pushed back on his head, are admiring some 竹 **take** (bamboo) which they may **Take** home; the cowboy in front is slouching, and both are eating **Chi**cken **Cut**lets

135. 横

PRONUNCIATIONS: yoko, ou*dan
MEANINGS: sideways, crooked **EXAMPLES:** 横 yoko = side; 横切る yokogiru = to cross or cut across; 横断する oudan suru = to cross (a street, etc.) **DESCRIPTION:** on the left, 木 ki (tree, # 118); at the right, a Cheshire cat belonging to Yoko Ono, with a plant radical (see # 43) at the top resembling prominent eye whiskers; below that, two large eyes, two large teeth, and extended front paws **CUES: Yoko**'s cat is 横 **yoko** (beside) this 木 (tree) in **O**saka **COMPARE:** 増(える) fueru = to increase, # 61; 贈(る) okuru = to give a present, # 84; 構(う) kamau = to mind, #141; 猫 neko = cat, # 72

136. 様

PRONUNCIATIONS: sama, you*su
MEANINGS: appearance, honorific form of address **EXAMPLES:** お客様 okyakusama = very honorable customer; 様子 yousu = condition, state **DESCRIPTION:** on the left, a 木 ki (tree, # 118); on the upper right, 羊 hitsuji (sheep, not included in this catalogue), an animal with 2 horns, 2 ears, 4 legs, and a tail – but the tail is absent here; on the lower right, 水 mizu (water, # 251) **CUES:** a **Yo**gurt seller named **Yo**landa 様 **sama** (very honorable Yolanda) will rescue the 羊 (sheep) that is drowning in 水 (water) beside this 木 (tree) because she is a Good **Sama**ritan **COMPARE:** 機 ki = machine, # 137

137. 機

PRONUNCIATION: ki **MEANING:** machine
EXAMPLES: 機械 kikai = machine; 飛行機 hikouki = airplane **DESCRIPTION:** on the left, 木 ki (wood, # 118), which tells us how to pronounce this; on the upper right, two 糸 (skeet shooters, #219); at the lower right, a platform supported by legs and transected by a halberd (combination lance and axe) **CUES:** this 機械 **ki**kai (machine), which can **Ki**ck you in the eye, is made from 木 **Ki** (wood) and supports two 糸 (skeet shooters) **COMPARE:** 様 sama = honorific form of address, # 136; 械 kai = machine, # 138

138. 械

PRONUNCIATION: kai **MEANINGS:** machine, gadget **EXAMPLE:** 機械 kikai = machine **DESCRIPTION:** on the left, 木 ki (wood, # 118); on the right, a halberd (combination lance and axe); in the center, reportedly, two hands tied together, i.e., a set of handcuffs **CUE:** the **Kai**ser owned this 機械 ki**kai** (machine) made from 木 (wood), featuring wooden handcuffs and a halberd to deal with criminals **COMPARE:** 機 ki = machine, # 137

139. 橋

PRONUNCIATIONS: hashi, bashi[1], kyou
MEANING: bridge **EXAMPLES:** 橋 hashi = bridge; 新橋 Shinbashi = district in Tokyo; 歩道橋 hodoukyou = pedestrian bridge
DESCRIPTION: on the left, 木 ki (wood,

118); on the upper right, a pregnant woman walking on what appears to be a bridge
CUES: a pregnant woman walks across a 橋 **hashi** (bridge) built with **Hashi** (chopsticks) made from 木 (wood) in **Kyou**to

140. 机

PRONUNCIATION: tsukue **MEANING:** desk
EXAMPLES: 机 tsukue = desk

DESCRIPTION: on the left, 木 ki (wood, # 118); on the right, a finished desk, which is high enough to accommodate a tsuitcase below it **CUE:** if we put a tsuitcase under a desk made from 木 (wood), the 机 **tsukue** (desk) is **TsuitCase no Ue** (above the suitcase)

141. 構

PRONUNCIATIONS: kou, kama*u, gama
MEANINGS: fine, to mind **EXAMPLES:** 結構 kekkou = fine, splendid, considerably; 構う kamau = to mind or care about; 心構え kokorogamae = a mental attitude

DESCRIPTION: on the left, 木 ki (wood, # 118); on the upper right, some tall bushes; on the lower right, 円 en (yen, # 39) with two additional lines drawn through it for extra support, suggesting a strong building
CUES: the people in **Ko**be used 木 (wood) when they built this 結構な kek**kou** na (fine) structure with tall bushes on the roof; because they 構う **kama**u (care about) strong buildings, they consulted the **Kama** Sutra, spent a lot of 円 (yen), and strengthened the building with additional lateral supports so that it would provide protection from **Gamma** rays
COMPARE: 横 yoko = side, # 135

142. 箱

PRONUNCIATION: hako, bako[1] **MEANING:** box **EXAMPLES:** 箱 hako = box; 靴箱 kutsubako = shoe box **DESCRIPTION:** on the left, 木 ki (wood, # 118); at the top, shortened 竹 take (bamboo, # 134), resembling clamps;

on the lower right, 目 me (eye, # 51), but this resembles a finished box
CUE: a 箱 **hako** (box), made from 木 (wood) and 竹 (bamboo), is on the lower right, and it contains a **Hat** and a **Coat**

Crossing

143. 父

PRONUNCIATIONS: chichi, tou, fu
MEANING: father **EXAMPLES:** 父 chichi = father; お父さん otousan = honorable father; 祖父 sofu = grandfather
DESCRIPTION: a father with thick eyebrows, sitting with crossed legs **CUES:** 父 **chichi** (father) has thick eyebrows, sits with crossed legs, dresses in a **Chichi** (chic) way, smokes **To**bacco, and cooks good **Foo**d

144. 交

PRONUNCIATIONS: kou, maji*waru, ka
MEANINGS: crossing, mingling **EXAMPLES:** 交通 koutsuu = traffic; 交差点 kousaten = traffic intersection; 交わる majiwaru = to keep company with; 交わす kawasu = to exchange **DESCRIPTION:** crossed roads under 六 roku (six, # 17) **CUES:** there is a 交差点 **kou**saten (traffic intersection) of 六 (six) roads in **Ko**rea where **Magi**c traffic signals keep **Ca**rs from colliding

145. 郊

PRONUNCIATION: kou*gai **MEANING:** suburb **EXAMPLE:** 郊外 kougai = suburbs
DESCRIPTION: on the left, 交 kou (crossing, # 144), which tells us how to pronounce this; on the right, ß beta from the Greek alphabet **CUE:** a Greek guy lives near a 交 **Kou** (crossing) in the 郊外 **kou**gai (suburbs), and he's a **Cold** guy, since his house is unheated

Mountain

146. 山

PRONUNCIATIONS: yama, san, zan

MEANING: mountain EXAMPLES: 山登り

yamanobori = mountain climbing; 富士山

fujisan = Mt. Fuji; 火山 kazan = volcano

DESCRIPTION: this mountain resembles a
volcano with lava spewing from the top

CUES: the Yak has Magic friends, such as

Santa Claus, who live on a volcanic 山 **yama**
(mountain) in Zanzibar

147. 出

PRONUNCIATIONS: shutsu, da*su, de*ru, shu

MEANINGS: to leave, to put out EXAMPLES:
外出する gaishutsu suru = to go out;

出す dasu = to put out; 出る deru = to

leave or go out; 出席 shusseki = attendance;

出張 shutchou = business trip; 出発

shuppatsu = departure DESCRIPTION: two

山 yama (mountains, # 146), suggesting two

volcanoes CUES: two volcanoes 出す **da**su

(put out) lava, which 出る **de**ru (emerges),
Shoots up into the air, **Da**shes down the slopes
and burns a **De**butante's **Sho**es NOTE:
consonants following 出 shu are doubled, or
"hardened" (see reference # 11 for a discussion
of 立, another kanji with this characteristic);
in the case of 出張 shutchou, we use "tc" to
denote a hard consonant, but shutchou could
also be spelled "shucchou" in romaji

Moon

148. 月

PRONUNCIATIONS: tsuki, getsu, gatsu

MEANINGS: moon EXAMPLES: 毎月

maitsuki = every month; 月曜日 getsuyoubi

= Monday; 二月 nigatsu = February

DESCRIPTION: 日 hi (day, or sun, # 32) with
two asymmetrical legs CUES: I packed a

Tsuitcase for the King to take to the 月 **tsuki**
(moon), where he hopes to Get Super rich by
Gathering Soot from moon volcanoes

149. 勝

PRONUNCIATIONS: shou, ka*tsu, ma*saru

MEANINGS: to win, victory

EXAMPLES: 優勝 yuushou = victory,

championship; 勝つ katsu = to win; 勝る

masaru = to outclass, to outdo

DESCRIPTION: on the left, 月 tsuki (moon,
148); on the upper right, a bonfire; on the

lower right, 力 chikara (force, # 107)

CUES: in order to put on a Show and achieve a

優勝 yuu**shou** (victory), the 月 (moon)

Shone its light with 力 (force) to ignite this

bonfire, and it 勝った **ka**tta (won) a
Catalogue and a Massage

150. 服

PRONUNCIATION: fuku MEANING: clothes

EXAMPLE: 洋服 youfuku = Western clothes

DESCRIPTION: on the left, 月 tsuki (moon,
148); on the right, a dressing room, with a
hook for hanging clothes; inside the dressing
room, 又 mata ("again," # 24), but this
resembles a simple dressing table

CUE: I will try on some 洋服 you**fuku**

(Western clothes) by the light of the 月

(moon) in **Fuku**oka, near a 又 (table), in a
dressing room with a clothes hook

COMPARE: 報(告) houkoku = report, # 386

151. 育

PRONUNCIATIONS: soda*teru, iku

MEANING: to bring up or raise a child

EXAMPLES: 育てる sodateru = to raise;

教育 kyouiku = education DESCRIPTION:
at the top, a pedaling leg, wearing a pointy hat;
at the bottom, 月 tsuki (moon, # 148)

CUES: a cyclist with a pointy hat sits on the
月 (moon), thinking that giving **soda** is

terrible when one 育てる **soda**teru (raises) a child, and that a child's 教育 kyou**iku** (education) should be mostly about **Ear Cooties**

152. 背

PRONUNCIATIONS: hai, se **MEANINGS:** back, height **EXAMPLES:** 背景 haikei = background, setting; 背が高い se ga takai = the height is tall; 背中 senaka = the back of the body **DESCRIPTION:** 北 kita (north, # 373) on top of a 月 tsuki (moon, # 148), but 北 could be two people sitting back-to-back, comparing their sitting heights **CUES:** in a **High** place on the 北 (north) side of the 月 (moon), two **S**ecretaries sit back-to-back and discover that they are both the same 背 **se** (height)

COMPARE: 皆 mina = all, everyone, # 597

153. 胃

PRONUNCIATION: i **MEANING:** stomach **EXAMPLES:** 胃 i = stomach; 胃癌 igan = stomach cancer **DESCRIPTION:** at the top, a 田(んぼ) tanbo (rice paddy, # 68); at the bottom, 月 tsuki (moon, # 148) **CUE:** in Iraq, a man in a 田 (rice paddy) rubs his 胃 **i** (stomach) while gazing at the 月 (moon)

154. 明

PRONUNCIATIONS: aka, ashi*ta, aki*raka, a*su, mei, myou*nichi **MEANINGS:** bright, obvious, tomorrow **EXAMPLES:** 明るい akarui = bright, cheerful; 明日 ashita = tomorrow; 明らかな akiraka na = obvious; 明日 asu = tomorrow; 明ける akeru = to end or expire, or to start; 説明 setsumei = explanation; 明日 myounichi = tomorrow; 明後日 myougonichi = the day after tomorrow; 明後日 asatte = the day after

tomorrow, usually written あさって **DESCRIPTION:** on the left, 日 hi (day, or sun, # 32); on the right, 月 tsuki (moon, # 148) **NOTE:** ashita, asu and myounichi are all spelled 明日, and they all have the same meaning; also, asatte and myougonichi are both spelled 明後日 and have the same meaning **CUES:** when the 日 (sun) and 月 (moon) shine together, the sky is 明るい **aka**rui (bright), and we can expect an 明るい **aka**rui (cheerful) person to come to the **Aca**demy 明日 **ashi**ta (tomorrow) and give an **Ashy** ashtray, **A Key** and some **Anchovies** to **May** the cat, who will **Meow** in response

155. 青

PRONUNCIATIONS: ao*i, sei **MEANINGS:** blue, fresh **EXAMPLES:** 青い aoi = blue; 青年 seinen = young man **DESCRIPTION:** at the top, compared to 土 tsuchi (dirt, # 59), this radical has an extra horizontal line, where an owl might perch; at the bottom, 月 tsuki (moon, # 148) **CUES:** an **O**wl perched on top of the 月 (moon) sees an 青い **ao**i (blue) sky and feels **Safe COMPARE:** 情(報) jouhou = information, news, # 156; 表 omote = surface, front, outside, # 582

156. 情

PRONUNCIATIONS: nasa*kenai, jou **MEANINGS:** emotion, feelings **EXAMPLES:** 情けない nasakenai = disappointing, regrettable; 愛情 aijou = love; 情報 jouhou = information, news **DESCRIPTION:** on the left, an erect astronaut from NASA named Joan of Arc; on the right 青(い) aoi (blue, # 155) **CUES:** NASA sent Joan the astronaut some 情けない **nasa**kenai (regrettable) 情報 **jou**hou (information), and she is feeling 青 (blue)

157. 前

PRONUNCIATIONS: mae, zen MEANINGS: front, before EXAMPLES: 二年前 ninen mae = 2 years ago; 駅前 eki mae = in front of the station; 午前九時 gozen kuji = 9:00 a.m. DESCRIPTION: on the top, an upside-down bench, with its legs sticking up; on the lower left, 月 tsuki (moon, # 148); on the lower right, the katakana character リ Ri, who is a maestro

CUES: a 月 (moon) and リ Ri the **Mae**stro are carrying a bench to a **Zen** temple, but the 月 is standing 前 **mae** (in front of) リ and will get to the temple 前 **mae** (before) リ

158. 消

PRONUNCIATIONS: ke*su, ki*eru
MEANINGS: to disappear, to erase

EXAMPLES: 消す kesu = to erase, turn off, extinguish, wipe out; 消える kieru = to go out (referring to, e.g., a fire) DESCRIPTION: on the left, a water radical (see # 12); on the right, 3 prongs, which resemble a switch, on 月 tsuki (moon, # 148) CUES: **Ke**n lives on the 月 (moon), where there is a 3-pronged switch that can 消す **ke**su (turn off) the water flow to Barbie, who lives in **Kie**v

COMPARE: 決(して) kesshite = never, # 180

159. 散

PRONUNCIATIONS: chi*ru, san*po

MEANING: to disperse EXAMPLES: 散る chiru = to disperse or scatter; 散歩 sanpo = a walk DESCRIPTION: on the upper left, some bushes; on the lower left, 月 tsuki (moon, # 148); on the right, a cheerful guy carrying a crutch over his head
CUES: a **Chee**rful disabled guy is going for a 散歩 **san**po (walk) in **San**d near some bushes by the light of the 月 (moon)

Evening

160. 夕

PRONUNCIATION: yuu MEANING: evening EXAMPLES: 夕方 yuugata = evening; 夕べ yuube = last night DESCRIPTION: this is a half 月 tsuki (moon, # 148), or a lesser moon, shining in the Yukon

CUE: a half 月 (moon) shines above the **Yu**kon during the 夕方 **yuu**gata (evening)

161. 多

PRONUNCIATIONS: oo*i, ta*bun

MEANING: many EXAMPLES: 多い ooi = a lot; 多分 tabun = probably

DESCRIPTION: two 夕 yuu (lesser moons, # 160) CUES: there are 多い **oo**i (many) Old Irregular 夕 (lesser moons) orbiting Jupiter, and I saw them on my **Ta**blet computer

162. 名

PRONUNCIATIONS: na*mae, mei, myou*ji

MEANING: name EXAMPLES: 名前 namae = name; 有名 yuumei = famous; 名字 myouji = family name DESCRIPTION: on the upper left, 夕 yuu (lesser moon, # 160); on the lower right, 口 kuchi (mouth, # 426), which resembles a card with names written on it CUES: **Na**poleon's maestro (teacher, in Spanish) called a **Ma**id into a **Mee**ting in **Yo**semite and wrote her 名前 **na**mae (name) on a card, which he hung from a 有名 yuu**mei** (famous) 夕 (lesser moon)

163. 外

PRONUNCIATIONS: soto, hoka, gai, hazu*su, ge*ka **MEANING:** outside **EXAMPLES:** 外 soto = outside; 外に hoka ni = besides, in addition; 外人 gaijin = foreigner; 外す hazusu = to remove; 外科 geka = surgery (medical specialty) **NOTE:** both soto and hoka are spelled 外 **DESCRIPTION:** on the left, 夕 yuu (evening, # 160); on the right, a radical that resembles the katakana character 卜 to, which reminds us of tomatoes **CUES:** in order to get tomatoes in the 夕 (evening), Justice **So**tomayor has to go 外 **soto** (outside) the **Hock**ey Arena and find a **Gui**de, who wears a **Ha**t and a **Zoo**t suit, and looks **Gay** **COMPARE:** 他(の) hoka no = another (undefined) object, # 505

164. 死

PRONUNCIATION: shi*nu, ji **MEANINGS:** to die, death **EXAMPLES:** 死ぬ shinu = to die; 死亡 shibou = death; 早死に hayajini = early death, dying young **DESCRIPTION:** at the top, a lid which could be a sheet; on the left, 夕 yuu (evening, # 160); on the right, the katakana character ヒ hi, which resembles a body curled up in a casket **CUE:** if a person 死ぬ **shi**nu (dies) in the 夕 (evening), they put the body under a **Shee**t and place it in a **Jee**p

165. 夢

PRONUNCIATIONS: yume, mu **MEANING:** dream **EXAMPLES:** 夢 yume = dream; 悪夢 akumu = nightmare **DESCRIPTION:** at the top, a plant radical (see # 43); in the middle, three eyes; at the bottom, 夕 yuu (evening, # 160), which helps us to pronounce this **CUES:** my 夢 **yume** (dreams) come from a third eye in my forehead and concern plants

from **U**tah and **Me**xico that bloom in the 夕 (evening) when the **Moo**n is shining

Master

166. 主

PRONUNCIATIONS: shu, omo, nushi, zu **MEANINGS:** lord, master, proprietor, main **EXAMPLES:** 主人 shujin = husband, master, landlord, landlady, proprietor, host or hostess; 主婦 shufu = housewife; 主な omo na = main, chief; 地主 jinushi = land owner; 坊主 bouzu = Buddhist monk **DESCRIPTION:** a man with broad shoulders, two arms and two legs, wearing a tiny cap **CUES:** the 主人 **shu**jin (master) wears a little cap, and he has nice **Sho**es; he uses an **O**ld **Mo**bile phone, his house has **New Shi**ngles, and he likes to visit the **Zoo** **COMPARE:** 玉 tama = ball, jewel, # 169; 王 ou = king, not included in this catalogue

167. 住

PRONUNCIATIONS: juu, su*mu **MEANING:** to reside **EXAMPLES:** 住所 juusho = address; 住む sumu = to reside **DESCRIPTION:** on the left, a man with a slanted hat; on the right, 主 shu (master, # 166) **CUES:** a man with a slanted hat, who drinks a lot of **Ju**ice and graduated **Su**mma cum laude, stands with his 主 (master) outside a house where they both 住む **su**mu (reside) **COMPARE:** 主任 shunin = foreman, # 166 and # 483; 注(意) chuui = caution, # 168

168. 注

PRONUNCIATIONS: chuu, soso*gu
MEANINGS: to pour carefully, to pay attention EXAMPLES: 注文する chuumon suru = to order; 注意する chuui suru = to warn; 注ぐ sosogu = to pour DESCRIPTION: on the left, a water radical (see # 12); on the right, 主 shu (master, # 166) CUES: while **Chew**ing gum, the 主 (master) 注ぐ <u>**soso**gu</u> (pours) water and often spills it, causing the carpet to become **So Soggy**, so 注意してください <u>**chuu**i</u> shite kudasai (please be careful) COMPARE: 住(む) sumu = to reside, # 167

169. 玉

PRONUNCIATIONS: dama, tama
MEANINGS: a round object, a jewel
EXAMPLES: 10 円玉 juuen dama = 10 yen coin; 玉 tama = ball, jewel; 玉ねぎ tamanegi = onion DESCRIPTION: reportedly this represents a vertical string of three jewels, but apparently one fell off the string CUES: people from **Dama**scus who like **Tama**les sometimes pay for them with 玉 <u>**tama**</u> (jewels) COMPARE: 主(人) shujin = husband, landlord, landlady, # 166; 国 kuni = country, # 170; 王 ou = king, not included in this catalogue

170. 国

PRONUNCIATIONS: kuni, koku, goku
MEANINGS: country EXAMPLES: 国 kuni = country; 韓国 kankoku = South Korea; 中国 chuugoku = China DESCRIPTION: a 玉 tama (jewel, # 169) in a box CUES: my 国 <u>**kuni**</u> (country) is like a 玉 (jewel) in a box, and it's full of **Cunn**ing people who drink a lot of **Coke** and **Gol**d **Kool**-Aid
COMPARE: (公)園 kouen = park, # 279; 困 (る) komaru = to be inconvenienced, # 280

Above & Below

171. 上

PRONUNCIATIONS: ue, a, jou, uwa*gi, nobo*ru MEANINGS: up, above, to raise, to give EXAMPLES: 上 ue = up; 上げる ageru = to give, or to raise something up; 上手 jouzu = skillful; 上着 uwagi = outer garment; 上る noboru = to go up

DESCRIPTION: compared to 土 tsuchi (dirt, # 59), 上 is asymmetrical and looks like a waiter holding a tray CUES: our **Ue**itaa (waiters) live 上 <u>**ue**</u> (above) the ground, from which they 上る <u>**nobo**ru</u> (rise) asymmetrically; working like **A**nts, they tell **J**okes, they sleep in **U**ber **Wag**ons, and **Nobo**dy can match them COMPARE: 登(る) noboru = to climb, # 297; 下 shita = below, # 172; 止(める) tomeru = to stop, transitive, # 173

172. 下

PRONUNCIATIONS: shita, sa*geru, ge, kuda, o*rosu, ka, he*ta MEANINGS: down, below, to hang down, to lower EXAMPLES: 下着 shitagi = undergarment; 下げる sageru = to lower, transitive, or to hang down; 下がる sagaru = to hang, intransitive; to step back, or go down; 下品な gehin na = vulgar; 下る kudaru = to descend; 下さる kudasaru = to give to me; 下ろす orosu = to withdraw money; 地下鉄 chikatetsu = subway; 下手 heta = unskillful DESCRIPTION: compared to 不 fu (negation, # 176), 下 is asymmetrical CUES: **Shi**gella live in **Tar**balls 下 <u>**shita**</u> (below) ground, from which they 下る <u>**kuda**ru</u> (descend) asymmetrically; when their spirits **Sag**, they **Get** assistance from barra**Cuda**s, who **O**blige them to **Ca**ll 911 for serious problems but **He**lp them with minor issues
COMPARE: 上 ue = above, # 171

173. 止

PRONUNCIATIONS: to, ya*meru, shi, do
MEANING: to stop **EXAMPLES:** 止まる
tomaru = to stop, intransitive; 止める
tomeru = to stop, transitive; 止める yameru
= to stop doing something, to give up; 中止
する chuushi suru = to cancel; 通行止め
tsuukoudome = road closed **NOTE:** tomeru
and yameru are both spelled 止める
DESCRIPTION: this resembles a barrier built
to keep traffic out of a farm
CUES: we put up a barrier so that cars will
止まる **to**maru (stop) before they run into
our **To**mato and **Ya**m farm; **Shee**p also cannot
enter, due to a **Do**mestic dispute
COMPARE: 正(しい) tadashii = correct,
174 ; 上(げる) ageru = to give to someone
of equal or higher status, # 171; 辞(める)
yameru = to resign a position, # 387

174. 正

PRONUNCIATIONS: tada*shii, shou*jiki, sei,
masa **MEANING:** correct **EXAMPLES:**
正しい tadashii = correct; 正直な
shoujiki na = honest; 正解 seikai = correct
answer; 正に masa ni = exactly, really
DESCRIPTION: 止(まる) tomaru (to stop,
173), with a cap added at the top
CUES: if a car 止 (stops) at the barrier and
everything is 正しい **tada**shii (correct), **T**ad
Dashes up and places a cap on top of the
barrier, **Show**ing that it is **Sa**fe for the car to
proceed to the **Massa**ge parlor

175. 政

PRONUNCIATION: sei **MEANINGS:** politics,
government **EXAMPLES:** 政治 seiji =
politics, government; 政治家 seijika =
politician **DESCRIPTION:** on the left,
正(しい) tadashii (correct, # 174); on the
right, a disabled person holding a crutch
CUE: 政治家 **sei**jika (politicans) should
pass 正 (correct) laws to encourage the
development of **Sa**fe **Jee**ps for disabled people,
like this person on the right who is holding a
crutch

176. 不

PRONUNCIATIONS: bu, fu **MEANING:**
negation **EXAMPLES:** 運動不足
undoubusoku = not enough exercise; 不便
fuben = inconvenient; 不足 fusoku =
insufficiency **DESCRIPTION:** compared to
下 shita (below, # 172), 不 descends into the
ground symmetrically, like a carrot divided
into three parts **CUES:** while walking around
in my **Boo**ts, I come across this symmetrical
three-part carrot, but it's 不足 **fu**soku
(insufficient) as a **Foo**d source

Knee

177. 年

PRONUNCIATIONS: nen, toshi **MEANING:**
year **EXAMPLES:** 三年 sannen = three
years; 今年 kotoshi = this year
DESCRIPTION: a disabled negative nephew is
sitting facing left, with a knee protruding and a
crutch over his head **CUES:** my **N**egative
Nephew is disabled and has been sitting here
for a 年 **nen** (year), playing with his **T**oy
Sheep and waiting for help
COMPARE: 念 nen = thought, # 314

178. 降

PRONUNCIATIONS: o*riru, fu*ru, kou, bu
MEANINGS: to precipitate, to step down
EXAMPLES: 降りる oriru = to get off a train etc.; 降る furu = to rain or snow; 下降 kakou = descent; 小降り koburi = light rain **DESCRIPTION:** on the left, ß beta, a character from the Greek alphabet; on the upper right, a dancer with a ponytail; on the lower right, a character similar to 年 nen (year, # 177), sitting facing left, with a knee protruding, but without a crutch

CUES: the dancer with a ponytail 降りる oriru (gets off) the Greek ship and leaps over the sitting figure to get some **O**reos, but then the rain 降る furu (precipitates) **F**uriously, she gets **C**old, and she puts on her **B**oots

179. 五

PRONUNCIATIONS: go, itsu*tsu **MEANING:** five **EXAMPLES:** 五人 gonin = 5 people; 五つ itsutsu = 5 items **DESCRIPTION:** unlike 年 nen (year, # 177) and 降(る) furu (to precipitate, # 178), the knee in 五 faces to the right; 五 contains five straight lines but is written with four strokes; it resembles a golfer staring down a fairway **CUES:** 五 go (five) **Go**lfers wearing **I**talian **Su**its are staring down a fairway

180. 決

PRONUNCIATIONS: ki, ketsu, ke*sshite
MEANINGS: to decide, to do decisively
EXAMPLES: 決める kimeru = to decide or arrange; 決まる kimaru = to be decided or arranged; 解決 kaiketsu = settlement, resolution, solution; 決して kesshite = never **DESCRIPTION:** on the left, a water radical (see # 12); on the right, compared to the left-facing knees in 年 nen (year, # 177) and 降(る) furu (to precipitate, # 178), this knee is facing right and is mounted on a stand, resembling a tiller, for steering a boat **CUES:** the pilot, who is wearing a **Ki**mono, 決める kimeru (decides) to turn the boat in the water, and he moves the tiller before pouring from a **Ket**tle into his **So**up, which he 決して kesshite (never) shares with **Ke**n and Barbie **COMPARE:** 消(す) kesu = to erase, turn off, # 158

181. 片

PRONUNCIATIONS: kata*zukeru, pen, hen
MEANINGS: one side, piece **EXAMPLES:** 片方 katahou = one side, the other side, one of a pair; 片手 katate = one hand or arm; 片付ける katazukeru = to put in order; 一片 ippen = a slice or piece; 破片 hahen = shard, fragment **DESCRIPTION:** reportedly this kanji depicts a tree divided in half vertically, so that only the roots and branches on the right side remain **CUES:** a person kneeling on one knee holds out a tray with a **Cata**logue of **Pen**s on it, but a **Hen** that is watching can only see 片方 katahou (one side) of it **COMPARE:** 方 kata = method, or honorable person, # 114; 方(がいい) hou ga ii = it would be better, # 114

Child

182. 子

PRONUNCIATIONS: su, ko, shi **MEANING:** child **EXAMPLES:** 様子 yousu = condition; 子供 kodomo = child; 男子 danshi = boy **DESCRIPTION:** a thin cold child, with a flat head

CUES: this thin 子 ko (child) from **Su**dan gets **C**old at night and sleeps under a **Shee**pskin **COMPARE:** 字 ji = character, # 183

183. 字

PRONUNCIATION: ji **MEANING:** character
EXAMPLE: 漢字 kanji = kanji
DESCRIPTION: at the top, a roof with a character protruding from it; at the bottom, 子 ko (child, # 182)
CUE: this 子 (child), whose name is **Jimmy Carter**, wrote a 字 **ji** (character) on the roof
COMPARE: 学 gaku = learning, # 184

184. 学

PRONUNCIATIONS: gaku, ga, mana*bu
MEANINGS: study, learning, science
EXAMPLES: 学のある人 gaku no aru hito = a learned person; 学校 gakkou = school; 学ぶ manabu = to learn **DESCRIPTION:** at the top, a roof with three characters protruding from it; at the bottom, 子 ko (child, # 182)
CUES: this **Gawk**y **U**ruguayan 子 (child) had the **Ga**ll to write three characters on the roof of the 学校 **ga**kkou (school) after he **Mana**ged to 学ぶ **mana**bu (learn) them
COMPARE: 字 ji = character, # 183

185. 厚

PRONUNCIATIONS: atsu*i, kou **MEANING:** thick **EXAMPLES:** 厚い atsui = thick; 濃厚 noukou = density, concentration
DESCRIPTION: on the left, a lean-to belonging to Superman; under the lean-to, 日 hi (sun, # 32), which looks like a heavy weight; under 日 hi, 子 ko (child, # 182)
CUES: this poor 子 (child) is getting crushed under a heavy weight **At Su**perman's lean-to, and he will likely become somewhat 厚い **atsu**i (thick, i.e., wide) as a result, but he will just have to **Co**pe with that
COMPARE: 暑(い) atsui = hot atmosphere, # 278; 熱(い) atsui = hot objects, # 65

186. 乳

PRONUNCIATIONS: nyuu, chichi
MEANING: milk **EXAMPLES:** 牛乳 gyuunyuu = cow's milk; 乳 chichi = milk
DESCRIPTION: on the upper left, a few drops of milk; on the lower left, a 子 ko (child, # 182); on the right, a breast
CUES: a 子 (child) at a mother's breast, drinking 乳 **nyuu** (milk) in **Nyuu**yooku (New York), while **Chichi** (father) looks on
COMPARE: 父 chichi = father, # 143

187. 教

PRONUNCIATIONS: oshi*eru, kyou, oso*waru **MEANING:** to teach **EXAMPLES:** 教える oshieru = to teach; 教室 kyoushitsu = classroom; 教わる osowaru = to be taught **DESCRIPTION:** this is a situation that concerns OSHA (the Occupational Safety and Health Administration): on the upper left, 土 tsuchi (dirt, # 59); below that, a pair of scissors; below the scissors, 子 ko (children, # 182); on the right, a person carrying a crutch
CUES: **OSHA I**nforms and 教える **oshi**eru (teaches) children and disabled people in **Kyou**to that they should stay out of the 土 (dirt), not play with scisssors, and not use **O**ld **Soy** sauce

Big

188. 大

PRONUNCIATIONS: tai, oo, dai, oto*na
MEANING: big **EXAMPLES:** 大変 taihen = terrible; 大きい ookii = big; 大学 daigaku = university; 大人 otona = adult
DESCRIPTION: 大 is a big character expanding in all directions, who is very tired
CUES: this 大きい **oo**kii (big) man is **T**ired and **O**verweight, and he lives on a **D**iet of **O**ld **T**omatoes

189. 天

PRONUNCIATIONS: ama, ten
MEANINGS: sky, heavens **EXAMPLES:**
天の川 ama no gawa = Milky Way; 天国
tengoku = heaven; 天気 tenki = weather
DESCRIPTION: compared to 大(きい) ookii
(big, # 188), this kanji has a tent above it
CUES: in the **Ama**zon, the 天 **ama** (sky) is
like a **Ten**t over a 大 (big) forest

190. 犬

PRONUNCIATIONS: inu, ken **MEANING:**
dog **EXAMPLES:** 犬 inu = dog; 番犬
banken = watchdog **DESCRIPTION:** 大(き
い) ookii (big, # 188), with a ball above its
right arm **CUES:** an 犬 **inu** (dog), which is
大 (big) and belongs to the **Inu**it tribe, chases
a ball that **Ken** threw to Barbie

191. 太

PRONUNCIATIONS: futo*ru, buto[1], tai*you
MEANINGS: to get fat, big, thick
EXAMPLES: 太る futoru = to get fat; 小太
り kobutori = plump; 太陽 taiyou = the sun
DESCRIPTION: 大(きい) ookii (big, # 188),
with a ball near its left leg
CUES: since this 大 (big) person 太る
futoru (gets fat), to the point that he has to
sleep on a **Futo**n with Ruth, he can only chase
balls near the floor, and he **Ti**res easily

192. 喫

PRONUNCIATION: kitsu*en, ki*ssaten
MEANING: to consume or smoke
EXAMPLES: 喫煙 kitsuen = smoking;
喫茶店 kissaten = coffee house
DESCRIPTION: at the top left, 口 kuchi
(mouth, # 426), suggesting smoking; in the
upper center, 主 shu (master, # 166); on the
upper right, 刀 katana (sword, # 102); at the
bottom, 大(きい) ookii (big, # 188)

CUES: I feel like a 大 (big) 主 (master) when
I make cigarettes using a **Kit** that I got from
Superman, and then I cut them in the **Ki**tchen
with this 刀 (sword), before smoking them
through my 口 (mouth) at a 喫茶店
kissaten (coffee shop)

193. 咲

PRONUNCIATION: sa*ku, za **MEANING:** to
blossom or bloom **EXAMPLES:** 咲く saku
= to blossom or bloom; 早咲き hayazaki =
early blooming **DESCRIPTION:** on the left,
口 kuchi (mouth, # 426); on the right, 大(き
い) ookii (big, # 188), with several extra lines
added near the top, suggesting blossoms
CUE: the 大 (big) tree 咲く **sa**ku (blossoms),
and we keep the flowers in a **Sack**; **Z**ach
makes tea from the blossoms, and we savor it
in our 口 (mouths) **COMPARE:** 呼(ぶ)
yobu = to call out, to summon, # 428

194. 狭

PRONUNCIATION: sema*i **MEANING:**
narrow **EXAMPLE:** 狭い semai = narrow,
cramped **DESCRIPTION:** on the left, a person
contorting her body; on the right, 大(きい)
ookii (big, # 188) with four extra arms,
suggesting a very big person **CUE:** inside a
Semi-truck, two people are trying to pass each
other in a 狭い **sema**i (narrow) space; the
lady on the left contorts her body in order to
accommodate the extremely 大 (big) person
on the right **COMPARE:** 猫 neko = cat, # 72

195. 実

PRONUNCIATIONS: jitsu, ji, mi, mino*ru
MEANINGS: real, fruit **EXAMPLES:** 実は
jitsu wa = as a matter of fact; 実行 jikkou =
practice, action, deed, performance, implementation; 木の実 kinomi = nut, fruit,
berry; 実る minoru = to bear fruit or ripen
DESCRIPTION: at the top, a roof; in the

middle, 士 shi (man, warrior, # 66); at the bottom, 大(きい) ookii (big, # 188)

CUES: this 大 (big) 士 (man) is a **Jittery Superstar** with a **Jeep** who raises 実の **jitsu** no (real) 木の実 kino**mi** (nuts) and **Meat** under the roof of his castle and shares them with his **Mino**taur

196. 険

PRONUNCIATIONS: kewa*shii, ken MEANINGS: steep, danger EXAMPLES: 険しい kewashii = steep; 危険 kiken = danger; 保険 hoken = insurance

DESCRIPTION: on the left, ß from the Greek alphabet; at the top right, a steep roof; under the roof, 大(きい) ookii (big, # 188), intersected by a horizontal keg, with a handle at the top CUES: this is a laundromat with a horizontally placed **Keg** stuck inside a 大 (big) **Wa**shing machine; the roof is too 険し い **kewa**shii (steep) to allow the Greek guy named **Ken** to climb the roof, grab the handle and fix the problem for Barbie

197. 漢

PRONUNCIATION: kan*ji MEANINGS: Chinese EXAMPLE: 漢字 kanji = Chinese character DESCRIPTION: on the left, a water radical (see # 12); at the upper right, a plant radical (see # 43); at the middle right, a pair of reading glasses; at the bottom right, 大(き い) ookii (big, # 188), with an extra pair of arms CUE: Chinese people come from over the water, they are fond of plants, they often wear glasses, they have 大 (big) hearts, and they print 漢字 **kan**ji (Chinese characters) on their **Can**dy wrappers COMPARE: 難(し い) muzukashii = difficult, # 198

198. 難

PRONUNCIATIONS: nan, muzuka*shii, gato, gata, niku*i MEANING: difficulty EXAMPLES: 困難 kon'nan = difficulty; 難しい muzukashii = difficult; 有難う arigatou = thank you; 有難い arigatai = grateful, but this is usually written ありがたい; 難い nikui = difficult to do, e.g., 読み難い yominikui = difficult to read, but this is usually written 読みにくい DESCRIPTION: at the upper left, a plant radical (see # 43); at the middle left, a pair of reading glasses; at the lower left, 大(きい) ookii (big, # 188), with an extra pair of arms; on the right, a cage CUES: **Nan**cy is a person with a 大 (big) heart who wears glasses and plant material on her head and wants to help the cats in this cage, which is 難しい **muzuka**shii (difficult) to penetrate; she wants to put a **Muzzle** on **Zu**ckerberg's **Cat**, which is inside the cage, along with another **Gato** (male cat, in Spanish), a **Gata** (female cat, in Spanish), and **Nick** the **Kool**-Aid vendor COMPARE: 漢(字) kanji = Chinese character, # 197

199. 笑

PRONUNCIATIONS: wara*u, e*gao, shou MEANINGS: to smile or laugh EXAMPLES: 笑う warau = to laugh; 笑顔 egao = smiling face; 爆笑 bakushou = burst of laughter DESCRIPTION: at the top, short 竹 take (bamboo, # 134) which resemble clamps; at the bottom, 大(きい) ookii (big, # 188), wearing a flat hat CUES: this 大 (big) **Warrior** named **Ra**ul Castro has bamboo clamps pinned to his eyebrows, and they made me 笑う **wara**u (laugh) during his **Excellent Show** COMPARE: 第 dai = order, # 530; 符 pu = tag, # 133

Cage

200. 曜

PRONUNCIATION: you*bi **MEANING:** day of the week **EXAMPLE:** 日曜日 nichiyoubi = Sunday **DESCRIPTION:** on the left, a 日 hi (sun, # 32) shining in Yosemite; on the upper right, feathers, suggesting a bird; on the lower right, a cage **CUE:** every 曜日 **you**bi (day of the week) in **Yo**semite, the 日 (sun) shines on a bird in a cage
COMPARE: 濯 taku = laundry, # 201

201. 濯

PRONUNCIATION: taku **MEANINGS:** laundry, wash **EXAMPLE:** 洗濯 sentaku = laundry **DESCRIPTION:** on the left, a water radical (see # 12); on the upper right, feathers, suggesting a bird; on the lower right, a cage **CUE:** using **Ta**p water and **Kool**-Aid, we wash our bird in a cage whenever we do the 洗濯 sen**taku** (laundry)
COMPARE: 曜 you = day of the week, # 200

202. 集

PRONUNCIATIONS: atsu, shuu*gou, tsudo*u **MEANINGS:** to collect, gather, congregate **EXAMPLES:** 集める atsumeru = to collect, transitive; 集まる atsumaru = to congregate, intransitive; 集合 shuugou = gathering, assembly, meeting; 集う tsudou = to gather or meet **DESCRIPTION:** at the top, a cage; at the bottom, 木 ki (tree, # 118)
CUES: a cage has been placed in a 木 (tree) to 集める **atsu**meru (collect) **Atsu**i (hot) flying mermaids, who travel without **Shoe**s and carry **Tsui**tcases full of **Dough**

203. 進

PRONUNCIATIONS: susu, susumu, shin **MEANING:** to move forward **EXAMPLES:** 進む susumu = to advance, make progress; 進める susumeru = to advance or promote, transitive; 進 Susumu = a boy's given name; 進出する shinshutsu suru = to advance or expand **DESCRIPTION:** at the left and the bottom, a snail; at the right, riding on the snail, a cage **CUES:** **Su**perman's **Su**mmer **Mu**sic program is like this cage on a snail which 進む **susu**mu (advances) slowly and collects donations for a **Shin**tou shrine
COMPARE: 勧(める) susumeru = to advise, not included in this catalogue

204. 準

PRONUNCIATION: jun*bi **MEANINGS:** standard, preparation **EXAMPLE:** 準備 junbi = preparation **DESCRIPTION:** at the upper left, a water radical (see # 12); at the upper right, a cage, which resembles a fish trap; at the bottom 十 juu (ten, # 18) **CUE:** 十 (ten) fishermen are placing their fish traps in water as 準備 **jun**bi (preparation) for **Jun**gle fishing

Cow

205. 牛

PRONUNCIATIONS: gyuu, ushi **MEANING:** cow **EXAMPLES:** 牛肉 gyuuniku = beef; 牛 ushi = cow **DESCRIPTION:** a depiction of the front half of a cow, seen from above; at the top, the head; below that, the horns, with an enlarged horn on the left; below that, the front legs and the back of the cow **CUES:** a **Gua**temalan **You**th, who is an **Us**her at an Indian theatre, has an 牛 **ushi** (cow) with one horn that is bigger than the other
COMPARE: 午 go = noon, # 207

206. 失

PRONUNCIATIONS: shitsu, ushina*u, shi*ppai **MEANINGS:** to lose; to slip away **EXAMPLES:** 失礼 shitsurei = discourtesy; 失業者 shitsugyousha = unemployed people; 失う ushinau = to lose; 失敗する shippai suru = to fail

DESCRIPTION: a fusion between 牛 ushi (cow, # 205) and 大(きい) ookii (big, # 188) CUES: our 大 (big) ushi (cow) always steps on our **Sheets**, and she is 失礼 **shitsu**rei (rude), but we have an **Ushi Now**, and also a **Shee**p, and we don't want to 失う **ushina**u (lose) them

207. 午
PRONUNCIATION: go MEANING: noon
EXAMPLES: 午前 gozen = in the morning; 午後 gogo = in the afternoon
DESCRIPTION: compared to 牛 ushi (cow, # 205), this cow is missing her head
CUE: the cow hides her head at 午 **go** (noon), when the **Go**lden sun shines brightest
COMPARE: 昼 hiru = noon, # 49

208. 生
PRONUNCIATIONS: i*kiru, u*mareru, sei, shou, jou, nama, ha*eru MEANINGS: to be born, to live EXAMPLES: 生きる ikiru = to live; 生まれる umareru = to be born; 先生 sensei = teacher; 一生 isshou = a lifetime; 誕生日 tanjoubi = birthday; 生 nama = raw; 生える haeru = to grow or sprout DESCRIPTION: at the top, 牛 ushi (cow, # 205); at the bottom, 土 tsuchi (dirt, # 59) CUES: after this 牛 (cow) 生まれる **u**mareru (is born), it rises out of the 土 (dirt), and it 生きる **i**kiru (lives), befriending **Ea**gles, driving for Uber, **Sa**ving its money, and going to **Sho**ws with **Joe Nama**th and his **Hac**ker friends
COMPARE: 性 sei = gender, # 209

209. 性
PRONUNCIATIONS: sei, shou MEANINGS: innate nature, sex, gender EXAMPLES: 性 sei = gender; 男性 dansei = man, male;

女性 josei = woman, female; 性格 seikaku = personality, character; 性能 seinou = efficiency; 相性 aishou = affinity, compatibility DESCRIPTION: on the left, an erect radical which could be a chromosome; on the right, 生(まれる) umareru (to be born, # 208) CUES: scientists **Say** that chromosomes determine one's 性 **sei** (gender) at the time one 生 (is born), and they can **Show** us these chromosomes under a microscope
COMPARE: (先)生 sensei = teacher, # 208

210. 産
PRONUNCIATIONS: san, u*mu, yage
MEANINGS: to give birth, to produce
EXAMPLES: 産業 sangyou = industry; 産む umu = to give birth, produce, lay an egg; お土産 omiyage = souvenir
DESCRIPTION: at the top, a bell resting on a lean-to, which is a sanitarium; inside the lean-to, 生(きる) ikiru (to live, # 208)
CUES: a **San**itarium with a bell on the roof, ringing to announce that medical researchers 生 (live) inside and suggesting that a 産業 **san**gyou (industry) will 産む **u**mu (give birth) to treatments for **Oo**zing wounds, such as **Ya**m and **Ge**kko-based ointments

Plants
211. 花
PRONUNCIATIONS: hana, bana[1], ka
MEANING: flower EXAMPLES: お花見 ohanami = honorable flower viewing; 生け花 ikebana = Japanese flower arrangement; 花粉 kafun = pollen
DESCRIPTION: at the top, a plant radical (see # 43); at the bottom, 化(学) kagaku (chemistry, # 487), which resembles flowers growing asymmetrically
CUES: **Hannah**'s 花 **hana** (flowers) grow asymmetrically on **Ca**bbage plants
COMPARE: 茶 cha = tea, # 212

438

212. 茶

PRONUNCIATIONS: cha, sa **MEANING:** tea
EXAMPLES: お茶 ocha = honorable tea;
喫茶店 kissaten = cafe **DESCRIPTION:** at
the top, a plant radical (see # 43); at the
bottom, a symmetrical bush growing under a
roof **CUES:** Prince **Cha**rles' 茶 **cha** (tea)
bushes grow in small houses and are
symmetrical, since he **Sa**ws them back every
year **COMPARE:** 花 hana = flower, # 211

Temple

213. 寺

PRONUNCIATIONS: tera, dera[1], ji
MEANING: temple **EXAMPLES:** 寺 tera =
temple; 清水寺 Kiyomizudera = a temple
in Kyoto; 寺院 jiin = temple
DESCRIPTION: at the top, 土 tsuchi (dirt,
59), which resembles a cross; at the bottom,
an asymmetrical structure with a terrace at the
top, suggesting that a building has been built
into the side of a hill **CUES:** this 寺 **tera**
(temple), which is built into the side of a hill,
features a cross at the top, as well as a **Terra**ce
and a **Jee**p **COMPARE:** 守(る) mamoru = to
protect, # 214

214. 守

PRONUNCIATIONS: su, mori, mamo*ru
MEANINGS: to protect, guard or defend
EXAMPLES: 留守 rusu = absence from a
house; 子守 komori = nanny, baby sitter;
守る mamoru = to protect **DESCRIPTION:**
at the top, a roof; at the bottom, an asymmetrical support structure, suggesting that a
building has been built into the side of a hill;
compared to 寺 tera (temple, # 213), the cross
at the top has been replaced by a roof **CUES:**
while the monks were 留守 ru**su** (absent),
Superman and **Maure**en took off the cross and
added a stronger roof to 守る **mamo**ru (protect) the temple from falling **Mamm**oths

215. 時

PRONUNCIATIONS: ji, to*kei, toki
MEANING: time
EXAMPLES: 時間 jikan = time; 時計 tokei
= clock, or watch ; 時 toki = time
DESCRIPTION: on the left, 日 hi (sun, # 32);
on the right, 寺 tera (temple, # 213) **CUES:**
the 日 (sun) shines on the 寺 (temple), and
the sundial tells the 時 **toki** (time), which is
一時 ichi**ji** (1:00), suggesting that it's time
to go out to the temple's **Jee**p and smoke
Tobacco; later, I can eat some **To**ast with
Quiche

216. 持

PRONUNCIATIONS: mo*tsu, ji **MEANINGS:**
to hold or possess **EXAMPLES:** 持つ motsu
= to hold or have; 持参する jisan suru = to
bring or take; 支持する shiji suru = to
support **DESCRIPTION:** on the left, a
crawling guy; on the right, 寺 tera (temple,
213) **CUES:** this guy crawls up to one of the
寺 (temple)'s **Mo**ats to say that he 持 **mo**tsu
(has) a **Jee**p that he wants to give to the monks
COMPARE: 待(つ) matsu = to wait, # 217

217. 待

PRONUNCIATIONS: ma*tsu, tai
MEANINGS: to wait or handle **EXAMPLES:**
待つ matsu = to wait; 招待 shoutai =
invitation **DESCRIPTION:** on the left, a man
with two hats; on the right, 寺 tera (temple,
213) **CUES:** a man with two hats 待 **ma**tsu
(waits) at the 寺 (temple) and asks for some
Mats to sit on, since he has traveled a long way
and is **Ti**red **COMPARE:** 持(つ) motsu = to
hold or have, # 216

218. 特

PRONUNCIATION: to, toku **MEANINGS:** special, notable **EXAMPLES:** 特急 tokkyuu = special express train; 特に toku ni = especially; 特別 tokubetsu = special **DESCRIPTION:** on the left, 牛 ushi (cow, # 205); on the right, 寺 tera (temple, # 213) **CUE:** a 特別な **toku**betsu na (special) 牛 (cow) and some **Toa**ds were given to the 寺 (temple) as **Tok**ens of **U**ber friendship

Skeet Shooter

219. 糸

PRONUNCIATION: ito **MEANING:** thread **EXAMPLES:** 糸 ito = thread, yarn; 糸目 itome = stitches **DESCRIPTION:** a gun mounted on a three-legged platform; this resembles a skeet shooter, a machine that launches clay targets into the air for target practice **CUE:** this skeet shooter has been repaired with 糸 **ito** (thread) and is used to fire at mosqu**Ito**s

220. 細

PRONUNCIATIONS: hoso*i, boso, koma*kai, sai **MEANINGS:** slender, detail **EXAMPLES:** 細い hosoi = thin; 心細い kokorobosoi = downhearted; 細かい komakai = minute, small; 詳細 shousai = details **DESCRIPTION:** on the left, a 糸 (skeet shooter, # 219); on the right, 田(んぼ) tanbo (rice paddy, # 68) **CUES:** a **Ho**me-schooled **So**ldier, who is just a **Boy So**ldier, and who is in a **Coma**, is **Si**lent as the 糸 (skeet shooter) shoots at the 細い **hoso**i (narrow) 田 (rice paddy) where he is hiding, leaving trails of smoke which are quite 細い **koma**kai (small)

221. 紙

PRONUNCIATIONS: kami, gami[1], shi **MEANING:** paper **EXAMPLES:** 紙 kami = paper; 折り紙 origami = Japanese paper-folding craft; 紙幣 shihei = paper money **DESCRIPTION:** on the left, a 糸 (skeet shooter, # 219); on the right, a pavilion with a flat roof **CUES:** the 糸 (skeet shooter) is firing skeets onto the flat 紙 **kami** (paper) roof of a pavilion, since it is occupied by **Commie**s (Communists) who are using paper **Shie**lds to protect themselves **COMPARE:** 低(い) hikui = low, # 222; 神 kami = god, # 273; (女)将 okami = landlady, # 374; 髪 kami = hair, # 501

222. 低

PRONUNCIATIONS: hiku*i, tei **MEANINGS:** low, short in stature **EXAMPLES:** 低い hikui = low; 最低 saitei = the worst **DESCRIPTION:** on the left, a guy with a slanted hat; on the right, a pavilion with a flat roof, as seen in 紙 kami (paper, # 221), but this pavilion is elevated on a flat rock **CUES:** the guy with a slanted hat has the **Hiccu**ps and is too 低い **hiku**i (low) to see over the paper pavilion, which has been **T**aped to a flat rock

223. 絵

PRONUNCIATIONS: kai*ga, e **MEANINGS:** picture, drawing, painting **EXAMPLES:** 絵画 kaiga = painting; 絵本 ehon = picture book **DESCRIPTION:** on the left, a 糸 (skeet shooter, # 219); on the right, 会(議) kaigi (meeting, # 293) **CUES:** a 糸 (skeet shooter) will have a meeting with the **Kai**ser to paint his 絵画 **kai**ga (painting), and he will sign his name near the **E**dge of the 絵 **e** (picture) that he paints

224. 経

PRONUNCIATIONS: ta*tsu, kei, he*ru
MEANING: to pass through   **EXAMPLES:**
経つ tatsu = to elapse or pass, referring to
time; 経験 keiken = experience; 経済
keizai = economics; 経る heru = to pass
(time), to go through or by way of
DESCRIPTION: on the left, a 糸 (skeet
shooter, # 219); on the upper right, 又 mata
("again," # 24), but this resembles a dog
groomer's table; on the lower right, 土 tsuchi
(dirt, # 59)
CUES: this 糸 (skeet shooter) gets some
経験 **kei**ken (experience) by shooting toward
a dog groomer's 又 (table) on some 土 (dirt),
where the dogs wear dog **Tags**, sit in **Ca**ges,
and **Help** themselves to dog food
COMPARE: 軽(い) karui = light, # 289

225. 約

PRONUNCIATION: yaku **MEANINGS:**
approximately, to promise, to shorten
EXAMPLES: 予約 yoyaku = reservation;
約束 yakusoku = promise; 契約 keiyaku =
contract; 約一年 yaku ichinen = approximately one year **DESCRIPTION:** on the left, a
糸 (skeet shooter, # 219); on the right, a giant
hook **CUE:** the giant hook, made from a **Yak**
horn, grabs the 糸 (skeet shooter) and binds
him to his 契約 kei**yaku** (contract)
COMPARE: 的 teki = having the
characteristics of, # 45

226. 続

PRONUNCIATIONS: tsuzu, zoku
MEANING: to continue **EXAMPLES:** 続く
tsuzuku = to continue, intransitive; 接続
setsuzoku = connection **DESCRIPTION:** on
the left, a 糸 (skeet shooter, # 219); on the
right, 売(る) uru (to sell, # 425), which

features a 士 shi (man, or warrior, # 66) on a
sturdy platform, who left his tsuitcase back at
the zoo **CUES:** the 糸 (skeet shooter) will
続く **tsuzu**ku (continue) shooting skeets at
the 士 (man) on the platform, and the 士
(man) will 続く **tsuzu**ku (continue) to get
more skeets from his **Tsu**itcase at the **Zoo** and
then sell them to the 糸 (skeet shooter), as
Zombies in **Ku**wait watch on TV
COMPARE: 読(む) yomu = to read, # 432

227. 緑

PRONUNCIATIONS: midori, ryoku*cha
MEANING: green **EXAMPLES:** 緑 midori =
green; 緑茶 ryokucha = green tea
DESCRIPTION: on the left, a 糸 (skeet
shooter, # 219); on the right, a green flag on a
miniature dory floating in 水 mizu (water,
251) **CUES:** the 糸 (skeet shooter) fires at a
緑 **midori** (green) flag on a **M**iniature **D**ory
floating in 水 (water) while his friend Pope
Leo drinks **Ko**ol-Aid and 緑茶 **ryoku**cha
(green tea) **COMPARE:** 線 sen (line), # 228

228. 線

PRONUNCIATION: sen **MEANING:** line
EXAMPLES: 線 sen = line; 二番線
nibansen = Track Number Two; 山手線
yamanote sen = Yamanote line
DESCRIPTION: on the left, a 糸 (skeet
shooter, # 219); on the right, 泉 izumi
(fountain, # 252) which consists of 白(い)
shiroi (white, # 44) above 水 mizu (water,
251) **CUE:** **Sen**ator 白 (White) is drowning
in water, and the 糸 (skeet shooter) shoots a
線 **sen** (line) to save him
COMPARE: 緑 midori = green, # 227;
(温)泉 onsen = hot spring, # 252

229. 練

PRONUNCIATIONS: ren, ne*ru **MEANINGS:** to practice or train **EXAMPLES:** 練習する renshuu suru = to practice; 練る neru = to knead or plan carefully **DESCRIPTION:** on the left, a 糸 (skeet shooter, # 219); on the right, 東 higashi (east, # 508) **CUES:** the 糸 (skeet shooter) 練習 **ren**shuu suru (practices) shooting 東 (east), since that's where its enemy the **Ren**t collector lives in **Ne**braska

230. 絡

PRONUNCIATION: raku **MEANING:** to get entangled with **EXAMPLE:** 連絡する renraku suru = to contact **DESCRIPTION:** on the left, a 糸 (skeet shooter, # 219); on the right, a dancer with a ponytail leaping over a box and raking it with her toes

CUE: someone 連絡する ren**raku** suru (contacts) the dancer with a ponytail about the approach of the 糸 (skeet shooter), and while she is escaping by leaping over this box, she **Rak**es the box with her toes

COMPARE: 終(わる) owaru = to finish, # 233; 落(語) rakugo = Japanese comic story telling, # 526; 楽 raku = pleasure, # 520

231. 結

PRONUNCIATIONS: ke, musu*bu **MEANINGS:** to tie, bind, organize, fasten **EXAMPLES:** 結果 kekka = result; 結婚 kekkon = marriage; 結局 kekkyoku = after all; 結ぶ musubu = bind, connect, conclude, organize, e.g., 手を結ぶ te wo musubu = to join hands **DESCRIPTION:** on the left, a 糸 (skeet shooter, # 219); on the upper right, 士 shi (man, or warrior, # 66); on the lower right, 口 kuchi (mouth, # 426)

CUES: the 糸 (skeet shooter) will 結婚する **ke**kkon suru (marry) the 士 (man), who is a **Ke**nnedy with **Mus**cles, and the 結果 **ke**kka (result) is that both of them will have to learn to control their mouths

232. 緒

PRONUNCIATIONS: cho, sho **MEANINGS:** rope, beginning **EXAMPLES:** 情緒 joucho = emotion; 一緒に issho ni = together **DESCRIPTION:** on the left, a 糸 (skeet shooter, # 219); on the right, 者 mono (person, # 276)

CUES: a 糸 (skeet shooter) has **Cho**sen a 者 (person) to marry, and she **Sho**ws up, and they are 一緒に is**sho** ni (together) at last

233. 終

PRONUNCIATIONS: o, shuu **MEANINGS:** to end or finish **EXAMPLES:** 終わる owaru = to finish, intransitive; 終える oeru = to finish, transitive; 最終電車 saishuu densha= last train **DESCRIPTION:** on the left, a 糸 (skeet shooter, # 219); on the right, 冬 fuyu (winter, # 234) **CUES:** the 糸 (skeet shooter)'s contract 終わる **o**waru (finishes) when 冬 (winter arrives), and he goes back to **O**saka, in order to **Sho**ot at his old enemies **COMPARE:** (連)絡 renraku = contact, # 230

234. 冬

PRONUNCIATIONS: tou*ki, fuyu **MEANING:** winter **EXAMPLES:** 冬期 touki = winter; 冬 fuyu = winter **DESCRIPTION:** a dancer with a pony tail jumps over a patch of ice **CUES:** a dancer with a ponytail escapes some **To**ries by taking a big leap over a patch of ice in 冬 **fuyu** (winter); I **Fo**oled **You**, she cries **COMPARE:** 終(わる) owaru = to finish, # 233; 久(しぶり) hisashiburi = after a long time, # 30

Female

235. 女

PRONUNCIATIONS: onna, jo, o*kami, me
MEANING: female **EXAMPLES:** 女の人
onna no hito = woman; 女性 josei = woman;
女将 okami = mistress, landlady, hostess,
proprietress; 乙女 otome = maiden
DESCRIPTION: at the top, a reclining
horizontal cross; at the bottom, an X-shaped
figure that resembles a person, carrying the
cross **CUES:** an **O**ld **Na**sty taskmaster is
forcing some 女の人 **onna** no hito (women)
named **Jo**an of Arc and **O**prah to carry this
cross to **Mex**ico

236. 安

PRONUNCIATIONS: an, yasu*i
MEANINGS: inexpensive, secure, peaceful
EXAMPLES: 安心する anshin suru = to
feel relieved; 安い yasui = cheap
DESCRIPTION: at the top, a roof; at the
bottom, an 女 onna (female, # 235) named
Queen Anne
CUES: Queen **Anne** is an 女 (female) in this
house who gives us 安心 **an**shin (relief) by
cooking 安い **yasu**i (cheap) **Yak Soup**
COMPARE: 案 an = plan, idea, # 120;
休(む) yasumu = to rest, # 122

237. 妻

PRONUNCIATIONS: tsuma, sai **MEANING:**
wife **EXAMPLES:** 妻 tsuma = wife; 夫妻
fusai = married couple **DESCRIPTION:** at the
top, a cross with a comb intersecting it; at the
bottom, 女 onna (female, # 235)

CUES: my 妻 **tsuma** (wife) is a 女 (female)
and a **Tsu**per **Ma** who is a **Sci**entist, and she
wears a cross and a comb in her hair

238. 要

PRONUNCIATIONS: you, i*ru **MEANING:**
important **EXAMPLES:** 要するに you
suru ni = in short; 必要 hitsuyou = necessary; 要る iru = to need **DESCRIPTION:** at
the top, three eyes suspended from a platform;
at the bottom, 女 onna (female, # 235)
CUES: because she has three eyes, this 女
(female) knows all of the 必要 hitsu**you**
(necessary) things that her family 要る **i**ru
(needs) to eat, such as **Yo**gurt and **Ee**ls
COMPARE: 悪(い) warui = bad, # 313

239. 好

PRONUNCIATIONS: su*ki, kono*mu,
kou*butsu **MEANING:** to like **EXAMPLES:**
好きです suki desu = I like it; 好み
konomi = liking, taste, choice; 好物
koubutsu = favorite food **DESCRIPTION:** on
the left, an 女 onna (female, # 235); on the
right, 子 ko (children, # 182)
CUES: when **Su**perman goes to **Su**kii (ski), he
好き **su**ki (likes) the way that 女 (females)
and 子 (children) hide their **Co**ld **No**ses in
their **Co**ats

240. 婚

PRONUNCIATION: kon **MEANING:**
marriage **EXAMPLE:** 結婚 kekkon =
marriage **DESCRIPTION:** on the left, 女
onna (female, # 235); on the upper right, the
leaning woman from 式 shiki (ceremony,
249) seems to be stuck in a box; on the
lower right, a 日 hi (sun, # 32) shining in the
Congo **CUE:** a 女 (female) from the **Con**go
will 結婚する kek**kon** suru (marry), and
she waits for the leaning woman to extricate
herself from the box so that they may start the
ceremony in the bright sun

241. 姉

PRONUNCIATIONS: ane, nee, shi*mai
MEANING: older sister **EXAMPLES:** 姉 ane
= older sister; お姉さん oneesan =
honorable older sister; 姉妹 shimai = sisters
DESCRIPTION: on the left, 女 onna (female,
235); on the right, 市 shi (city, # 242),
which looks like a spinning lady with wide
hips **CUES:** compared to 妹 (little sister), 姉
ane (big sister) has wider hips, tells more
Anecdotes, eats more **N**ectarines, and is more
Chic, since she lives in the 市 (city)
COMPARE: 妹 imouto = little sister, # 244

242. 市

PRONUNCIATIONS: shi, ichi*ba
MEANINGS: market, city, municipal
EXAMPLES: 都市 toshi = city; 市長
shichou = mayor; 市場 ichiba = market
DESCRIPTION: a spinning lady with wide hips
named Bo Peep, who owns sheep and wears a
pointy hat **CUES:** Bo Peep has wide hips and
spins around the 都市 to**shi** (city) looking for
her **Shee**p who are **Itch**ing to see her
COMPARE: 姉 ane = older sister, # 241

243. 帽

PRONUNCIATION: bou*shi **MEANINGS:**
cap, headgear **EXAMPLE:** 帽子 boushi =
hat **DESCRIPTION:** on the left, Bo Peep, a
spinning lady with wide hips; compared to 市
shi (city, # 242), she is not wearing her pointy
hat; on the upper right, 日 hi (sun, # 32); on
the lower right, 目 me (eye, # 51); 日 and
目 resemble two tall hats **CUES:** Bo Peep,
who is not wearing her pointy hat, is trying to
decide between these two **Bo**dacious 帽子
boushi (hats) **COMPARE:** 慣(れる) nareru
= to get used to, # 92

244. 妹

PRONUNCIATIONS: imouto, mai
MEANING: younger sister **EXAMPLES:** 妹
imouto = younger sister; 姉妹 shimai =
sisters **DESCRIPTION:** on the left, 女 onna
(female, # 235); on the right, 木 ki (tree,
118), with an extra horizontal line forming
two arms, and this might represent a little sister
CUES: compared to 姉 (big sister), 妹
imouto (little sister) has narrow hips, she has
relatively **Immo**bile **Toe**s which make it
difficult for her to spin, and she plays with
Mice **COMPARE:** 味 aji = taste, # 245; 姉
ane = big sister, # 241

245. 味

PRONUNCIATIONS: aji, mi **MEANING:** taste
EXAMPLES: 味 aji = taste; 意味 imi =
meaning; 趣味 shumi = hobby; 地味な
jimi na = subdued, inconspicuous, unattractive
DESCRIPTION: on the left, 口 kuchi (mouth,
426), but this resembles a mirror; on the
right, an aging 木 ki (tree, # 118), with an
extra horizontal line forming two arms
CUES: this tree with two arms is **Ag**ing, but
when it looks in this **Mir**ror, it sees that it still
has good 味 **aji** (taste) in clothes
COMPARE: 妹 imouto = little sister, # 244

Crafted Object

246. 工

PRONUNCIATIONS: kou, ku **MEANING:**
crafted object **EXAMPLES:** 工場 koujou =
factory, 大工 daiku = carpenter
DESCRIPTION: an I-beam, seen on end, used
in coal mines
CUES: this 工 **kou** (crafted object) resembles
an I-beam, seen on end, which is used inside
Coal mines and in **Coo**ling towers
COMPARE: the katakana character エ e

247. 紅

PRONUNCIATIONS: kou, beni MEANINGS: scarlet, red EXAMPLES: 紅茶 koucha = black tea; 紅 beni = red, rouge, lipstick; 口紅 kuchibeni = lipstick

DESCRIPTION: on the left, a 糸 skeet shooter (# 219); on the right, 工 kou (crafted object, # 246), which helps us to pronounce this CUES: the 糸 (skeet shooter) shoots 紅茶 **kou**cha (black tea) at the 工 (crafted object)'s **Coat**, at a time when the 工 is wearing 口紅 kuchi**beni** (lipstick) and is about to leave for **Beni**hana (a brand of teppanyaki restaurants)

248. 空

PRONUNCIATIONS: su*ku, a*ku, kuu*sha, kara, sora MEANINGS: sky, empty
EXAMPLES: 空く suku = to become empty; 空く aku = to become vacant; 空き地 akichi = vacant lot; 空港 kuukou = airport; 空車 kuusha = free taxi; 空 kara = empty; 空 sora = sky NOTE: suku and aku are both spelled 空く; in addition, kara and sora are both spelled 空 DESCRIPTION: at the top, a super-sized soaring bird; at the bottom, 工 kou (crafted object, # 246), which could be part of a vacant cooling tower CUES: a **S**uper-sized **A**lbatross rebounds from an 空いている **a**ite iru (vacant) 工 (crafted object) **Coo**ling tower near the 空港 **kuu**kou (airport) in **Cara**cas and **Soar**s into the 空 **sora** (sky)

249. 式

PRONUNCIATION: shiki MEANINGS: ceremony, formula EXAMPLE: 結婚式 kekkon shiki = wedding ceremony
DESCRIPTION: a woman leans over a 工 kou (crafted object, # 246) CUE: this woman, who is participating in a 式 **shiki** (ceremony), leans over a 工 (crafted object), and she sees that it is a **Shift Key**

Water

250. 川

PRONUNCIATIONS: kawa, sen, gawa MEANING: river EXAMPLES: 川 kawa = river; 河川 kasen = river; 小川 ogawa = brook DESCRIPTION: a flowing river provides water to a car wash CUES: this 川 **kawa** (river) supplies water for a **Car Wa**sh in the **Cen**ter of a town, where there is a **Gas War**

251. 水

PRONUNCIATIONS: mizu, sui*youbi MEANING: water EXAMPLES: 水 mizu = water; 水曜日 suiyoubi = Wednesday
DESCRIPTION: a waterfall flowing between two cliffs at a miniature zoo CUES: outside the cafeteria at a **Mi**niature **Zoo**, 水 **mizu** (water) was flowing between two cliffs, and we ordered **Swee**t yogurt COMPARE: 小(さい) chiisai = small, # 253

252. 泉

PRONUNCIATIONS: sen, izumi MEANING: fountain EXAMPLES: 温泉 onsen = hot spring; 泉 izumi = spring (of water)
DESCRIPTION: at the top, 白(い) shiroi (white, # 44); at the bottom, 水 mizu (water, # 251) CUES: **Sen**ator 白 (White) bathed in the 温泉 on**sen** (hot spring) which was supplied by white 水 (water) from a natural 泉 **izumi** (spring) at the **E**agle **Zoo** in **Mi**chigan COMPARE: 線 sen = line, # 228

253. 小

PRONUNCIATIONS: chii*sai, shou, ko, o*gawa **MEANING:** small **EXAMPLES:** 小さい chiisai = small; 小学校 shougakkou = elementary school; 小鳥 kotori = little bird; 小川 ogawa = brook

DESCRIPTION: like 水 mizu (water, # 251), 小 contains a central line with a curve at the bottom, but the secondary lines surrounding this middle line are smaller and straighter in 小, which resembles a chimpanzee wearng a coat **CUES:** 小さい <u>chii</u>sai (small) **Chi**mpanzees sign up and then **Show** up wearing **Coa**ts at the 小学校 <u>shou</u>gakkou (elementary school) in **O**saka

COMPARE: 川 kawa = river, # 250; 少(し) sukoshi = a little, # 254

254. 少

PRONUNCIATIONS: suku*nai, suko*shi, shou **MEANING:** small amount **EXAMPLES:** 少ない sukunai = a little; 少し sukoshi = a little; 少々 shoushou = a little

DESCRIPTION: this kanji adds a disparaging slash to 小 shou (small, # 253), suggesting that something is 少ない <u>suku</u>nai (a few) or 少し <u>suko</u>shi (a little)

CUES: our **Succu**lent plants are 少ない <u>suku</u>nai (few), but **Su**perman and his **Co**-workers got 少し <u>suko</u>shi (a little) pleasure from them when they came to our plant **Show**

255. 泳

PRONUNCIATIONS: oyo*gu, ei **MEANING:** to swim **EXAMPLES:** 泳ぐ oyogu = to swim; 水泳 suiei = swimming

DESCRIPTION: on the left, a water radical (see # 12), suggesting swimming; on the right, 水 mizu (water, # 251), with two small lines added above it, representing some yogurt and some ale belonging to Oprah

CUES: **O**prah eats **Yog**urt before she 泳ぐ <u>oyo</u>gu (swims), and she drinks **A**le after her 水泳 su<u>iei</u> (swimming) is finished

256. 浴

PRONUNCIATIONS: yu*kata, a*biru, yoku*shitsu **MEANING:** to bathe **EXAMPLES:** 浴衣 yukata = summer kimono; 浴びる abiru = to bathe; 浴室 yokushitsu = bathroom **DESCRIPTION:** on the left, a water radical (see # 12); on the right, a bathroom containing a bathtub, with water vapor rising from the top, which looks like a good place to drink a biiru (beer) **CUES:** a **You**thful person puts on a 浴衣 <u>yu</u>kata (summer robe), drinks **A** biiru (a beer), and 浴びる <u>a</u>biru (bathes) in this **Yoku** (well)-made 浴室 <u>yoku</u>shitsu (bathroom)

COMPARE: 冷(める) sameru = to cool off, # 299

257. 温

PRONUNCIATIONS: atata, on **MEANING:** warm objects **EXAMPLES:** 温かい atatakai = warm (water etc.); 温める atatameru = to heat up water, etc., transitive; 温度 ondo = temperature; 温泉 onsen = hot spring **DESCRIPTION:** on the left, a water radical (see # 12); on the upper right, a warm 日 hi (sun, # 32) shining; on the lower right, 皿 sara (bowl, # 567) **CUES:** **Ata**turk with a **Tan** is the **Own**er of this bathhouse, where the 日 (sun) shines on water in a 皿 (bowl) and produces 温かい <u>atata</u>kai (warm) water vapor

COMPARE: 暖(かい) atatakai = warm atmosphere, # 38; 塩 shio = salt, # 60

258. 薄

PRONUNCIATIONS: usu*i, haku*jou
MEANINGS: dilute, thin, weak EXAMPLES:
薄い usui = pale, thin, light, watery, dilute,
weak (taste); 薄情 hakujou = cruel, heartless,
uncaring DESCRIPTION: on the left, a water
radical (see # 12); at the top, a plant radical
(see # 43); at the bottom, 寺 tera (temple,
213), but 田(んぼ) tanbo (rice paddy,
68) has been inserted into the middle of 寺
CUES: combining water with rice, our 寺
(temple) 田 (rice paddy) is producing 薄い
usui (thin) rice tea appropriate for Usurers and
Hackers

259. 済

PRONUNCIATIONS: zai, su, sai MEANING:
to finish EXAMPLES: 経済 keizai =
economy; 済む sumu = to end (intransitive),
to manage, to do without; 済ます sumasu =
to finish, transitive; 救済 kyuusai = help,
rescue, relief DESCRIPTION: on the left, a
water radical (see # 12), which suggests water
near a beach; on the right, 又 mata ("again,"
24) wearing a pointy hat, above a truncated
月 tsuki (moon, # 148)
CUES: 又 ("again"), wearing a pointy hat, is
disappointed to find only a truncated moon at
this beach in Zaire; "Soon my vacation will
済む sumu (finish)," she Sighs

260. 活

PRONUNCIATIONS: katsu, ka*kki
MEANINGS: life, lively, activity
EXAMPLES: 生活 seikatsu = life, livelihood;
活躍 katsuyaku = great efforts; 活気 kakki
= liveliness DESCRIPTION: on the left, a
water radical (see # 12); on the upper right, a
forked tongue; on the lower right, 口 kuchi
(mouth, # 426) CUES: my 生活 seikatsu
(livelihood) is to cook safe ton Katsu (breaded
pork cutlet) and Cabbage, and I add water to

the sauce and taste it with my forked tongue
before serving it

Rain

261. 雨

PRONUNCIATIONS: ame, u*ryou
MEANING: rain EXAMPLES: 大雨 ooame
= heavy rain; 雨量 uryou = amount of rain
DESCRIPTION: this resembles rain drops on
two window panes
CUES: in American Urban areas, the 雨 ame
(rain) varies depending on the location

262. 雪

PRONUNCIATIONS: setsu, yuki MEANING:
snow EXAMPLES: 新雪 shinsetsu = new
snow; 雪 yuki = snow DESCRIPTION: at
the top, 雨 ame (rain, # 261); under 雨, there
are three layers of ice CUES: since there are
three layers of ice on the ground, this 雨 (rain)
must be 雪 yuki (snow), which some of our
Settlement's Super pioneers find Yucky
COMPARE: 電(気) denki = electricity, # 263

263. 電

PRONUNCIATION: den MEANING:
electricity EXAMPLES: 電気 denki =
electricity; 電話 denwa = telephone
DESCRIPTION: at the top, 雨 ame (rain,
261); at the bottom, 田(んぼ) tanbo (rice
paddy, # 68), with a wire emerging from it,
suggesting an electrical transformer
CUE: a wire is emerging from the transformer
under this 雨 (rain), suggesting that 電気
denki (electricity) is being generated from
lightning strikes in Denmark
COMPARE: 雪 yuki = snow, # 262

264. 雲

PRONUNCIATION: kumo **MEANING:** cloud
EXAMPLE: 雲 kumo = cloud
DESCRIPTION: at the top, 雨 ame (rain, #261); at the bottom, Governor Cuomo's leg pedaling a bicycle **CUE:** these 雲 **kumo** (clouds) suggest that 雨 (rain) is coming, so Governor **Cu**omo had better pedal his bike home quickly **COMPARE:** 曇(り) kumori = cloudy, not included in this catalogue, which adds a small 日 hi (sun, #32) to the top of 雲

265. 震

PRONUNCIATIONS: shin, furu*eru
MEANINGS: to tremble or shake
EXAMPLES: 地震 jishin = earthquake; 震える furueru = to tremble
DESCRIPTION: at the top, 雨 ame (rain, #261); at the bottom, a Shintou shrine which is a platform supported by the katakana character エ and the letter Y
CUES: 雨 (rain) is falling during a 地震 ji**shin** (earthquake), and since only エ and Y are supporting this platform, this **Shin**tou shrine will 震える **furu**eru (tremble) and collapse into **Fu**ll-blown **Ru**in

Sound

266. 音

PRONUNCIATIONS: oto, on, in, ne*iro
MEANING: sound **EXAMPLES:** 音 oto = sound; 音楽 ongaku = music; 母音 boin = vowel; 音色 neiro = timbre
DESCRIPTION: at the top, an Ottoman era bell; at the bottom, 日 hi (day, or sun, #32), which resembles a two-drawer cabinet
CUES: during the **Otto**man era, people discovered that a bell on a two-drawer cabinet full of **On**ions makes an **In**credible 音 **oto** (sound) and can annoy the **N**eighbors

267. 部

PRONUNCIATIONS: he*ya, bu, be
MEANINGS: part, section **EXAMPLES:**
部屋 heya = room; 全部 zenbu = entirely;
部長 buchou = division manager;
子供部屋 kodomobeya = child's room
DESCRIPTION: on the left, compared to 音 oto (sound, #266), this bell is on a box instead of appearing on a cabinet; on the right, ß from the Greek alphabet, suggesting that Helen, a Greek citizen, owns the bell
CUES: **He**len uses her 部屋 **he**ya (room) for **Bu**ddhist ceremonies; she is a Greek 部長 **bu**chou (division manager), and she keeps a **Be**ll on a box for the ceremonies

268. 暗

PRONUNCIATIONS: kura*i, an*ji
MEANING: dark **EXAMPLES:** 暗い kurai = dark; 暗示 anji = hint **DESCRIPTION:** on the left, 日 hi (sun, #32); on the right, 音 oto (sound, #266), which features a bell on a cabinet, where curry rice is stored **CUES:** even when the 日 (sun) shines on this bell, there are 暗い **kura**i (dark) places in the cabinet below it, where we keep **Cu**rry **Ri**ce, but **An**ts are getting into it **COMPARE:** 晴(れる) hareru = to clear up (weather), #37

269. 倍

PRONUNCIATION: bai **MEANINGS:** to double or multiply **EXAMPLES:** 三倍の sanbai no = three times as much; 倍増する baizou suru = to double **DESCRIPTION:** on the left, a man with a slanted hat; on the right, a bell on a box **CUE:** this man wants to **Buy** the bell on the box, and he hopes to resell it for 倍増 **bai**zou (double) the price
COMPARE: 部(屋) heya = room, #267

270. 位

PRONUNCIATIONS: i, kurai MEANINGS: rank, place, approximately EXAMPLES: 第一位 dai ichi i = first place; 位 kurai = rank DESCRIPTION: on the left, a man with a slanted hat; on the right, an Easter bell CUES: a man with a slanted hat who plays this Easter bell won 第一位 dai ichi **i** (first place) in a bell-ringing competition, received a prize of **Kool**-Aid and **Ri**ce, and was awarded a high 位 **kurai** (rank)

COMPARE: 暗(い) kurai = dark, # 268

Shah

271. 社

PRONUNCIATIONS: sha, ja MEANINGS: shrine, company of people EXAMPLES: 会社 kaisha = company; 社員 shain = company employee; 神社 jinja = Shintou shrine DESCRIPTION: on the left, the Shah, wearing a crown; on the right, 土 tsuchi (dirt, # 59) CUES: the **Sha**h is looking at some 土 (dirt), where he plans to build a 会社 kai**sha** (company) with **Ja**ck Nicholson

272. 祖

PRONUNCIATION: so MEANING: ancestral EXAMPLES: 祖父 sofu = grandfather; 祖母 sobo = grandmother; 祖先 sosen = ancestor DESCRIPTION: on the left, the Shah (see # 271); on the right, 目 me (eye # 51) on a broad base, but this looks like a solar panel CUE: the Shah is praying at the tomb of his 祖父 **so**fu (grandfather), which resembles a **So**lar panel

273. 神

PRONUNCIATIONS: jin*ja, shin*tou, kami MEANINGS: gods, mind, soul EXAMPLES: 神社 jinja = shintou shrine; 神道 Shintou = a Japanese religion; 神 kami = god DESCRIPTION: on the left, the Shah (see

271), wearing skinny jeans; on the right, what appears to be a car but, compared to 車 kuruma (car, # 283), this car is missing its wheels CUES: the **Sha**h stands in his skinny **Jean**s, praying to a **Shin**y car without wheels which he regards as a 神 **kami** (god), but a **Commie** (Communist) is watching COMPARE: 押(す) osu = to push, # 592; 紙 kami = paper, # 221; (女)将 okami = mistress, landlady, # 374; 髪 kami = hair, # 501

274. 祝

PRONUNCIATIONS: iwa*u, shuku, shuu MEANING: to celebrate EXAMPLES: 祝う iwau = to celebrate; 祝日 shukujitsu = national holiday; 祝儀 shuugi = celebration, wedding, gratuity DESCRIPTION: on the left, the Shah (see # 271); on the right, 兄 ani (big brother, # 420) CUES: the Shah **iwau** 祝う (celebrates) with 兄 (big brother); they are happy that eels are on the menu and say "**Ee**ls? **Wow!**" as they **Shuck** corn for the feast and **Shoot** off fireworks

275. 礼

PRONUNCIATION: rei MEANINGS: to bow; propriety; a gift in token of gratitude EXAMPLES: お礼 orei = gratitude, thanks; 礼 rei = a bow, or gratitude; 失礼 shitsurei = discourtesy DESCRIPTION: on the left, the Shah (see # 271); on the right, the letter L, which represents a Lady CUE: the Shah feels お礼 o**rei** (gratitude) to this **La**dy, who helped him even after the Shah was 失礼 shitsu**rei** (rude) to her

Person

276. 者

PRONUNCIATIONS: mono, sha MEANING: person EXAMPLES: 悪者 warumono = villain; 学者 gakusha = scholar DESCRIPTION: at the top, 土 tsuchi (dirt,

59); in the middle, a pair of scissors; at the bottom, 日 hi (sun, # 32), which resembles a two-drawer cabinet **CUES:** a 者 **mono** (person) is playing a **Mono**tonous game with **Shar**p scissors that he keeps in this cabinet

277. 都

PRONUNCIATIONS: tsu*gou, to, miyako **MEANING:** capital **EXAMPLES:** 都合 tsugou = circumstances, convenience; 都市 toshi = city; 京都 Kyouto = city in Japan; 都 miyako = capital **DESCRIPTION:** on the left, 者 mono (person, # 276), who plays with scissors as if they were toys; on the right, ß beta, from the Greek alphabet, suggesting that this is a Greek 者 (person)
CUES: 都合がいい **tsu**gou ga ii (it is convenient) for this Greek 者 (person) to carry a **Tsu**itcase containing scissors to the big 都市 **to**shi (city), where he hopes to buy better **Toy**s and **Meet Yak Ow**ners

278. 暑

PRONUNCIATION: atsu*i **MEANING:** hot atmosphere **EXAMPLES:** 暑い日 atsui hi = hot day **DESCRIPTION:** at the top, 日 hi (sun, # 32); at the bottom, a 者 mono (person, # 276) named Superman **CUE:** compared to 者 (person), this kanji has two 日 (suns), suggesting that the weather **At Su**perman's house is doubly 暑い **atsu**i (hot)
COMPARE: 熱(い) atsui = hot objects, # 65; 厚(い) atsui = thick, # 185

Complicated Boxes

279. 園

PRONUNCIATIONS: en, zono, sono
MEANINGS: park, spacious garden
EXAMPLES: 公園 kouen = park; 花園 hanazono = flower garden; 園子 Sonoko = a

girl's given name **DESCRIPTION:** on the perimeter, a fence, suggesting a park; at the top, 土 tsuchi (dirt, # 59); at the bottom, a machine on a tripod, with a speaker extending to the right, which could be a megaphone **CUES:** an **En**gineer is using this megaphone to tell children playing in the 土 (dirt) in the 公園 kou**en** (park) to enter the **Z**one to the North, and have **Sono**grams done
COMPARE: 遠(い) tooi = far, # 351; 国 kuni = country, # 170; 困(る) komaru = to be inconvenienced, # 280

280. 困

PRONUNCIATIONS: koma*ru, kon*nan
MEANING: in trouble **EXAMPLES:** 困る komaru = to be troubled, inconvenienced; 困難 kon'nan = difficult **DESCRIPTION:** a 木 ki (tree, # 118) stuck in a box **CUES:** while this 木 (tree) was in a **Coma**, someone built a box around it, so that it 困っている **koma**tte iru (is in trouble), and **Con**an says that this is a 困難な **kon**'nan na (difficult) situation **COMPARE:** 国 kuni = country, # 170; (公)園 kouen = park, # 279

281. 図

PRONUNCIATIONS: zu, to*shokan
MEANINGS: drawing, to plan **EXAMPLES:** 図 zu = drawing; 地図 chizu = map; 図書館 toshokan = library **DESCRIPTION:** a framed drawing of two people riding on a giraffe **CUES:** this is a 図 **zu** (drawing) of two people riding on a giraffe, returning from the **Zoo**, where they saw some **Toa**ds, to the 図書館 **to**shokan (library)
COMPARE: 以(下) ika (less than), # 601

282. 面

PRONUNCIATIONS: omo*shiroi, ji, men*dou
MEANINGS: mask, face, features
EXAMPLES: 面白い omoshiroi = interesting; 真面目な majime na = sincere; 面倒 mendou = annoyance; 地面 jimen = the surface of the earth, the ground
DESCRIPTION: this resembles an old limousine with an antenna, seen from the back, with 目 me (eye, # 51) imprinted on it
CUES: this **O**ld **Mo**torcar is a **Jee**p, and the working 目 (eye) on its back panel is an 面白い **omo**shiroi (interesting) innovation that protects it from 面倒な **men**dou na (annoying) **Men** without dough

Car

283. 車

PRONUNCIATIONS: kuruma, sha
MEANING: car EXAMPLES: 車 kuruma = car, wheel; 自転車 jitensha = bicycle
DESCRIPTION: a two-wheeled car seen from the top, with a wheel on each side, which belongs to the Shah
CUES: this **C**urvy, **R**oomy, **M**agnificent 車 **kuruma** (car) belongs to the **Shah**
COMPARE: 重(い) omoi = heavy, # 284

284. 重

PRONUNCIATIONS: omo*i, kasa*neru, chou, juu MEANINGS: heavy, layer EXAMPLES: 重い omoi = heavy; 重ねる kasaneru = to pile up; 慎重な shinchou na = cautious, prudent; 体重 taijuu = a person's weight
DESCRIPTION: a 車 kuruma (car, # 283), with extra hubcaps added to each wheel
CUES: this 車 (car) is 重い **omo**i (heavy) because **O**ld **Mo**ses added extra hubcaps to each wheel, and **Casa**nova and Margaret **Cho** 重ねる **kasa**neru (pile up) even more weight by adding **Ju**ice to the trunk

285. 転

PRONUNCIATIONS: koro*bu, ten
MEANING: to roll EXAMPLES: 転ぶ korobu = to fall; 自転車 jitensha = bicycle
DESCRIPTION: on the left, a 車 sha (vehicle, # 283); on the right, a pedaling leg, with a line above it suggesting a bicycle basket CUES: a 車 (vehicle) with a pedaling leg, suggesting a 自転車 ji**ten**sha (bicycle), from which one may 転ぶ **koro**bu (fall down) if one's **Coro**nary arteries **B**urst while riding in **Ten**nessee
COMPARE: 伝(える) tsutaeru = to convey, # 345; (自)動(車) jidousha = car, # 286

286. 動

PRONUNCIATIONS: dou, ugo MEANING: to move EXAMPLES: 自動車 jidousha = car; 動く ugoku = to move, intransitive; 動かす ugokasu = to move, transitive
DESCRIPTION: on the left, 重(い) omoi (heavy, # 284); on the right, 力 chikara (force, # 107) CUES: this is a 重 (heavy) 自動車 ji**dou**sha (car) which 動く **ugo**ku (moves) under its own 力 (force) to escape **D**oberman dogs and Uber **Go**phers
COMPARE: (自)転(車) jitensha = bicycle, # 285; 働(く) hataraku = to labor, # 287

287. 働

PRONUNCIATIONS: hatara*ku, dou
MEANINGS: to work, operate EXAMPLES: 働く hataraku = to labor; 労働者 roudousha = laborer DESCRIPTION: on the left, a man with a slanted hat; on the right, 動(く) ugoku (to move, # 286)
CUES: as the man with a slanted hat 働く **hatara**ku (labors) making **H**ats for **Ara**bians, he 動 (moves) hats from one place to another and gets paid good **Dough** for doing so

288. 輸

PRONUNCIATION: yu **MEANING:** to transport **EXAMPLES:** 輸入する yunyuu suru = to import; 輸出する yushutsu suru = to export **DESCRIPTION:** on the left, a 車 kuruma (car, # 283); at the top right, a peaked roof suggesting a house in the Yukon; at the lower right, 月 tsuki (month, # 148) and the katakana character リ Ri

CUE: リ Ri, working from his house in the **Yu**kon, 輸入する **yu**nyuu suru (imports) and 輸出する **yu**shutsu suru (exports) 車 (cars) every 月 (month)

289. 軽

PRONUNCIATIONS: karu*i, kei **MEANING:** light weight **EXAMPLES:** 軽い karui = light; 軽自動車 keijidousha = a lightweight car **DESCRIPTION:** on the left, 車 kuruma (car, # 283); on the right, 又 mata ("again," # 24), but this resembles an athlete leaping over 土 tsuchi (dirt, # 59) **CUES:** like **Caru**so, who was said to have a light voice, this athlete is 軽い **karu**i (light) enough to jump out of a 車 (car) and over a pile of 土 (dirt), even after eating a whole **C**ake **COMPARE:** 経験 keiken = experience, # 224

290. 乾

PRONUNCIATIONS: kawa*ku, kan*denchi **MEANING:** to get dry **EXAMPLES:** 乾く kawaku = to get dry; 乾電池 kandenchi = dry cell battery **DESCRIPTION:** the radical on the left is not the same as 車 kuruma (car, # 283), since the axle doesn't travel all the way through, so let's call this a California wagon; on the right, a snake holding a crutch **CUES:** there are disabled snakes outside our **C**alifornia **Wa**gon, so let's stay inside, where 乾いている **kawa**ite iru (it's dry), and we can eat from **Can**s **COMPARE:** 朝 asa = morning, # 291; 渇(く) kawaku = to get thirsty, not included in this catalogue, e.g., 喉が渇く nodo ga kawaku = to get thirsty

291. 朝

PRONUNCIATIONS: sa, chou*shoku, asa **MEANING:** morning **EXAMPLES:** 今朝 kesa = this morning; 朝食 choushoku = breakfast; 朝 asa = morning **DESCRIPTION:** the radical on the left is not the same as 車 kuruma (car, # 283), since the axle doesn't travel all the way through, so let's call this a wagon; on the right, 月 tsuki (moon, # 148) **CUES:** I'm sitting in a wagon in the early 朝 **asa** (morning), watching the 月 (moon) fade away, feeling **Sa**d that I was **Cho**sen for early morning watch duty, and hoping that the day will get warm **ASA**P **COMPARE:** 乾(く) kawaku = to get dry, # 290

Now

292. 今

PRONUNCIATIONS: ima, kon, k*you, ko*toshi, ke*sa **MEANING:** now **EXAMPLES:** 今 ima = now; 今度 kondo = this time, next time; 今日 kyou = today; 今年 kotoshi = this year; 今朝 kesa = this morning **DESCRIPTION:** at the top, a roof, with a ceiling under it; at the bottom, the number 7 **CUES:** Imagine that 今 **ima** (now) it is 7:00, and it's time for the **Con**ductor to turn the **Key**, start the **C**ommuter train and settle back to drink a **Ke**g of beer **COMPARE:** 会(う) au = to meet, # 293; 合(う) au = to harmonize, # 294

293. 会

PRONUNCIATIONS: kai, gai, a*u
MEANING: to meet (people) EXAMPLES:
会社 kaisha = company; 会議 kaigi =
meeting; 運送会社 unsougaisha = moving
company; 会う au = to meet someone
DESCRIPTION: at the top, a roof, with a
ceiling under it, but this could be the Kaiser's
hat; at the bottom, a leg pedaling a bicycle in
Austria
CUES: the Kaiser will travel by bike in order
to 会う au (meet) a Guide, who will take
him to a 会議 kaigi (meeting) in Austria
COMPARE: 今 ima = now, # 292; 合(う)
au = to harmonize, # 294

294. 合

PRONUNCIATIONS: ai, gou, a*u, ga*ssen
MEANING: to match or harmonize, to come
together EXAMPLES: 具合 guai =
condition, state; 会合 kaigou = meeting,
assembly; 都合 tsugou = circumstances,
convenience; 合う au = to come together, to
match or suit; 合わせる awaseru = to put
together, combine or harmonize; 合戦
gassen = battle DESCRIPTION: at the top, a
roof, with a ceiling under it, but this could be a
lid for a box; at the bottom, a cold box full of
ice CUES: this kanji shows a lid fitting neatly
on a box under a roof, suggesting that our
plans to market Ice-cold Goat milk will 合う
au (come together) in Australia, if 都合が
いい tsugou ga ii (circumstances are good),
and if we can buy Gas for our refrigerators
COMPARE: 今 ima = now, # 292; 会(う)
au = to meet, # 293

295. 答

PRONUNCIATION: kota*eru MEANING: to
answer a question EXAMPLE: 答える
kotaeru = to reply DESCRIPTION: at the top,
two shortened 竹 take (bamboo, # 134), which
could represent a question on the left and a
corresponding answer on the right; at the
bottom, 合(う) au (to match or suit, # 294)
CUE: when I consult with my Colorado Tax
attorney, my questions and her 答え kotae
(answers) 合 (match) each other
COMPARE: (内)容 naiyou = content, # 296

296. 容

PRONUNCIATION: you MEANINGS: content,
to let in EXAMPLE: 内容 naiyou = content
DESCRIPTION: at the top, a hovering bird; at
the bottom, a box containing yogurt, with a
roof; compared to 合(う) au (match, # 294)
and 答(え) kotae (answer, # 295), there is no
ceiling between the box and the roof
CUE: a hovering bird is trying to get into the
内容 naiyou (contents) of this box under a
roof, which consist of Yogurt

Bench Hats

297. 登

PRONUNCIATIONS: nobo*ru, to*zan
MEANING: to climb EXAMPLES: 登る
noboru = to climb; 登山 tozan = mountain
climbing DESCRIPTION: at the top left and
top right, two radicals that resemble upside-
down benches; let's call them bench hats; at
the bottom, a climber with a big 口 kuchi
(mouth), standing on a broad base CUES: this
climber with a big 口 (mouth) wears two
bench hats; he can 登る noboru (climb) like
Nobody else, but certain Tortoises from
Zanzibar can also climb well
COMPARE: 上(る) noboru = to rise, # 171;
発(表) happyou = presentation, # 298

298. 発

PRONUNCIATIONS: ha, hatsu*mei, patsu[1], ho*ssa MEANINGS: departure, to disclose EXAMPLES: 発表 happyou = presentation; 発明 hatsumei = invention; 東京発 toukyou hatsu = departing from Tokyo; 出発する shuppatsu suru = to depart; 発作 hossa = attack or fit, e.g., 心臓発作 shinzou hossa = heart attack DESCRIPTION: at the top left and top right, two radicals that resemble upside-down benches; let's call them bench hats; at the bottom, a happy expansive guy with a long right leg CUES: a **H**appy yodeler, wearing two bench **H**ats, gives a 発表 **ha**ppyou (presentation) with his right leg extended, but the sock on his right foot has a **H**ole in it COMPARE: 登(る) noboru = to climb, # 297

Peaked Roof

299. 冷

PRONUNCIATIONS: rei*zouko, tsume*tai, hi*yasu, sa*meru MEANING: cold object (not cold atmosphere) EXAMPLES: 冷蔵庫 reizouko = refrigerator; 冷たい tsumetai = cold object; 冷やす hiyasu = to chill; 冷める sameru = to cool off DESCRIPTION: on the left, a water radical (see # 12) which suggests rain; on the right, a house with a peaked roof and a wobbly table on the ground floor, which we rent from Melvin CUES: when it **R**ains, Melvin's house leaks water, and the walls are 冷たい **tsume**tai (cold), so we will **Tsue Me**lvin to get him to **He**at the house, and hire some **Sa**murai to fix the roof COMPARE: 浴(びる) abiru = to bathe, # 256

300. 全

PRONUNCIATIONS: matta*ku, sube*te, zen MEANINGS: all, entire EXAMPLES: 全く mattaku = entirely; 全て subete = all, everything; 全部 zenbu = all, everything; DESCRIPTION: at the top, a Zen temple with a peaked roof; under the roof, 王 ou (king, not included in this catalogue); compared to 金 kane (money, # 301), 全 is missing two short lines at the bottom CUES: a **Mata**dor and a **Sub**editor come to this **Zen** temple to talk about 全部 **zen**bu (everything) with the 王 (king) COMPARE: 主(人) shujin = master, # 166

301. 金

PRONUNCIATIONS: kin*youbi, kane, kana*mono MEANINGS: money, gold, metal EXAMPLES: 金曜日 kinyoubi = Friday; 金属 kinzoku = metal; お金 okane = money; 金物 kanamono = hardware DESCRIPTION: a well-supported symmetrical house that could be a kindergarten; compared to 全 zen (everything, # 300), 金 includes an additional line on each side of the ground floor, which may represent money or gold belonging to the kindergarten CUES: my **Kin**dergarten teacher gave me some お金 o**kane** (money) to buy sugar **Cane** to feed the **Cana**ries

302. 銀

PRONUNCIATION: gin MEANING: silver EXAMPLES: 銀行 ginkou = bank; 銀 gin = silver DESCRIPTION: on the left, 金 kane (money, # 301); at the top right, 日 hi (sun, # 32); at the bottom right, the letters L and y which remind us of "friendly" CUE: when I went to the 銀行 **gin**kou (bank) to get 金 (money) for **Gin**, a friend**L**y 日 (sun) was shining

303. 良

PRONUNCIATIONS: ryou, yo*i, ra
MEANING: good **EXAMPLES:** 不良 furyou
= delinquent, poor condition; 良い yoi =
good; 良かった yokatta = it was good;
奈良 Nara = a city in Japan **DESCRIPTION:**
at the top, 白(い) shiroi (white, # 44); at the
bottom, the letters L and y which remind us of
"friendly" **CUES:** Pope **Leo** is 白 (white)
guy who is a **Yo**gurt eater, and he's a 良い
yoi (good) friend**Ly** person who also eats a lot
of 白 (white) **Ra**men (egg noodles)
COMPARE: 銀 gin = silver, # 302; 長(い)
nagai = long, # 502

304. 鉄

PRONUNCIATION: tetsu **MEANING:** iron
EXAMPLES: 地下鉄 chikatetsu = subway;
鉄製 tetsusei = made of iron
DESCRIPTION: on the left, 金 kane (metal,
301); on the right, 失(礼) shitsurei
(discourtesy, # 206) which is a fusion of 牛
ushi (cow, # 205) and 大きい ookii (big,
188) **CUE:** this 大 (big) 牛 (cow) stepped
on some rusty 金 (metal), and the **Tet**anus
shot that **Su**perman gave her was delivered via
a 鉄 **tetsu** (iron) needle

305. 館

PRONUNCIATION: kan **MEANING:** large
building **EXAMPLES:** 旅館 ryokan =
Japanese inn; 図書館 toshokan = library
DESCRIPTION: on the left, 食(事) shokuji
(meal, # 398); on the right, a 2-story building,
under a roof **CUE:** this is a 旅館 ryo**kan**
(Japanese inn), where 食 (meals) are made in
the kitchen on the left, and the 2-story
dormitory on the right is lighted by **Can**dles

Heart

306. 心

PRONUNCIATIONS: kokoro, shin
MEANINGS: heart, mind **EXAMPLES:**
心 kokoro = heart; 心配する shinpai suru
= to worry **DESCRIPTION:** the small line on
the left represents one ventricle of the heart,
the large curved line represents the other
ventricle, and the two lines at the upper right
represent shingles, protecting the heart of a
man named Roy **CUES:** don't throw **Co**conuts
at **Roy**'s **Shin**gles, since you may damage his
心 **kokoro** (heart)

307. 必

PRONUNCIATIONS: kanara*zu, hitsu
MEANINGS: without fail, necessary
EXAMPLES: 必ず kanarazu = without fail;
必要 hitsuyou = necessary
DESCRIPTION: a 心 kokoro (heart, # 306)
belonging to a Canadian rat, sliced in half
CUES: if you want the **Cana**dian **Ra**t from the
zoo to expire 必ず **kanara**zu (without fail), it
is 必要 **hitsu**you (necessary) to slice its 心
(heart) in two, before it **Hits U** with its tail

308. 思

PRONUNCIATION: omo*u, shi **MEANINGS:**
to think, thought **EXAMPLE:** 思う omou =
to think/feel; 思想 shisou = thought, idea
DESCRIPTION: at the top, 田(んぼ) tanbo
(rice paddies, # 68); at the bottom, 心 kokoro
(heart, # 306), but these could be four legs on a
sheep **CUE:** **O**saka **Mo**squitoes breed in
田 (rice paddies), and we 思う **omo**u (think)
that they bite four-legged **Shee**p

309. 恥

PRONUNCIATIONS: ha*zukashii, haji
MEANINGS: shame, dishonor **EXAMPLES:**
恥ずかしい hazukashii = embarrassed,
shy, ashamed; 恥 haji = shame, dishonor
DESCRIPTION: on the left, 耳 mimi (ears,

57); on the right, 心 kokoro (heart, # 306) CUES: it's 恥ずかしい **ha**zukashii (embarrassing) that 耳 (ears) are located next to 心 (hearts) in a back room at Prince Harry's zoo, which is cashing in on body parts, according to **H**acker **J**immy **C**arter

310. 忘

PRONUNCIATIONS: wasu*reru, bou*nenkai **MEANING:** to forget **EXAMPLES:** 忘れる wasureru = to forget; 忘年会 bounenkai = end-of-year party **DESCRIPTION:** at the top, a fish hook; at the bottom, 心 kokoro (heart, # 306) **CUES:** there was a **W**ar in the **Su**ez canal involving patrol **Bo**ats, but a wizard put a fish hook into my 心 (heart) to make me 忘れる **wasu**reru (forget) about it

311. 窓

PRONUNCIATIONS: mado, sou **MEANING:** window **EXAMPLES:** 窓 mado = window; 同窓会 dousoukai = reunion of graduates **DESCRIPTION:** at the top, a bird soaring; in the middle, ム mu (the sound made by a cow), so the bird must be a cowbird; at the bottom, 心 kokoro (heart, # 306) **CUES:** when I was living in a **Mars Do**me, I looked through a 窓 **mado** (window) and saw a **So**aring ム (cow) bird, causing my 心 (heart) to flutter

312. 急

PRONUNCIATIONS: kyuu, iso **MEANING:** to hurry or rush **EXAMPLES:** 急に kyuu ni = suddenly; 急ぐ isogu = to hurry **DESCRIPTION:** at the top, a cute fish head that seems isolated; in the middle, some stream-lining, suggesting speed; at the bottom, 心 kokoro (heart, # 306) **CUES:** this **Cu**te fish is **Iso**lated from the others, but he has a lot of 心 (heart), and

急に **kyuu** ni (suddenly) he can 急ぐ **iso**gu (hurry)

313. 悪

PRONUNCIATIONS: waru*i, aku **MEANING:** bad **EXAMPLES:** 悪い warui = bad; 悪 aku = evil **DESCRIPTION:** at the top, three eyes, sandwiched between two platforms; at the bottom, 心 kokoro (heart, # 306) **CUES:** **W**ar **Ru**ined the health of this 悪い **waru**i (bad) three-eyed pirate with an 悪 **aku** (evil) 心 (heart), but he is getting **Ac**upuncture treatments **COMPARE:** 要(る) iru = to need, # 238

314. 念

PRONUNCIATION: nen **MEANINGS:** thought, to ponder **EXAMPLES:** 残念 zannen = too bad; 信念 shinnen = belief **DESCRIPTION:** at the top, 今 ima (now, # 292); at the bottom, 心 kokoro (heart, # 306); together they look like a negative nephew, moving to the right **CUE:** 今 (now), my **N**egative **N**ephew's 心 (heart) is driving him to the right of the political spectrum, and that's 残念 zan**nen** (too bad) **COMPARE:** 年 nen = year, # 177

315. 息

PRONUNCIATIONS: musu*ko, iki, soku **MEANINGS:** son, breath, respiration **EXAMPLES:** 息子 musuko = son; 息 iki = breath, respiration; 休息 kyuusoku = rest, relief, relaxation **DESCRIPTION:** at the top, 自 ji (self, # 55), which resembles a rib cage or perhaps a stringed musical instrument; at the bottom, a 心 kokoro (heart, # 306) **CUES:** my 自 (self)'s 息子 **musu**ko (son) is a **Mus**ical **U**ber driver, and he has a good 心 (heart), but he's so thin that you can see his ribs, his 息 **iki** (breath) is **Icky**, and he's always **So**aked with sweat

316. 娘

PRONUNCIATION: musume **MEANINGS:** daughter, young woman **EXAMPLE:** 娘 musume = daughter **DESCRIPTION:** on the left, 女 onna (female, # 235); on the right, 良(い) yoi (good, # 303) **CUE:** our 娘 **musume** (daughter) is a 良 (good) girl who worked at the **Mu**seum during the **Summer**

317. 意

PRONUNCIATION: i
MEANINGS: meaning, intention, mind
EXAMPLES: 意味 imi = meaning; 意見 iken = opinion; 注意 chuui = attention; 用意する youi suru = to prepare
DESCRIPTION: at the top, 音 oto (sound, # 266); at the bottom, 心 kokoro (heart, # 306) **CUE:** this 音 (sound) in my 心 (heart) sounds **E**erie and must have some kind of 意味 **i**mi (meaning)
COMPARE: 億 oku = 100 million, # 318

318. 億

PRONUNCIATION: oku **MEANING:** one hundred million **EXAMPLE:** 五億 go oku = 500 million **DESCRIPTION:** on the left, a man standing erect; on the right, 意 (mind, # 317), which features a bell at the top **CUE:** the man is standing erect and ringing 意 (mind)'s bell, which can play 一億の ichi**oku** no (100 million) **O**ld **Ko**ol-Aid jingles

319. 怒

PRONUNCIATIONS: oko*ru, ika*ri, do
MEANING: angry **EXAMPLES:** 怒る okoru = to get angry; 怒り ikari = anger, fury; 激怒 gekido = fury, outrage
DESCRIPTION: at the upper left, 女 onna (female, # 235); at the upper right, 又 mata ("again," # 24), but this resembles a leaping

athlete named **O**klahoma **Ru**th; at the bottom, 心 kokoro (heart, # 306) **CUES:** **O**klah**O**ma **Ru**th is an athletic 女 (female) with 心 (heart) who 怒った **oko**tta (got angry) at **I**ca**r**us, the **Do**pe who flew too close to the sun

X's

320. 区

PRONUNCIATION: ku **MEANINGS:** ward, section **EXAMPLES:** 区役所 kuyakusho = ward office; 区別する kubetsu suru = to distinguish or differentiate **DESCRIPTION:** a building in Kuwait that is open on one side, resembling a storefront, containing an X
CUE: this 区役所 **ku**yakusho (ward office) in **Ku**wait is a storefront, and X marks the spot where citizens from the ward are served
COMPARE: 医 i = medicine, # 325

321. 気

PRONUNCIATIONS: ki, ge, gi, ke
MEANINGS: spirit, air
EXAMPLES: 天気 tenki = weather; 気持ち kimochi = feeling; 気が付く ki ga tsuku = to notice, to regain consciousness; 何気ない nanigenai = casual; 風邪気味 kazegimi = a bit of a cold (upper respiratory infection); 寒気 samuke = a chill
DESCRIPTION: at the top and to the right, a lean-to with a triple roof; at the bottom, an X representing the spirit of a king
CUES: the 気 **ki** (spirit) of a **K**ing, **Ge**nghis **K**han, who played the **Gui**tar in **Ke**nya, is represented by an X and is protected by a lean-to with a triple roof

322. 歳

PRONUNCIATION: sai, zai[1] **MEANINGS:** age, year **EXAMPLE:** 十六歳 juurokusai = 16 years old; 万歳 banzai = "10,000 years," i.e., "long live!" **DESCRIPTION:** at the top, 止(まる) tomaru (to stop, # 173); below 止, a lean-to intercepted by a long halberd (combination lance and axe); on the lower left, a nail flanked by two pieces of gum; this kanji resembles a math problem in division, as seen in constructions like $3 \overline{\smash{\big)}\, 12x} = 4x$

CUE: 歳 **sai** (age) is a number, and it is divisible, but I remain **Si**lent about my age and 止 (stop) speaking before revealing it

American Indian Chief

323. 知

PRONUNCIATIONS: shi*ru, chi **MEANINGS:** to know; knowledge

EXAMPLES: 知る shiru = to know; 知り合い shiriai = acquaintance; 知識 chishiki = knowledge; 知人 chijin = acquaintance **DESCRIPTION:** on the left, an American Indian chief, wearing a war bonnet; on the right, the 口 kuchi (mouth, # 426) of a sheep **CUES:** this American Indian chief is a veterinary dentist specializing in **Shee**p who 知る **shi**ru (knows) a lot about the 口 (mouth), and his prices are **Chea**p

COMPARE: 短(い) mijikai = short, # 324

324. 短

PRONUNCIATIONS: mijika*i, tan

MEANING: short **EXAMPLES:** 短い mijikai = short; 長短 choutan = length **DESCRIPTION:** on the left, a midget American Indian chief, wearing a war bonnet; on the right, a gasoline pump **CUES:** this American Indian chief is a **Mi**dget who owns a **Jee**p **Car**; he has a good **Tan**, but he is too 短い **mijika**i (short) to see over this gas pump

COMPARE: 知(る) shiru = to know, # 323

325. 医

PRONUNCIATION: i **MEANING:** medicine **EXAMPLES:** 医者 isha = medical doctor **DESCRIPTION:** an American Indian chief, wearing a war bonnet, in a building that is open on one side **CUE:** this American Indian chief is an 医者 **i**sha (doctor) standing in his storefront clinic, which is open on one side **COMPARE:** 区(役所) kuyakusho = ward office, # 320

Uncooked Rice

326. 米

PRONUNCIATIONS: kome, bei, mai **MEANINGS:** rice, America **EXAMPLES:** 米 kome = uncooked rice; 米国 beikoku = U.S.A.; 白米 hakumai = white rice **DESCRIPTION:** this resembles an eight-sided comet **CUES:** 米 **kome** (uncooked rice) grains can be arranged into an eight-sided **Com**et, **Ba**ked in an oven and fed to the **Mi**ce **COMPARE:** 来(る) kuru = to come, # 327; 奥(さん) okusan = someone else's wife, # 532; 歯 ha = tooth, # 533

327. 来

PRONUNCIATIONS: ki*masu, ko*nai, ku*ru, rai **MEANINGS:** to come, next **EXAMPLES:** 来ます kimasu = to come; 来ない konai = will not come; 来る kuru = to come; 来年 rainen = next year; 来日する rainichi suru = to visit Japan **DESCRIPTION:** compared to 米 kome (rice, # 326), this adds a horizontal line at the top, which could represent a package of Kool-Aid **CUES:** the **K**ey to getting **C**onan to 来る **ku**ru (come) for dinner 来週 **rai**shuu (next week) is to promise to serve plenty of **K**ool-Aid with **R**ice

328. 番

PRONUNCIATION: ban **MEANINGS:** watch, turn, order **EXAMPLES:** 一番 ichiban = number one; 交番 kouban = police box; 番号 bangou = number **DESCRIPTION:** at the top, 米 kome (rice, # 326), with a slash drawn over it; at the bottom, a 田(んぼ) tanbo (rice paddy, # 68) in Bangladesh **CUE:** the horizontal slash at the top indicates that it's the 番 **ban** (turn) of this 田 (rice paddy) in **Ban**gladesh to supply 米 (rice)

329. 隣

PRONUNCIATION: rin*jin, tonari **MEANINGS:** neighbor, next door **EXAMPLES:** 隣人 rinjin = neighbor; 隣 tonari = next door **DESCRIPTION:** on the left, ß beta from the Greek alphabet; at the top, 米 kome (rice, # 326); at the bottom left, 夕(方) yuugata (evening, # 160); at the bottom right, a left-facing knee, suggesting a sitting person **CUE:** a **Lean** Greek named **T**obias in **Nari**ta lives 学校の隣 gakkou no **tonari** (next door to a school) and sits in the evenings, sorting through his rice **COMPARE:** 降(りる) oriru = to exit a vehicle, # 178

Sheep

330. 洋

PRONUNCIATION: you **MEANINGS:** ocean, abroad **EXAMPLES:** 西洋 seiyou = the western part of the world; 洋服 youfuku = Western clothes; 東洋 touyou = the eastern part of the world **DESCRIPTION:** on the left, a water radical (see # 12); on the right, 羊 hitsuji (sheep, not included in this catalogue), an animal that has two horns, two ears, four legs and a tail; compared to 半 han (half, middle, # 331), 羊 hitsuji (sheep) has a Y at the top, which could stand for 洋 **you** (abroad)

CUE: 西洋 sei**you** (the western part of the world) is across the water, where a lot of people keep 羊 (sheep) and eat **Yo**gurt **COMPARE:** 遅(い) osoi = late, # 350

331. 半

PRONUNCIATIONS: naka*ba, han **MEANINGS:** half, middle **EXAMPLES:** 半ば nakaba = half, the middle; 一時半 ichijihan = half past 1:00; 半分 hanbun = half, or a ½ share **DESCRIPTION:** compared to 羊 hitsuji (sheep), the radical seen on the right in 洋 you (abroad, # 330), 半 adds a head but removes the sheep's two back legs **CUES:** if you look at this kanji and have the **Knack** of **A**bandoning useless thought, **Han**sel says that you will see that 半分 **han**bun (half) of this 羊 (sheep) is missing

332. 業

PRONUNCIATIONS: gyou, waza **MEANINGS:** hard work, skills **EXAMPLES:** 卒業 sotsugyou = graduation; 工業 kougyou = industry; 授業 jugyou = class; 仕業 shiwaza = deeds, acts **DESCRIPTION:** at the bottom, an ordinary 木 ki (tree, # 118); above this tree are several extra branches, capped by a tray carrying four lights, resembling a Christmas tree **CUES:** 卒業 sotsu**gyou** (graduation) is a celebration that reminds us of Christmas, since it's an occasion when we can eat **Gyo**za (pot stickers) and **Wa**tch **Za**chary open his graduation presents **COMPARE:** 僕 boku = I (male), # 333

333. 僕

PRONUNCIATION: boku **MEANING:** I (male) **EXAMPLE:** 僕 boku = I (male) **DESCRIPTION:** on the left, a man with a slanted hat, who is bony; on the right, compared to 業 gyou (hard work, # 332), this radical is missing its central trunk at the bottom **CUE:** 僕 **boku** (I) am a **Bony Kool**-

Aid salesman, and ever since I cut the central trunk from 業 gyou (hard work), I stay in bed all day, not wearing my slanted hat

Man with a Double Hat

334. 行

PRONUNCIATIONS: i*ku, kou, okona*u, gyou*ji, yu*ki **MEANINGS:** to go, carry out, conduct a business **EXAMPLES:** 行く iku = to go; 銀行 ginkou = bank; 行う okonau = to conduct; 行事 gyouji = event; 東京行き toukyou yuki = bound for Tokyo
DESCRIPTION: on the left, a man from Italy with a double hat; on the right, this J-shaped radical is a nail, with a line above it which could represent a hammer
CUES: the man with a double hat from **I**taly has a **Co**ld, but he will 行く **i**ku (go) to **O**klah**O**ma **N**ow, carrying a hammer and a nail, to get some **Gyo**za for the **Yu**le celebration

335. 後

PRONUNCIATIONS: ushi*ro, go, ato, nochi*hodo **MEANINGS:** behind, later, rear
EXAMPLES: 後ろ ushiro = behind; 午後 gogo = afternoon; 後で ato de = later; 後ほど nochihodo = afterward, later; 明後日 asatte = the day after tomorrow
NOTE: it isn't practical to divide 明後日 asatte (the day after tomorrow, also pronounced myougonichi) into three component pronunciations; fortunately, it is usually written あさって **DESCRIPTION:** on the left, a man with a double hat; on the right, a dancer with a ponytail who is an usher, holding a gun over her head, similar to the gun of a 糸 (skeet shooter, # 219) **CUES:** next to the man with the double hat, we see a dancer who is an **Ush**er from **Iran**, pointing a gun to the 後ろ **ushi**ro (rear); she will spend **Go**ld in the 午後 **go**go (afternoon) to buy an **Ato**mic clock, and 後で **ato** de (later) she

will eat some g**Nocchi** **COMPARE:** 係(り) kakari = person in charge, # 492

Every

336. 毎

PRONUNCIATIONS: mai, goto **MEANING:** every **EXAMPLES:** 毎週 maishuu = every week; 三日毎に mikka goto ni = every three days **DESCRIPTION:** at the top, a crutch belonging to Michael Jackson; at the bottom, 田(んぼ) tanbo (rice paddy, # 68)
CUES: 毎日 **mai**nichi (every day), **M**ichael grabs his crutch, loads the **Go**ats into the **To**yota, and goes out to the 田 (rice paddy)
COMPARE: 海 umi = ocean, # 337

337. 海

PRONUNCIATIONS: umi, kai **MEANINGS:** ocean, sea, beach **EXAMPLES:** 海 umi = ocean; 海外 kaigai = overseas
DESCRIPTION: on the left, a water radical (see # 12), suggesting the ocean; on the right, 毎 mai (every, # 336) **CUES:** 毎 (every) year I go to the 海 **umi** (ocean) to watch **U**ber **M**ilitary exercises with the **Kai**ser

What

338. 何

PRONUNCIATIONS: nan, nani **MEANING:** what **EXAMPLES:** 何人 nannin = how many people; 何 nani = what
DESCRIPTION: on the left, a man with a slanted hat watching over a mysterious box under a lean-to
CUES: seeing this box, **Nan**cy and her **Nan**ny ask, "何ですか **nan** desu ka" (what is it?)
COMPARE: 同(じ) onaji = the same, # 339; 向(こう) mukou = opposite (side), # 340; 伺(う) ukagau = to humbly visit, # 341; 荷(物) nimotsu = luggage, # 342

339. 同

PRONUNCIATIONS: ona*ji, dou
MEANINGS: the same, the said EXAMPLES:
同じ onaji = the same; 同情 doujou =
sympathy, pity DESCRIPTION: compared to
何 nani (what, # 338), this kanji is 同じ
onaji (the same) on both the right and the left,
i.e., it is symmetrical CUES: there is an Old
Nasty Doughnut above the box, which is
probably 同じ onaji (the same) as whatever
is inside the box COMPARE: 向(こう)
mukou = opposite (side), # 340; 伺(う)
ukagau = to humbly visit, # 341

340. 向

PRONUNCIATIONS: mu, kou MEANINGS:
to face, opposite side EXAMPLES: 向く
muku = to face toward; 向かう mukau = to
go toward; 向こう mukou = the other side;
方向 houkou = direction DESCRIPTION:
compared to 同 ona (the same, # 339), the line
above the box has moved to the opposite side
of the upper fence CUES: the ground is
Mucky and Cold on the 向こう mukou
(opposite) side of the upper fence
COMPARE: 何 nani = what, # 338; 伺(う)
ukagau = to humbly visit, # 341

341. 伺

PRONUNCIATION: ukaga*u MEANINGS: to
pay respects, visit, inquire EXAMPLE: 伺う
ukagau = to ask humbly, to visit humbly
DESCRIPTION: compared to 何 nani (what,
338), there is a line above the box CUE: an
Uber California Gambler 伺う ukagau
(humbly visits) in order to 伺う ukagau
(humbly inquire) about this line above the box,
before betting on the contents of the box
COMPARE: 同(じ) onaji = the same, # 339;
向(く) muku = to face toward, # 340

342. 荷

PRONUNCIATIONS: ni*motsu, ka
MEANINGS: to carry, luggage EXAMPLES:
荷物 nimotsu = luggage; 出荷する
shukka suru = to ship or send DESCRIPTION:
at the top, a plant radical (see # 43); at the
bottom, 何 nani (what, # 338)

CUES: Question: 何 (what) is your Niece
carrying in her 荷物 nimotsu (luggage)?
Answer: it's Cabbage, which is plant material.

Bicycle

343. 去

PRONUNCIATIONS: kyo*nen, sa*ru, ko
MEANINGS: to leave, past EXAMPLES:
去年 kyonen = last year; 去る saru = to
leave; 過去 kako = the past

DESCRIPTION: at the top, 土 tsuchi (dirt,
59), which looks like a cross; at the bottom,
the katakana character ム mu under a
horizontal line, which looks like a pedaling leg
CUES: after buying a bicycle in Kyoto 去年
kyonen (last year), Saruman decided to 去る
saru (depart), so he put on his cross and rode
his bike to Kobe, where he had lived in the 過
去 kako (past)
COMPARE: 法(律) houritsu = law, # 344

344. 法

PRONUNCIATIONS: hou, pou MEANING:
law EXAMPLES: 法律 houritsu = law;
方法 houhou = method; 文法 bunpou =
grammar, syntax DESCRIPTION: on the left,
a water radical (see # 12); on the right, 去
(る) saru (to leave, # 343), which reminds us
of Saruman wearing a cross and riding a bike
CUES: Saruman leaves, but since there's a
Hole in the bridge, his bike falls into the water,
and he decides to pass a 法律 houritsu (law)
telling the Police to prohibit bikes on the
bridge

345. 伝

PRONUNCIATIONS: den, tsuta*eru, tsuda
MEANINGS: to convey, transmit, hand down
EXAMPLES: 伝言 dengon = message;
伝える tsutaeru = to convey or hand down;
手伝う tetsudau = to help DESCRIPTION:
on the left, a man with a slanted hat from
Denmark; at the top right, a horizontal line
which could represent a bicycle's basket; at
the bottom right, a pedaling leg, representing a
bicycle CUES: a man with a slanted hat from
Denmark rides a bike with a 伝言 **den**gon
(message) in the basket which he will
伝える **tsuta**eru (convey); he usually wears
a Tsuit and Tails, but the Tsuit got Damaged

Snail

346. 週

PRONUNCIATION: shuu MEANING: week
EXAMPLE: 来週 raishuu = next week
DESCRIPTION: on the lower left, a snail; the
snail carries a tent containing 土 tsuchi (dirt,
59) near the top and a package containing
shoes at the bottom, hidden under the dirt
CUE: our **Sho**es arrive 毎週 mai**shuu** (every
week) in a box hidden under some 土 (dirt),
carried by snail mail COMPARE:
調(べる) shiraberu = to check, # 441

347. 達

PRONUNCIATIONS: tachi, dachi, tatsu
MEANINGS: plural, friend EXAMPLES:
人達 hitotachi = people; 友達 tomodachi =
friend; 速達 sokutatsu = express mail
DESCRIPTION: on the lower left, a snail; on
the snail, a tower with 5 levels for attaching
notices CUES: the snail carries a tower with 5
levels, enough to hold many 人達 hito**tachi**
(people), who are at**Tach**ing political notices
with **D**ark **Chee**se to the tower; this is titsu for
Tatsu, since the other political party is doing
the same thing to them COMPARE: 幸 sachi
(happiness, # 385), which has only 4 levels

348. 送

PRONUNCIATIONS: oku*ru, sou MEANING:
to send EXAMPLES: 送る okuru = to send,
or to drop off; 放送 housou = broadcast
DESCRIPTION: on the lower left, a snail; on
the snail, an 大(きい) ookii (big, # 188)
person named Oklahoma's Uber Ruth, wearing
a hat with two antennae
CUES: on a snail, **Ok**lahoma's **U**ber **Ru**th, a
big person wearing antennae, runs left and
right, 送る **oku**ru (sends out) packages, and
放送する hou**sou** suru (broadcasts) **So**rdid
electronic messages with her antennae

349. 道

PRONUNCIATIONS: tou, dou, michi
MEANINGS: road, street, direction
EXAMPLES: 神道 shintou = a Japanese
religion based on animism and ancestor
worship; 道路 douro = road; 道 michi =
street DESCRIPTION: on the lower left, a taxi
snail from Michigan; on the snail, 首 kubi
(neck, # 56) CUES: this snail is carrying a 首
(neck) to its **T**ony **D**ormitory, but there is a
bottleneck in this 道 **michi** (street) in
Michigan COMPARE: 通(る) tooru = to
pass through, # 365, and 通(り) doori = in
accordance with, or Avenue, # 365

350. 遅

PRONUNCIATIONS: oso*i, oku*reru, chi*koku MEANINGS: slow, late

EXAMPLES: 遅い osoi = late, slow; 遅れる okureru = to be delayed; 遅刻する chikoku suru = to be tardy

DESCRIPTION: on the lower left, a snail, which is carrying a lean-to with a double roof; under the lean-to, Oscar the oily 羊 hitsuji (sheep, not included in this catalogue – an animal with two horns, two ears, four legs and a tail) is returning from the oil fields

CUES: the snail carries Oscar the Oily 羊 (sheep), plus a double roof above Oscar, causing the snail to move slowly, and it appears that Oscar will be 遅い osoi (late) to work, he will 遅れる okureru (be delayed) to the Occult museum, and he will 遅刻する chikoku suru (be tardy) on his trip to the Cheese factory

351. 遠

PRONUNCIATIONS: too*i, en*ryo, doo

MEANING: distant, far EXAMPLES: 遠い tooi = far; 遠慮 enryo = reserve; 待ち遠しい machidooshii = long for, look forward to DESCRIPTION: on the lower left, a snail; at the top, 土 tsuchi (dirt, # 59), but this looks like a t, which could stand for "tooi" (distant); at the bottom, a machine on a tripod, with a speaker extending to the right, which could be a toy megaphone CUES: this snail carries a megaphone, hidden under some 土 (dirt), which looks like a Toy but which an advertiser can use to speak to people in 遠い tooi (distant) places, Encouraging them to eat Doughnuts COMPARE: (公)園 kouen = park, # 279

352. 選

PRONUNCIATIONS: era*bu, sen MEANING: to choose EXAMPLES: 選ぶ erabu = to choose; 選挙 senkyo = election; 選手 senshuu = athlete DESCRIPTION: on the lower left, a snail; on the snail's back, at the top, two backward S's, which may represent two senators standing for election in the era of Bush, elevated on a high platform

CUES: the snail is a 選挙 senkyo (election) van, carrying two candidates for the Senate, from which one had to 選ぶ erabu (choose) during the Era of Bush

COMPARE: 替(える) kaeru = to replace or to exchange money, # 551

353. 連

PRONUNCIATIONS: ren, tsu*rete MEANINGS: linking, accompanying

EXAMPLES: 連絡する renraku suru = to contact; 連れて行く tsurete iku = to bring a person along DESCRIPTION: on the lower left, a snail; above the snail, a rental 車 kuruma (car, # 283)

CUES: my Rental car broke down, and after I 連絡した renraku shita (contacted) the agency, they sent this snail to pick up the car, after which they 連れて行った tsurete itta (took me along) to my destination, but I forgot my Tsuitcase in the rental car

COMPARE: 運(ぶ) hakobu = to carry, # 354

354. 運

PRONUNCIATIONS: hako*bu, un MEANINGS: to transport, luck EXAMPLES: 運ぶ hakobu = to carry or transport; 運動 undou = exercise, 運転する unten suru = to operate or drive; 運 un = luck, fortune

DESCRIPTION: on the lower left, a snail; on the right, 車 kuruma (car, # 283), covered by a lid, which also serves as a hat on cold days CUES: the snail can 運ぶ hakobu (carry) this 車 (car), and the car can 運ぶ hakobu (carry) this lid, which also serves as a Hat on Cold days; Undoubtedly the hat also protects us from rain when we 運動する undou suru (exercise) COMPARE: 連(絡) renraku = contact, # 353

355. 違

PRONUNCIATIONS: chiga*u, i*han
MEANINGS: to differ, wrong **EXAMPLES:**
違う chigau = different; 違反 ihan =
violation, offense **DESCRIPTION:** on the
lower left, a snail, carrying a radical that looks
about the same whether it is right side up or
upside down; reportedly this represents two
feet facing in opposite directions

CUES: two feet on a snail that are 違う
chigau (different) in that they face in opposite
directions; both feet have been been bitten up
by **Chig**gers and **A**nts, not to mention **Ee**ls

356. 返

PRONUNCIATIONS: kae, hen **MEANING:** to
return something **EXAMPLES:** 返す kaesu
= to return an item; 返事 henji = reply
DESCRIPTION: on the lower left, a snail; on
the right, a large F over a smaller X **CUES:**
when I get an F on my paper, or have it marked
with an X, I put it on this snail and 返す
kaesu (return it) to the teacher, but the teacher
Calls **E**sther, my mother, and sends the paper
back to us on a **Hen COMPARE:** (ご)飯
gohan = meal, cooked rice, # 400

357. 込

PRONUNCIATION: ko*mu, komi
MEANING: to get crowded **EXAMPLES:**
込む komu = to get crowded; 申込書
moushikomisho = application form
DESCRIPTION: on the lower left, a commuter
snail; on the right, 入(る) hairu (to enter,
14) **CUES:** many people 入 (enter) the
snail bus in order to **Commute** to work, but it
込む **ko**mu (gets crowded), often **Com**ically
so **NOTE:** recently, Japanese people are more
likely to use an alternative spelling, 混む, for
komu when it appears by itself and means "to
get crowded"; they use 込む in compound
words, like 飛び込む tobikomu = to dive

358. 迎

PRONUNCIATIONS: muka*eru, gei
MEANING: to welcome **EXAMPLES:**
迎える mukaeru = to greet/welcome;
歓迎する kangei suru = to welcome
DESCRIPTION: on the lower left, a snail; on
the snail, two standing figures who could be
Moonies **CUES:** two **Moo**nies **Ca**ll to
potential donors as they ride on a snail to the
station, where they will 迎える **muka**eru
(greet and welcome) a colleague **Gai**ly

359. 速

PRONUNCIATIONS: haya*i, soku
MEANING: fast **EXAMPLES:** 速い hayai =
fast; 速達 sokutatsu = express mail;
高速道路 kousokudouro = expressway;
早速 sassoku = immediately
DESCRIPTION: on the lower left, a snail
heading to Prince Harry's yacht; riding on the
snail, (約)束 yakusoku (promise, # 99)

CUES: 束 (soku), which looks like a tree
wearing glasses, is 速い **haya**i (fast), in spite
of using a snail for transport, since his glasses
allow him to see far ahead and avoid obstacles;
he is heading to Prince **H**arry's **Ya**cht, where
he will **Soak** in the tub

360. 遊

PRONUNCIATIONS: aso*bu, yuu*enchi
MEANINGS: to play, have fun **EXAMPLES:**
遊ぶ asobu = to play; 遊園地 yuuenchi =
playground **DESCRIPTION:** on the lower left,
a snail; above the snail, 方 kata (honorable
people, # 114), a crutch, and 子 ko (child,
182) **CUES:** an **Asso**ciate boot maker allows
his handicapped 子 (child) to 遊ぶ **aso**bu
(play) with 方 (honorable people) on snails in
the **Yu**kon

361. 過

PRONUNCIATIONS: su, ka, ayama*chi
MEANINGS: to pass through, excessively
EXAMPLES: 食べ過ぎる tabesugiru = to overeat; 過ぎる sugiru = to pass by; 過去 kako = the past; 過ち ayamachi = fault, error DESCRIPTION: on the lower left, a snail; on the right, two boxes which each contain a smaller package holding Superman's geese; in the upper box, the inner package has slipped out of place CUES: I placed these two packages containing Superman's geese into the center of larger boxes for transport on this snail, but I やり過ぎた yarisugita (overdid it) by piling them so high, and the package that was in the center of the upper box slipped out of place, resulting in a Cacophony of honking, and the Ayatollah got Mad

362. 辺

PRONUNCIATIONS: hen, ata*ri, nabe, be
MEANINGS: area, around, peripheral, edge
EXAMPLES: この辺 kono hen = around here; その辺り sono atari = around there; 田辺 Tanabe = family name; 水辺 mizube = waterside DESCRIPTION: on the lower left, a snail; on the right, a 刀 katana (sword, #102) used to guard hens

CUES: I keep my 刀 (sword) on the back of my snail when guarding the Hens in this hen 辺 (area) near the Atari company; Nancy and Betty are my favorites, and then there is Betsy

363. 建

PRONUNCIATIONS: ta*teru, tate*mono, ken
MEANING: to erect a building EXAMPLES: 建てる tateru = to build; 建物 tatemono = building; 建築 kenchiku = architecture
DESCRIPTION: the radical seen at the left and bottom of this kanji is different from the snail radical seen earlier in this section; we can call it a "3x snail," since it consists of a 3 intersected at the bottom to form an X; on the right, a three-fingered hand has been placed across

the top of a telegraph pole, and this is similar to the three-fingered hand in 書く kaku (to write, #415) CUES: before they 建てる tateru (erect) a Taxi garage for a Tall Techie, Ken and Barbie must review their plans 3x and write them down

Fence

364. 用

PRONUNCIATION: you, mochi MEANINGS: errand, to use EXAMPLES: 用事 youji = errand; 利用する riyou suru = to use; 用いる mochiiru = to use DESCRIPTION: a Japanese fence, made from pieces of bamboo and tied together with rope CUES: we will 利用する riyou suru (use) this fence to enclose a cow, so that we can make our own Yogurt and stop Mooching from the neighbors

365. 通

PRONUNCIATIONS: too*ru, tsuu, doo, kayo*u
MEANING: to pass through EXAMPLES: 通う kayou = to commute; 通る tooru = to pass through; 通り toori = street, way; 通学する tsuugaku suru = to commute to school; 通り doori = in accordance with, Avenue DESCRIPTION: on the lower left, a snail; at the upper right, the katakana character マ ma, which represents a mammoth; at the lower right, 用 you (errand, #364) which resembles a fence

CUES: a マ (mammoth) on (or inside) its 用 (fence) 通う kayou (commutes) on a snail to its job at a lakeside hotel, where mammoths 通る tooru (pass through) the lobby Towing Tsuitcases, guests arrive in Dories, and Coyotes roam the grounds

COMPARE: 踊(る) odoru = to dance, #366; 痛(い) itai = painful, #368; 道 tou, or dou, = road, street, direction, #349

366. 踊

PRONUNCIATION: odo*ru **MEANINGS:** to dance or skip **EXAMPLE:** 踊る odoru = to dance **DESCRIPTION:** on the left, a square head on 正(しい) tadashii (correct, # 174), suggesting a correct gentleman; on the right, the katakana character マ ma, which represents a mammoth, on (or perhaps inside) 用 you (errand, # 364), which resembles a fence **CUE:** a 正 (correct) gentleman and a マ (mammoth) in its 用 (fence) 踊る **odo**ru (dance) together, which leaves a distinctive **Odor** of mammoth on the gentleman **COMPARE:** 通(う) kayou = to commute, # 365; 痛(い) itai = painful, # 368

367. 備

PRONUNCIATIONS: sona*eru, bi **MEANINGS:** to be prepared or equipped with **EXAMPLES:** 備える sonaeru = to prepare, have, be equipped with; 準備 junbi = preparation; 設備 setsubi = equipment, facility **DESCRIPTION:** on the left, a man with a slanted hat; at the top right, some bushes above a lean-to; at the bottom right, 用 you (errand, # 364), which resembles a fence **CUES:** a man with a slanted hat uses **Sonar** to monitor the **B**ingo games that are held in his 設備 setsu**bi** (facility), which is a lean-to under a roof garden, with a fence around it

Vertical Bed

368. 痛

PRONUNCIATIONS: ita*i, tsuu **MEANING:** pain **EXAMPLES:** 痛い itai = painful; 頭痛 zutsuu = headache **DESCRIPTION:** on the upper left, a bed shown vertically, with legs pointing to the left and a headboard at the top; in the bed, 用 you (errand, # 364), which resembles a fence, with the katakana character マ ma, which could represent a mammoth,

above it **CUES:** the マ (mammoth) on the 用 (fence), who comes from **Ita**ly and is wearing a **Tsu**it, is being squeezed against this headboard, which 痛い **ita**i (hurts) **COMPARE:** 通(う) kayou = to commute, # 365; 踊(る) odoru = to dance, # 366

369. 病

PRONUNCIATIONS: ya*mai, byou **MEANINGS:** illness, disease, sick **EXAMPLES:** 病 yamai = illness; 病気 byouki = illness **DESCRIPTION:** on the upper left, a bed shown vertically, with legs pointing to the left and a headboard at the top; inside the bed, 内 uchi (within, # 396), suspended from a horizontal beam, resembling a chest x-ray of a yak, with ribs superimposed on lungs **CUES:** the chest x-ray of a **Ya**k on a bed suggests a 病気 **byou**ki (illness) which could be **B.O.** (bacterial overgrowth)

370. 疲

PRONUNCIATIONS: tsuka*reru, hi*rou **MEANINGS:** to get tired, fatigue **EXAMPLES:** 疲れる tsukareru = to get tired; 疲労 hirou = fatigue, weariness **DESCRIPTION:** on the upper left, a bed shown vertically, with legs pointing to the left and a headboard at the top; in the bed, at the top, an arrow pointing to the right, intersected by a vertical line, representing a guy named Straight Arrow, who has a long cape that trails down to the end of the bed on the left; at the bottom, 又 mata ("again," # 24), but this looks like Straight Arrow's springy legs **CUES:** Straight Arrow 疲れた **tsuka**reta (got tired) and is sleeping in this bed; he left his **Tsu**it in the **Car**, but he's still wearing his **Hero**'s cape **COMPARE:** 彼 kare = he, # 371

371. 彼

PRONUNCIATIONS: kare, kano*jo
MEANINGS: he, she **EXAMPLES:** 彼 kare = he; 彼女 kanojo = she **DESCRIPTION:** on the left, a man with a double hat; at the upper right, an arrow pointing to the right, intersected by a vertical line, representing a guy named Straight Arrow, who has a long cape on the left that trails down to the floor; at the lower right, 又 mata ("again," # 24), but this looks like Straight Arrow's springy legs **CUES:** the man with a double hat and Straight Arrow are males who eat a lot of **Kare**e (curry) made with **Cano**la oil, and either of them can be referred to as 彼 **kare** (he) **COMPARE:** 疲(れる) tsukareru = to get tired, # 370

372. 寝

PRONUNCIATIONS: ne*ru, shin*shitsu
MEANINGS: to sleep or lie down
EXAMPLES: 寝る neru = to go to bed, to sleep; 寝室 shinshitsu = bedroom
DESCRIPTION: on the left, a bed shown vertically; there is a roof at the top; on the right, long hair belonging to Nervous Ruth, streaming to the left, above a platform that is resting on 又 mata ("again," # 24), but this looks like Ruth's springy legs

CUES: **Ne**rvous Ruth **ne**ru 寝る (sleeps) in this bed, with her long hair falling to the left, after saying her **Shin**to prayers

373. 北

PRONUNCIATIONS: kita, ho, boku
MEANING: north **EXAMPLES:** 北 kita = north; 北海道 hokkaidou = Hokkaido; 敗北 haiboku = defeat **DESCRIPTION:** on the left, a bed, shown vertically; on the right, the katakana character ヒ hi, which resembles a king lying in bed; together, these two radicals seem to point north **CUES:** a **K**ing reviews his **Ta**x code while lying in bed, with his head pointing 北 **kita** (north), where he keeps a **Ho**me at the North Pole; the home is nice, and as a **Bo**nus he stays **Coo**l

374. 将

PRONUNCIATIONS: kami, shou
MEANINGS: future, army general
EXAMPLES: 女将 okami = mistress, landlady, hostess, proprietress; 将来 shourai = future; 大将 taishou = a general in the military **DESCRIPTION:** on the left, a bed shown vertically; at the upper right, several floating lines that suggest dreams floating in the air; at the lower right, a Commie (Communist) lying in the bed, with an object next to her feet, which could be *Das Kapital* **CUES:** a **Commie** lying on a bed sees visions of the 将来 **shou**rai (future) dancing above her head; she believes that these dreams **Show Life** as it will be after the Revolution

COMPARE: 紙 kami = paper, # 221; 神 kami = god, # 273; 髪 kami = hair, # 501

Citizen
375. 民

PRONUNCIATION: min **MEANING:** people
EXAMPLES: 市民 shimin = citizen; 国民 kokumin = people of a nation, citizens
DESCRIPTION: on the upper left, a lean-to with a double roof; at the lower right, a mean bending person trying to squeeze into it

CUE: these 市民 shi**min** (citizens) are squeezed into their lean-to's like sardines in a can, which is one reason that they are so **Mean**

COMPARE: 眠(る) nemuru = to sleep, # 376; 宅 taku = home, # 21

376. 眠

PRONUNCIATIONS: nemu*ru, min
MEANING: to sleep **EXAMPLES:** 眠る nemuru = to sleep; 眠い nemui = sleepy; 睡眠を取る suimin wo toru = to get some sleep **DESCRIPTION:** on the left, 目 me (eye, # 51); on the right, (市)民 shimin (citizen, # 375) **CUES:** the 目 (eyes) of this citizen are wide open, since he can't 眠る **nemu**ru

(sleep), because his **N**eighbors' **Mu**sic ruins his rest, and this makes him **Mean**

Festival

377. 祭

PRONUNCIATIONS: sai, matsu*ri
MEANINGS: festival, to worship
EXAMPLES: 祭日 saijitsu = holiday; 祭り matsuri = festival
DESCRIPTION: a spinning pavilion with a peaked roof; on the left roof, a three-legged bench; on the right roof, a slice of pizza
CUES: as we admired this spinning pavilion decorated for a **Sci**entific 祭り **matsu**ri (festival), we sat on the **Mat** that **Su**perman brought and enjoyed seeing the three-legged bench and the pizza slice on the roof
COMPARE: 途(中) tochuu = on the way, # 378; (国)際 kokusai = international, # 379

378. 途

PRONUNCIATION: to*chuu **MEANINGS:** route, way **EXAMPLE:** 途中 tochuu = on the way **DESCRIPTION:** on the lower left, a snail; at the upper right, a pavilion spinning like a tornado, with a peaked roof; unlike 祭 matsu (festival, # 377), this pavilion carries no decorations **CUE:** a snail carries this pavilion which spins like a **T**ornado 途中 **to**chuu (on the way) to its destination

379. 際

PRONUNCIATIONS: sai, giwa, kiwa*datsu
MEANINGS: contact, edge of an area
EXAMPLES: 国際 kokusai = international; 手際 tegiwa = skill; 際立つ kiwadatsu = to stand out or be conspicuous
DESCRIPTION: on the left, ß from the Greek alphabet, suggesting Greek science; on the right, 祭 (り) matsuri (festival, # 377)
CUES: this festival has a 国際 koku**sai** (international) flavor; it includes exhibits on Greek **Sci**ence and **Gee**ky **W**arriors, and it is **Kee**nly **Wa**tched by the world

Horse

380. 駅

PRONUNCIATION: eki **MEANING:** train station **EXAMPLE:** 東京駅 toukyou eki = Tokyo station **DESCRIPTION:** on the left, reportedly this represents a horse; on the right, the square mounted high above the ground reportedly represents a "watchful eye"
CUE: this refers to the old custom of changing horses at the imperial 駅 **eki** (station) under the watchful eye of **E**dward the **K**ing
COMPARE: 訳 wake = reason, # 437

381. 駐

PRONUNCIATION: chuu **MEANING:** to park a vehicle **EXAMPLES:** 駐車する chuusha suru = to park a vehicle **DESCRIPTION:** on the left, reportedly this represents a horse; on the right, 主(人) shujin (master, # 166)
CUE: the master 駐車する **chuu**sha suru (parks) his horse and carriage, while the horse **Chews** hay

382. 験

PRONUNCIATION: ken **MEANING:** to examine **EXAMPLES:** 試験 shiken = examination; 経験 keiken = experience
DESCRIPTION: on the left, reportedly this represents a horse; on the right, a laundromat with a peaked roof, containing a keg stuck sideways in a washing machine **CUES:** **Ken** and his horse have arrived from **Ken**tucky to visit Barbie, and he will 経験する kei**ken** suru (experience) the stuck-keg problem when he does his laundry **COMPARE:** 険(しい) kewashii = steep, # 196

Needle

383. 親

PRONUNCIATIONS: oya, shin, shita*shii
MEANINGS: parent, intimate **EXAMPLES:**
親 oya = parent; 両親 ryoushin = parents;
親しい shitashii = intimate, close

DESCRIPTION: on the left, 木 ki (tree, # 118)
topped by an additional pair of branches and a
bell which, taken together, resemble a needle
with a syringe; on the right, 見(る) miru (to
look, # 53) **CUES:** when 親 <u>oya</u> (parents) say
Oyasuminasai (good night) to their kids, they
should look at their beds and check for **Shin**y
needles and **Shin**y **T**acks

COMPARE: 新 shin = new, # 389

384. 辛

PRONUNCIATIONS: kara*i, tsura*i
MEANINGS: spicy, bitter, hot, salty
EXAMPLES: 辛い karai = spicy, hot; 辛い
tsurai = painful, tormenting **NOTE:** karai and
tsurai are both spelled 辛い **DESCRIPTION:**
a needle and syringe; compared to the needle
in 新 shin (new, # 389), 辛 is missing two
handles near the bottom **CUES:** while singing
Karaoke and eating 辛い <u>kara</u>i (spicy) food
at a dude ranch, I found a needle in the food, so
I **Tsu**ed the **R**anch **COMPARE:** 幸(せ)
shiawase = happiness, # 385

385. 幸

PRONUNCIATIONS: shiawa*se, sachi, saiwa*i,
kou MEANINGS: happiness, good luck
EXAMPLES: 幸せ shiawase = happiness;
幸子 Sachiko = a girl's given name; 幸い
saiwai = lucky, happy; 幸福 koufuku =
happiness DESCRIPTION: 幸 has 4 levels,
compared to 辛(い) karai (spicy, # 384),
which has only 3 levels; also, 幸 has an
antenna at the top **CUES:** I live in a **Sh**ia
country torn by **W**ar, and there are some **Sa**d
Children here, and a lot of spicy food, but if I

can take **S**ilent **W**alks, fight off **C**olds, and
keep this antenna on my roof, that means
幸せ <u>shiawa</u>se (happiness) for me, and I feel
幸い <u>saiwa</u>i (lucky) **COMPARE:** 達 tachi
(plural, # 347), where the tower has 5 levels

386. 報

PRONUNCIATION: hou MEANINGS: report,
news EXAMPLES: 報告 houkoku = report;
予報 yohou = forecast DESCRIPTION: on
the left, 幸 sachi (happiness, # 385),
resembling a syringe with a needle; on the
right, a dressing room, with a hook for hanging
clothes **CUES:** we received a 報告 <u>hou</u>koku
(report) about a **Ho**rnet with a needle-like
stinger near the **Hoo**k in the dressing room
COMPARE: 服 fuku = clothes, # 150

387. 辞

PRONUNCIATIONS: ji*sho, ya*meru
MEANINGS: word, to resign **EXAMPLES:**
辞書 jisho = dictionary; 辞める yameru =
to resign a position DESCRIPTION: on the
left, 口 kuchi (mouth, # 426), with a forked
tongue emerging from it; on the right, 辛(い)
karai (spicy, # 384) **CUES:** **J**immy Carter
showed us his forked tongue after he finished
his work tasting **Ya**m recipes; the recipes were
too 辛 (spicy) for him, so he will start
working on a 辞書 <u>ji</u>sho (dictionary) project
and 辞める <u>ya</u>meru (resign) from his tasting
job **COMPARE:** 止(める) yameru = to stop
doing something, to give up, # 173

388. 南

PRONUNCIATIONS: minami, nan
MEANING: south EXAMPLES: 南 minami =
south; 南米 nanbei = South America
DESCRIPTION: at the sides and top, a weather
station, with an antenna on top; inside the
weather station, a needle pointing south
CUES: in the weather station located near the
Minaret of **Mi**ckey's mosque, the compass

needle points 南 **minami** (south), rather than north, according to Mickey's **Nan**ny

Pliers

389. 新

PRONUNCIATIONS: atara*shii, shin
MEANINGS: new, fresh   EXAMPLES:
新しい atarashii = new, fresh; 新聞 shinbun = newspaper   DESCRIPTION: on the left, 木 ki (tree, # 118) topped by an additional pair of branches and a bell; this resembles a shiny syringe and needle; on the right, a pair of pliers   CUES: I store my **Atara**x (allergy medicine) with an 新しい **atara**shii (new) **Shin**y needle and a pair of pliers
COMPARE: 親 shin = parent, # 383

390. 近

PRONUNCIATIONS: chika*i, kin*jo
MEANING: near, close   EXAMPLES: 近い chikai = close; 近所 kinjo = neighborhood; 最近 saikin = recently   DESCRIPTION: on the lower left, a snail from Chicago; on the snail, a pair of pliers   CUES: this snail is an electrician from **Chica**go who carries a pair of pliers that he uses on wires that are 近い **chika**i (near) the **Kin**dergarten where he works

391. 所

PRONUNCIATIONS: tokoro, dokoro[1], jo, sho
MEANING: place   EXAMPLES: 所 tokoro = place; 台所 daidokoro = kitchen; 近所 kinjo = neighborhood; 場所 basho = place
DESCRIPTION: on the left, under a roof, a P, which could stand for "Place"; on the right, a pair of pliers   CUES: after **T**ony Bennett had a **Coro**nary, **Jo**an of Arc used pliers to fix up his 所 **tokoro** (place) for a **Show**

Old

392. 古

PRONUNCIATIONS: furu*i, go, ko
MEANINGS: old, referring to things
EXAMPLES: 古い furui = old; 名古屋 Nagoya = city in Japan; 古代 kodai = ancient times
DESCRIPTION: a box with a cross on it
CUES: I was **Fu**rious when they **Ru**ined that 古い **furu**i (old) tomb with a **Go**ld cross on top, where the **Co**debreaker was buried

393. 苦

PRONUNCIATIONS: niga*i, ku, kuru*shii
MEANINGS: bitter, painful   EXAMPLES:
苦い nigai = hard, painful; 苦手 nigate = weak point; 苦労 kurou = hardship; 苦しい kurushii = hard, painful
DESCRIPTION: at the top, a plant radical (see # 43), representing Nigerian apple trees; at the bottom, 古(い) furui (old, # 392)   CUES: it's 苦い **niga**i (bitter) to see 古 (old) tombs overgrown with **Nig**erian **A**pple trees, and it's even worse when rac**Coo**ns dig up the levee, and the river's **Current Ru**ins the cemetery

394. 故

PRONUNCIATIONS: ko, yue   MEANINGS: past, to cause   EXAMPLES: 事故 jiko = accident; 故障 koshou = breakdown; 故に yue ni = therefore   DESCRIPTION: on the left, 古(い) furui (old, # 392); on the right, a guy holding a crutch   CUES: an 古 (old) car from **Co**lombia was involved in a 事故 j**iko** (accident), and now the driver is crippled and has to fly home by **U.A.** (United Airlines)

395. 個

PRONUNCIATION: ko **MEANINGS:** individual, counter for eggs, etc. **EXAMPLES:** 卵三個 tamago sanko = three eggs; 個人 kojin = individual **DESCRIPTION:** on the left, a man with a slanted hat; on the right, 古(い) furui (old, # 392), inside a cold box **CUE:** the man with a slanted hat keeps 卵一個 tamago ik**ko** (one egg) in a **Co**ld box, but the egg is getting 古 (old) **COMPARE:** 週 shuu = week, # 346

Inside

396. 内

PRONUNCIATIONS: nai, uchi **MEANING:** inside **EXAMPLES:** 国内 kokunai = inside the country; 家内 kanai = my wife; その内に sono uchi ni = before long **DESCRIPTION:** a person extending her head through a hole in the roof of a building **CUES:** a 家内 ka**nai** (wife) with a **Kni**fe and some **Uber Chee**se is 内 **uchi** (inside) a dwelling, with her head protruding through a hole in the roof **COMPARE:** 家 uchi = home, # 405; 病(気) byouki = illness, # 369; 肉 niku = meat, # 397

397. 肉

PRONUNCIATION: niku **MEANING:** meat **EXAMPLE:** 肉 niku = meat **DESCRIPTION:** these look like ribs on an chest x-ray, surrounded by meat **CUE: Ni**cholas in **Ku**wait sent us some 肉 **niku** (meat) which was x-rayed in Customs **COMPARE:** 内 uchi = within, # 396

Eat

398. 食

PRONUNCIATIONS: ta*beru, shoku, ku*u **MEANING:** to eat **EXAMPLES:** 食べる taberu = to eat; 食事 shokuji = meal; 食う kuu = to eat (rough speech) **DESCRIPTION:** at the top, a peaked roof, suggesting a tabernacle; at the bottom, 良(い) yoi (good, # 303) **CUES:** after I 食べる **ta**beru (eat) near the **Ta**bernacle, I usually **Show** some **Koo**l-Aid packages to my 良 (good) **Koo**ky friends **COMPARE:** 娘 musume = daughter, # 316; 飲(む) nomu = to drink, # 399; (ご)飯 gohan = meal, cooked rice, # 400

399. 飲

PRONUNCIATIONS: no*mu, in **MEANINGS:** to drink or swallow **EXAMPLES:** 飲む nomu = to drink or swallow; 飲食 inshoku = drinking and eating **DESCRIPTION:** on the left, 食(べる) taberu (to eat, # 398); on the right, an oil derrick which drinks oil from the ground **CUES:** when the **No**mads on the moon 食 (eat), they 飲む **no**mu (drink) oil from the ground and then act **In**sane **COMPARE:** (ご)飯 gohan = meal, cooked rice, # 400

400. 飯

PRONUNCIATIONS: han, meshi **MEANING:** a meal **EXAMPLES:** ご飯 gohan = meal, cooked rice; 冷や飯 hiyameshi = cold rice **DESCRIPTION:** on the left, 食(事) shokuji (meal, # 398); on the right, an X under an F **CUES:** this ご飯 go**han** (cooked rice) 食 (meal) that **Han**sel made is **Me**ssy, and it gets an F; we're also marking it with an X **COMPARE:** 返(す) kaesu = to return something, # 356

Various

401. 物

PRONUNCIATIONS: motsu, butsu, bu*kka, mono **MEANINGS:** stuff, tangible things
EXAMPLES: 荷物 nimotsu = luggage; 動物 doubutsu = animal; 物価 bukka = price of goods; 物 mono = thing
DESCRIPTION: on the left, 牛 ushi (cow, # 205); on the right, this radical reportedly represents a variety of streamers, or "assorted things," which may produce a monotonous sound when the wind blows **CUES:** when we sit by the **Moats**, cows, old **Boots**, empty **Boo**ze bottles and other assorted 物 **mono** (things) make **Mono**tonous noise in the wind

402. 易

PRONUNCIATIONS: yasa*shii, eki, i **MEANINGS:** easy, fortune telling
EXAMPLES: 易しい yasashii = easy; 貿易 boueki = trade; 安易な an'i na = easy **DESCRIPTION:** at the top, 日 hi (sun, # 32); at the bottom, a variety of streamers which reportedly represent simple, various things, implying that things under the sun are simple and easy **CUES:** a **Ya**k **Sa**w a Shiite in the **Eki** (station) and told him that writing 日 (sun) and some streamers to form the character 易 yasa (easy) is 易しい **yasa**shii (**Ea**sy), compared to writing 優 yasa (kind)
COMPARE: 場(所) basho = place, # 403; 湯 yu = hot water, # 404; 駅 eki = station, # 380; 優(しい) yasashii = kind, # 528

403. 場

PRONUNCIATIONS: jou, ba **MEANING:** place **EXAMPLES:** 会場 kaijou = site of an event; 場所 basho = place
DESCRIPTION: on the left, 土 tsuchi (dirt, # 59) conveys the idea of place; on the right, 易(しい) yasashii (easy, # 402), with wide roots like those of banana trees
CUES: **Joa**n of Arc likes **Ba**nanas, and it's 易 (easy) for her to grow them in the 土 (dirt) in this 場所 **ba**sho (place)
COMPARE: 湯 yu = hot water, # 404

404. 湯

PRONUNCIATIONS: yu, tou **MEANINGS:** hot water, hot bath **EXAMPLES:** お湯 oyu = honorable hot water; 熱湯 nettou = boiling water **DESCRIPTION:** on the left, a water radical (see # 12); on the right, 易(しい) yasashii (easy, # 402), with long roots like those of yucca plants
CUES: growing **Yu**cca plants is 易 (easy); after giving them water, I relax in 湯 **yu** (hot water), and stretch my **Toe**s
COMPARE: 場(所) basho = place, # 403

405. 家

PRONUNCIATIONS: ie, uchi, ke, ka, ya*nushi **MEANINGS:** house, person **EXAMPLES:** 家 ie = house; 家 uchi = home, but Japanese people usually spell this うち, to avoid confusion with ie (house); 田中家 tanakake = the Tanaka family; 家族 kazoku = family; 家内 kanai = my wife; 家主 yanushi = landlord **DESCRIPTION:** at the top, a roof; at the bottom, this radical is also found in 豚 buta (pork, not included in this catalogue); it is not the same as the radicals seen in 物 mono (thing, # 401) and in 易(しい) (easy, # 402), although they are similar
CUES: this roof with a **Ye**llow pig under it is a 家 **ie** (house), where they make Uber **Chee**se, **Ke**n parks his **Ca**r, and Barbie grows **Ya**ms

Rocker-bottom

406. 参

PRONUNCIATIONS: mai*ru, san*ka
MEANINGS: to humbly come or go, to visit a temple or shrine **EXAMPLES:** 参る mairu = to humbly come or go; 参加 sanka = participation **DESCRIPTION:** at the top, the katakana character ム mu (the sound made by a cow); at the bottom, a rocker-bottom shoe **CUES:** wobbling on rocker-bottom shoes, a ム (cow) travels many **Mai**ru (miles) as she 参ります **mai**rimasu (humbly goes) to **San** Francisco **COMPARE:** 珍(しい) mezurashii = unusual, rare, # 407

407. 珍

PRONUNCIATION: mezura*shii
MEANINGS: rare, strange **EXAMPLE:**
珍しい mezurashii = unusual, rare
DESCRIPTION: on the left, 王 ou (king, not included in this catalogue); on the right, a rocker-bottom shoe **CUE:** when the 王 (king) visited a 珍しい **mezura**shii (unusual) **Me**xican **Zoo** to see **Ra**ccoons, he wore his rocker-bottom shoes **COMPARE:** 参(る) mairu = to humbly come or go, # 406

408. 歩

PRONUNCIATIONS: aru*ku, po, ho*dou
MEANINGS: to walk, step **EXAMPLES:**
歩く aruku = to walk; 散歩する sanpo suru = to walk, 歩道 hodou = sidewalk
DESCRIPTION: at the top, 止(める) tomeru (to stop, # 173); at the bottom, 少(し) sukoshi (a little, # 254); taken together, these resemble a rocker-bottom shoe with an ankle above it **CUES:** wearing my rocker-bottom shoes in **Aru**ba, I will 歩く **aru**ku (walk) for the Clean Air Trust fundraiser, in order to help stop **Po**llution a little, near my **Ho**me

Gate

409. 門

PRONUNCIATION: mon **MEANINGS:** gate, doors **EXAMPLE:** 門 mon = gate
DESCRIPTION: two swinging doors that form a gate **CUE:** I watch the 門 **mon** (gate) on **Mon**days

410. 問

PRONUNCIATIONS: mon, to*u **MEANINGS:** to question or inquire **EXAMPLES:** 問題 mondai = a problem; 質問 shitsumon = a question; 問う tou = to ask, question, inquire, to charge (with a crime) **DESCRIPTION:** compared to 門 mon (gate, # 409), this adds 口 kuchi (mouth, # 426), but 口 could be a Monet painting displayed inside a gate **CUE:** when we hang our **Mon**et painting under this gate, the **T**one of the colors changes, but this is only a small 問題 **mon**dai (problem)

411. 間

PRONUNCIATIONS: aida, ken, gen, kan, ma
MEANINGS: duration of time, between
EXAMPLES: 間 aida = duration, between; 世間 seken = society, other people; 人間 ningen = human being; 時間 jikan = time, hour; 間違える machigaeru = to make a mistake; 間もなく mamonaku = before long **DESCRIPTION:** compared to 門 mon (gate, # 409), this adds 日 hi (day, or sun, # 32), suggesting time **CUES:** standing near this gate, **Ida**, **Ken** and **Gen**ghis **Khan** can measure the 間 **aida** (duration) of time by **Ma**tching the shadows the 日 (sun) casts against marks on the ground **COMPARE:** 聞(く) kiku = to hear or ask, # 412

412. 聞

PRONUNCIATIONS: bun, ki*ku **MEANINGS:** to listen, hear, ask **EXAMPLES:** 新聞 shinbun = newspaper; 聞く kiku = to hear or ask **DESCRIPTION:** compared to 門 mon (gate, # 409), this adds 耳 mimi (ears, # 57) **CUES:** sitting under a 門 (gate) out in the **Boon**docks, we read 新聞 shin**bun** (newspapers) on our **Ki**ndles, open our 耳 (ears) to 聞く **ki**ku (listen) to gossip, and 聞く **ki**ku (ask) each other questions **COMPARE:** 間 aida = duration, between, # 411

413. 開

PRONUNCIATIONS: a, kai, hira **MEANINGS:** to open, to begin **EXAMPLES:** 開ける akeru = to open, transitive; 開く aku = to open, intransitive; 開発 kaihatsu = development; 開く hiraku = to open or unfold, transitive **NOTE:** both aku and hiraku are spelled 開く **DESCRIPTION:** compared to 門 mon (gate, # 409), 開 adds Achilles standing in the gate, who has a welcoming stance **CUES:** Achilles is standing in the gate with a welcoming stance, signaling that he will 開ける **a**keru (open) the gate so that people may bring their **Ki**tes inside, where they can **Hear Ra**p music **COMPARE:** 閉(める) shimeru = to close, transitive, # 414

414. 閉

PRONUNCIATIONS: to*jiru, shi, hei **MEANING:** to close **EXAMPLES:** 閉じる tojiru = to close; 閉める shimeru = to close, transitive; 閉鎖する heisa suru = to close down **DESCRIPTION:** compared to 門 mon (gate, # 409), 閉 adds a Tory standing in the gate, who has a forbidding stance **CUES:** a **Tory** in the gate extends a leg like a **Shie**ld to block passage, signifying that the gate 閉ま

っている **shi**matte iru (is closed) to people who want to harvest **Hay** **COMPARE:** 開 (ける) akeru = to open, # 413

Trident

415. 書

PRONUNCIATIONS: ka*ku, sho **MEANING:** to write **EXAMPLES:** 書く kaku = to write; 辞書 jisho = dictionary **DESCRIPTION:** at the top, a three-fingered hand that resembles a trident is grasping a vertical brush, which is writing on a table supported by a two-drawer cabinet **CUES:** I'm using a brush to 書く **ka**ku (write) a story about how I took a **Ca**n of Kool-Aid to a Broadway **Show**

416. 事

PRONUNCIATIONS: koto, goto, ji **MEANINGS:** an intangible thing or matter **EXAMPLES:** 事 koto = matter; 仕事 shigoto = work; 用事 youji = errand **DESCRIPTION:** the vertical line with a curve at the bottom represents a cylinder containing intangible things, and a three-fingered hand, which resembles a trident, is seen near the bottom, grasping the cylinder **CUES:** some 事 **koto** (things) are intangible, like **Koto** (Japanese harp) music, **Gho**st **To**es and **Ge**nius **COMPARE:** 言(葉) kotoba = words, # 430

417. 律

PRONUNCIATIONS: ritsu, richi*gi **MEANING:** law **EXAMPLES:** 法律 houritsu = law; 律儀な richigi na = conscientious **DESCRIPTION:** on the left, a man with a double hat named Richie; on the right, a telephone pole; the three-fingered trident near the top of the pole is pointed at the man, as though threatening him **CUES:** 法律 hou**ritsu** (laws) are more than **Writ**ten **Sugg**estions; they threaten men like **Richie** if they don't obey **COMPARE:** 静(か) shizuka = quiet, # 418; 君 kimi = you, # 419

418. 静

PRONUNCIATIONS: shizu*ka, sei
MEANINGS: quiet, serene **EXAMPLES:**
静か shizuka = quiet, serene; 安静 ansei =
rest **DESCRIPTION:** on the left, 青(い) aoi
(blue, # 155); on the right, a monster with a
fish head that someone has stabbed with a
trident **CUES:** the sky is blue, and it's 静か
shizuka (quiet), now that a **Shee**p herder from
Zurich stabbed this fish monster, and we are
Safe **COMPARE:** 君 kimi = you, # 419;
(法)律 houritsu = law, # 417

419. 君

PRONUNCIATIONS: kun, kimi **MEANING:**
suffix for (usually) male names of younger
people **EXAMPLES:** 石田君 ishida kun =
young man Ishida; 君 kimi = you (informal
male speech) **DESCRIPTION:** at the top,
someone named Kimmy has been stabbed in
the face with a trident; at the bottom, 口
kuchi (mouth, # 426) **CUES:** "hey 君 **kimi**
(you)! a **Cun**ning person has stabbed **Kimmy**
with a trident, and his 口 (mouth) is wide
open" **COMPARE:** (法)律 houritsu = law,
417; 静(か) shizuka = quiet, # 418

Sturdy Legs

420. 兄

PRONUNCIATIONS: ani, nii, kyou*dai, kei
MEANINGS: older brother, male elder
EXAMPLES: 兄 ani = my older brother;
お兄さん oniisan = your older brother;
兄弟 kyoudai = siblings; 父兄 fukei =
parents, guardians **DESCRIPTION:** this
square head on sturdy legs could belong to an
animal **CUES:** 兄 **ani** (older brother) has a
square head and sturdy legs, and he ate like an
Animal when he visited his **Niec**e in **Kyou**to,
where she offered him some **C**ake

421. 元

PRONUNCIATIONS: moto, gen, gan*jitsu
MEANINGS: base, origin, source

EXAMPLES: 元 moto = base, origin, source;
元気 genki = cheerful, healthy; 元日
ganjitsu = January 1 **DESCRIPTION:** a table
on sturdy legs, with a strong line over it

CUES: this sturdy table suggests a solid 元
moto (base or source) for a 元気な **gen**ki na
(healthy) lifestyle, such as the ones
exemplified by the **Moto**rcycle gang led by
Genghis and **Gan**dalf

422. 先

PRONUNCIATIONS: sen, ma*zu, saki
MEANINGS: previous, before **EXAMPLES:**
先生 sensei = teacher; 先ず mazu = first of
all; 先ほど sakihodo = a while ago
DESCRIPTION: a senator, standing on a
platform with sturdy legs, holding a shield on
the left **CUES:** the **Sen**ator, who used to be a
先生 **sen**sei (teacher), is standing on a
platform with sturdy legs at the **Ma**ll and
holding a shield, which he keeps in a **Sack** that
he bought in **I**ndia, to shield himself from
accusations about things that happened
先ほど **saki**hodo (a while ago)

COMPARE: 洗(う) arau = to wash, # 423;
(報)告 houkoku = report, # 429

423. 洗

PRONUNCIATIONS: sen, ara*u **MEANING:**
to wash with water **EXAMPLES:** 洗濯
sentaku = laundry; 洗う arau = to wash
DESCRIPTION: on the left, a water radical
(see # 12); on the right, 先 **sen** ("previous,"
422)
CUES: a **Sen**ator from Saudi **Ara**bia stands on
platform with sturdy legs; he holds his shield
out to the water and 洗う **ara**u (washes) it
COMPARE: 先(生) sensei = teacher, # 422;
(報)告 houkoku = report, # 429

424. 院

PRONUNCIATION: in **MEANING:** institution
EXAMPLE: 病院 byouin = hospital
DESCRIPTION: on the left, ß beta from the Greek alphabet; at the upper right, a roof; at the lower right 元 moto (base, # 421)
CUE: Greek doctors put a roof on a sturdy base and made a 病院 byouin (hospital), to care for people with **In**dustrial injuries

425. 売

PRONUNCIATIONS: u*ru, bai, uri
MEANING: to sell **EXAMPLES:** 売る uru = to sell; 販売 hanbai = sales; 読売 Yomiuri = name of a newspaper in Japan
DESCRIPTION: at the top, a statue of a (兵)士 heishi (soldier, # 66) made from uranium; at the bottom, a base with sturdy legs that resembles 元 moto (base, # 421)
CUES: we 売る uru (sell) this Uranium soldier statue mounted on a sturdy base, which you may also **Buy** from our 販売機 han**bai**ki (vending machines) located near the **Ur**inals in the bathrooms
COMPARE: 読(む) yomu = to read, # 432

Mouth

426. 口

PRONUNCIATIONS: kuchi, kou, guchi
MEANING: mouth **EXAMPLES:** 口 kuchi = mouth; 人口 jinkou = population; 入り口 iriguchi = entrance **DESCRIPTION:** a square mouth belonging to a person from Kuwait
CUES: in **Ku**wait they eat **Chee**se with their 口 **kuchi** (mouths), and they carry **Corn** in **Gucci** handbags
COMPARE: the katakana character ロ ro

427. 吸

PRONUNCIATIONS: su*u, kyuu*shuu
MEANING: to suck **EXAMPLES:** タバコを吸う tabako wo suu = to smoke tobacco; 吸収する kyuushuu suru = to absorb or digest **DESCRIPTION:** on the left, 口 kuchi (mouth, # 426); on the right, a graph of breathing patterns **CUES:** the mouth on the left and the graph of breathing patterns on the right remind us of a baby named **Sue** who cannot 吸う **suu** (suck) properly, but is very **Cu**te **COMPARE:** 吹(く) fuku = to blow, breathe, whistle, # 537

428. 呼

PRONUNCIATIONS: yo*bu, ko*kyuu
MEANINGS: to call out, exhale **EXAMPLES:** 呼ぶ yobu = to call out, to summon; 呼び名 yobina = given name, alias; 呼吸 kokyuu = breathing, respiration
DESCRIPTION: on the left, 口 kuchi (mouth, # 426); on the right, a person throwing up her arms in frustration as she calls a tardy companion **CUES:** I open my mouth when I 呼ぶ **yo**bu (call out) to say that the **Yo**gurt burned, together with my **Coat** **COMPARE:** 咲(く) saku = to blossom, # 193

429. 告

PRONUNCIATIONS: koku, tsu*geru
MEANINGS: to proclaim, to inform
EXAMPLES: 広告 koukoku = advertisement; 報告 houkoku = report; 告げる tsugeru = to inform **DESCRIPTION:** at the top, a person extending a shield to the left; at the bottom, 口 kuchi (mouth, # 426) **CUES:** a big mouth speaks 広告 kou**koku** (advertisements), claiming that drinking **Coke**, as well as **Tsou**p (soup), can shield us from unpopularity **COMPARE:** 先 saki = previously, # 422; 洗(う) arau = to wash, # 423

430. 言

PRONUNCIATIONS: i*u, koto, gen, gon
MEANINGS: words, to say **EXAMPLES:**
言う iu = to speak; 言葉 kotoba = words;
言語 gengo = language; 伝言 dengon =
message **DESCRIPTION:** at the top, four
horizontal lines that represent words; at the
bottom, 口 kuchi (mouth, # 426) **CUES:** an
Indian from Utah 言う **iu** (speaks) four
言葉 **koto**ba (words) about **Koto** (intransitive
things) to **Gen**ghis Khan, but soon the words
are **Gone COMPARE:** 事 koto = intransitive
things, # 416

431. 信

PRONUNCIATION: shin **MEANINGS:** to
believe, to trust, letter **EXAMPLES:**
信じる shinjiru = to believe; 信号
shingou = stoplight; 信念 shinnen = belief;
信徒 shinto = a follower or believer
DESCRIPTION: on the left, a man with a
slanted hat; on the right, 言(う) iu (to speak,
430) **CUE:** the man with a slanted hat
信じる **shin**jiru (believes) in **Shin**tou, and
he 言 (speaks) about his 信念 **shin**nen
(beliefs) **COMPARE:** 神(道) Shintou = a
Japanese religion, # 273

432. 読

PRONUNCIATIONS: doku, yo*mu, tou,
yomi*uri **MEANING:** reading **EXAMPLES:**
読書 dokusho = reading; 読む yomu = to
read; 句読点 kutouten = punctuation marks;
読売 Yomiuri = name of a newspaper in
Japan **DESCRIPTION:** on the left, 言(う) iu
(to speak, # 430); on the right, 売(る) uru (to
sell, # 425) **CUES:** in a **Docu**mentary about
Yosemite, a man stands on his **Toe**s, 読む
yomu (reads) from a transcript and 言
(speaks) to promote a lifestyle in which one
can practice **Yo**ga and **Mee**t single people

COMPARE: 続(く) tsuzuku = to continue,
226

433. 話

PRONUNCIATIONS: hana, hanashi, banashi[1],
wa **MEANING:** to speak **EXAMPLES:**
話す hanasu = to talk; 話 hanashi = story;
昔話 mukashibanashi = folklore, remini-
scence; 会話 kaiwa = conversation
DESCRIPTION: on the left, 言(う) iu (to
speak, # 430); at the upper right, a forked
tongue; at the lower right, 口 kuchi (mouth,
426) **CUES:** **Hannah** 話す **hana**su (talks)
and 言 (speaks), while **Hannah**'s **Sheep** lick
salt with their forked tongues and **Wa**lk around

434. 計

PRONUNCIATIONS: haka*ru, kei
MEANINGS: to measure or count
EXAMPLES: 計る hakaru = to measure;
時計 tokei = clock, watch; 計画 keikaku =
plan **DESCRIPTION:** on the left, 言(う) iu
(to speak, # 430); on the right, 十 juu (ten,
18) **CUES:** I 言 (speak) about my 計画
keikaku (plan) to buy a 時計 to**kei** (clock)
with the ten dollars I earned in the last
Hackathon, which we held in a **Ca**ve

435. 語

PRONUNCIATIONS: go, kata*ru, gatari
MEANINGS: words, to talk **EXAMPLES:**
英語 eigo = English; 語る kataru = to talk;
物語 monogatari = tale, story, legend
DESCRIPTION: on the left, 言(う) iu (to
speak, # 430); on the right, 五 go (five,
179), which helps us to pronounce this,
standing on a box and resembling a golfer
staring down a fairway **CUES:** this man
knows **Go** (five) words in 英語 ei**go**
(English), but he only likes to 語る **kata**ru
(talk) and 言 (speak) about **Go**lf; he has to

stare because he has **Cata**racts, and he drinks a lot of **Gatari**de (instead of Gatorade)

436. 試

PRONUNCIATIONS: tame*su, shi, kokoro*miru MEANINGS: to test, a trial
EXAMPLES: 試す tamesu = to attempt; 試験 shiken = examination; 試みる kokoromiru = to attempt DESCRIPTION: on the left, 言(葉) kotoba (words, # 430); on the right, 式 shiki (ceremony, # 249); under the arm of the leaning woman is a 工 kou (crafted object, # 246), which is a model of her tame sheep CUES: a woman, who has **Tame**d a **Shee**p and has a big **Kokoro** (heart), 試す **tame**su (tries) to leap over 言 (words) during a 試験 **shi**ken (test) for her dance class

437. 訳

PRONUNCIATIONS: wake, yaku
MEANINGS: reason, translation
EXAMPLES: 訳 wake = reason, interpretation; 言い訳 iiwake = excuse; 通訳 tsuuyaku = interpreter, interpretation
DESCRIPTION: on the left, 言(葉) kotoba (words, # 430); on the right, a square eye on long legs; we called this a "watchful eye" when describing 駅 eki (station, # 380), but it could also be considered a "wakeful eye"
CUES: the 訳 **wake** (reason) that the **Wake**ful eye is watching these 言 (words) is to check the accuracy of the 通訳 tsuu**yaku** (interpretation) being done for a **Yaku**za (gangster)

438. 議

PRONUNCIATION: gi MEANING: to discuss
EXAMPLE: 会議 kaigi = meeting
DESCRIPTION: on the left, 言(う) iu (to speak, # 430); at the top right, 羊 hitsuji (sheep, not included in this catalogue), which has both horns, both ears and all four legs, but is missing its tail; at the lower right, a crawling guy and a halberd (combination lance and axe), containing an X, which represents the missing tail CUE: the purpose of this 会議 kai**gi** (meeting) is to 言 (speak) about the **Gee**se that ran off with this 羊 (sheep)'s tail, represented by an X, after the crawling guy cut it off with his halberd

439. 説

PRONUNCIATION: setsu MEANINGS: to explain, opinion EXAMPLES: 説明 setsumei = explanation; 小説 shousetsu = novel DESCRIPTION: on the left, 言(う) iu (to speak, # 430); on the right, 兄 ani (older brother, # 420), wearing rabbit ears
CUE: 兄 (older brother), who is wearing rabbit ears, 説明する **setsu**mei suru (explains) and 言 (speaks) about how he **Set** up a **Su**per rabbit farm

440. 誰

PRONUNCIATION: dare MEANING: who
EXAMPLES: 誰 dare = who DESCRIPTION: on the left, 言(う) iu (to speak, # 430); on the right, a cage CUE: 誰 **dare** (who) **Dare**s to 言 (speak) from the cage?

441. 調

PRONUNCIATIONS: chou, shira*beru
MEANINGS: to investigate, condition
EXAMPLES: 調子 choushi = condition; 調べる shiraberu = to check
DESCRIPTION: on the left, 言(う) iu (to speak, # 430); on the right, a tent; inside the tent, 土 tsuchi (dirt, # 59) above 口 kuchi (mouth, # 426), which resembles a box CUES: a detective has been **Cho**sen, and he 言 (says) that he will 調べる **shira**beru (check) this box hidden below the 土 (dirt) inside the tent to see whether it contains **Shee**p or **Ra**bbit food
COMPARE: 週 shuu = week, # 346

442. 研

PRONUNCIATIONS: ken, to*gu **MEANINGS:** to hone, to sharpen by grinding **EXAMPLES:** 研究 kenkyuu = research; 研ぐ togu = to sharpen, to wash rice **DESCRIPTION:** on the left, a pointed instrument, with a handle, above 口 kuchi (mouth, # 426); on the right, a tall person named Ken who is standing on his toes **CUES: Ken** is a tall dentist who uses a sharp instrument to do 研究 **ken**kyuu (research) into diseases of the 口 (mouth), with help from Barbie, and this keeps him on his **Toe**s

Fire

443. 火

PRONUNCIATIONS: hi, bi[1], ka **MEANING:** fire **EXAMPLES:** 火 hi = fire; 花火 hanabi = fireworks; 火事 kaji = fire; 火曜日 kayoubi = Tuesday **DESCRIPTION:** 人 hito (person, # 13) with flames leaping from both sides **CUES:** a 人 (person) who gets lost in the **H**imalayas can use a signal 火 **hi** (fire) to **Ca**ll for help

444. 灰

PRONUNCIATION: hai **MEANING:** ash **EXAMPLES:** 灰 hai = ash; 灰色 haiiro = grey **DESCRIPTION:** on the upper left, a lean-to; inside the lean-to, a high 火 hi (fire, # 443) **CUE:** if you light a **High** 火 (fire) inside a lean-to, you will generate 灰 **hai** (ash) and make the inside of the lean-to 灰色 **hai**iro (grey)

445. 秋

PRONUNCIATIONS: aki, shuu **MEANING:** autumn **EXAMPLES:** 秋 aki = autumn; 晩秋 banshuu = late fall **DESCRIPTION:** on the left, this is a grain plant with a ripe head; on the right, 火 hi (fire, # 443)

CUES: Achilles visited us in 秋 **aki** (autumn) to admire our ripe grain and 火 (fire)-like leaves, and also to show us his new **Shoe**s

446. 焼

PRONUNCIATIONS: ya*ku, shou*kyaku **MEANING:** to burn
EXAMPLES: 焼く yaku = to grill, toast, etc.; 焼き鳥 yakitori = grilled skewered chicken; 焼却 shoukyaku = incineration
DESCRIPTION: on the left, 火 hi (fire, # 443); on the right, 元 moto (base, # 421), supporting three pieces of chicken on skewers
CUES: 焼き鳥 **ya**kitori (grilled chicken) is grilled with 火 (fire) on a base and often eaten by **Ya**kuza (gangsters) during movie **Show**s

447. 赤

PRONUNCIATIONS: aka*i, ka, seki*dou
MEANING: red **EXAMPLES:** 赤い akai = red; 赤ちゃん akachan = baby; 真っ赤 makka = bright red; 赤道 sekidou = equator
DESCRIPTION: at the top, 土 tsuchi (dirt, # 59); at the bottom, a fire **CUES:** this fire under the 土 (dirt) at the **Aca**demy Awards is 赤い **aka**i (red), it's about to start a **Car** fire, and the smoke from it is causing a **Seki** (cough) **COMPARE:** 咳 seki = cough, not included in this catalogue

448. 光

PRONUNCIATIONS: hika*ru, hikari, kou
MEANING: light **EXAMPLES:** 光 hikari = light; 光る hikaru = to shine, glitter, stand out; 日光 nikkou = sunlight; also, 日光 Nikkou = a town in Japan **DESCRIPTION:** 3 streams of light emerging from a fire on a sturdy base, similar to 元 moto (base, # 421) **CUES:** the **Hick Ka**rl and his friend, the **Hick Carrie**, who were feeling **Co**ld, lit a fire that 光る **hika**ru (shines) on a sturdy base

Foot

449. 足

PRONUNCIATIONS: ashi, a*dachi, ta*riru, soku **MEANINGS:** leg, foot, to suffice **EXAMPLES:** 足 ashi = leg or foot; 足立 Adachi = a ward in Tokyo; 足りる tariru = to suffice; 不足 fusoku = not sufficient **DESCRIPTION:** at the bottom left, a foot radical; above the foot, a square that resembles a kneecap, connecting to the foot via a "T" on its side, which may represent the Tibia **CUES:** I tripped on an **Ash**y ashcan and hurt my 足 **ashi** (leg), and this **A**ccident 足りた **ta**rita (sufficed) to keep me from going to work at the **Ta**riff office; I then saw an Uber car and kicked water at it to **Soak** the Uber, but my efforts were 不足 fu**soku** (insufficient)

450. 走

PRONUNCIATIONS: hashi*ru, sou **MEANING:** to run **EXAMPLES:** 走る hashiru = to run; 脱走 dassou = desertion, escape **DESCRIPTION:** at the bottom, a foot radical; above the foot, horizontal lines representing knees, hips, and shoulders **CUE:** after smoking **Hashi**sh in the **So**viet Union, this guy could really 走る **hashi**ru (run)

COMPARE: 足 ashi = leg or foot, # 449

451. 徒

PRONUNCIATION: to **MEANINGS:** follower, pupil **EXAMPLES:** 生徒 seito = student; 信徒 shinto = follower, believer **DESCRIPTION:** on the left, a man with a double hat, who resembles 行(く) iku (to go, # 334); on the right, 走(る) hashiru (to run, # 450) **CUE:** after he finishes his **Toa**st, the 生徒 sei**to** (student) 走 (runs) after his teacher, and they 行 (go) to school

452. 起

PRONUNCIATION: o*kiru, ki*ritsu **MEANINGS:** to get up, to arise **EXAMPLES:** 起きる okiru = to get up; 起こす okosu = to wake someone up; 起こる okoru = to occur, to happen; 起立する kiritsu suru = to stand up **DESCRIPTION:** at the left and bottom, 走(る) hashiru (to run, # 450); on the right, a snake from Okinawa **CUES:** in **O**kinawa, if a snake appears at the end of my foot, I 起きる **o**kiru (get up), grab my **Key**s and 走 (run)

453. 越

PRONUNCIATION: ko, koshi **MEANINGS:** to cross or go over **EXAMPLES:** 引っ越す hikkosu = to move one's residence; 越える koeru = to go across; 三越 Mitsukoshi = name of a department store **DESCRIPTION:** at the left and bottom, 走(る) hashiru (to run, # 450); on the right, a halberd (combination of an axe and a lance), belonging to a Coast Guardsman **CUES:** the **Co**ast Guardsman has 引っ越した hik**ko**shita (moved his residence), and he 走 (runs) with his halberd, since now he has to 越える **ko**eru (go across) town in order to go to work with his **Co-Ship**mates

454. 題

PRONUNCIATION: dai **MEANINGS:** title, topic **EXAMPLES:** 問題 mondai = problem; 題名 daimei = title; 話題 wadai = topic **DESCRIPTION:** at the bottom, a foot radical, which looks like a boat; at the front of the boat, a lantern; at the back of the boat, a boatman who is missing his head, like the radical on the right in 頭 atama (head, # 93) **CUE:** the 話題 wa**dai** (topic) of today's discussion is the headless boatman who will ferry me across the River Styx after I **Die**; this sounds like a real 問題 mon**dai** (problem)

455. 定

PRONUNCIATIONS: tei, sada*meru
MEANINGS: to decide, to be fixed
EXAMPLES: 予定 yotei = plan; 定食 teishoku = set meal; 定年 teinen = retirement age; 定める sadameru = to decide or prescribe **DESCRIPTION:** at the top, a roof; in the middle, a taser weapon; at the bottom, a foot radical **CUES:** my 予定 yo**tei** (plan) was to mount a **Ta**ser on my foot and hide from **Sadda**m under this roof

Hugging

456. 左

PRONUNCIATIONS: hidari, sa **MEANING:** left **EXAMPLES:** 左手 hidari te = left hand; 左折 sasetsu = left turn **DESCRIPTION:** on the left, a hugging person named Robert E. Lee; on the right, 工 kou (crafted object, # 246) **CUES:** when Robert E. Lee makes a 工 (crafted object), he needs to hug it with his 左 **hidari** (left) arm, but that's difficult now, since a **HideA**way bed hit **Lee**'s left arm after a **Sa**xophone player bumped into it

COMPARE: 右 migi = right, # 457

457. 右

PRONUNCIATIONS: migi, u*setsu, yuu
MEANING: right **EXAMPLES:** 右側 migigawa = right side; 右折 usetsu = right turn; 左右 sayuu = left and right
DESCRIPTION: on the left, a hugging person; on the right, 口 kuchi (mouth, # 426)

CUES: when I eat, I use my 右 **migi** (right) hand to grasp food and bring it to my mouth, but some **Mean Gee**se and an **U**ber strike in the **Yu**kon are making it hard for me to focus on eating

COMPARE: 左 hidari = left, # 456; 石 ishi = stone, # 458; 若(い) wakai = young, # 461

458. 石

PRONUNCIATIONS: ishi, seki, shaku, se*kken
MEANING: stone **EXAMPLES:** 小石 koishi = pebble; 一石 isseki = one stone; 磁石 jishaku = magnet; 石鹸 sekken = soap
DESCRIPTION: compared to 右 migi (right, # 457), 石 ishi is missing a vertical line at the top, and it seems that someone may have removed a stone from its roof

CUES: compared to 右 (right), a stone is missing from the top of 石 **ishi** (stone), because an **In**donesian **Shi**p was ordered by a **Se**lfish **Ki**ng to transport it to a **Shack** for a **Se**cretary to sit on

459. 友

PRONUNCIATIONS: yuu*jin, tomo*dachi
MEANING: friend **EXAMPLES:** 友人 yuujin = friend; 友達 tomodachi = friend
DESCRIPTION: on the left, a hugging person; on the right, 又 mata ("again," # 24), but this resembles a simple table

CUES: my **You**thful 友達 **tomo**dachi (friend) is hugging a 又 (table) that he made; **Tomo**rrow he will make another one for me

460. 有

PRONUNCIATIONS: a*ru, ari, yuu*mei
MEANINGS: to exist, to have **EXAMPLES:** 有る aru = to exist, but Japanese people usually spell this ある; 有難う arigatou = thank you; 有名 yuumei = famous
DESCRIPTION: on the left, a hugging person; on the right, 月 tsuki (moon, # 148)
CUES: **Ar**thur, an **Ari**stocrat from the **Yu**kon, symbolically hugs the 有名 **yuu**mei (famous) 月 (moon) which 有る **a**ru (exists), and he says 有難う **ari**gatou (thank you)

461. 若

PRONUNCIATION: waka*i **MEANING:** young **EXAMPLE:** 若い wakai = young **DESCRIPTION:** at the top, a plant radical (see # 43); at the bottom, 右 migi (right, # 457) **CUE:** when I was 若い **wakai** (young), I played **Whack-A-**mole under the bushes on the 右 (right) side of our house

462. 存

PRONUNCIATIONS: zon*jiru, son*zai **MEANINGS:** to sustain, to humbly know or think **EXAMPLES:** 存じる zonjiru = to humbly know; 存在 sonzai = existence, presence **DESCRIPTION:** on the left, a hugging person, plus an additional vertical line; on the right, 子 ko (child, # 182) **CUES:** when I'm in the **Zone**, I hug a 子 (child), who plays games that are made by **Son**y, as I 存じる **zon**jiru (humbly know)

463. 怖

PRONUNCIATIONS: kowa*i, fu **MEANINGS:** dreadful, to be frightened **EXAMPLES:** 怖い kowai = afraid, scary; 恐怖 kyoufu = fear, horror **DESCRIPTION:** on the left, an erect guy who could be a koala; on the upper right, a hugging person; on the lower right, 市 shi (city, # 242) **CUES:** a **Koa**la is next to us, and I **Foo**lishly hug my friend from the 市 (city) because I'm 怖い **kowa**i (scared)

West

464. 西

PRONUNCIATIONS: nishi, zai, sei*ou **MEANING:** west **EXAMPLES:** 西 nishi = west; 東西 touzai = East and West; 西欧 seiou = Western Europe **DESCRIPTION:** at the top, a balcony in Zaire (former name of the Congo) supported by two legs; at the bottom,

四 yon (four, # 6) **CUES: Nietzche** lived in a house with four sides and high balconies in 西 **nishi** (west) **Zai**re, where he felt **Sa**fe **COMPARE:** 酒 sake, # 465

465. 酒

PRONUNCIATIONS: sake, zake[1], shu, saka*ya **MEANING:** alcohol **EXAMPLES:** 酒 sake = alcoholic beverage; 冷酒 hiyazake = cold sake, but this is usually pronounced "reishu"; 日本酒 nihonshu = Japanese sake; 洋酒 youshu = foreign liquor; 酒屋 sakaya = liquor store **DESCRIPTION:** on the left, a water radical (see # 12), suggesting liquid; on the right, 西 nishi (west, # 464), with an added basement **CUES:** while drinking 酒 **sake** in the basement of this house, I **Saw Kay**, so I put on my **Shoe**s and went outside to play **Sakkaa** (soccer) **COMPARE:** 西 nishi = west, # 464

466. 配

PRONUNCIATIONS: kuba*ru, hai, pai **MEANINGS:** to distribute, hand out, arrange **EXAMPLES:** 配る kubaru = to deliver, distribute, hand out; 宅配便 takuhaibin = home delivery; 心配する shinpai suru = to worry **DESCRIPTION:** on the left, 酒 sake (# 465), missing its water radical; on the right, a twisted backwards letter "S" **CUES:** a **Cool Ba**rmaid named **Hi**awatha has brought a **Pie** to the house with the sake cellar, but since no one is at home, she is twisted with 心配 shin**pai** (worry) that it will spoil

Kangaroo

467. 汚

PRONUNCIATIONS: o*sui, yogo*su, kitana*i, kega*su **MEANINGS:** dirty, soiled

EXAMPLES: 汚水 osui = sewage; 汚す yogosu = to soil; 汚い kitanai = dirty; 汚す kegasu = to sully or disgrace

DESCRIPTION: on the left, a water radical (see # 12); on the right, a kangaroo from oosutorariya (Australia), with a powerful leg for jumping

CUES: a kangaroo from **O**osutorariya (Australia) jumps away from 汚水 <u>o</u>sui (sewage), causing me to spill **Yo**gurt made from **Goat**'s milk on my suit and 汚す <u>yogo</u>su (soil) it; the kangaroo also bumps into a **Kit**ten **At Nigh**t and gets it 汚い <u>kitana</u>i (dirty), and it spills a **Kega** (keg of) beer

468. 写

PRONUNCIATIONS: utsu*su, sha

MEANING: to copy **EXAMPLES:** 写す utsusu = to copy; 写真 shashin = photograph

DESCRIPTION: at the top, a roof; at the bottom, a kangaroo, up to his calves in water, with a powerful leg for jumping

CUES: this kangaroo flooded the darkroom while trying to 写す <u>utsu</u>su (copy) some 写真 <u>sha</u>shin (photos) of people **U**tilizing **Su**bmarines, which he wanted to take back to his **Sha**ck

469. 考

PRONUNCIATIONS: kanga*eru, kou

MEANING: to think thoroughly **EXAMPLES:** 考える kangaeru = to think; 思考 shikou = consideration, thought **DESCRIPTION:** compared to 者 mono (person, # 276), this kanji has powerful legs like a kangaroo and, like 者, it plays with scissors

CUES: this human-**Kanga**roo hybrid 考える <u>kanga</u>eru (thinks) about how to **C**ope with the cuts that he gets from scissors, but he continues to play with them

470. 号

PRONUNCIATION: gou **MEANINGS:** to call in a loud voice, number **EXAMPLES:** 番号 bangou = number; 信号 shingou = traffic light; 六号車 rokugousha = car number six

DESCRIPTION: at the top, 口 kuchi (mouth, # 426); at the bottom, a kangaroo with a powerful leg for kicking, which resembles a soccer player who can score goals

CUE: the 口 (mouth) at the top may represent a 番号 ban<u>gou</u> (number, i.e., the number "0") which this kangaroo soccer player wears on his uniform when he scores **Goa**ls

Feathers

471. 弱

PRONUNCIATIONS: yowa*i, jaku

MEANING: weak **EXAMPLES:** 弱い yowai = weak; 弱点 jakuten = weak point, weakness **DESCRIPTION:** these two radicals represent feathers, reportedly

CUES: the two feathers that **Y**our **W**ife and **Jack** Nicholson placed next to each other are 弱い <u>yowa</u>i (weak)

472. 習

PRONUNCIATIONS: nara*u, shuu

MEANINGS: to learn, learning by repeating

EXAMPLES: 習う narau = to learn; 練習 renshuu = practice; 習字 shuuji = calligraphy practice

DESCRIPTION: at the top, these two radicals represent feathers, reportedly; at the bottom, 白(い) shiroi (white, # 44)

CUES: the two feathers plus 白 (white) suggest that a 白 (white) bird was using its feathers to 習う <u>nara</u>u (learn) to fly in **Nara**, until someone threw a **Shoe** at it

Fish Head

473. 色

PRONUNCIATIONS: iro, shiki **MEANINGS:** color, amorous **EXAMPLES:** 茶色 chairo = brown; 景色 keshiki = view
DESCRIPTION: at the top, a fish head; in the middle, a horizontal 日 hi (day, or sun, # 32), but this looks like two eyes; at the bottom, a snake **CUES:** this snake with two eyes and a fish head has an 色 **iro** (color) like **Iron**; he is sitting up high and has a good 景色 ke**shiki** (view) of a **Sheep**ish **King**

474. 勉

PRONUNCIATION: ben **MEANING:** exerting oneself **EXAMPLE:** 勉強 benkyou = study
DESCRIPTION: at the upper left, a fish head; below this, a horizontal 日 hi (day, or sun, # 32), but this looks like two eyes; at the lower left, two long tentacles, one of them bent, possibly belonging to an octopus; at the right, 力 chikara (force or power, # 107)
CUE: the octopus **Ben**ds a tentacle and kneels, using his power of concentration to 勉強する **ben**kyou suru (study)

475. 触

PRONUNCIATIONS: fu*reru, sawa*ru, shoku **MEANINGS:** contact, touch, feel
EXAMPLES: 触れる fureru = to touch; 触る sawaru = to touch; 接触する sesshoku suru = to touch or contact
DESCRIPTION: at the upper left, a fish head; below this, 田(んぼ) tanbo (rice paddy, # 68), on legs, which resembles a person's body; on the right, 虫 mushi (insect, # 9)
CUES: a **Foo**lish fish-head guy is sidling up to 触る **sawa**ru (touch) the insect which he **Saw Wa**lking down the road, but the insect will **Shock** him with its stinger

Pull

476. 引

PRONUNCIATIONS: hi*ku, in, hiki, biki[1]
MEANING: to pull **EXAMPLES:** 引く hiku = to pull; 引っ越す hikkosu = to move; 引っ張る hipparu = to pull; 引力 inryoku = attraction, gravitational pull, magnetism; 取引 torihiki = business deal; 割引 waribiki = discount **DESCRIPTION:** on the left, a bow, reportedly, but this could also be a twisted hickory tree; on the right, a rope **CUES:** since this **Hickory** tree was uber twisted, I 引いた **hi**ita (pulled) it down with this rope, but the rope **In**jured my skin, and now I have a **Hickey**

477. 張

PRONUNCIATIONS: chou, ha, pa
MEANINGS: to stretch, pull or extend
EXAMPLES: 出張 shutchou = business trip; 張り合う hariau = to compete or contend with; 引っ張る hipparu = to pull
DESCRIPTION: on the left, a bow, reportedly, but this could represent something twisted; on the right, 長(い) nagai (long, # 502); together, these two radicals suggest a long twisted story **CUES:** on 出張 shut**chou** (business trips), businessmen who are **Cho**sen by their managers sit around the **Har**bor, beg each other's **Par**don, and tell long twisted stories while they 引っ張る hip**pa**ru (pull) on their noses
COMPARE: 引(く) hiku = to pull, # 476

478. 強

PRONUNCIATIONS: tsuyo*i, kyou
MEANINGS: strong, to force **EXAMPLES:**
強い tsuyoi = strong; 勉強 benkyou =
study **DESCRIPTION:** on the left, a bow,
reportedly, which resembles 引(く) hiku (to
pull, # 476); at the upper right, the katakana
character ム mu; at the lower right, 虫 mushi
(insect, # 9), but these two radicals on the right
look like a barbell **CUES:** my **Tsu**itcase is **Yo**i
(good), but it popped open, and the barbell that
I was carrying in it fell into a hole in **Kyou**to;
it will take a 強い **tsuyo**i (strong) person to
pull it out

479. 風

PRONUNCIATIONS: fuu, fu, kaze
MEANINGS: wind, manner, style
EXAMPLES: 台風 taifuu = typhoon;
風 kaze = wind; 風呂 furo = hot bath;
日本風 nihon fuu = Japanese style
DESCRIPTION: the continuous line on the left,
top and right side of this kanji suggests wind,
blowing from left to right; under this line of
wind, a 虫 mushi (insect, # 9) is wearing a flat
hat and seems to be dropping into someone's
food **CUES:** when a 台風 tai**fuu** (typhoon)
occurs, it creates 風 **kaze** (wind) which may
blow 虫 (insects) into our **Foo**d or damage
our **Caze**tte (cassette) collection

Man with a Slanted Hat

480. 使

PRONUNCIATIONS: tsuka*u, shi
MEANINGS: to use; servant **EXAMPLES:**
使う tsukau = to use; 使用 shiyou = use,
employment; 大使 taishi = ambassador
DESCRIPTION: on the left, a man with a
slanted hat; on the right, a servant wearing
ordinary glasses, rather than bifocals, as seen
in 便(利) benri, # 481

CUES: a man with a slanted hat 使う **tsuka**u
(uses) this servant, who wears ordinary glasses

(not bifocals), and has a **Tsu**itcase in his **Car**,
where he keeps fresh **Shee**ts

COMPARE: (兵)士 heishi = soldier, # 66;
仕(様) shiyou = means, method, # 67;
私(用の) shiyou no = private, # 510

481. 便

PRONUNCIATIONS: tayo*ri, ben, bin
MEANINGS: service, convenient
EXAMPLES: 便り tayori = news, letter;
便利 benri = convenient; 郵便 yuubin =
mail **DESCRIPTION:** on the left, a tall
Yorkshire man with a slanted hat; on the right,
a servant named Ben Franklin; compared to
使う tsukau (to use, # 480), Ben is wearing
bifocals, which he invented **CUES:** the man
with a slanted hat is a **Ta**ll **Yo**rkshire man,
with a servant named **Ben** who wears bifocals,
which are more 便利 **ben**ri (convenient)
when reading the small print in **Bin**go
instructions

482. 作

PRONUNCIATIONS: tsuku*ru, saku, sa
MEANINGS: to create or make **EXAMPLES:**
作る tsukuru = to make; 作文 sakubun =
written composition; 作品 sakuhin =
creation, work of art or literature; 作家
sakka = writer; 作動 sadou = functioning,
operation; 発作 hossa = attack or fit, e.g.,
心臓発作 shinzou hossa = heart attack
DESCRIPTION: on the left, a man with a
slanted hat; on the right, a serrated axe, small
enough to fit into a tsuitcase from Kuwait
CUES: a man with a slanted hat is using a
serrated axe that he carried in his **Tsu**itcase
from **Ku**wait to 作る **tsuku**ru (make) a 作
品 **saku**hin (creation), which he will keep in a
Sack whenever he is playing the **Sa**xophone
COMPARE: 昨(晩) sakuban = last night,
41

483. 任

PRONUNCIATIONS: maka*seru, nin
MEANINGS: to take up a burden;
responsibility EXAMPLES: 任せる
makaseru = to entrust; 主任 shunin =
foreman DESCRIPTION: on the left, a man
with a slanted hat; on the right, 王 ou (king,
not included in this catalogue), but 王 looks
like pieces of macaroni arranged in a pattern
CUES: the man with a slanted hat will
任せる makaseru (entrust) responsibility
for this Macaroni to the 主任 shunin
(foreman), since he's a Ninja
COMPARE: 住(む) sumu = to reside, # 167

484. 価

PRONUNCIATIONS: ka, atai MEANINGS:
value, price EXAMPLES: 物価 bukka =
price; 価値 kachi = value; 価 atai = value,
price DESCRIPTION: on the left, a man with
a slanted hat; on the right, a carry-on suitcase
with its handle extended CUES: the man is
Calculating the 物価 bukka (price) of this
Carry-on suitcase that A Thai guy is selling

485. 借

PRONUNCIATIONS: ka*riru, shaku*ya,
sha*kkin MEANING: to borrow
EXAMPLES: 借りる kariru = to borrow or
rent; 借家 shakuya = rented house; 借金
shakkin = debt DESCRIPTION: on the left, a
man with a slanted hat; on the right, 昔
mukashi (olden days, # 33), which looks like a
bank teller's window CUES: in 昔 (the olden
days), the man with a slanted hat stood outside
a bank teller's window to 借りる kariru
(borrow) money which he Carried home to his
Shack in Shanghai

486. 供

PRONUNCIATIONS: domo, kyou, tomo*ni
MEANINGS: together, both EXAMPLES:
子供 kodomo = child; 提供する teikyou
suru = to offer, provide, sponsor; 共に
tomoni = together DESCRIPTION: on the left,
a man with a slanted hat; on the right, some
bushes balanced on a dome
CUES: the man watches as 子供 kodomo
(children) play 共に tomoni (together) in
bushes balanced on a Dome in Kyouto, and he
makes Tomograms of their knees

487. 化

PRONUNCIATIONS: ke*shou, ka MEANING:
to change EXAMPLES: 化粧 keshou =
makeup; 化学 kagaku = chemistry; 文化
bunka = culture DESCRIPTION: on the left, a
man with a slanted hat; on the right, the
katakana character ヒ hi; these two radicals
resemble a map of Canada, i.e., on the left, we
see a straight west coast, topped by Alaska; on
the right, we see Hudson Bay and the Maritime
provinces CUES: Ken creates 化粧 keshou
(makeup) for Barbie at his job in the 化学
kagaku (chemistry) industry in Canada,
COMPARE: 科(学) kagaku = science, # 511

488. 件

PRONUNCIATION: ken MEANINGS: case,
matter, counter for houses EXAMPLES:
その件 sono ken = the matter being
discussed; 事件 jiken = incident; 四件
yonken = four houses DESCRIPTION: on the
left, a man with a slanted hat named Ken; on
the right, 牛 ushi (cow, # 205) CUES: Ken
investigates a 事件 jiken (incident) at the
Kentucky Derby involving Barbie's cow

489. 夜

PRONUNCIATIONS: yoru, yo, ya MEANING: night EXAMPLES: 夜 yoru = night; 夜中 yonaka = middle of the night; 今夜 konya = tonight DESCRIPTION: at the top, a roof; at the lower left, a man with a slanted hat; at the lower right, this appears to be a yoke designed to fit around the neck of a yak

CUES: this man eats **Yo**gurt under his **Roof** at 夜 **yoru** (night), and then he repairs this **Yo**ke for his **Ya**k

490. 側

PRONUNCIATIONS: gawa, soba
MEANINGS: side, close by EXAMPLES: 右側 migigawa = right side; 側に soba ni = close to; however, 側 soba is usually written そば, to avoid confusion with gawa
DESCRIPTION: on the left, a man with a slanted hat; in the middle, 見(る) miru (to see, # 53); on the right, the katakana character リ Ri CUES: the man with the slanted hat and リ Ri are on the opposite 側 **gawa** (sides) of 見, but there is a **Ga**udy **Wa**gon 側に **soba** ni (close by), at which they are both able to buy **Soba** (noodles)

491. 宿

PRONUNCIATIONS: shuku, yado, juku
MEANING: inn EXAMPLES: 宿題 shukudai = homework; 宿 yado = inn; 新宿 Shinjuku = a ward in Tokyo
DESCRIPTION: at the top, a roof; at the lower left, a man with a slanted hat; at the lower right, 百 hyaku (hundred, # 47) CUES: 百 (100) guys showed up to help the man with his 宿題 **shuku**dai (homework), which he completed using **Shoe** polish and **Koo**l-Aid; the guys are staying at the 宿 **yado** (inn), in the **Ya**rd by the **Do**or, next to the **Ju**kebox

492. 係

PRONUNCIATIONS: kakari, kei MEANING: person in charge EXAMPLES: 係 kakari = person in charge; 関係 kankei = relationship
DESCRIPTION: on the left, a man with a slanted hat; on the right, a 糸 (skeet shooter, # 219), with a cape draped across his head
CUES: the man with a slanted hat is a 係員 **kakari** in (person in charge), and he shows that he **Can Carry** his weight in his 関係 kan**kei** (relationship) with the skeet shooter by giving him a **Cape** COMPARE: 後 ato = later, #335

Lean-to

493. 店

PRONUNCIATIONS: mise, ten MEANINGS: shop, store EXAMPLES: 店 mise = store; 店員 ten'in = store clerk
DESCRIPTION: on the upper left, a lean-to; inside the lean-to, a well with a handle
CUES: this is a **Mise**rable 店 **mise** (store) under a lean-to, where people come to buy water from a 店員 **ten**'in (store clerk) who also plays **Ten**nis

494. 広

PRONUNCIATIONS: hiro*i, biro, kou
MEANINGS: spacious, wide EXAMPLES: 広い hiroi = wide, spacious; 背広 sebiro = man's suit; 広告 koukoku = advertisement
DESCRIPTION: on the upper left, a lean-to, with a small sign on the top; inside the lean-to, the katakana character ム mu (the sound made by a cow) CUES: this ム (cow) has a 広い **hiro**i (wide and spacious) lean-to; the sign at the top says that it is intended for **Hero**s who eat a lot of **Bean Ro**lls (burritos) and drink **Co**la

495. 庭

PRONUNCIATIONS: niwa, tei **MEANING:** garden **EXAMPLES:** 庭 niwa = garden; 裏庭 uraniwa = back yard; 庭園 teien = formal Japanese garden **DESCRIPTION:** on the upper left, a lean-to; inside the lean-to, the radical at the lower left is different from the snail radical seen in many kanji, e.g., 週 shuu (week, # 346); we can call it a "3x snail," since it consists of a 3 intersected at the bottom to form an X; let's also call it a wagon, since an 王 ou (king, not included in this catalogue) is riding in it **CUES:** the 王 (king) likes neon lighting, and he rides in his **Ne**on-lit **Wa**gon under a lean-to in his 庭 **niwa** (garden), where he is guarded with **Ta**sers

496. 席

PRONUNCIATION: seki **MEANING:** seat **EXAMPLES:** 席 seki = seat; 出席 shusseki suru = to attend; 座席 zaseki = the seat of a chair **DESCRIPTION:** on the upper left, a lean-to; inside the lean-to, an infant seat resting on a 3-legged stool **CUE:** before feeding the baby, I put him in an infant 席 **seki** (seat) on top of a 3-legged stool in my lean-to, but he has a **Seki** (cough) and can't eat **COMPARE:** 両(方) ryouhou = both, # 579; 座(る) suwaru = to sit on a zabuton, # 497; 咳 seki = cough, not included in this catalogue

497. 座

PRONUNCIATIONS: za, suwa*ru **MEANINGS:** to sit, seat **EXAMPLES:** 座布団 zabuton = floor cushion for sitting; 口座 kouza = account (bank); 座る suwaru = to sit on a zabuton **DESCRIPTION:** on the upper left, a lean-to; inside the lean-to, 土 tsuchi (dirt, # 59); on each side of the upper deck of 土 (dirt), a person is sitting **CUE:** if you 座る **suwa**ru (sit) on the 土 (dirt) in a restaurant in **Za**mbia, they serve you **Sou**p and **Wa**ter **COMPARE:** 席 seki = seat, 496

498. 度

PRONUNCIATIONS: do, tabi, taku **MEANINGS:** time, degree **EXAMPLES:** 今度 kondo = this time or next time; 百度 hyakudo = 100 degrees; 転勤の度 tenkin no tabi = transfer's occasion; 支度 shitaku = preparation **DESCRIPTION:** on the upper left, a lean-to belonging to Dorothy; inside the lean-to, a pot of food over 又 mata ("again," # 24), but this resembles a simple table **CUES:** 毎度 mai**do** (every time) **Do**rothy prepares food for the Wizard of Oz in her lean-to, she also feeds it to her **Ta**bby cat at this 又 (table), together with **Ta**p water and **Koo**l-Aid

499. 渡

PRONUNCIATION: wata, to*bei **MEANINGS:** to cross, to hand over **EXAMPLES:** 渡る wataru = to cross; 渡す watasu = to hand over; 渡米 tobei = going to America **DESCRIPTION:** on the left, a water radical (see # 12); on the right, 度 do (time, # 498) **CUE:** every time that Napoleon would 渡る **wata**ru (cross) the bridge at **Wate**rloo, he had to 渡す **wata**su (hand) money to the **To**ll collector

500. 岸

PRONUNCIATIONS: gan, kishi **MEANINGS:** beach, shore **EXAMPLES:** 海岸 kaigan = beach; 岸 kishi = beach, shore **DESCRIPTION:** at the top, 山 yama (mountain, # 146); below 山, a kitschy lean-to; inside the lean-to, a telephone pole **CUES:** **Gan**dalf visits a 海岸 kai**gan** (beach) under a 山 (mountain), and talks on the telephone in a **Kitschy** lean-to

Hair

501. 髪

PRONUNCIATIONS: kami, hatsu, ga
MEANING: hair **EXAMPLES:** 髪 kami = hair; 白髪 hakuhatsu = white or grey hair; 白髪 shiraga = white or grey hair

DESCRIPTION: on the upper left, 長(い) nagai (long, # 502); on the upper right, three lines suggesting hair strands; at the bottom, 友(達) tomodachi (friend) **CUES:** my friend, who is a **Cam**bodian **I**mmigrant, has long 髪 **kami** (hair) which she covers with **H**ats that she bought in **Ga**za **COMPARE:** 紙 kami = paper, # 221; 神 kami = god, # 273; (女)将 okami = landlady, # 374

502. 長

PRONUNCIATIONS: naga*i, chou
MEANINGS: long, chief, principal
EXAMPLES: 長い nagai = long; 社長 shachou = company president
DESCRIPTION: at the top, long flowing hair; at the bottom; the letters L and y which remind us of "friendly" **CUES:** this friend**L**y 社長 sha**chou** (president) with long hair owns **Naga**ina, a 長い **naga**i (long) cobra who was **Cho**sen to represent her tribe
COMPARE: (出)張 shutchou = business trip, # 477; 良(い) yoi = good, # 303

Scorpion

503. 地

PRONUNCIATIONS: ji, chi **MEANINGS:** ground, soil **EXAMPLES:** 地震 jishin = earthquake; 地下鉄 chikatetsu = subway

DESCRIPTION: on the left, 土 tsuchi (dirt, # 59); on the right, this is reportedly a scorpion, with a long stinging tail
CUES: **J**ittery scorpions live under the 地 **chi** (ground), where they eat **Chee**se

COMPARE: 池 ike = pond, # 504; 他 hoka = another, # 505

504. 池

PRONUNCIATIONS: ike, chi **MEANING:** pond **EXAMPLES:** 池 ike = pond; 乾電池 kandenchi = battery **DESCRIPTION:** on the left, a water radical (see # 12); on the right, this is reportedly a scorpion, with a long stinging tail **CUES:** scorpions lived near the 池 **ike** (pond) on **Ike**'s (Eisenhower's) farm and ate his **Chee**se **COMPARE:** 地 chi = ground, # 503; 他 hoka = another, # 505

505. 他

PRONUNCIATIONS: hoka, ta*nin
MEANING: others **EXAMPLES:** 他の hoka no = another (undefined) object; 他人 tanin = other people, outsiders **DESCRIPTION:** on the left, a man with a slanted hat; on the right, this is reportedly a scorpion, with a long stinging tail **CUES:** ordinary men with flat hats ride in unmarked vehicles, but 他の **hoka** no (other) men with slanted hats ride in **H**opped-up **Ca**rs marked with scorpion decals, which is why they are considered 他人 **ta**nin (outsiders), in spite of their nice **Tan**s
COMPARE: 外(に) hoka ni (besides, # 163); 別(の) betsu no = another (defined) object, # 561; 地 chi = ground, # 503; 池 ike = pond, # 504

Skirts

506. 春

PRONUNCIATION: haru **MEANING:** spring **EXAMPLE:** 春休み haruyasumi = spring break **DESCRIPTION:** at the top, a 人 hito (person, # 13), with the number 三 san (three, # 3) inscribed across it; at the bottom, 日 hi (sun, # 32), which appears to be under the skirts of the 人 **CUE:** during the first 春 **haru** (spring) when King **Ha**rold **Ru**led, many people gave birth to 三つ子 mitsugo (triplets), with 日 (sun)-like (i.e., sunny) dispositions

507. 寒

PRONUNCIATION: samu*i, kan*ki
MEANING: cold atmosphere EXAMPLES: 寒い samui = cold atmosphere; 寒気 kanki = a chill, but this can also be pronounced "samuke" DESCRIPTION: at the top, a roof; under the roof, a samurai's wife, wearing a corset, with legs spread apart, sheltering some children under her skirt

CUE: when it's 寒い samui (cold), this Samurai's wife stays in her house in Canada and gathers her children under her skirt

East

508. 東

PRONUNCIATIONS: higashi, tou
MEANING: east EXAMPLES: 東 higashi = east; 東京 toukyou = Tokyo

DESCRIPTION: 日 hi (sun, # 32) seen behind a 木 ki (tree, # 118) in the morning, telling us that this tree is east of us CUES: in a High Gash on the 東 higashi (east) side of a 木 (tree) in 東京 toukyou (Tokyo), there is a family of tree Toads that watches the 日 (sun) rise COMPARE: 乗(る) noru = to get aboard or ride, # 509

509. 乗

PRONUNCIATIONS: jou, no*ru MEANINGS: to ride, to get aboard EXAMPLES: 乗客 joukyaku = passenger; 乗る noru = to get aboard or ride DESCRIPTION: compared to 東 higashi (east, # 508), 乗 has a roof on top, suggesting a vehicle with a roof; the structure overlapping the 木 ki (tree, # 118) in 乗 has protrusions on both sides, suggesting that it is a vehicle, not the sun CUES: Joan of Arc is waiting because she wants to be a 乗客

joukyaku (passenger) on this vehicle behind the 木 (tree), but when she tries to 乗る noru (board), there is No room

Grain Plants

510. 私

PRONUNCIATIONS: watakushi, watashi, shi*you MEANINGS: I, personal, private
EXAMPLES: 私 watakushi = I; 私 watashi = I; 私用の shiyou no = private
DESCRIPTION: on the left, a grain plant with a ripe head; on the right, an arm bent to claim what belongs to me CUES: 私 watakushi (I) am a Washington Takushii (taxi) driver, and I use a lawyer named Wallace to create Tax Shields for my Sheep farm, where I bend my arm to clutch the ripe grain that is mine

COMPARE: 仕(様) shiyou = means, method, # 67; 使(用) shiyou = use, employment, # 480

511. 科

PRONUNCIATION: ka MEANINGS: section, category EXAMPLES: 科学 kagaku = science; 科学者 kagakusha = scientist; 教科書 kyoukasho = textbook; 歯科 shika = dentistry DESCRIPTION: on the left, a grain plant with a ripe head, but let's call this a scientist with a flat-top haircut; on the right, a shelf holding two bottles of calcium

CUE: a 科学者 kagakusha (scientist) with a flat-top haircut searches a shelf for some Calcium to use in his research

COMPARE: 課 ka = section, # 587; 化(学) kagaku = chemistry, # 487; 料(理) ryouri = cuisine, # 512

512. 料

PRONUNCIATION: ryou **MEANINGS:** food, fee, provisions **EXAMPLES:** 料理 ryouri = cuisine; 無料 muryou = free of charge; 料金 ryoukin = fee **DESCRIPTION:** on the left, Pope Leo, a pet owner with messy hair; on the right, a shelf holding two cans of food **CUE:** Pope **Leo**, a fuzzy-haired pet owner, is about to open one of two cans of pet 料理 **ryou**ri (cuisine) on the shelf **COMPARE:** 科(学) kagaku = science, # 511

513. 和

PRONUNCIATIONS: wa, yawa*ragu **MEANING:** harmony **EXAMPLES:** 和食 washoku = Japanese food; 温和 onwa = mild, calm, gentle; 和らぐ yawaragu = to soften or become less severe **DESCRIPTION:** on the left, grain plants with ripe heads; on the right, 口 kuchi (mouth, # 426), suggesting eating **CUES:** when the grain plants get ripe, we eat 和食 **wa**shoku (Japanese food) served from a **Wa**gon, experience 平和 hei**wa** (peace), **Ya**wn and **Wa**sh the dishes

Capital

514. 京

PRONUNCIATION: kyou **MEANING:** capital **EXAMPLES:** 京都 kyouto = Kyoto; 東京 toukyou = Tokyo **DESCRIPTION:** a castle with a roof, set on a hill **CUE:** the **Key** that the **Yo**deler gave me fits this castle on a hill in 京都 **kyou**to (Kyoto) **COMPARE:** 涼(しい) suzushii = cool, # 515

515. 涼

PRONUNCIATION: suzu*shii **MEANINGS:** cool **EXAMPLE:** 涼しい suzushii = cool **DESCRIPTION:** on the left, a water radical (see # 12); on the right, 京 kyou (capital, # 514) **CUE:** when it rains in the 京 (capital),

it gets 涼しい **suzu**shii (cool), and it's a good time to eat **Su**perman's **Z**ucchini

516. 景

PRONUNCIATIONS: ke*shiki, kei **MEANINGS:** fine view, scene **EXAMPLES:** 景色 keshiki = view, scenery; 風景 fuukei = view, scenery, landscape **DESCRIPTION:** at the top, 日 hi (sun, # 32); at the bottom, 京 kyou (capital, # 514)

CUES: when the sun shines above the 京 (capital), the 景色 **ke**shiki (scenery) is lovely, and we drink from a **Ke**g provided by our sheepish king and eat **Ca**ke

Tsutomeru

517. 勤

PRONUNCIATIONS: tsuto*meru, kin **MEANINGS:** to be employed, to serve **EXAMPLES:** 勤める tsutomeru = to be employed; 通勤する tsuukin suru = to commute to work; 出勤する shukkin suru = to attend work **DESCRIPTION:** at the upper left, a plant radical (see # 43); at the lower left, a sincere man wearing glasses; on the right, 力 chikara (force, # 107) **CUES:** a sincere man wearing glasses with plants dangling over his head **Tsu**ki **To**meru (moon parks) his moon buggy at the place where he 勤めている **tsuto**mete iru (is being employed), and he expends a lot of 力 (force) taking care of plants at a moon **Kin**dergarten **COMPARE:** 務(める) tsutomeru = to discharge one's duty, # 518; 努(める) tsutomeru = to make an effort, # 519; 野(菜) yasai = vegetable, # 545

518. 務

PRONUNCIATIONS: mu, tsuto*meru **MEANING:** to discharge one's duty **EXAMPLES:** 公務員 koumuin = public servant; 事務所 jimusho = office;

491

務める tsutomeru = to discharge one's duty
DESCRIPTION: this is a portrait of the workers at an office on the moon: at the upper left, the katakana character マ ma, representing Ma (mother); at the lower left, a barbed nail; at the upper right, a guy carrying a crutch; at the lower right, 力 chikara (force, # 107)

CUES: マ (Ma), a guy with a barbed wit, a disabled guy, and a forceful guy work at a 事務所 jimusho (office) on the **Mo**on, where they **Tsu**ki **To**meru (moon park) their moon buggies and then **tsuto**meru 務める (discharge their duties) **COMPARE:** 勤(める) tsutomeru = to be employed, # 517; 努(める) tsutomeru = to make an effort, # 519

519. 努
PRONUNCIATIONS: tsuto*meru, do*ryoku
MEANING: to try hard **EXAMPLES:** 努める tsutomeru = to make an effort; 努力 doryoku = effort **DESCRIPTION:** at the upper left, 女 onna (female, # 235); at the upper right, 又 mata ("again," # 24), but this resembles a table where doughnuts are made; at the bottom, 力 ryoku (force, # 107)

CUES: this 女 (female) **Tsu**ki **To**meru (moon parks) her moon buggy and 努める **tsuto**meru (makes an effort) for her job on the moon, where she expends 努力 **do**ryoku (effort) making **Dough**nuts on a 又 (table) **COMPARE:** 勤(める) tsutomeru = to be employed, # 517; 務(める) tsutomeru = to discharge one's duty, # 518

Pleasant
520. 楽
PRONUNCIATIONS: tano*shii, gaku, raku
MEANINGS: happy, enjoyable, without difficulty **EXAMPLES:** 楽しい tanoshii = pleasant; 音楽 ongaku = music; 楽 raku =

comfort, pleasure, relief **DESCRIPTION:** a loudspeaker belonging to Tanya Tucker has been mounted at the top of a 木 ki (tree, # 118), and music is emerging from it
CUES: Tanya **Ow**ns the loudspeaker on a tree that plays 楽しい **tano**shii (pleasant) 音楽 on**gaku** (music) for **Gaku**sei (students) during their **Rack**etball games

COMPARE: 薬 kusuri = medicine, # 521; 絡 raku = contact, # 230; 落(語) rakugo = Japanese comic story telling, # 526

521. 薬
PRONUNCIATIONS: kusuri, gusuri[1], ya*kkyoku, yaku*hin **MEANINGS:** medicine, pharmaceutical **EXAMPLES:** 薬 kusuri = medicine; 眠り薬 nemurigusuri = sleeping medicine; 薬局 yakkyoku = pharmacy; 薬品 yakuhin = medicine, drug
DESCRIPTION: at the top, a plant radical (see # 43); at the bottom, 楽(しい) tanoshii (pleasant, # 520)

CUES: 薬 **kusuri** (medicines), which a doctor will prescribe after a **Curs**ory exam, come from plants like **Ya**ms and sometimes have pleasant side-effects, such as causing people to **Yak** (talk) too much

Dancer
522. 夏
PRONUNCIATIONS: natsu, ka **MEANING:** summer **EXAMPLES:** 夏 natsu = summer; 初夏 shoka = early summer
DESCRIPTION: at the top, a radical similar to 百 hyaku (hundred, # 47), but with one additional horizontal line; like 百, this resembles a limousine with an antenna, seen from the back; at the bottom, a dancer with a ponytail **CUES:** in 夏 **natsu** (summer), this dancer with a ponytail wears a **Nat**ty **Sui**t and is driven around in a limousine **Car**

COMPARE: 愛 ai = love, # 523

523. 愛

PRONUNCIATION: ai **MEANING:** love
EXAMPLES: 愛しています ai shite imasu = I love you; 愛情 aijou = love
DESCRIPTION: at the top, the upper portion of 受(ける) ukeru (to take an exam, # 577), which resembles a cloth covering three exam booklets on a tablecloth; in the middle, 心 kokoro (heart, # 306); at the bottom, a dancer with a ponytail **CUE:** this dancer with a ponytail is an **I**ce dancer and a student; when she takes her exams, she puts a lot of 心 (heart) into them because of the 愛情 **ai**jou (love) that she feels for knowledge
COMPARE: 夏 natsu = summer, # 522

524. 客

PRONUNCIATION: kyaku **MEANINGS:** guest, customer **EXAMPLES:** お客 okyaku = honorable guest; 観客 kankyaku = audience; 乗客 joukyaku = passenger
DESCRIPTION: at the top, a roof; in the middle, a leaping dancer with a ponytail; at the bottom, a box **CUE:** a dancer with a ponytail leaps over a box under a roof, for a 客 **kyaku** (customer) who is a **Kayak**er
COMPARE: (連)絡 renraku = contact, # 230; (道)路 douro = road, # 525

525. 路

PRONUNCIATION: ro **MEANING:** road
EXAMPLE: 道路 douro = road
DESCRIPTION: on the left, a square head above 正(しい) tadashii (correct, # 174), suggesting a correct gentleman, as seen in 踊(る) odoru (to dance, # 366); on the right, a dancer with a ponytail leaping over a box, as seen in 客 kyaku (customer, # 524)
CUE: the 正 (correct) gentleman and the dancer with a ponytail are **Roa**ming on a

道路 dou**ro** (road) **COMPARE:** 絡 raku = contact, # 230; 落(す) otosu = to drop, # 526

526. 落

PRONUNCIATIONS: o, raku **MEANINGS:** to fall or drop **EXAMPLES:** 落とす otosu = to knock down or drop; 落ちる ochiru = to fall; 落語 rakugo = Japanese comic story telling **DESCRIPTION:** at the top, a plant radical (see # 43); on the lower left, a water radical (see # 12); on the lower right, a dancer from the Ottoman era, with a ponytail, leaping over a box of old cheese
CUES: during the **O**ttoman era, when this dancer jumps over a box of **O**ld cheese to escape a river, her head **Rak**es some leaves and 落とす **o**tosu (knocks them down) so that they 落ちる **o**chiru (fall), and her toes **Rak**e the box as well, scratching it
COMPARE: 絡 raku = contact, # 230; 楽 raku = comfort, pleasure, relief, # 520; 客 kyaku = customer, # 524; 路 ro = road, # 525

527. 復

PRONUNCIATION: fuku **MEANINGS:** again, to repeat **EXAMPLES:** 復習 fukushuu = review; 回復 kaifuku = recovery
DESCRIPTION: this is a pleasant scene from Fukuoka: on the left, a man in a double hat, who is a therapist; at the top right, a crutch; at the middle right, 日 hi (sun, # 32); at the bottom right, a dancer with a ponytail
CUE: in **Fuku**oka, injured dancers are helped by therapists; they use crutches, they sit in the 日 (sun), and they gradually experience 回復 kai**fuku** (recovery)

528. 優

PRONUNCIATIONS: yasa*shii, yuu, sugu*reru
MEANINGS: actor, excellent, graceful

EXAMPLES: 優しい yasashii = kind; 優秀 yuushuu = excellent; 優勝 yuushou = victory; 優れる sugureru = to excel

DESCRIPTION: on the left, a man with a slanted hat; at the top right, a radical that looks like 百 hyaku (hundred, # 47) but with one more horizontal line, resembling a limousine with an antenna; at the middle right, 心 kokoro (heart, # 306); at the bottom right, a youthful dancer with a ponytail CUES: this man is 優しい **yasa**shii (kind), he wears a **Ya**nkee **Sa**sh, he rides in a 優秀な **yuu**shuu na (excellent) limousine, he acts from his 心 (heart), his girlfriend is a **You**thful dancer with a ponytail, and they will **Soo**n buy a **Goo**se

Twisted

529. 弟

PRONUNCIATIONS: otouto, dai, tei, de*shi
MEANING: younger brother EXAMPLES: 弟 otouto = younger brother; 兄弟 kyoudai = sibling; 子弟 shitei = younger people; 弟子 deshi = disciple, apprentice

DESCRIPTION: younger brother, wearing two antennae on his head, appears to have twisted himself around a 木 ki (tree, # 118), which is missing a branch on the lower right CUES: 弟 **otouto** (younger brother) eats only **O**ld **TomaTo**es, which is a strange **Di**et, and he has twisted himself around a 木 (tree) which he wants to make into a **Ta**ble for a **De**butante

COMPARE: 第 dai = order, number, # 530

530. 第

PRONUNCIATION: dai MEANING: order
EXAMPLES: 第三課 daisanka = section number three; 次第に shidai ni = gradually; 次第で shidai de = depending on

DESCRIPTION: at the top, 竹 take (bamboo, # 134), which resembles two clamps; at the bottom, 弟 otouto (younger brother, # 529), without his antennae CUE: 弟 (younger brother) has two 竹 (bamboo) clamps in his hair, indicating that he is 第二 **dai** ni (Number Two) in line at Weight Watchers; he wants to go on a **Di**et, and he will get to the front of the queue 次第に shi**dai** ni (gradually)

COMPARE: 切符 kippu = ticket, # 133; 笑(う) warau = to laugh, # 199

531. 沸

PRONUNCIATIONS: wa, fu*ttou
MEANINGS: to seethe, boil EXAMPLES: 沸く waku = to boil, intransitive; 沸かす wakasu = to boil, transitive; 沸騰する futtou suru = to boil DESCRIPTION: on the left, a water radical (see # 12); on the right, twisted radiator pipes CUES: the **Wa**ter is cool before it enters these twisted pipes, but then it 沸く **wa**ku (boils) and cooks our **Foo**d

Deep Inside

532. 奥

PRONUNCIATION: oku MEANING: deep inside EXAMPLES: 奥のほう oku no hou = toward the back; 奥さん okusan = someone else's wife DESCRIPTION: a box on top of a two-legged table, containing 米 kome (uncooked rice, # 326)

CUES: the 奥さん **oku**san (honorable wife), who went to **Ok**lahoma University, stores 米 (rice) by placing it 奥のほう **oku** no hou (toward the back) of this **Oak** box

COMPARE: 歯 ha = tooth, # 533

533. 歯

PRONUNCIATIONS: ha, ba, shi*ka
MEANING: tooth
EXAMPLES: 歯 ha = tooth; 虫歯 mushiba
= decayed tooth; 歯科 shika = dentistry
DESCRIPTION: at the top, 止(める) tomeru
(to stop, # 173); at the bottom, 米 kome
(uncooked rice, # 326), in a box; together
these radicals resemble irregular teeth arising
from a gum containing dental roots
CUES: my two 歯 **ha** (teeth) can be seen
above the gum line, with the roots below, and
they are rather irregular, since my false 歯 **ha**
(teeth) are in the **Ha**ll, in a **Ba**g, where my
Sheepdog left them **COMPARE:** 奥(さん)
okusan = someone else's wife, # 532

Oil Derrick

534. 歌

PRONUNCIATIONS: ka*shu, uta*u
MEANINGS: to sing, a song **EXAMPLES:**
歌手 kashu = singer ; 歌う utau = to sing
DESCRIPTION: on the left, two song sheets
hanging from racks; on the right, an oil derrick
from Utah
CUES: the oil derrick is a 歌手 **ka**shu
(singer) who likes to eat **Ca**shew nuts, and she
reads from a music stand with two song sheets
when she 歌う **uta**u (sings) in **Uta**h

535. 欲

PRONUNCIATIONS: ho*shii, yoku
MEANINGS: greed, wanting more
EXAMPLES: 欲しい hoshii = to desire ;
欲張り yokubari = greed; 食欲
shokuyoku = appetite **DESCRIPTION:** at the
upper left, some droplets of water; at the lower
left, a yoku (well) made house; on the right, an
oil derrick **CUES:** the oil derrick 欲しい
hoshii (desires) a **H**orse that she saw on a **Sh**ip,
as well as this **Yoku** (well) made house, which
she is drooling over

536. 次

PRONUNCIATIONS: tsugi, ji*kai, shi*dai
MEANING: next **EXAMPLES:** 次に tsugi ni
= next; 次回に jikai ni = next time;
次第に shidai ni = gradually
DESCRIPTION: on the left, a water radical
(see # 12); on the right, an oil derrick
CUES: the oil derrick, who is wearing a **Tsu**it
(suit) and carrying a **Gui**tar, waits by the
water; 次に **tsugi** ni (next), it will be her
turn to cross the river; after that comes a **Jee**p,
and then some **Shee**p

537. 吹

PRONUNCIATIONS: fu*ku **MEANINGS:** to
blow, to breathe **EXAMPLE:** 吹く fuku = to
blow, breathe, whistle **DESCRIPTION:** on the
left, 口 kuchi (mouth, # 426); on the right, an
oil derrick in Fukuoka **CUES:** in **Fu**kuoka, an
oil derrick extracts oil and then 吹く **fu**ku
(blows) it out through its 口 (mouth)
COMPARE: 吸(う) suu = to suck, # 427;
服 fuku = clothes, # 150; 復(習) fukushuu
= review, # 527

Platform

538. 台

PRONUNCIATIONS: dai, tai*fuu
MEANING: platform **EXAMPLES:** 台 dai =
platform; 台所 daidokoro = kitchen; 二台
nidai = two machines, cars etc.; 台風 taifuu =
typhoon **DESCRIPTION:** at the top, the
katakana character ム mu (the sound made by
a cow); at the bottom 口 kuchi (mouth, # 426),
but this could be a platform
CUES: a ム (cow) rests on a 台 **dai**
(platform); she is on a **Di**et, and she is **Ti**red
of it

539. 治

PRONUNCIATIONS: nao, chi*an, osa*meru, ji
MEANINGS: to govern, control, cure
EXAMPLES: 治す naosu = to heal; 治る naoru = to recover from illness; 治安 chian = safety; 治める osameru = to govern or reign; 政治 seiji = politics DESCRIPTION: on the left, a water radical (see # 12); on the right, 台 dai (platform, # 538), which consists of ム mu (the sound made by a cow) above a 口 kuchi (mouth, # 426) CUES: Naomi 治した naoshita (cured) ム (cows) Cheaply by putting pills with water into their 口 (mouths), but Osama bin Laden Jeered her efforts

COMPARE: 直(す) naosu = to correct, repair or restore, # 570; 直(る) naoru = to be corrected, repaired or restored, # 570

540. 始

PRONUNCIATIONS: haji, shi MEANING: to begin EXAMPLES: 始める hajimeru = to begin; 開始する kaishi suru = to begin
DESCRIPTION: on the left, 女 onna (female, # 235); on the right; 台 dai (stand, # 538)
CUES: a 女 (female) leaves her Hat in her Jeep and 始める hajimeru (begins) her job examining Sheep on a 台 (stand)

COMPARE: 初(めて) hajimete = for the first time, # 104

Hanging Bucket

541. 甘

PRONUNCIATION: ama*i MEANING: sweet
EXAMPLES: 甘い amai = sweet; 甘やかす amayakasu = to pamper
DESCRIPTION: a bucket hanging from a rod, half-full of liquid CUE: Amanda bought half a bucket of 甘い amai (sweet) molasses

542. 世

PRONUNCIATIONS: se, yo, sei*ki
MEANINGS: a world, a generation
EXAMPLES: 世界 sekai = the world; 世話をする sewa wo suru = to take care of; 世の中 yo no naka = life, society, world; 世紀 seiki = century
DESCRIPTION: a bucket hanging from a rod supported by a stand CUES: since the 世界 sekai (world) is hanging in a bucket and might fall any Second, people are consulting Yogis to find out how to keep it Safe

543. 葉

PRONUNCIATIONS: ha, you, ba MEANING: leaf EXAMPLES: 葉 ha = leaf; 紅葉 kouyou = autumn colors; 言葉 kotoba = word DESCRIPTION: at the top, a plant radical (see # 43); in the middle, 世 se (world, # 542) which includes a hanging bucket; at the bottom, a 木 ki (tree, # 118) in Hawaii CUES: in Hawaii, a Yogi came out of a Bar and saw these 葉 ha (leaves) hanging in a bucket on a 木 (tree)

Rotated M

544. 予

PRONUNCIATION: yo MEANINGS: to prepare, preliminary EXAMPLES: 予定 yotei = plan, schedule; 予約 yoyaku = reservation DESCRIPTION: an M rotated 45° to the right, representing Mom, balanced on a nail CUE: M (Mom) has good balance, she has a 予定 yotei (plan), and she has made 予約 yoyaku (reservations) for a Yoga class

545. 野

PRONUNCIATIONS: no, ya **MEANINGS:** field, outside, outsider **EXAMPLES:** 野原 nohara = field; 野村 Nomura = a family name; 野菜 yasai = vegetable; 野球 yakyuu = baseball **DESCRIPTION:** at the upper left, 田(んぼ) tanbo (rice paddy, # 68); at the lower left, 土 tsuchi (dirt, # 59); together these resemble a sincere guy wearing bifocals; on the right, 予(定) yotei (plan, # 544), resembling an M rotated 45° to the right, which reminds us of a mom, balanced on a nail **CUES:** this sincere guy with bifocals and his M (mom) live in Norway, and they have a plan to grow some 野菜 yasai (vegetables) for their Yak **COMPARE:** 勤(める) tsutomeru = to be employed, # 517

546. 柔

PRONUNCIATIONS: juu*dou, yawa*rakai **MEANINGS:** tender, gentleness, softness **EXAMPLES:** 柔道 juudou = judo; 柔らかい yawarakai = soft, tender, limp **DESCRIPTION:** at the top, an M rotated 45° to the right, which represents Mom; at the bottom, 木 ki (tree, # 118) **CUES:** M (Mom) knows 柔道 juudou and can climb a tree, although this activity is rather Juvenile; she is 柔らかい yawarakai (tender and soft), even to Yakuza (gangster) Warlords **COMPARE:** 予(定) yotei = plan, # 544

Snake

547. 危

PRONUNCIATIONS: abu*nai, ki*ken **MEANING:** danger **EXAMPLES:** 危ない abunai = dangerous; 危険 kiken = danger **DESCRIPTION:** at the top, an abused fish head; under the fish head, a lean-to; under the lean-to, a snake **CUES:** this fish head, who has been Abused, sits on a lean-to and

tries to escape the 危ない **abu**nai (dangerous) snake lurking inside, which has already **Ki**lled Ken but spared Barbie

548. 包

PRONUNCIATION: hou*sou, tsutsu*mu, zutsumi **EXAMPLES:** 包装 housou = wrapping; 包む tsutsumu = to wrap; 小包 kozutsumi = a package sent by mail **MEANING:** to wrap **DESCRIPTION:** at the top, J-shaped packaging; below, contents shaped like a backward "S" **CUES:** the Hostess will 包む **tsutsu**mu (wrap) this J-shaped or S-shaped package, which contains Tsuits piled on Tsuits, including Zoot Suits for our Meeting

549. 港

PRONUNCIATIONS: minato, kou **MEANING:** port **EXAMPLES:** 港 minato = port; 空港 kuukou = airport **DESCRIPTION:** on the left, a water radical (see # 12); at the upper right, a broad tower on sturdy legs; at the bottom right, a snake **CUES:** at this 港 **minato** (port), which is controlled by Mighty NATO, there is a tower on the upper right that supports cranes used to load ships bound to Cologne, and there is a big snake in the water below

550. 記

PRONUNCIATION: ki **MEANING:** to record **EXAMPLES:** 記事 kiji = newspaper article; 日記 nikki = diary; 記入 kinyuu = entry, filling in forms **DESCRIPTION:** on the left, 言(葉) kotoba (words, # 430); on the right, a killer snake **CUE:** I read a 記事 **ki**ji (article) containing a lot of 言 (words) about a snake that almost Killed Jimmy Carter

Kaeru & Kawaru

551. 替

PRONUNCIATIONS: ka*eru, gae, ga **MEANINGS:** to replace, or to exchange money **EXAMPLES:** 替える kaeru = to replace or exchange money; 両替 ryougae = money exchange; 着替える kigaeru = to change clothes **DESCRIPTION:** at the top, two 大(きい) ookii (big, # 188) men, named Carl Ericson and Guy Ericson, each with an extra pair of arms; at the bottom, a 2-drawer cabinet **CUES:** since **Car**l Ericson and **Guy E**ricson are two 大 (big) men who are almost identical, there is no **Ga**p between them, and we can 替える **ka**eru (exchange) one for the other **COMPARE:** 選(ぶ) erabu = to choose, # 352

552. 代

PRONUNCIATIONS: dai, ka, yo
MEANINGS: people changing, generations
EXAMPLES: 時代 jidai = era; 代わる kawaru = to take the place of; 代わりに kawari ni = in place of; 千代田 Chiyoda = a ward in Tokyo **DESCRIPTION:** on the left, the man with a slanted hat is the president; on the right, the woman leaning on him is the vice president **CUES:** if the man with the slanted hat **Die**s, the leaning woman will start a new 時代 ji**dai** (era) in government; she will **Ca**ll the War Department, 代わる **ka**waru (take the place) of the president, and order people to eat more **Yo**gurt

553. 変

PRONUNCIATIONS: hen, ka **MEANINGS:** to change something; strange, extraordinary
EXAMPLES: 変な hen na = strange ; 大変 taihen = terrible; 変える kaeru = to change, transitive; 変わる kawaru = to change, intransitive
DESCRIPTION: at the top, a swooping hen; at the bottom, a dancer with a ponytail
CUES: I just saw a 変な **hen** na (strange) sight: a large **Hen** swooped down over a dancer with a ponytail and tried to 変える **ka**eru (change) her; let's **Ca**ll erudite Eric to witness this

554. 換

PRONUNCIATIONS: ka*eru, kan
MEANINGS: to replace or exchange
EXAMPLES: 乗り換える norikaeru = to change trains; 交換する koukan suru = to exchange **DESCRIPTION:** on the left, an erudite crawling guy; on the right, a Canadian general with a fish head, who wears two decorations on his chest
CUES: we have **Ca**lled an erudite crawling guy to 換える **ka**eru (exchange) the decoration on the right side of the **Can**adian general's chest for the one on the left

Bird

555. 鳥

PRONUNCIATIONS: tori, chou **MEANING:** bird **EXAMPLES:** 小鳥 kotori = small bird; 白鳥 hakuchou = swan **DESCRIPTION:** this 鳥 tori (bird) has a little tuft on its head, feathers, and strangely, five toes **CUES:** this 鳥 **tori** (bird) with five toes belongs to a **Tory** who was **Cho**sen to serve in Parliament **COMPARE:** 島 shima = island, # 556

556. 島

PRONUNCIATIONS: shima, jima[1], tou
MEANING: island **EXAMPLES:** 島 shima = island; 広島 Hiroshima = city in Japan; 桜島 Sakurajima = a volcano in southern Kyushu; 半島 hantou = peninsula
DESCRIPTION: compared to 鳥 tori (bird, # 555), four of the bird's toes have been replaced by 山 yama (mountain, # 146)
CUES: 鳥 (birds) that live on 山 (mountains) that arise on 島 **shima** (islands), such as those near Hiro**Shima**, sometimes lose their **Toe**s to predators

Yak or Sword on a Table

557. 役

PRONUNCIATION: yaku **MEANINGS:** role, service **EXAMPLES:** 役に立つ yaku ni tatsu = to make use of; 区役所 kuyakusho = ward office **DESCRIPTION:** on the left, a man with a double hat; on the right, π (the Greek letter pi, which represents a pious yak here), standing on 又 mata ("again,"# 24), but this resembles a simple table **CUE:** the pious **Yak** is performing a 役 **yaku** (service) by standing on this 又 (table) and serving as a lookout for the man with the double hat **COMPARE:** 投(げる) nageru = to throw, # 558; 段(々) dandan = gradually, # 559

558. 投

PRONUNCIATION: tou, na*geru **MEANING:** to throw **EXAMPLES:** 投資 toushi = investment; 投げる nageru = to throw **DESCRIPTION:** on the left, a crawling guy; on the right, π (the Greek letter pi), standing on 又 mata ("again," # 24), but this resembles a table **CUE:** this crawling guy wants to make some **Toa**st and has been **Nagging** π to get off the 又 (table); next, he plans to 投げる **na**geru (throw) π off **COMPARE:** 役 yaku = role, service, # 557; 段(々) dandan = gradually, # 559

559. 段

PRONUNCIATION: dan **MEANINGS:** step, paragraph, case **EXAMPLES:** 階段 kaidan = stairs; 段々 dandan = gradually; 普段 fudan = usual, every day **DESCRIPTION:** on the left, a ladder with four steps; on the right, π (the Greek letter pi), a pious yak belonging to Daniel Boone, standing on a 又 mata ("again," # 24), but this resembles a simple

table **CUE: Dan**iel uses the 階段 kai**dan** (steps) on the left to climb up and down and give food to the pious yak on the 又 (table) **COMPARE:** 役 yaku = role, service, # 557; 投(げる) nageru = to throw, # 558; 作(る) tsukuru = to make, # 482

560. 招

PRONUNCIATIONS: mane*ku, shou **MEANING:** to invite **EXAMPLES:** 招く maneku = to invite; 招待 shoutai = invitation **DESCRIPTION:** on the left, a crawling guy; on the right, a 刀 katana (sword, # 102) on a box **CUES:** the crawling guy wants to write a letter to 招く **mane**ku (invite) a **Manne**quin to a Broadway **Show**, but first he has to remove the 刀 (sword) from his writing box **COMPARE:** 投(げる) nageru = to throw, # 558

Ri

561. 別

PRONUNCIATIONS: betsu, waka*reru **MEANING:** to separate **EXAMPLES:** 別に betsu ni = particularly; 別の betsu no = another (defined) object; 別れる wakareru = to separate **DESCRIPTION:** on the left, Betsy, who has a square head resting on 万 man (ten thousand, # 113); on the right, the katakana character リ Ri **CUES: Bets**y with her square head doesn't like リ Ri with his pointy toes 別に **betsu** ni (particularly), and they 別れる **waka**reru (break up) after リ Ri **Wa**lks on the **Cat COMPARE:** 他(の) hoka no = another (undefined) object, # 505

562. 割

PRONUNCIATIONS: wa*ru, wari, katsu **MEANINGS:** to divide, apportion **EXAMPLES:** 割る waru = to break glass and wood, transitive; 割れる wareru = to break, intransitive; 4 割る 2 yon waru ni = 4 divided by 2; 割に wari ni = relatively; 分割する bunkatsu suru = to divide or split **DESCRIPTION:** on the left, 王 ou (king, not included in this catalogue), wearing a wide crown; he is standing on a box, which might be a warrior's tomb; on the right, the katakana character リ Ri, which looks like some kind of tool **CUES:** a 王 (king), wearing a wide crown, is **Wa**lking on the **Warri**or's tomb with his **Ca**ts and digging with the リ Ri tool, trying to 割る **wa**ru (break) the tomb

563. 倒

PRONUNCIATIONS: tao*reru, tou*san, dou **MEANINGS:** overthrow, fall, collapse, breakdown, become bankrupt **EXAMPLES:** 倒れる taoreru = to fall, collapse, drop, fall senseless; 倒す taosu = to bring down, knock down, defeat; 倒産 tousan = bankruptcy; 面倒 mendou = annoyance, difficulty, care **DESCRIPTION:** on the left, a man with a slanted hat; in the center, a tower composed of a pedaling leg balanced on 土 tsuchi (dirt, # 59); on the right, the katakana character リ Ri **CUES:** if either the man or リ Ri moves, the **Tow**er will 倒れる **tao**reru (fall), and that will cause **To**tal 面倒 men**dou** (annoyance) to the people who paid good **Dou**gh to put it up

564. 利

PRONUNCIATIONS: ri **MEANINGS:** useful, sharp **EXAMPLES:** 利用する riyou suru = to use; 便利 benri = convenient; 有利 yuuri = advantageous; 利益 rieki = profit **DESCRIPTION:** on the left, a grain plant with a ripe head; on the right, the katakana character リ Ri , which tells us how to pronounce this **CUES:** リ **Ri** 利用する **ri**you suru (uses) ripe grain to make meals

565. 刻

PRONUNCIATIONS: koku, kiza*mu **MEANINGS:** to tick away, to cut into pieces **EXAMPLES:** 遅刻する chikoku suru = to be tardy; 時刻 jikoku = time; 刻む kizamu = to cut, mince, carve **DESCRIPTION:** on the left, this is said to be the skeleton of a wild boar; on the right, the katakana character リ Ri **CUES:** after リ Ri carved up the boar, he stopped to drink a **Co**ke, and to **Ki**d **Za**ch about not helping him, and therefore he will 遅刻する chi**koku** suru (be tardy)

566. 帰

PRONUNCIATIONS: kae*ru, ki*taku **MEANINGS:** to go home, to return **EXAMPLES:** 帰る kaeru = to return home; 帰宅 kitaku = a return to one's home **DESCRIPTION:** on the left, the katakana character リ Ri; at the upper right, long hair streaming to the left; at the lower right, the face of an elephant, with low-hanging ears and a long trunk **CUES:** as リ Ri watches, a **Ca**t **E**nters my home, and I will 帰る **kae**ru (return), riding my elephant, with my long hair streaming to the left, to **Ki**ck the cat out

Vertical Storage

567. 皿

PRONUNCIATION: sara, zara[1] **MEANING:** plate, dish, saucer **EXAMPLES:** 皿 sara = plate, dish or saucer; 大皿 oozara = large dish **DESCRIPTION:** three rolls of Saran wrap, positioned vertically on a shelf **CUE:** I put my left-over food on 皿 **sara** (plates) and cover it with **Sara**n wrap **COMPARE:** 温(かい) atatakai = warm object, # 257; 冊 satsu = counter for books, # 568

568. 冊

PRONUNCIATION: satsu
MEANING: counter for books
EXAMPLE: 三冊 sansatsu = three books
DESCRIPTION: a box divided into six compartments for storing satisfying Superman novels CUE: only six 冊 **satsu** (volumes) of **Sat**isfying **Su**perman novels will fit into this bookcase
COMPARE: 皿 sara = plate or dish, # 567

Corner

569. 置

PRONUNCIATIONS: o*ku, chi MEANINGS: to place, to leave something EXAMPLES: 置く oku = to place something; 位置 ichi = position DESCRIPTION: at the top, a thick double handle, with the upper level divided into three sections; below this, a three-drawer oak box; at the bottom, a shelf with a back wall, seen from the side CUES: we use this thick double-handled tool to 置く **o**ku (place) heavy items, like **Oa**k storage boxes of **Chee**se, at the backs of our shelves
COMPARE: 直(す) naosu (to correct, #570)

570. 直

PRONUNCIATIONS: nao, su, jiki, choku, tada*chi MEANINGS: straight, direct, to correct EXAMPLES: 直す naosu = to correct or repair something; 真っ直ぐ massugu = straight; 正直 shoujiki = honest; 直面 chokumen = confrontation; 直ちに tadachi ni = immediately DESCRIPTION: at the top, a thin handle; below this, a three-drawer box; at the bottom, a shelf with a back wall, seen from the side CUES: **Nao**mi and **Su**perman say that if we use this thin-handled tool to place lighter items, like **Jee**p **Key**s and Margaret **Cho**'s **Kool**-Aid packets, at the backs of our shelves, we can 直す **nao**su (correct) our storage problems, and we think that they are **Tada**shii (correct) COMPARE: 置(く) oku = to place, # 569; 治(す) naosu = to heal,
539; 治(る) naoru = to recover, # 539; 値(段) nedan = price, # 571; 正(しい) tadashii = correct, # 174

571. 値

PRONUNCIATIONS: atai, chi, ne*dan
MEANING: value EXAMPLES: 価 atai = value, price; 価値 kachi = value; 値段 nedan = price DESCRIPTION: on the left, a man with a slanted hat; on the right, 直(す) naosu (to correct, #570), which looks like a thin handle on a box, stored at the back of a shelf CUES: the man with a slanted hat, who is **A Thai** person, thinks that, in order to 直 (correct) our storage policy, we should store our **Chea**p lightweight items, like **Ne**cklaces, in boxes with thin handles at the backs of our shelves, but the 値段 **ne**dan (prices) that he charges for his advice are high

572. 県

PRONUNCIATION: ken MEANING: prefecture EXAMPLE: 県 ken = prefecture; 広島県 hiroshima ken = Hiroshima prefecture DESCRIPTION: compared to 直(す) naosu (to correct, # 570), this shelf that Ken & Barbie designed has three legs and can walk around; for that reason, they have no need for a handle at the top of the three-drawer box CUE: **Ken** and Barbie like to move around in their 県 **ken** (prefecture), and they keep their maps in a three-drawer box on this three-legged self-propelled shelf

Tower

573. 形

PRONUNCIATIONS: katachi, gyou, kei*tai, kata **MEANING:** shape **EXAMPLES:**
形 katachi = shape; 人形 ningyou = doll; 形態 keitai = form, shape, system; 形見 katami = keepsake, memento **DESCRIPTION:** on the left, a tower, which could be part of a catapult; on the right, these three lines look like spare cords for the catapult
CUES: this tower 形 **katachi** (shape) is part of a **Cata**pult for launching **Chee**se tubs at enemies who steal our **Gyo**za and **Ca**ke, and it can be bought from a **Cata**log

574. 飛

PRONUNCIATIONS: hi*kouki, to*bu
MEANING: to fly **EXAMPLES:** 飛行機 hikouki = airplane; 飛ぶ tobu = to fly
DESCRIPTION: on the left, a toy tower that is slightly different from the one found in 形 katachi (shape, # 573); on the right, two propellers, but these can also be seen as waves of heat arising from the tower
CUES: when waves of **Hea**t start rising from this tower, the two propellers will start turning, and a **Toy** 飛行機 **hi**kouki (airplane) will start to 飛ぶ **to**bu (fly)

Vertical Lines

575. 並

PRONUNCIATION: nara **MEANINGS:** to line up; row **EXAMPLES:** 並ぶ narabu = to line up, intransitive; 並べる naraberu = to line up, transitive
DESCRIPTION: various lines on a temple wall in Nara, most of which line up fairly well; compared to 普(通) futsuu (ordinary, # 576), the stove at the bottom is missing
CUE: these lines **nara**bu 並ぶ (line up) on the wall of a temple in **Nara**

576. 普

PRONUNCIATION: fu **MEANINGS:** universal, ordinary **EXAMPLES:** 普通 futsuu = ordinarily, usually, generally; 普段 fudan no = usual, casual, everyday **DESCRIPTION:** at the top, 並(ぶ) narabu (to line up, # 575), but this looks like four burners on a stove for cooking food, with the two center burners producing a higher flame; at the bottom, 日 hi (sun, # 32), but this is the body of the stove
CUE: this is just a 普通 **fu**tsuu (ordinary) stove, with four burners for cooking **Foo**d

577. 受

PRONUNCIATIONS: u*keru, ju*ken
MEANING: to receive **EXAMPLES:** 受ける ukeru = to receive, to take or pass an exam or class; 受験する juken suru = to take an academic exam **DESCRIPTION:** at the top, a cloth covering three exam booklets; below that, a tablecloth; at the bottom, 又 mata ("again," # 24), an exam table **CUES:** when you 受ける **u**keru (take or receive) an exam in the U.K., three exam booklets are covered with cloth and placed on top of a tablecloth covering a table, on which you may keep a bottle of **Juice COMPARE:** 授(業) jugyou = class, # 578; 愛 ai = love, # 523

578. 授

PRONUNCIATIONS: ju, sazu*karu
MEANINGS: to grant or bestow **EXAMPLES:** 授業 jugyou = class instruction; 教授 kyouju = professor; 授かる sazukaru = to be endowed with, be blessed with
DESCRIPTION: on the left, a crawling guy; on the right, 受(ける) ukeru (to take, or pass, an exam or class, # 577) **CUES:** the crawling guy is a 教授 kyou**ju** (professor) who keeps **Juice** in his 授業 **ju**gyou (class); his students take exams about the animals living in the San Diego **Z**oo **COMPARE:** 愛 ai = love, # 523

579. 両

PRONUNCIATION: ryou **MEANINGS:** both, two **EXAMPLES:** 両方 ryouhou = both; 両親 ryoushin = both parents
DESCRIPTION: this resembles a chair lift seat, hanging from a cable **CUE:** 両方 **ryo**hou (both) Pope **Leo** and his hobo friend can fit onto this chair lift seat when they go skiing
COMPARE: 席 seki (seat), # 496; (映)画 eiga = movie, # 77

エ & Y

580. 製

PRONUNCIATION: sei **MEANING:** to manufacture **EXAMPLES:** 日本製 nihonsei = Japanese product; 製品 seihin = finished product; 手製の tesei no = handmade, homemade **DESCRIPTION:** above the line, 牛 ushi (cow, # 205), who is the boss, sits on a revolving chair, next to リ Ri the supervisor; below the line, the katakana character エ and the letter Y are the workers in the factory
CUES: エ and Y follow orders given by the cow and リ Ri and manufacture 製品 **sei**hin (finished products) to be sold at **S**afeway stores

581. 袋

PRONUNCIATION: bi, fukuro, bukuro[1]
MEANINGS: sack, bag, pouch **EXAMPLES:** 足袋 tabi = Japanese-style socks; 袋 fukuro = sack, bag; 手袋 tebukuro = gloves; 紙袋 kamibukuro = paper bag **DESCRIPTION:** above the line, the katakana character イ and the leaning woman from 式 shiki (ceremony, # 249), who appears to be carrying a handbag; below the line, the katakana character エ and the letter Y are the workers in a factory in Fukuoka **CUE:** エ and Y manufacture 袋 **fukuro** (bags) for the privileged class, who use them to carry **Bee**r on **Fuku**oka **Roa**ds

582. 表

PRONUNCIATIONS: omote, pyou, arawa*su, hyou **MEANINGS:** surface, outside, front, to make public **EXAMPLES:** 表 omote = surface, front, outside; 発表する happyou suru = to announce, publish, reveal, make a presentation; 表す arawasu = to signify, represent or express; 表現 hyougen = expression **DESCRIPTION:** above the line, a double cross above an omotel (honorable motel); below the line, the katakana character エ and the letter Y **CUES:** in this **Omote**l (honorable motel), there are many straight 表 **omote** (surfaces), such as the ones in the double cross seen on the roof; at the bottom, エ and Y are the owners and, like the Lone Ranger, they often greet guests from **Pyo**ngyang, or **Ara**bian guests like **W**a**l**i and Sultan, by saying "**Hi Yo**"
COMPARE: 青(い) aoi = blue, # 155

Net

583. 無

PRONUNCIATIONS: mu, bu*ji, na*kusu **MEANINGS:** nothing, to not exist
EXAMPLES: 無理 muri = impossible, unreasonable; 無料 muryou = free of charge; 無駄な muda na = useless, wasteful; 無事 buji = safety, peace, health, good condition; 無くす nakusu = to lose; 無くなる nakunaru = to run out or disappear; 無い nai = does not exist, usually written ない
DESCRIPTION: a large net running on four legs; this could be a drunk wagon
CUES: **Mu**riel says that it's 無理 **mu**ri (impossible) for the **Boo**zers to escape from this net-like drunk wagon while it's running along, unless they have a **Kna**ck for doing so

584. 舞

PRONUNCIATIONS: ma*u, bu*tai, mai
MEANING: to dance **EXAMPLES:** 見舞い
mimai = visit to a sick person; 舞う mau =
to dance; 舞台 butai = stage, setting, scene;
舞 mai = a dance **DESCRIPTION:** at the top,
a net; at the lower left, 夕(方) yuugata
(evening, # 160); on the lower right, a sitting
person, with a knee extending to the left
CUES: Ma is caught in a net of illness, so I
will お見舞いする omi**mai** suru (pay a
visit to a sick person) in the evening, sit by her
bedside, drink **Boo**ze, and listen to **M**ichael
Jackson music

Shaky Table

585. 亡

PRONUNCIATIONS: na*kunaru, bou
MEANINGS: to pass away, to die
EXAMPLES: 亡くなる nakunaru = to die;
死亡 shibou = death **DESCRIPTION:** a
shaky table **CUES:** there's a **Kna**ck to balan-
cing this shaky table; if we seat **Bo**no at it, it
might fall on him, and he may 亡くなる
nakunaru (die) **COMPARE:** 忙(しい)
isogashii = busy, # 586

586. 忙

PRONUNCIATIONS: isoga*shii, bou
MEANING: busy **EXAMPLES:** 忙しい
isogashii = busy; 多忙 tabou = very busy
DESCRIPTION: on the left, an man standing
erect; on the right, 亡(くなる) nakunaru (to
die, # 585), which resembles a shaky table
CUES: there is an **Iso**lated **Ga**dfly on this
shaky table on a **Boa**t, and this man is
忙しい **iso**gashii (busy), trying to keep it all
from falling down

Fruit

587. 果

PRONUNCIATIONS: kuda*mono, ha*tasu, ka
MEANINGS: fruit, reward **EXAMPLES:**
果物 kudamono = fruit; 果たす hatasu =
to accomplish, realize, perform; 結果 kekka
= result **DESCRIPTION:** at the top,
田(んぼ) tanbo (rice paddy, # 68), which
resembles four fruits available for harvesting;
at the bottom, 木 ki (tree, # 118)
CUES: my **Cool Da**d saw these four 果物
kudamono (fruits) growing on a tree, so he
Harvested them, and **Ca**rved them up
COMPARE: 課 ka = section, # 588; 菓(子)
kashi = candy, # 589

588. 課

PRONUNCIATION: ka **MEANINGS:** to assign,
lesson, section **EXAMPLES:** 課長 kachou =
section manager; 第一課 dai ikka = section
1 **DESCRIPTION:** on the left, 言(う) iu
(to speak, # 430); on the right, 果(物)
kudamono (fruit, # 587) **CUE:** in his 課 **ka**
(section) at a fruit company, **Ka**rl Marx, the
課長 **ka**chou (section manager), 言 (speaks)
about fruit
COMPARE: 菓子 kashi = candy, # 589

589. 菓

PRONUNCIATION: ka*shi, ga **MEANING:**
sweets **EXAMPLES:** お菓子 okashi =
pastry, confectionery, candy; 和菓子
wagashi = Japanese sweets **DESCRIPTION:**
at the top, a plant radical (see # 43); at the
bottom, 果(物) kudamono (fruit, # 587);
together these may represent a cashew tree
CUE: we often eat 菓子 **ka**shi (candy) that is
made from fruit and **Ca**shew nuts, but
sometimes it gives us **Ga**s
COMPARE: 課 ka = section, # 588

Crawling Person

590. 打

PRONUNCIATIONS: u, da*geki **MEANING:** to hit **EXAMPLES:** 打つ utsu = to hit or strike; 打ち合わせ uchiawase = a planning meeting; 打撃 dageki = shock, impact **DESCRIPTION:** on the left, a crawling guy wearing an uber tsuit (suit); on the right, a nail, which looks like a dagger **CUES:** the crawling guy is a gangster who wears Uber tsuits (suits) and sometimes 打つ **u**tsu (strikes) his enemies with a **D**agger

591. 払

PRONUNCIATION: hara*u **MEANINGS:** to pay, to brush away **EXAMPLES:** 払う harau = to pay; 支払い shiharai = payment **DESCRIPTION:** on the left, a crawling guy; on the right, the katakana character ム mu (the sound made by a cow when it is harassed) **CUE:** the crawling guy is crawling over to see if he can 払う **hara**u (pay) for this ム (cow), which is being **Hara**ssed

592. 押

PRONUNCIATION: o*su, oshi **MEANINGS:** to press or push **EXAMPLES:** 押す osu = to push; 押入れ oshiire = closet **DESCRIPTION:** on the left, a crawling guy; on the right, 田(んぼ) tanbo (rice paddy, # 68), on a pole, but this looks like a sign in oosutorariya (Australia) **CUE:** the crawling guy 押す **o**su (pushes) on this sign in **O**osutorariya (Australia) and knocks it down, causing it to fall onto some **O**ld **Shee**p **COMPARE:** 神 kami = god, # 273

593. 拝

PRONUNCIATIONS: oga*mu, hai*ken **MEANINGS:** to worship, to revere, to do something humbly **EXAMPLES:** 拝む ogamu = to assume the posture of prayer with hands held together, to revere; 拝見する haiken suru = to humbly read or see **DESCRIPTION:** on the left, a crawling person named Oprah; on the right, a high stalk of flowers **CUES:** before **O**prah **Ga**mbles, she 拝む **oga**mu (prays humbly) to a god, and since she is holding these flowers **High**, people say that they 拝見する **hai**ken suru (humbly see) them

594. 捨

PRONUNCIATION: su*teru **MEANING:** to throw away **EXAMPLE:** 捨てる suteru = to throw away **DESCRIPTION:** on the left, a crawling person named Superman; at the top right, a peaked roof; at the middle right, 土 tsuchi (dirt, # 59), which resembles a cross; at the bottom right, 口 kuchi (mouth, # 426), which could be a platform for the cross **CUE:** **Su**perman is a terrible crawling person who is approaching our house and wants to 捨てる **su**teru (throw away) our cross **COMPARE:** 拾(う) hirou = to pick up, # 595

595. 拾

PRONUNCIATION: hiro*u **MEANING:** to pick up **EXAMPLE:** 拾う hirou = to pick up **DESCRIPTION:** on the left, a crawling person who is a hero; at the top right, a peaked roof; at the middle right, a horizontal line, which could be the ceiling of the house; at the bottom right, 口 kuchi (mouth, # 426), which could be a box **CUE:** this **H**ero is a crawling guy who is approaching the enemy's storehouse and trying to 拾う **hiro**u (pick up) a box of food **COMPARE:** 捨(てる) suteru = to throw away, # 594

596. 掛

PRONUNCIATION: ka*keru **MEANINGS:** to hang, suspend, or depend **EXAMPLES:** 掛ける kakeru = to hang (a picture, etc.), to sit on a chair, to take (time or money), to make a phone call, to multiply, to put on (glasses), to pour or sprinkle, and many other meanings

DESCRIPTION: on the left, a crawling guy; in the middle, two 土 tsuchi (dirt, # 59), but these look like chairs; on the right, the katakana character ト to, which reminds us of a toboggan
CUE: the crawling guy is a diplomat who 掛ける **ka**keru (hangs) two chairs on a wall next to a toboggan at a Nordic diplomatic reception and then **Ca**lls John Kerry

Everyone

597. 皆

PRONUNCIATION: mina MEANINGS: all, everyone EXAMPLE: 皆 mina = everyone
DESCRIPTION: at the top, two people are sitting facing in the same direction; at the bottom, 白(い) shiroi (white, # 44) CUE: 皆 **mina** (everyone) is sitting on a white snowy hill in **Mina**sota (Minnesota)
COMPARE: みんな minna = everyone, spelled with hiragana; 階(段) kaidan = stairs, # 598; 背 se = height, # 152

598. 階

PRONUNCIATION: kai MEANINGS: story or floor of a building, counter for stories or floors of a building EXAMPLES: 階段 kaidan = stairs; 四階 yonkai = the fourth floor
DESCRIPTION: on the left, the Greek letter ß which represents a Greek guy with a kite; on the right, 皆 mina (everyone, # 597)
CUE: a Greek guy, who owns a **K**ite, and everyone else live on the 三階 san**kai** (third floor) of our building

Nurse

599. 喜

PRONUNCIATIONS: yoroko*bu, ki*geki
MEANINGS: to feel pleased or happy
EXAMPLE: 喜ぶ yorokobu = to be delighted; 喜劇 kigeki = comedy

DESCRIPTION: at the top, (兵)士 heishi (soldier, # 66) which resembles a cross worn by a nurse; in the middle, the nurse himself, wearing a white nurse's cap; at the bottom, a square which is the nurse's white coat CUES: this nurse 喜ぶ **yoroko**bu (gets delighted) in the **Yoro**pean (European) city of **Colo**gne when a **K**ing gives him an award COMPARE: 嬉(しい) ureshii = pleased, # 600

600. 嬉

PRONUNCIATION: ureshi*i MEANINGS: glad, pleased EXAMPLES: 嬉しい ureshii = pleased DESCRIPTION: on the left, 女 onna (female, # 235); on the right 喜ぶ yorokobu (to get delighted, # 599), which resembles a nurse wearing a cross and a white cap CUES: this 女 (female) nurse is 嬉しい **ureshi**i (pleased) about her patient with kidney failure and the **Urea She** is excreting (urea is a major component of urine)
COMPARE: 喜(ぶ) yorokobu = to be delighted, # 599

Miscellaneous

601. 以

PRONUNCIATIONS: i, mo MEANINGS: starting point, by means of EXAMPLES: 以前に izen ni = a long time ago; 以後 igo = after, since, or from now on; 三人以上 sannin ijou = three people or more; 以下 ika = below, less than; 五分以内に gofun inai ni = within 5 minutes; 以外 igai = other than; 前以て maemotte = beforehand, in advance
DESCRIPTION: this resembles someone sliding off the back of a giraffe
CUES: this person used to ride a giraffe, a giant **E**el and a **Mo**torcycle 以前に **i**zen ni (a long time ago)

602. 船

PRONUNCIATION: fune, bune[1], funa, sen

MEANINGS: ship, boat EXAMPLES: 船 fune = ship, boat; 釣り船 tsuribune = fishing boat; 船便 funabin = ship mail; 船長 senchou = captain of a ship DESCRIPTION: on the left, a boat, seen from above, with a pointed prow, and fore and aft compartments, but it is missing a stern in the back; on the right, 八 hachi (eight, # 15), above 口 kuchi (mouth, # 426), which could represent a dock CUES: this 船 **fune** (boat) is wide open at the rear, and it looks **Fune**y (funny) to **Foo**lish **Na**ncy, but there are 八 (eight) guys on the dock who were **Sen**t to work on the problem

603. 靴

PRONUNCIATION: kutsu MEANING: shoe

EXAMPLE: 靴 kutsu = shoe DESCRIPTION: on the left, this looks like a needle, with a syringe; on the right, 化(学) kagaku (chemistry, # 487), but this resembles a map of Canada – see # 487 CUE: these 靴 **kutsu** (shoes) that Superman bought in Canada are too narrow, and it feels as though needles are **Cut**ting **Su**perman's feet

604. 寄

PRONUNCIATIONS: yo*ru, ki*fu

MEANINGS: to be inclined to, to stop by

EXAMPLES: 寄る yoru = to drop in at, to gather, to go closer; 年寄り toshiyori = elderly person; 寄付 kifu = donation DESCRIPTION: above the floor, a big bird; under the floor, a box CUES: if you don't mind the big bird and want to 寄る **yo**ru (stop by) some **Yo**ru (night), you can see the box containing 寄付 **ki**fu (donations) under the floor, where we also **Kee**p food

COMPARE: 夜 yoru = night, # 489

605. 残

PRONUNCIATIONS: noko*su, zan

MEANINGS: to remain, cruel EXAMPLES: 残る nokoru = to remain; 残す nokosu = to leave behind; 残念 zannen = regrettable; 残業 zangyou = overtime DESCRIPTION: reportedly the radical on the left is an axe, and the one on the right is a halberd (combination lance and axe), sliced by 4 cuts CUES: a **No**ble **Co**de allows warriors to 残す **noko**su (leave behind) victims of axe and halberd attacks, but this is considered cruel and 残念 **zan**nen (regrettable) behavior in **Zan**zibar

606. 球

PRONUNCIATION: kyuu MEANINGS: ball, sphere EXAMPLES: 野球 yakyuu = baseball; 地球 chikyuu = the Earth

DESCRIPTION: on the left, 玉 tama (ball, or jewel, # 169), which looks like a long cucumber; on the right a tall t, with a y under its right arm, which stands for "thank you" CUE: I received a long green jewel, which looks like a **Cu**cumber, and I wrote, "ty (thank you) very much for the jewel; I plan to sell it in order to buy equipment for my 野球 ya**kyuu** (baseball) team"

607. 寿

PRONUNCIATION: su*shi, ju*myou

MEANINGS: life, longevity EXAMPLES: 寿司 sushi = raw fish slices on rice; 寿命 jumyou = lifespan, longevity DESCRIPTION: at the lower right, 寺 tera (temple, # 213), but the cross at the top of 寺 is partially hidden beneath a very long slanting t, which is superimposed on 寺 and represents time CUES: the **Su**pervisor of the sheep at the temple says that it's time to eat 寿司 **su**shi with some **J**uice

608. 司

PRONUNCIATION: shi **MEANINGS:** official, to administer **EXAMPLES:** 寿司 sushi = raw fish slices on rice; 司会 shikai = master of ceremonies; 上司 joushi = one's superior (in a company) **DESCRIPTION:** compared to

伺う ukagau (to visit or ask, # 341), 司 is missing the man with a slanted hat
CUE: when the man with the slanted hat wandered off to look for some 寿司 su**shi**, his 上司 jou**shi** (superior) examined this box to see whether it contained any **Shee**p food

508

Hiragana Review

わ wa	ら ra	や ya	ま ma	は ha	な na	た ta	さ sa	か ka	あ a
	り ri		み mi	ひ hi	に ni	ち chi	し shi	き ki	い i
を wo	る ru	ゆ yu	む mu	ふ fu	ぬ nu	つ tsu	す su	く ku	う u
	れ re		め me	へ he	ね ne	て te	せ se	け ke	え e
ん n	ろ ro	よ yo	も mo	ほ ho	の no	と to	そ so	こ ko	お o

Here's a mnemonic that may help you to remember the order of the top row of characters, from right to left:

A, Ka, Sa, Ta, Na, Ha, Ma, Ya, Ra, Wa.

A King Saw The Nurse Hiding Milky Yellow Rabbits, Wow!

The following 48 words and sentences contain all of the phonetic combinations of hiragana that you might realistically encounter. Please use a piece of paper or your thumb to cover the answers in the right column while you read the hiragana on the left.

1. びょうき	Byouki (sickness)
2. さんびゃく	Sanbyaku (three hundred)
3. じゃない	Ja nai (something isn't something else)
4. はっぴゃく	Happyaku (eight hundred)
5. こんぴゅうたー	Konpyuutaa (computer)
6. はっぴょう	Happyou (presentation, announcement)
7. じゅんこ	Junko (a girl's given name)
8. かのじょ	Kanojo (she)

9. ぎゅう	Gyuu (cow)
10. じゅぎょう	Jugyou (class, lesson)
11. りゃく	Ryaku (abbreviation, omission)
12. りゅうがく	Ryuugaku (study abroad)
13. りょうきん	Ryoukin (fee, charge)
14. みょうな	Myou na (strange)
15. ひゃく	Hyaku (one hundred)
16. ひょうばん	Hyouban (popularity, reputation)
17. しんにゅうしゃいん	Shinnyuushain (newly entered employee)
18. にょう	Nyou (urine)
19. おちゃ	Ocha (honorable tea)
20. ちゅうごく	Chuugoku (China)
21. ちょっと	Chotto (a moment)
22. せんしゅう	Senshuu (last week)
23. しょくじ	Shokuji (meal)
24. きゃく	Kyaku (customer)
25. きゅうねん	Kyuu nen (nine years)
26. ゆうびんきょく	Yuubinkyoku (post office)
27. がっこうから	Gakkou kara (from school)
28. ぬれる	Nureru (to get wet)
29. よろしい	Yoroshii (polite word meaning good)
30. りっぱなおたく	Rippa na otaku (a splendid honorable home)
31. てんぷら	Tenpura (tempura)
32. ぺらぺら	Perapera (fluent)

33. しっぽ — Shippo (tail)

34. だいぶとおいです。 — Daibu tooi desu. (it's quite far)

35. かたづける — Katazukeru (to straighten up)

36. あのえいがはどうでしたか。 — Ano eiga wa dou deshita ka. (as for that movie over there, how was it?)

37. ありがとうございます。 — Arigatou gozaimasu. (thanks a lot)

38. ぷーるでおよぎます。 — Puuru de oyogimasu. (I swim in the pool)

39. はずかしい — Hazukashii (embarrassed or embarrassing)

40. ぜひいちどきてみてください。 — Zehi ichido kite mite kudasai. (certainly one time please come and see)

41. ほんでしらべてみます。 — Hon de shirabete mimasu. (I will check from a book and see)

42. こーひーをこぼしました。 — Koohii wo koboshimashita. (I spilled coffee)

43. いっかげつぐらいです。 — Ikkagetsu gurai desu. (it's about one month)

44. どうぞおだいじに。 — Douzo odaiji ni. (go ahead, take care – said to a sick person)

45. ひとりでなにもかもしようとおもわないほうがいいですよ。 — Hitori de, nanimokamo shiyou to omowanai hou ga ii desu yo. (by yourself, it's better not to think that you shall do everything, for sure)

46. あめがやむまでまって、じゅうじごろでたんです。 — Ame ga yamu made matte, juuji goro detan desu. (I wait until the rain will stop, and I left about 10 o'clock)

47. こんどすしやへいくときおさそいします。 — Kondo sushiya e iku toki osasoi shimasu. (next time, when I go to the sushi place, I will humbly invite you along)

48. とうきょうのちかてつはふべんですか。 — Toukyou no chikatetsu wa, fuben desu ka. (as for the Tokyo subway, is it inconvenient?)

Katakana Review

ワ wa	ラ ra	ヤ ya	マ ma	ハ ha	ナ na	タ ta	サ sa	カ ka	ア a
	リ ri		ミ mi	ヒ hi	ニ ni	チ chi	シ shi	キ ki	イ i
ヲ wo	ル ru	ユ yu	ム mu	フ fu	ヌ nu	ツ tsu	ス su	ク ku	ウ u
	レ re		メ me	ヘ he	ネ ne	テ te	セ se	ケ ke	エ e
ン n	ロ ro	ヨ yo	モ mo	ホ ho	ノ no	ト to	ソ so	コ ko	オ o

The following 48 words and sentences contain all of the phonetic combinations of katakana that you might realistically encounter. Please use a piece of paper or your thumb to cover the answers in the right column while you read the katakana on the left.

Of course, most of the words in this list should not actually be written in katakana, since katakana is primarily used for words with foreign origins.

Please note that certain counting words, such as 1 ヶ月 ikkagetsu (one month), contain a small ヶ ke which is pronounced ka and has the effect of doubling, or hardening, the consonant that follows it. Words like this can also be written with a small カ ka, e.g., 1 カ月 ikkagetsu.

1. ビョウキ — Byouki (sickness)
2. サンビャク — Sanbyaku (three hundred)
3. ジャナイ — Ja nai (something isn't something else)
4. ハッピャク — Happyaku (eight hundred)
5. コンピューター — Konpyuutaa (computer)
6. ハッピョウ — Happyou (presentation, announcement)
7. ジュンコ — Junko (a girl's given name)
8. カノジョ — Kanojo (she)

9. ギュウ	Gyuu (cow)
10. ジュギョウ	Jugyou (class, lesson)
11. リャク	Ryaku (abbreviation, omission)
12. リュウガク	Ryuugaku (study abroad)
13. リョウキン	Ryoukin (fee, charge)
14. ミョウナ	Myou na (strange)
15. ヒャク	Hyaku (one hundred)
16. ヒョウバン	Hyouban (popularity, reputation)
17. シンニュウシャイン	Shinnyuu shain (newly entered employee)
18. ニョウ	Nyou (urine)
19. オチャ	Ocha (honorable tea)
20. チュウゴク	Chuugoku (China)
21. チョット	Chotto (a moment)
22. センシュウ	Senshuu (last week)
23. ショクジ	Shokuji (meal)
24. キャク	Kyaku (customer)
25. キュウネン	Kyuu nen (nine years)
26. ユウビンキョク	Yuubinkyoku (post office)
27. ガッコウカラ	Gakkou kara (from school)
28. ヌレル	Nureru (to get wet)
29. ヨロシイ	Yoroshii (polite word meaning good)
30. リッパナオタク	Rippa na otaku (a splendid honorable home)
31. テンプラ	Tenpura (tempura)
32. ペラペラ	Perapera (fluent)
33. シッポ	Shippo (tail)

34. ダイブトオイデス 。

Daibu tooi desu. (it's quite far) \

35. カタヅケル

Katazukeru (to straighten up)

36. アノエイガハドウデシタカ 。

Ano eiga wa dou deshita ka. (as for that movie over there, how was it?)

37. アリガトウゴザイマス。

Arigatou gozaimasu. (thanks a lot)

38. プールデオヨギマス 。

Puuru de oyogimasu. (I swim in the pool)

39. ハズカシイ

Hazukashii (embarrassed or embarrassing)

40. ゼヒイチドキテミテクダサイ。

Zehi ichido kite mite kudasai. (certainly one time please come and see)

41. ホンデシラベテミマス。

Hon de shirabete mimasu. (I will check from a book and see)

42. コーヒーヲコボシマシタ。

Koohii wo koboshimashita. (I spilled coffee)

43. イッカゲツグライデス。

Ikkagetsu gurai desu. (it's about one month)

44. ドウゾオダイジニ 。

Douzo odaiji ni. (go ahead, take care – said to a sick person)

45. ヒトリデナニモカモシヨウトオモ ワナイホウガイイデスヨ。

Hitori de, nanimokamo shiyou to omowanai hou ga ii desu yo. (by yourself, it's better not to think that you shall do everything, for sure)

46. アメガヤムマデマッテ、ジュウジ ゴロデタンデス。

Ame ga yamu made matte, juuji goro detan desu. (I wait until the rain will stop, and I left about 10 o'clock)

47. コンドスシヤヘイクトキオサソイ シマス。

Kondo sushiya e iku toki osasoi shimasu. (next time, when I go to the sushi place, I will humbly invite you along)

48. トウキョウノチカテツハフベンデ スカ。

Toukyou no chikatetsu wa, fuben desu ka. (as for the Tokyo subway, is it inconvenient?)

Rendaku

Rendaku is a phenomenon that can affect the pronunciations of kanji in compound words, when kanji appear in the middle or at the end of a word. Kanji pronunciations that contain the consonants shown in the following table can change as shown here.

ch → j (e.g., chi → ji)	k → g (e.g. koto → goto)
f → b (e.g., fun → bun)	s → z (e.g., sushi → zushi)
f → p (e.g., fuku → puku)	sh → j (e.g., sha → ja)
h → b (e.g., hito → bito)	t → d (e.g., toki → doki)
h → p (e.g., hai → pai)	ts → z (e.g., tsukai → zukai)

If you cannot find a kanji pronunciation that you are seeking in the Pronunciation Index starting on the next page, it may have been affected by rendaku. If so, you may be able to use the table above to help you find it.

In this book we provide retrieval cues for most, but not all, of the alternative pronunciations associated with the rendaku phenomenon. For this reason, you will sometimes see a kanji pronunciation without an accompanying cue in the Kanji Catalogue starting on page 401. For example, 百 hyaku, reference # 47, can also be pronounced "byaku" or "pyaku," but only one retrieval cue is provided ("the **Hackers** own 百 **hyaku** (100) limousines"). In reference # 47 and some other kanji references, we use a superscripted "1" to identify pronunciations for which no retrieval cues are provided, such as byaku[1] and pyaku[1]. The footnote to which this number refers appears only on page 408.

In some words, two Japanese kanji are repeated, one after the other, and the second kanji is replaced by the repetition symbol 々. If this repetition occurs with kanji pronunciations that are affected by rendaku, the second kanji may be pronounced differently from the first one, in accordance with the rules of rendaku. For example, 木々 kigi = many trees, 人々 hitobito = people, 口々 kuchiguchi = every mouth, 久々 hisabisa = a long time ago, 日々 hibi = every day, 国々 kuniguni = countries, 時々 tokidoki = sometimes, 様々 samazama = various and 花々 hanabana = flowers.

For some words containing the repetition symbol 々, like 少々 shoushou (a little) and 次々 tsugitsugi (one after the other), the rules of rendaku are not applied, and both kanji are pronounced in the same way. Words like 色々 iroiro (various), which doesn't contain any of the consonants listed above, are obviously not affected by rendaku.

Kanji Pronunciation Index

The following list of kanji pronunciations has been alphabetized by a computer. Many of the pronunciations contain asterisks, to indicate that the pronunciation of the kanji in question ends at the asterisk and also that another pronunciation, shown after the asterisk, often follows it. Note that the computer places blank spaces first, then asterisks, and then the letter "a," followed by the other letters in alphabetical order.

Japanese people use kanji combinations for some words without breaking the words into separate pronunciations for each kanji. In spite of that, we have chosen to break such words into separate component pronunciations for each kanji, so that it will possible for students to look them up readily in this Index.

For example, 土産 mi*yage is recognized as a single word by Japanese people, not as a combination of two kanji with different pronunciations that can be combined. The same thing is true for 今日 k*you, 明日 a*su, 明日 a*shita, 一日 tsui*tachi, 昨日 ki*nou, 大人 oto*na, and so forth. The asterisks that we have placed in these words are only intended to help people who are looking them up in this Index, and they have no other significance.

A 当– 31
A 上– 171
A 明– 154
A 開– 413
A*biru 浴– 256
A*dachi 足– 449
A*ku 空– 248
A*ru 有– 460
A*u 会– 293
A*u 合– 294
Abu*nai 危– 547
Ai 合– 294
Ai 愛– 523
Aida 間– 411
Aji 味– 245
Aka 明– 154
Aka*i 赤– 447
Aki 秋– 445
Aki*raka 明– 154
Aku 悪– 313
Ama 天– 189
Ama*i 甘– 541

Ame 雨– 261
An 案– 120
An 安– 236
An*ji 暗– 268
Ane 姉– 241
Ani 兄– 420
Ao*i 青– 155
Ara*u 洗– 423
Arawa*su 表– 582
Ari 有– 460
Aru*ku 歩– 408
Asa 朝– 291
Ashi 足– 449
Ashi*ta 明– 154
Aso*bu 遊– 360
Ata*ri 辺– 362
Atai 価– 484
Atai 値– 571
Atama 頭– 93
Atara*shii 新– 389
Atata 暖– 38
Atata 温– 257

Ato 後– 335
Atsu 集– 202
Atsu*i 熱– 65
Atsu*i 厚– 185
Atsu*i 暑– 278
Ayama*chi 過– 361
Ba 場– 403
Ba 歯– 533
Ba 葉– 543
Bai 売– 425
Bai 倍– 269
Bai*bai 買– 89
Bako 箱– 142
Ban 晩– 35
Ban 万– 113
Ban 番– 328
Bana 花– 211
Banashi 話 – 433
Bashi 橋– 139
Bayashi 林– 125
Be 部– 267
Be 辺– 362

Fu*ru 降– 178
Fu*sai 負– 87
Fu*ttou 沸– 531
Fuku 服– 150
Fuku 復– 527
Fukuro 袋– 581
Fun 分– 105
Funa 船– 602
Fune 船– 602
Furu*eru 震– 265
Furu*i 古– 392
Futa 二– 2
Futo*ru 太– 191
Futsu 二– 2
Fuu 風– 479
Fuyu 冬– 234
Ga 画– 77
Ga 学– 184
Ga 髪– 501
Ga 替– 551
Ga 菓– 589
Ga*ssen 合– 294
Gae 替– 551
Gai 外– 163
Gai 会– 293
Gaku 学– 184
Gaku 楽– 520
Gama 構– 141
Gami 紙– 221
Gan 顔– 95
Gan 岸– 500
Gan*bou 願– 94
Gan*jitsu 元– 421
Gao 顔– 95
Gata 方– 114
Gata 難– 198
Gatari 語– 435
Gato 難– 198
Gatsu 月– 148
Gawa 川– 250
Gawa 側– 490
Ge 下– 172
Ge 気– 321

Ge*ka 外– 163
Gei 迎– 358
Gen 間– 411
Gen 元– 421
Gen 言– 430
Getsu 月– 148
Gi 着– 52
Gi 木– 118
Gi 気– 321
Gi 議– 438
Gi*ru 切–103
Gin 銀– 302
Giwa 際– 379
Go 五– 179
Go 午– 207
Go 後– 335
Go 古– 392
Go 語– 435
Goku 国– 170
Gon 言– 430
Goro 頃– 96
Goto 毎– 336
Goto 事– 416
Gou 合– 294
Gou 号– 470
Gu 具– 100
Guchi 口– 426
Gusuri 薬– 521
Gyo 魚– 80
Gyou 業– 332
Gyou 形– 573
Gyou*ji 行– 334
Gyuu 牛– 205
Ha 八– 15
Ha 発– 298
Ha 張 – 477
Ha 歯– 533
Ha 葉– 543
Ha*eru 生– 208
Ha*reru 晴 – 37
Ha*tasu 果– 587
Ha*zukashii 恥– 309
Hachi 八– 15

Haha 母– 50
Hai 背– 152
Hai 灰– 444
Hai 配– 466
Hai*ken 拝– 593
Hai*ru 入– 14
Haji 初– 104
Haji 恥– 309
Haji 始– 540
Haka*ru 計– 434
Hako 箱– 142
Hako*bu 運– 354
Haku 白– 44
Haku 泊– 46
Haku*jou 薄– 258
Han 半– 331
Han 飯– 400
Hana 花– 211
Hana 話– 433
Hana*su 放– 117
Hanashi 話 – 433
Har*umi 晴– 37
Hara*u 払– 591
Haru 春– 506
Hashi 橋– 139
Hashi*ru 走– 450
Hatara*ku 働– 287
Hatsu 髪– 501
Hatsu*ka 二– 2
Hatsu*koi 初– 104
Hatsu*mei 発– 298
Haya*i 早– 34
Haya*i 速– 359
Hayashi 林– 125
Hazu*su 外– 163
He*ru 経– 224
He*ta 下– 172
He*ya 部– 267
Hei*sa 閉– 414
Hen 片– 181
Hen 返– 356
Hen 辺– 362
Hen 変– 553

Ka 夏– 522	Kan*ji 漢– 197	Ken 犬– 190
Ka 代– 552	Kan*ki 寒– 507	Ken 険– 196
Ka 変– 553	Kana*mono 金– 301	Ken 建– 363
Ka 果– 587	Kanara*zu 必– 307	Ken 験– 382
Ka 課– 588	Kane 金– 301	Ken 間– 411
Ka*eru 替– 551	Kanga*eru 考– 469	Ken 研– 442
Ka*eru 換– 554	Kano*jo 彼– 371	Ken 件– 488
Ka*keru 掛– 596	Kao 顔– 95	Ken 県– 572
Ka*kki 活– 260	Kara 空– 248	Ketsu 決– 180
Ka*ku 書– 415	Kara*i 辛– 384	Kewa*shii 険– 196
Ka*riru 借– 485	Karada 体– 124	Ki 木– 118
Ka*shi 菓– 589	Kare 彼– 371	Ki 機– 137
Ka*shu 歌– 534	Karu*i 軽– 289	Ki 決– 180
Ka*su 貸– 90	Kasa*neru 重–284	Ki 気– 321
Ka*tsu 勝– 149	Kata 方– 114	Ki 記– 550
Ka*u 買– 89	Kata 形– 573	Ki*eru 消– 158
Kaa*san 母– 50	Kata*ru 語– 435	Ki*fu 寄– 604
Kado 角– 81	Kata*zukeru 片– 181	Ki*geki 喜– 599
Kae 返– 356	Katachi 形– 573	Ki*ken 危– 547
Kae*ru 帰– 566	Katana 刀– 102	Ki*ku 聞– 412
Kai 回– 4	Katsu 活– 260	Ki*masu 来– 327
Kai 界– 69	Katsu 割– 562	Ki*nou 昨– 41
Kai 貝– 83	Kawa 川– 250	Ki*ritsu 起– 452
Kai 械– 138	Kawa*ku 乾– 290	Ki*ru 着– 52
Kai 会– 293	Kayo*u 通– 365	Ki*ru 切–103
Kai 海– 337	Kaze 風– 479	Ki*ssaten 喫– 192
Kai 開– 413	Ke 気– 321	Ki*taku 帰– 566
Kai 階– 598	Ke 結– 231	Kimi 君– 419
Kai*ga 絵– 223	Ke 家– 405	Kin 勤– 517
Kakari 係– 492	Ke*sa 今– 292	Kin*jo 近– 390
Kaku 画– 77	Ke*shiki 景– 516	Kin*youbi 金– 301
Kaku 角– 81	Ke*shou 化– 487	Kishi 岸– 500
Kaku*go 覚– 54	Ke*sshite 決– 180	Kita 北– 373
Kama*u 構– 141	Ke*su 消– 158	Kitana*i 汚– 467
Kami 紙– 221	Kega*su 汚– 467	Kitsu*en 喫– 192
Kami 神– 273	Kei 経– 224	Kiwa*datsu 際– 379
Kami 将– 374	Kei 軽– 289	Kiza*mu 刻– 565
Kami 髪– 501	Kei 兄– 420	Ko 子– 182
Kan 慣– 92	Kei 計– 434	Ko 小– 253
Kan 館– 305	Kei 係– 492	Ko 去– 343
Kan 間– 411	Kei 景– 516	Ko 古– 392
Kan 換– 554	Kei*tai 形– 573	Ko 故– 394
Kan*denchi 乾– 290	Ken 見– 53	Ko 個– 395

Mi 味– 245
Mi*ru 見– 53
Mi*yage 土– 59
Michi 道– 349
Midori 緑– 227
Miga*ku 磨– 126
Migi 右– 457
Mijika*i 短– 324
Mimi 耳– 57
Min 民– 375
Min 眠– 376
Mina 皆– 597
Minami 南– 388
Minato 港– 549
Mino*ru 実– 195
Mise 店– 493
Miyako 都– 277
Mizu 水– 251
Mizuka*ra 自– 55
Mo 以– 601
Mo*tsu 持– 216
Mochi 用– 364
Modo*ru 戻– 75
Moku 目– 51
Moku*youbi 木– 118
Mon 文– 25
Mon 門– 409
Mon 問– 410
Mono 者– 276
Mono 物– 401
Mori 森– 127
Mori 守– 214
Moto 本– 123
Moto 元– 421
Motsu 物– 401
Motto*mo 最– 42
Mou*su 申– 10
Moushi 申– 10
Mu 夢– 165
Mu 向– 340
Mu 務– 518
Mu 無– 583
Mu*ttsu 六– 17

Mui*ka 六– 17
Muka*eru 迎– 358
Mukashi 昔– 33
Mura 村–131
Mushi 虫– 9
Musu*bu 結– 231
Musu*ko 息– 315
Musume 娘– 316
Muzuka*shii 難– 198
Myou*ji 名– 162
Myou*nichi 明– 154
Na 人– 13
Na*geru 投– 558
Na*ku 泣– 12
Na*kunaru 亡– 585
Na*kusu 無– 583
Na*mae 名– 162
Na*reru 慣– 92
Nabe 辺– 362
Naga*i 長– 502
Nai 内– 396
Naka 中– 8
Naka*ba 半– 331
Nama 生– 208
Nan 男– 109
Nan 難– 198
Nan 何– 338
Nan 南– 388
Nana 七– 20
Nani 何– 338
Nano 七– 20
Nao 治– 539
Nao 直– 570
Nara 並– 575
Nara*u 習– 472
Nasa*kenai 情– 156
Natsu 夏– 522
Ne 熱– 65
Ne*dan 値– 571
Ne*iro 音– 266
Ne*ru 寝– 372
Ne*ru 練– 229
Nee 姉– 241

Nega*u 願– 94
Neko 猫– 72
Nemu*ru 眠– 376
Nen 年– 177
Nen 念– 314
Netsu 熱– 65
Ni 二– 2
Ni 日– 32
Ni*motsu 荷– 342
Nichi 日– 32
Niga*i 苦– 393
Nii 兄– 420
Niku 肉– 397
Niku*i 難– 198
Nin 人– 13
Nin 任– 483
Nishi 西– 464
Niwa 庭– 495
No 野– 545
No*mu 飲– 399
No*ru 乗– 509
Nobo*ru 上– 171
Nobo*ru 登– 297
Nochi*hodo 後– 335
Noko*su 残– 605
Nou 日– 32
Nushi 主– 166
Nyuu 入– 14
Nyuu 乳– 186
O 男– 109
O 終– 233
O 落– 526
O*gawa 小– 253
O*kami 女– 235
O*kiru 起– 452
O*ku 置– 569
O*riru 降– 178
O*rosu 下– 172
O*su 押– 592
O*sui 汚– 467
O*u 負– 87
Obo*eru 覚– 54
Odo*ru 踊– 366

Oga*mu 拝– 593
Oko*ru 怒– 319
Okona*u 行– 334
Oku 憶– 318
Oku 奥– 532
Oku*jou 屋– 63
Oku*reru 遅– 350
Oku*ru 贈– 84
Oku*ru 送– 348
Omo 主– 166
Omo*i 重– 284
Omo*shiroi 面– 282
Omo*u 思– 308
Omote 表– 582
On 温– 257
On 音– 266
Ona*ji 同– 339
Onna 女– 235
Oo 大– 188
Oo*i 多– 161
Ooyake 公– 16
Osa*meru 治– 539
Oshi 押– 592
Oshi*eru 教– 187
Oso*i 遅– 350
Oso*waru 教– 187
Oto 音– 266
Oto*na 大– 188
Otoko 男– 109
Otouto 弟– 529
Ou*dan 横– 135
Oya 親– 383
Oyo*gu 泳– 255
Pa 張– 477
Pai 配– 466
Patsu 発– 298
Pen 片– 181
Pin 品– 5
Po 歩– 408
Pon 本– 123
Pou 法– 344
Pu 符– 133
Pun 分– 105

Pyaku 百– 47
Pyou 表– 582
Ra 良– 303
Rai 頼– 98
Rai 来– 327
Raku 絡– 230
Raku 楽– 520
Raku 落– 526
Rei 礼– 275
Rei*zouko 冷– 299
Ren 練– 229
Ren 連– 353
Ri 人– 13
Ri 理– 78
Ri 利– 564
Ri*ppa 立– 11
Richi*gi 律– 417
Riki*saku 力– 107
Rin 林– 125
Rin*jin 隣– 329
Ritsu 立– 11
Ritsu 律– 417
Ro 呂– 7
Ro 六– 17
Ro 路– 525
Roku 六– 17
Ru*su 留– 71
Rui 類– 97
Ryo 旅– 116
Ryoku 力– 107
Ryoku*cha 緑– 227
Ryou 良– 303
Ryou 料– 512
Ryou 両– 579
Ryuu*gaku 留– 71
Sa 茶– 212
Sa 朝– 291
Sa 左– 456
Sa 作– 482
Sa*geru 下– 172
Sa*ku 咲– 193
Sa*meru 覚– 54
Sa*meru 冷– 299

Sa*ru 去– 343
Sa*ssoku 早– 34
Sachi 幸– 385
Sada*meru 定– 455
Sai 切– 103
Sai 菜– 121
Sai 細– 220
Sai 妻– 237
Sai 済– 259
Sai 歳– 322
Sai 祭– 377
Sai 際– 379
Sai*sho 最– 42
Saiwa*i 幸– 385
Saka*ya 酒– 465
Sakana 魚– 80
Sake 酒– 465
Saki 先– 422
Saku*ban 昨– 41
Saku*hin 作– 482
Sama 様– 136
Samu*i 寒– 507
San 三– 3
San 山– 146
San 産– 210
San*ka 参– 406
San*po 散– 159
Sara 皿– 567
Sasa 支– 26
Satsu 冊– 568
Sawa*ru 触– 475
Sazu*karu 授– 578
Se 背– 152
Se 世– 542
Se*kken 石– 458
Sei 声– 40
Sei 勢– 110
Sei 青– 155
Sei 正– 174
Sei 政– 175
Sei 生– 208
Sei 性– 209
Sei 静– 418

Sei 製– 580	Shi*mai 姉– 241	Shou 性– 209
Sei*ki 世– 542	Shi*meru 閉– 414	Shou 小– 253
Sei*ou 西– 464	Shi*nu 死– 164	Shou 少– 254
Sei*ten 晴– 37	Shi*ppai 失– 206	Shou 将– 374
Sei*za 星– 48	Shi*ru 知– 323	Shou 招– 560
Seki 石– 458	Shi*you 私– 510	Shou*jiki 正– 174
Seki 席– 496	Shi*zen 自– 55	Shou*kyaku 焼– 446
Seki*dou 赤– 447	Shiawa*se 幸– 385	Shu 手– 23
Sema*i 狭– 194	Shichi 七– 20	Shu 首– 56
Sen 千– 22	Shiki 式– 249	Shu 出– 147
Sen 線– 228	Shiki 色– 473	Shu 主– 166
Sen 川– 250	Shima 島– 556	Shu 酒– 465
Sen 泉 – 252	Shin 申– 10	Shu*toku 取– 58
Sen 選– 352	Shin 真–101	Shuku 祝– 274
Sen 先– 422	Shin 進– 203	Shuku 宿– 491
Sen 洗– 423	Shin 震– 265	Shutsu 出– 147
Sen 船– 602	Shin 心– 306	Shuu 終– 233
Setsu 切–103	Shin 親– 383	Shuu 祝– 274
Setsu 雪– 262	Shin 新– 389	Shuu 週– 346
Setsu 説– 439	Shin 信– 431	Shuu 秋– 445
Sha 社– 271	Shin*rin 森– 127	Shuu 習– 472
Sha 者– 276	Shin*shitsu 寝– 372	Shuu*gou 集– 202
Sha 車– 283	Shin*tou 神– 273	So 卒– 27
Sha 写– 468	Shina 品– 5	So 祖– 272
Sha 借– 485	Shio 塩– 60	Soba 側– 490
Shaku 石– 458	Shira 白– 44	Soda*teru 育– 151
Shaku*ya 借– 485	Shira*beru 調– 441	Soku 束– 99
Shi 四– 6	Shiro*i 白– 44	Soku 息– 315
Shi 支– 26	Shita 下– 172	Soku 速– 359
Shi 士– 66	Shita*shii 親– 383	Soku 足– 449
Shi 仕– 67	Shitsu 室– 62	Son 村– 131
Shi 資– 91	Shitsu 質– 86	Son*zai 存– 462
Shi 止– 173	Shitsu 失– 206	Sona*eru 備– 367
Shi 子– 182	Shizu*ka 静– 418	Sono 園– 279
Shi 紙– 221	Sho 初– 104	Sora 空– 248
Shi 市– 242	Sho 緒– 232	Soso*gu 注– 168
Shi 思– 308	Sho 所– 391	Soto 外– 163
Shi 試– 436	Sho 書– 415	Sotsu 卒– 27
Shi 使– 480	Shoku 食– 398	Sou 窓– 311
Shi 始– 540	Shoku 触– 475	Sou 送– 348
Shi 司– 608	Shou 勝– 149	Sou 走– 450
Shi*dai 次– 536	Shou 笑– 199	Sou*tai 早– 34
Shi*ka 歯– 533	Shou 生– 208	Su 日– 32

Tsui*tachi 一 – 1
Tsuka 支– 26
Tsuka*eru 仕– 67
Tsuka*reru 疲– 370
Tsuka*u 使– 480
Tsuke 付– 132
Tsuki 月– 148
Tsuku 作– 482
Tsukue 机– 140
Tsuma 妻– 237
Tsume*tai 冷– 299
Tsuno 角– 81
Tsura*i 辛– 384
Tsuta*eru 伝– 345
Tsuto*meru 勤– 517
Tsuto*meru 務– 518
Tsuto*meru 努– 519
Tsutsu*mu 包– 548
Tsuu 通– 365
Tsuu 痛– 368
Tsuyo*i 強– 478
Tsuzu 続– 226
U 打– 590
U*keru 受– 577
U*mareru 生– 208
U*mu 産– 210
U*ru 売– 425
U*ryou 雨– 261
U*setsu 右– 457
Uchi 内– 396
Uchi 家– 405
Ue 上– 171
Ugo 動– 286
Ukaga*u 伺– 341
Umi 海– 337
Un 運– 354
Uo 魚– 80
Ureshi*i 嬉– 600
Uri 売– 425
Ushi 牛– 205
Ushi*ro 後– 335
Ushina*u 失– 206
Usu*i 薄– 258

Uta*u 歌– 534
Utsu*su 映– 36
Utsu*su 写– 468
Uwa*gi 上– 171
Wa 話– 433
Wa 和– 513
Wa 沸– 531
Wa*karu 分– 105
Wa*ru 割– 562
Waka*i 若– 461
Waka*reru 別– 561
Wake 訳– 437
Wara*u 笑– 199
Wari 割– 562
Waru*i 悪– 313
Wasu*reru 忘– 310
Wata 渡– 499
Watakushi 私– 510
Watashi 私– 510
Waza 業– 332
Ya 屋– 63
Ya 夜– 489
Ya 野– 545
Ya*kkyoku 薬– 521
Ya*ku 焼– 446
Ya*mai 病– 369
Ya*meru 止– 173
Ya*meru 辞– 387
Ya*nushi 家– 405
Ya*ttsu 八– 15
Yado 宿– 491
Yage 産– 210
Yaku 約– 225
Yaku 訳– 437
Yaku 役– 557
Yaku*hin 薬– 521
Yama 山– 146
Yasa*shii 易– 402
Yasa*shii 優– 528
Yasu*i 安– 236
Yasu*mu 休– 122
Yawa*ragu 和– 513
Yawa*rakai 柔– 546

Yo 四– 6
Yo 夜– 489
Yo 世– 542
Yo 予– 544
Yo 代– 552
Yo*bu 呼– 428
Yo*i 良– 303
Yo*mu 読– 432
Yo*ru 寄– 604
Yogo*su 汚– 467
Yoko 横– 135
Yoku 欲– 535
Yoku*shitsu 浴– 256
Yomi*uri 読– 432
Yon 四– 6
Yoroko*bu 喜– 599
Yoru 夜– 489
You 日– 32
You 要– 238
You 容– 296
You 洋– 330
You 用– 364
You 葉– 543
You*bi 曜– 200
You*ka 八– 15
You*su 様– 136
Yowa*i 弱– 471
Yu 由– 73
Yu 輸– 288
Yu 湯– 404
Yu*kata 浴– 256
Yu*ki 行– 334
Yue 故– 394
Yuki 雪– 262
Yume 夢– 165
Yuu 由– 73
Yuu 夕– 160
Yuu 右– 457
Yuu 優– 528
Yuu*enchi 遊– 360
Yuu*jin 友– 459
Yuu*mei 有– 460
Za 咲– 193

528

Kanji Groups, in the Order of Appearance

Kanji Groups, Alphabetized

Made in the USA
Middletown, DE
03 February 2017